Canadian Parties in Transition

Canadian Parties in Transition

Recent Trends and New Paths for Research

FOURTH EDITION

EDITED BY
Alain-G. Gagnon and A. Brian Tanguay

UNIVERSITY OF TORONTO PRESS

LIBRARY AND ARCHIVES CANADA CATALOGUING IN PUBLICATION

Canadian parties in transition : recent trends and new paths to research / edited by Alain-G. Gagnon
and A. Brian Tanguay.—Fourth edition.

Includes bibliographical references and index.

Issued in print and electronic formats.

ISBN 978-1-4426-3471-8 (hardback).—ISBN 978-1-4426-3470-1 (paperback).—
ISBN 978-1-4426-3473-2 (pdf).—ISBN 978-1-4426-3472-5 (html).

1. Political parties—Canada. 2. Political parties—Canada—History. 3. Canada—Politics and
government. 4. Representative government and representation—Canada. 5. Elections—Canada.
I. Gagnon, Alain-G. (Alain-Gustave), 1954–, editor II. Tanguay, A. Brian (Andrew Brian), 1954–,
editor.

JL195.C28 2016   324.271   C2016-900507-0
                                                 C2016-900508-9

We welcome comments and suggestions regarding any aspect of our publications—please feel free to
contact us at news@utphighereducation.com or visit our Internet site at www.utppublishing.com.

North America
5201 Dufferin Street
North York, Ontario, Canada, M3H 5T8

2250 Military Road
Tonawanda, New York, USA, 14150

ORDERS PHONE: 1–800–565–9523
ORDERS FAX: 1–800–221–9985
ORDERS E-MAIL: utpbooks@utpress.utoronto.ca

UK, Ireland, and continental Europe
NBN International
Estover Road, Plymouth, PL6 7PY, UK
ORDERS PHONE: 44 (0) 1752 202301
ORDERS FAX: 44 (0) 1752 202333
ORDERS E-MAIL: enquiries@nbninternational.com

Every effort has been made to contact copyright holders; in the event of an error or omission,
please notify the publisher.

This book is printed on paper containing 100% post-consumer fibre.

The University of Toronto Press acknowledges the financial support for its publishing activities of
the Government of Canada through the Canada Book Fund.

Printed in Canada

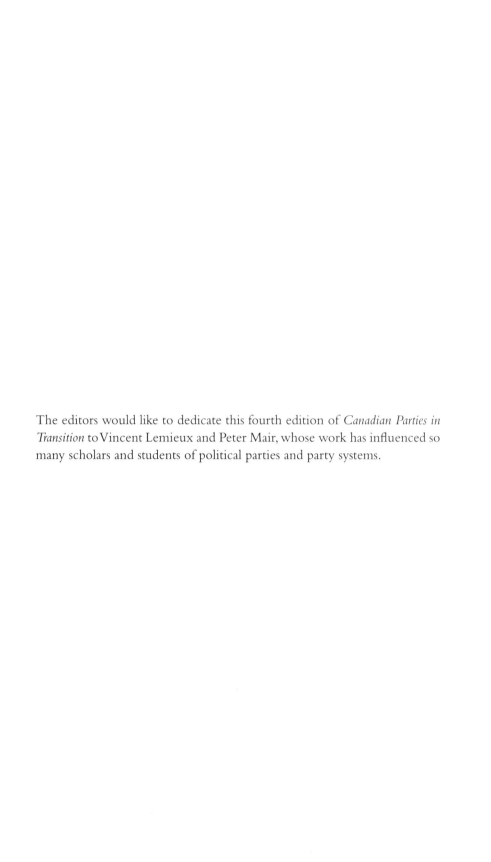

The editors would like to dedicate this fourth edition of *Canadian Parties in Transition* to Vincent Lemieux and Peter Mair, whose work has influenced so many scholars and students of political parties and party systems.

Contents

Part III: Representation and Democracy

Part IV: New Paths for Research

     Changing Nature of Party Politics in Canada   343
     ALEX MARLAND AND THIERRY GIASSON

17   Political Campaigning   364
     RICHARD NADEAU AND FRÉDÉRICK BASTIEN

18   Two Decades of Digital Party Politics in Canada:
     An Assessment   388
     TAMARA A. SMALL

19   Participation, Mobilization, and the Political Engagement
     of the Internet Generation   409
     HENRY MILNER

20   Municipal Political Parties: An Answer to Urbanization or
     an Affront to Traditions of Local Democracy?   432
     KRISTIN R. GOOD

     Statistical Appendix   465
     List of Contributors   473
     Index   479

Preface

Tʜᴇ ꜰɪʀsᴛ ᴇᴅɪᴛɪᴏɴ ᴏꜰ *Canadian Parties in Transition* was published over 25 years ago, in 1989, and it is reasonable to ask whether Canada's political parties and party system(s) could have been "in transition" for this entire period. The short answer is "yes"—unequivocally—as the chapters in this fourth edition of the book will demonstrate. It might well be that the federal election of 19 October 2015 restored the partisan status quo ante, with a dominant Liberal Party, the Conservative Party (whatever epithet it uses to label itself) as the principal opposition, and the NDP trailing the other two as a potential third option. But perhaps the existing party system is not exactly the same as the old one(s), with the partisan allegiances of Quebec's voters still up for grabs, the question of possibly significant electoral reform on the agenda at the federal level for the first time in decades, and the ongoing impact of new communications and campaign technologies on power relations both within party organizations and among the parties themselves. The contributions to the fourth edition of *Canadian Parties in Transition* help shed light on the possible futures of this country's political parties and party system.

The chapters are organized into four parts. The first explores the morphology of the existing party system and the principal factors that will shape its future evolution. Part II examines the nature of ideological competition in the Canadian party system and provides detailed portraits of each of the main parties along with the main third-party competitors that have periodically challenged their monopoly on representation. The chapters in Part III focus on both *how* interests are represented in contemporary democracies—voting systems, social movement and civil society alternatives to the parties, and the various mechanisms of direct democracy—as well as how effectively key groups and political communities in Canadian society (women and Québécois, for instance) are represented by the existing system of partisan competition. Part IV is an entirely new and innovative feature of this fourth edition: each of the chapters here sketches out an important new path for future research in the disciplinary subfield of party politics. This section will be particularly useful for graduate students in need of new vistas for their own research projects.

All but 5 of the 20 chapters in this collection are entirely new, and the five that remain from the third edition have been substantially revised and updated to take into account the major political developments since the last edition appeared in 2007. The book ends with a statistical appendix containing the federal election results from 1925 to 2015 and a graph displaying voter turnout in federal elections from Confederation to the present. Emily Mann undertook these revisions for the fourth edition.

PART I

Origins and Evolution of the Canadian Party System

1

The Evolution of the Canadian Party System: From Brokerage to Marketing-Oriented Politics

STEVE PATTEN

WHILE POLITICAL SCIENTISTS ARE IN AGREEMENT that the patterns of competition and interrelationships between political parties are central to what we mean by the notion of a party system (Epstein 1975, 234), scholars of Canadian politics argue that focusing too narrowly on the number of parties, party competition, and the associated alignment of voters in support of those parties ignores much of what is interesting and revealing regarding the character of a party system (Carty, Cross, and Young 2000, 4). There is, in Canada, a tradition of embracing a more detailed conception of the party system and also a richer approach to studying the system's historical evolution (Koop and Bittner 2013, 310). In this chapter, the party system is understood as defined by a range of organizational, legal, ideological, and political features, all of which are significant to the nature of party competition and the historical evolution of that system.

The distinctive features of Canada's party system include the organizational structure and operational character of political parties—including, among other things, their method of leadership selection and policy development—and the legal framework of rules governing matters such as the franchise, the conduct of elections, party financing, and the operations of parliamentary politics. The party system is also characterized by accepted norms and practices regarding styles of leadership, campaign behaviour, and media relations. At the ideological level, the party system is defined by a set of ideas—a discursive framework—that delimits the boundaries of political debate by offering up a particular conception of Canada and the core issues, interests, and identities that should animate partisan competition. Finally, as a system of political representation that is central to the nature of governance, the party system is defined by, first, its relations to other representative systems—such as interest groups and social movements—and, second, by the unique relationship that exists between governing, partisanship, and campaigning. Incorporating all these elements into one's understanding of the party system and looking beyond the changing patterns of party competition is essential to a fruitful examination of the historical evolution of a party system (Ladd 1990).

While some degree of party system change is ever-present, there are periods of more dramatic transformations, as well as periods when change slows, stability sets in, and the party system takes on characteristics that become widely accepted and normalized as a unique historical configuration of the Canadian party system. It was election studies scholars who first conceptualized party system change in this way, arguing that periodically a "critical election" realigns the distribution of party support and inaugurates a new "electoral era" (Blake 1979, 263–64). But, for those embracing a richer conception of the party system, it was David Smith's (1985) exploration of the history of party-government in Canada and Ken Carty's (1988) interpretation of the historical development of national politics that focused scholars' collective minds on the notion that there have been a series of historical epochs in which the characteristics of Canadian party politics congeal and form distinct systems of partisan politics. By the 1990s it was widely accepted that since 1867 four identifiable historical conjunctures had been associated with four distinct Canadian party systems—known as the first, second, third, and fourth party systems (se. Table 1.1; Bickerton, Gagnon, and Smith 1999; Carty et al. 2000; MacIvor 2006).

To understand the processes of party system change one must recognize that each new party system does not always follow on the heels of the previous system. Not all aspects of the party system change at the same time or rate and, if we are true to our richer conception of the party system and avoid fixating on critical elections and changes in party competition to the exclusion of other features of the party system, it is difficult to identify the precise beginning and end of each party system. In fact, there can be periods between party systems when change itself is the order of the day, as if we are groping toward a new, yet to congeal, system of party politics. There will also always be aspects of the party system that seem out of step, more in tune with a previous (or future) party system than with the current system. As such, it is useful to think of Canada's party systems as having gone through a period of emergence followed by the system's heyday—when its logic

Table 1.1 Canadian Party Systems in History

Party System	Period of Emergence	Heyday	Period of Unravelling
First	1867–1887	1896–1911	1911–1917
Second	1918–1921	1935–1957	1957–1962
Third	1963–1967	1968–1984	1985–1987
Fourth	1988–1993	1995–2003	2003–2006
Fifth	2006–2013	2015–	

and character are most evident—and, finally, a period when the old system unravels, change accelerates, and transition to a new party system begins. In this chapter I argue that the lead up to the 2015 general election marked the beginning of the heyday of Canada's fifth party system (Koop and Bittner 2013; Walchuk 2012). The remainder of this chapter will examine some of the core characteristics and evolution of Canada's five party systems. This examination will demonstrate that the adage that "Canadian politics is brokerage politics" must be re-examined in light of the marketing orientation that dominates in Canada's fifth party system (Carty, Cross, and Young 2013; Marland and Giasson in this volume).

Canada's First Party System

It took two to three decades following Confederation for Canada's first party system to take shape. Initially, parties were little more than loose coalitions that took their form more from the institutions of Parliament than electoral competition. As party labels lacked nationwide relevance and party organization played only a minor role in bringing coherence to electoral competition, elections were "conceived as a series of discrete constituency contests" (Carty 2001, 17). In the first three general elections as many as a quarter of all Members of Parliament (MPs) were acclaimed to office and so many candidates were "loose fish"—individuals who sought office without being clear about which partisan grouping they supported—that following the 1872 election, the Toronto *Globe* and the Montreal *Gazette* disputed the party affiliation of fully 35 of the 200 newly elected MPs (Reid 2001, 13). The MPs who sat as members of Sir John A. Macdonald's nominally Conservative coalition actually ran under a variety of labels, ranging from Conservative to Liberal-Conservative, Nationalist Conservative, Independent Conservative, and, in one case, Conservative Labour. But Macdonald was skilled at using power, patronage, and the perks of government in support of building the Conservative Party into a coherent national institution, which advantaged him over the Liberals, who were initially little more than an alliance of regionally based rivals of Macdonald's governing coalition. It wasn't until the years after 1887, when Wilfrid Laurier became Liberal leader, that the Liberals and Conservatives could both be said to exist as truly national parties, unified and politically relevant in all regions (Reid 2001, 14; Underhill 1999, 79). But even as the Conservative–Liberal rivalry defined the core of partisan competition in the heyday of Canada's first party system (1896 to 1911), the partisan landscape was complicated by the election of a small number of Labour, Nationalist, McCarthyite, and Patrons of Industry MPs.[1]

To appreciate the nature of party politics we must remember that the era of the first party system was, by modern standards, pre-democratic. Until 1874 there was no guarantee of secret ballots, and the governing party used staggered election dates to create a sense of momentum in favour of its re-election. The right to vote was restricted to a limited class of socially and economically privileged men. Women lacked political rights, and until the late 1890s many men were prohibited from voting by property and income qualifications and restrictions that excluded those who were non-British and foreign-born (Eagles 1996). Even when the franchise was expanded to something approximating universal manhood suffrage, most adult Canadians lacked political rights. The organization and financing of political parties also fell short of modern democratic standards. Parties were creatures of Parliament, existing to facilitate the functioning of a Westminster-style Parliament in which the government of the day faced an Official Opposition in parliamentary debate. There were no extra-parliamentary party organizations or organized constituency associations. Outside of Parliament, the parties were no more than private networks of supporters and financial backers. But the major newspapers were highly partisan—supporting either the Conservatives or the Liberals—and this ensured the parties a presence in local political life. Still, without an organized base of party members, party leaders were simply the leaders of their parliamentary caucuses; as such, they were selected by their caucus colleagues in closed-door caucus meetings (Blake, Carty, and Erickson 1996, 214).

Party leaders were responsible for raising money to ensure their re-election and supplement the funds raised by the party's candidates. This was difficult for a party out of power, but the government party (first the Conservatives, then the Liberals) received generous contributions from larger corporations, particularly the railways and the banks. Of course, since the extra-parliamentary parties did not formally exist, this fundraising was unregulated and no official records were kept. Beginning in 1874 there were legal requirements for candidates to disclose their campaign spending, and between 1908 and 1930 there were restrictions on candidates receiving corporate or union donations. But these regulations were not carefully enforced, and they ignored the fundraising activities of the parties and their leaders (Carty et al. 2000, 131–32). In essence, political parties were considered private associations rather than public institutions and, therefore, they were not recognized (or regulated) in law.

In terms of the discursive framework and public policy preoccupations of the first party system, political debate revolved around what has come to be called the "National Policy," which was a package of policies designed to facilitate the development of the Canadian economy and the maturation of an economically independent Canadian nation with strong cultural and governing ties to Britain. These policies included a system of protective tariffs instituted to foster investment and protect domestic industry, railway construction, Western land settlement schemes, and the 1876 Indian Act, among others (Brodie 1990). Macdonald's nation-building vision, which was initially opposed by nineteenth-century Liberals, allowed the Conservatives to organize and behave as a brokerage party—a party with a strong leader who articulates a unifying national vision that supposedly accommodates social divisions sufficiently well to appeal to (nearly) the entire electorate (Carty et al. 2013). But after Macdonald's death in 1891, intraparty conflicts revealed that the Conservatives were no longer fully accommodating of Roman Catholics, while the Laurier-led Liberals were making peace with the National Policy and articulating a political vision that appealed to corporate backers and spanned religious and linguistic divides sufficiently well to ensure their electoral success throughout the heyday of the first party system (1896 to 1911).

By 1911, however, Prime Minister Laurier abandoned the National Policy in favour of free trade with the United States. This and other issues—including the contentious Naval Service Bill—were fuelling regional, linguistic, and class divisions and testing the capacity of either national party to represent all sections of the nation. These tensions ultimately precipitated the unravelling of the National Policy, the system of partisan competition, and other features of the first party system (Thorburn 2001, 3–4).

Canada's Second Party System

Important changes occurred within the Canadian party system in the years following World War I. In 1918 Canada took another step closer to universal adult suffrage by granting women the right to vote and run in federal elections, but continued restrictions on the voting rights of foreign-born citizens, the Inuit, and Status Indians meant that Canada's modern liberal democracy remained incomplete. In 1919 Wilfrid Laurier passed away and the Liberals held Canada's first leadership convention, selecting Mackenzie King to lead their party. Also that year. Thomas Crerar, Robert Borden's minister of agriculture, resigned to lead the new Progressive Party, a party of agrarian protest that challenged the very foundations of the first party system by contesting the privilege of Canada's two established parties, opposing the tariff and rail policies of the National Policy, decrying government patronage, and criticizing the influence of large industrial and financial interests in party politics (Carty 2001, 21; Morton 1950). The Progressives' success in the 1921 election—winning the second-most parliamentary seats—dealt a fatal blow to Canada's two-party system and opened the door to an era in which third parties would ensure new voices were heard in the partisan arena (Azoulay 1999a, 161). Of course, we must be cautious about overstating third party influence. Traditional parties, particularly the Liberals, continued to dominate national politics, and third parties had only limited impact on the discursive and policy content of Canadian politics throughout the second party system (Brodie and Jenson 1988).

In terms of partisan electoral competition, the second party system was an era of Liberal political hegemony. Other than a few months of Conservative government in 1926, the Liberal Party was out of power for just one term (1930 to 1935). Even with the rise of third parties, the Liberals never dropped below 40 per cent popular support in an election, and in the system's heyday (1935 to 1957) the party won five consecutive majority governments. The Conservatives were transformed into a party of perpetual opposition status, often trailing the Liberals by 10 or more percentage points in general elections. The Liberals emerged as Canada's "natural governing party" and a true brokerage party capable of controlling the political agenda, defining the maturing Canadian nation, and limiting the possibility of other partisan voices being electorally successful (Whitaker 1977). Strong leaders—King and then Louis St. Laurent—shaped the party, but its organizational structure was more stratarchical than hierarchical,[2] thus allowing for powerful regional ministers, local organizational independence, and the brokering of competing interests within the cabinet and party caucus (Carty et al. 2013). Indeed, as leader of a minority government after the 1921 election, Mackenzie King rejected any suggestion of forming a coalition and moved instead to entice the less-experienced and less-disciplined Progressive MPs to cross the floor with minor changes to tariff and freight rate policies and, for some, an opportunity to sit at the cabinet table.

Those Progressives who adhered to group and interest representational strategies that were incompatible with Liberal brokerage politics eventually joined forces with a small bloc of United Farmer and Labour MPs to form the Ginger Group, a parliamentary coalition that, in 1932, helped establish the Co-operative Commonwealth Federation (CCF) as one of two important third parties of the second party system. As a coalition of socialists and farm and union activists, the CCF—which later transformed into the New Democratic Party (NDP)—articulated a progressive critique of capitalism and the dominant governing paradigm, but never managed to receive more than 15 per cent of the popular vote and at its peak in 1945 elected only 28 MPs. The other significant third party to emerge in this era was the Social Credit Party, a right-wing Alberta-based grouping of populist farmers and independent entrepreneurs. While Social Credit managed to win a small number of seats in Saskatchewan and British Columbia, the party was really an Alberta phenomenon, and most of the 10 to 17 seats it won in each election in this era were located in that province.

Liberal and Conservative party organizations developed considerably during the second party system. Local associations and national extra-parliamentary organizations were established, and party offices were set up. But, particularly in the case of the Liberals, the parliamentary leadership continued to play a central role (Azoulay 1999b, 30). Powerful regional cabinet ministers coordinated political organizing, raised funds, identified potential candidates, and brokered competing political interests. In power, the Liberals continued to use the perks of government to attract corporate donations, even relying on a "contract levy system" linking financial support to government business (Whitaker 1977, 403–5). Where possible, the opposition Conservatives followed the Liberal example, establishing a formal extra-parliamentary organization and opting to select their leaders at leadership conventions. But in many ways these organizational advances were hindered by the continued control exercised by the parties' parliamentary leadership. Party organizations served the leaders' wishes, and leadership conventions were "managed" and "uncompetitive" affairs (Blake et al. 1996, 218–19). Still, conventions were open enough to allow provincial politicians like John Bracken and George Drew to jump from provincial politics to lead the national Conservative Party, but the outgoing leader and the party establishment never really relinquished control of the process. Moreover, for all the advances in organization and leadership selection, the question of how to remove a leader from office was never addressed, leaving the issue of when to leave office in the hands of the leader and, to a certain extent, his caucus colleagues. Interestingly, it was the selection of Bracken, the former Progressive premier of Manitoba, that led the Conservatives, in 1942, to change their name to the Progressive Conservative Party of Canada.

By the dawn of the second party system, the policy orientation and priorities that had shaped the model of governance since the 1870s were under challenge, and not only by the Progressives and other opposition politicians. King hinted at an expanded role for government in social welfare during his 1919 campaign for the Liberal leadership, but during the 1920s changes in this direction were limited (Guest 1985). Even when the Great Depression hit, Conservative Prime Minister R.B. Bennett was hesitant to abandon timeworn policies of limited spending and a traditional economic policy framework, including selective tariff increases to protect Canadian industry and jobs. However, the experience of economic depression eventually altered views and, in 1935, Bennett went on radio to pronounce the failure of laissez-faire capitalism and traditional models of social and economic

policy and to propose a New Deal of social welfare and marketing legislation, including national unemployment insurance.

When the Conservatives lost the 1935 election Bennett's New Deal
was abandoned, but there was clear momentum toward a new policy paradigm. The Liberals established a national system of unemployment insurance in 1941, and in 1943 the Marsh Report on social security called for
family allowances, paid maternity leave, and a national system of health
insurance. Progress toward a new national governing paradigm was slow,
but by the 1950s the governing Liberals, the CCF, and even some Conservatives were moving toward a new consensus that ensured social policy
innovations, and the interventionist economic policies of technocratic
Keynesianism would alter the discursive framework of party politics and
underpin a welfare state governing paradigm for much of the third party
system (Bradford 1998).

Canada's Third Party System

The emergence of the third party system marked important changes to
the structure of partisan competition, particularly in Quebec and Western
Canada. The Liberals had dominated Quebec politics since Laurier first led
the party. Between 1896 and 1957 Liberal candidates won, on average, 58
per cent of the vote in Quebec. Over the next three elections, however,
Liberal dominance in Quebec was challenged—first by the Diefenbaker-led
Progressive Conservatives (PCs) in 1958, then by an unprecedented upsurge
in support for Quebec-based Social Credit candidates in 1962 and 1963. As
the contours of the third party system were solidifying in the mid-1960s, the
Liberal Party regained its dominant position in Quebec, but Diefenbaker and
the Social Credit (known as the *Ralliement des créditistes* in the 1965 and 1968
elections) demonstrated the electoral potential of more conservative forces
within the province. In the West, the Liberals dominated Manitoba and Saskatchewan, placed a respectable second place to the Social Credit in Alberta,
and competed almost equally with the PCs and CCF in British Columbia
throughout the second party system. But in 1958 Diefenbaker's PCs won
all but five Western seats—those being won by the CCF. The Liberals and
Social Credit were devastated, and the stage was set for the PCs to dominate
prairie politics and compete strongly in British Columbia throughout the
third party system. Although the Liberals were dominant during the heyday
of the third party system (1968 to 1984), they were a reduced party, regularly forming minority governments and relying heavily on Quebec and the
party's base of French-speaking and Catholic voters to mask their long-term
decline (Bickerton et al. 1999; Johnston 2013).

The landscape of third party politics began to change with the defeat of the entire slate of Social Credit candidates in 1958. Then, in 1961, the CCF formalized its relationship with organized labour and transformed into the New Democratic Party. Between 1963 and 1984 the NDP won between 17 and 32 seats, mostly in Ontario, Saskatchewan, and British Columbia. The Social Credit managed to win four to five seats in British Columbia and Alberta in the 1962, 1963, and 1965 elections but have been unsuccessful on the Prairies at the federal level since then. The most surprising, although short-lived, development in this period was the Social Credit bursting onto the Quebec political scene, winning 26 seats in 1962 and then between 6 and 15 seats in every election until 1979 (Pinard 1975).

In terms of the institutions and structures of party organization, the third party system witnessed an expansion of parties' extra-parliamentary wings and the development of more professional modern campaign organizations. While the PCs were in power (1957 to 1963), the National Liberal Federation and local Liberal constituency associations were strengthened, and the party's national headquarters was also enlarged (Wearing 1981). After regaining power, Liberal Prime Minister Lester Pearson continued building the extra-parliamentary wing of the party. By ordering his ministers to focus on parliamentary and executive responsibilities and spend less time on party affairs, Pearson hastened the end of the brokerage-style ministerialism that saw powerful regional ministers controlling central aspects of party organization and financing (Azoulay 1999b, 31). Under Pearson, and then Pierre Trudeau, the Prime Minister's Office (PMO) was strengthened, both in terms of its executive power as a key central agency and with regard to the leader's power within the Liberal Party. Indeed, by the 1970s the upper echelons of the party bureaucracy were so closely tied to the PMO they formed a highly centralized and hierarchical political machine. The PCs developed in similar directions during this era. Out of power for all but nine months during the heyday of the third party system (1968 to 1984), they were less able to raise money to fund expansion of the party bureaucracy, and the Office of the Leader of the Opposition is typically less capable of centralizing power. But, relying on Ontario's Big Blue Machine, a small coterie of professional fundraisers and political managers with expertise in advertising and polling, the PCs built a sophisticated team of political operatives that rivalled Trudeau's Liberal team. This was an important development, with its roots in the trend toward seeking technical campaign advice from advertising professionals and public opinion pollsters beginning in the 1950s and 1960s. By the 1980s, parties were increasingly controlled by new political entourages of professional managers, consultants, and strategists (Noel 1996). This new power elite of party politics added significantly to the power of party leaders.

Professionalization was also evident in the campaigns mounted to win the leadership of Canada's major political parties. The third party system marked the zenith of delegated leadership conventions. Beginning with the conventions that selected Robert Stanfield as PC leader (1967) and Pierre Trudeau as Liberal leader (1968), the number of candidates, the competitiveness of the races, and the amount being spent on campaigns increased significantly (Blake et al. 1996). Organizing to select delegates and win votes became highly sophisticated, with campaigns running slates of delegates and employing refined delegate-tracking systems to influence each and every convention vote. By the early 1980s the cost of a successful leadership race surpassed $2 million. Equally important were changes in the role of the party membership in calling a leader's reign to an end. Prior to the third party system the power to remove a leader remained with the leader and, to a certain extent, with the parliamentary caucus, which could put pressure on a leader to resign. But in 1966, despite Diefenbaker's stated desire to stay on as PC leader, the party's president put forward a proposal for a leadership convention before a meeting of the party's National Association. It passed with 73 per cent support, marking the first time a leadership convention had been forced when the position was not vacant (Perlin 1980). Over the next decade the principle of "leadership review" was entrenched in all the major parties' constitutions, giving the party membership some control over the timing of future leadership conventions.

Important steps in the democratization of the legal framework of party politics were taken during the third party system. By the early 1960s, changes to electoral boundaries and amendments to the Elections Act ensured the Inuit of Canada's North and Status Indians had full political rights. Then, the entrenchment of the political right to vote in the 1982 Charter of Rights and Freedoms forced the removal of any remaining restrictions on voting rights—including those that disenfranchised mentally disabled patients and prisoners in correctional facilities (Eagles 1996). It was the 1974 Elections Expenses Act that had the greatest impact on the operation of party politics, however. After decades of virtually unregulated fundraising and campaign spending and ongoing evidence of patronage and kickback schemes being used to solicit contributions, Parliament acted to limit spending and provide public oversight of fundraising (Stanbury 2001). Parties were required to report to Elections Canada on their fundraising and campaign spending. Limits were placed on the amounts national parties and local candidates could spend during campaigns, there were restrictions on the amount of prime-time radio and TV advertising parties could purchase, all donations of $100 or more were to be made public, and public financing of parties and campaigns was instituted through tax credits on contributions and partial reimbursements of election expenses. The new regulations took Canada's political parties an important step closer to being quasi-public institutions, rather than merely private associations.

The discursive framework and governing paradigm of the third party system built on the commitment to Keynesian economic and social welfare policies that began to emerge in the latter years of the second party system. By the late 1960s, Canada's Keynesian welfare state was defined by relative openness to foreign investment; social policy measures in the areas of income maintenance, health, education, and social services; and a commitment to macroeconomic demand management. Although social welfare and government intervention to shape and protect the Canadian economy and culture were contentious, they came to form the basis of a political consensus that animated partisan policy debates (Cameron 1989). There also emerged a national narrative rooted in Canada's colony-to-nation story. Under Liberal governments of the 1960s to early 1980s, the idea of Canada as a middle power peacekeeper and a multicultural and bilingual political community of rights-bearing citizens took hold in the public consciousness and the Canadian party system.

Canada's Fourth Party System

The third party system came under strain shortly after Brian Mulroney's 1984 landslide election victory. Particularly during the Mulroney PCs' second term in office (1988 to 1993), a combination of political tensions associated with constitutional politics, regionalism, intensified ideological debate, and public cynicism set in motion changes in the partisan landscape that became strikingly apparent in the general election of 1993. The governing PCs were reduced to just two seats, the NDP elected only nine MPs, the Liberals were returned to power, and the fledgling Bloc Québécois and Reform Party both won over 50 seats, establishing themselves, at least temporarily, as Canada's principal opposition parties.

The core features of electoral competition in the fourth party system were regionalization, multiparty electoral competition, and Liberal dominance. Of course, regionalism was not entirely new to Canadian party politics (see Bickerton, in this volume). Pan-Canadian electoral strategies aiming at national competitiveness defined partisan competition during the third party system (Carty 1988), but even the governing Liberals relied on historical support among Eastern Canadian Catholics and Quebec voters to maintain power (Bickerton et al. 1999; Bickerton and Gagnon 2004, 250). During the 1990s, however, the regionalized character of party competition intensified, clarifying the existence of regional party subsystems in Atlantic

Canada, Quebec, Ontario, and the West. The PCs were largely uncompetitive in all regions other than Atlantic Canada; the NDP's pockets of strength were in Saskatchewan and Nova Scotia; the Liberals had some strength in several regions, but relied on winning almost every Ontario seat to maintain power; the Bloc dominated Quebec; and the Reform Party and, later, the Canadian Alliance swept Alberta and was competitive in other Western provinces. "Given this balkanization in party competition, no party could effectively campaign on the same message in each part of the country" (Carty, Cross, and Young 2002, 27). Even the governing Liberals, long Canada's party of regional accommodation and pan-Canadian brokerage-style politics, abandoned pretenses of national competitiveness, writing off any chance of winning Albertan and British Columbian constituencies other than a small number in Edmonton and Vancouver/Victoria.

The fourth party system also witnessed new developments in leadership selection and the legal regulation of party financing. With regard to leadership selection, there were developments in two contrary directions. First, a new enthusiasm for grassroots democracy resulted in a turn away from traditional leadership conventions and the adoption of various forms of universal membership vote (UMV), in which all party members can participate directly in the leader selection process (Carty et al. 2000, 123–29; Preyra 2001). While UMV serves the cause of democracy in Canada's extra-parliamentary parties, developments associated with increasingly costly and sophisticated leadership campaigns ran counter to meaningfully open and democratic leadership selection (Patten 2006). When the Liberal Party held its final traditional delegated leadership convention in 1990, just as the fourth party system emerged, Jean Chrétien built an unprecedented nationwide organization that allowed him to literally "capture" the party and win the leadership at delegate selection meetings rather than on the campaign trail or the convention floor (Carty et al. 2000, 78). In 2003, after the Liberals adopted procedures that blended a convention with a UMV that gave rank-and-file members direct control over the outcome of the first ballot, Paul Martin adopted and extended Chrétien's strategy. His team raised over $11 million and put such a lock on local Liberal associations that all but one potential rival bowed out of the race, ensuring a Martin coronation supported by over 90 per cent of member-controlled delegate votes. The process was far from meaningfully open and democratic.

The ability of Paul Martin's strategists—many of whom were professional campaigners, pollsters, and media and government relations consultants—to take over the Liberal Party revealed the extent to which party organizations are, increasingly, hollow shells with little in the way of an ideological or policy essence and little organic connection to civil society. Reg Whitaker (2001) argues Canadian parties have become "virtual parties" that have little political or ideological character beyond the leader's personal image and a related agenda that is arrived at based on polling analysis and media strategy. Of course, Canadian parties have a long history of strong leaders who shape their party's character and appeal. What is new is the extent to which, despite objectively democratic reforms like the UMV, both a party's grassroots and its parliamentary caucus are increasingly unimportant to the party's ideological and policy agenda. Even the Liberals, Canada's traditional party of brokerage politics, no longer serve as a vehicle for accommodating competing interests: the party is "neither the elite-run 'ministerialist' party of the King-St. Laurent era, nor the 'participatory' party of the Pearson-Trudeau era" (Whitaker 2001, 19). During the fourth party system the trend toward abandoning pan-Canadian strategies in favour of strategic electoral appeals to clusters of old and new supporters, the hollowness of the virtual party, and the exceptional capacity of new leaders to redefine their parties revealed a continued departure from the tradition of brokerage politics in the Canadian party system (Carty et al. 2013).

In early 2003, as the fourth party system was beginning to show signs of unravelling, Prime Minister Jean Chrétien seemed increasingly concerned that his legacy would be tainted by scandal. There were accusations that he had influenced government decisions that ensured he profited from a real estate deal and, perhaps more significantly, a 2002 report of the Auditor General had revealed widespread rule-breaking in the awarding of government advertising contracts (an affair now known as the sponsorship scandal). To cleanse himself of the growing impressions that corporations and money had too much influence in Liberal Party politics (LeDrew 2005), Chrétien introduced party and election financing legislation that placed significant new limitations on the sources and size of contributions. Under the new legal framework, individuals could give no more than $5,000 annually to any registered political party, candidate running in a federal election, local party constituency association, contestant seeking a local nomination, or leadership contestant. Moreover, corporations, trade unions, and associations were forbidden from contributing to national parties or leadership campaigns and were restricted to a maximum $1,000 contribution to local candidates, party constituency associations, or nomination contestants. To compensate for the loss of corporate and union contributions to national parties, the legislation instituted an annual public allowance set, for 2004, at $1.75 for each vote the party received in the last general election. While Chrétien's reforms turned out to be only the first step in a series of reforms that would be extended (and partially transformed) under Stephen Harper during the emergence of the fifth party system, they were significant for the way in which they extended the logic of understanding parties as public institutions that, by definition, are legitimate targets of both public regulation and public financing. In fact, implicit in Chrétien's regulatory framework was the assumption that there is a public good associated with putting parties on a somewhat more level playing field in terms of financing and spending.

The emergence of the fourth party system was marked by increased ideological polarization and conflict (Koop and Bittner 2013). The 1988 election played out as a virtual referendum on Brian Mulroney's proposed Canada–United States Free Trade Agreement. Over the next half decade, while social movement organizations related to the environment, feminism, and anti-racism were involved in unprecedented levels of political activity and engagement with partisan politics, the Reform Party emerged to champion its unique blend of neoliberal challenges to the size and cost of government and socially conservative populist critiques of progressive social change (Laycock 2002). Reform also challenged the notion that Canadians are well served by a governing paradigm that understands Canada to be a socially liberal, multicultural, and bilingual political community, and by constitutional reforms that focus on responding to the demands of Québécois and Aboriginal nationalists (Patten 1999). In the 1993 election, as the PCs defended their agenda of free trade and aggressive reductions in social expenditures (Rice and Prince 1993), the Liberals campaigned on a progressive platform that raised doubts about Canada's entry into the North American Free Trade Agreement (NAFTA), emphasized the stimulative power of the state, and promised infrastructure programs and public spending in support of economic growth and job creation (Liberal Party of Canada 1993). But over the next two years the Chrétien Liberals moved to embrace economic globalization and support the processes of continentalization within NAFTA (Clarkson and Lachapelle 2006). Then, in February 1995, Finance Minister Paul Martin shocked observers by introducing what was arguably the most economically conservative budget of the postwar era. That budget championed the idea of attacking the federal deficit through structural changes in the operation of government and implementing major cuts to federal transfers to fund health, postsecondary education, and social services (Department of Finance 1995). The Liberal government had embraced the neoliberal revolution, and even Stephen Harper declared the Chrétien government to be "more conservative on most issues than the previous Progressive Conservative government" of Brian Mulroney (Harper and Flanagan 1996–97, 39). Thus, ideological conflict and polarization faded, and the heyday of the fourth party system (1995 to 2003) came to be defined by a right-leaning neoliberal governing paradigm. Long after the deficit was slain and aggressive attacks on the Keynesian welfare state were no longer required, a neoliberal discursive frame guided core social and economic policies, even proposals for social reinvestment.

Canada's Fifth Party System

When the Canadian Alliance and the PCs merged and formed the Conservative Party of Canada (CPC) in 2003, many observers assumed that the reuniting of partisan conservatives marked the further congealment of Canada's fourth party system. Today, however, there is a developing consensus that 2003 actually marked the end of that system's heyday. Between 2003 and 2013 the fourth party system unravelled and a new fifth party system emerged (Koop and Bittner 2013). In terms of the contours of electoral competition, the Harper Conservatives successfully reduced the governing Liberals to minority status in 2004, won minority governments in 2006 and 2008, and in 2011 formed the first Conservative majority government since the Mulroney era. While the new Conservative Party was gaining electoral strength under the leadership of Stephen Harper, the Liberals transitioned from an era defined by the long-term leadership of Prime Minister Jean Chrétien to a period of rapid leadership changes: Paul Martin (2003–06), Stéphane Dion (2006–08), Michael Ignatieff (2008–11), and Bob Rae (2011–13). The elections of 2006, 2008, and 2011 saw the CPC's electoral support grow from 36.3 per cent to 39.6 per cent, giving Harper just enough support to form a majority government. Even more striking was the shifting balance of support for the opposition parties. The once powerful Liberal Party saw its support drop from 30.2 per cent in 2006 to a historic low of 18.9 per cent in 2011, while NDP support grew from 17.5 per cent to 30.6 per cent of the vote, winning 103 seats and Official Opposition status in 2011. The Bloc, for its part, was devastated in 2011: after winning between 38 and 54 Quebec seats in each election since 1993, the party was reduced to a mere four seats. Adding to the historic character of the 2011 election was the election of the first Green Party MP, Elizabeth May. This historic realignment was at least as significant as the 1993 election. In fact, the apparent reduction in the number of electorally competitive parties in 2011 led some scholars to speculate that the fifth party system might be a two-party system in which a united right (Conservative) would be pitted against a united left (NDP) (Koop and Bittner 2013, 316). But, in an era of virtual parties whose character and electoral prospects can be transformed by a simple change of leader, the death of NDP leader Jack Layton in 2011 and the selection of Justin Trudeau as Liberal leader in 2013 were game-changers.

Despite the effective parliamentary performance of the new NDP leader Tom Mulcair, excitement generated by Trudeau's selection as Liberal leader boosted the Liberal Party into first place in opinion polls during 2013–14, while the NDP sank, once again to third place. In this context the Liberal Party was able to rebuild its campaign and fundraising organizations. But, as the 2015 campaign approached, large numbers of flexible partisans were rethinking their preferences. Polls indicated at least two-thirds of Canadians wanted to vote for change but were increasingly uncertain which alternative they preferred. At the same time, almost one-third of the electorate strongly supported the Harper Conservatives and rejected all other available alternatives. One month out from the 19 October election, the three main parties were virtually tied in opinion polls. As election day approached, however, Justin Trudeau gained the momentum required to be seen as the preferred agent of change. The Liberals won 39.5 per cent of the vote—more than double what they won in 2011—and secured 184 seats in the House of Commons, enough for a solid majority. The NDP dropped to 19.7 per cent of the vote, which is still at the high end of their historic levels of support. For their part, the Harper Conservatives dropped from 39.6 per cent to 31.9 per cent support. While the Bloc and Greens both won seats—10 and 1, respectively—there was no sense that either party was set to be anything more than a fairly marginalized minor party. As such, the results brought the Harper era to an end, producing a distribution of votes and seats that, superficially, was similar to many elections of the third party system.

Despite the altered character of partisan competition and shifts in the relative strength of the parties, the 2015 campaign reinforced many of the distinct characteristics of Canada's fifth party system and, indeed, may mark the beginning of the heyday of that system. Although media analysis often maintains that, at the discursive level, the Trudeau Liberals' commitment to fund investments in public infrastructure by running modest short-term deficits marked a decisive break from the Harper Conservatives' neoliberal agenda, consideration of the full range of major party policy positions reveals that the fifth party system, like the fourth, continues to be defined by competing versions of an essentially neoliberal governing paradigm. True, the commitments of "rollback neoliberalism"—which dominated policy in the 1990s and continue to motivate many Conservatives—have been superseded by "roll-out neoliberalism" (Patten 2013). Still, the core assumptions of the neoliberal model of governance remain largely intact.

The most novel and significant features of the fifth party system are marketing-oriented politics and the permanent campaign. The idea of the permanent campaign refers to much more than the sort of constant campaign readiness, pseudo-campaigning, and intensified partisanship that is often observed during minority parliaments, when parties are forced by circumstance to be prepared for an election at any time. The permanent campaign is, for parties and governments, a state of being in which the strategies and tactics of elections are used between elections regardless of how unlikely it is that an election could be called. The now-powerful campaign and media professionals of party leaders' entourages serve to reinforce the hyper-partisan politics of the permanent campaign. They ensure parties engage in perpetual fundraising and employ media and advertising strategies that give the party, its leader, and its messages prominence in the news media, on the Web, and in social media. They ensure that the lens of strategic political communications and message control determines even the most mundane activities of politicians and their parties (Flanagan 2014). The permanent campaign has transformed the relationship between partisanship, campaigning, and the processes of governance. It has been increasingly common for government resources to be deployed in support of electoral goals. Policy making, government communications, and senior public service appointments have been progressively politicized, and partisan political staffs have emerged as a major force in governance (Aucoin 2012). The need for organizational discipline in support of strategic precision in an era of permanent campaign has reinforced the empowerment of strong leaders supported by an almost military-style hierarchy in the organizational structure and operations of parties (Flanagan 2013).

Marketing-oriented politics, as Marland and Giasson explain in this volume, has emerged as modern electoral–professional parties developed the capacity to employ polling and big data analytics to develop the sort of fine-grained understanding of the electorate that allows researchers to identify the characteristics, interests, and political attitudes of clusters of like-minded voters. As in the world of consumer marketing, parties now employ research to develop "market intelligence" in the task of "market segmentation" and, importantly, they are willing to alter not only their rhetoric but also their policies and programs to appeal to those segments of the electorate that, when mobilized, have the potential to alter election results. Canadian parties' embrace of a marketing orientation disrupts many aspects of traditional brokerage politics, including the focus on accommodating regional interests within a unified conception of the national interest, as well as the desire to appease flashpoints of political tension and avoid the ideological fringes. It is not, however, identical to the catch-all politics of big-tent parties that strive to use persuasive campaigns to attract the support of as many voters as possible by targeting appeals to a range of traditional supporters and new electoral groupings who could be enticed to come on board (Carty et al. 2013). Instead, marketing-oriented parties are unique in, first, their willingness to shift from a focus on persuasion to designing and framing policies that appeal to key segments of the electorate and, second, their embrace of the notion that the easiest and most stable route to political power is to build a "minimum winning coalition" of deeply committed supporters (Flanagan 2014, 71). In the context of Canada's winner-take-all single-member plurality electoral system with multiple competitive parties, it is accepted that as little as 39 per cent of the vote is enough to form a majority government—indeed, with only two-thirds of Canadians regularly turning out to vote, a party that carefully targets appeals to key segments of the electorate might be able to achieve a minimum winning coalition with even fewer votes. Thus, rather than producing catch-all parties, a marketing orientation might be consistent with what could be called "catch-enough politics." This realization is transforming the strategic orientation of parties, including their approach to political communication, their embrace of data-driven microtargeting, and, for some, their willingness to engage in wedge politics.

Wedge politics involves strategic political interventions that are purposefully divisive and polarizing. The goal is to galvanize core party supporters who can be counted on for fundraising and electoral support, even if opponents are enraged (and demonized) in the process (Toner and McKee 2014). Employing wedge politics—as the Conservative Party has done with its repeal of the long-gun registry, much of its tough-on-crime agenda, and the 2015 promise to ban the wearing of niqabs at citizenship ceremonies—is risky because the outcomes of inflaming flashpoints of political tension are unpredictable. As such, while the market orientation of parties in the fifth party system makes wedge politics more likely, this sort of divisive politics is not inevitable.

The impact of the permanent campaign and market-oriented politics on the way parties approach strategic political communications, news management, and political marketing is centrally important to the character of the fifth party system. Parties now view the media as a means to an end. In an effort to limit the capacity of news organizations to set the agenda, they will snub or bypass media outlets that are viewed as negatively predisposed to their leader or message. The Conservatives, when in power, carefully limited and managed the media's access to ministers and members of caucus. No one spoke publicly without fairly high-level approval. Harper himself regularly avoided the parliamentary press gallery while making himself available to more conservative talk radio programs, regional radio and television programs, and specialized news media, such as OMNI Television, which serve identifiable ethnic communities that have become a target market for the Conservative Party (Ditchburn 2014). In their efforts to create positive news stories and manage the longevity and political fallout of potentially negative stories, all parties have become quite proficient at providing the news media with "information subsidies" in the form of prewritten quotes, pseudo-events, and photo opportunities that are little more than prepackaged political news stories (Marland 2014). Moreover, when in government the Harper Conservatives displayed an unprecedented willingness to allow strategic political goals to trump the legitimate governing purposes of government—not party—communications (Thomas 2013).

As the fifth party system was emerging, the Harper Conservatives were at the forefront of a revolution in political campaigning: the rise of data-driven microtargeting. All of Canada's major parties now rely on massive databases, data analytics and predictive modelling, and data-driven microtargeting to maximize their capacity to identify and mobilize key clusters of voters. The Conservatives were first to develop their database, the Constituent Information Management System (CIMS), in 2004. In the 2006 and 2008 general elections the CIMS database was effectively employed in battleground constituencies where centrally coordinated voter contact programs were used to identify and get supporters to the polls. By 2011 all three major parties had roughly similar databases, but the Conservative database contained considerably more personal information on voters and it was employed most effectively. Thus, as they prepared for the 2015 election, the NDP and Liberals overhauled their databases (known as Populus and Liberalist, respectively) and invested heavily in training local campaign teams to collect and employ data in voter persuasion and mobilization. Both parties developed in-house analytics operations, with the Liberals spending three times what they had invested in data and data analytics in 2011 (Patten, in press). Developing and mining party databases allows campaign teams to identify target markets of voters to whom they can tailor boutique policy commitments and political communications (Delacourt 2013). With this increased market intelligence, parties are shifting from emphasizing broad appeals to narrowcasting targeted appeals that will, increasingly, rely on communications via social media. When market research and voter databases are used in highly focused direct voter contact programs, a local candidate's support can increase by 5 to 10 percentage points on election day, enough to ensure victory in a battleground constituency (Flanagan 2010).

As the fifth party system took shape, the Conservatives' effective use of database technology and targeted messages in fundraising motivated changes to the legal regulation of party financing. Just two years after the Chrétien government's dramatic 2003 overhaul of the regulations, Harper instituted an all-out ban on corporate and union contributions to political parties, even at the local level, and further reduced the maximum contributions individuals can make to parties, candidates, constituency associations, and contestants in local nomination and leadership races; as of 2015, that limit was $1,500. Then, as Young explains in this volume, the Conservative government made changes to the structure of public financing of parties. While leaving tax credits for donations and the partial reimbursements of campaign expenses in place, they committed to phasing out the annual per-vote public subsidy. The last of these subsidies was paid in April 2015. The net effect of these changes is to require parties to be more aggressive at seeking out large numbers of small and mid-size contributions. Wealthy donors, corporations, and unions are no longer able to support parties or fund campaigns with the large donations that were once common. Thus, the most successful parties will be those who effectively use databases and speedy electronic communications to encourage multiple donations, sometimes in response to controversies that arise around divisive wedge issues.

Conclusion

Canadian political scientists have dedicated considerable energy to elaborating a rich and encompassing conception of the party system, one that looks beyond the number of parties, party competition, and the alignment of voters in support of those parties. The distinctive features of the party system include the organizational structure and operational character of our parties; the legal framework of rules governing parties and party politics; the accepted norms of leadership, campaigning, and media relations; the relationship of parties and campaigning to governance and other systems of political representation; and finally the discursive framework that defines the dominant conception of the Canadian political community and the core issues, interests, and identities that are relevant to political debate. This chapter's review of the evolution of Canada's five party systems could only provide a partial and limited overview of each system. But the glimpses into the character of these systems reveal a lot about the changing character of party politics in Canada. One observation was stressed above others: after generations of students being taught about brokerage politics and brokerage parties, this chapter highlighted the fact that developments related to the new marketing orientation of political parties have disrupted the tradition of brokerage-style party politics. Today, in the era of the fifth party system, Canadian politics is no longer accommodative brokerage politics. Carty et al. (2013) contend that Canadian parties have been, for some time, catch-all rather than brokerage parties. Now, with the rise of the permanent campaign and the development of sophisticated database technologies and microtargeting, party politics in Canada is being shaped by a new marketing-oriented politics—and catch-enoughism—rather than brokerage politics.

Suggested Readings

Blake, Donald. 1979. "1896 and All That: Critical Elections in Canada." *Canadian Journal of Political Science* 12 (2): 259–80. http://dx.doi.org/10.1017/S0008423900048113

Carty, R. Kenneth. 1988. "Three Canadian Party Systems: An Interpretation of the Development of National Politics." In *Party Democracy in Canada: The Politics of National Party Conventions,* edited by G. Perlin, 16–32. Scarborough, ON: Prentice-Hall Canada.

Cody, Howard, and Jamie Gillies. 2015. "The Canadian Party System and the Leadership of Stephen Harper." *New England Journal of Political Science* 8 (1): 2–49.

Koop, Royce, and Amanda Bittner. 2013. "Parties and Elections after 2011: The Fifth Canadian Party System?" In *Parties, Elections, and the Future of Canadian Politics,* edited by Amanda Bittner and Royce Koop, 308–31. Vancouver: University of British Columbia Press.

Smith, David. 1985. "Party Government, Representation and National Integration in Canada." In *Party Government and Regional Representation in Canada,* edited by Peter Aucoin, 1–68. Toronto: University of Toronto Press.

Walchuk, Brad. 2012. "A Whole New Ballgame: The Rise of Canada's Fifth Party System." *American Review of Canadian Studies* 42 (3): 418–34. http://dx.doi.org/10.1080/02722011.2012.705867

Notes

1   The Patrons of Industry was a farmers' organization that nominated candidates for election in a number of federal and Ontario provincial elections during the 1890s. The McCarthyites were a slate of candidates who supported the anti-French and anti-Catholic views of the Canadian parliamentarian Dalton McCarthy and his Imperial Federation League.

2   Stratarchical parties are characterized by a diffusion of power among and within different strata (or levels) of the party organization. Rather than all aspects of the party being shaped by centralized command and control, there is tolerance of autonomy, local initiative, and intraparty competition. Lines of communication and control between branches of the party are weaker than would be found in a hierarchical organization (Eldersveld 1964).

References

Aucoin, Peter. 2012. "New Political Governance in Westminster Systems: Impartial Public Administration and Management Performance at Risk." *Governance: An International Journal of Policy, Administration and Institutions* 25 (2): 177–99. http://dx.doi.org/10.1111/j.1468-0491.2012.01569.x

Azoulay, Dan. 1999a. "The Emergence of Protest Parties, 1918–1945: Introduction." In *Canadian Political Parties: Historical Readings,* edited by D. Azoulay, 159–73. Toronto: Irwin Publishing.

Azoulay, Dan. 1999b. "The Evolution of Party Organization in Canada, 1900–1984." In *Canadian Political Parties: Historical Readings,* edited by D. Azoulay, 27–50. Toronto: Irwin Publishing.

Bickerton, James, and Alain-G. Gagnon. 2004. "Political Parties and Electoral Politics." In *Canadian Politics,* 4th ed., edited by James Bickerton and Alain-G. Gagnon, 239–62. Peterborough, ON: Broadview Press.

Bickerton, James, Alain-G. Gagnon, and Patrick J. Smith. 1999. *Ties That Bind: Parties and Voters in Canada.* Toronto: Oxford University Press.

Blake, Donald. 1979. "1896 and All That: Critical Elections in Canada." *Canadian Journal of Political Science* 12 (2): 259–80. http://dx.doi.org/10.1017/S0008423900048113

Blake, Donald, R. Kenneth Carty, and Lynda Erickson. 1996. "Coming and Going: Leadership Selection and Removal in Canada." In *Canadian Parties in Transition,* 2nd ed., edited by A. Brian Tanguay and Alain-G. Gagnon, 213–37. Toronto: Nelson Canada.

Bradford, Neil. 1998. *Commissioning Ideas: Canadian National Policy Innovation in Comparative Perspective.* Toronto: Oxford University Press.

Brodie, Janine. 1990. *The Political Economy of Canadian Regionalism.* Toronto: Harcourt Brace Jovanovich.

Brodie, Janine, and Jane Jenson. 1988. *Crisis, Challenge and Change: Party and Class in Canada Revisited.* 2nd ed. Ottawa: Carleton University Press.

Cameron, Duncan. 1989. "Political Discourse in the Eighties." In *Canadian Parties in Transition: Discourse, Organization, and Representation,* edited by Alain-G. Gagnon and A. Brian Tanguay, 64–82. Toronto: Nelson Canada.

Carty, R. Kenneth. 1988. "Three Canadian Party Systems: An Interpretation of the Development of National Politics." In *Party Democracy in Canada: The Politics of National Party Conventions,* edited by G. Perlin, 15–30. Scarborough, ON: Prentice-Hall Canada.

Carty, R. Kenneth. 2001. "Three Canadian Party Systems: An Interpretation of the Development of National Politics." In *Party Politics in Canada,* 8th ed., edited by Hugh G. Thorburn and Alan Whitehorn, 16–32. Toronto: Prentice Hall.

Carty, R. Kenneth, William Cross, and Lisa Young. 2000. *Rebuilding Canadian Party Politics.* Vancouver: University of British Columbia Press.

Carty, R. Kenneth, William Cross, and Lisa Young. 2002. "A New Canadian Party System." In *Political Parties, and Electoral Democracy in Canada,* edited by William Cross, 15–36. Toronto: Oxford University Press.

Carty, R. Kenneth, William Cross, and Lisa Young. 2013. "Has Brokerage Politics Ended? Canadian Parties in the New Century." In *Parties, Elections, and the Future of Canadian Politics,* edited by Amanda Bittner and Royce Koop, 10–23. Vancouver: University of British Columbia Press.

Clarkson, Stephen, and Erick Lachapelle. 2006. "Jean Chrétien's Continental Legacy: From Commitment to Confusion." In *The Chrétien Legacy: Politics and Public Policy in Canada,* edited by Lois Harder and Steve Patten, 102–23. Montreal: McGill-Queen's University Press.

Delacourt, Susan. 2013. *Shopping for Votes: How Politicians Choose Us and We Choose Them.* Madeira Park, BC: Douglas & McIntyre.

Department of Finance. 1995. "Budget Speech." Ottawa: Queen's Printer.

Ditchburn, Jennifer. 2014. "Journalistic Pathfinding: How the Parliamentary Press Gallery Adapted to News Management under the Conservative Government of Stephen Harper." Master of Journalism thesis, Carleton University, Ottawa.

Eagles, Munroe. 1996. "The Franchise and Political Participation in Canada." In *Canadian Parties in Transition,* 2nd ed., edited by A. Brian Tanguay and Alain-G. Gagnon, 307–27. Toronto: Nelson Canada.

Eldersveld, Samuel J. 1964. *Political Parties: A Behavioral Analysis.* Chicago: Rand McNally.

Epstein, Leon D. 1975. "Political Parties." In *The Handbook of Political Science,* vol. 4, edited by Nelson W. Polsby and Fred I. Greenstein, 229–77. Lexington, MA: Addison-Wesley.

Flanagan, Tom. 2010. "Campaign Strategy: Triage and the Concentration of Resources." In *Elections,* edited by Heather MacIvor, 155–72. Toronto: Emond Montgomery Publications.

Flanagan, Tom. 2013. "Something Blue: The Harper Conservatives as Garrison Party." In *Conservatism in Canada,* edited by James Farney and David Rayside, 79–94. Toronto: University of Toronto Press.

Flanagan, Tom. 2014. *Winning Power: Canadian Campaigning in the Twenty-First Century.* Montreal: McGill-Queen's University Press.

Guest, Dennis. 1985. *The Emergence of Social Security in Canada.* 2nd ed. Vancouver: University of British Columbia Press.

Harper, Stephen, and Tom Flanagan. 1996–97. "Our Benign Dictatorship." *Next City,* Winter, 34–42.

Johnston, Richard. 2013. "Situating the Canadian Case." In *Parties, Elections, and the Future of Canadian Politics,* edited by Amanda Bittner and Royce Koop, 284–307. Vancouver: University of British Columbia Press.

Koop, Royce, and Amanda Bittner. 2013. "Parties and Elections after 2011: The Fifth Canadian Party System?" In *Parties, Elections, and the Future of Canadian Politics,* edited by Amanda Bittner and Royce Koop, 308–31. Vancouver: University of British Columbia Press.

Ladd, Everett Carll. 1990. "Like Waiting for Godot: The Uselessness of 'Realignment' for Understanding Change in Contemporary American Politics." *Polity* 22 (3): 511–25. http://dx.doi.org/10.2307/3234761

Laycock, David. 2002. *The New Right and Democracy in Canada: Understanding Reform and the Canadian Alliance.* Toronto: Oxford University Press.

LeDrew, Stephen. 2005. "Political Parties, Money, and Public Policy." *Policy Options,* October 1, 69–71.

Liberal Party of Canada. 1993. *Creating Opportunity: The Liberal Plan for Canada.* Ottawa: Author.

MacIvor, Heather. 2006. *Parameters of Power: Canada's Political Institutions.* 4th ed. Scarborough, ON: Thomson Nelson.

Marland, Alex. 2014. "Political Communication in Canada: Strategies and Tactics." In *Canadian Politics,* 6th ed., edited by James Bickerton and Alain-G. Gagnon, 309–26. Toronto: University of Toronto Press.

Morton, William. 1950. *The Progressive Party in Canada.* Toronto: University of Toronto Press.

Noel, S.J.R. 1996. "Patronage and Entourages, Action-Sets, Networks." In *Canadian Parties in Transition,* 2nd ed., edited by A. Brian Tanguay and Alain-G. Gagnon, 252–80. Toronto: Nelson Canada.

Patten, Steve. 1999. "The Reform Party's Re-imagining of the Canadian Nation." *Journal of Canadian Studies* 34 (1): 27–51.

Patten, Steve. 2006. "Jean Chrétien and a Decade of Party System Change." In *The Chrétien Legacy: Politics and Public Policy in Canada,* edited by Lois Harder and Steve Patten, 321–34. Montreal: McGill-Queen's University Press.

Patten, Steve. 2013. "The Triumph of Neoliberalism within Partisan Conservatism." In *Conservatism in Canada,* edited by James Farney and David Rayside, 59–76. Toronto: University of Toronto Press.

Patten, Steve. In press. "Databases, Microtargeting and the Permanent Campaign: A Threat to Democracy?" In *Permanent Campaigning in Canada,* edited by Anna Esselment, Thierry Giasson, and Alex Marland. Vancouver: University of British Columbia Press.

Perlin, George. 1980. *The Tory Syndrome: Leadership Politics in the Progressive Conservative Party.* Montreal: McGill-Queen's University Press.

Pinard, Maurice. 1975. *The Rise of a Third Party: A Study in Crisis Politics.* Montreal: McGill-Queen's University Press.

Preyra, Leonard. 2001. "From Conventions to Closed Primaries? New Politics and Recent Changes in National Party Leadership Selection in Canada." In *Party Politics in Canada,* 8th ed., edited by Hugh G. Thorburn and Alan Whitehorn, 443–59. Toronto: Prentice Hall.

Reid, Escott M. 2001. "The Rise of National Parties in Canada." In *Party Politics in Canada,* 8th ed., edited by Hugh G. Thorburn and Alan Whitehorn, 9–15. Toronto: Prentice Hall.

Rice, James J., and Michael J. Prince. 1993. "Lowering the Safety Net and Weakening the Bonds of Nationhood: Social Policy in the Mulroney Years." In *How Ottawa Spends: A More Democratic Canada . . .? (1993–1994),* edited by Susan D. Phillips, 381–416. Ottawa: Carleton University Press.

Smith, David. 1985. "Party Government, Representation and National Integration in Canada." In *Party Government and Regional Representation in Canada,* edited by Peter Aucoin, 1–68. Toronto: University of Toronto Press.

Stanbury, W.T. 2001. "Regulating Federal Party and Candidate Finances in a Dynamic Environment." In *Party Politics in Canada,* 8th ed., edited by Hugh G. Thorburn and Alan Whitehorn, 179–205. Toronto: Prentice Hall.

Thomas, Paul G. 2013. "Communications and Prime Ministerial Power." In *Governing: Essays in Honour of Donald J. Savoie,* edited by James Bickerton and B. Guy Peters, 53–84. Montreal: McGill-Queen's University Press.

Thorburn, Hugh G. 2001. "The Development of Political Parties in Canada." In *Party Politics in Canada,* 8th ed., edited by Hugh G. Thorburn and Alan Whitehorn, 1–8. Toronto: Prentice Hall.

Toner, Glen, and Jennifer McKee. 2014. "Harper's Partisan Wedge Politics: Bad Environment Policy and Bad Energy Policy." In *How Ottawa Spends, 2014–2015: The Harper Government—Good to Go?* edited by G. Bruce Doern and Christopher Stoney, 108–24. Montreal: McGill-Queen's University Press.

Underhill, Frank. 1999. "The Development of National Political Parties in Canada." In *Canadian Political Parties: Historical Readings,* edited by Dan Azoulay, 65–82. Toronto: Irwin Publishing.

Walchuk, Brad. 2012. "A Whole New Ballgame: The Rise of Canada's Fifth Party System." *American Review of Canadian Studies* 42 (3): 418–34. http://dx.doi.org/10.1080/02722011.2012.705867

Wearing, Joseph. 1981. *The L-Shaped Party: The Liberal Party of Canada 1958–1980.* Toronto: McGraw-Hill Ryerson.

Whitaker, Reg. 1977. *The Government Party: Organizing and Financing the Liberal Party of Canada 1930–1958.* Toronto: University of Toronto Press.

Whitaker, Reg. 2001. "Virtual Political Parties and the Decline of Democracy." *Policy Options,* June 1, 16–22.

2
Money, Politics, and the Canadian Party System

LISA YOUNG

T HE CANADIAN PARTY SYSTEM IN 2015 looks, at least on the surface, remarkably like the party system Carty (1992) coined the "third party system," which spanned the period from 1963 to 1993. After two decades of experimenting with a five-party Parliament, Canadian voters have returned to the three parties of the third party system: the Liberals, New Democrats, and (no longer Progressive) Conservatives, with the Liberals in 2015 resuming their traditional role as national governing party.

Moving beyond this superficial similarity, however, the contemporary party system differs in important ways from its twentieth-century predecessor. This chapter examines the transition from the third party system to the current day with a focus on money in politics. While recognizing that the forces that shape party systems are far more diverse and complex than election law and the source of party funds, an examination of how Canadian parties have structured the rules governing political finance, and where they get the money they require to operate, helps to illuminate some of the dynamics of party system change and helps us understand the structure of political competition. Through this lens, it appears that the parties contesting the 2015 election were different from those of the third party system in important ways, shaped by the imperative to thrive in an environment that demands populist political finance. The dynamic of the party system has also changed, marked by a polarization between the Conservative Party on the one hand and a grouping of parties, notably the Liberals and New Democrats, that define themselves in opposition to the Conservatives.

Party Organization, Party Systems, and Election Finance Law

The focus of this chapter is on the interrelationship of party organization, party systems, and the laws governing election and party finance. The term *party system* has taken on many meanings in the political science literature, but refers generally to the number of competitive parties within a political system and their competitive relations with one another. Some accounts of party systems focus solely on the number of parties (i.e., two-party, multi-party), while others include competitive dynamics (i.e., single-party dominant, multi-polar).

As Patten notes in Chapter 1, within Canadian political science there has been a focus on historical analysis and periodization of the party system, initiated in Carty's (1992) characterization of three party systems from Confederation to the early 1990s, and then Carty, Cross, and Young's (2000) argument that the 1993 election ushered in a period of transition. Political scientists have different interpretations of when the third party system ended. While Carty, Cross, and Young date the change to 1993, Patten suggests it ended in 1988. Likewise, Patten and others suggest that the fourth party system has come and gone, while I would argue that it is only just taking shape. Ultimately, it will fall to later generations of political scientists to make this determination, should they find it relevant, since they will benefit from a historical perspective that we currently lack. Regardless of these debates over periodization, there is a strong consensus that much has changed in the Canadian party system over the past 20 years or so and that we must grapple with these changes if we are to understand the dynamics of party competition in our national politics.

Party organization refers to the characteristics of individual political parties, focusing on the role and influence of various groups within the party, notably members and leaders. The most influential narrative has suggested an evolution from elite "cadre" parties, to more inclusive and internally democratic "mass parties," to hybrid "catch-all" parties that are ideologically flexible, electorally focused, and leader driven but constituted as modestly internally democratic membership organizations. The Canadian political science literature has tended to use the term *brokerage* to describe parties that would otherwise be called catch-all. Embedded in the notion of brokerage, beyond the idea of ideological flexibility and electoral focus, is the idea that national parties broker across deep cleavages, most notably between Quebec and the rest of Canada.

Party and election finance law refers to the legal rules governing who can contribute to candidates and parties, how much candidates and parties can spend, and setting out the formulas governing the transfer of money from the public treasury to parties or candidates, if any.

The most comprehensive effort to theorize the linkages between these concepts to date has been Katz and Mair's (1995) cartel party thesis. The thesis proceeded from the observation that parties in many established democracies were struggling to recruit volunteers and raise sufficient funds from private donors to mount competitive campaigns. The increasing costs associated with advertising and polling exacerbated these difficulties. In the face of these pressures, Katz and Mair observed, parties in many established democracies were turning to the state for financial support. This required collusion among the major parties, causing them to form a "cartel." For economists, a cartel is a group of producers that would normally compete but instead collude to set the price of a product to increase their own profits. For Katz and Mair, agreement among all the major political parties in a system formed a parallel system in which the parties agreed to access public funds for their own political purposes. Such an arrangement would be difficult to sustain if one of the major parties opted out and criticized the others for passing laws providing public funds to parties, suggesting that a cartel of some sort is a necessary precondition for extensive public funding of parties. Just as the companies in an economic cartel stop competing with one another, Katz and Mair suggest that parties in a cartel also stop competing as vigorously, instead sharing the spoils of power. This notion of sharing power is, of course, more compelling in the context of a multiparty system in which coalition governments are the norm. One of the key functions of the cartel, according to Katz and Mair, is to ensure the longevity of the parties that compose it. To preserve its members, the cartel should establish rules for election finance that constitute barriers to entry for new parties, making it difficult for them to displace the cartel members.

Parties in these cartels, no longer dependent on members for voluntary labour or donations, moved closer to the state, weakening their ties to civil society. Ultimately, these weaker ties to civil society reshaped parties' organizational form. This new party form, the "cartel party," was characterized by professionalization with a limited role for party members, volunteers, and donors since public funds allow the party to replace these voluntary contributions of time and money.

In essence, Katz and Mair suggest that electoral finance rules shape both the party system and party organization. For them, the more salient relationship is between regulations and party organization, as they are focused on proposing the emergence of a new type of party form. Party system change is a mechanism, in this view. The formation of the cartel, characterized as it is by collusion among the parties, must occur to spawn other changes: the turn to the state results in public funding, which in turn exacerbates parties' distance from civil society.

In this chapter, the focus is on both party organization and the interplay between election finance and party system dynamics. It will trace changes to election finance law from the 1970s to the present, asking whether there is evidence of the formation of a cartelized party *system* in Canada. To say that the party system is cartelized would require both evidence of collusion (cooperation among parties to turn to public funds to contest elections and run regular operations) as well as some decline in competitiveness or an increase in willingness to cooperate on critical issues. This latter criterion is less rigorous than that proposed by Katz and Mair, who look for evidence of sharing power. In the context of a Westminster system with a single-member plurality electoral system this is highly unlikely and too rigorous a test. Finally, cartels imply a desire to protect the interests of their members by creating barriers to the emergence of competitors. This chapter argues that the third party system displayed some, but not all, characteristics of a cartel, but that the post-1993 system does not.

Party Finance in the Third Party System

Carty's third party system, which stretched from 1963 to 1993 (although there is no consensus around these dates, as illustrated by Patten's chapter in this volume), was characterized by "pan-Canadian politics" as political parties sought to "define a national agenda and to mobilize Canadians, as individual participating citizens, in support of their competing visions for the country" (Carty, Cross, and Young 2000, 21). Although the three major parties of the third party system—the Liberals, Progressive Conservatives, and New Democrats—differed on many questions of public policy, they shared a commitment to pan-Canadian (as distinct from regionalist) politics and generally agreed on the basic "rules of the game" for politics. Notably, the three parties shared a belief that national politics should be a contest among national political parties, an idea that embodied the pan-Canadian consensus during this period. Toward this end, the parties passed and defended legislation that required a registered political party to run candidates in at least 50 electoral districts. This rule remained in place until it was struck down by the Supreme Court in 2003. In its decision in *Figueroa v. Canada,* the Supreme Court rejected the government's argument that the benefits of registered party status—which included access to reimbursement of election expenses, ability to put the party's name on the ballot by the candidate's name, and ability to issue tax receipts to contributors—should be limited to parties that could nominate at least 50 candidates.

The major parties' consensus regarding how politics should operate included a remarkable degree of agreement around how money should—and should not—be regulated in political competition. The first element of consensus held that these rules should be negotiated among and agreed on by the major parties. The 1964 Committee on Election Expenses (the Barbeau Committee) included representation from the three major parties (Aucoin 1993). Its recommendations were not implemented until 1974, but when they were it was with the support of all three major parties. Reforms to the Canada Elections Act in 1983, including limits on advocacy group expenditures, relaxing spending limits, and changing reimbursement formulas, were drafted by an ad hoc committee of representatives from the three parties advising the chief electoral officer (CEO) at the time, and the reforms received multiparty support in Parliament (see Young 1998, 348). Faced with controversy over expenditures by businesses and advocacy organizations in the 1988 election, and calls from the CEO to amend the legislation, the Mulroney government appointed a Royal Commission on Electoral Reform and Party Financing in 1989, comprising commissioners representing the three major parties. It would be naive to suggest that parties did not act in self-interested ways through this period. However, their established practices of seeking consensus and turning to external experts for advice—or at least legitimization—marks an approach based on an understanding that election law has a status different than other policy domains because it shapes political competition in future elections.

A product of the cross-partisan consensus on the approach to political finance during this period was the development of strong institutions of electoral administration to underpin and enforce the regulatory regime. The office of the CEO, an officer of Parliament, is a position that was first created in 1920. As the regulation of elections and electoral finance became more extensive, the role of the CEO expanded significantly. From the 1970s until 2006, the role grew steadily, with the addition of enforcement of political finance, creation and maintenance of the permanent voters' list, and by the late 1990s an emerging role in addressing declines in voter turnout (Kingsley 2004). Through the 1970s and 1980s, the major political parties exercised considerable influence over the CEO through the mechanism of an ad hoc committee with representatives from all the major parties, which influenced the outcome of regulatory decisions related to political finance. Jean-Pierre Kingsley, appointed to the role in 1990, put an end to this committee, replacing it with an advisory group with representation from the major parties (Kingsley 2004). This marked the emergence of the role of the CEO as a strong, autonomous, nonpartisan actor in the administration of Canadian elections and election finance, garnering international recognition (Pastor 2004).

One might argue that the party finance regime put in place during the third party system constituted what Katz and Mair would describe as a cartelized party system. Heather MacIvor (1996) argued that between the 1960s and 1993 the established parties used their control of the House of Commons to exclude or impede new or smaller parties, and that parties used state subsidies in their own self-interest. The rule requiring that a party run 50 candidates to qualify for registration, for example, can be seen as a barrier to entry constructed by the major parties to make it more difficult for new or regionally based parties to emerge. Other accounts (Young 1998) held that the collusion focused less on the provision of state subsidies and more on an agreement among the parties to halt the upward spiral of election spending by legislating caps on election expenditures. While acknowledging that there were elements of cartel-like behaviour among the three parties during this period, I argue that the parties "used their 'cartel' power to lessen the stringency of the rules they set for themselves, not to draw more heavily on the state" (Young 1998, 350).

During the third party system, the regulation of political finance concentrated on limiting campaign spending by both candidates and national parties through legislated spending limits. Public funds were provided both in the form of reimbursement of a substantial proportion of election expenses plus an indirect subsidy through the political contribution tax credit. By limiting expenditures and partially subsidizing the cost of mounting election campaigns, the regulatory regime in place through most of the third party system weakened demand for money in politics but did not eliminate it.

In the absence of limits on either the size or source of contributions to parties or candidates, parties tended to rely on sizable contributions from corporate or union donors. The two "brokerage" parties that rotated in and out of office (the Liberals and Progressive Conservatives) relied predominantly on corporate donations, while the NDP was financed through contributions from trade unions, although to a lesser extent. For instance, in 1993 59 per cent of the funds raised by the Progressive Conservative Party were from corporations, as were 56 per cent of the dollars raised by the Liberal Party. The NDP was less reliant on unions, with 35 per cent of its dollars coming from that source (Elections Canada 2015). If we accept the underlying assumption of Katz and Mair's model—that parties are responsive to their funders—then Canadian parties during the third party system were closer to the state and to the corporate and union sectors than to the electorate.

Cooperation among parties in the third party system extended beyond election finance. Certainly by the end of the third party system there is evidence of parties cooperating on key policy issues, at least in the domain of national unity. All three of the national parties came together to support the Charlottetown Accord in 1992, a constitutional agreement patched together in the aftermath of the collapse of the Meech Lake Accord in 1990. The major parties combined forces to staff the "Yes" committee in a national referendum on the Charlottetown Accord, perhaps the clearest example of cooperation among the national parties in defence of the pan-Canadian vision of the country. The defeat of the "Yes" committee in the referendum spoke to the growing gulf between the major parties and the Canadian electorate in the early 1990s, culminating in the 1993 election, in which the Progressive Conservative Party was decimated and two new regionally based "outsider" parties (the Bloc Québécois and the Reform Party) shattered the pan-Canadian consensus and the party system that supported it. Much as the established parties had used their place in Parliament to erect legislative and financial barriers to entry to new parties, the groundswell of popular support for the new parties overcame them and the third party system came to an abrupt end.

Party Finance in the Contemporary Party System

Regardless of whether one argues that the period from 1993 to the present represents two party systems (as Patten asserts in Chapter 1) or that these years mark the transition into a new fourth party system, it is evident that the story of party system change is intertwined with changes to the regulatory regime governing political finance. A consistent element of this story has been the role of the Conservative Party, and its Reform/Canadian Alliance predecessors, as the "cartel buster." The Reform Party burst onto the national scene in 1993, promising to change how politics is done in Canada. While some elements of the approach taken by the contemporary Conservative Party might be foreign to the early Reformers, several elements remain constant, most notably a rejection of established consensus around political finance and a commitment to populism. It is this consistent role of the Conservatives as drivers of change, bolstered by their self-perception as outsiders (even after a decade in government), that supports my notion that we still find ourselves in the fourth party system.

While the third party system was characterized by a consensus among parties around a pan-Canadian vision, no such consensus can be found in the contemporary party system. The rise of regional parties (the Reform and the Bloc) shattered the former system, and although the regional parties have either waned or morphed into more national parties, the pan-Canadian consensus has not reappeared. Certainly, the Liberal Party continues to articulate echoes of pan-Canadianism and the NDP articulates a more robust role for the national government. But the political movement that has thus far dominated and driven change in the fourth party system—the Reform/Alliance/Conservative Party—has demonstrated that Canada can be governed by a party with little or no representation from Quebec (Bakvis 2014, 63) and has worked to downplay the role of the national government in some aspects of Canadian politics, notably the area of social policy, where the federal government tended to be very active throughout the third party system.

Pan-Canadianism is not the only element of consensus that collapsed with the end of the third party system. The three major parties' consensus on how the rules governing political finance should be determined and on what those rules should be is another relic. Replacing this consensus, the parties in Parliament since 1993 have disagreed profoundly on the appropriate role of the state in funding political parties and the rules governing who can contribute to parties and candidates. As a result, interpartisan conflicts over political finance have been intertwined with the story of the evolving Canadian party system throughout much of this period. Arguably, the Liberal Party let the genie out of the bottle with its reforms to the Canada Elections Act in 2004, but it has been the Conservative Party that has driven more recent legislative changes that have profoundly reshaped the partisan political landscape. In the realm of election finance, this has resulted in a bipolar array of parties, with the Conservatives at one pole and a "syndicate" of the Liberals, New Democrats, the Bloc, and Greens on the other (Jansen and Young 2011).

Act 1: Toward State-Financed Parties

For the first decade after the 1993 election, the regulation of political finance received relatively little attention. The Liberal Party, which appeared poised to continue its domination of Canadian politics through the Chrétien years and beyond, made no significant changes to the regulatory regime governing political finance, and there was relatively little discussion of issues related to political finance in the public realm during this period. Then, in 2003, while his government was beset with scandals, Jean Chrétien introduced an "ethics package" that included legislation making significant changes to political finance (Young and Jansen 2011, 4). This legislation banned contributions from corporations and unions, allowing only individuals to contribute to parties and candidates, albeit at a relatively high level ($5,000). To replace the lost income, registered political parties that had won at least 2 per cent of the vote nationally, or 5 per cent in the districts where the party ran candidates, would be paid a quarterly allowance, its amount calculated by the number of votes the party had won during the most recent election. The legislation was calibrated to ensure that the Liberal Party would replace its lost corporate income with state funds (Clark 2003, cited in Young and Jansen 2011, 9). In effect, this legislation marked an intention on the part of the Liberal Party to turn from corporate donors to the state as the primary financial backer for national political parties.

Unlike earlier reforms, this measure did not reflect any effort to develop consensus among the major political parties. Instead, it was an initiative from the Prime Minister's Office and was to be implemented even over objections from within Prime Minister Chrétien's own party (Stewart 2005). For the Bloc Québécois, which had a limited fundraising base, the legislation was a godsend. The New Democrats also agreed with it. Both the Progressive Conservatives and the Canadian Alliance (which later merged to form the Conservative Party) opposed the legislation based on objections to the extensive state funding. Canadian Alliance leader Stephen Harper articulated this in Parliament: "The worst idea in the legislation is new direct stipends to parties themselves based on previous electoral performance. In this case not only would parties be isolated from the feelings they may have from their own former supporters, but frankly even people who never supported them would be asked to support the party" (Hansard, 11 February 2003).

Despite the lack of consensus, the Liberal government pressed ahead with these reforms, comfortable in the assumption that the Liberal Party would continue to benefit from the largest share of the vote and continue to govern. The prospect that another party might turn the legislation to its advantage by embarking on ambitious fundraising from individuals did not appear to concern the party's leadership at the time.

Not long after this legislation was passed, however, the Canadian Alliance and Progressive Conservative parties merged, bringing together the direct-mail fundraising expertise of the PCs with the populist base and sensibility of the Alliance. This merger created a fundraising juggernaut that quickly established an active and successful fundraising program for the newly formed Conservative Party.

One of the peculiarities of the quarterly allowance, during the relatively brief period it was in place, was the effect it had on the party system. Figure 2.1 shows the source of income, by party, in 2010 and 2014, both nonelection years. In 2010, the allowance composed just over one-third of the revenue of the Conservative Party, as compared to just under half the revenue for the Liberal Party, just over half for the New Democrats and Greens, and fully three-quarters for the Bloc Québécois. The public funds bolstered the electoral strength of the Bloc, which was able to effectively contest federal elections in Quebec without engaging in any substantial fundraising efforts. The Green Party won enough votes in the 2004 election to benefit from the quarterly allowance and was able to parlay this new source of income into a stronger electoral presence and a more robust fundraising operation (Jansen and Young 2011, 95).

Act 2: Populist Political Finance

Once elected with a minority government in 2006, the Conservative Party quickly moved to pass its Federal Accountability Act, which reduced the

Figure 2.1 Party Revenues, 2010 and 2014

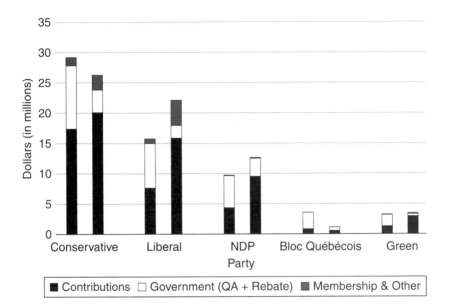

maximum amount an individual could contribute to a political entity from $5,000 to $1,000. This reform played to the Conservatives' strength in soliciting relatively small contributions from individuals and harmed the Liberals, who had continued to emphasize larger contributions from a relatively small number of elite donors as the core of their fundraising strategy. The Conservatives continued their aggressive fundraising efforts and, as the party that had won the most votes in the 2006 election, also benefited from receiving the largest state subsidy.

Driven by its objection to the idea of per-vote state funding, and secure in the Conservative Party's significant advantage in fundraising from individuals, the Harper government in 2008 moved to abruptly end the per-vote quarterly allowance. Elected with a minority in 2008, the Conservatives introduced legislation addressing the international financial crisis that had occurred during the 2008 campaign. Included in this legislation, most of which focused on stimulating the economy, was a measure to immediately eliminate the quarterly allowance. This move would have been catastrophic for the other parties, all of which were heavily reliant on public funds, particularly given the prospect of needing to fight another election at any time. They banded together in an attempt to defeat the minority Harper government in the House of Commons and govern with a Liberal–NDP coalition that would be supported by the Bloc Québécois. Writing about this cooperation among the parties, Jansen and Young (2011) argued that these parties formed a *syndicate*—a term referring to a group of companies cooperating to try to control a market. A syndicate is less comprehensive than a cartel, both in the inclusion of players and in the more limited ambition of the group.

Ultimately, Harper foiled this plan by asking the governor general to prorogue Parliament, and he withdrew the idea of eliminating the quarterly allowance. Public reaction to the idea of a coalition government, particularly one supported by the Bloc, was generally negative and was raised by the Conservatives as a concern in the 2011 election, which resulted in a Conservative majority government.

Once elected with its majority, the Harper government again moved to eliminate the quarterly allowance, this time by gradually phasing it out. The final instalment of the allowance was paid in April 2015, making the 2015 election the last contest between predominantly state-funded parties. Unless new legislation is brought in, Canadian political parties will be wholly reliant on contributions from individual donors, plus partial reimbursement of campaign expenses, from the 2015 election on. Figure 2.1 illustrates the impact of the gradual elimination of the quarterly allowance on party revenue. The Liberals, New Democrats, and Greens all increased their fundraising revenues substantially while the amount of the allowance declined. As a result these parties were already substantially less reliant on public money by 2014, with only the Bloc remaining reliant on government dollars for most of its income.

In 2014 the Conservatives introduced legislation—the Fair Elections Act—that included a provision to exempt from spending limits any fundraising efforts involving an individual who had donated at least $20 to a party over the previous five years. This provision proved controversial, as observers suggested that it would be difficult to enforce and would effectively increase the spending cap for parties. Faced with controversy on this and several other provisions of the legislation, the government withdrew it and amended its bill. It did, however, leave in a provision that would increase the maximum allowable expenditures by parties and candidates when election campaigns stretched longer than the legislated minimum of 36 days. When Prime Minister Harper called the 2015 federal election, scheduled by law to fall on October 19, several weeks early, he stretched the official campaign period to 78 days. As a result, the maximum amount parties and candidates could spend doubled from what would have been the case for a 36-day campaign, and all expenditures made during that period became eligible for partial reimbursement (at a rate of 50 per cent for parties and 60 per cent for candidates).

Money and Politics in the Contemporary Party System

From 2003 to the present, party and election finance has been a controversial policy issue in national politics. Amendments to the Canada Elections Act have driven change in both party organization and the party system. In both respects, the contrasts to the patterns of the third party system are noteworthy.

The first striking contrast lies in the collapse of the norm that significant changes to the rules governing political finance should be legitimized through consultation with experts and efforts to achieve consensus among major parties. Instead, political finance reform in the emerging party system has been characterized by independent action by parties. The Liberal Party unleashed this by proceeding with the implementation of the quarterly allowance over the objection of the right-of-centre parties, and the Conservatives have continued by pursuing a series of reforms over the objections of their competitors. Of all the major legislative changes discussed above, only the 2006 Federal Accountability Act was supported by all parties. None of the changes were preceded by consultations of any kind, whether with experts or the public.

With the breakdown of the consensus, the nonpartisan administration of elections has also come under pressure. Throughout their time in government, the Harper Conservatives had an uneasy relationship with the office of the chief electoral officer. In the 2006 election, the Conservatives found creative means to circumvent the spending limits. In 2006, the "in and out" scheme saw the party transferring money to candidates to pool together to purchase ads, thereby effectively circumventing the spending limit. While maintaining that the scheme did not circumvent the law as they interpreted it, the Conservatives eventually admitted to exceeding the spending limit and filing an inaccurate election return and paid fines for the violation (Postmedia News 2012). Following both the 2008 and 2011 elections, the CEO initiated investigations into several Conservative candidates, including one who was convicted of spending over the authorized limit in 2008.

The Harper government's uneasy relationship with Elections Canada may have influenced the content of the initial version of the Fair Elections Act of 2014, which included measures that would prevent the CEO from communicating with the public except to indicate where and when to vote. Under this legislation, the CEO would have been prevented from advertising to encourage Canadian voters or undertaking any research or surveys (Mas 2014). In the face of considerable criticism, including from the CEO, the government amended the Bill. Nonetheless, it demonstrated a deliberate effort to curtail the role of the CEO.

A second striking contrast is the emergence of the *permanent campaign* in Canadian politics. The influx of cash to parties—both public dollars via the quarterly allowance and then private dollars raised by the parties—has facilitated the emergence of a permanent campaign in Canadian federal politics, in which parties engage in election-oriented behaviour such as advertising and polling both during and between elections. This phenomenon is not unique to Canada, nor is it new. It was first identified in the United States in the late 1970s. However, a series of factors have combined to amplify the appearance of a permanent campaign in Canadian politics over the past two decades. The series of minority governments from 2004 to 2011 meant that parties had to be prepared to fight frequent elections, thereby focusing party leaders' attention on electoral strategies and tactics and keeping the parties on an election-ready footing at all times. The public funding that was in place throughout this period left the parties better off financially than they would otherwise have been and accelerated the permanent campaign. This has been particularly evident for the Conservative Party, which was able to supplement its public funding with significant income from donors. Flanagan (2012) observes that from 2004 on, the Conservative Party has engaged in extensive campaign-style advertising outside the election period. The other major parties have followed suit, but with less well-resourced efforts. Flanagan argues convincingly that the regulatory regime governing political finance from 2004 to 2015 resulted in a significant influx of money to the parties that fuelled their advertising and other campaign efforts between elections.

Finally, we have entered into a period of "popular finance" of Canadian political parties. Unless the Liberal Party reverses the decision to cut the quarterly allowance, Canadian parties will be funded by a combination of state funds, paid primarily either through reimbursements of election expenses and subsidies to donors through the political contribution tax credit (PCTC), and relatively small donations from individuals. The form of the public funds does little to insulate parties from their donors—the PCTC is valuable only for parties that can effectively solicit contributions from individuals, and the reimbursement of campaign expenses is tied to the ability to raise and borrow funds. This regulatory regime favours parties with a populist base willing to fund the party. It also encourages parties to structure their appeals with the party's donor base in mind. Parties in such a system are presumably responsive to supporters who are or who might be donors. In such a system, we would expect to see some polarization as parties appeal to donors motivated by ideological appeals.

We know relatively little about what motivates donors to Canadian political parties. By analyzing aggregate data (total donations for parties in a census district and census data regarding household income), Carmichael and Howe (2014) found that donors are more likely to live in neighbourhoods with higher median household income. This tells us little about donors' motivations or behaviour, which will become an increasingly important question for political scientists in an era of populist political finance.

The ability of parties to raise money from individuals will be all the more important to the extent that demand for money in politics increases. The Conservative Party's recent efforts to increase the spending limit for election campaigns by extending the writ period signals a frustration with these limits, at least from that party. To the extent that these limits are increased or eliminated altogether, demand for money in politics would increase, and the imperative to raise money through populist political finance will be all the stronger.

Conclusion

The three parties that animate Canadian politics—the Conservatives, Liberals, and New Democrats—appear superficially to be the parties that competed during the third party system. Those late twentieth-century parties, however, converged in their understanding of the norms of democratic competition and were relatively content to rely on businesses or unions to fund their activities with significant supplementation from the state. The parties competing in 2015 have been moulded by a 20-year period of relative political instability, during which the Reform Party and its successors have reshaped Canadian politics.

At the level of the party system, there is no evidence of a cartel of political parties. The parties have been polarized in their views of the appropriate role of the state in funding political activity, with the Conservatives rejecting a role for the state in providing direct support and the other parties supporting the idea (although with no stated intention to act on this belief). The party system has been characterized by intense competition, played out through a "permanent campaign" in which parties engage in election-style activities both between and during elections. It remains to be seen whether the permanent campaign will persist beyond 2015 and whether a consensus will emerge among the parties regarding reliance on individual contributions to fund partisan activity.

At the level of party organization we see few of the characteristics of "cartelized" parties. Parties must seek the support of civil society as they seek out the donors that will fund the perpetual campaign. Party members play a limited role, as is the case for the cartel party, but their role is usurped not by the state but by donors (who may or may not hold party memberships) and supporters who might be converted into donors.

Election finance has not been the sole driver of change between the third and current party systems, but it has played a role both in structuring the third party system and in the construction of the fourth. Changes in the source of financial support for parties have resulted in an evolution of those parties, loosening their ties to business and union backers and moving them closer to their donor base. The state remains an important source of funds, but one that is effective only for those parties that can effectively mobilize individuals to provide financial support.

Suggested Readings

Carty, R. Kenneth. 1992. "Three Canadian Party Systems." In *Canadian Political Party Systems, 1978–1984,* edited by R. Kenneth Carty, 563–86. Peterborough, ON: Broadview Press.

Jansen, Harold J., and Lisa Young. 2011. "Cartels, Syndicates, and Coalitions: Canada's Political Parties after the 2004 Reforms." In *Money, Politics, and Democracy: Canada's Party Finance Reforms,* edited by Lisa Young and Harold J. Jansen, 82–104. Vancouver: University of British Columbia Press.

Katz, Richard, and Peter Mair. 1995. "Changing Models of Party Organization and Party Democracy: The Emergence of the Cartel Party." *Party Politics* 1 (1): 5–28. http://dx.doi.org/10.1177/1354068895001001001

References

Aucoin, Peter. 1993. "The Politics of Electoral Reform." *Canadian Parliamentary Review* 7: 7–13.

Bakvis, Herman. 2014. "Canada: A Crisis in Regional Representation?" *Tocqueville Review* 35 (2): 51–77. http://dx.doi.org/10.1353/toc.2014.0013

Carmichael, Brianna, and Paul Howe. 2014. "Political Donations and Democratic Equality in Canada." *Canadian Parliamentary Review* 37(1):16–20. Academic OneFile.

Carty, R. Kenneth. 1992. "Three Canadian Party Systems." In *Canadian Political Party Systems, 1978–1984,* edited by R. Kenneth Carty, 563–86. Peterborough, ON: Broadview Press.

Carty, R. Kenneth, William Cross, and Lisa Young. 2000. *Rebuilding Canadian Party Politics.* Vancouver: University of British Columbia Press.

Elections Canada. 2015. http://www.elections.ca/ecFiscals/1993/table03_e.html. Accessed July 7.

Figueroa v. Canada (Attorney General) [2003] 1 S.C.R. 912, 2003 SCC 37.

Flanagan, Tom. 2012. "Political Communication and the 'Permanent Campaign.'" In *How Canadians Communicate IV: Media and Politics,* edited by David Taras and Christopher Waddell, 129–48. Athabasca, AB: Athabasca University Press.

Jansen, Harold J., and Lisa Young. 2011. "Cartels, Syndicates, and Coalitions: Canada's Political Parties after the 2004 Reforms." In *Money, Politics, and Democracy: Canada's Party Finance Reforms,* edited by Lisa Young and Harold J. Jansen, 82–104. Vancouver: University of British Columbia Press.

Katz, Richard, and Peter Mair. 1995. "Changing Models of Party Organization and Party Democracy: The Emergence of the Cartel Party." *Party Politics* 1 (1): 5–28. http://dx.doi.org/10.1177/1354068895001001001

Kingsley, Jean-Pierre. 2004. "The Administration of Canada's Independent, Non-Partisan Approach." *Election Law Journal* 3 (3): 406–11. http://dx.doi.org/10.1089/1533129041492268

MacIvor, Heather. 1996. "Do Canadian Political Parties Form a Cartel?" *Canadian Journal of Political Science* 29 (2): 317–34. http://dx.doi.org/10.1017/S0008423900007733

Mas, C. Susana. 2014. "Election Reform Bill an Affront to Democracy, Marc Mayrand Says." *CBC News,* February 8. http://www.cbc.ca/news/politics/election-reform-bill-an-affront-to-democracy-marc-mayrand-says-1.2527635

Pastor, Robert A. 2004. "Improving the US Electoral System: Lessons from Canada and Mexico." *Election Law Journal* 3 (3): 584–93. http://dx.doi.org/10.1089/153312904323216186

Postmedia News. 2012. "Conservatives Drop Appeal of 'In-and-Out' Ruling." *National Post,* March 6. http://news.nationalpost.com/news/canada/conservatives-drop-appeal-of-in-and-out-ruling

Stewart, Ian. 2005. "Bill C-24: Replacing the Market with the State?" *Electoral Insight.* January. http://www.elections.ca/res/eim/article_search/article.asp?id=127&lang=e&frmPageSize=

Young, Lisa. 1998. "Party, State and Political Competition in Canada: The Cartel Model Reconsidered." *Canadian Journal of Political Science* 31 (2): 339–58. http://dx.doi.org/10.1017/S000842390001982X

Young, Lisa, and Harold J. Jansen. 2011. "Reforming Party and Election Finance in Canada." In *Money, Politics, and Democracy: Canada's Party Finance Reforms,* edited by Lisa Young and Harold J. Jansen, 1–18. Vancouver: University of British Columbia Press.

3

Parties and Regions: Representation and Resistance

JAMES BICKERTON

THE REGIONALIZATION OF CANADIAN POLITICS associated with the changes wrought by the 1993 federal election results—changes that were reflected in several subsequent elections—confirmed the profound influence of region on Canadian politics and on the Canadian party system. Many voters in these elections turned their backs on pan-Canadian parties that had pursued national integration through the construction of grand coalitions spanning Canada's regional, linguistic, and class divides. In effect, they were rejecting that particular mode of interparty competition and political representation that Carty, Johnston, and others have referred to as the third party system (see Bickerton, Gagnon, and Smith 1999; Carty 1988; Johnston 1992).

What this interpretation suggests is that the organizational and ideological character, voter bases, electoral fortunes, and competitive dynamics of the party system can only be understood as components of a broader political system. Successive party systems in Canada have been demarcated as historical epochs during which a competitive equilibrium has been attained, wherein the competing parties, voter alignments, and the overall pattern of competition and cooperation is stable and predictable. Each of these historical party systems, however, was subjected to tensions and forces that intensified from time to time, sometimes leading to the complete breakdown of the party system and its replacement by a new one featuring a different array of parties, ideologies, voter alignments, and organizational characteristics. The upshot was a new partisan dynamic or competitive logic that structured electoral and political competition between all parties within the system—in short, a new party system.

From this perspective, a fourth party system emerged in Canada after 1993, one that featured two new regional parties and the displacement of one of the country's traditional national parties. What were the characteristics that differentiated this new party system? Most obviously regional fragmentation had replaced national integration as the predominant motif of political representation. This development was widely interpreted as a kind of party system failure precipitated by the crisis of a particular type of party (the national brokerage party) and hegemonic discourse (centrist, welfarist, bilingual, multicultural, pan-Canadianism). This type of party and political discourse, which anchored a broad national consensus that had persisted for decades, formed the foundations of the third party system.

Of course, this assessment of what happened in 1993 downplays the degree to which region and regionalism had always been an important factor in Canadian party politics. While the third party system may appear to have been a "nationalized" one, that system too was anchored in a regionalized language of politics, with party strategies, support bases, and policy orientations shaped by regional identities and interests. To a not inconsiderable extent, then, parties in the third party system remained tethered to the regionalized politics they inherited and in turn perpetuated, either unwilling or simply unable to escape its particular competitive logic. (For a discussion of party system continuity and change, see Mair 1997.)

It should be noted at this point that the extent of the collapse of the national brokerage party model in 1993 was far from complete. Although it is certainly true to say that its "easy hegemony" was "cracked" (Carty, Cross, and Young 2000–01, 25), it appears to have been overlaid rather than completely superseded by new types of parties and ideologies. Still, there is no denying that the relationship between parties and regions was fundamentally altered by the shock of two new regionally dominant parties (the Bloc Québécois and Reform Party) and the sharply reduced capacity of the traditional parties to represent regional interests and identities, and therefore any legitimacy they might claim to be truly national. All parties had been reduced to being regional ones, though not necessarily regional in the same way. Indeed, in contrast to the third party system, the main antagonists in the fourth harboured distinctly different national visions and aspirations. National consensus had been replaced by political dissensus.

Regionalization of the Party System

Canada has long been something of an exception among comparable political systems in terms of its propensity to support "third parties" (see Bélanger, Chapter 10, in this volume). Although only two parties have ever formed the government in Canada (Liberal and Conservative, or some variant thereof), the party system since 1921 has included three to five parties with elected Members of Parliament (MPs). Most of the smaller parties have had distinct regional bases of support, even those presenting themselves as national alternatives with candidates in all regions. Others have had no such pretensions beyond their narrow regional appeal.[1]

Various explanations have been offered for this characteristic of the Canadian party system. Some have been case or situation specific, such as C.B. Macpherson's (1962) interpretation of Alberta's unusual "quasi-party" tradition, the origins of which, he argued in the 1950s, lay in its neocolonial relationship with Eastern Canada and its homogeneous agrarian class structure. Other perspectives on third-party formation have been more generally applicable, such as Maurice Pinard's (1975) theory of minor-party formation that identifies two factors that are structurally conducive to third-party formation: sustained one-party dominance joined with conditions of societal strain that discredits both the long-governing party as well as the traditional alternative. For their part, Gagnon and Tanguay (1996) cite a more general composite factor at work in third-party formation and success: the "nonresponsiveness" of the national party system to particular regional interests and concerns.

The concept of nonresponsiveness in this context suggests a kind of systemic failure of the brokerage role played by Canada's national parties. At least one scholar has directly faulted the parties themselves for this shortcoming (D.E. Smith 1985), but others have targeted the interaction of the party system with other institutions in the political system: the executive dominance and strict party discipline typical of Westminster-style parliamentary democracy, the inadequacies of the Canadian Senate as a forum for regional representation, the perverse workings of the first-past-the-post electoral system, and Canada's highly decentralized form of federalism.

Canada's parliamentary system has been widely criticized for its democratic failings. The biggest knock against it is the dominant position assumed by the political executive, and more particularly the prime minister. To some critics, the concentration of power in the hands of the prime minister, the doctrine of cabinet and caucus secrecy, and the strict enforcement of party discipline effectively turn elected members of the House of Commons into "trained seals" rather than true representatives of their constituents (Simpson 2001). Relatively powerless and rigidly bound by party discipline, MPs are ill-suited to the task of effective regional representation. Further, the federal cabinet—once a primary venue for regional accommodation, and still constructed to give every region an appropriate share of ministerial posts—is a shadow of its former self as ministerial autonomy and power has faded relative to the prime minister and the central agencies that provide him or her with information and advice (Bakvis 2000–01; Savoie 1999).

The poor design of the House of Commons for regional representation is not balanced by Canada's other chamber of Parliament. Almost alone among comparable federal states—witness the substantive role of senates in the United States, Australia, and Germany—the Canadian Senate has never been an effective forum for regional representation within the national Parliament (Sayers 2002). As prime ministerial appointees, its members have neither the democratic legitimacy nor the personal inclination to act as articulators and defenders of regional interests within the legislative process. Though the bearer of significant constitutional powers, popular and scholarly opinion holds that Canada's Senate has always been a rather dysfunctional and largely irrelevant institution. To make matters worse, spending and corruption scandals have swept away whatever residual respect and support it could claim (Collenette 2014; Geddes 2013). With the Senate seemingly reduced to a diseased appendix within the nation's body politic (and a constitutionally inoperable one at that), it is the ill-suited House of Commons that continues to bear the full burden of regional representation within Parliament (Bickerton 2007; Sayers 2002; Smiley and Watts 1986).

A similarly long-standing vein of criticism has been levelled at the electoral system, which distorts regional interests and identities by frequently misrepresenting regional voter preferences within Parliament. It does this by overrepresenting the strongest parties in regions (the "winners") and underrepresenting weaker ones (the "losers"), often out of all proportion to the actual levels of voter support enjoyed by each party. Minor parties with regional bases of support are rewarded, while minor parties with diffuse national support are punished. Parties find themselves bereft of seats in some regions and oversupplied in others. Regions poorly represented within the caucuses of particular parties are more likely to become alienated from those parties and less likely to vote for them in the future, creating a self-perpetuating cycle of regionalized party politics (Cairns 1968; Gibbins 2005). The high degree of regionalization encouraged by the electoral system is also a factor in the sustained downturn in voter participation. Regionalization—whereby particular parties dominate whole regions—reduces political competitiveness in many districts, which over time suppresses voter turnout as some voters tire of the futility of casting a ballot in elections that have a forgone conclusion.

Finally, Canada's form of federalism is a constitutional arrangement that turns provinces into powerful subnational governments and the dominant "voice of region" in Canadian politics. As highly autonomous political arenas with their own discrete party systems, provinces can become regional platforms capable of sustaining parties at the federal level, especially if those parties (or affiliated versions thereof) have been successful in capturing power at the provincial level (Cairns 1977; Simeon 1975). There can be no question that the impact of federalism on party organization and behaviour has been far-reaching. Several parties have existed primarily or exclusively at only one level, creating gaps and discontinuities between federal and provincial party systems (Johnston 2010).[2] Parties at each level have evolved to be separate and distinct, even if they share a party label; indeed, federal and provincial parties of the same name can be quite hostile toward each other.[3]

This lack of national integration reduces the capacity of the party system to secure political stability through the intraparty accommodation of diverse regional interests, a vital role performed by party systems in most other federations (Bickerton 2007; Tanguay 2003).

While the regionalized character of the party system has tended to exacerbate regional conflict and widen regional divisions, regional parties of protest should nonetheless be given their due. It can be argued that their resilience and surprising success historically has been important for the vibrancy of Canadian democracy. For instance, they have been key sources of both policy and organizational innovation. The traditional mainstream parties have been poor performers when it comes to policy development and innovation, traditionally relying on government-appointed royal commissions to advise them (Bradford 1999). Regional parties, on the other hand, have brought radical proposals for change to the table, and when they gain power at the provincial level they have often conducted "policy experiments" as innovators of new policies and programs (Thorburn 1991).[4]

Regional parties have also been innovators in terms of party organization, fundraising techniques, and election campaign tactics and have done so in ways that have internally democratized parties and extended their popular reach. Such changes have a "contagion effect" on others in the party system who attempt to emulate and counter the introduction of any successful innovation by a competitor (Duverger 1951). The effective use of radio by the populist Social Credit, the class-based appeal of the socialist CCF, the affirmative action initiatives of the NDP, the leader selection process introduced by the Parti Québécois, and the new fundraising techniques employed by the Reform Party are all examples of innovations introduced by regional parties in Canada (Bickerton, Gagnon, and Smith 1999; Cross 2004). Finally, regional parties have acted as a safety valve for Canadian democracy—an institutional outlet for channelling voter frustration, anger, or disillusionment into the electoral arena. And once part of the "national conversation" themselves, regional parties have tended to absorb, contain, and moderate the more radical or extreme elements within their own support base (Gagnon and Tanguay 1996).

This interactive cycle of third-party insurgency followed by systemic response provides part of the explanation for the findings of Richard Johnston, who argues that the rise of regional parties in 1993 is consistent with the unfolding of a recurring cycle of protest in Canadian history. This happens when protest-party success results in regional fragmentation, followed by gradual reconsolidation and "renationalization" of the party system. This is not an unchanging loop, however. Johnston's findings indicate that reconsolidation of the party system occurs at a higher level of fragmentation than existed before the spasm of regional protest, which translates into a diminishing capacity over time to perform the function of securing national political integration (Johnston 2005).

Regionalism: Three Modes of Representation and Resistance

In Michael Keating's analysis of the political economy of regionalism, he defines three forms of regionalism that coexist within many countries (Keating 1997). These forms of regionalism can be adapted for the purpose of describing modes of regional representation and resistance within Canada's national party system. So, while *integrative regionalism* is associated with regional attempts to adapt to change and is propelled by a motivation to reinsert the region into a changing national political economy, it will usually express itself as a political strategy of influence within the governing party, congruent with the existing national policy paradigm and political consensus. In contrast, a posture of *defensive regionalism* is adopted as a means to resist change that is perceived to be threatening to regional economies and cultures; it may also be the catalyst for developing a critical and counterdiscursive strategy that embodies a competing national project and vision. The third variant identified by Keating is *autonomist regionalism*. This tends to be linked to a region's historical claims to nation status and its search for a distinctive path to the future that combines political autonomy-seeking with cultural promotion and a regional economic strategy. Autonomist regionalism is rooted in a high degree of alienation and disengagement from the national identity and political system.

These three forms of regionalism are not mutually exclusive. They can and do "bleed into" and overlap one another, depending on changes in regional political economies and shifts in short-term political circumstances and conditions. Each of the three forms can be observed in Canadian politics, and each has its own political advantages and limitations from the point of view of effective regional representation and resistance. Finally, as suggested earlier, each of these forms of regionalism is profoundly influenced by the institutional and systemic biases and constraints that limit the capacity of parties and the political system more generally to effectively integrate Canada's diverse regions.

What is the relationship between various forms of regionalism on the one hand and regional parties and voting patterns on the other? Rather than assuming a simple one-to-one correspondence, the type of regionalism being expressed by and through the party system can best be apprehended through the ideological discourse, programs, objectives, and aspirations of the parties that succeed in gaining regional support. With this in mind, it can be ascertained that the "two-party" competitive model of party politics will normally be associated with integrative regionalism, but also (sometimes) with defensive regionalism. Similarly, the voter strategy of consolidating support behind a party in a position to win or at least contest for power—the "one-party dominant" model—can at times be a manifestation of integrative regionalism, but also can be indicative (depending on the region's circumstances and its own conception of its "political weight") of a defensive strategy. Finally, the third-party protest model can represent either defensive or autonomist regionalism, which is usually apparent in the type of party being supported. In every case, the variants of regionalism that find expression through the party system are linked to evolving regional political economies, shifting demographics, and contested political discourses. It is the historical circumstances of regions defined by these factors (and others) that primarily determine stability and change in the content and character of Canada's diverse regionalisms.

The Two-Party Competitive Model

In Atlantic Canada, the classic two-party system fuelled by competitive voting has persisted relatively intact throughout Canadian history, with the regional caucus of the governing party and regional ministers in the federal cabinet acting as the primary policy and program lobby as well as the political conduit for various sorts of government benefits (infrastructure, regionally sensitive program modifications, pork barrel spending, etc.). The persistence of this model has surprised many observers of Canadian politics as something of an anomaly. The Atlantic region would appear to have had valid reasons for rejecting the traditional parties if economic deprivation or inequality is understood to be a cause or ingredient in political alienation and protest. So what explains this apparent conundrum?

Until recently, the most common explanation for Atlantic Canada's adherence to the traditional two-party system was a cultural one, the argument being that traditionalism and conservatism were dominant features of the region's political culture, producing stable and enduring lines of partisan cleavage (Beck 1972, 1981; Bellamy 1976; MacKinnon 1972; J. Smith 1988). A variation on this refers to the continued sway exerted over the political loyalties of the population by the political elite's use of patronage and clientelist politics (Adamson and Stewart 1985; Fitzpatrick 1972; Rawlyk 1969). More recent analyses reject such images of cultural and political conservatism as outdated or misdirected in their reliance on culture to explain the region's politics (Bickerton 1989, 1990b; Milne 1992; Ornstein 1986). Alternative lines of inquiry have focused on the effects of economic underdevelopment

(Brodie and Jenson 1980; Brym 1979) and dependence (Bickerton 1990a; Brodie 1990; Ornstein, Stevenson, and Williams 1980). Putting aside this debate over why Atlantic Canada hasn't produced regional protest parties, how well has the region been served by a competitive two-party system?

During the twentieth century, the Atlantic region was truly marginalized within Canada, both in terms of its role within the national economic strategy and its political importance to successive federal governments. To make matters worse for the region, it did not often find political allies for its political concerns. When early in the twentieth century the Maritime provinces demanded the restoration of the Confederation bargain with its transportation and tariff concessions to the region, the West was strongly opposed while Quebec and Ontario were either hostile or uninterested (Forbes 1979). When in the interwar period regional politicians lobbied hard for federal aid to improve the region's deteriorating fiscal and economic situation, the larger provinces again resisted the kind of federal action that would have been required. And in the post–World War II period, when state power was centralized in Ottawa and economic power in Central Canada, widening regional disparities continued to go largely unchecked by any policies aimed at redistributing a portion of growing national wealth to less advantaged regions (Bickerton 1990a). Under these less-than-propitious circumstances for Atlantic Canada, the national party system provided some access to the political power and state resources needed to defend and modernize the region, even if insufficient to reverse its relative decline.

Only in the 1960s and 1970s did political circumstances for the region dramatically improve: partisan alignments during this period were unsettled, revaluing political support in the region; the ideology of governing elites had shifted leftward toward egalitarian and social welfare concerns; and the Quiet Revolution in Quebec changed that province's political culture and policy orientation, giving Atlantic Canada an important ally on questions of regional redistribution and federal transfers for social programs (Bickerton 1989, 1990a). These policies resulted in the economic, social, and political integration of the region into the national economy and society, and in the wake of this long-overdue development, the region's often defensive posture gave way to an enthusiastic integrative regionalism. However, these halcyon days of regional development did not last. A short quarter-century after the first regional development initiatives, the political opportunity structure for Atlantic Canada became much less favourable. In the 1990s, an Ontario-dominated Liberal caucus, the sudden rise of the ideologically right-wing Reform Party, and the accompanying demise of the social welfarist, Keynesian policy paradigm facilitated deep federal cuts in social and regional development spending. This federal retreat did trigger a regional political backlash in 1997, producing the first significant advance for the third-party protest model. Though for the most part this departure from traditional voting patterns was not sustained in subsequent elections, the region has not returned to its former unalloyed attachment to the two-party system.[5]

The underlying forms of regionalism in Atlantic Canada have been both defensive and integrative. With little political leverage and marginalized economically within Confederation, party politics became a contest for access to the distribution of social benefits, partisan spoils, and federal government support to help sustain and modernize traditional economic sectors. Stakes such as these increased the importance of party politics and the political realm as a source of resources for hard-pressed communities. Given this context, the two-party competitive system served Atlantic Canada about as well as could be expected. When the political opportunity structure turned in the region's favour, as it did in the 1960s, its ministerial contingent succeeded in obtaining a significantly increased level of federal resources and favourable adjustments to national policies (Bickerton 1990a). Neither the third-party protest model nor one-party dominance was a particularly attractive alternative for voters who had learned to be pragmatic about their region's economic role and prospects and the marginal political influence they could hope to exert. Party appeals and voter responses were shaped by these assumptions and perceived limits. Staying within the boundaries of traditional two-party politics may not have altered the region's place within Confederation, but no other model of party representation was likely to do so either. Recognition of this state of affairs led voters to view the party system as a vital two-way conduit to the political centre. Given the region's circumstances, this may well have been an optimal political strategy for Atlantic Canadians.

The One-Party Dominant Model

Prior to the 1990s, the one-party dominant model of party competition was most in evidence in the case of Quebec, where party politics at the federal level saw francophone voters coalescing behind the governing party. When defined as a particular party capturing 75 per cent or more of the seats, Quebec voted as a block on 23 of 31 occasions before 1993, compared with only four times for Ontario (Thomas 1991, 200). The explanation that is usually made for this tendency is that as a linguistic and cultural minority, francophones adopted a strategy of not fragmenting their vote among different parties (Jackson and Jackson 1990, 445). Whatever might have been its cause, the propensity to politically concentrate their votes gave the Québécois a key role in deciding federal elections because of their demographic weight within Canada; it also made it highly likely that any party commanding the support of Quebec would form the government, giving Quebec MPs a strong presence in both the cabinet and the caucus of the governing party.

Generally there has been a greater level of elite consensus in Quebec politics than elsewhere, and this has translated into a more cohesive electorate. One obvious reason for this is the role of nationalist ideology in providing Quebecers with common values and a shared frame of reference (Rioux 1979). Commenting upon this, Pierr. Trudeau argued that the uses made of nationalism in Quebec politics ultimately undermined democracy by discouraging independent thinking on political, moral, and social questions. It also had the effect of encouraging support for only one party at the federal level, and until 1984 that was the Liberals, who repeatedly reminded the francophone electorate that they were the only trustworthy representatives of their interests (Trudeau 1968). Between 1984 and 1993, the windfall of Quebec seats because of this effect crossed the floor of the House of Commons to Brian Mulroney's Progressive Conservatives. But regardless which of the governing parties was the beneficiary of this coalescing voter behaviour, political scientists have noted that one-party dominance in Quebec was largely a function of the electoral system rather than a thoroughgoing single-mindedness on the part of voters (Bakvis and Macpherson 1995; Cairns 1968).

Once Liberal dominance became established in Quebec, voters became progressively alienated from the perpetually-in-opposition Conservatives, causing that party to atrophy in Quebec, both organizationally and at the polls. This only increased the likelihood that the dominant Liberal Party would remain unchallenged until some sort of "strain" or combination of strains mobilized discontented voters behind a third-party alternative, as happened with the Créditistes in Quebec in 1962 (Bélanger 2004; Pinard 1975). It also can be argued that since the rise of the independence movement in the late 1960s, political debate in Quebec has tended to revolve around the choice between federalism and separatism and that in this polarized situation there was room for only one party on the federalist side of the political spectrum. Whitaker (1984, 42), for example, has argued that it was rational if not shrewd for Quebec voters to play both sides against the other by providing themselves with strong federalist representation in Ottawa balanced by equally strong nationalist representatives in Quebec City.

The one-party dominant model of regional representation as illustrated by the Quebec case reflected an underlying regionalism that was primarily integrative in economic terms but defensive in cultural terms. There can be little doubt that for many years Quebec consistently benefited from strong regional representation at the centre. With large cohesive government caucuses and ministerial contingents and continuity in key party personnel,

Quebec's interests could never be ignored. Official bilingualism, powerful cabinet positions for francophones, and significant levels of federal spending in Quebec were three indicators of "French power in Ottawa." But the successful exercise of regional influence through the ministerialist system did not guarantee Quebec's prosperity. Once at the centre of the Canadian economy during the heyday of the National Policy, the province struggled to stave off economic marginalization within a progressively more integrated North American economy (Gagnon and Montcalm 1990). Nor was Quebec able to successfully conclude a new constitutional arrangement with the rest of Canada, despite three decades of discussion and negotiation (Gagnon 1994).

Beyond its evident political advantages for a large and powerful region like Quebec, there are some limitations and drawbacks to the one-party dominant model. It can only work on a consistent basis when the region has enough seats to determine the outcome of elections; conferring an abundance of regional seats on an opposition party is not a recipe for effective political influence at the centre, as the West discovered during long periods of Liberal rule without much Western support. Beyond this, electing regional representatives primarily from one party limits the range of regional opinion that can be reflected within Parliament; some groups within the one-party dominant region will be excluded from representation. Finally, over time continued one-party dominance within a region will inevitably foster a rather blasé attitude on the part of governing elites, leading to declining responsiveness to voter concerns.

The Third-Party Protest Model

The third-party protest model is most closely associated with Western Canada, where the traditional parties as early as the 1920s were unsuccessful in containing regionalist sentiment. Fuelled by policy grievances and a sense of regional alienation, protest voting in the West supported the formation of a range of third parties: the Progressives, Social Credit, CCF-NDP, and most recently the Reform and Canadian Alliance parties. The historic pattern of party politics in Western Canada, where third parties and protest voting have been a common and sometimes predominant theme, has been unique. Much scholarly attention has been accorded to this phenomenon, with a range of explanations proffered. (In this connection, see Bélanger, Chapter 10, in this volume.) Wood's (1975) analysis of the Progressives stressed the history of farm protest movements across the North American plains and the infectious spread of its political ideas and ideals. Lipset's (1971) study of the Saskatchewan CCF, which formed the first socialist government in North America, dwelt on the importance of farmers' organizations and the cooperative movement. Macpherson's (1962) study of the Alberta Social Credit argued that the province's party system was a result of class homogeneity (farmers) and a colonial relationship with Eastern Canada. Wiseman (1991) has suggested that one can understand the different party systems that developed in the West by looking at the political cultures associated with each province's "founding fragments": the place of origin, cultural backgrounds, and political values of its early settlers.

A resource hinterland for much of its history, the overriding importance of export agriculture to the Prairies gave that region's protest movements a policy focus and organizational base for which there was no equivalent in other regions. A national policy framework perceived to be discriminatory toward the West, but to which both traditional parties were wedded, gave substance to arguments that the region needed its own political party or that the system as a whole had to be overhauled and placed on a new foundation. National policies that incited disagreement and backlash in the West—tariffs, energy policy, official bilingualism—left the region feeling victimized by "issue nonresponsiveness" on the part of the traditional parties, whereby their fundamental interests and preferences were sacrificed to those of Central Canada.

Beyond this, the West's willingness to send to Ottawa a majority of their parliamentary contingent who were not members of the governing party has been a reflection of their confidence regarding the importance of their region's economic role and its buoyant long-term prospects. This optimism raised expectations and generated impatience and discontent with a party system and political process that often seemed more an obstacle than a benefit to Western progress. Western resources remained a viable if volatile source of independence and a potential fount of prosperity. This allowed the regional electorate to look upon party politics as a chance to demonstrate their disdain for the old-line parties and push their demands for sweeping institutional and policy change. This orientation to politics has been the common denominator in the electoral success of all third parties in the West.

The West's "third-party" model of regional representation is primarily a manifestation of defensive regionalism. The third parties that were created, including the Reform Party that replaced the Progressive Conservatives in the West after 1993, sought sweeping reforms to national institutions and policies to make them more congruent with Western political values and interests. Reform's rallying cry of "The West Wants In" was a succinct statement of not only its own motivation and objectives but those of the regional parties that preceded it. What it wanted "In" to, however, was not traditional party politics as usual, which it profoundly rejected. It sought power at the national level not to simply replace one set of elites with another, but to install a wholly different politics that was fuelled by a new ideology and national vision. When Stephen Harper's Conservative victory in 2006 finally gave them a version of this, it allowed the West to usurp Quebec's traditional place within Canada: a one-party dominant region that is central to the governing party's power base, with its attendant advantages of enhanced regional representation at the centre.

To return for a moment to the "electoral earthquake" of 1993, when the West was reverting to its familiar third-party model of regional representation by embracing the Reform-cum-Canadian Alliance Party, Quebecers were breaking decisively with their political past. For almost two decades (until the election of 2011), the separatist Bloc Québécois would win between one-half and two-thirds of the province's seats, even serving for a time as the Official Opposition (1993–97). Later, under conditions of minority government (2004–2011), the party would exercise a degree of political influence of the sort that accrues to those that hold or can contribute to the balance of power. More to the point, the continuing strength of the provincial Parti Québécois and the ongoing threat of another referendum kept the question of Quebec's relationship with the rest of Canada high on the federal government's agenda. The underlying regionalism that triggered the rise of the Bloc and supported its dominant position with francophone voters was clearly autonomist in form, seeking regional devolution and disengagement from national political institutions with outright sovereignty for Quebec as the ultimate goal. Under these circumstances, the third-party model arguably provided more influence for Quebec at the centre than was ever the case for Western Canada. Quebec's dramatic turn away from the Bloc in 2011, when most of the latter's seats were transferred to the NDP, suggests yet another significant shift in voter sentiment, this time away from an autonomist strategy toward a mixed variant of integrative and defensive regionalism. With Quebec voting behaviour since the 1980s displaying successive shifts between and overlaps among all three variants of regionalism, it remains to be seen which will gain ascendance in the years to come.

Conclusion

In Canada, the political importance of regions and regionalism is most obviously institutionalized through federalism and intergovernmental relations. But such a primal and primary force in Canadian politics has also made itself felt in national party politics, and in more than one fashion. To be sure, regional support for third parties, especially those that have explicitly represented themselves as regional protest parties, is the most dramatic and attention-grabbing expression of regionalism in the Canadian party system. But depending on its particular party expression, regional protest of this sort can be understood to reflect quite different underlying forms of regionalism. Further, regional representation and resistance through party politics does not limit itself to just this third-party model. It can also take the form of consolidated (block) voting in support of the governing party, and even through the traditional two-party system, where the representation of regional interests and grievances can occur through the regional caucus and regional minister, regardless of which of the traditional governing parties happens to be in power.

The foregoing discussion of parties and regions argues that the party system has been made susceptible to periods of regional fragmentation by the combined and interactive effects on the party system of national political institutions—the electoral system, Parliament (especially the unreformed Senate), cabinet government, executive federalism—that are dysfunctional from the perspective of facilitating the systematic, effective, and equitable representation of regions. This set of institutional deficiencies—so clearly corrosive to the process of national integration—represents a serious failing for a political system that must manage a decentralized federal state and highly regionalized society.

Regions and regional interests must be represented continuously and equitably in national government and politics. Otherwise, "national" policies will be developed and a "national interest" articulated that amounts to little more than a reflection of powerful interests at the centre—that is, the most populous regions and most important interest groups. This inevitably leads to mounting political tensions that, left unmediated, foment regional alienation and erode national unity. If some equilibrium is to be found between centralism and regionalism, between policy centralization and territorial representation, all reasonable measures should be taken and means employed to make it possible for regional concerns to be adequately voiced and considered within national political institutions. The party system, because it is territorially rooted, necessarily becomes a key mechanism for regional representation and resistance. But the party system operates within a wider set of political institutions, the design of which can either hinder or facilitate the regional role of political parties.

It seems clear that over time the national party system has suffered a diminished capacity for binding Canada's regions together. Perhaps most helpful to sustaining a stable and effective party system would be to find ways to redistribute the representational weight that it has been forced to carry, a heavy burden that it has shown itself to be less and less adept at shouldering. This can really only be accomplished by finally biting the bullet of institutional reform, specifically with regard to the electoral system and the Senate. Doing the former would reduce the distortions of regional representation created by the current first-past-the-post system, which frequently turns a national electorate only moderately divided along regional lines into a regionally fractured and polarized House of Commons. It might also reduce inflated regionalist rhetoric in Canadian politics by paying fewer electoral dividends to parties choosing to use this strategy. Senate reform would provide institutional support to the poorly equipped House of Commons and federal cabinet, where the regional representation role has withered. It would provide Parliament with a purposively designed forum for regionally sensitive policy deliberation and brokerage, as well as an important legitimating mechanism for the federal government.

There is no doubt that other bases of representation and modes of political integration have begun to displace region. The Charter of Rights and Freedoms, multicultural groups, and new social movements have caused many people to view themselves politically as rights-bearing individuals or as members of nonterritorial groups rather than as residents of a particular region. Parties have been forced to reorient themselves to tap into these new identities and bases of representation. In the process, they tend toward becoming ideological alternatives rather than defenders of regional interests, and in this fashion alternative foundations of political stability and national unity can be constructed. Yet Canada's regions will not be easily sidelined; more likely is that they will remain at or near the centre of Canadian politics for as long as there is a Canada. Finding ways to effectively represent the concerns, identities, and aspirations of regions in national politics will continue to challenge and preoccupy each political party and the national party system as a whole.

Suggested Readings

Bakvis, Herman, and A. Brian Tanguay. 2012. "Federalism, Political Parties and the Burden of National Unity: Still Making Federalism Do the Heavy Lifting?" In *Canadian Federalism,* 3rd ed., edited by Herman Bakvis and Grace Skogstad, 96–115. Toronto: Oxford University Press.

Bickerton, James, and Alain-G. Gagnon. 2014. "Regions." In *Comparative Politics,* 3rd ed., edited by Daniele Caramani, 252–66. Oxford: Oxford University Press.

Bickerton, James, Alain-G. Gagnon, and Patrick Smith. 1999. *Ties That Bind: Parties and Voters in Canada.* Toronto: Oxford University Press.

Brodie, Janine. 1990. *The Political Economy of Canadian Regionalism.* Toronto: Harcourt Brace Jovanovich.

Carty, R. Kenneth, William Cross, and Lisa Young. 2000–01. "Canadian Party Politics in the New Century." *Journal of Canadian Studies* 35 (4): 23–39.

Gibbins, Roger. 2005. "Early Warning, No Response: Alan Cairns and Electoral Reform." In *Insiders and Outsiders: Alan Cairns and the Reshaping of Canadian*

Citizenship, edited by Gerald Kernerman and Phillip Resnick, 39–50. Vancouver: University of British Columbia Press.

Keating, Michael. 1997. "The Political Economy of Regionalism." In *The Political Economy of Regionalism,* edited by Michael Keating and John Loughlin, 17–40. London: Routledge.

Koop, Royce, and Amanda Bittner. 2013. "Parties and Elections after 2011: The Fifth Canadian Party System?" In *Parties, Elections and the Future of Canadian Politics,* edited by Amanda Bittner and Royce Koop, 308–31. Vancouver: University of British Columbia Press.

Web Links

Three Hundred and Eight:

www.threehundredeight.com
A website that compiles and analyzes polling data on Canadian political parties and elections.

Regional Federal Studies:

www.tandfonline.com/loi/frfs20#.VtXmH5wrJXi
Website for the journal *Regional and Federal Studies,* the publishing outlet for the Standing Group on Regionalism, part of the European Consortium for Political Research (ECPR).

Party Politics:

www.partypolitics.org
Website for the journal *Party Politics,* an international journal for the study of political parties and official journal of the Political Organizations and Parties section of the American Political Science Association.

Notes

1   Examples of the former include the CCF-NDP and the Reform Party; of the latter, the Social Credit and Bloc Québécois.

2   For example, the United Farmers, Social Credit, CCF, NDP, and Saskatchewan Party in Western Canada; the NDP in Ontario; the Union Nationale and Parti Québécois in Quebec.

3   For example, this was the case for decades with the federal and provincial Liberal parties in Quebec, while in the 2008 federal election the provincial Conservative government in Newfoundland and Labrador ran an ABC (anyone but Conservative) campaign against their federal counterpart.

4   Such was the case, for instance, with regard to Canada's system of public health care, which was first instituted by an NDP government in the province of Saskatchewan. Likewise, family policy innovations were pioneered by the Parti Québécois, and the Western-based Reform Party was the first to fully embrace the neoliberal critique of big government, prescribing lower taxes, spending cuts, deregulation, and decentralization as the cure for Canada's ills.

5   Atlantic Canadians have almost always enjoyed a level of political representation within the government caucus that has been greater than or commensurate with the region's share of federal seats. Election results since the 1930s indicate that there have been only four occasions when this did not hold.

References

Adamson, Agar, and Ian Stewart. 1985. "Politics in the Mysterious East." In *Party Politics in Canada,* 5th ed., edited by Hugh Thorburn, 319–33. Scarborough, ON: Prentice-Hall.

Bakvis, Herman. 2000–01. "Prime Minister and Cabinet in Canada: An Autocracy in Need of Reform?" *Journal of Canadian Studies* 35 (4): 60–79.

Bakvis, Herman, and Laura G. Macpherson. 1995. "Quebec Block Voting and the Canadian Electoral System." *Canadian Journal of Political Science* 28 (4): 659–92.

Beck, J. Murray. 1972. "The Party System in Nova Scotia: Tradition and Conservatism." In *Canadian Provincial Politics,* edited by Martin Robin, 168–97. Scarborough, ON: Prentice-Hall.

Beck, J. Murray. 1981. "An Atlantic Region Political Culture: A Chimera." In *Eastern and Western Perspectives,* edited by David J. Bercuson and Phillip A. Buckner, 147–68. Toronto: University of Toronto Press.

Bélanger, Éric. 2004. "The Rise of Third Parties in the 1993 Canadian Federal Election: Pinard Revisited." *Canadian Journal of Political Science* 37: 581–94.

Bellamy, David. 1976. "The Atlantic Provinces." In *The Provincial Political Systems,* edited by David J. Bellamy, Jon Pammett, and Donald C. Rowat, 3–18. Toronto: Methuen.

Bickerton, James. 1989. "The Party System and the Representation of Periphery Interests: The Case of the Maritimes." In *Canadian Parties in Transition: Discourse, Organization, Representation,* edited by Alain-G. Gagnon and A. Brian Tanguay, 461–84. Toronto: Nelson Canada.

Bickerton, James. 1990a. *Nova Scotia, Ottawa, and the Politics of Regional Development.* Toronto: University of Toronto Press.

Bickerton, James. 1990b. "Creating Atlantic Canada: Culture, Policy, and Regionalism." In *Canadian Politics: An Introduction to the Discipline,* edited by Alain-G. Gagnon and James P. Bickerton, 325–44. Peterborough, ON: Broadview Press.

Bickerton, James. 2007. "Between Integration and Fragmentation: Political Parties and the Representation of Regions." In *Canadian Parties in Transition,* 3rd ed., edited by Alain-G. Gagnon and A. Brian Tanguay, 411–35. Toronto: Nelson.

Bickerton, James, Alain-G. Gagnon, and Patrick Smith. 1999. *Ties That Bind: Parties and Voters in Canada.* Toronto: Oxford University Press.

Bradford, Neil. 1999. "Innovation by Commission: Policy Paradigms and the Canadian Political System." In *Canadian Politics,* 3rd ed., edited by James P. Bickerton and Again-G. Gagnon, 541–60. Peterborough, ON: Broadview Press.

Brodie, Janine. 1990. *The Political Economy of Canadian Regionalism.* Toronto: Harcourt Brace Jovanovich.

Brodie, Janine, and Jane Jenson. 1980. *Crisis, Challenge, and Change: Party and Class in Canada.* Toronto: Methuen.

Brym, Robert J. 1979. "Political Conservatism in Atlantic Canada." In *Underdevelopment and Social Movements in Atlantic Canada,* edited by Robert J. Brym and R. James Sacouman, 59–80. Toronto: New Hogtown Press.

Cairns, Alan C. 1968. "The Electoral System and the Party System in Canada, 1921–1965." *Canadian Journal of Political Science* 1 (1): 55–80. http://dx.doi.org/10.1017/S0008423900035228

Cairns, Alan C. 1977. "The Governments and Societies of Canadian Federalism." *Canadian Journal of Political Science* 10 (4): 695–726.

Carty, R. Kenneth. 1988. "Three Canadian Party Systems: An Interpretation of the Development of National Politics." In *Party Democracy in Canada: The Politics of National Party Conventions,* edited by George Perlin, 15–31. Scarborough, ON: Prentice-Hall.

Carty, R. Kenneth, William Cross, and Lisa Young. 2000–01. "Canadian Party Politics in the New Century." *Journal of Canadian Studies* 35 (4): 23–39.

Collenette, Penny. 2014. "Senate Scandal's 'Quiet Damage' Ripples across Canada." *Globe and Mail,* February 5.

Cross, William. 2004. *Political Parties.* Vancouver: University of British Columbia Press.

Duverger, Maurice. 1951. *Political Parties: Their Organization and Activity in the Modern State.* New York: Wiley.

Fitzpatrick, Peter. 1972. "The Politics of Pragmatism." In *Canadian Provincial Politics,* edited by Martin Robin, 116–33. Scarborough, ON: Prentice-Hall.

Forbes, Earnest R. 1979. *The Maritime Rights Movement, 1919–1927.* Montreal: McGill-Queen's University Press.

Gagnon, Alain-G. 1994. "Quebec: Variations on a Theme." In *Canadian Politics,* 2nd ed., edited by James Bickerton and Alain-G. Gagnon, 450–68. Peterborough, ON: Broadview Press.

Gagnon, Alain-G., and Mary-Beth Montcalm. 1990. *Quebec: Beyond the Quiet Revolution.* Toronto: Nelson Canada.

Gagnon, Alain-G., and A. Brian Tanguay. 1996. "Minor Parties of Protest in Canada: Origins, Impact and Prospects." In *Canadian Parties in Transition,* 2nd ed., edited by Alain-G. Gagnon and A. Brian Tanguay, 106–35. Toronto: Nelson.

Geddes, John. 2013. "Canada's Senate: Chamber of Disrepute." *Maclean's,* March 8.

Gibbins, Roger. 2005. "Early Warning, No Response: Alan Cairns and Electoral Reform." In *Insiders and Outsiders: Alan Cairns and the Reshaping of Canadian Citizenship,* edited by Gerald Kernerman and Phillip Resnick, 39–50. Vancouver: University of British Columbia Press.

Jackson, Robert J., and Doreen Jackson. 1990. *Politics in Canada: Culture, Institutions, Behaviour, and Public Policy.* 2nd ed. Toronto: Prentice-Hall.

Johnston, Richard. 1992. "The Electoral Basis of Canadian Party Systems, 1878–1984." In *Canadian Political Party Systems,* edited by R. Kenneth Carty, 587–623. Peterborough, ON: Broadview Press.

Johnston, Richard. 2005. "The Electoral System and the Party System Revisited." In *Insiders and Outsiders: Alan Cairns and the Reshaping of Canadian Citizenship,* edited by Gerald Kernerman and Phillip Resnick, 51–64. Vancouver: University of British Columbia Press.

Johnston, Richard. 2010. "Political Parties and the Electoral System." In *The Oxford Handbook of Canadian Politics,* edited by J.C. Courtney and D.E. Smith, 91–207. New York: Oxford University Press.

Keating, Michael. 1997. "The Political Economy of Regionalism." In *The Political Economy of Regionalism,* edited by Michael Keating and John Loughlin, 17–40. London: Routledge.

Lipset, Seymour Martin. 1971. *Agrarian Socialism*. Rev. ed. Berkeley: University of California Press.

MacKinnon, Frank. 1972. "Big Engine, Little Body." In *Canadian Provincial Politics,* edited by Martin Robin, 240–61. Scarborough, ON: Prentice-Hall.

Macpherson, C.B. 1962. *Democracy in Alberta*. 2nd ed. Toronto: University of Toronto Press.

Mair, Peter. 1997. *Party System Change: Approaches and Interpretations*. Oxford: Clarendon Press.

Milne, David. 1992. "Challenging Constitutional Dependency: A Revisionist View of Atlantic Canada." In *The Constitutional Future of the Prairie and Atlantic Regions of Canada,* edited by James N. McCroirie and Martha L. MacDonald, 308–17. Regina: Canadian Plains Research Center.

Ornstein, Michael D. 1986. "Regionalism and Canadian Political Ideology." In *Regionalism in Canada,* edited by Robert J. Brym, 47–88. Richmond Hill, ON: Irwin.

Ornstein, Michael D., H. Michael Stevenson, and H. Paul Williams. 1980. "Region, Class and Political Culture in Canada." *Canadian Journal of Political Science* 13 (2): 227–72. http://dx.doi.org/10.1017/S000842390003300X

Pinard, Maurice. 1975. *The Rise of a Third Party*. Enlarged ed. Montreal: McGill-Queen's University Press.

Rawlyk, George A. 1969. "The Maritimes and the Canadian Community." In *Regionalism in the Canadian Community 1867–1967,* edited by Mason Wade, 100–16. Toronto: University of Toronto Press.

Rioux, Marcel. 1979. "The Development of Ideologies in Quebec." In *The Canadian Political Process,* 3rd ed., edited by Richard Schultz, Orest M. Kruhlak, and John C. Terry, 98–114. Toronto: Holt, Rinehart, Winston.

Savoie, Donald. 1999. *Governing from the Centre: The Concentration of Power in Canadian Politics*. Toronto: University of Toronto Press.

Sayers, Anthony. 2002. "Regionalism, Political Parties, and Parliamentary Politics in Canada and Australia." In *Regionalism and Party Politics in Canada,* edited by Lisa Young and Keith Archer, 209–21. Toronto: Oxford University Press.

Simeon, Richard. 1975. "Regionalism and Canadian Political Institutions." *Queen's Quarterly* 82 (4): 499–511.

Simpson, Jeffrey. 2001. *The Friendly Dictatorship*. Toronto: McClelland and Stewart.

Smiley, Donald, and Ronald L. Watts. 1986. *Intrastate Federalism in Canada*. Vol. 39, Research Studies: Royal Commission on the Economic Union and Development Prospects for Canada. Toronto: University of Toronto Press.

Smith, David E. 1985. "Party Government, Representation, and National Integration in Canada." In *Party Government and Representation in Canada,* edited by Peter Aucoin, 1–68. Vol. 36, Research Studies: Royal Commission on the Economic Union and Development Prospects for Canada. Toronto: University of Toronto Press.

Smith, Jennifer. 1988. "Ruling Small Worlds: Political Leadership in Atlantic Canada." In *Prime Ministers and Premiers: Political Leadership and Public Policy in Canada,* edited by Leslie A. Pal and David Taras, 126–36. Scarborough, ON: Prentice-Hall.

Tanguay, A. Brian. 2003. "Political Parties and Canadian Democracy: Making Federalism Do the Heavy Lifting." In *Canadian Federalism,* edited by Herman Bakvis and Grace Skogstad, 296–315. Toronto: Oxford University Press.

Thomas, Paul G. 1991. "Parties and Regional Representation." In *Representation, Integration, and Political Parties in Canada,* edited by Herman Bakvis, 179–252. Vol. 14 of the Research Studies: Royal Commission on Electoral Reform and Party Financing. Toronto: Dundurn Press.

Thorburn, Hugh. 1991. "Interpretations of the Canadian Party System." In *Party Politics in Canada,* 6th ed., edited by Hugh Thorburn, 114–24. Scarborough, ON: Prentice-Hall.

Trudeau, Pierre Elliott. 1968. "Some Obstacles to Democracy in Quebec." In *Federalism and the French Canadians,* 103–23. Toronto: Macmillan.

Whitaker, Reginald. 1984. "The Quebec Cauldron." In *Canadian Politics in the 1980s,* 2nd ed., edited by Michael S. Whittington and Glen Williams, 33–57. Toronto: Methuen.

Wiseman, Nelson. 1991. "The Pattern of Prairie Politics." In *Party Politics in Canada,* 6th ed., edited by Hugh Thorburn, 414–32. Toronto: Prentice-Hall.

Wood, L.A. 1975. *A History of Farmers' Movements in Canada: The Origins and Development of Agrarian Protest 1872–1924.* Toronto: University of Toronto Press.

4
Polarized Pluralism in the Canadian Party System

RICHARD JOHNSTON

CANADA'S PARTY SYSTEM IS A BUNDLE OF seeming contradictions: multiparty competition but single-party government; durable cabinets but massive electoral volatility; roots that are deep but archaic and possibly irrelevant; tight agenda control but inflammatory rhetoric; and sharp discontinuities between federal and provincial elections within many provinces. Not surprisingly, claims about the system's essential character are as contradictory as the empirical patterns. I want to argue that the patterns are not so much contradictory as complementary and that a single model accounts for much of what we see. As with any good model, it raises as many questions as it answers.

In brief, the Canadian party system must be seen as an example of polarized pluralism, an ideal type first conceptualized by Giovanni Sartori (1966, 1976).[1] He saw it as a rare and unhealthy form of party competition, which juxtaposes multipartism to domination by a party of the centre. Ironically, the very power of the centre party gives the rest of the system a centrifugal logic. All of Sartori's examples were of proportional representation (PR) systems. He regarded Canada as a garden-variety two-party system, as would be expected under our first-past-the-post (FPP) electoral formula. Even as Sartori was writing, however, the Canadian system was starting to exhibit pathologies that now must be recognized as symptomatic of the syndrome. Recognition of this is aided by events of the last two decades, in particular the electoral earthquake of 1993.

My argument operates at the level of the party system. In doing so, it attempts to revive a mode of analysis that was never very fashionable, and for Canadians in the past 30 years almost nonexistent. The pedigree is distinguished, however, as the first volume of the *Canadian Journal of Political Science* featured two remarkably influential articles pitched at the systemic level, Alan Cairns's (1968) "The Electoral System and the Party System in Canada, 1921–1965" and Jean Blondel's (1968) "Party Systems and Patterns of Government in Western Democracies." These articles are widely cited and influential, but they stand out as exceptional even for their time. In the decades since, focus on party systems as systems has been rare, and not just in the Canadian literature (Bardi and Mair 2008). Cairns certainly spawned controversy (Bakvis and Macpherson 1995; Johnston and Ballantyne 1977;

Lovink 1970) and inspired reform proposals (Irvine 1979), but further contributions were more about geographic incentives in the electoral system
than about the fundamental structure of party competition. There is also a
Canadian literature about the succession of social bases and organizational
forms on the partisan landscape (Carty 1988; Johnston et al. 1992; Smith
1985). Individuals' behaviour and individual parties continue to be objects of
study. Debate over the psychology of Canadian voters, as affected by stylized
facts about the party system, has been a cottage industry. But little of this
work considers systemic causes of systemic effects.

The Electoral System and the Number of Parties

The main exception is the study of the impact of the electoral system on the
number of parties. This is a question in comparative politics, for claims about
systemic cause and effect require comparison across systems. The driving
force of the literature is elaboration on Duverger's Law and Hypothesis
(Duverger, [1954] 1963).[2] The law states that FPP always produces two-party
politics, or at least produces dynamic tendencies pointing in that direction.
The hypothesis, a weaker statement, says that PR may produce multipartism.[3] The standing claim is that a complex social structure can produce a
complex party system only if the electoral system allows it to (Amorim Neto
and Cox 1997; Ordeshook and Shvetsova 1994). And only "weak" electoral
systems—systems that do not punish coordination failure among kindred
political groups or parties (PR, basically)—allow this to happen.[4] This also
makes PR a necessary but not a sufficient condition for multipartism. A
"strong" electoral system—a system that does punish coordination failure—
constrains the number of parties to slightly more than two, regardless of the
complexity of the underlying social structure. As Amorim Neto and Cox
(1997, 167) put it, "A polity can tend toward bipartism either because it has
a strong electoral system or because it has few cleavages. Multipartism arises
as the joint product of many exploitable cleavages and a permissive electoral
system." The problem with Canada, of course, is that it fits none of these
boxes. It combines the quintessentially strong electoral system, FPP, with a
high level of electoral fractionalization.[5]

The extent of fractionalization appears in Figure 4.1, which shows the
"effective number of parties" in every election since 1878. It is no longer
conventional to represent the number by a simple integer or by fractional
approximations, such as Blondel's (1968) "two-and-a-half" category. Now
the indicator of choice is a continuous one, the "effective number of parties"
(Laakso and Taagepera 1979). The indicator captures the intuition that the
fractionalization of a party system reflects not just the number of discrete

Figure 4.1 Components of Electoral Fractionalization

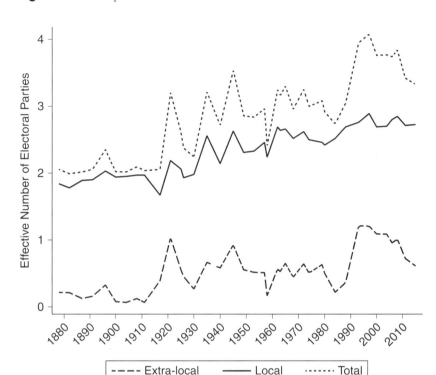

party labels but their relative sizes as well.[6] The magic number is, of course, two, the theoretical ideal of parties in an FPP system.

Before 1921, the effective number of parties in the Canadian electorate oscillated right around that magic number.[7] The number surged in 1921 with the Progressive breakthrough, fell back as the Conservative Party recovered, and grew permanently in 1935 when the system acquired the equivalent of roughly one extra party. In fact, two discrete parties—the Co-operative Commonwealth Federation (CCF) and Social Credit—appeared and endured. In the 1990s, the equivalent of one more party was added to the system. Again, several new players—most notably the Bloc Québécois and Reform/Alliance—gained prominence. The system consolidated slightly in 2000 and more significantly after 2008.

The scale of fractionalization made Canada an outlier. Although all comparable systems fragmented in the 1910s and 1920s, all subsequently purged themselves, so to speak, as parties on the centre and right consolidated to block the threat from the labour/social democratic left. This reconsolidation is dramatic evidence of the power of Duverger's Law. In Canada, however, multipartism became a way of life. Down to the 1970s, the gap between Canada and its comparators was about one party. Some gaps then closed, but the Canadian system pulled away from its remaining comparators again in the 1990s.[8]

All this happened notwithstanding a powerful and continuing contrary effect from the translation of votes into seats. As in other FPP systems, Parliament is less fractionalized than the electorate, reflecting what Duverger ([1954] 1963) called the system's mechanical effect.[9] The Canadian mechanics do not seem unusual.

What is unusual is the apparent weakness of the follow-on psychological effect, also posited by Duverger. Electoral system theory says that a strong system induces strategic action to move the number of electoral parties down, such that sooner or later voters and parties will consolidate into two roughly coequal blocs.[10] There is a hint in Figure 4.1 that the system exhibits Duvergerian equilibration in that sudden gains in the effective number of parties (ENP) are mitigated eventually—at least, one can impose such a reading on the data.[11] But electoral consolidation arrives late and typically lasts for only one Parliament. As the ensuing breakup is usually greater than the preceding consolidation, and each successive mitigation is weaker than the last one, electoral and parliamentary fractionalization have each ratcheted upward. In the electorate, the system went from two parties to four. In Parliament, the effective number increased from two parties to three.

Unpacking Fractionalization

The standing explanation for Canada's embarrassment of parties starts with the observation that although governments are formed nationally, votes are counted locally. Lipset (1954) made this point as early as the 1950s and it lies at the heart of Cairns's (1968) critique. Rae (1971) put the Canadian case front and centre in the comparative literature as the exception that proves the Duverger rule. His stylization of the Canadian pattern—local bipartism, national multipartism—has stuck. It hints that Duverger's Law works only at the constituency level, a proposition now taken as canonical.[12] By implication, coordination across locales requires some other force. The critical extra-local factor may be the centralization of the policy agenda, as argued by Cox (1987). In most countries power has flowed to the centre, such that partisan coordination across geographic subunits becomes imperative. In Canada this logic turns on its head: the decreasing importance of the federal government weakens the imperative for cross-district coordination. Thus it is possible for Duverger's Law to apply even as the national party system breaks down.

This argument has been made most forcefully by Chhibber and Kollman (2004). Although they admit there are difficulties with the Canadian case, they stare the difficulties straight in the face and pass on by. They notice some local fractionalization—contra Duverger—and also admit that the flux in cross-district breakdown does not admit an unambiguous interpretation. Figure 4.1 puts the problem front and centre by splitting total fractionalization into local and extra-local components. The line labelled "local" is the average constituency-level ENP. Cross-district failure is indicated by the "local–national" gap.[13] Local coordination failure is indicated by the difference between the observed local ENP values and the theoretically indicated ENP of two. On the Duvergerian account, the local line should exhibit no net upward movement. The big shifts should be on the extra-local side, and these shifts should explain most of the gains on the national line.

In a word, they do not. In fact, each component explains about half the total fractionalization gain. The typical constituency harboured one more "party" at the end of the century than at the beginning. Before 1921—really, before 1935—the effective number of parties within a typical riding was under two, as riding contests were often one-sided to the point of acclamation. From 1935 on, however, the local ENP was always larger than two. By the turn of the century it was about 2.8. Likewise, the extra-local contribution grew by about one "party." The extra-local value is positive right from the start, as it is arithmetically required to be. The real excitement starts with a large gain in 1921. The line dips over the next few years but surges again in 1935. The 1945 election brought another pulse, and the surge in 1993 is stunning.

The two components of fractionalization exhibit qualitatively different dynamics, and each dynamic reveals a puzzle. Local fractionalization, notwithstanding modest discontinuities, follows a trend. The dynamic force behind this trend is the CCF-NDP. The appearance of the CCF was the biggest contributor to the 1935 lift in the local line, since from the beginning the party contested about 60 per cent of all ridings.[14] Starting in 1962, the NDP completed the move toward universal tripartism, and by 1968 it, like the traditional parties, was contesting every seat. The spread of candidacies induced a spread of votes. In this respect, the CCF and NDP merely extended a late nineteenth-century pattern of diffusion initiated by the Conservatives and Liberals. Relative to the early years of the twentieth century, the vote for the system's three core parties has become more nationalized, consistent with the pattern identified by Caramani (2004) for Europe. Extra-local flux, in contrast, is episodic. And critically, there are four elections—1930, 1958, 1984, and 1988—where the gain in the extra-local component relative to the nineteenth-century starting point is effectively zero.

The narrative poses difficult questions. The spread of local tripartism arguably has only expanded the total volume of electoral futility. Why would Liberals and Conservatives divide the centre-right and risk capture of seats by the left? Why would the Liberals and NDP divide the centre-left and risk capture of seats by the right? Equally hard to square with the usual Duvergerian story is the system's episodic extra-local dynamic. The just-mentioned four elections that take sectional differences back to the nine-teenth-century starting point are also the instances, referred to earlier in this chapter, of modest equilibration. If so, the equilibration is not what we would expect from the current formulation of Duvergerian logic. On that logic, consolidation should occur locally, where the coordination problem seems more tractable and where the penalty for coordination failure is immediate. Instead, when Canadian parties and voters get their act together, they do so through convergence among regions, leaving local tripartism largely untouched. And each moment of extra-local convergence has one thing in common: these are the only elections between 1917 and 2011 to produce Conservative majority governments.

The Historically Dominant Centre

Both peculiarities—local fractionalization and episodic extra-local flux—stem from the historical dominance of the system by the Liberal Party. And the critical thing about the Liberal Party is that it is a party of the centre, the only such party to dominate an FPP-based consolidated party system.[15] Liberals command the centre on at least two key dimensions of choice: the left–right ideological axis and the "national question." Left and right are conventional categories, organizing a big fraction of party politics almost everywhere. Most countries also have a form of national question, often a variant that poses a fundamental challenge to their territorial integrity. But no other country forces secessionist and anti-secessionist politics through the FPP electoral formula.

A two-dimensional stylization of party preference is outlined with the 2004 and 2006 Canadian Election Study survey data shown in Figure 4.2. The figure locates party supporters rather than the parties, for my argument requires that I split party support groups up. The horizontal axis deploys an indicator of left–right self-placement. The vertical axis displays support for Quebec's aspirations.[16] For visual simplicity, each measure is scaled to a −1, +1 range. Because one dimension is framed in terms of Quebec, party supporters are separated into Quebecers and non-Quebecers.

Each point indicates the mean position of each party support group simultaneously on the left/right and pro/anti-Quebec axes. Scanning

Figure 4.2 The Policy Space, 2011

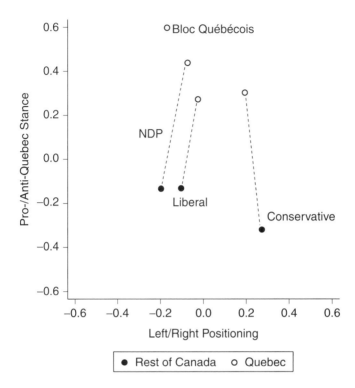

horizontally, we see that each party's supporters locate themselves from left to right "correctly."[17] Distances among party support groups seem small, especially in Quebec. This is a fairly standard finding, however; in most electorates, supporters are not as polarized as party elites.

In this context, the width of Quebec/non-Quebec gaps within parties is all the more striking. In itself this should not be surprising, given the question. The Bloc, of course, is the most pro-Quebec; if things were otherwise we would distrust the indicator. Within Quebec, NDP and Liberal supporters hardly differ over left and right but diverge sharply over the Quebec question. For Liberal and Conservative supporters the opposite is true. Outside Quebec, the gap between Conservative supporters and the others is sharp, as is the left–right gap. Most critically, although each pan-Canadian party group is sharply divided internally, the Liberals are the least divided. On this dimension the Liberals may not be the only party to seek the centre, but they have the least difficulty holding it.[18]

The Idea of Polarized Pluralism

All this is to say that party competition in Canada takes the form of polarized pluralism. The most extended account of this "ideal type" of party competition is Sartori (1976).[19] The model is not deductive but instead emerges from Sartori's meditation on Weimar Germany, postwar Italy, Fourth-Republic France, and pre-1973 Chile. Its pivotal feature is that a large party controls the centre.[20] This point cannot be stressed too much. In the standing theory of committees and elections, the centre exerts a powerful attraction for political competitors. This is the fundamental Downsian point in spatial analyses (Downs 1957; Enelow and Hinich 1984). Empirically, however, the attractive power of the centre is exerted on parties or ideological families that bracket the centre; they do not actually occupy it. Here is Duverger ([1954]1963, 215) on the point:

> Political choice takes the form of a choice between two alternatives. A duality of parties does not always exist, but there is almost always a duality of tendencies. . . . This is equivalent to saying that the center does not exist in politics. . . . The term "center" is applied to the geometrical spot at which the moderates of opposed tendencies meet. . . . Every Center is divided against itself and remains separated into two halves, Left-Center and Right-Center. For the Center is nothing more than the artificial grouping of the right wing of the Left and the left wing of the Right. The fate of the Center is to be torn asunder.

So if parties are typically pulled to the centre by competitive considerations, they rarely start there.[21] But the centre is exactly where the Liberal Party of Canada starts.

Where a major party commands the centre, opposition is forced to be bilateral, coming from both ends of an ideological or policy spectrum. For Sartori, because the centre is occupied, it is "out of competition" in that "the very existence of a center party . . . discourages . . . the centripetal drives of the political system" (1976, 135). Oppositions are likely to be irresponsible and engage in a politics of outbidding. In itself this may not be bad if in the long run emptying the centre creates the conditions for the ideal form of competition—that is, off-centre parties responding to the pull of the centre. But also typifying polarized pluralism, indeed probably a critical factor in its very existence, is the presence of one or more "anti-system" parties. Such parties do not see themselves as engaged in the struggle for power under the existing rules but rather as committed to changing those rules. Classic examples are communist and fascist parties. Votes and seats for these parties are subtracted from the zone of true competition, yet their presence limits the scope for coalition building. At the same time, their threat to the system encourages concentration on the centre by voters concerned about maintaining the overarching polity. Even so, the centre cannot hold: "centrifugal drives [prevail] over centripetal ones," leading to "enfeeblement of the centre, a persistent loss of votes to one of the extreme ends (or even to both)" (Sartori 1976, 136).[22]

Sartori did not see any of this applying to Canada. For him, the critical thing about Canada is that governments are formed by one party only. The fact that some of these are minority governments testifies all the more to the powerful logic of the Westminster system: "This pattern [minority governments] attests ... to the force of the inner, systemic logic of twopartism. One could also say—with respect to the 'conventions' of the constitution—that the Canadians are more British than the British themselves" (Sartori 1976, 188–89). Much of what Sartori saw as characterizing the Canadian case still holds. Governments are still formed by only one party, and only five times since he wrote has the governing party been in the minority. But many features of the polarized pluralism model echo recent—in some cases, abiding—tendencies in Canadian politics. And it is the key to understanding both peculiarities—the rise of riding-level three-party competition and the cycles in sectionalism—embedded in Canadian multipartism.

Left–Right Ideology and Local Tripartism

Earlier I alluded to the risks of coordination failure on the centre-right and centre-left. In fact, before 2011 such risks were low. Failure on the centre-right has never produced a federal government of the left. Conservatives may complain that the Liberal Party really sits on the left, not at the centre, but that is not a complaint about a failure to coordinate. The NDP typically finished first or second (usually second) in about one riding in four, or one in three outside Quebec. So the centre-right rarely faces a threat from the left. The threat from the right is usually greater. The 1990s aside, Conservatives, Progressive, or otherwise finish first or second in 60 to 80 per cent of ridings, 80 to 90 per cent outside Quebec. The Conservatives did even better in 1984 and 1988. And Conservative majorities, when they occur, are usually so overwhelming that coordination elsewhere on the spectrum hardly seems relevant. Only in 1988 and 2011 was it plausible that centre-left coordination failure yielded a perverse result. For all that, the Liberals routinely did best of all: they used to win or place second in 70 to 90 per cent of all ridings, even when their backs were to the wall. Voters who prefer the Liberal Party rarely needed to move to block an unacceptable outcome.

Ironically, Liberal Party strength permits voters on the right to support a conservative alternative without risking victory by the party furthest left. The Liberals do the same for voters on the left, although less often. When there is a real threat from the right, it has tended to be the Liberals, not the NDP, who benefit from strategic consolidation.

In most of Canada, the only other strategic option available to Conservatives and New Democrats was to combine with each other. Merely to say this is to restate the problem: the presence of the strong, centrist Liberals. To the extent that politics is organized on a left–right basis, an NDP–Conservative combination is implausible, Red Tory nostalgia notwithstanding. In general, supporters of parties that are ideologically disconnected (i.e., separated from each other by one or more intermediate parties) do not coalesce. The Liberals are the "Condorcet winner," the party that beats all others in a straight fight. As such, they have been the coordination point when either ideological extreme threatens to take power.

The centre has shrunk, however, consistent with the polarized pluralism's logic. Liberal vote shares shrank after 1960, even though the party continued to win seat majorities. Compared to earlier winning years, the Liberal share shrank further in 1993. Thereafter, Liberal parliamentary majorities rested on a narrower electoral base than formerly had typified minority governments, and the tiniest of perturbations would have deprived them of their majorities.

The National Question and Governmental Succession

By its very existence as a strong party of the centre, the Liberal Party was also responsible for the system's peculiar sectional dynamics. This is a story about the national question, if we admit that the question takes us beyond the boundaries of Quebec. The dynamics partake of two things: the existence of anti-system parties or tendencies, and the continuing imperative, given FPP, of single-party governments.

Figure 4.3 shows how cyclical sectionalism maps onto the history of Conservative success and failure. It does so by portraying the geographic basis of party coalitions in three parliamentary situations. The horizontal axis arrays the provinces from west to east; the vertical axis gives average values of the federal vote within each province. The portrayal is for all years from 1908, the completion of the nine-province system (with Newfoundland dating from 1949), to 2008, inclusive. The nuance washed over by such draconian pooling is not central to my argument. Besides, surprisingly little nuance is lost: the picture remains remarkably stable over many temporal groupings.

Figure 4.3 Geographical Inclusiveness of Electoral Coalitions

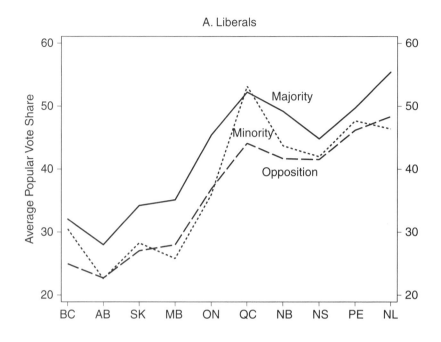

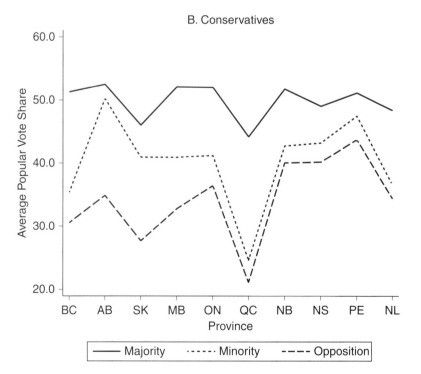

To underscore just how remarkable the Conservative pattern is, consider first the Liberal one. The popular basis of Liberal governments has always been highly differentiated geographically. The East–West gradient steepened in the second half of the twentieth century, but changes since 1921 have been modest. When the Liberals retreat from power, differences sharpen only at the margin. When they lose their majority but hold on as a minority government, losses are typically outside Quebec, and Quebec sustains them in power. Only when they suffer a Quebec reversal do they actually lose power. Although this pattern may not indicate healthy, broad support for a purportedly national government, its dynamics are at least moderate and contained.

The Conservative Party, in contrast, constantly flirted with the edge. When in opposition, Conservative support followed an East–West gradient altogether like that for the Liberals. This was least true from 1963 to 1984, although even in those years Conservative support was lower in Manitoba, Saskatchewan, and British Columbia than in Atlantic Canada. Conservative support seems more uniform when the party forms minority governments. This reflects the fact that all Conservative minorities postdate 1957.[23] Indeed, Conservative strength in the West seems to be a necessary condition for the party even to approach power.

The West did not suffice to give Conservatives parliamentary majorities, however. For that, capturing Quebec was the necessary final step. True, in achieving majority status the party makes gains generally proportional to former weaknesses. But the gains in Quebec are always stunning. This was the pattern for the 1984 Conservative landslide: a Quebec swing of 38 points, compared to 10 points elsewhere. The 1984 pattern magnified but otherwise repeated earlier episodes: in 1958 the Quebec gain was 19 points, compared to 15 elsewhere; in 1930, 10 points, compared to 2; and in 1911, 5 points, compared to 2.5. Figure 4.3 portrays not just gains but losses as well, and the flipside of stunning growth can be sudden collapse. With the partial exception of 1957–63, each Conservative experience of power left the party worse off.

The asymmetry between the parties implies that Conservative gains and losses come in exchange not so much with the Liberals as with third parties, in particular with parties representing sectional interests. Many of these parties qualify for Sartori's designation as "anti-system." The parties that qualify, some only barely, include the Progressives (especially the United Farmers of Alberta), Reconstruction, Social Credit, the Bloc populaire canadien, the Bloc Québécois, and the Reform (but probably not the Alliance).[24] The key, in my view, is not that these parties always reject Westminster parliamentarism or the Canadian union. It is that at critical moments these parties dangle a metacritique of the system and voters rise to the bait, whether or not these voters know what they are doing or intend much by the act. The rhetoric is, in Sartori's terms, one of outbidding. Even if little comes of the rhetoric, the bar is raised for the next round. Under FPP, anti-system insurgency can have a compounded effect (Cairns 1968). And as long as an anti-system party persists, it compresses the scope for government formation.[25]

Reflections

To recapitulate, the key to the puzzle of Canadian elections is their historical domination by a party of the centre. At the riding level this accounts for three-party competition, where outside Quebec the centrist Liberals dominate a left–right ordering. Given strategic circumstances, the only option for consolidation involves an ends-against-the-middle coalition, and this is unrealistic. Such coalition building is possible across regions, however, as the Conservative record shows. Joining the opposites sometimes involves absorbing anti-system parties or anti-system tendencies. The resulting incoherence accounts for the short life and commonly dire fate of Conservative majority governments. The fall of Conservative governments is often the midwife of anti-system parties, with the Bloc and Reform as only the most recent examples. Conservative boom and bust is the source of the episodic volatility in Canadian elections and is, in fact, the complement of Liberal longevity.

The logic outlined in this chapter also helps account for federal–provincial divergence. The three-party dynamic in federal constituencies does not extend to provincial ones, at least not in most provinces. Where circumstances favour growth on the left, as they first did in the West, jockeying will ensue for survival on the centre-right and only one party can remain as an alternative to the NDP. Where circumstances do not favour the NDP, as has traditionally been the case in Atlantic Canada, no centre-right consolidation is required in provincial elections, but neither is three-party competition the norm.

Why does a party of the centre survive? Many voters are undoubtedly happy that it does, and its survival makes Canada the sole majoritarian system in which the governing party routinely covers the median (Powell 2000). It also makes Canada the only system among the obvious comparators not dominated by a party of the right. Most likely, the key to Liberal dominance is the national question. It is commonplace to observe that the Liberals have been historically better than others at managing that question. But their survival as a dominant player requires that they control a pole on at least one major dimension of choice and, as I have shown for the electorate as a whole, they do not control such a pole, not even on the national question. The electorate is not a unitary entity, however; it is segmented between, at a minimum, Quebec and the rest of Canada. If Liberal supporters are a guide, their party controls a pole within each segment but the opposite one between segments: the pro-Quebec pole outside Quebec; the pro-Canada one inside Quebec. This does not require the Liberals to be peculiarly inconsistent, only that the electorate be segmented.

The origins lie, I believe, in the period in which the national question was outward looking—Canada in Empire—and the Liberal Party controlled the anti-imperial pole. Imperial relations were the only policy domain in which party and religious interests aligned cleanly. All other issues with linguistic or religious content divided each party against itself (Brown 1975; Crunican 1974; Miller 1979). Although Quebec was the chief locus of anti-imperial sentiment, it was so as the most Catholic place. Outside Quebec, Catholic people and places also gravitated to anti-imperial appeals. The 1900 election, with the South African War on its agenda, was the test run for the twentieth century. Even when external relations dominated party choice, the potential for polarized pluralism was detectable. The 1911 election is commonly thought of as mainly about commercial policy, the failed Canada–US Reciprocity Treaty. But it was also a referendum on imperial relations more generally, with the 1910 Naval Service Bill as a case in point. The Laurier government's creation of the Canadian Naval Service was a compromise between British demands for dreadnoughts and Quebec's resistance to any naval policy whatsoever. Outside Quebec, the policy was castigated as insufficiently imperialist; in Quebec, it was condemned for opposite reasons. The beneficiary of both critiques was the Conservative Party: ends against the middle.[26]

This pattern became clearer as the national question turned inward, to the place of Quebec in or out of Canada. The Liberal Party was able to cash out its older record on continuing credibility in Quebec, at least for a time. But with the inward turn came a "stretching," so to speak, of the Quebec end of this dimension, and options hitherto unimaginable—or at least unspeak-able—became concrete possibilities. This still leaves the Liberals in the centre. But can the Liberals sustain their position? As mentioned, the middle has been shrinking. Perhaps a centre party can remain a major player only so long as it is the dominant one. If so, the Conservative objective must be to keep the Liberals out long enough that their claim to superiority in managing the Que-bec–Canada relationship sinks on the mere fact of distance from power.

If I am right for the Canadian case, then it follows that comparative analy-sis must move beyond studying electoral systems in a context- and history-free vacuum. It does not suffice to invoke the mere fact of diversity, even in an interactive setup in the manner of Ordeshook and Shvetsova (1994) or Amorim Neto and Cox (1997). After all, the Canadian case does not feature a weak electoral system that accommodates diversity. Rather, the Canadian sys-tem punishes coordination failure as severely as any in the world, and yet such failure persists. Comparative analysis should also, on my argument, address systemic relations among parties. Does a strong party of the centre necessitate centrifugal appeals by the other players, or does that logic apply only to anti-system parties? Or is it the presence of credible anti-system parties or of potentially exploitable anti-system tendencies that in turn privileges the centre? To the extent that two-party competition remains normative among our comparators, understanding its breakdown is necessary to identifying the contingencies that underpin bipartism where it survives. These contingencies may be disappearing, such that multipartism will become the norm even under strong electoral systems. If so, it is all the more critical to understand Canada, the country ahead of the curve.

Acknowledgements

An earlier version of this chapter was given as the presidential address to the 2008 Annual Meeting of the Canadian Political Science Association. Many colleagues have contributed to this address, often without knowing it, but special mention must be made of Amanda Bittner and Scott Matthews. Thanks to the University of Pennsylvania for material support. Data from the 2011 Canadian Election Survey (CES) were gathered by the Institute for Social Research, York University, and put in circulation by the CES team. The surveys were funded by Elections Canada and the Social Sciences and Humanities Research Council of Canada. Co-investigators were Patrick Fournier, Fred Cutler, Dietlind Stolle, and Stuart Soroka. None of these individuals or institutions is responsible for the analyses and interpretations presented here. The address was dedicated to the memory of Bill Irvine.

Suggested Readings

Cairns, Alan C. 1968. "The Electoral System and the Party System in Canada, 1921–1965." *Canadian Journal of Political Science* 1 (1): 55–80. http://dx.doi.org/10.1017/S0008423900035228

Chhibber, Pradeep K., and Ken Kollman. 2004. *The Formation of National Party Systems: Federalism and Party Competition in Canada, Great Britain, India, and the United States.* Princeton, NJ: Princeton University Press.

Cox, Gary W. 1997. *Making Votes Count: Strategic Coordination in the World's Electoral Systems.* Cambridge: Cambridge University Press. http://dx.doi.org/10.1017/CBO9781139174954

Duverger, Maurice. (1954) 1963. *Political Parties: Their Organization and Activity in the Modern State.* Translated by Barbara North and Robert North. New York: Wiley.

Sartori, Giovanni. 1966. "European Political Parties: The Case of Polarized Pluralism." In *Political Parties and Political Development,* edited by Joseph LaPalombara and Myron Weiner, 137–76. Princeton, NJ: Princeton University Press.

Notes

1 I am not the first to make this claim for Canada. Pride of place goes to William Dobell (1986).

2 Although Duverger was not the first to formulate the proposition that FPP constrains party systems to a low number, he did claim law-like status for it (Riker 1982).

3 Rae (1971) provided the first systematic empirical demonstration. Taagepera and Shugart (1989) shifted emphasis among electoral institutions and raised the level of empirical sophistication several notches. Lijphart (1994) produced the most complete inventory of patterns. Cox (1994) supplied the pivotal theoretical elaboration, and Cox (1997) provided the complementary empirics.

4 The notion of an electoral system's strength or weakness originates with Sartori (1968).

5 Riker (1982) and Benoit (2006) offer key intellectual histories of the Duvergerian idea, and this paragraph depends heavily on these accounts. Also important is the careful summary in Chhibber and Kollman (2004).

6 The calculation is as follows:

$$ENP_t = 1 \,/\, (\Sigma_i \, p_{it}^{\,2})$$

where: ENP_t is the effective number of parties in the election at t; and p_{it} is the i-th party's proportion of seats or votes in the election at t;

$$0 < p_{it} < 1 \; ; \Sigma_i \, p_{it} = 1$$

The intuition behind the indicator is exactly the same as in Rae's (1971) index of fractionalization. If p_{it} gives the probability of randomly selecting a supporter of the i-th party at t, $p_{it}^{\,2}$ gives the probability of selecting a supporter of that party on successive independent draws. If the system has two parties of exactly equal size, the probability of choosing one party's supporter on a given draw is 0.5 and of choosing such individuals on successive draws is 0.25. In this situation, the same probabilities hold for the other party. The sum of the two probabilities is 0.5: One has a 0.50 probability of choosing supporters of the same party, 0.25 for each party. If the system has two parties but one is larger than the other, the probability of choosing two supporters of the same party is greater than 0.5; on the arithmetic, the diminished probability of choosing supporters of the smaller party is more than offset by the enhanced probability of selecting from the larger group. Contrariwise, if the number of alternatives is more than two, the probability of choosing from the same party is diminished, all the more so as the number of alternatives increases and as each alternative approaches equiprobability with the others. If we now take all this logic and, literally, turn it on its head, by taking the reciprocal of $\Sigma_i \, p_{it}^{\,2}$, we get an indicator with a minimum value of one. Where $\Sigma_i \, p_{it}^{\,2} = 0.5$, its reciprocal equals 2, and so on. For an acerbic critique of ENP, see Dunleavy and Boucek (2003).

7 For the record, the effective number for the first few elections is smaller in my series than in the series reported in Chhibber and Kollman (2004). This reflects coding decisions about partisan affinities among candidates: I tend to see

affinities, where Chhibber and Kollman do not. The difference matters little for the argument in this chapter, which is about trends over the twentieth century, by which point my series and the Chhibber–Kollman one coincide.

8   For all this, Canada was not the extreme case among FPP systems. Over the postwar period, the Indian electorate was even more fractionalized than Canada's. Generally speaking, India's ENP averaged about 4 when Canada's ENP averaged about 3. The further fractionalization of the Canadian system in the 1990s closed the gap considerably (but not entirely, especially as the Indian system fractionalized a bit more in the 1990s).

9   Over the full period since 1878, the electoral system dismissed the equivalent of 0.5 parties. Since 1935, 0.75 parties have been stripped, and in two periods—1935 to 1958 and 1984 to 2000—the electoral system dismissed the equivalent of more than one party.

10 The empirical number seems to be 2.5 (Taagepera and Shugart 1989).

11 The 1930 election undid nearly all of the 1921 damage, 1958 did so for much of the 1935 breakdown, 1984 corrected some of 1962, and 2000 reversed a small part and 2011 a large part of 1993.

12 It was made so by Riker (1982) and Cox (1994, 1997).

13 Strictly speaking, cross-district failure could occur as much within provinces as between them, but as Chhibber and Kollman (2004), Figure 6–6 shows, within-province variation in ENP has decreased.

14 Social Credit was also a factor, but only in a handful of places.

15 This is not quite—or not always—true. Until the consolidation of the Bharatiya Janata Party (BJP), Congress controlled the middle of the Indian party spectrum and posed its rivals with a coordination challenge similar to that in Canada. This was a central point in Riker (1976), which contrasted Canadian and Indian multipartism. Canada has now converged on the Indian case, or the countries have switched places.

16 The left–right indicator is based on the following item in the 2011 Canadian Election Study (CES):

> "In politics people sometimes talk of left and right. Where would you place yourself on the scale below?"

The scale ranges from 0 to 10. The indicator of support for Quebec is

> "How much do you think should be done for Quebec: much more, somewhat more, about the same as now, somewhat less, or much less?"

This question was asked of 2011 CES respondents in a postelection telephone wave. Party preference is indicated by respondents' reported 2011 vote, which was also included in the CES postelection telephone wave.

17 The ordering conforms to the patterns for party platforms in Budge et al. (2001) and Benoit and Laver (2006).

18 Benoit and Laver (2006) have a "Quebec" dimension that locates parties as pro- or anti-sovereignty and place all parties other than the Bloc at the same

spot. The Bloc and the Liberal Party are coded as placing more emphasis on the issue, however.

19 The first account, however, seems to be Sartori (1966).

20 The centre is not defined by some absolute standard but by relative positioning: "when one speaks of a centre-based system, one is concerned only with a centre positioning, not with centre doctrines, ideologies, and opinions—whatever these may be" (Sartori 1976, 134).

21 This is the dynamic tension captured by Aldrich (1983).

22 The pattern can appear only when there are more than two parties. Indeed, Sartori's conjecture, based on PR examples, is that at least six (nominal, not "effective") parties are required. The Canadian case does not quite reach this threshold, especially in the early years, but I want to argue that this particular threshold is not critical.

23 The short-lived 1926 Meighen government does not count as an exception for my purposes, since the party was in opposition for the bulk of the relevant Parliament.

24 Flanagan (1995) shows that the Reform program had other elements in contradiction with this aim and these other elements ultimately prevailed, as did the imperative to coordinate the right-wing vote across provinces.

25 The Canadian picture of massive, recurring swings has particular affinities with one of Sartori's polarized pluralism cases, Chile: "The election of the president by universal suffrage imposes alliances that—in a polarized system—generate strong tensions within the centre group of parties and induce acrobatic ideological leaps along the left-right dimension" (Sartori 1976, 159). The critical fact about Chile is that, unlike the other three cases, it is a true presidential system—that is, a system with a directly elected national office. Strictly speaking, where no candidate received an outright majority (the usual case) Congress was required to choose between the top-two vote-getters. But no matter how close the vote or what might have been the second choices of supporters of the eliminated candidates, Congress always chose the first-place candidate. This produced striking dynamics and the eventual election, with 37 per cent of the vote, of Salvador Allende. So the Chilean formula is, in effect, FPP for its most important office.

26 See, in particular, Brown (1975, 163ff., 235 passim).

References

Aldrich, John H. 1983. "A Downsian Spatial Model with Party Activism." *American Political Science Review* 77 (4): 974–90. http://dx.doi.org/10.2307/1957570

Amorim Neto, Octavio, and Gary W. Cox. 1997. "Electoral Institutions, Cleavage Structures, and the Number of Parties." *American Journal of Political Science* 41 (1): 149–74. http://dx.doi.org/10.2307/2111712

Bakvis, Herman, and Laura G. Macpherson. 1995. "Quebec Block Voting and the Canadian Electoral System." *Canadian Journal of Political Science* 28 (4): 659–92. http://dx.doi.org/10.1017/S000842390001934X

Bardi, Luciano, and Peter Mair. 2008. "The Parameters of Party Systems." *Party Politics* 14 (2): 147–66. http://dx.doi.org/10.1177/1354068807085887

Benoit, Kenneth. 2006. "Duverger's Law and the Study of Electoral Systems." *French Politics* 4 (1): 69–83. http://dx.doi.org/10.1057/palgrave.fp.8200092

Benoit, Kenneth, and Michael Laver. 2006. *Party Policy in Modern Democracies.* London: Routledge.

Blondel, Jean. 1968. "Party Systems and Patterns of Government in Western Democracies." *Canadian Journal of Political Science* 1 (2): 180–203. http://dx.doi.org/10.1017/S0008423900036507

Brown, Robert Craig. 1975. "Robert Laird Borden." *Biography* I: 1854–914.

Budge, Ian, Hans-Dieter Klingemann, Andrea Volkens, Judith Bara, and Eric Tanenbaum. 2001. *Mapping Policy Preferences: Estimates for Parties, Electors, and Governments, 1945–1998.* Oxford: Oxford University Press.

Cairns, Alan C. 1968. "The Electoral System and the Party System in Canada, 1921–1965." *Canadian Journal of Political Science* 1 (1): 55–80. http://dx.doi.org/10.1017/S0008423900035228

Caramani, Daniele. 2004. *The Nationalization of Politics: The Formation of National Electorates and Party Systems in Western Europe.* Cambridge: Cambridge University Press. http://dx.doi.org/10.1017/CBO9780511616662

Carty, R. Kenneth. 1988. "Three Canadian Party Systems: An Interpretation of the Development of National Politics." In *Party Democracy in Canada,* edited by G.C. Perlin, 16–32. Toronto: Prentice-Hall.

Chhibber, Pradeep K., and Ken Kollman. 2004. *The Formation of National Party Systems: Federalism and Party Competition in Canada, Great Britain, India, and the United States.* Princeton, NJ: Princeton University Press.

Cox, Gary W. 1987. *The Efficient Secret: The Cabinet and the Development of Political Parties in Victorian England.* Cambridge: Cambridge University Press. http://dx.doi.org/10.1017/CBO9780511571473

Cox, Gary W. 1994. "Strategic Voting Equilibria under the Single Nontransferable Vote." *American Political Science Review* 88 (3): 608–21. http://dx.doi.org/10.2307/2944798

Cox, Gary W. 1997. *Making Votes Count: Strategic Coordination in the World's Electoral Systems.* Cambridge: Cambridge University Press. http://dx.doi.org/10.1017/CBO9781139174954

Crunican, Paul. 1974. *Priests and Politicians: Manitoba Schools and the Election of 1896.* Toronto: University of Toronto Press.

Dobell, William M. 1986. "Updating Duverger's Law." *Canadian Journal of Political Science* 19 (3): 585–95. http://dx.doi.org/10.1017/S0008423900054603

Downs, Anthony. 1957. *An Economic Theory of Democracy.* New York: Harper and Row.

Dunleavy, Patrick, and Françoise Boucek. 2003. "Constructing the Number of Parties." *Party Politics* 9 (3): 291–315. http://dx.doi.org/10.1177/1354068803009003002

Duverger, Maurice. (1954) 1963. *Political Parties: Their Organization and Activity in the Modern State.* Translated by Barbara North and Robert North. New York: Wiley.

Enelow, James N., and Melvin J. Hinich. 1984. *The Spatial Theory of Voting: An Introduction.* Cambridge: Cambridge University Press.

Flanagan, Thomas. 1995. *Waiting for the Wave: The Reform Party and Preston Manning.* Toronto: Stoddart.

Irvine, William P. 1979. *Does Canada Need a New Electoral System?* Kingston: Queen's University Institute for Intergovernmental Relations.

Johnston, Richard, and Janet Ballantyne. 1977. "Geography and the Electoral System." *Canadian Journal of Political Science* 10 (4): 857–66. http://dx.doi.org/10.1017/S0008423900050927

Johnston, Richard, André Blais, Henry E. Brady, and Jean Crête. 1992. *Letting the People Decide: Dynamics of a Canadian Election.* Montreal: McGill-Queen's University Press.

Laakso, Markku, and Rein Taagepera. 1979. "Effective Number of Parties: A Measure with Application to West Europe." *Comparative Political Studies* 12: 3–27.

Lijphart, Arend. 1994. *Electoral Systems and Party Systems: A Study of Twenty-seven Democracies.* Oxford: Oxford University Press. http://dx.doi.org/10.1093/acprof:oso/9780198273479.001.0001

Lipset, Seymour Martin. 1954. "Democracy in Alberta." *Canadian Forum* (December): 196–98.

Lovink, J.A.A. 1970. "On Analyzing the Impact of the Electoral System on the Party System in Canada." *Canadian Journal of Political Science* 3 (4): 497–516. http://dx.doi.org/10.1017/S0008423900025932

Miller, J.R. 1979. *Equal Rights: The Jesuits' Estates Act Controversy.* Montreal: McGill-Queen's University Press.

Ordeshook, Peter C., and Olga Shvetsova. 1994. "Ethnic Heterogeneity, District Magnitude, and the Number of Parties." *American Journal of Political Science* 38 (1): 100–23. http://dx.doi.org/10.2307/2111337

Powell, G. Bingham. 2000. *Elections as Instruments of Democracy: Majoritarian and Proportional Visions.* New Haven, CT: Yale University Press.

Rae, Douglas W. 1971. *The Political Consequences of Electoral Laws.* 2nd ed. New Haven, CT: Yale University Press.

Riker, William H. 1976. "The Number of Political Parties: A Re-examination of Duverger's Law." *Comparative Politics* 9 (1): 93–106. http://dx.doi.org/10.2307/421293

Riker, William H. 1982. "The Two-Party System and Duverger's Law: An Essay on the History of Political Science." *American Political Science Review* 76 (4): 753–66. http://dx.doi.org/10.1017/S0003055400189580

Sartori, Giovanni. 1966. "European Political Parties: The Case of Polarized Pluralism." In *Political Parties and Political Development,* edited by Joseph LaPalombara and Myron Weiner, 137–76. Princeton, NJ: Princeton University Press.

Sartori, Giovanni. 1968. "Political Development and Political Engineering." In *Public Policy,* vol. XVII, edited by John D. Montgomery and Albert O. Hirschmann, 261–98. Cambridge: Cambridge University Press.

Sartori, Giovanni. 1976. *Parties and Party Systems: A Framework for Analysis.* Cambridge: Cambridge University Press.

Smith, David E. 1985. "Party Government, Representation, and National Integration in Canada." In *Party Government and Regional Representation in Canada,* edited by Peter Aucoin, 1–68. Toronto: University of Toronto Press.

Taagepera, Rein, and Matthew Soberg Shugart. 1989. *Seats and Votes: The Effects and Determinants of Electoral Systems.* New Haven, CT: Yale University Press.

5

The Waning of Political Parties?

GRANT AMYOT

ARE POLITICAL PARTIES NECESSARY? For at least the past 20 years, political scientists have noted the signs of parties' decline. In the developed democracies, party loyalties among voters are weakening and party membership is falling as more and more citizens take up an independent stance and electorates are increasingly volatile from one election to the next. The policies of the competing parties differ less on fundamental issues, and in any case major decisions appear to be made by bureaucrats and international bodies, far from the reach of democratic processes. All too often the range of acceptable solutions has been set very narrowly by the ruling discourse. Most recently, party organizations have lost even a large part of their role in fighting elections to staffs of pollsters, fundraisers, and strategists. These professionals serve the leaders and candidates, who seem to overshadow their parties as never before. Many citizens, especially the young, have become disenchanted not just with the existing parties, but with parties themselves. Many parties have been tarnished by scandals, and most seem less able to represent the many diverse identities of their voters. Suggestions for more free votes in the House of Commons, greater accountability of individual Members of Parliament (MPs) to their constituents, or the use of referendums on major issues all recall the populist attacks of a century ago that labelled party government corrupt and unresponsive to the will of the people. Have parties in fact outlived their usefulness? Are they destined to be replaced by a new politics, a nonparty form of democracy characterized by independent voters, charismatic leaders, and opinion polling? And would such a new politics be a good thing? An investigation of some of the reasons for the decline of parties will help to answer these questions.

Parties in Democratic Theory

The notion of nonparty democracy is not as outlandish as it may seem; in spite of their major role in modern democratic politics, parties do not have a firm footing in the tradition of liberal–democratic political thought that has underpinned it. In this tradition, the concepts of the individual, the people, and the state bulk large, but parties are rarely mentioned, and when they are it is often in negative terms. For classical liberal thinkers, parties in the modern sense were unnecessary and indeed harmful. Politics was concerned with the rational pursuit of the public interest, and liberals believed that all individual citizens, if they used their faculty of reason, would arrive at roughly similar conceptions of that interest. Correct reasoning would tend to create unity in the polity rather than division. Not all classical liberals, of course, went as far as Rousseau in his antipathy to "factions" that would distract the citizens from their search for the General Will, but his opinion illustrates this facet of their thought in an extreme form. Generally speaking, liberals believed that reason would dictate a framework of human laws that reflected natural law and would preserve the rights of the citizens vis-à-vis the state; legislators were meant to work together to formulate this framework.

Politics for classical liberals, then, was not primarily about the struggle of conflicting interests, for the public interest was beyond particular concerns. Therefore, legislators were to be chosen for their highly developed powers of reason and their disinterestedness, rather than as delegates or representatives of their constituents. As Edmund Burke said in his often-quoted speech to the voters of Bristol, "Parliament is a deliberative Assembly of one Nation, with one Interest, that of the whole; where, not local Purposes, not local Prejudices ought to guide, but the general Good, resulting from the general Reason of the whole" (Burke [1774] 1996, 69; Beer 1969, 20–22). While Burke defended the parties of his day—the Whig "connexions"—his conception of politics does not allow for strong party organization or discipline. In his view, each individual MP (and each citizen) has to be free to follow his own reason in the pursuit of the public interest, although the ideal situation would be unanimity around one conception of that interest. Burke's famous definition of party— "a body of men united for promoting by their joint endeavours the national interest upon some particular principle in which they are all agreed" ([1770] 1981, 317)—suggests something quite different from the disciplined parties of today, which are held together by more substantial links than shared principle alone. When only principle binds a group of citizens together, there is always the potential for differing individual interpretations of that principle (Burke [1770] 1981, 319–20); indeed, individual freedom is necessary to the search for the true common good. Hence the revulsion of one of the first students of political parties, Moisei Ostrogorski, at the development of party organization in the United States and Britain, because it limited the independence of the party's members and representatives. As a classical liberal, he favoured instead temporary parties organized around great questions of the day; once these were resolved, their members would once again be able to express their views free from the constraints of party discipline (Ostrogorski 1902, 651–71).

One of the greatest principles that early liberals thought a fit and noble basis for the organization of parties was the struggle against "tyranny." In Burke's case, this meant the attempts of the ministers of George III to rule in disregard of constitutional traditions:"nothing but a firm combination of public men against this body [the Court faction]. . . can possibly get the better of it" (Burke [1770] 1981, 321). Later, utilitarians like Jeremy Bentham viewed democracy itself principally as a means of controlling the government, which otherwise might use its powers to oppress the people. While the common good remained the goal—and, indeed, Bentham had a somewhat technocratic view of how government should function on a day-to-day basis—the utilitarians recognized that both reason and desire inhabit human nature, particularly when men and women are placed in positions of power. Today, however, when all political actors accept the democratic system and when elected leaders rather than technocrats are expected by democratic theory to formulate policy, parties have a role that goes far beyond checking governmental "tyranny."

Other liberal–democratic thinkers, such as John Stuart Mill, shared these views but at the same time laid greater emphasis on citizen participation as a goal in itself. However, Mill's favoured forums for this participation were local government and the workplace, which he thought could allow for direct democracy. Only in the work of some scholars in the tradition of Mill, such as C.B. Macpherson (1977), are parties seen as the principal vehicles for citizen participation, and this is definitely a minority tendency in liberal–democratic theory.

In the twentieth century, thinking about democracy shifted its emphasis from the politics of principle to the politics of interests. This was partly a consequence of longer experience with actual democratic government, especially in the United States. Pluralist writers, like Arthur Bentley ([1908] 1967), began to argue that politics was the struggle of a multiplicity of different interest groups, each striving to attain its goals in a process of conflict and bargaining with the others. In the pure pluralist scenario, interest groups occupy centre stage, with parties relegated to a secondary role of brokers and mediators between them. In the United States Congress we have often observed this type of politics: major bills are passed by cross-party coalitions of senators and representatives, who vote in response to the pressures of lobbies rather than according to the party line. Many key parts of the American government, furthermore, seem to have been captured by the interests that they are supposed to be regulating. In a political world inhabited by pressure groups and political entrepreneurs, American parties for many years seemed to survive only thanks to institutional and legal mechanisms such as the rules for party primaries, voter registration, and campaign contributions. While pluralist theory may have envisaged a certain creative role for parties in fashioning policy packages that would appeal to as many interest groups as possible, the American example seemed to show that in a pluralist world parties are of secondary importance. As we shall see below, the increasingly bitter partisan conflict that has marked the past 20 years, and particularly Barack Obama's presidency, is itself a manifestation of the relatively weak and undisciplined character of American parties.

Only if we accept a thesis such as the Marxist belief that there are a limited number of interests in society can the politics of interests produce a system of stable disciplined parties. For Marxists, there are only two fundamental interests: that of the workers and that of the capitalists. Since for Marxism these interests are radically opposed to each other, there can be no "common good" in a capitalist society and it can embrace the idea of the political party and partisanship without reservations. For Gramsci (1971, 227), the Italian Communist theorist, parties are the "nomenclature for classes," and Marxists believe that the working class has a particular need for a strong party: "In its struggle for power the proletariat has no other weapon but organization" (Lenin [1904] 1967, 440).

Marxism, however, is not part of the mainstream of liberal–democratic theory that has historically justified contemporary democracy, though Marxists are right to point out that pressure from the working class for a share in the polity was a major factor in the extension of the democratic franchise (Rueschemeyer, Stephens, and Stephens 1992, 59, 270). Nor, as Marxists would admit, do all parties represent distinct social classes in a clear-cut fashion. Of the other contemporary varieties of democratic theory, the only one that gives parties a key role is Joseph Schumpeter's "competitive elitist" theory—arguably one of the most impoverished from a normative point of view, though it claims the virtue of a greater correspondence with empirical reality. For Schumpeter, the mass of the citizenry are uninformed and irrational, and elites must rule, but party competition within the elite is necessary to simplify the electorate's decision, to prevent tyranny, and to legitimize the system by giving the voters the illusion of consumer choice (Schumpeter 1950, 269–83).

Competitive elitism is a far from morally compelling form of democracy, and the role it reserves for parties, while necessary, is not particularly noble. In response to the lack of ethical appeal of competitive elitism and pluralism, and the individualist bias of classical liberalism, academic critics have not only taken up Mill's advocacy of citizen participation but often proposed a return to the republican virtue of citizen involvement in politics that is so highly valued by a major strand of Western political thought, from Aristotle to the present. But, as in the case of Rousseau, this tradition emphasizes public-spiritedness, devotion to the common good, and participation as an individual virtue; hence, it is often hostile or indifferent to "factions" or parties.

More recently, pluralism has been rejuvenated and given a new form by the contributions of postmodern thought. Postmodernism emphasizes the multiplicity of identities that people have in the contemporary world (e.g., religion, ethnicity, and gender) and stresses the fact that each individual partakes in several of these identities. This leads to the claim that politics must take account of each of these, allowing it a voice. As in the pluralist framework, parties are not taken as the primary vehicles for these multiple identities and are usually seen as attempts to homogenize differences under platforms designed to appeal to a majority. Similarly, the notion of "deliberative democracy," proposed by Jürgen Habermas (1996) and since developed by many others, calls for the participation of citizens in a serious discourse in which they are asked to reassess their conception of their own interests in light of the values and interests of others. Rather than taking interests as pre-formed, it seeks to shape them through a reasoned discussion. While formal political institutions such as parties have a certain role in his schema, Habermas's emphasis is on the direct involvement of individuals as members of civil society.

The Roots of Parties

Given the lack of a strong justification for parties in liberal–democratic theory, what accounts for their ubiquity in modern democracies? In fact, parties first arose not to advance shared principles, or even to aggregate various interests, but rather to secure continuity of support for government. Of course, shared ideology (in the case of the Whigs, the principles of the Glorious Revolution of 1688) and interests also had a role in creating party loyalty, but they did not account for the formation of the parties: once governments came to depend on a majority in Parliament (in England by the eighteenth century), the need for a form of party organization that could ensure a stable majority became overwhelming. As the constitutional maxim has it, "The King's government must be carried on." At that time, the problem was chiefly one of organizing a sufficient body of MPs, as elections were locally centred affairs; the cabinet, chosen in name and sometimes in fact by the king, sought to win over as many MPs as possible directly, but it also used its patronage and influence to try to ensure a majority for itself at elections. The general election of 1835 was arguably the first where the incumbent cabinet "lost."

When the franchise was limited, local notables were able to secure their own election on the basis of family prestige, economic power, or favours. As it expanded, party organization became necessary not only in Parliament but to run election campaigns (see Blyth and Katz 2005, 34–36). Organization gives a great advantage when fighting an election in terms of money, volunteer labour, advertising, and public image; furthermore, it is a virtual necessity if one is to contest the American presidency seriously or aim at a majority in the House of Commons. In forming electoral coalitions, parties also ideally organize the alternatives offered to voters into a small number of well-publicized, coherent packages; these are valuable in reducing voters' "information costs," especially since the parties tend to adhere to similar programs over time. For example, if an autoworker puts his or her interests as a worker first in politics and identifies the New Democratic Party (NDP) as the party most favourable to workers, he or she can in principle rationally vote for that party without troubling to find out its positions on each issue in each election.

This simplifying role of parties is especially useful because it permits accountability to the electorate: where there is no party discipline, it is too hard for many voters to study their representative's individual voting record; even when they do, it is too easy for representatives to excuse themselves for failing to carry out their promises by claiming that there was no majority support. (This is why factors like incumbency and name recognition are so important in Canadian municipal elections, where there are usually no party organizations.) Parties also often perform many of the other functions indicated by liberal–democratic theory: advocating competing principles, representing and aggregating interests, and checking governmental high-handedness. They may also provide a useful way for citizens to participate in politics. From the point of view of competitive elitism, parties are valuable because they recruit, select, and train leaders.

However, parties retain their historical role as links between state and society, and this means that organization still often proceeds from the top down, as governments seek to ensure majority support. This is especially so where organizations of civil society are particularly weak. In countries such as Italy and Japan, for example, lengthy occupation of government in the postwar period gave ruling parties the opportunity to build bases of support with patronage and spending on local projects or particular interests. Elsewhere, not only institutional arrangements like the cabinet system or the election of the American president, but electoral systems such as proportional representation based on lists of candidates or electoral laws such as the American laws regulating primaries, as well as the public funding of parties, have strongly encouraged the formation of parties. In Canada, provisions for the assignment of broadcast time and the funding of elections and political activity led in the 1970s to the institutionalization of parties, which had previously been only informal entities with no precise legal status (Courtney 1978, 34, 36).

The Decline of Parties

In spite of their lack of a strong theoretical justification, political parties therefore grew and flourished with the extension of enfranchisement. The existing parliamentary-based parties grew "downwards" to form mass organizations, and mass parties formed to represent the newly enfranchised groups in society, most notably manual workers but also religious denominations, farmers, and ethnic minorities. The classic mass political party enjoyed a heyday from the late nineteenth century to the early 1970s; of course, it did not prevail everywhere, and in many cases its mass character was more a façade for an elite-dominated structure or was watered down in an effort to appeal to a broader electorate (the "catch-all party" phenomenon).

But for the past 30 years, several tendencies have set in that are seriously weakening parties as we know them. This decline has more than one dimension, though each reinforces the other: on the governmental side, they are losing their power as originators and advocates of policy; on the electoral side, they are losing their hold on voters as the number of loyal party supporters declines and the number of uncommitted or disinterested floating voters increases. Even as organizers of elections, they are losing ground to pollsters and consultants who are typically professionals rather than party militants. The late Peter Mair (2013) has provided an excellent account of the various dimensions of this decline of political parties in his book *Ruling the Void*. The increasing distance between parties and citizens, he argues, means that parties and elections are no longer an effective channel for legitimating political decisions; instead, technocratic decision making and "output legitimacy," graphically illustrated by the European Union, are taking their place. Mair identifies the narrowing of the range of policy alternatives as a major cause of this increasing irrelevance of parties for voters, while also suggesting that the parties themselves share responsibility for their own failure to adapt to changed circumstances (16). In fact, at the root of these dimensions of party decline, two major sets of processes seem to be at work. On the one hand, structural changes in the economies and political systems of the developed democracies are limiting the parties' room to manoeuvre in policy terms; on the other hand, sociological changes are undermining their former bases of support among the voters. The latter, of course, are also the product of long-term economic and social changes, such as the shrinking of the manufacturing working class.

Structural Changes

It is convenient today to attribute the structural changes that limit parties' policy choices to "globalization," an all-purpose term that has been used to explain so many phenomena of the past generation. In fact, the end of the long postwar boom in the early 1970s, though in part caused by heightened competition between domestic and imported products, preceded the take-off of the process of internationalization of the world's major economies. Simultaneous with the spread of globalization, neoliberal ideology and practices have gained increasing sway. Whatever the exact causal sequence, it is undeniable that in today's world economy governments have fewer easy policy choices; in particular, they have less freedom to engage in public spending, as deficit financing is frowned upon and punished by international financial markets (and international organizations such as the International Monetary Fund [IMF] and the World Bank). All governments of the developed world were forced to embrace deficit spending during the financial crisis of 2008–2009, but what is striking is how quickly they reverted to spending cuts and efforts to balance their budgets after the worst was past. And if carried out by a single government, deficit spending is no longer as effective a policy tool: the stimulus that, according to Keynes's theory, it gives to the economy is reduced by the fact that much of it is now spent on imports rather than creating domestic employment. And monetary policy is also constrained by the fact that developed democracies have all abolished controls on the movement of capital into and out of the country: lowering interest rates too far, or other moves that do not please investors, will result in a capital outflow and pressure on the country's currency.

Globalization also brings higher levels of foreign investment. While governments in capitalist countries have always had to pay close attention to the interests of the business community for fear of a capital strike and the flight of investment abroad, foreign capitalists are more likely to choose not to invest (or even to withdraw their investment) if they find the conditions for doing business unfavourable. Hence, governments feel intense pressure to implement policies that will attract these investors, including incentives for new investment, flexible labour market policies, and so on. And heightened trade competition means that, in the interests of both domestic and foreign-owned businesses, all governments feel they must pursue a "competitiveness agenda." The result of all these processes is that political parties of all stripes are compelled to adopt these business-friendly policies and thus seem as though they are not offering the voters a real policy choice.

Some scholars have questioned the degree to which globalization has in fact constrained governments, but there can be no doubt that the policy space has been reduced, with major implications for party competition. The most striking early demonstration of the new climate occurred in France. In 1981, the Socialist François Mitterrand was elected president, the first time the left had come to power under the Fifth Republic, and he introduced a radical leftist program of public spending to stimulate the economy. However, the other major capitalist powers were pursuing the opposite policies, so that "Keynesianism in one country" did not work: money began to flee from France in search of higher interest rates, and higher public expenditures created a balance of payments deficit that threatened the franc. Within less than two years, Mitterrand was forced to execute a U-turn, bringing in restrictive measures to control spending. Had he persisted, his government would have had to take measures to insulate France from the world economy, with unpredictable consequences. His failure to keep his promise to deal with unemployment created cynicism in the voters' minds about parties in general. In subsequent years, the French coined the phrase *pensée unique* ("single thought") to describe the consensus between the major parties of left and right on the main lines of economic policy; the current president, François Hollande, campaigned as an opponent of austerity in 2012 but has since embraced balanced budgets and economic deregulation. The actual choice available at elections seemed to be limited—except for that offered by the extreme-right National Front, which was unacceptable to many voters. French politics have always retained a strong traditional localistic flavour—in which notables with territorial power bases compete for power on the national stage—and the persistence of this localism has been favoured by the decline of the parties' role in presenting meaningful national alternatives. The phenomenon of *pensée unique* is also evident in the current "grand coalition" of the two major parties in Germany: since 2013 the largest party, the Christian Democrats, and the second-largest party, the Social Democrats, have governed together. The two parties have agreed on the need for austerity policies to solve the Eurozone crisis and other key issues. In Britain, too, both the Conservatives and the Labour Party vied for the "centre ground" in the run-up to the 2015 election, both promising spending cuts to eliminate the deficit. When the Conservatives won a surprising majority victory, many Labour voices argued that the problem was that the party's campaign had not embraced the new consensus in favour of austerity wholeheartedly enough, and when a leftist critic of austerity, Jeremy Corbyn, was chosen as leader in 2015, they continued to maintain that he was "unelectable"; whether they are right remains to be seen.

The United States appears to be the exception to the rule: partisan rivalry has become so intense in recent years that we have seen a virtual stalemate between a Democratic president and a Republican House of Representatives. But American parties are in fact particularly weak: because of the presidential system, strong party discipline is not a feature of American politics, and furthermore the campaign finance regime makes individual candidates beholden to the interests that contribute the most to their campaigns. Powerful interest groups have a much freer hand in the US political system than elsewhere. For example, the Tea Party, a faction within the Republican Party that has benefited from financial contributions from wealthy interests like the Koch brothers, has contributed a great deal to the polarization of American political discourse: it has challenged not only the Democrats but also mainstream Republicans whom it considers too "liberal." This freer, more porous party system has allowed business interests and the right to push American politics and policy further in a neoliberal direction, toward deregulation and tax cuts for the rich, than has been the case in many other developed states. The United States has thus adapted to and in many cases led the structural changes in the world economy, following a different route than most other states: on the one hand, as the hegemonic power in the world economy, it has had more freedom to manoeuvre than others, and on the other hand, the strength of business in the Democratic coalition has ensured that Democrats as well as Republicans have supported the major steps toward deregulation and tax cuts, notwithstanding the appearance of partisan conflict. At the same time, as many commentators have recognized, the American party system can become dysfunctional and prevent the United States from responding successfully to the challenges of the global economy, as evidenced by episodes like the shutdown of the federal government in 2013.

A major institutional development connected to economic globalization is the increasing "externalization" (Blyth and Katz 2005, 43–44), or delegation, of many areas of policy from governments to independent agencies such as central banks, to international bodies such as the European Union (EU), to subnational institutions through devolution, or to private managers of formerly public services. (The failure of the EU itself to develop effective organs of electoral democracy based on party competition is one of the themes most lucidly discussed by Mair [2013, Chapter 4].) While parties may not have consciously promoted such externalization to reduce their responsibility for outcomes, as Blyth and Katz suggest, the result nevertheless has been to limit the number of policies over which they have control. The move to increase the independence of central banks has been noteworthy in the past 35 years. An independent central bank is held in much of the economic literature (and in the minds of investors) to be a guarantee against inflation and irresponsible government spending: if governments overspend, or trade unions make inflationary wage demands, an independent bank can teach them a lesson by raising interest rates and choking growth. This strong anti-inflationary stance is of course very much in the interests of holders of financial assets, whose power has been increasing since the 1970s; the financial sector is the real constituency of the central banks. The German Bundesbank was the model central bank in this regard; from 1974 on, it gave priority to controlling inflation in spite of the consequences for full employ-ment and growth. The new European Central Bank (ECB), which manages the euro, was patterned on it; its independence is further enhanced by the fact that it has no single national government that could potentially interfere with its mandate. Along with control over interest rates and the money sup-ply, central banks have de facto gained the power to manage the currency and the exchange rate. Their autonomy also deprives governments of the tool of devaluation, especially since a strong anti-inflationary stance is likely, on the contrary, to promote the appreciation of the currency.

The countries of the Eurozone, by adopting a single currency under the control of the ECB, gave up the ability to devalue their currencies in cases of economic difficulty. The serious consequences of this restriction became evident with the financial crisis of 2008. When the downturn that began in the United States hit Europe, states with difficulty servicing their public debt could not devalue to stimulate their economies—instead they had to accept bailouts by the EU, the ECB, and the IMF, which, following the model insisted on by Germany and the Bundesbank, imposed stringent austerity programs on the bailed-out countries, notably Greece, Portugal, and Ireland. Other states with significant deficits, such as Italy and Spain, were required by the EU to follow similar, if less severe, policies. These austerity policies failed to achieve their objectives, as they held back economic growth and imposed great hardship on the peoples affected; furthermore, they were a serious limitation of national sovereignty and severely restricted the ability of voters in those countries to choose their own way out of the crisis. In the meantime, the EU has embraced austerity even more enthusiastically by enacting tighter controls on member states' budgets in an effort to prevent the recurrence of high levels of debt. Only in the case of Greece, which has suffered more than any of the others with six straight years of recession and unemployment over 25 per cent, has a major party, Syriza (the Coalition of the Radical Left), given voice to the people's suffering and opposed the aus-terity policies of Germany and the EU. Syriza, previously a minor party that brought together a disparate collection of leftist groups, rapidly gained sup-port because both of the established parties had signed the bailout deals and pushed through austerity; its victory in the January 2015 election seemed to give hope that elections and parties could make a difference. This hope was soon dashed, however: after five months of negotiations and a referendum in which 61 per cent of voters rejected the austerity package that the EU was insisting on, the Syriza-led government was driven to accept an even harsher package to obtain a further bailout that was needed to stave off eco-nomic collapse. As in the case of France in 1981, there was an alternative for Greece: leaving the euro and re-establishing a national currency. The more radical ministers were prepared to contemplate this strategy, but Prime Minister Tsipras and the rest of Syriza judged the risks of economic disruption too high for them to take this route.

The Greek case seems emblematic of the growing impotence of national parties and electorates in the face of the imperatives of international bodies and the world economy. On the other hand, the intense politicization of the issue meant that the opposition of the EU, led by Germany, to relaxing the harsh terms imposed on Greece was not the result of impersonal economic forces or technocratic rules, but explicit choices in favour of an economic policy of austerity by EU governments, with some backing from their own parties and electorates. Indeed, many economists decried the policy of austerity as counterproductive, and even the IMF believed that Greece needed a debt reduction. For these reasons, the Eurozone crisis, which is still ongoing as this book is being written, is somewhat unique. But at a minimum it illustrates how entering into a supranational arrangement such as the euro can limit a government's room to manoeuvre in major ways.

All of the above factors—neoliberalism, globalization, and the externalization of policy decisions—have led to a growing inability of political parties to deliver on their promises to the voters. Mitterrand's U-turn in France is only the most spectacular example. A striking instance in Canada was the Trudeau government's introduction of wage and price controls in the fall of 1975, after it had just won an election the previous year by campaigning against the Progressive Conservatives' proposal of just such a plan (Meisel 1979, 130). In 1993, the Ontario NDP government, in response to a mounting deficit caused by the economic downturn, introduced a series of cuts in public spending, including imposed reductions in public sector pay (the "Rae days"). In each of these cases there were alternatives possible, but the pressure on these governments to renege on their previous policy commitments was tremendous. The logic of the situation, as interpreted by policy advisers and powerful lobbies, seemed to point in a single direction; it would have taken considerable courage and commitment, and solid backing from the government's supporters, to defy it. Human agency has its limits in the face of structural pressures of this sort. Nevertheless, it would perhaps be more accurate to say that these severe tests revealed the latent weaknesses of these parties: the absence of a strong mass base, the lack of solid ties between their constituencies and their leaders, and the absorption of the latter into the dominant networks of power.

In other cases, parties have not been forced into U-turns but simply failed to implement their promises to create jobs, improve social services, or cut taxes. As a master of public relations, Silvio Berlusconi (then leader of the opposition in Italy) sensed the growing popular disillusionment with broken promises and countered it with a brilliant media coup when he signed, on prime-time television, a document containing five promises to the Italian people. While he won that election in 2001, his record of implementing the commitments was spotty. These failures led him to sharply criticize the European Union, accusing it of preventing his government from keeping its promises. These protests only underscored the inability of the national government to achieve many of the objectives the voters favoured. Throughout the advanced democracies, these disappointments fuel cynicism about the democratic process itself, and often about parties as such. Party loyalties are strained; citizens become floating voters—and often angry protest voters— ready to give their votes to new movements and leaders.

Syriza itself appeared on the left as a major party to represent protest against the EU's austerity program; in Spain Podemos is now bidding to play the same role. The election of Corbyn as Labour leader and Bernie Sanders's campaign for the 2016 Democratic nomination are similar signs of opposition to globalization and austerity from the left. Elsewhere in Europe, far-right parties have arisen to challenge *pensée unique* and give voice to voters' unease about globalization, the growing power of the EU, and immigration. In the 2014 election to the European Parliament, the National Front in France and the UK Independence Party in Britain each received the largest percentage of the vote. In Italy, the Five Star Movement led by the comedian Beppe Grillo won 25 per cent of the vote in 2013 on a program that, rather than right-wing, was anti-politician and anti-EU. We could argue that these parties, even if we find them extremist, show that political parties are still able to offer meaningful choices to voters. At the moment they do not all appear seriously capable of governing, and Syriza's experience shows the difficulty they would have in reversing the migration of powers from the nation-state, but their future development is still open to various possibilities.

Social Changes

The above structural changes that have severely limited parties' room for manoeuvre in policy terms have been paralleled by the weakening of their traditional bases of support among voters. Writers on political parties, looking primarily to European models, have noted how they tended to be based on social groups defined by historical "cleavages" (Lipset and Rokkan 1967), such as a region, a social class, or a religious denomination. The largest and most successful of these developed into mass parties that stood at the centre of subcultural networks of associations, including trade unions, recreational clubs, youth groups, and so on. The networks promoted a particular worldview as well as loyalty to the party. Rapid social and economic change and secularization of values have undermined these subcultures. Economic globalization has only hastened these processes, causing the shrinking of the industrial pro-letariat in the developed world. Traditional working-class neighbourhoods have changed character with deindustrialization, and upward mobility has also weakened links to the socialist movement. The new jobs generated by the service economy are not giving rise to the same kind of class identity or organization as the manual working class had (Crouch 2004, Chapter 4). Like the traditional self-employed petty bourgeoisie, this group is highly open to manipulation by parties, leaders, and the media.

Another important factor has been the change in lifestyles, as free time is spent more often in the home in front of electronic media rather than, for instance, at the pub with workmates or neighbours. The decline of associa-tional life and sociability in general, noted by Robert Putnam (2000) in his famous study *Bowling Alone,* has naturally loosened the ties between voters and parties as well; isolated individuals or families are more likely to be open to media persuasion in choosing how to vote. The fall in church attend-ance is simply the outward sign of secularization, resulting from rationalistic criticism of premodern values, and it has weakened the religious bases of Christian Democratic parties. These trends are at work in Canada as well; for instance, the Liberal Party has relied on the traditional loyalty of certain ethnic groups, a loyalty that is destined to fade as they become integrated into the mainstream of Canadian society and as the Conservatives move away from their own traditional support base to court them.

In place of these traditional identities (worker, Catholic, Italo-Canadian), many younger voters, better educated than their parents, have sought political meaning in new social movements, such as environmentalism and feminism. Postmodernist theory registers this fragmentation of traditional identities and the multiplication of new ones, linking it to the opening up of new channels of communication and the availability of new discourses on which identities are based. Typically, the established parties have seemed unwelcoming to the new movements, already in the hands of other groups, and unable to offer the type of participatory politics they seek. Therefore, voters have often chosen to act outside party politics as nonpartisan lobby groups or by direct action (see Newman, Chapter 12 in this volume).

The exceptions to this pattern are interesting. In Germany, the Green Party was founded in 1980 as the political arm of several social movements that had flourished in the 1970s. Today it has spent seven years in federal government in coalition with the Social Democrats, is currently the major governing party in the state of Baden-Württemberg and a coalition part-ner in nine other states, and is regarded by many of its original supporters as having compromised too much in exchange for a share of power. This experience would suggest that there is a large gap between the requirements of governing, such as cabinet solidarity, and the aspirations of the social movements. In Canada, on the other hand, the NDP has been more successful than most of its sister social-democratic parties in forging co-operative links with the new movements, as manifested in the election of Jack Layton as leader in 2004. Layton was well known for his support for environmental causes and other social movements and succeeded in building bridges to them. Nevertheless, the movements often prefer to maintain a nonpartisan stance for tactical reasons, and since Layton's death in 2011 ties with the NDP have not been as close.

Changes in Party Organization

There has been a coincidence in the past 35 years of these two sets of factors that have weakened the role of parties. From above, structural changes in the world economy have limited the apparent room for manoeuvre of governments, and hence of parties; from below, social changes have loosened the ties of voters to parties. In the face of these developments, however, parties have also changed in an attempt to preserve themselves, resorting to technology, new sources of funding, and above all the appeal of charismatic leaders.

In fact, the use of television and other electronic media in election campaigns pre-dates the decline in party membership and loyalty. While the print media (party newspapers, etc.) required a corps of dedicated militants to sell and distribute them, radio and television advertising requires only money plus a small technical staff that can be hired. As party membership has declined, it has become necessary to rely more on media messages; and as the actual policy differences between parties have shrunk, the "packaging" of their messages by public relations experts (e.g., by emphasizing the leader's personal qualities) has become increasingly important. The apparatus of pollsters, strategists, and political consultants, with skills very different from those of traditional party activists, has grown.

Social media, such as Facebook and Twitter, has begun to change this picture slightly; Barack Obama, for instance, used these platforms to great advantage in his presidential campaigns. Social media involves large numbers of activists and ordinary supporters in spreading the campaign message, and also allows for mass fundraising. However, this involvement of larger numbers of voters has not translated into an infusion of support for a revival of the Democratic Party as an organization, and it remains to be seen if social media signifies a real change in the character of party politics rather than another channel by which the party strategists can reach the electorate (see Small, Chapter 18 in this volume, and Milner, Chapter 19 in this volume).

Of course, this increased reliance on the media means that parties and candidates have an increased need for campaign funding; membership dues and other traditional sources of finance are often not sufficient to pay for television time and professional staffs. Hence, parties have had to resort to new approaches: outside donors, as in the American case, corruption, or state support. Some parties that have used corruption, such as the Italian Christian Democrats and Socialists and the Japanese Liberal Democrats, have suffered serious consequences in the form of scandals that, in the Italian case, led to the demise of the parties themselves. And elsewhere corruption scandals are becoming more frequent, from the case of Helmut Kohl in Germany to that of Jacques Chirac in France to the "sponsorship scandal" in Canada. Needless to say, this form of financing has contributed to public disenchantment with parties. Another strategy has been to resort to increased public financing of political parties; this is one of a series of developments that led Katz and Mair (1995) to identify a new type of party, the "cartel party." As the name implies, it denotes a member of a group of established parties that agrees to vote themselves state financing with the aim in part of erecting barriers to new parties.

Other characteristics of cartel parties are policy convergence and reduced control by the mass membership over the leaders (Blyth and Katz 2005, 45–46). The cartel party strategy may be a reasonable response by parties to their changed circumstances, but it will not necessarily secure loyalty on the part of voters if they are increasingly seen as interchangeable and compete largely on the basis of the image and managerial skills of their leaders. In fact, with the decline of the traditional mass party and the reduction of opportunities for patronage and politically targeted spending in the current economic climate, parties are now facing their original problem in a new form: how to secure stable support for government. In eighteenth-century Britain, the task was to keep a large enough group of MPs together behind the government; today, it is a question of establishing a link between the individual voter and the party and also uniting a sufficient number of political leaders to support the government. As we pointed out above, the type of link required varies from one political system to another. However, as traditional forms of voter–party links are weakening, another type is becoming more important: the personal appeal of the leader (Blondel et al., 2010).

Though strong leaders have often featured in democratic politics, the new importance of leadership first became apparent in the late 1970s, when governments were faced with novel economic challenges. Among the prescriptions suggested by the increasingly current neoliberal theories were wrenching policy innovations, such as deflationary economic policies and cuts in government spending, and these often involved challenging established interests. Where parties could not provide the fund of legitimacy for these shifts, strong leaders with broad popular appeal, such as Ronald Reagan in the United States and Margaret Thatcher in Britain, filled the gap. Both fought the traditional establishments of their own parties, and both garnered votes beyond their parties' traditional constituencies on the basis of their own personal appeal and their own perception of the public mood. Both could be viewed as examples of "Bonapartism." This term refers to the rule of leaders who are able to override even dominant interests in the name of their particular vision of the long-term national good. They generally come to power in times of acute conflict between dominant groups, or with the subordinate classes, or when the country is faced with extraordinary challenges; they typically have the charisma that allows them to appeal for support directly to the masses. They rise above parties, replacing them as sources of policy formation and political legitimacy. General Charles de Gaulle, for example, made no secret of his contempt for partisan politics.

Reagan and Thatcher were less paradigmatic cases of Bonapartism than de Gaulle. Both, however, received mandates not only to attack the working class and the poor but also to ignore the interests of many segments of business and industry. Thatcher came to power when Britain's economic decline had reached an acute stage and when the working class appeared in need of a short, sharp lesson, having brought down the Heath government in 1974 and undone Labour Prime Minister James Callaghan's efforts to create an incomes policy. But her monetarism also imposed real hardship on much of British manufacturing; the deindustrialization of Britain hit some sectors of British business very hard. She dominated the Conservative Party, as its constitution allowed her to do, and placed her own supporters in key positions of power while excluding as far as possible her "wet" critics. When she came into acute conflict with the dominant sector of business—the City of London—over European integration, however, she lost power. Reagan, similarly, ignored orthodox business opposition to his deficit spending and was deaf to the cries of many segments of American manufacturing for protection as he pursued trade liberalization.

Both leaders forged a direct personal link with the electorate based on an appeal to traditional values and racial insecurity. Reagan, the "Great Communicator," drew heavily on the support of the Christian right, while Thatcher stressed the Protestant virtues of hard work and self-reliance; both combined these with strident patriotism, an aggressive posture in foreign policy, and support for a strong state to oppose crime and disorder.

In Canada too, party leaders, even those without the outstanding characteristics of Thatcher or Reagan, have come more and more to overshadow their parties, both in campaigning and in policy making (Carty 1988, 24–8).

John Diefenbaker may have initiated the trend, but Pierre Elliott Trudeau illustrated it best. Trudeau had had no connection with the Liberal Party until his election to Parliament in 1965, yet three years later he was party leader and prime minister, winning an election with a highly personalized campaign. In power, he showed little interest in party affairs or Parliament, formulating policy with the aid of the civil service and a few trusted advisers (Meisel 1979, 129). It was after his return to office in 1980 that "Bonapartist" tendencies became most pronounced, as initiatives such as the National Energy Policy alienated the most important sectors of Canadian business. And Trudeau's son Justin became leader of the Liberal Party with the help of his father's name and personality, and his 2015 electoral victory hinged in significant measure on his own personality, as he was able to project his attractive features while sufficiently countering accusations that he lacked experience.

The most extreme example of the predominance of leaders over parties is the phenomenon of the personal party created by its leader. A forerunner was Ross Perot, the American billionaire who ran for president in 1992 and 1996. He was able to finance his own campaign, buying the services of experienced political consultants as well as large blocks of media time, and garnered 19 per cent of the popular vote in his first run. He decided to create a party to bring together his supporters almost as an afterthought.

The most noteworthy case of a leader who has created his own party is former Italian Prime Minister Silvio Berlusconi. He is a media magnate, owner of the three largest private television networks in Italy as well as many other interests. In January 1994 he announced his entry into politics, and within three months he had set up his own party, Forza Italia ("Go Italy"), which won enough votes to make him prime minister as head of the largest party in a coalition government. Berlusconi did not need to raise funds since his companies and television channels provided money, media time, and the technical staff needed to run the campaign. At the "grassroots" level, he had the sales representatives of his advertising and public relation company set up local clubs modelled on the clubs of supporters of AC Milan, Berlusconi's soccer team. There was no conventional party structure: "There are no policy committees, elected leaderships, or votes. Policy is decided from on high and fine-tuned through extensive market research" (Jacques 1994, 4.1). In the intervening years, of course, Forza Italia has developed into something that looks more like a traditional party. While its first membership list consisted of those who had mailed in coupons printed in the TV guide published by Berlusconi's company, it was also forced to recruit candidates for Parliament and later for local offices, which led to an influx of local notables. Initially marginalized, these representatives of Forza Italia began to demand some say in party affairs, but Berlusconi remained the undisputed master of his party. In 2001, he returned to power with a campaign that was centred even more strongly on his own personality: he personally signed the five promises to the voters, and Forza Italia's major piece of campaign literature, sent to every home in Italy, was a biography of Silvio Berlusconi.

Berlusconi's success was all the more remarkable because, in spite of his record as a successful self-made businessman (stressed in the campaign biography) and a certain personal appeal, his image was tarnished by a series of trials that saw him accused of crimes from tax evasion to corrupting judges. Even after his conviction in 2013 on charges of tax evasion and falsifying records and the defection of several of his former associates, he remains at 79 the leader of the largest opposition party. The principal explanation lies in the fact that the Italian right, after the massive corruption investigations of 1992–93 had discredited the then-governing parties beyond repair, was in desperate need of a source of cohesion—and Berlusconi was able to provide it. Not only did he have the resources to construct a new right-wing party, he was also perhaps the only one able to attract and hold the other fragments of the right in a stable coalition. In fact, Berlusconi's 2001–05 government, despite much internal friction, holds the postwar record for length of time in office in Italy without a cabinet crisis. Berlusconi and Forza Italia demonstrate how, when traditional party allegiances fade in the electorate, the attraction of a leader often provides the necessary link between government and voters. (The relative weakness of Forza Italia in local elections demonstrates how Berlusconi "carries" the rest of the party.)

Outside of the developed world, the cleavage patterns that provide the social bases of parties have had much less relevance, and personal parties are much more common, for instance, in Latin America and East Asia. Since the Thatcher–Reagan era, there have also been several other examples of charismatic leaders in the developed world, such as Jean-Marie Le Pen in France or (in a different style, to be sure) Junichiro Koizumi in Japan, who promoted a major change in the hitherto immobile Japanese political economy: the privatization of the post office and its huge savings bank.

In many other countries, however, the difficult transition to neoliberalism was accomplished some time ago, and now the predominance of personality over party is due more to the twin phenomena outlined earlier in this chapter: the narrowing of the space for policy disagreement, which leads parties to compete predominantly on the basis of the managerial competence of their leaders, and the dissolution of the traditional loyalties of voters to parties, which are replaced by the appeal of the personality of the leader. Clearly, the media have played a role in the increased importance of leaders. They tend to personalize issues, to seek the human side of them, as well as to rely on authoritative spokespersons, and this often involves highlighting the leaders. And the media are predominantly national in focus, so they tend to concentrate on the national leaders as opposed to local candidates. The practice of televised debates has shone the spotlight even more intensely on the leaders. Nevertheless, the other structural and sociological factors I have outlined above have played the major role in enhancing leaders' importance vis-à-vis their parties.

The evolution of British parties, particularly the Labour Party, is the most emblematic of many of the factors we have outlined that have contributed to the transformation of parties. This is not surprising: Britain has always been a highly open and internationalized economy, dependent on the overseas earnings of its financial sector; it has also experienced the most striking process of deindustrialization and tertiarization in the developed world. On becoming leader in 1994. Tony Blair re-baptized the Labour Party "New Labour" and moved it decisively toward the political centre, stressing the need to appeal to the middle class and business. He reduced the role of the party membership in policy making while he made sophisticated use of the media, giving major weight to public relations considerations in many of the acts of his government, as the prominent role of "spin doctors" such as Alastair Campbell attests. Under Blair, private donations from business-people first became an important source of Labour Party funding. Initially his own personality and image of competence were a major ingredient in New Labour's appeal; even his decision to participate in the invasion of Iraq, which proved so damaging to his personal popularity, was consistent with his political project in that it further narrowed the policy differences between his government and the opposition Conservatives. Since the party's defeat in 2010, and the hardship caused by the austerity policies of David Cameron's Conservative government, there has been a reaction against Blairism, culminating in the surprising election of Jeremy Corbyn as leader in 2015, but the proponents of the "New Labour" strategy remain strong within the party.

All of these factors—increasing disenchantment with parties that do not seem able to deliver, weakening of the social bases of traditional party loyalties, and the enhanced role of leaders—have, over the past 35 years or so, produced increases in electoral volatility as well as reduced turnout at elections. New parties have been formed after a period when the party systems of the developed world appeared to be frozen. Old parties, being cautious and often unwieldy, have lagged in adapting to new circumstances. One of the most extreme cases of volatility was the 1993 Canadian federal election, in which the Progressive Conservatives fell from 43 per cent to 16 per cent of the popular vote and the NDP from 20 per cent to 7 per cent, while the new Bloc Québécois received 14 per cent and the Reform Party rose from barely

2 per cent to 19 per cent. Italy had seen the sudden rise of the Northern League even before Forza Italia broke onto the scene, and in 2013 saw the equally meteoric rise of the Five Star Movement. In Japan, the scandals of the early 1990s generated several new reforming parties. All of these new formations rejected party politics as it had been conducted (and party politicians as well) while at the same time they were markedly leader-centred. Interestingly, though, the last few years have seen a certain stabilization and return to past patterns: the Canadian right has reunited, and the Liberal Democrats are back in power in Japan, though with a different type of opposition. While each national situation is unique, we can suggest that part of the explanation lies in the efforts of politicians to stabilize the party system through "cartel"-like behaviour.

Conclusion

We have seen how the modern form of capitalism, characterized by neoliberalism and globalization, has seriously undermined parties as sources of policy innovation. At the same time, social changes, many caused by the same economic trends, have undermined the traditional bases of parties. Communications technologies, which are generally credited as a cause rather than an effect of globalization, have also played a role in hollowing out the party organizations and enhancing the role of leaders. The prospect, in other words, is one of continued decline of parties as leaders take on increasing prominence.

Yet this decline is not inevitable; the purported ineluctability of the process of "globalization" is part of the ideology that fuels it. In fact, resistance to its logic, when it is not in citizens' interests, is possible but requires strong organizations with committed members, not electoral fan clubs for media-hyped leaders. Otherwise, the demands of the market economy and the most powerful interest groups will prevail.

Experiments with nonparty democracy have shown its weaknesses. At the turn of the twentieth century, American Progressives advocated "nonpartisan" city government in reaction to corrupt urban political machines. They saw local government in largely technocratic terms, and their attempt to depoliticize it served to mask underlying conflicts of interest rather than eliminate them. Well-organized interest groups were able to impose their agendas with relatively little competition or scrutiny. Without party labels, councillors were harder to hold to account, voters had to expend effort to inform themselves about their records, and turnout fell—elected officials became less, not more, responsible to the electorate.

Parties are not only necessary to organize choice in a representative system and provide stable support for government, they can also play a positive role in enhancing democracy. They can provide the vehicle through which ordinary citizens can affect the course of policy; they can be agencies for political mobilization and participation. Parties can aggregate disparate interests around common purposes, forcing single-issue groups to engage in deliberation and take into account other viewpoints and considerations. Nor are they simply passive aggregators and brokers of existing interests— they can also create new interests and worldviews, and shape existing ones, achieving the highest goals of democratic theory. A democracy without parties, on the other hand, would be a weak and impoverished democracy.

Suggested Readings

Duverger, Maurice. 1959. *Political Parties: Their Origin and Activity in the Modern State.* London: Methuen.

Garrett, Geoffrey. 1998. *Partisan Politics in the Global Economy.* Cambridge: Cambridge University Press. http://dx.doi.org/10.1017/CBO9780511625633

Ginsborg, Paul. 2004. *Silvio Berlusconi: Television, Power, and Patrimony.* London: Verso.

Gunther, Richard, J. R. Montéro, and Juan J. Linz, eds. 2002. *Political Parties: Old Concepts and New Challenges.* New York: Oxford University Press. http://dx.doi.org/10.1093/0199246742.001.0001

Gunther, Richard, and Larry Diamond. 2003. "Species of Political Parties: A New Typology." *Party Politics* 9 (2): 167–99. http://dx.doi.org/10.1177/13540688030092003

Hay, Colin, and Ben Rosamond. 2002. "Globalization, European Integration and the Discursive Construction of Economic Imperatives." *Journal of European Public Policy* 9 (2): 147–67. http://dx.doi.org/10.1080/13501760110120192

Hix, Simon. 2008. *What's Wrong with the European Union and How to Fix It.* Cambridge: Polity.

Katz, Richard, and Peter Mair. 1997. *Party System Change: Approaches and Interpretations.* Oxford: Clarendon.

Katz, Richard, and Peter Mair. 2009. "The Cartel Party Thesis: A Restatement." *Perspectives on Politics* 7 (4): 753–66. http://dx.doi.org/10.1017/S1537592709991782

Kirchheimer, Otto. 1966. "The Transformation of West European Party Systems." In *Political Parties and Political Development,* edited by J. Lapalombara and M. Weiner, 177–200. Princeton, NJ: Princeton University Press.

Mair, Peter. 2014. *On Parties, Party Systems, and Democracy.* Edited by Ingrid van Biezen. Colchester, UK: ECPR Press.

Ross, George. 1996. "The Limits of Political Economy: Mitterrand and the Crisis of the French Left." In *The Mitterrand Era: Policy Alternatives and Political Mobilization in France,* edited by Anthony Daley, 33–55. London: Macmillan. http://dx.doi.org/10.1007/978-1-349-13699-5_2

Russell, Meg. 2005. *Building New Labour: The Politics of Party Organization.* Basingstoke, UK: Palgrave Macmillan. http://dx.doi.org/10.1057/9780230513167

Special Issue in Memory of Peter Mair. 2014. *West European Politics* 37 (2).

References

Beer, Samuel. 1969. *British Politics in the Collectivist Age*. New York:Vintage.

Bentley, Arthur. (1908) 1967. *The Process of Government*. Cambridge, MA: Harvard University Press. http://dx.doi.org/10.4159/harvard.9780674733657

Blondel, Jean, and Jean-Louis Thiébault, with K. Czernicka, T. Inoguchi, U. Pathmanand, and F. Venturino. 2010. *Political Leadership, Parties and Citizens*. London: Routledge.

Blyth, Mark, and Richard Katz. 2005. "From Catch-all Politics to Cartelisation: The Political Economy of the Cartel Party." *West European Politics* 28 (1): 33–60. http://dx.doi.org/10.1080/0140238042000297080

Burke, Edmund. (1770) 1981. "Thoughts on the Cause of the Present Discontents." In *The Writings and Speeches of Edmund Burke*, vol. 2, edited by P. Langford, 251–322. Oxford: Clarendon Press.

Burke, Edmund. (1774) 1996. "Speech at the Conclusion of the Poll" (3 November). In *The Writings and Speeches of Edmund Burke*, vol. 3, edited by W.M. Olofson with J.A. Woods, 64–70. Oxford: Clarendon Press.

Carty, R. Kenneth. 1988. "Three Canadian Party Systems." In *Party Democracy in Canada*, edited by George Perlin, 15–30. Scarborough, ON: Prentice-Hall.

Courtney, John C. 1978. "Recognition of Canadian Political Parties in Parliament and in Law." *Canadian Journal of Political Science* 11 (1): 33–60. http://dx.doi.org/10.1017/S0008423900038750

Crouch, Colin. 2004. *Post-Democracy*. Cambridge: Polity.

Gramsci, Antonio. 1971. *Selections from the Prison Notebooks*. Edited by Q. Hoare and G. Nowell Smith. London: Lawrence and Wishart.

Habermas, Jürgen. 1996. *Between Facts and Norms*. Cambridge: Polity.

Jacques, Martin. 1994. "Big Brother." *Sunday Times*, 3 April: 4.1–4.2.

Katz, Richard, and Peter Mair. 1995. "Party Organization, Party Democracy, and the Emergence of the Cartel Party." *Party Politics* 1 (1): 5–28. http://dx.doi.org/10.1177/1354068895001001001

Lenin, Vladimir I. (1904) 1967. "One Step Forward, Two Steps Back." *Selected Works*, vol. 1. New York: International Publishers.

Lipset, Seymour M., and Stein Rokkan. 1967. "Cleavage Structures, Party Systems, and Voter Alignments: An Introduction." In *Party Systems and Voter Alignments*, edited by Seymour M. Lipset and Stein Rokkan, 1–64. New York: Free Press.

Macpherson, C.B. 1977. *The Life and Times of Liberal Democracy*. Oxford: Oxford University Press.

Mair, Peter. 2013. *Ruling the Void:The Hollowing of Western Democracy*. London:Verso.

Meisel, John. 1979. "The Decline of Party in Canada." In *Party Politics in Canada*, 4th ed., edited by Hugh Thorburn, 119–35. Scarborough, ON: Prentice-Hall.

Ostrogorski, Moisei. 1902. *Democracy and the Organization of Political Parties*, vol. 2. New York: Macmillan.

Putnam, Robert. 2000. *Bowling Alone:The Collapse and Revival of American Community*. New York: Simon and Schuster. http://dx.doi.org/10.1145/358916.361990

Rueschemeyer, Dietrich, Evelyn H. Stephens, and John Stephens. 1992. *Capitalist Development and Democracy*. Chicago: University of Chicago Press.

Schumpeter, Joseph. 1950. *Capitalism, Socialism, and Democracy*. 3rd ed. New York: Harper and Row.

PART II

Ideologies and Party Politics

6

Ideological Competition in the Canadian Party System

NELSON WISEMAN

The Nature and Origins of Ideology

The ideology of a political party helps to give it purpose and direction. Ideology energizes the emotions of partisans and feeds their intellects, and successful ideologies will embed themselves in the political culture of a society. An essential characteristic of a party's ideology is its grounding in the past as it is made relevant to contemporary conditions. Followers of a political party's ideology have a sense of being part of a tradition that began before them and will continue after they are gone. Parties, however, must constantly re-examine and reinterpret their ideological underpinnings if they are to remain relevant. Successful political parties modernize their ideologies as the temper of the times change. If a party is to survive and thrive, its ideology must evolve as popular notions of the good society and the nature of government evolve. It must recalibrate its message so that those who identify with it remain faithful and those who have previously shunned it may be won over. Parties therefore may be seen as developing ideological arcs as the social and historical contexts in which they operate change.

Ideology is as old as the ancients. Plato, Aristotle, and others through the centuries have offered interpretations of the relationship between the individual and society: what that relationship is and what it ought to be. For followers and opponents of a political party, ideology offers a prism through which to evaluate issues and policies. Political parties wield ideological terms to justify their policies and to vilify those of their opponents. Societal change contributes to shaping and reshaping commonly used ideological terms such as *conservatism, liberalism, socialism, populism,* and *nationalism*. Conservatism and liberalism, for example, have meant different things in different centuries and in different societies. Context also informs the use of *left* and *right,* the most common ideological categorizations. Canada has had "left" and "right" conservatives, liberals, socialists, populists, and nationalists, and political parties have reflected these orientations.

The terms *ideology* as well as *left* and *right* emerged during the French Revolution when a group of philosophers known as the *idéologues* hailed the triumph of reason over tradition as the revolution's greatest accomplishment

(Lichtheim 1967, 6–7). Committed to freethinking, the *idéologues* rejected the aristocratic and conservative *ancien régime*. They believed that reason must govern as the ultimate authority; they thought ideas could be studied in the way that chemistry or geology and other sciences are studied with the best ideas, in the form of discoverable laws, used to construct progressive, superior, and harmonious social and political orders.

During the revolution, the king's conservative supporters in the National Assembly sat to the speaker's right, and the radical innovative groups sat to his left. Britain and its colonies adopted this arrangement, and it continues in Canadian legislatures (except in Newfoundland[1]). In the nineteenth century, *left* and *right* became associated with the interests of socioeconomic classes; the right became identified with society's dominant and upper classes, the landed and privileged, and the defence of established institutions and prerogatives; the left became identified with those lower on the socioeconomic ladder, the less advantaged, and those contesting the entrenched order in pursuit of greater equality. On a left–right spectrum, the "centre" is associated with the middle classes, a broad amorphous group straddling the middle of a societal hierarchy. The spatial dimension of the left–right spectrum makes it easy to grasp conceptually, although much of the public does not think in terms of "left" and "right" and is confused about or ignorant of them; in 2004, only 47 per cent of respondents to a survey placed the right-wing Canadian Alliance party to the right of the New Democratic Party (NDP), while 18 per cent placed it to its left (*National Post* 2004).

In contemporary politics, rightists disparage dependence on governments as undermining personal dignity; leftists espouse using the instrumentality of government to secure the dignity and well-being of the people. Contemporary rightists value negative liberty: the freedom from government intrusion. Leftists value positive liberty: using government and collective action to liberate groups and individuals from oppressive conditions (Berlin 1969). The media often classify policies such as tax cuts, balanced budgets, military spending, privatization, deregulation, streamlining of government programs, and social spending restraint as right-wing policies, and policies such as government spending, nationalization, and social programs as left-wing. This approach cannot account for the large deficits and debts—the largest in Canadian history in the case of Stephen Harper's Conservatives—run up by right-wing governments and the closure of hospitals and deficit and debt cutting by left-wing governments such as Roy Romanow's Saskatchewan NDP.

Ideology ought not to be conflated with policy. What counts is the motivation behind policy. Is a social welfare program, for example, designed to solidify the status quo, or to bring about greater equality of economic and political power? Vital at the ideological level, therefore, is not policy per se but the rationale for it. The distinction between ideology and policy is, of course, not absolute and is susceptible to dissipation, but a party's long-term values are better guides than an election platform in taking the measure of the party's ideology.

Conservatism, Liberalism, Socialism, Populism, Nationalism

Conservatism, liberalism, and socialism are constellations of normative principles, an assembly of values. Classical conservatives place a premium on respecting traditional authority and established institutions. Skeptical of experimentation, classical conservatives hark back to the past and the wisdom of the ages. They caution people to do and think as their ancestors did. They value social order and stability because they see humans as born flawed and imperfect. They believe in a hierarchically structured society of rank and subordination with amity among social groups. In this communitarian cosmology, distinct social classes cooperate for the common good under the leadership of the higher classes. Classical conservatives believe in an organic, integrated, and inherited intergenerational social order. Class harmony prevails among hierarchically differentiated and unequal classes.

Classical liberalism arose as an ideology antithetical to conservatism. At its heart are the primacy and freedom of the individual. Classical liberals would have the citizen left at liberty to pursue his or her own idea of the good life without state interference. They prize the self-determination, potential, skills, wits, and ambitions of the individual, whom they see as infinitely perfectible. They believe, as Adam Smith did, that the "invisible hand" of the market produces the greatest happiness for the greatest number of people. In the ken of classical liberals, an innate possessive individualist outlook drives man. They uphold the freedom of individuals to acquire and accumulate, to have, to hold, and to be free to pass on their holdings to whomever they wish. Liberals also value the equality of individuals—everyone deserves an equal opportunity to find fulfillment in his own way. They place less faith in the wisdom of government than in the wisdom of individuals. Classical liberals view competition as both natural and good, and they assess social, economic, and political relations in that light. They wish to shrink the state to a minimum and oppose centralized planning by government—they see it as a foolhardy attempt at social and economic engineering. Liberals also champion technology and associate it with human progress.

Classical socialism synthesizes elements of classical conservatism and classical liberalism. Like classical conservatives, classical socialists are communitarians. Both see individuals as shaped by their class or group backgrounds, but unlike classical conservatives classical socialists pursue social equality and the elimination of class distinctions. Like classical liberals, they subscribe to the principles of freedom and equality, but they contend that the concept of a free individual is empty if she or he lacks the necessities of a good life. In the ken of classical socialists, true freedom must include freedom from restraints such as illiteracy, malnourishment, and homelessness. To socialists, poverty is the result of injustice and it is incumbent on the state to alleviate it. The destitute in this view are not necessarily accountable for their condition, and socialists do not perceive the receipt of social welfare as demeaning to personal dignity. Like classical liberals but unlike classical conservatives, classical socialists oppose hierarchy. Where the classical conservative accepts class divisions as natural and where the classical liberal denies the importance of class, the classical socialist upholds the solidarity of a single class, the working class, whose interests should take primacy.

All three of these classical ideologies evolved with societal change. Conservatism has adapted in two stages. First, a liberalized conservatism made its peace with modernity and capitalism and embraced free market economics and then political democracy in the form of an expanded franchise. However, it retained from its pre-capitalist past a readiness to care for "the condition of the people" (O'Kell 2013, 259–60)[2] through the welfare state and other innovations. In Canada, it called itself "progressive conservatism." Second, and more recently, modern conservatism has abandoned this progressive moment and become neoconservative, a variant of classical liberalism. Contemporary conservatives, like classical liberals, give priority to the individual over the community, and they define community as little more than the sum of its self-governing, free-willed individuals.

With the exception of the state's capacity to wage war and to police, contemporary conservatives preach circumscribed government. They treasure the negative liberties or private freedoms associated with classical liberalism. Contemporary conservatives, like classical liberals, view people as autonomous actors and see society as a one-class citizenry. Unlike classical conservatives like Edmund Burke, though, who thought of politicians as public trustees to be judged on their stewardship, neoconservatives insist that those elected behave as delegates obligated to voice the unmediated views of their electors. What is generally termed neoconservatism in the United States is termed neoliberalism in Europe. In Canadian usage, as in Canadian grammar and spelling, the terms are interchangeable.

Contemporary liberalism, like classical liberalism, considers every individual as having a uniquely special dimension, a potential to be realized. To the classical and contemporary liberal, the individual must be free to pursue his own definition of what is good and what makes him happy. Where contemporary liberalism departs from classical liberalism is in its view of the role of the state. Contemporary liberalism advocates a more active and interventionist state on behalf of individuals' welfare than did classical liberalism; it may be described as welfare liberalism. For contemporary liberals, welfare programs and public education facilitate individual development. Liberalism's primary focus, however, remains individual self-realization. Contemporary liberals embrace diversity and affirmative action programs to aid the advancement of individuals from underrepresented and less-privileged groups. Contemporary conservatives, like classical liberals, look askance at such initiatives and dismiss them as judging individuals not on their merits but by the groups to which they belong.

Socialism has evolved as well. Classical socialism stressed the state's determinative role. Some socialists (communists) speak of revolutionary change and government by the waged working class; others (social democrats or democratic socialists) prefer the evolutionary transformation of the economy and the steady amelioration of unjust and inequitable conditions. Communists believe that socialism will inevitably triumph over capitalism; democratic socialists think legislation could transform it gradually. For contemporary socialists, the government continues to have a seminal role in combating inequality, and they support, as did classical socialists, people's cooperative endeavours. Contemporary socialists, or social democrats, are more reconciled to society's class divisions and they court the middle as well as working classes. They accept a mixed economy where capital goods are in both private and public hands. They believe in attaining socialist objectives by regulating private corporations. Theirs is the path of indirect management, or "functional socialism" (Adler-Karlson 1970). Like classical socialists, contemporary socialists consider freedom and equality as mutually dependent and they express concern for those on the margins of society. Unlike classical socialists, however, they also see class lived as race, ethnicity, gender, and sexual orientation, adding these dimensions of exclusion and exploitation to the older socialist analysis of economic class.

Philosophical disputes exist among ideological kin as well as among ideological antagonists. Among contemporary conservatives, for example, libertarians reject the legislation of morality while social conservatives demand it to some degree. Some contemporary liberals still see government as an obstacle to individual advancement while others consider government an instrument to enable it. Among contemporary socialists, some believe in centralized planning, others in decentralized local initiatives.

As with "left" and "right," there are pitfalls in mechanistically linking the policies and programs of conservatives, liberals, and socialists with ideology. Consider the nationalization of industry. It is a policy identified with socialism, but conservatives and liberals who have governed federally and provincially have brought industries such as railroads, banks, hydroelectric power, telephone service, and broadcasting under public ownership. This does not make their nationalization policy either socialist or non-ideological. The indicative tests for ideology are motivation and aspiration: were the industries nationalized for nation-building purposes (a possible classical conservative rationale), to accommodate private interests (a classical liberal concern), or as a transitional step away from capitalism (social democracy)? The federal Conservatives created the CBC for nation-building, British Columbia's Social Credit government nationalized hydropower to facilitate private enterprise, and the Saskatchewan Co-operative Commonwealth Federation (CCF) created a large stable of Crown corporations to redistribute wealth more equitably. Similarly, consider public health care, supported by all of Canada's political parties. A classical conservative may endorse medicare out of a sense of *noblesse oblige,* the obligation of the higher classes to assist those less fortunate. A contemporary liberal may support medicare because he recognizes that illness impedes the individual's opportunity to succeed through no fault of her own. In further contrast, a socialist considers medicare a manifestation of the community collectively caring for all its members in solidarity, an expression of the socialist principle of equality of condition.

Populism and nationalism are two ideologies that may have right-wing, left-wing, conservative, liberal, or socialist manifestations. Populism, an egalitarian orientation that champions the rights and power of ordinary people against privileged elites, is a notoriously slippery concept (Canovan 1981). In celebrating the wisdom, worth, and political supremacy of common folk, populism may have a collectivist hue as it has in Saskatchewan—its provincial motto is "From Many Peoples Strength"—or an individualist shade as it has in Alberta—its provincial motto is "Strong and Free." Some see populism as a threat to democratic politics and associate it with mobs and demagoguery; to others, populism represents the common sense of the common people.

Nationalism, a sentiment based on shared cultural characteristics that bind a group, such as language and ethnicity, also cross-cuts conservatism, liberalism, socialism, left, and right. It is a form of devotion to the culture or interests of one's nation. Each of conservatism, liberalism, and socialism expresses a different nationalist face. Classical conservative nationalism views the nation-state as organic and cooperative, where citizens and groups have duties to one another and to the state. Liberal or civic nationalism repudiates xenophobic nationalism as intolerant and posits a nationalist vision compatible with the equality, freedom, and rights of individuals (Kymlicka 1995). Socialist nationalism has an anti-colonial and anti-imperialist tenor. It prizes national self-determination in the context of an international brotherhood of free and equal nations. Right-wing nationalism includes cultural conservatives who may talk of race, religion, and culture as their nation's fundamental or essential identity, while left-wing nationalists focus on social equality, self-determination, and popular sovereignty.

The Nineteenth Century: Loyalist, Tory, Reformer, Grit, Conservative, Liberal, Bleu, and Rouge

The ideas propelling Canada's parties have been European in origin but American in evolution. Statism—the doctrine of centralized government control over economic planning and policy—has had more prominence in Canada than in the United States. Canada, very much a product of the creation of the United States, represented an ideological counter-narrative to the radical liberalism of the American Revolution. Republican Americans called the decamped Loyalists—those loyal to the British Crown harried from their American farmsteads and mansions—"Tories." Although the ascendant ideology of nineteenth-century liberalism grounded the thinking of the Tories, some classical conservative notions did flavour their liberalism. They subscribed to a more hierarchical and commanding state than did classical liberals; they believed it made for a more orderly and less chaotic society than the society emerging in the United States. Tories characterized the American system of government as mobocracy and identified it with the Jacobins, the radical French revolutionaries and their Reign of Terror. Tories believed a superior polity fused the executive and legislative branches of government with a constitutional monarchy that represented all social classes and hovered above the partisan fray. Tory ideology rejected the American idea of popular will driving government. Devoted to British institutions, the Loyalists bitterly opposed republicanism.[3] However, as North Americans accustomed to economic mobility and representative government, they were no less passionate about individual liberty.

The War of 1812, which pitted Britain against the United States, reinforced Tory conservatism in Canada. Upper Canada's leading Tories, the Family Compact (a privileged group of colonial administrators, financiers, landed gentry, ranking lawyers, judges, and clergymen) were the governor's advisers and the main beneficiaries of his patronage. In opposition, the more liberal Reformers arose in the 1820s to form the largest group in the legislative assembly, but the unelected upper house, the Tory-dominated legislative council, blocked their aspirations for democratic reforms. Reformers wanted a more egalitarian polity with an expanded franchise and a government accountable to elected representatives.

After the Reformers divided over the British colonial connection and free trade with the United States, the Tory and more radical Reformer ideological visions clashed in the Upper Canada Rebellion of 1837. A decade later, the coming of responsible government undid the high Tory right by requiring the government to secure the confidence of the popularly elected assembly. In contrast to the Americans who sought liberty through independence, Canadians achieved it through self-government within the Empire. Radical left-wing liberal reformers, largely farmers drawn from southwestern Ontario known as Clear Grits, considered the moderate Reformers who held office as too accepting of the Tory conception of a hierarchical society.

Even before the arrival of the decamped Loyalists, classical conservative thinking had underpinned French Canada's quasi-feudal society. After the Conquest of 1760, the very conservative Roman Catholic Church served as the object of French Canadians' collective allegiance, but it was Lower Canada's version of the elite Family Compact, the anglophone Château Clique, who advised the governor. French Canada was more like preliberal, prerevolutionary France than like its revolutionary successor. In exchange for clerical fealty during the Lower Canada Rebellion of 1837–38, the British left the conservative Catholic leadership undisturbed as the political and cultural elite of French-Canadian society. A mutually reinforcing arrangement had the economically dominant British using a strong centralized state to control industry, finance, and commerce, while the economically subordinate French Canadians looked to their religion for spiritual inspiration to preserve their traditional rural ways. French Canada's illiterate *habitants* identified with the rebellion's anti-British nationalists, but they could not fathom the republican and anti-clerical ideas of some of its leaders. Populism was the common denominator in both the Upper and Lower Canada rebellions, but in both cases rebellion faltered.

The conservative–liberal dynamic in Upper Canada had a Lower Canada counterpart, but liberalism was much weaker there. The liberal ideas of some of the rebellion's leaders inspired the creation of the Institut Canadien and the Parti Rouge. In reaction, the Church-endorsed Parti Bleu appeared. The complementary liberal orientations of English Canada's Grits and French Canada's Rouges provided a common ideological basis for what eventually emerged as the national Liberal Party, while the corresponding ideological outlooks of the Tories and Bleus provided the basis for the creation of the national Conservatives. The colours of those pre-Confederation parties—red, traditionally associated with left-wing radicals, and blue with conservative parties—continue to serve as the colours of today's Liberal and Conservative parties.

The symmetry among the partisan factions of English and French Canada reflected another ideological difference between British North America and the United States. The latter constitutionally separated religion and the state amidst a proliferation of nonconformist, individualist-oriented Protestant sects. A somewhat more hierarchical British Canada, in contrast, granted constitutional status, land, and control over education to the hierarchically organized Anglican and Catholic churches, which were closely identified with the conservative English and French political parties. Canada recognized ethnic, linguistic, and denominational particularisms as group rights; the United States denied them in favour of universal individual rights. This spoke to the relative strength of classical conservatism in Canada.

Although the Conservative and Liberal parties have undergone great changes, their ideological origins lie in the pre-Confederation period. John A. Macdonald's aptly titled party at the time of Confederation, the Liberal-Conservatives, displayed a liberalism tinted by classical conservatism. After Confederation, the Conservatives represented the Tory ideological tradition and the Liberal Party, which only emerged in the 1870s, represented the more radical Reform–Grit orientation. As the parties adapted to changing conditions, their ideological orientations evolved.

Rooted in nineteenth-century British conservatism, Canadian conservatism had both left and right faces. As in Britain, those with wealth, rank, and authority identified with the Conservatives, but their party was in some sense a left-wing force in that it recognized that the welfare of the weaker classes was vital to maintaining social order and deference to the primacy of the higher classes. Macdonald twinned the interests of labour and capital by wooing workers with a Trade Union Act in the 1870s that undercut the Liberals. Devoted to classical liberal ideals, their most influential spokesman, Toronto *Globe* publisher George Brown, opposed both the nine-hour day and the Toronto typographers' strike, the century's most notable strike. Toronto's conservative newspaper, the *Leader,* supported the typographers, and labour rallies and working-class candidates appeared in support of the Conservatives (Creighton 1943, 362–76; Kealey 1991, 216).

Classical liberalism, at the core of Liberal Party thinking, counterposed the individual with the state. Canada's classical liberals, like those of Britain, championed negative liberty and business liberalism. They proffered free markets as the solution for policy problems, placing individual freedom ahead of the interests of collectives such as the nation and social classes. The Liberals prized individuals' competitiveness and acquisitiveness over efforts to manage the economy or to harmonize the interests of distinct economic classes. As classical liberals, they discounted both economic class and cultural distinctions such as ethnicity, religion, and language. They considered the state a product of wilful individuals acting freely.

The Liberal Party, however, accommodated Canada's cultural distinctions and, like the Liberals in Britain, accepted the hierarchical Canadian political system with its monarch and unelected Senate. On economic issues, the Liberals favoured free trade and opposed the 1879 National Policy of the Conservatives, whose objective was to grow Canada's nascent industries by protecting them from American competition. The Conservatives were more state- and British-oriented than the Liberals, who were skeptical of the Tory notion of the state as societal cement. The Liberals preferred to see Canada as a North American state unencumbered by Britain's class hierarchies. Tinged by English Canada's Tory and French Canada's quasi-feudal foundations, however, the Liberals were not as market oriented, ruggedly individualist, egalitarian, or fiercely hostile toward centralized federalism and welfare liberalism as were their American counterparts. The Liberals sided with defenders of provincial rights in disputes between Canada's two orders of government, a position consistent with both their suspicion of big government and their newfound affiliation with Quebec.

The Twentieth Century

Two elections near the turn of the century highlighted partisan and ideological differences about Canada's place in the world. In both the 1891 and 1911 campaigns the issue of free trade with the United States featured prominently. Conservatives cheered Canada's membership in a globally federated and heterogeneous British Empire; they dwelled on the emotional attachments of English-speaking Canadians to Britain, and they rejected truck or trade with the Americans. The Liberals, led by Wilfrid Laurier, were more moderate imperialists. They looked more favourably upon enhancing ties between Canada and its southern neighbour. Laurier's French-Canadian compatriots cared little for British imperialism. They saw Quebec and Canada as their only home and the rallying point of their nationalism.

The Liberals prevailed in the 1896 election, but their failure to act aggressively on free trade, the subsequent dislocations occasioned by World War I, and farmers' anxieties about the emergence of an industrial, urbanized Canada led to the rural-based Progressive Party becoming the second-largest party in Parliament in the 1920s. The Progressives represented the foremost populist upsurge in the first half of the century. Formerly Liberals, the Progressives felt the Liberal Party had betrayed them by maintaining tariffs, which made farm equipment unnecessarily expensive and favoured central Canadian industries. Influenced by American agrarian movements such as the populist People's Party, the Progressives wanted to jettison many parliamentary conventions, including party discipline. They proposed citizen-initiated referendums and recall legislation as antidotes to the power of parties and party leaders. They also found fault with the first-past-the-post electoral system. Governing in Manitoba and Alberta as farmers' parties, they adopted the single transferrable vote in the largest cities and the alternative vote in the rural constituencies.[4]

The Progressives resented the financial–industrial power of the barons of Montreal's St. James and Toronto's Bay streets. They were hostile to the banks, the railroads, and elites generally. Within the decade, however, most of the federal Progressives returned to their Liberal roots. Provincially, Alberta's Social Credit movement inherited the radical liberal populism of the Progressives that stressed individual initiative. Saskatchewan's CCF represented populism's socialist manifestation.

The Depression broadened Canada's ideological spectrum, and the upshot of World War II subsequently narrowed it. English-Canadian communists and French-Canadian radical right-wing Catholics had offered polar alternatives to the failures of capitalist liberal democracy in the 1930s when both of these radical creeds and the parties and movements that expounded them attained their zenith. However, both ideologies and their partisans shrank as political forces with the defeat of Nazism and the onset of the Cold War. In contrast, democratic socialism or social democracy successfully implanted itself during the Depression. Unlike the communists, who served as ideological loudspeakers for Moscow, the CCF's British labour and Christian roots imparted a solid cultural legitimacy to their message; it protected the party against the charge of preaching an alien ideology (Robin 1968, 276).

Unlike conservatives and liberals, social democrats lauded social and economic planning by government. The CCF's *Regina Manifesto,* formulated during the darkest days of the Depression as capitalist ideology floundered under its own weight, had a hyperbolic ring—"No C.C.F. Government will rest content until it has eradicated capitalism. . . ."—but the party's policy proposals were more moderate. To avoid the appearance of being too radical, the widely read book by the party's brain trust, *Social Planning for Canada,* avoided the word *socialism* in its 524 pages (League for Social Reconstruction 1935) at a time when both Nazis and Soviets described themselves as "socialists."

A muted ideological climate prevailed during the Cold War and toward the end of the Liberals' long hold on power that had begun in the early 1920s. Except for an interregnum during the Depression, it lasted until the late 1950s. Under Mackenzie King and Louis St. Laurent, the Liberals and the state's senior bureaucrats increasingly merged, becoming "an instrument for the depoliticization" of Canadian politics (Whitaker 1977, 420). Postwar prosperity, unlike the aftershocks of World War I, led social democrats to take stock and modernize their program. The CCF's *Winnipeg Declaration* of 1956 made a kind of peace with capitalism, modified the party's position on nationalization, and emphasized the "need for private enterprise which can make a useful contribution to the development of our economy" (Socialist History Project, 2014b). The transformation of the CCF into the New Democratic Party in 1961 confirmed its ideological reorientation; where the CCF described itself as a federation of "farmer-labour-socialist," the NDP described itself as appealing to labour, farmers, and "liberally minded Canadians." Welfare liberalism and social democracy were converging.

To recast their image as an establishment party of white Anglo-Saxon Protestants opposed to agrarian interests and to counter the growing popularity of the CCF, a Conservative conference in Port Hope adopted what may be termed a red tory platform during World War II. Rooted in classical conservatism, red toryism inclines more toward the commonweal than the free market system. After Conservative Prime Minister and millionaire corporate lawyer R.B. Bennett presaged the shift with his New Deal proposals in the 1930s in an unsuccessful deathbed gesture to avoid defeat, the Conservatives drafted Manitoba's Progressive Premier John Bracken to lead them. They renamed themselves Progressive Conservatives and pledged a range of expansive social security measures consistent with social democratic prescriptions. Elected in 1943 on a platform of "economic and social security from the cradle to the grave," pensions, mothers' allowances, and "the fairest and most advanced labour laws" (*Globe and Mail* 1943, quoted in Dyck 1996, 338), Ontario's Progressive Conservatives went on to govern for 42 uninterrupted years.

During this period, the federal Progressive Conservatives under John Diefenbaker and Robert Stanfield both modernized and retained some traditional conservative principles. Diefenbaker fanned his party's historical animus to the United States and celebrated the British Commonwealth and royal symbols. His government's Bill of Rights codified the rights of individuals to life, liberty, personal security, and enjoyment of property, but unlike the Liberals' subsequent Charter of Rights, the Bill of Rights was not constitutionally entrenched. Stanfield honed the Conservatives' red tory image, reminding his caucus that Conservatives had pioneered federal trade union legislation and campaigning for a guaranteed annual income for society's most vulnerable citizens. He cited classical conservative Edmund Burke and noted that while conservatives supported free enterprise, unlike liberals they did not worship at its altar (Stanfield 1987, 376–81). Stanfield's successor, Joe Clark, defined Canada as a "community of communities" (Christian and Campbell 1983, 229)—a contrast to the liberal notion of a political community of undifferentiated individuals as well as a distinctly un-American formulation.

Liberal thinking also evolved. In 1919, the Liberals had endorsed a social welfare agenda including health, old-age, and unemployment insurance programs. They implemented only a primitive old-age pension program, making it contingent on provincial participation and only after being pressured by two socialist MPs. The Depression led the Liberals, as it had the Conservatives, to recognize that preserving capitalism required some redistribution of wealth and the creation of a welfare floor. Welfare liberalism now complemented the unvarnished business liberalism of the Liberals' earlier years with the party launching and expanding Canada's modern welfare state between the late 1940s and late 1960s.

This permitted the Liberals to fend off socialist challenges from the left. When the temper of the times took a turn in a contemporary conservative direction, as it did in the 1970s and 1990s, the Liberals responded in a rightward direction, imposing wage controls and cutting transfers for provincial social programs. While the Conservatives and NDP often prided themselves as being parties of principle, the Liberals boasted that they were non-ideological, some in an exaggerated manner. For example, in the words of Liberal MP Pierre Gimaiel:

> To be a Liberal is first and foremost to be . . . a person whose leitmotif, whose supreme will, is to provide opportunities for development and progress for all Canadians. In such a situation, anything can be justified. If the development of individual Canadians is to be achieved through socialization, the Liberal party can turn socialistic. If the development of individual Canadians is to be achieved through a turn to the right through a strengthening in the industry, the Liberal party can move to the right. If in order to promote our development the Liberal party thinks we have to be communistic, we shall be communistic. This is what it is all about to be a Liberal. (*Globe and Mail* 1982, 8)

In 1969, a leftist group known in the NDP as the Waffle adopted an assertive nationalist position. It harked back to the *Regina Manifesto,* calling for "the public ownership of the means of production" but in a new context of combating American corporate capitalism, which it defined as the "major threat to Canadian survival" (Socialist History Project 2014a). The Waffle soon faded away, but its emergence against the backdrop of Canada's centenary coincided with new nationalist stirrings in the older parties. As British power ebbed internationally, English-speaking Canadians' Britishness evaporated. With English-speaking Canadians lacking a common sense of identity as a coherent national community, each party strove to define the national community in its own way.

Elected in the 1980s, Brian Mulroney's Conservatives voiced both business liberal and some red tory sentiments. Before coming to office, Mulroney had decried welfare programs and "the tragic process of the Swedenizing of

Canada" (quoted in Cohen 1998, 334). On the hustings, however, he described those programs as a "sacred trust not to be tampered with" (Bashevkin 2002, 28). The media offered "blue tories"—essentially Conservatives advocating business liberalism or contemporary conservatism—as a term counterposing red tories, but "blue tories" are not true ideological tories because they are free of the tory notion of giving priority to the community. Blue tory-ism or neoconservatism—opposition to government intervention in the economy—proved a stronger force among Conservatives who, turning their back on their history, pursued a free trade agreement with the United States. The Liberals also changed their historical posture vis-à-vis the United States, opposing the initiative.

Mulroney's coalition of Québécois nationalists and blue tory Western fiscal conservatives led the Conservatives to backtrack on their promise to use only business criteria in awarding government contracts. Although a Western Canadian bid was cheaper, technologically superior, and recom-mended by the nonpartisan bureaucracy, the government awarded a major military contract to a Quebec firm. This triggered the creation of the pop-ulist conservative Reform Party. Composed mainly of disillusioned Con-servatives, it dismissed Mulroney as an ideological apostate. Reform went on to capture the Conservatives' Western support in the 1990s.

Led by former Social Crediter Preston Manning, the Reform Party reimagined Canada by offering a discourse challenging the "politics of cultural recognition"—initiatives such as affirmative action programs—with the principle of "universal citizenship"; it denigrated special status for Quebec, bilingualism, multiculturalism, and Indigenous self-government (Patten 1999). Echoing the Progressives of the 1920s, Reform proposed direct democracy in the form of citizen initiatives, referendums, and recall. Representing an ideological counterpoint to Reform's pan-Canadian nationalism and capturing the Mulroney Conservatives' Quebec base, the Bloc Québécois led by Lucien Bouchard and then Gilles Duceppe advanced Québécois nationalism and Quebec's secession from Canada. Mulroney's coalition of Québécois nationalists and Western conservatives unravelled in the 1993 election, effectively replaced by the Bloc and Reform.

The Twenty-First Century

The new century began as the last one ended: a fragmented five-party system in Parliament and a broadened ideological spectrum. Soon, however, Reform's successor party, the Canadian Alliance, merged with the remnants of the enfeebled Progressive Conservatives. Some Conservative red tories, including Joe Clark and former cabinet minister Flora MacDonald, objected, but to no avail. A flashback to the older conservatism came on the eve of the merger when Senator Lowell Murray, a former chief of staff to Stanfield and Mulroney cabinet minister, pleaded with Progressive Conservative leader Peter MacKay to resist the union. He noted that true conservatives

> believe that government's job is to provide stability and security against the excesses of the market. Democratic politics must define the public interest and ensure it always prevails over more private ambitions. To that extent the forces of technology and globalization need to be tamed. . . . Reform conservatism which is what the Alliance practises relies on people's fear of moral and economic decline. . . . It spoils all the good arguments for the market economy by making a religion of it, pretending there are market criteria and market solutions to all of our social and political problems. (Murray 2003)

Nevertheless, the new Reform-cum-Conservative party exhibited some traces of the older conservative ideology and its symbols. In government, they reattached the use of "Royal," a term the Liberals had detached, to the titles of both the Canadian Air Force and Navy; they opened joint Canada–British diplomatic missions abroad; and they hung the Queen's portrait, after a lengthy absence, at the headquarters of the Department of Foreign Affairs. In contrast, Liberal Deputy Prime Minister John Manley had called for an end to the monarchy, and over one-third of Liberal convention delegates voted to study severing ties with the "British Crown" (Taber 2012). In Quebec, support for the Bloc Québécois indicated that its nationalist message had successfully cut across the conservative–liberal–socialist ideological triad despite the party styling itself as social democratic. Although the Bloc was decimated in the 2011 election, Québécois nationalism persists, expressed by the separatist Parti Québécois and Québec solidaire and, less stridently, by Quebec's other parties.

Ideological fault lines persist among Canada's political parties, but the current century shows evidence of attenuated ideological and partisan fidelity among voters. There is perhaps an increasing mixture of once more clearly distinguishable ideological positions among the parties. The constitutions of the major parties, however, continue to demarcate philosophic differences. The Conservatives offer the neoconservative "belief that the best guarantors of . . . prosperity and well-being . . . are: the freedom of individual Canadians to pursue their enlightened and legitimate self-interest within a competitive economy; [and] . . . to enjoy the fruits of their labour to the greatest possible extent" (Conservative Party of Canada 2011). The Liberals commit themselves to "individual freedom, responsibility and human dignity in the framework of a just society, and political freedom in the framework of meaningful participation by all persons" (Liberal Party of Canada 2011, 1). In contrast to the right-wing orientation of the Conservatives and the more centrist articulation of the Liberals, the preamble to the NDP constitution refers unabashedly to the party's "social democratic and democratic socialist traditions" and its work "to build a more just, equal, and sustainable Canada within a global community" (New Democratic Party of Canada 2013).

Conclusion

Changing circumstances in the world and in Canada in recent years have produced newer "isms" that conservative, liberal, and socialist ideologues have had to address and incorporate into their ideological frames. They have been compelled to specify their orientations to issues such as identity and diversity politics, feminism, environmentalism, and globalization. The latter imposes new limits on the state's behaviour and on the capacity of a political party, whatever its ideology, to affect in any great measure the course of events. The rise and studies of left- and right-wing think tanks such as the Fraser Institute and the Canadian Centre for Policy Alternatives represent another and newer dimension to ideological competition; they inform and buttress the policies of political parties.

In the 1950s and 1960s, many social scientists argued that ideology had died, that managerial and technical expertise had rendered the differences between leftists and rightists, between conservatives, liberals, and socialists obsolete; technology and technocrats could engineer the "good society" (Waxman 1968). In the 1990s, with the demise of the Soviet Union, Francis Fukuyama (1992) argued that liberal individualism and free markets represented the terminus of history, the irreversible triumph of liberal democratic capitalism. Competing ideologies, however, will most likely remain an integral feature of political parties and party systems. Ideological postures become apparent when one reads the lines and between the lines of parties' professed principles and platforms. Ideas always flourish, and ideological competition is likely to persist so long as people organize as political parties.

Suggested Readings

Ball, Terence, Richard Dagger, William Christian, and Colin Campbell. 2012. *Political Parties and the Democratic Ideal*. 3rd ed. Toronto: Pearson Education.
Campbell, Colin, and William Christian. 1996. *Parties, Leaders, and Ideologies in Canada*. Toronto: McGraw-Hill Ryerson.
Fierlbeck, Katherine. 2005. *The Development of Political Thought in Canada: An Anthology*. Peterborough, ON: Broadview Press.
Forbes, H.D. 1985. *Canadian Political Thought*. Toronto: Oxford University Press.

Monière, Denis. 1981. *Ideologies in Quebec.* Toronto: University of Toronto Press.
Noël, Alain, and Jean-Philippe Thérien. 2008. *Left and Right in Global Politics.* Cambridge: Cambridge University Press. http://dx.doi.org/10.1017/CBO9780511790751

Notes

1   The peculiar arrangement in Newfoundland, where the government sits on the left, arose in the 1850s when the ruling legislators decided to sit closer to the heaters located to the left of the governor's chair in the Colonial Building.
2   British Conservative Prime Minister Benjamin Disraeli used the term in his novel *Sybil* to refer to the "degradation of the multitude."
3   Republicanism is a belief in a system of government in which citizens elect their head of state rather than being his or her subjects.
4   See Dennis Pilon's chapter in this book.

References

Adler-Karlson, Gunnar. 1970. *Reclaiming the Canadian Economy: A Swedish Approach through Functional Socialism.* Toronto: Anansi.
Bashevkin, Sylvia. 2002. *Welfare Hot Buttons: Women, Work, and Social Policy Reform.* Toronto: University of Toronto Press.
Berlin, Isaiah. 1969. "Two Concepts of Liberty." In *Isaiah Berlin: Four Essays on Liberty.* Oxford: Oxford University Press.
Canovan, Margaret. 1981. *Populism.* New York: Harcourt Brace Jovanovich.
Christian, William, and Colin Campbell. 1983. *Political Parties and Ideologies in Canada: Liberals, Conservatives, Socialists, Nationalists.* Toronto: McGraw-Hill Ryerson.
Cohen, Daniel. 1998. "The Political Legacy of Neoconservative Rhetoric and Governance: A Comparative Study of the Impact of Political Leadership on Consumer Sentiment in Canada and the United States." Doctoral dissertation, Department of Political Science, Carleton University, Ottawa.
Conservative Party of Canada. 2011. *Constitution.* As amended by the delegates to the National Convention on June 11. As consolidated by the National Constitution Committee and approved by National Council. http://www.conservative.ca/media/2012/06/Sept2011-Constitution-E.pdf
Creighton, Donald G. 1943. "George Brown, Sir John A. Macdonald, and the 'Workingman.'" *Canadian Historical Review* 24 (4): 362–76. http://dx.doi.org/10.3138/CHR-024-04-03
Dyck, Rand. 1996. *Provincial Politics in Canada.* 3rd ed. Scarborough, ON: Prentice-Hall.
Fukuyama, Francis. 1992. *The End of History and the Last Man.* New York: Free Press.
Globe and Mail. 1943. "The Constructive Platform of the Progressive Conservative Party in the Province of Ontario," July 3.
Globe and Mail. 1982. "The Ottawa Scene," March 1.
Kealey, Gregory S. 1991. *Toronto Workers Respond to Industrial Capitalism, 1867–1892.* Toronto: University of Toronto Press.
Kymlicka, Will. 1995. *Multicultural Citizenship: A Liberal Theory of Minority Rights.* Oxford: Clarendon Press.

League for Social Reconstruction. 1935. *Social Planning for Canada.* Toronto: Nelson.

Liberal Party of Canada. 2011. *Constitution.* As adopted and amended at the Biennial Convention on November 30 and December 1, 2006, further amended at the Biennial Convention in Vancouver on May 2, 2009, and at the Extraordinary Convention on June 18, 2011, and ratified by the National Board of Directors on July 9, 2011. https://www.liberal.ca/files/2010/05/lpc-2009-constitution-en.pdf

Lichtheim, George. 1967. *The Concept of Ideology and Other Essays.* New York: Vintage Books.

Murray, Lowell. 2003. "Don't Do It, Peter." *Globe and Mail,* June 23.

National Post. 2004. "Canadians Confused by Left and Right." November 16. http://www.canada.com/national/features/mandate/story.html?id=5F5BDF34–59FF-4F8E-9BA4–72C0F483324A

New Democratic Party of Canada. 2013. *Constitution.* http://xfer.ndp.ca/2013/constitution/2013_CONSTITUTION_E.pdf

O'Kell, Robert. 2013. *Disraeli: The Romance of Politics.* Toronto: University of Toronto Press.

Patten, Steve. 1999. "The Reform Party's Re-imagining of Canada." *Journal of Canadian Studies* 34 (1): 27–51.

Robin, Martin. 1968. *Radical Politics and Canadian Labour, 1880–1930.* Kingston: Industrial Relations Centre, Queen's University.

Socialist History Project. 2014a. "The Waffle Manifesto: For an Independent Socialist Canada." Accessed July 5. http://www.socialisthistory.ca/Docs/Waffle/WaffleManifesto.htm

Socialist History Project. 2014b. "The Winnipeg Declaration of Principles (1956)." Accessed June 27. http://www.socialisthistory.ca/Docs/CCF/Winnipeg.htm

Stanfield, Robert L. 1987. "Conservative Principles and Philosophy." In *Politics: Canada,* 6th ed., edited by Paul W. Fox and Graham White, 376–81. Toronto: McGraw-Hill Ryerson.

Taber, Jane. 2012. "Ottawa Notebook." *Globe and Mail,* January 16. http://www.theglobeandmail.com/news/politics/ottawa-notebook/liberals-vote-to-keep-monarchy-legalize-pot-at-convention/article620760/#dashboard/follows/

Waxman, Chaim I., ed. 1968. *The End of Ideology Debate.* New York: Funk and Wagnalls.

Whitaker, Reginald. 1977. *The Government Party: Organizing and Financing the Liberal Party of Canada, 1930–58.* Toronto: University of Toronto Press.

7

The Liberal Party of Canada: Rebuilding, Resurgence, and Return to Power

BROOKE JEFFREY

Introduction

When the dust had settled after the May 2011 federal election, the once mighty Liberal Party of Canada found itself on the outside looking in. With only 34 seats in the House of Commons, the party that built modern Canada and governed for most of the twentieth century was reduced, for the first time ever, to third-party status. This astonishing reversal of fortunes was all the more surprising given that the Liberals under Jean Chrétien had only recently formed three successive majority governments. Many observers had assumed the party was firmly entrenched in power for the foreseeable future. Indeed, after their third electoral victory in 2000 the Liberals' future appeared so secure that political scientist Bruce Doern wrote "Jean Chrétien stands astride the Canadian political scene without much effective opposition." Doern further speculated about "the degree to which a one-party state is congealing at the federal level under the Liberals" (Doern 2003, 3).

Yet little more than a decade later, the Liberals under Michael Ignatieff were humiliated. Ignatieff lost his own seat in the 2011 election and promptly resigned, throwing the party into further disarray as it faced its third leadership contest in five years. With so few seats in Parliament, the funding for the Liberal caucus and leader's office was dramatically reduced. The party's public visibility through question period and media scrums also decreased sharply. Meanwhile, the party organization was in shambles, and the steep drop in revenue from public and private sources made attempts to rebuild difficult if not impossible.

The situation appeared to be so serious that many observers predicted the imminent demise of the party and the emergence of a more polarized two-party system at the federal level, one pitting the new right-wing Conservative Party of Stephen Harper against the socialist NDP. Former NDP leader Ed Broadbent, for one, declared that there was no longer any room for the Liberals and their "mushy middle" (Jeffrey 2010, 10). Pollster Darrell Bricker and *Globe and Mail* Ottawa Bureau Chief John Ibbitson, whose book *The Big Shift* (Bricker and Ibbitson 2013) declared "the centre isn't there anymore," also concluded "the odds are good" that the Liberals would die. Their views were echoed by noted political pundit and journalist Peter Newman (2012), who by late 2011 had penned *When the Gods Changed: The Death of Liberal Canada*. In various interviews promoting his book, Newman declared darkly that not only the Liberal Party but liberalism itself was finished as a political force in Canada.

To appreciate the full extent of this devastating turnaround, it is worth noting that even after this rout the Liberal Party of Canada remained the most successful political machine in the Western democratic world, albeit on the strength of past performance. The party had obtained more votes than any other party in 13 of the 17 federal elections held between 1945 and 2000. Until 2006, every Liberal leader with one exception (Edward Blake) had served as prime minister. Four Liberal leaders—Mackenzie King (21.5 years), Pierre Trudeau (15.5 years), Wilfrid Laurier (15 years), and Jean Chrétien (10 years)—were among the longest serving prime ministers in Canadian history. In fact, the party had been so successful that it was commonly referred to as "the natural governing party," leading political scientist John Meisel to declare at one point that "the line between the Liberal Party and the government has become tenuous" (Meisel 1972). An exasperated Alliance Leader Stephen Harper reinforced this view when he declared "You can be a good Canadian and not vote Liberal!" (Jeffrey 2015, 331).

The obvious question, then, is what went wrong for the Liberals? The answer is less clear-cut. On the one hand, there were several glaring immediate problems that cost the party dearly in the federal elections of 2006, 2008, and 2011. On the other hand, some of the reasons for the party's seemingly precipitous fall from grace were actually the result of a long but steady decline caused by its failure to address several important underlying problems. In the end, the more fundamental question facing the Liberal Party as it attempted to rebuild was whether these problems were insurmountable, as so many observers speculated, or whether it was instead undergoing another temporary "interlude" and the Liberal brand was still strong.

The following analysis examines the party's progress since 2011 in addressing both these immediate and underlying issues as the Liberals introduced a range of rebuilding measures that directly contributed to their remarkable turnaround in the 2015 election. It then concludes by outlining how the Liberals overcame their third-place standing when the writ was dropped with a near-perfectly executed campaign, one that returned them to power with a substantial majority, suggesting that liberalism and the Liberal Party are indeed resurgent.

The Leadership Issue

Among the most obvious short-term mistakes made by the Liberal Party was its choice of leaders. Beginning in November 2003 with Paul Martin, a former finance minister under Jean Chrétien, the party proceeded to choose three leaders within the space of five years, each of whom was fatally flawed.

Martin had long been viewed as the heir apparent and party saviour, and his victory in the November 2003 leadership race was frequently referred to as a coronation. Yet once in power Martin's performance, perhaps falling victim to unrealistically high expectations, did not impress. His perceived inability to make decisions, epitomized by the "Mr. Dithers" label he was soon awarded by the press, was problematic in itself and not something expected of Liberal leaders. Nor was his continued and highly public vendetta against those in the party who had supported his predecessor, Jean Chrétien, thereby delivering a serious blow to the party's legendary reputation for internal unity. Coupled with Martin's ill-fated decision to launch a public inquiry into the sponsorship scandal in the form of the Gomery Commission and his poor personal performance in the election campaigns of June 2004 and January 2006, the Liberals' majority quickly fell to a minority and then a loss, relegating the party to the Official Opposition with only 95 seats. Martin then surprised many by stepping down as leader immediately, forcing a leadership race under trying circumstances.

His unexpected successor in the December 2006 leadership vote was the politically inept Stéphane Dion, a former political science professor and staunch federalist from Quebec. Dion had been appointed directly to a cabinet post and given a safe seat by Chrétien after the 1995 Quebec referendum, to help him implement his Plan B approach to national unity that resulted in the Clarity Act. Dion was undeniably effective as the sherpa for the act in his role as minister of intergovernmental affairs. Then he moved to the environment portfolio shortly afterwards, where he became a well-known proponent of government action to combat climate change. The popular support he received for this stance led him to throw his hat into the ring in the 2006 leadership race, where he won an upset victory in the party's first contest held under controversial new constitutional rules.[1] However, his lack of political experience and shallow roots within the party, to say nothing of his poor communication skills in English, were highly problematic in a national leader of the party—constraints that became evident long before his disastrous performance in the October 2008 election, which saw the Liberals reduced by a further 20 seats to 77. Nevertheless, and unlike Paul Martin, Dion attempted to stay on as leader. But within two months he had created another political landmine for the Liberal Party in the form of a botched attempt to form a coalition government with the NDP, thus handing Conservative Prime Minister Stephen Harper a weapon to be used repeatedly against Dion's successors. Dion himself resigned shortly after, having been urged to do so by several of the party's key organizers and elder statesmen.

By now the party was in severe difficulty. Rather than launch yet another leadership race immediately, a decision was made to appoint the second-place finisher in the last race, Michael Ignatieff, as interim leader. Then, in another extraordinary and unprecedented move, the party decided not to hold an official leadership race but instead "confirmed" Ignatieff at its scheduled biennial conference in Vancouver in May 2009.

Unfortunately, Ignatieff, who was first elected as a Member of Parliament (MP) in 2008, had equally shallow roots within the Liberal Party and soon demonstrated an equal lack of political acumen as well.[2] In addition, although he was a widely regarded academic and public intellectual, Ignatieff had resided outside of the country for decades before being encouraged to return and take on the leadership role in the party, a strategy that promptly backfired as Conservative attack ads began labelling him an "outsider" and telling voters "he did not come back for you." Over the next two years he proved unable to establish any real rapport with Canadians, and although he performed far better than expected in the 2011 campaign, many observers argued that he had effectively lost the election before it began (Ibbitson 2011).

This rapid succession of unconvincing leaders was particularly traumatic for the Liberals, given their long history of success. It was also symptomatic of a deeper leader-centric problem. In the past Liberal leaders had served for lengthy periods, most for a decade or more. This was true even when the leader did not win an election or failed to deliver a majority, as the case of Lester Pearson proved. The tradition of long service by Liberal leaders was accompanied by a culture of loyalty to the leader and a deep-seated commitment to party unity by the party grassroots and caucus members alike. In the second half of the twentieth century this Liberal tradition stood in stark contrast to that of the Progressive Conservative Party. The Liberals' only real opposition capable of forming a government at the federal level, the Tories engaged in numerous highly publicized leadership coups that severely damaged their credibility, a phenomenon so well-known that it was referred to as the Tory syndrome (Perlin 1979). Interestingly, this pattern of leadership struggles was also followed in the early days by the new Reform and Canadian Alliance parties.

Yet with the selection of John Turner to succeed the venerable Pierre Trudeau as leader in 1984, this tradition, which had served the party so well in the past, began to crumble. Throughout his brief and troubled leadership, Turner was beset by numerous challenges to his stewardship by supporters of Jean Chrétien, some of which became public. Nevertheless, Turner was able to choose the time and place of his leaving, but his successor, Jean Chrétien, was not so lucky. Despite delivering an unprecedented three successive majority governments, Chrétien was ultimately forced to step down as the result of a palace coup orchestrated by supporters of his former leadership opponent, Paul Martin.

However, Martin failed to deliver for the party. As many critics noted, the Liberals' long-standing success had apparently engendered an expectation of a quick return to power even when they inevitably lost after lengthy periods in office. As Jon Pammett et al. (2010) put it, the history of federal elections had been one of Liberal "dynasties" and Progressive Conservative "interludes." This in turn had increasingly led Liberal elites and grassroots members in the post-Trudeau era to assume that a change in leadership would be a sufficient remedy to ensure the party's restoration to its proper place governing the country. As a result, both party unity and loyalty to the leader, which had been sorely tried during Martin's lengthy campaign to unseat Chrétien, were unceremoniously replaced by an increasingly frantic search for a new messiah to lead the party out of the wilderness. Moreover, the failure of any leader to achieve that turnaround quickly was increasingly considered unacceptable, truncating their terms of office and leading to the unprecedented number of costly and politically problematic leadership contests in such a short space of time.

Meanwhile the internecine warfare begun during the Martin–Chrétien era continued by proxy throughout the Dion and Ignatieff leaderships and threatened to become an entrenched feature of the party's organizational culture. This public show of disunity, in turn, was widely perceived as yet another indication that the party was not ready to govern.

The Fundraising Issue and Party Finances

Both Stéphane Dion and Michael Ignatieff were further hampered during their leadership by a significant lack of financial resources to fight their campaigns. Indeed, the Liberals' money woes became an issue during both elections. In 2008, for example, lack of funds played a significant role in the party's failure to secure a traditional campaign plane for the Leader's Tour. This problem was widely publicized at the time and led to an image of incompetence before the election even started. The party limped along with a 30-year-old Boeing 737 leased from Air Inuit, after spending the first week of the campaign travelling on buses while the aircraft was undergoing repairs. In addition, the Liberals' failure to respond to the increasingly aggressive attack ads launched by the Conservatives was attributed to their lack of funds, a point specifically reiterated by a bitter Dion after the loss.

Despite Dion's experience, the same problem occurred during the Ignatieff leadership, although the party's finances were in better shape than they had been in 2008. This time the party attempted to downplay the significance of the Conservative attack ads by declaring that they were taking the high road and ignoring the Harper team's negative approach. However, party officials later admitted that a lack of funds had played a key role in their strategy. Nor did the Liberals under Ignatieff have the resources to mass produce the kind of platform document made popular with the introduction of the Red Book by Jean Chrétien in 1993, relying instead on brief pamphlets that were not available in sufficient quantities to distribute widely.

The importance of this financial quandary can be seen by comparing the Liberals' fundraising efforts with those of the new Conservative Party, whose mastery of direct-mail campaigns and ability to raise funds from special interest groups has long been widely recognized. In April 2008, for example, just months before the next federal election, Elections Canada revealed that the Liberals had raised only $846,129 from a total of 10,169 contributors. Meanwhile, in the same period, the Conservatives had accumulated $4.9 million from 44,345 donors, and the NDP had also outperformed the Liberals, reporting fundraising revenue of $1.1 million from 13,329 individuals.

There were several immediate causes of the Liberals' financial woes. The first was the inevitable difficulty faced by any party trying to raise funds during three successive leadership races, when potential contributions are instead siphoned off to the various leadership camps. The second was the traditional difficulty in attracting significant contributions that parties face when out of power.

A third, unexpected cause was the tactically clever decision by Stephen Harper to reduce the limit on individual contributions permitted under the controversial party financing legislation introduced by Jean Chrétien.[3] Although Chrétien's legislation was widely praised as a timely effort to level the playing field among political parties and to prevent Canadian elections from deteriorating into the American-style free-for-alls that now dominate that political system, it also was criticized for its potentially disproportionate impact on the Liberal Party. This criticism, in turn, was directly related to the Liberals' well-known and long-standing inability to reduce dependence on corporate contributions and large donations from wealthy individuals. Its failure to adapt to modern fundraising practices meant it was incapable of compensating for the loss of large donations by increasing the number of smaller contributions from individual party members as well as the general public. Here again the comparison is instructive. In 2006 the Conservatives received contributions from roughly 50 per cent of their members, but only 5 per cent of Liberal Party members contributed financially. In addition, the Conservatives raised unprecedented amounts of money from special interest groups, while the Liberals had made little or no progress in this area (Flanagan and Jansen 2009; Grenier 2011).

The Liberals' failure to modernize their fundraising techniques had been the subject of internal party discussion for more than a decade, but efforts to remedy the problem while Chrétien was in power had come to naught. Still, there was a widespread expectation that the $5,000 cap on individual contributions mandated by his legislation would provide the party with a sufficient level of funding, a point on which even maverick party president Stephen LeDrew, who had originally opposed the legislation, agreed. But Harper's sudden move to lower the cap to only $1,000 per individual had a devastating effect on those expectations, adding to the Liberals' growing financial difficulties.

The fourth cause of the Liberals' financial woes was the commitment by Stephen Harper to eliminate public subsidies for political parties, another unexpected blow that affected the opposition parties—notably the Liberal Party—far more than the Conservatives. The move was widely criticized by experts, including the former chief electoral officer, because it reduced fairness and equity in the electoral system and reversed the trend toward increased public funding for political parties that is prevalent in almost all Western democracies. It was also widely seen as a blatantly partisan attempt to hobble the Liberal Party (Nicholls 2011). The plan was so potentially damaging that the opposition parties attempted to unseat the Harper minority and form a coalition government in late 2008. Their scheme ultimately failed when the governor general granted Harper's request for a prorogation, but he prudently put the proposal on the back burner until he finally obtained a majority in 2011. Shortly after that victory Harper once again introduced his legislation to eliminate the public subsidy, although as a minor concession he agreed to phase in the withdrawal of funding over a three-year period. This meant that the scheduled 2015 election would be fought by all parties without any public monies. Given that Elections Canada tables indicated that only 18 per cent of the funding for the Liberals' 2011 election campaign came from sources other than this public funding, the potential gravity of their situation was immediately apparent.[4]

The Organization Issue and Regional Collapse

For more than 50 years the Liberal Party of Canada enjoyed a reputation as a highly skilled and well-oiled political machine. Its senior backroom organizers had orchestrated a succession of meticulously planned and professionally managed election campaigns, resulting in the nickname "the Big Red Machine" (Clarkson 2005). But, as several observers noted, by the 2006 election the image far exceeded the reality (Jeffrey 2009).

Nor did the situation improve. Instead, the 2006 and 2008 elections were arguably among the least competent and most poorly managed in the party's long history. In fairness, the disorganized desperation of the Martin Liberals' 2006 campaign was also driven by unanticipated events, such as the RCMP's extraordinary announcements concerning income trusts and the shooting of an innocent bystander in a downtown Toronto gang war (Jeffrey 2010). Both events proved a windfall for the Conservatives, which the Liberals were powerless to contain. No such explanation can be provided for the party's inept and self-inflicted performance in 2008, which at the national level included poorly attended events, last-minute schedule changes or cancellations, and a Leader's Tour that never got off the ground. Moreover, across the country Liberal riding associations had been allowed to atrophy, resulting in a shrinking number of party workers on the ground to provide support for local campaigns.

Underlying this deterioration in the party's election readiness machinery was another more significant problem. Over time the party's base, which once had been truly national, had been shrinking as well. The most obvious and long-standing example was in Western Canada, where the party's support had been steadily eroding for decades (Smith 1981). Although Paul Martin in particular had recognized this problem publicly and pledged to address it during his time in office, the results he hoped for were not forthcoming during his short tenure as leader. This was partly due to the emergence of the Western-based Reform/Alliance Party and its eventual achievement of national party status with the takeover of the Progressive Conservative Party. But that party's success could only have been possible within the context of prolonged Liberal inaction and inattention to the West.

Meanwhile in Quebec, the greatest of the Liberal bastions, the party's image as the guardian of national unity had provided overwhelming electoral support for decades. However, there had been a dramatic decline in Liberal fortunes under the leadership of John Turner and the emergence of the separatist Bloc Québécois during the Mulroney era. Still, that decline had appeared to be temporary. The return of the Chrétien Liberals in 1993 saw the party increase its Quebec representation in each of the three elections that delivered majority governments. By 2003, when Chrétien left office, the party held 40 of the 75 seats in Quebec and the organizers for his successor, Paul Martin, were openly predicting an increase to 60 seats in the 2006 election. Indeed, their entire Quebec strategy was based on the premise that this was not only possible but likely.

Yet their approach was one that had not worked for John Turner, and it was surprising that they would try to repeat his mistake of wooing the so-called soft separatists instead of tackling the Bloc Québécois head-on. Abandoning the party's image as the guardian of national unity, pan-Canadianism, and strong federalism, they instead recruited a former maverick Liberal MP and co-founder of the Bloc, Jean Lapierre, to serve as Martin's Quebec lieutenant and organize the province for the election. In short order Lapierre had disowned the Clarity Act and recruited a further eight former Bloc MPs to run for the Liberals in that province. By the time the national campaign team realized this approach was proving disastrous, the party had fallen to third place in the polls and was in danger of losing many of the 40 seats it already held. Lapierre was replaced by Stéphane Dion late in the campaign, but not before considerable damage had been done. In the end, the Liberals were reduced to 21 seats, their second-worst showing ever in that province, only exceeded by Turner's dismal 17 seats in 1984.

This debacle produced an organizational vacuum that neither Stéphane Dion nor Michael Ignatieff was able to fill. First, Dion caused considerable dissension in Quebec Liberal ranks by ignoring veteran organizers and by personally appointing inappropriate candidates for several by-elections, which the party subsequently lost. (One of those losses, in Outremont, provided the NDP with their second-ever Quebec MP, Tom Mulcair.) Public criticism of the leader by prominent Quebec Liberals then led Dion's Quebec lieutenant, Marcel Proulx, to resign, and Dion was further humiliated when several of his choices to replace Proulx declined his offer. Not surprisingly, in the 2008 election Liberal fortunes in their former stronghold plummeted once again. Had the Conservatives not created problems of their own, when the prime minister cavalierly dismissed his government's cuts to cultural programs as window-dressing in a province committed to them, the situation might have been even worse. As it was, the Liberals held on to only 14 seats.

Dion's successor, Michael Ignatieff, had already created even more confusion about the party's federalist stance by declaring his support for the idea that Quebec was a nation. Under his leadership the party organization continued to wither, and a highly public dispute with his Quebec lieutenant, Denis Coderre, led the latter to resign as well. The almost total lack of organization on the ground that followed, along with numerous disputed nomination battles, further contributed to the party's precipitous drop in popular support. The 2011 federal election saw many traditional Liberal voters stay home, while others turned in desperation to the NDP as the most likely way to defeat the Conservatives.

The Liberals took only seven seats in Quebec as an unprecedented Orange Wave swept across the province, allowing the NDP to take the lead as the new federalist party of choice in Quebec. The loss of their Quebec fortress was costly for the Liberals, but it was not their only problem. They had lost seats and suffered a drop in popular support across the country, including their last remaining base in Ontario. There the Conservatives had captured much of the seat-rich 905 area-code region surrounding Toronto, while the NDP had taken some inner city seats. Indeed, it appeared to many observers that the Liberals had been reduced to an urban rump based primarily in the wealthier sections of Toronto, Montreal, and Vancouver. Journalist Peter Newman summed up the party's dilemma succinctly but brutally: "They have no power base. Every party must have a power base—a geographic base where they feel at home. . . . They've lost their Toronto fortress, their Maritime fortress and Quebec fortress, and they haven't been out west in a while" (*CBC News,* 2011).

Yet some analysts, Newman among them, felt this actually was not the most serious challenge facing the party. Instead, they argued the fundamental problem was the Liberals' failure to spell out a meaningful vision for the country, or one that differed sufficiently from that of their opponents.

The Vision Issue

Certainly in the short term there was some justification for these arguments. The Martin campaigns of 2004 and 2006 were disorganized in terms of policy as well as organization. Although platforms had been drafted, they were rarely referenced by Martin or his candidates during the campaigns. Worse still, many of the platform planks had already been announced in advance of the elections, sometimes more than once. From the health care and equalization deals with the provinces to the commitment to resolve the "democratic deficit" in Parliament, Paul Martin had been promising these items since the early days of the 2003 leadership race, and they could not be repackaged successfully to capture the imagination of voters during the election, a fact campaign co-chair David Herle later admitted (Jeffrey 2010). Even the Kelowna Accord (a landmark federal–provincial agreement on funding and support for a wide range of Indigenous programs that was arguably Paul Martin's single most important achievement) was viewed as a *fait accompli* during the 2006 election, even though it was later annulled by the victorious Harper Conservatives. Instead, it was the Conservatives' platform of anti-corruption and accountability measures, so salient in light of the Gomery Commission, that set the agenda for the campaign and leaders' debates. Many observers believed there was little Martin could have done to counter that agenda, particularly as the Liberals had by then been in power for 13 years and the "interlude" impulse among voters was strong.

An entirely different problem arose during the 2008 election campaign, when Stéphane Dion put all of his eggs into the climate change basket. Rather than a typically broad-based platform covering many policy areas and built around traditional Liberal themes, Dion's platform was narrowly focused on environmental protection and sustainable development. Still, the Green Shift package, announced by the Liberals long before the start of the election, was initially well-received. But the devil was in the details. It soon became bogged down in controversy as various aspects were challenged by academics or special interest groups. And with so much lead time, the Conservatives were able to launch a full frontal assault on the Green Shift in the form of a negative ad campaign, which was highly effective in shaping public opinion, even though the ads featured several technically incorrect statements. For example, although the Green Shift was actually designed to be accompanied by a variety of tax breaks and was revenue neutral overall, the Conservative communications machine convinced many voters that the opposite was true. They positioned it as a tax grab that would cripple the economy and represent a costly sacrifice for most Canadians, an accusation that was fatal in tough economic times. Support for the Green Shift turned to widespread rejection, and as a result the Liberals entered the campaign far behind the Conservatives. Their situation deteriorated throughout the next six weeks. Not even a document signed by more than 100 economists stating that the plan's claim to be revenue neutral was correct could convince Canadians that the Liberal platform was anything but an albatross around the party's neck, and, with no other substantive planks to offer, the leader was seen as a one-trick pony.

Evidently wary of repeating this mistake, the party's 2011 platform under Michael Ignatieff appeared to offer something for everyone. Indeed, an important group of planks was often referred to as the "Family Pack," because it contained measures for all age groups—universal child care, financial assistance to low-income students for postsecondary education, lifelong learning for workers, and improved pensions for seniors. Initial reviews of the platform were consistently positive. Many observers saw it as a worthy successor to the Chrétien Red Book. Perhaps equally important, the various measures in the platform were organized around a broad liberal theme—equality of opportunity—which had been specifically recommended by Liberal policy icon Tom Kent in an editorial shortly before (Kent 2011).

Unfortunately, several tactical errors quickly reduced both the importance and the impact of this platform. To begin with, it was rarely seen or mentioned by Ignatieff after its release early in the campaign. Instead, the leader focused on specific planks, providing a painstaking amount of detail that often left audiences mystified. Moreover, the release of the entire platform at such an early stage in the election meant that it was soon forgotten by the media. And, with no hard copies to distribute to candidates or voters at the door, its virtual presence on the party website was ignored. And it, too, became a target for negative Conservative ads attacking its credibility. Last, but hardly least, after the press conference releasing the platform, Ignatieff rarely referred to the theme of equality of opportunity again, leaving most voters to conclude the platform was once again a disparate collection of specific planks with little or nothing to unite them and representing no overarching vision for the country. This was effectively the opposite of Jean Chrétien's successful approach, which had involved carrying the Red Book around at all times, waving it enthusiastically, and speaking in general terms about liberal themes and values while leaving the plank details to others to explain.

An underlying and even more serious problem with this Liberal platform was indeed its lack of fiscal credibility. Evidently Ignatieff was determined to avoid the label of a "tax and spend" Liberal, and the platform went to great lengths to demonstrate that this would not be the case. Yet it was unconvincing. On the one hand, the Liberals were proposing a significant number of new and often costly initiatives. On the other hand, they were arguing that there would be no increase in taxes—either income tax or the GST—and no return to deficit financing. Clearly this attempt to square the circle was disingenuous, and both the media and the Conservatives were quick to point this out. As a result Ignatieff was frequently placed on the defensive, forced to speak about the cost implications of his proposals rather than their underlying purpose. This dilemma was the direct result of a lengthy period in which the Liberals had been reluctant to challenge the neoconservative discourse on taxation and the costs of government. Having implicitly accepted the right-wing argument that deficits were unacceptable, even in economic downturns, and equally that taxes should not be raised and ideally should be lowered, the Liberals found themselves caught in a trap of their own making.

It was also apparent that Canadians were increasingly convinced by the conservative discourse, or at the very least they were concerned that the Liberals had been unable to present a compelling argument for their opposing point of view. Indeed, the Liberals seemed incapable even of defending their own fiscal record, which was arguably far superior to that of the Harper Conservatives. It was Jean Chrétien and his then finance minister, Paul Martin, who had turned the massive federal deficit they inherited from Brian Mulroney in 1993 into a string of surpluses beginning in 1997, leaving the Conservatives with a $13 billion surplus when they arrived in power in 2006.[5] Yet, despite the Conservative record of quickly turning that surplus into a series of ever-increasing deficits, they had somehow managed to frame the Liberals as the poor economic managers.

This, in turn, led numerous observers to argue, as Peter Newman did, that liberalism itself was in serious trouble in Canada. Liberalism, he argued, was a spent force. Perhaps worse still, several scholars concluded that most Canadians now took for granted the original programs of the welfare state that had been introduced by Liberals, so the party could no longer count on their support for that reason. In *The Big Shift,* for example, pollster Darrell Bricker and journalist John Ibbitson argued that Canadian society had moved far to the right, as Western populists and new conservative-minded immigrants came to dominate national politics, replacing the traditional Central Canadian elites. In fact, the authors went so far as to predict that the Harper Conservatives would be in power for several decades, if not several generations. "We believe that the Conservative party will be to the twenty-first century what the Liberal party was to the twentieth," the authors wrote, "the perpetually dominant party, the natural governing party" (Bricker and Ibbitson 2013, 126).

This familiar argument from 1984 had also played out in reality in the United States more than a decade before, as John Kenneth Galbraith and Christopher Lasch have outlined (Galbraith 1992; Lasch 1995). Yet in the end it produced what Robert Reich (1989) has described as a liberal resurgence, epitomized by the presidencies of Bill Clinton and Barack Obama. Similarly, and long before Prime Minister Stephen Harper had dropped the writ for the 2015 election, there were signs that this resurgence might be occurring in Canada as well. The concluding sections of this chapter therefore explore the measures taken by the Liberal Party of Canada to address the issues responsible for its decline—measures that ultimately led to its remarkable turnaround and return to power on 19 October 2015.

The Liberal Rebuilding Process

With the Liberals' unprecedented third-place finish in the 2011 election, it was obvious that the party would need time to regroup before making any significant decisions. As a result, the leadership race was delayed until 2013. This decision proved to be crucial to the Liberal Party's chances of recovery. Although initially it did not appear that many potential candidates were planning to throw their hat in the ring, in the end there was a crowded field of sitting and former MPs as well as some newcomers. By the deadline of January 2013, a field of nine candidates had registered, although three of these subsequently withdrew before the April 14 vote. That vote saw rookie MP Justin Trudeau elected as leader, a dramatic turn of events that quickly drew the attention of the Harper Conservatives, who launched negative attack ads about Trudeau within days of his selection as leader.

Trudeau, the son of former Prime Minister Pierre Trudeau, subsequently enjoyed a lengthy honeymoon period with the Canadian public despite several minor gaffes and missteps. As many observers noted, the selection of Trudeau was risky in terms of his lack of experience, but it also proved to be inspired in terms of his ability to reflect a significantly different leadership style and personality from that of Prime Minister Harper. As former Prime Minister Brian Mulroney remarked in an interview, Trudeau's most important advantage was that "he's not Harper. My point to the Conservatives was be very careful in the manner in which you treat this fellow. Because you're not dealing with a Stéphane Dion. You're not dealing with a Michael Ignatieff here. You're dealing with a different generation, a different product of that life" (Kennedy 2014). Indeed, Mulroney predicted that leadership change could become the most important issue in the 2015 election campaign, a factor that would hugely favour the Liberals over not only the Conservatives but also the NDP, whose leader, Tom Mulcair, has proved unable to strike a chord with ordinary Canadians.

Trudeau's leadership campaign was so successful in raising money that he was able to turn over a significant amount of unused funds to the party. Here, too, it soon became clear that the leadership choice had a beneficial impact on the party's fortunes. A concerted effort by the new executive to embrace direct mail and focus on individual contributions from party members quickly paid off. By fall 2013 the party had surpassed even the Conservatives in the total number of donors at 30,000, compared with 21,000 for Harper's party. In 2014 the Liberals' revenue increased by 40 per cent over the previous year, for a total of $15.8 million, or double the amount raised by the NDP despite the latter's Official Opposition status. The importance of this differential can hardly be overemphasized in light of the Conservatives' unexpected decision in 2015 to conduct one of the longest and most expensive campaigns in history.

Meanwhile, considerable progress was made on the organizational front as well. The Liberals' intensive use of their recently achieved national membership list (Liberalist) and their advanced use of digital technology to communicate with those members paid off in terms of the party's ability to marshal both funds and workers for several federal by-elections in 2013 and 2014. The results were encouraging. Two decisive wins for the Liberals in Ontario by-elections in June 2014 led pollster Nik Nanos to declare that the Liberals "have a real shot" at forming a government in 2015, particularly as several of his own and other polls consistently showed the Liberals taking the lead in public opinion in the crucial 905 region of exurban Toronto. Subsequently, the consensus of five polling experts in late summer 2014 suggested Harper could not hope for more than a minority in the next election and could very easily find his party relegated to the Official Opposition by the Liberals. This optimism was reinforced by two very close by-election races in late 2014, which suggested, at a minimum, the growing strength of the Liberals and the rapidly declining position of the NDP as the key opposition to the Harper government.

Indeed, the Liberal Party occupied first place for much of 2014 and early 2015. Still, there were ongoing concerns about the leader's lack of experience (fuelled by Conservative attack ads claiming Trudeau was "just not ready") and the party's lack of policy substance. Trudeau's controversial decision to support the Conservatives' anti-terror bill (Bill C-51) added to doubts and contributed to the NDP's emergence as the frontrunner by May 2015, while the Liberals fell once more to third place. Fears resurfaced among Liberals that the NDP would become the preferred alternative for "Anybody but Harper" voters, which represented some 65 per cent of the electorate. Indeed, by the start of the 2015 campaign talk centred on the real possibility of an NDP federal government.

These concerns were heightened by the party's ongoing regional problems, notably in Quebec and the West. In November 2014, for example, pollster Éric Grenier had struck a sombre note with his analysis of the Liberals' weak situation in the province of Quebec, where they needed to regain a significant number of seats to win. According to Grenier (2014), although the NDP at that time was trailing badly in national polls, it was "still the party to beat in Quebec." And in May 2015, with the unprecedented election of an NDP provincial government in Alberta, the Liberals' apparent lack of penetration in the West was once again highlighted as well, despite considerable efforts by Trudeau to connect with voters in British Columbia and urban Alberta.

Nevertheless the party could take considerable comfort from repeated national polls showing that Canadians had not only failed to move to the right, but if anything had actually become more liberal in the years that Stephen Harper was in power (Adams 2013). Thus the challenge, once again, was to attract the majority of those voters to the Liberal banner, rather than splitting the "progressive" vote with the NDP. At the same time, it was also evident from polls that Canadians continued to see the Conservatives and Stephen Harper as competent managers of the economy. This too was something that most observers agreed would need to be confronted directly by the Liberals along with the neoconservative discourse that had become so prevalent, primarily by offering what Robert Reich (1989) referred to as an alternative narrative. Finally, as the campaign neared, it became clear that the Liberals would need to present something dramatic to voters in the way of a platform if they were to distinguish themselves from the NDP as the real alternative to the Conservatives.

The Remarkable Liberal Comeback

The remarkable comeback of the Liberal Party in the 2015 election is significant for many reasons. The reality—that the Liberals moved from third place in the polls on August 2, when the writ was dropped, to capture a convincing majority of 184 seats and nearly 40 per cent of the popular vote in only 11 weeks—is an exceptional accomplishment by any standard. But this is far from the whole story, impressive though it may be.

With rejuvenated riding organizations, state-of-the-art technology, and a massive fundraising effort under their belt, the Liberals still went into the 2015 campaign as underdogs, underestimated by everyone, including their political opponents. But as Justin Trudeau demonstrated from the first leaders' debate, the emperor did have clothes and he, like his party, was ready. Similarly, the Liberals' dramatic victory made a mockery of the argument that the party could never again be a truly national party. The election results produced Liberal MPs in every region of the country, and most importantly new Liberal seats in Alberta and British Columbia as well as a majority of seats in Quebec, including francophone ridings; this was the best result in Quebec since Pierre Trudeau's 1980 election victory.

The Liberal campaign was pitch perfect. Its positive and effective advertising, credible platform, and strong team of candidates, to say nothing of Trudeau's winning performances in the leaders' debates, all contributed to the steady building of momentum that saw the party overtake first the NDP and then the Conservatives in public opinion polls. Certainly the Liberals ran a polished, professional campaign (due in no small measure to their ample war chest), but they also ran an optimistic and positive one that stressed fundamental liberal values. Leader Justin Trudeau's "sunny ways" were in sharp contrast to the petty partisanship of the Conservatives. More importantly, he consistently reiterated the notion of liberal values and beliefs in his speeches and leaders' debates, epitomized by the slogan "In Canada, better is always possible." Moreover, with the NDP fatally determined to balance budgets rather than demonstrate significant change, the Liberals took advantage by outflanking that party on the left, staking out their own economic platform of modest deficits and infrastructure expenditures as one way of offering "real change" that Canadians found credible and convincing. At the same time, following the suggestions of Reich acolyte and Liberal adviser Larry Summers, they tackled the Conservative discourse on taxation by arguing for reduced taxes on the middle class and a modest tax increase for the wealthiest Canadians, another move that outflanked the NDP while also heightening the credibility of their platform.

Meanwhile, the Conservatives—who had spent two years creating low public expectations of Trudeau—must surely have regretted that strategy as the Liberal leader effortlessly exceeded those low expectations time and time again, just as they must have come to regret their decision to conduct such a long election campaign, allowing the Liberals and their leader enough time to define themselves and change public perceptions. No doubt the Conservatives must also have questioned the wisdom of their efforts to make the niqab a central issue of the campaign, since it had the inadvertent effect of sinking NDP fortunes in Quebec and consequently ensuring that the Liberals were seen across the country as the best choice to prevent another Harper government.

With the Liberal Party's convincing electoral victory on October 19, the party appears to have demonstrated once again that it is the natural home for most Canadians. At a minimum its rebuilding efforts and superior election campaign have proven that the party and its brand should never be dismissed as a political force in Canada. However, the Liberals will face many new and unexpected challenges in power, particularly with a new and untested leader. Many observers have argued that the implementation of many of the Liberals' electoral commitments will be difficult if not impossible, while others have noted that the new Liberal government will also be required to expend considerable time and effort undoing or eliminating many Conservative measures as promised. Whether liberalism is truly resurgent, and to what degree the party benefited from the strong anti-Conservative sentiment among voters rather than a positive attachment to liberalism, may only become evident after the Trudeau Liberals' first term in office.

Suggested Readings

Carty, R. Kenneth. 2015. *Big Tent Politics: The Liberal Party's Long Mastery of Canada's Public Life*. Vancouver: University of British Columbia Press.

Clarkson, Stephen. 2005. *The Big Red Machine: How the Liberal Party Dominates Canadian Politics*. Vancouver: University of British Columbia Press.

English, John. 2009. *Just Watch Me: The Life of Pierre Elliott Trudeau, 1968–2000*. Toronto: Knopf.

Jeffrey, Brooke. 2010. *Divided Loyalties: The Liberal Party of Canada 1984–2008*. Toronto: University of Toronto Press.

McCall-Newman, Christina. 1983. *Grits: An Intimate Portrait of the Liberal Party*. Toronto: Macmillan.

Notes

1   Among the many changes were the transition to a two-pronged selection process, in which voting took place at the riding level as well and far in advance of the national convention, allowing significant time for leadership-camp side agreements. Further, delegate selection became a more crucial element because delegate votes were binding on the first ballot.

2   Upon his return to private life, Ignatieff admitted as much in his memoirs (Ignatieff 2013).

3   The Chrétien legislation had placed a cap of $5,000 on individual contributions, an amount eventually reduced to $1,000 by Harper, with devastating consequences for the Liberals.

4   See Elections Canada, Political Financing, Data and Expenditure Tables, at http://elections.ca/content.aspx?section=fin&lang=e

5   It should be noted that the means used by Martin to eliminate the deficit were often problematic, involving both cuts to federal transfers and retention of the Mulroney GST, which provided considerably increased revenue.

References

Adams, Michael. 2013. "The Myth of Conservative Canada." *Policy Options,* September.   http://www.environicsinstitute.org/uploads/michael-adams/16sept. mythofconservativecanada.policyoptions.pdf.

Bricker, Darrell, and John Ibbitson. 2013. *The Big Shift: The Seismic Change in Canadian Politics, Business and Culture and What It Means for Our Future.* Toronto: Harper Collins.

CBC News. 2011. "Peter C. Newman on the Death of the Liberal Party." November 19.   http://www.cbc.ca/news/politics/peter-c-newman-on-the-death-of-the-liberal-party-1.1042535

Clarkson, Stephen. 2005. *The Big Red Machine: How the Liberal Party Dominates Canadian Politics.* Vancouver: University of British Columbia Press.

Doern, G. Bruce. 2003. "The Chretien Liberals' Third Mandate." In *How Ottawa Spends 2002–3,* edited by G. Bruce Doern. Toronto: Oxford.

Flanagan, Tom, and Harold Jansen. 2009. "Election Campaigns under Canada's Party Finance Laws." In *The Canadian General Election of 2008,* edited by Jon H. Pammett and Christopher Dornan, 194–216. Toronto: Dundurn Press.

Galbraith, John Kenneth. 1992. *The Culture of Contentment.* Boston: Houghton Mifflin.

Grenier, Éric. 2011. "How Much Will Killing per Vote Subsidy Stack Odds in Tory Favour?" *Globe and Mail,* June 13.

Grenier, Éric. 2014. "NDP Still the Party to Beat in Quebec." *Hill Times,* November 24.

Ibbitson, John. 2011. "Tory Attack Ads Pack a Punch That Leaves Liberals Reeling." *Globe and Mail,* February 21.

Ignatieff, Michael. 2013. *Fire and Ashes: Success and Failure in Politics.* Toronto: Random House. http://dx.doi.org/10.4159/harvard.9780674729650

Jeffrey, Brooke. 2009. "Missed Opportunity: The Invisible Liberals." In *The Canadian Federal Election of 2008,* ed. Jon Pammett and Christopher Dornan, 63–97. Toronto: Dundurn Press.

Jeffrey, Brooke. 2010. *Divided Loyalties.* Toronto: University of Toronto Press.

Jeffrey, Brooke. 2015. *Dismantling Canada: Stephen Harper's New Conservative Agenda.* Montreal: McGill-Queen's University Press.

Kennedy, Mark. 2014. "Mulroney Cautions Tories to Tread Carefully on Trudeau." *Ottawa Citizen,* September 4.

Kent, Tom. 2011. "A Few Questions for Ignatieff and the Liberals." *Globe and Mail,* July 2, A13.

Lasch, Christopher. 1995. *The Revolt of the Elites.* New York: Norton and Company.

Meisel, John. 1972. *Working Papers on Canadian Politics.* Montreal: McGill-Queen's University Press.

Nicholls, Gerry. 2011. "Kill the Subsidy, Not the Party." *Ottawa Citizen,* May 24.

Newman, Peter C. 2012. *When the Gods Changed: The Death of Liberal Canada.* Toronto: Random House.

Pammett, Jon H., Lawrence LeDuc, Judith I. Mackenzie, and André Turcotte. 2010. *Dynasties and Interludes.* Toronto: Dundurn Press.

Perlin, George C. 1979. *The Tory Syndrome: Leadership Politics in the Progressive Conservative Party.* Montreal: McGill-Queen's University Press.

Reich, Robert. 1989. *The Resurgent Liberal.* New York: Random House.

Smith, David E. 1981. *The Regional Decline of a National Party: Liberals on the Prairies.* Toronto: University of Toronto Press.

8
The Conservatives: Rebuilding and Rebranding, Yet Again

PETER WOOLSTENCROFT

F OR THE CONSERVATIVE PARTY OF CANADA (CPC), victory in the 2015 election would have been historic. It would have been the first time the party had won four consecutive elections (minority or majority) since the late 1800s.[1] Will its defeat be consistent with its electoral record, where a winning electoral coalition is brought together, but the party soon has problems maintaining its base? Then, upon defeat it struggles to rebuild or, worse, fragments. This chapter discusses the CPC as an electoral entity through two prisms. How did the party respond to new political demands? And how was the party organized? The answers speak to old and contemporary Canada.

From 1867 to 1917, the CPC was dominant in a two-party system, winning six of ten elections, although closely challenged by the Liberals. From 1921 on it has generally been the second party, with the Liberals being so strong (primarily because of its hegemonic Quebec base) that they were dubbed "Canada's natural governing party." Conservative victories were episodic and spasmodic, though the party could claim Canada's most impressive triumphs in 1958 and 1984.[2]

Since the modern party system's beginnings in 1921 (understood as more than two parties winning seats), the Conservatives formed government 10 times (five as a minority, five as a majority) out of 29 elections. These mediocre results were offset by the fact that the party won over half of the vote in 1958 and 1984—the two biggest electoral landslides in Canadian history. The 1958 triumph was frittered away in 1962, with the Conservatives first relegated to a minority until the 1968 election, after which they remained out of office until the brief Joe Clark interregnum of 1979–80. The 1984 victory, with a majority of seats in every province and territory, was a singular achievement. However, two elections later, in 1993, in one of the world's greatest electoral tsunamis, the party was almost extinguished, winning just two seats and 16 per cent of the vote.

Following a decade-long fight between the Reform/Canadian Alliance parties and the Progressive Conservatives (PC), a disputed merger produced the CPC in 2003, which Stephen Harper led to defeat in 2004. The party, slowly improving its electoral strength, won minority governments in 2006 and 2008 and a majority in 2011, but only reached the high 30s in voter support.

Two questions about Harper's electoral legacy were answered in 2015: Would he recalibrate electoral metrics to make the CPC the new dominant party (Wells 2013)? And would the new "national" party include Quebec? To do so would be doubly remarkable.

The Political Party

Here the party will be understood as an organization that nominates candidates to contest an election to form government or influence those who do. And there is a broader matter: for Canada, lacking many national symbolizations, "one of the chief and most important latent functions of the political parties and the party system is to foster and develop a sense of national unity and of national being" (Meisel 1963, 370). But does the party add to or undercut the nation?

Downs (1957, 25–30) famously understood a party to be a coalition whose members agree on all goals and "formulate policies in order to win elections." Other analysts, while accepting the power premise, argue that members commit time and resources for myriad reasons (Eldersveld 1964, 220–44). One motivation is ideas about society's organization and prospects. These matters, fundamentally political, may clash with power seeking. Canadian conservatives have been riven by ideological disputes undercutting their electoral purposes. "Blue Tories" subscribe to frugality in spending, balanced budgets, and prefer markets over governments in economics. "Red Tories" believe in British institutional traditions and, suspicious of "the market is supreme" and individualistic arguments, will use state instruments for collective purposes. More recently, the latter category of Tory encompasses those with liberal rather than traditional views on social issues. The anti-statism of the "Blues" means there is both suspicion of the state and high regard for the United States; for the "Reds" the state is an important nation- and community-building force, and the United States commands both respect and suspicion.[3]

Liberal democracy generally allows for the unimpeded formation of parties and for citizens to choose freely. Any party, then, is in a highly competitive situation, ordinarily having to face traditional rivals but at times also confronting insurgents, perhaps even drawn from its own ranks. Moreover, the environment in which the party operates is highly contingent; uncertainties arise either from long-term changes in society, which the party may reject, welcome, or be oblivious to, or from immediate events, such as a sudden economic crisis or some explosive mid-campaign revelation, which may derail a well-prepared and well-resourced campaign even if the claim is unsubstantiated.

Electoral success requires that a vote-seeking party address five organizational issues: (1) prepare its resources for optimal application; (2) raise money to support its infrastructure and messaging; (3) develop a clear and accessible presentation of its ideas, old in terms of its mythic public purposes and new in terms of how it will address social and economic changes; (4) establish sustaining connections with "friends"—those social groups and institutions supportive of the party's being and efforts; and (5) develop a strategy to define "enemies" and repel their attacks. The competitive rhythm of continuity and change in part reflects a party's management of its organizational challenges, which contain another issue: How does the party connect its "top" with its "bottom"? What is the role of members?

The parliamentary system built on disciplined parties poses a fundamental issue. How are the disparate voices and interests across Canada to be represented in such a tight system? One answer is that the traditional party had two important elements. The national party organization (the dominant part) defined its central character—policies, leaders, communication strategies and appeals, and organizational infrastructure—while individual units (constituency associations, the weaker part) allowed for local interests and concerns to be expressed and to mount the local campaign (Carty 2002, 731–32).

The party, as a coalition of voluntary members coming together for various interests and perspectives, suffers the danger of members and supporters exiting. The party is a means for winning power, but it also contains forces seeking to replace those who lead, if not now then tomorrow. The logic of democracy has led parties to open themselves up to increasing involvement of members in party life, notably in the selection of leaders.

While every party faces intraparty contests over its direction and its leadership, Conservatives have been particularly susceptible to factionalism—in Perlin's phrasing, "disruption from within"—and coalition fracturing (Perlin 1980, 28–57). No other Canadian party has spawned more competitors, and no other party has had to rebuild more often.

The party's ability to compete successfully in the contingent electoral game is greatly affected by changes in its political environment. Canada, as with other long-established democracies, has gone through enormous changes. How has the CPC comprehended what is happening and responded to the inevitable grievances, demands, and interests intertwined in change?

The Canadian Political Environment

Since 1867, Canada has undergone great territorial expansion and experienced enormous population growth and diversification, along with rapid and extensive industrialization and urbanization. Social and economic changes created new electoral marketplaces and challenges: How to simultaneously represent traditional interests and values while engaging emerging social forces?

The political system itself has changed enormously. To summarize a complicated history, from 1867 on the secular trend has been Ottawa's decline and the rise of the provinces. Macdonald's vision was of Canadians imbued with a British-centred nationalism identifying strongly with a dominant central government; now the national government operates alongside provinces as "interdependent political competitors" (Cairns 1977) with Canadians holding "limited identities" (Careless 1969) and living in "small worlds," viewing politics through prisms of place, ethnicity, and language rather than monochromatically (Elkins and Simeon 1980). For parties, the consequence was that national appeals were hard to construct; what might work well in one region might be repellent elsewhere.

The party system has also changed enormously. John English (1977, 15) notes that Macdonald's dream of a "hegemonic national party system . . . was largely the work of Laurier and (Robert) Borden" from 1896 to 1917. However, since 1921 not only has there been a gradual increase in the number of parties winning seats (over the seven Parliaments from 1993 to 2015, the mean number of parties was 4.7, with more registered by Elections Canada) but the very idea of a "national party system" has been challenged (see Patten's chapter in this volume).

In Confederation's first five decades, both the Conservatives and the Liberals were nationally competitive; one party's area of strength also elected the other's Members of Parliament (MPs). Since 1921, the major parties have had regional areas of strength and weakness. Themes of regional domination and subordination have underlain much of the party system's evolution. Instead of an integrated party system crossing jurisdictions, clear discontinuities between the national and provincial systems have developed. Only two parties have won national office, but in seven provinces (Quebec to British Columbia plus Nova Scotia) other parties have formed government. In some provinces one or both of the Liberals and Conservatives have disappeared as viable contenders. Provincialization produced increasing separation between the national and subnational parties of the same name. Activists have been identified as working for different federal and provincial parties (Koop 2011, 186–87). At times the electoral necessity for a party to be seen as advancing its jurisdiction's interests would drive it to oppose its namesake at the other level, ordinarily the national (Walchuk 2008).

One important difference between American and Canadian electoral politics is that successful presidential candidates are often drawn from the ranks of former governors. In Canada, however, no provincial premier has won a federal election after becoming the national party's leader. Does provincial political success create resistance from voters in other provinces? The structure of the Canadian party system undercuts the ability of parties to be nation-builders.

The last change is communications. In Canada's first election, voting was spread over weeks; Macdonald did not leave his constituency, and there was no platform (Beck 1968, 1–12). Just as the parties learned to use print, radio, and television, they now use many communication technologies. One overarching feature of the 2015 election is that, for most voters, it was conducted on a screen.

In this world of continuing electoral contingency, the Conservative Party, so often proud of its founding role and its early public purposes, has struggled with honouring its past while confronting issues arising from socioeconomic changes. Consider the 1891 election, held just months before Macdonald's death. The party's winning slogan—"The Old Flag, The Old Policy, The Old Man"—artfully heralded its mythologizing of its past and imagery of Canada built on the British connection, resistance to assimilation with the United States, and the building of an industrial heartland in Ontario and Quebec through the National Policy (Pennington 2012). How would the messaging be understood and appreciated by the enormous number of immigrants, mostly drawn from outside of France and the British Isles, entering Canada through the immigration policy of the Liberal government elected in 1896 and mostly settling in Western Canada? All policies entail differential costs and benefits; the National Policy promised industrialization for Ontario and Quebec while requiring Western Canada to be a food supplier. The electoral legacy for the Tories was that the Prairies were uncongenial territory until 1957. Conservative politicians until the 1970s would make tradition and the British connection central to their rhetoric, highlighted by opposition to the new Canadian flag in 1965. How would that messaging be understood and appreciated in Quebec?

The party's origins and its development through Canada's first decades defined it as an electoral entity, led to its success, and limited its future. In the first six elections it fought, the party won almost 60 per cent of Quebec's seats and 70 per cent of Ontario's. Since 1896, Quebec has been the pivot point of electoral politics for both the Liberals and Conservatives. In the 36 elections from 1896 to 2015, Quebec has elected 2,493 MPs; the Liberals have won 63.4 per cent of them, the Conservatives only 15.4 per cent. The Tory record is worse than presented, as three elections produced 45 per cent of their seats. The fundamental fact of electoral politics has been the Liberal dominance of Quebec and the failure of the Conservatives to do better than intermittent strong showings. The Conservative problem of establishing a sustainable Quebec base was exacerbated by the polarized federalism–separatism debate from the 1970s onward, with the Liberals holding the federalist flag until the sudden rise of the NDP and the precipitous fall of the Bloc Québécois in 2011.

Outside of Quebec, the Tories are much more competitive, winning 47 per cent of the seats from 1896 to 2015, compared to the Liberals' 40 per cent. The 13 per cent won by "others" are concentrated in the West, which meant, depending on the province and the time, two or three "other" parties compete with the Tories and Grits. For the Liberals, the drive for a majority rests on its Quebec heartland and winning seats elsewhere, usually in Ontario. The Conservatives have electoral lockjaw: Quebec only comes on board when they are doing very well elsewhere, and there are limited opportunities, generally, for the party to win a massive number of seats elsewhere.

Canada's electoral bifurcation produced a strategic conundrum for the party. How should resources be allocated? A national risk/reward calculation either by electoral district or by province would have disproportionately limited resources for one province over another, or even selected constituencies. However, perhaps the party had to "overinvest" in Quebec, since it would be problematic for national unity for the party not to campaign in the province.

The Conservatives and the Early Game

The CPC's birth in 1854 resulted from a meeting of political leaders to address another of the recurring political crises related to the use of the governor's executive powers, along with issues related to religion and English–French differences. The roots of Canadian political culture were deeply established at that time: sharp partisanship, pervasive patronage, premium on a strong leader, and a strong state orientation. And underlying Canada's development was strong localism flowing from the nature of social organization. "Political parties did not create localistic attitudes, but by their use of them, they entrenched localism in the Canadian political tradition" (Stewart 1986, 97). Lipset (1989) argues that the American Revolution created two different political systems. The United States was built on republican and liberal ideas that emphasized "life, liberty, and the pursuit of happiness," while British North America reflected monarchical beliefs and Tory values expressed in "peace, order, and good government." While the notion of path dependency is highly contested, it seems indisputable that pre-Confederation politics influenced the formation of the Canadian state and the subsequent practice of party politics. The widespread and widely accepted use of state resources to reward friends and punish foes was the heart of party organization in the post-Confederation period. Supplicants applied not to the department "but to the executive committee of the local Conservative association" whose recommendations were made to Macdonald, who passed advice to the pertinent minister (Pennington 2012, 24–25). The effect was to reinforce localistic tendencies: local committees considered local people for what were mostly local jobs. Borden's 1917 civil service reform, which introduced merit employment, "nationalized" the party system (English 1977).

How, then, to understand Canadian conservatism? Interpreters of Canada's early political development produced three analytical approaches—materialism, brokerage politics, and the primacy of the great leader—that have continuing pertinence for contemporary politics.

First, the materialist interpretation centres on the relations between private economic enterprises and parties. Colonial politicians' close ties with business entities imbued the development of representative institutions and early political life in Canada. Underhill (1960, 177) argued that Confederation was the work of Tory politicians and Montreal–Toronto capitalists. Stevenson (1989, 24) described capitalists as hegemonic since there were few countervailing interests (labour or middle class). Conservatives, dependent on election monies from business and industrial concerns (famously in the railway scandal of the 1870s), became perceived as closely connected with large-scale private economic interests (Williams 1956, 144). Recent electoral law changes have severely limited the reliance of all parties on private economic interests for election monies.

Second, André Siegfried's examination of how parties addressed French–English relationships provided the influential account of "brokerage politics." Parties, being primarily interested in their continuance, tend "to become agencies for the conquest of power," thereby discarding ideals and principles to be "a machine for winning elections" (Siegfried 1907, 112–13). It is not just a cynical game that is played, however, but one that reflects the perception that Canada's racial (ethnolinguistic) and religious divisions are so incendiary that "prudent and far-sighted" politicians avoid them. It is a bittersweet heritage, because the resulting heterogeneous parties avoid sharp positions but also lower political discussion as people focus on material advantage, especially through patronage. For Siegfried the irony is deep: conflicts are depoliticized, yet elections produce unparalleled "fury and enthusiasm" with contests of "great gusto." Politics is poorly served because the parties do not represent points of view but simply combine different views into bland compromise. Brokerage politics was well practised by Macdonald's Conservatives in the first decades of Confederation; but increasingly, after his death, the party lost its ability to play the brokerage game effectively.

Macdonald, who for most Canadians belongs in the "great leader" category, is the basis of the third interpretation. He is credited for his political vision and practice that took Canada in new and, for most, better directions. Although flawed, as are all human beings, his central role in the building of Canada is indisputable. As a politician, his approach from his early days was to find common ground between Roman Catholic French and Protestant English. He dismissed those he regarded as having "pre-adamite" views and called for progressive conservatism to underpin the party's thinking.

And his appeal to many was indisputable. Canadians were forgiving of Macdonald's drinking and eager to hear him. Plamondon (2009, 57) references crowds of 5,000 in Belleville, Ontario, and 50,000 in Montreal. Conservatives took Macdonald to validate their belief in the strong leader for the well-being of the nation (Morton 1962, 287). Embedded in that belief is the necessity to find a leader with the right electoral stuff.

One Light in the Dark Decades: From 1921 to 1953

From 1921 to 1953, the Conservatives fought eight elections under five different names; it also had nine leaders (two interim) and considerable battles over its platform, reflecting both the leader's influence and the party's efforts to find a winning formula. Only the 1930 campaign produced a victory.

The party's dismal record was contoured by the 1917 Unionist victory. Fought on the necessity of conscription, it produced a bifurcated electorate, with Quebec against and the rest of Canada for. Macdonald's coalition, challenged in the 1890s but showing life in the 1900s, was seriously undercut. Moreover, the party was grappling with issues relating to postwar social unrest, a rapidly urbanizing and industrializing society, and the 1930s Depression.

The Tories were confronted with three strategic challenges. First, economic protectionism dominated the party's discourse through the decades: How to present a persuasive appeal across the land, not just in the party's strongholds? The party's "Red Tory" and "Blue Tory" divide was manifest. Second, Quebec was inhospitable, with Tories castigated as anti-French by the Liberals. What would be the party's message? Finally, did the party have the organizational capacity—active local associations and successful fundraising—to produce victory?

The 1930 triumph reflected a well-organized campaign that effectively used radio, mass mailings, and printed media to communicate the party's messages, both nationally and locally (Beck 1968, 191–205; Glassford 1992, 72–97). Noteworthy innovations included using the leader's sister on a gramophone recording and delivering quick responses to Liberal announcements and questions posed by citizens. The campaign was well funded, primarily because of large amounts of money provided by business interests (mostly from Montreal) and the leader, R.B. Bennett (Glassford 1992, 85–89).[4]

The construction of a "national" election campaign provides an important insight. How did the party plan to improve on its base in the Maritimes, Ontario, and British Columbia, where there were few prospects for gains? Should they focus on Ontario and the Prairies? Or Ontario and Quebec? With Bennett, a Calgary lawyer, as leader and a platform designed for the West, the choice was clear: "Quebec was not written off completely, but no substantial improvement was expected. If all went as planned, none was needed" (Glassford 1992, 75). The Conservatives did better in Quebec than expected (but not so well elsewhere) in 1935, but from that year until Diefenbaker's breakthrough in 1958, the party failed to win more than a handful of seats in the province in any election.

The party, mindful that Westerners were not sympathetic to protectionism, virtually dropped the term. In Quebec, moreover, the party engaged in symbolic shuffling: its slogan was "Canada first, then the Empire," but in Quebec the message was different: "*Canada d'abord*" (Glassford 1992, 79). Muddying of messages is at the heart of brokerage politics, but the party's approach also presaged its contemporary emphasis on symbolic presentation and branding.

The 1930 victory also contained a lesson for future successes. Five Tory provincial governments strongly supported the Conservative campaign. The road to Ottawa was seen to be through provincial capitals, and certainly the party had considerable provincial support in 1957, 1958, and 1979; in some defeats, such as 1921 and 1935, Conservatives were weak provincially.

The party's organizational strengths were soon undercut by Bennett's inattention, financial shortfalls (Glassford 1992, 132–34), and the intraparty debate driven by the deepening Depression. One side, comprising traditional business and commercial interests, insisted on free market solutions. Bennett's side (eventually) committed itself to an expansive state role in economic transactions, akin to the American New Deal. The debate's effect was to create two new (albeit short-lived) parties that eroded the Conservative base.

The 1935 election set the stage for the next 20 years and four elections in which Conservatives won only 239 of 1,017 seats as the Liberals rolled to consecutive majorities. Almost two-thirds of the party's parliamentary caucus came from Ontario. Conservatives before World War I worked quietly with Quebec nationalist groups, and a similar approach was taken in the province during this period as the Tories worked with the Union Nationale until its disappearance in 1985.

Party leaders at a 1938 conference made vigorous affirmations about being British subjects and about ensuring "the safety of the Commonwealth," which riled Quebec's delegation (Glassford 1992, 219). The 1940 party, led by Robert Manion, was attacked for being hostile to business, socialist in its aspirations, and unsympathetic to its traditional support of British-centred policies (Plamondon 2009, 178–79). The 1943 Port Hope Conference affirmed conscription, the Empire, and free enterprise, but argued also for state intervention in the event of market failures and for "extraordinary resolutions" supporting a wide range of welfare state components, including (in essence) medicare (Granatstein 1967, 134). The party then turned to John Bracken, Manitoba's premier, who had the party adopt the name "Progressive Conservative" as a condition of his leadership, reflecting his political history and Macdonald's terminology. However, Bracken moved away from the progressivism of Port Hope and recommitted to conscription, while the Liberals co-opted much of the Conservative agenda as well as that of the Co-operative Commonwealth Federation. For the Tories, 1945 was not only lost but it represented the nadir of its Quebec weakness, with only 29 candidates nominated in the province's 75 ridings.

Notwithstanding Ontario's long-standing centrality for the party, since World War II only one Ontario politician (George Drew, from 1948 to 1956) has become leader. There also has been a reduction in the number of Ontario-based candidates. In the party's first two leadership races Ontario politicians were prominent: three of six candidates in 1927 and four of five in 1938. In 1942, however, there were no Ontarians. In the seven leadership races from 1956 to 2003, only twice did an Ontarian reach the final ballot.[5] Quebec, surprisingly, given the Conservative weakness in the province, has produced two leaders, Brian Mulroney and Jean Charest. Of the party's 13 elected leaders since 1927, nine came from outside of Ontario and Quebec. The two Drew campaigns (1949 and 1953) were uninspired efforts, and the party was weaker after 1953 than it was after 1945. Overall, the party, while looking for leaders to transcend its narrow base, lacked a clear understanding of its place in rapidly changing mid-century Canada.

John Diefenbaker, Robert Stanfield, and Joe Clark

With John Diefenbaker at the helm and building on his 1957 minority, the 1958 victory might have been a "critical election" in the sense of a recalibration of the parties' competitive positions as large sections of the electorate migrated to a new party (Key 1955). In contrast to the patrician George Drew, Diefenbaker's populist style changed the party's base, especially in rural and small-town Canada. Quebec and the Prairies moved strongly to the Tories, reflecting their unusual election commitments to increased government spending and economic intervention, which were portrayed as moving the party from established Eastern business interests (now close to the Liberals) to neglected and less prosperous groups and regions (Meisel 1963, 377).

However, what is almost universally seen as an incompetent administration put the Conservatives into a minority in 1962 (Newman 1963). Massive Quebec losses were followed by weakening vote shares and fewer seats in the province through the seven elections until 1984, despite evident sympathies from Robert Stanfield and Joe Clark, Diefenbaker's successors. The Prairies, historically hostile, became the party's unyielding heartland until 1993 and Diefenbaker's electoral heritage.

One big internal issue was the relationship between the leader and the party. The use of delegated conventions, first by the Liberals in 1919 then by the Conservatives in 1927, considerably reduced the caucuses' role in choosing party leaders from within their ranks. Conventions raised two questions: To which body—parliamentary caucus or extra-parliamentary party—is the leader accountable? And how should conflicts between the two entities be resolved? Part of the problem is that the caucus is a continuing institution while the party does not have a fixed meeting schedule. For the Conservatives, the leader "gives symbolic expression to the party in the country" and "the role of the leader is endowed with transcendent authority in the structure of the party" (Perlin 1980, 27). Yet many party members were deeply unhappy with Diefenbaker's leadership. Prolonged fratricidal fighting over the question of how and where the party could withdraw confidence in the leader resulted in the party-in-convention, after the 1965 loss, deciding there would be a leadership convention. Diefenbaker was a candidate in the subsequent contest, which chose Stanfield.[6]

Another issue centred on the campaign in Quebec. Money in 1957 was not allocated to the province on the calculation that prospects were better elsewhere (Perlin 1980, 55), a decision that was interpreted by some as reflecting bias and by others as a "one Canada" view, a perspective that was to reappear in 2004. In 1958 the message to Quebec was simple: "N'ISOLONS PAS LE QUÉBEC."

The failed Stanfield campaigns of 1968, 1972, and 1974 represented generally a "Red Tory" approach supported by an attempt to modernize the party. Opposition to official bilingualism by a duly nominated candidate led Stanfield to refuse to sign the appropriate papers as required by Elections Canada. This marked the beginning of centralization of power in the party, as before that associations were on their own. The development of mass fundraising marked further centralization in party life, and as continued in the first Joe Clark regime (1976 to 1983) improved the party's finances, setting the stage for a revolution in party life in subsequent decades.

The convention system created an arena where opposing forces clashed in some measure publicly. Stanfield's victory was essentially polarized between pro- and anti-Diefenbaker forces, while Clark's win was underlain with "Blue" and "Red" divisions. Both winners suffered from winning the convention but not the caucus, especially Clark, who had continuing problems with the party's right wing.[7] Quebec Conservatives, with two candidates (Brian Mulroney and Claude Wagner) losing to Clark, were generally unsupportive despite Clark's openness to Quebec. Anti-Clark voices were many and public after the 1979 and 1980 elections: the former produced a minority Conservative government, but an election following a lost confidence motion nine months later returned the Liberals to power. A leadership review convention gave Clark two-thirds support, which he took to be insufficient. Mulroney bested Clark at the ensuing leadership convention.

The Mulroney Conservatives

Mulroney's appeal was historically compelling: Liberals could not be beaten unless their Quebec base was destroyed. Mulroney, a fluently bilingual Quebecer, led his party to a smashing victory in 1984, winning 80 per cent of Quebec's seats and 50 per cent of its vote. The idea that his victory would restructure the Canadian party system was seemingly confirmed in 1988 with increases in Quebec's seats and votes. Although other Conservatives, even Joe Clark, often described as a Red Tory, spoke encouragingly about various neoliberal ideas popularized by conservatives in the United Kingdom and the United States, it was the Mulroney government that transformed the party's posture through privatization of Crown corporations (Petro-Canada and Air Canada, for instance); changes in the Canadian tax system through an introduction of a consumption tax, the GST; cuts to various Keynesian-type social programs; and free trade agreements with the Americas. On the other hand, Mulroney committed the party to state-centred health care insurance coverage, declaring the Canada Health Act to be a sacred trust.

As for the party, members, expressing considerable angst over perceived control of local affairs by party officials and those around Mulroney, resented just being "cheerleaders and fundraisers" (Woolstencroft 1996). A familiar pattern of Canadian politics reappeared: members attracted by a contested nomination soon drifted away; in Quebec, almost 90 per cent of members left from 1984 to 1985 (Woolstencroft 1996, 292). Carty (1991, 101) found in 1990 that while the Liberals and Conservatives were national organizations, the Quebec Conservatives had only one "paper branch"; the 1993 election (which produced one Tory seat, a drop of 62 from 1988) eviscerated the party's electoral base. In 1997, when the strong campaign by new leader Jean Charest resonated well in the polls, the party lacked the ability to mobilize potential voters (Woolstencroft 1997, 85–86). A decade later only one-third of PC associations met the national party's goals for organizational readiness—and only

16 per cent of Quebec's associations did so (Woolstencroft 2001, 255–59). The party's efforts to take advantage of opportunities were handicapped by its flaccid infrastructure.

Quebec was decisive. Mulroney sought to rectify Quebec's refusal to sign the 1982 Constitution, but intraparty disputes over the Meech Lake Accord led to the formation of the Bloc Québécois, which dominated Quebec from 1993 to 2011. Western Canada, angered that a technically superior and cheaper aircraft maintenance contract was moved from Winnipeg to Montreal and then energized by discussions seen as giving Quebec special constitutional standing, migrated to the fledging Reform Party, which (along with its successor, the Canadian Alliance) dominated Western Canada from 1993 to 2000. Mulroney's dream of a coalition reminiscent of Macdonald's imploded in less than a decade.

The New Conservatives: Harper's Party and Government

The 2003 merger between the Progressive Conservatives and the Canadian Alliance (CA) was the culmination of many frustrated attempts to unite two parties whose continued existence seemingly offered the Liberals an easy path to government.[8] Following Clark's resignation as PC leader,[9] Peter MacKay won the 2003 leadership after publicly signing a document stipulating that he would not engage in merger talks with the CA. A precipitating event for the CA was its 2003 by-election defeat to the PCs in a putatively winnable district (Marland and Flanagan 2015, 280–81). Long-term factors—changes in party financing laws, the parliamentary weakening of the PCs from 1997 to 2000, and the underrepresentation of each parliamentary party as a result of the single-member electoral system—generated merger pressures (Bélanger and Godbout 2010). The following talks quickly led to agreement and acceptance by each party's members.[10] One immediate issue during the merger negotiations was the party's name and the CA caucus's unhappiness "over the policy symbolism of the colour of the maple leaf in the CPC logo" (Marland and Flanagan 2013, 952). Harper won the subsequent leadership contest.

Three questions can be asked about the new party: How did it present itself as an electoral competitor to Canadians? What was the significance of its internal organization? What was its electoral base?

Following the disappointing 2004 election (in which the CPC received 29.6 per cent of the vote compared to 37.7 per cent for the CA and PCs in 2000), the party at the next year's convention confronted the Liberals' framing of the CPC as extremist and harbouring a secret agenda on social-conservative issues. Right-to-life advocates were the most dangerous from the perspective of the party's image. Harper, ironically given his Reform

Party history and its advocacy of candidates and MPs speaking freely, developed strict controls over messaging and policy positioning and declared that the party would not have an abortion plank. The convention's resolutions on a wide range of issues reflected more PC than CA antecedents (Ellis and Woolstencroft 2006, 62–65).

The 2004 election revealed a modern electoral danger. "Bozo" eruptions—unorthodox or incendiary pronouncements by candidates—that rapidly circulated through social media, were cited by opponents as revealing the true party.[11] The party developed an imperfect system to approve those seeking the party's nomination.[12]

Changes in election law were arguably to the CPC's advantage. The Liberal government's 2004 election financing reforms, which radically limited corporate and union donations, benefited the CPC, which had inherited the PC's well-developed direct-mail system that, with their own innovations, put the party in a strong financial position. The 2007 amendment to the Canada Elections Act to set election dates, designed to limit prime ministerial power, had the effect of reproducing in Canada the permanent campaign characteristic of American politics. The CPC used its ample resources to run commercials to blacken the Liberal leaders, Stéphane Dion in 2008, Michael Ignatieff in 2011, and, less successfully, Justin Trudeau after he became Liberal leader in 2013. Changes introduced by the CPC to eliminate per-voter subsidies in 2015 also benefited the party, as it has a wider contribution base than the other parties.[13] The last systemic advantage for the Conservatives was the addition of 30 seats to the House of Commons, mostly located in suburban areas where the party had made significant gains in 2011.

The new party introduced a different mode of organization into Canada. The first parties, centred in Parliament with the caucus at their heart, paid little attention to riding associations except for the expectation they would organize the local campaign.

The 1983 PC leadership race led to charges that candidates' campaigns were manipulating the buying of memberships and running delegate selection meetings. The party began to develop rules regarding issuance of memberships, keeping of records, and procedures for nomination meetings and election of delegates to leadership conventions. Constituency autonomy was lost as the central party assumed control.

Centralization of party life also appeared through mass fundraising, as appeals to individual donors bypassed local associations. Intraparty life was complicated in that donations could be made through the national party or local association, but the former did not share lists with the latter lest the association "poach." Another complication was that donating to the party did not constitute membership. Donors to the national party would appear at local nomination or delegate selection meetings to participate, but they were denied standing since they were not party members.

The new party committed itself to an organizational philosophy unusual in Canadian politics until recent times. The Progressive Conservative Party, as with other national parties, had maintained formal organizational ties with its provincial counterparts, but the Canadian Alliance had no such links. The new Conservative Party "operates at a single level and remains organizationally distinct from the existing PC parties in the provinces" (Pruysers 2014, 243). Perlin (1980) argued that the federal system necessitated a national party's organization that reflected Canada's institutional and political features, which served to mediate between people in provinces and regions. Such an organizational system was conducive to brokerage politics. The CPC's image of a "national" party was to create an organization free of subnational linkages, one that did not need to build and sustain relationships with provincial or territorial parties.

A similar issue, one that vexed the merger discussions, concerned the organization of the party's members. Is one a member through the local association, or through the party as a whole? The PCs, based on the first definition, held leadership conventions on a points system: each association had 100 points, regardless of the number of members, which were awarded to candidates on the basis of their showing in the district. The CA system was based on Canada as the organizing unit. The PC system created "rotten boroughs," but also encouraged the party to establish "franchises" across the country and for candidates to organize where they could; otherwise they would focus on large population centres. The CPC has accepted the PC model, but only after fierce debates at conventions. At its core are two concepts of national party building: the PC system goes through local associations, the CA model through individual members, that is, the nation reflected by people's ideas and preferences, wherever they happen to live.

Overall, then, two organizational features are at the heart of the CPC. It is a highly centralized entity except for the holding of memberships. Second, it lacks institutional ties with parties centred in the provinces and territories. In 2011, civil servants received a memorandum from the Prime Minister's Office that henceforth "The Government of Canada" would be termed "The Harper Government."

New and old Canada challenged the party. The CA's 2000 election campaign suffered from advertising that was tone deaf to Quebec's political dynamics (Flanagan 2009, 148). The 2004 election reflected the party's continuing weakness in Quebec as well as its failure to win ridings with large numbers of new Canadians or in non-prairie metropolitan areas. Harper and his colleagues invested time and resources to build strength in these weak areas in the knowledge that winning office was not otherwise possible, and showed gains in subsequent elections, especially in districts with large numbers of new Canadians.[14]

In 2011 the party's slogan was "Here for Canada." Harper's victory speech heralded "a strong, stable, national majority government." The unanswered question was whether the CPC was a national party. Certainly seats were won in every subnational jurisdiction, but how well did the party do across the country?

Table 8.1 shows the CPC vote proportional to subnational jurisdictions' populations for each of the elections in which Harper led the party. The logic underlying the data in Table 8.1 is that a "national" party would draw its vote in proportion to the population in the various jurisdictions. Parties with regionalized or provincialized appeals will do proportionally better in some areas and disproportionately worse elsewhere. The CPC campaigns in the five elections produced four significant features. The area from Ontario to the West and the northern territories overcontributed to the party's showing; to the East, the results were uneven, most striking being its sustained weakness in Quebec. In 2011, the CPC elected five MPs out of a possible

Table 8.1   Conservative Party Vote, by Province and Territory, Canadian Federal Elections 2004–2015

	2004	2006	2008	2011	2015
NL	+0.1	+0.3	−0.9	−0.5	−1.0
PE	+0.2	+0.1	+0.1	+0.2	−0.1
NS	+0.3	−0.2	−0.6	0.0	−0.9
NB	−1.0	+0.8	+0.9	+1.0	−0.1
QC	−13.9	−4.5	−6.3	−10.6	−10.4
ON	+1.3	−1.7	+0.2	+3.5	+2.3
MB	+1.0	+0.5	+0.8	+0.9	+0.4
SK	+1.4	+0.8	+1.3	+1.4	+1.6
AB	+8.6	+6.3	+4.8	+5.0	+9.8
BC	+2.5	−0.5	+2.2	+1.5	−0.5
Territories★	+1.2	+0.3	+0.1	+0.1	−0.1

★ Nunavut, Northwest Territories, and Yukon, combined.

Source: Elections Canada, *Official Voting Results* (various years); Statistics Canada.

Entries in each cell represent the following calculation:
The CPC vote in a province (territory) as a percentage of the national CPC vote compared to the jurisdiction's share of the national population. For Ontario in 2011, the calculation is as follows:
Conservative vote as a percentage of the party's national vote: 42.1
Ontario's population as a percentage of Canada's population: 38.6
Difference: +3.5

75 in Quebec. The difference between the CPC's minorities and its 2011 majority was Ontario. And, from 2004 to 2015, the party did not expand its base beyond Alberta and (rural/small-town) Ontario.

Meisel's national unity premise requires parties to make inroads in areas strongly dominated by other parties. The old system had parties thinking of regional interests and regional support bases. Generally, Canadian politics historically has involved the articulation and accommodation of interests with a considerable, if not high, degree of spatial content.

Contemporary Canada's electorate is highly regionalized, as it has been since 1921, yet the rhetoric and policy positioning of parties, especially the CPC, are predicated on winning "middle class" voters wherever they are, while being seemingly indifferent to a divergent and regionalized electorate.

Conservatives, maintaining a long-term pattern, are more likely to be supported by older than younger voters. Polls also show a consistent pattern of men rather than women, in any socioeconomic category, supporting the CPC, a gender divide in support for the leftist and rightist parties that is ordinarily found elsewhere. However, from the perspective of comparative electoral behaviour, the CPC base contains an uncommon characteristic. Polls during the 2015 election showed that voters with lower levels of educational attainment were more likely to be Conservative voters than higher educated voters (EKOS 2015).

Since its birth the CPC has brought its resources together efficiently and effectively (Ellis and Woolstencroft 2011). Ample financial resources have been available for party work. Modern politics comprises an electorate with about 60 per cent voting in elections in which many parties fragment political space;[15] the CPC benefits since it has no serious enemies to its right and, as the 2015 election showed, could count on an electoral base that stayed largely loyal despite enormous negative publicity. In some ways the party plays the centrist game well by avoiding extreme positions on economic issues (Stevenson 2014). Its opponents are to the left (more mushy than hard, to be sure), with all playing to the amorphous "middle class" (Walchuk 2012). The CPC uses its control of government to "reward" its base by adopting right-wing policies that most do not care or know about (Frenette 2014). The CPC has developed the art of crafting niche policies that appeal to small slices of the electorate but who matter enormously in an electoral system that handsomely rewards a winning margin no matter how low its support level. The CPC's 2011 comfortable majority came from 39.6 per cent of the 61.1 per cent of Canadians who voted.

Its strongest public commitments were lower taxes, followed by personal and state security, but under the radar the policy has been a gradual reduction of federal government spending in Canada as a proportion of the gross national product. A generation ago PC politicians lamented the absence of market-centred think tanks; in 2015 the CPC has many ideological friends.[16] It has avoided free market rhetoric, focusing more on the virtue of lowering taxes, but clearly "Blue" Tories won the day and "Red" Tories drifted away.

The Harper government's many actions and postures had created deep-seated animosity by the time the 2015 election was called; polls showed that two-thirds of voters wanted change, and only about 40 per cent would even consider voting Conservative. Its two leading opponents vied to lead the charge but with campaigns that avoided ideological crusades; like the Conservatives they focused on the "middle class," and the "change" they offered seemed more of personnel and style than a significant alteration of the socioeconomic structure. In that sense, then, the Conservatives, despite their defeat, had changed the substance of political discourse.

Rebuilding and Rebranding, Yet Again

With Harper's resignation as leader, the party awaits a leadership convention. How will the CPC in its newest incarnation handle the transition to its second leader? Every party has its factions, but the Conservatives, for much of their history, have been marked by internecine battles. The CPC under Harper had successfully tamped down the fractiousness of Conservatives, but the party's leadership conventions have been seriously riven. How will the party's social-conservative and moderate wings view each other? Leader-centred politics means that the new leader will be able to put his or her stamp on the party's branding. However, the legacy of Harper's steely-eyed populism will be difficult to overcome in the near-term future.

With support of 32 per cent of voters, 99 MPs in the House of Commons, and no foe on the right, CPC partisans will think it is in a strong position to fight the next election. Moreover, contemporary electorates, lacking firm commitments and party loyalties, move easily from one party to another. Recent electoral history has seen weak parties make enormous gains, sometimes vaulting from obscurity into office. Nonetheless, the sobering thought for Conservatives is what to do about their poor showing in urban districts in Quebec and especially Ontario and British Columbia, where the party had invested much to gain some profit that has subsequently disappeared.

One traditional road to office was through building support with provincial parties. At the end of 2015 no Conservative provincial party was in office (though the Saskatchewan Party is a successor to the province's former Conservative Party). Does the party's centralized structure allow for spatially based issues to be heard in its processes? Moreover, if electoral reform is put into place, as promised by the Liberals for the 2019 election, the electoral calculus will have been fundamentally changed. How will the Conservatives play that game?

Suggested Readings

English, John. 1977. *The Decline of Politics: The Conservatives and the Party System, 1901–20.* Toronto: University of Toronto Press.

Flanagan, Tom. 2009. *Harper's Team: Behind the Scenes in the Conservative Rise to Power.* 2nd ed. Montreal: McGill-Queen's University Press.

Glassford, Larry A. 1992. *Reaction and Reform: The Politics of the Conservative Party under R.B. Bennett, 1927–1938.* Toronto: University of Toronto Press.

Granatstein, J.L. 1967. *The Politics of Survival: The Conservative Party of Canada, 1939–1945.* Toronto: University of Toronto Press.

Perlin, George C. 1980. *The Tory Syndrome: Leadership Politics in the Progressive Conservative Party.* Montreal: McGill-Queen's University Press.

Plamondon, Bob. 2009. *Blue Thunder: The Truth about Conservatives from Macdonald to Harper.* Toronto: Key Porter Books.

Notes

1   In its long history the party has had many names:

Liberal-Conservative (1867–1917)
Unionist (1917–22)
National Government (1940)
Progressive Conservative (1942–2003)
Conservative (1922 to 1940; 2003 to present)
"Tory" and "Conservative" will be used at times for stylistic reasons.

2   Overwhelming victories can be problematic. What led so many to support the party? And what will maintain their support? In discussing the electoral virtue of the minimum winning coalition, Tom Flanagan (2014, 71) points to 1958 and 1984 as being fragile because of the incompatible expectations of supporters in Quebec and elsewhere.

3   There is a voluminous literature on this subject. For a cogent recent discussion, see Stevenson (2014). Taylor (1984) presented a literary examination of various luminaries with "Red Tory" inclinations.

4   Although the 1930 election nicely illustrates Flanagan's (2014) argument, he does not make any reference to it.

5   The 1967 leadership convention had five Ontario candidates out of 11; there were five rounds of voting, but no Ontario candidate lasted beyond the third.

6   Diefenbaker was a candidate and spoke about his opposition to the "Deux Nations" interpretation of Quebec and Canada and the importance of the British connection.

7   In 1977, Jack Horner, a long time MP and fellow Albertan, crossed the floor to join the Liberals; he was one of many hostile to Clark.

8   The complex history from 1973 to 2003 has been covered by many; the best single source is Flanagan (2009). See also Ellis and Woolstencroft (2004).

9   Clark, who left politics in 1993, returned to become leader of the PCs in 1998 and won a seat in 2000. He resigned as leader in 2003, and not only did he not join the CPC, he became a continuing critic.

10   Negotiations on the PC side were carried out by people chosen by Peter MacKay without the involvement of Bruck Easton, party president since 2000.

11   To be sure, all parties have had to deal with candidates saying politically incendiary things; in some cases the words are from many years ago. In the electronic world, anything is fair game for one's opponents, as we saw in the 2015 campaign.

12   Control extended deep into the party. A student of the author's was interviewed for an internship with the party; two employees from the Prime Minister's Office attended the interview.

13   The subsidy was based on a certain sum paid to a party for each vote it received. It means that people, in effect, are donating to a party when they vote for it.

14   See the various essays by Ellis and Woolstencroft on the CPC's campaigns. Flanagan (2009) speaks to Harper's work on learning French and various outreach undertakings.

15   The turnout of over 68 per cent in 2015 seemingly played to the CPC's disadvantage.

16   Principally, the Fraser Institute, Macdonald-Laurier Institute, Atlantic Institute for Market Studies, C.D. Howe Institute, Frontier Centre for Public Policy, Manning Centre, and Canadian Taxpayers Federation.

References

Beck, J.M. 1968. *Pendulum of Power*. Scarborough, ON: Prentice-Hall.

Bélanger, Éric, and Jean-François Godbout. 2010. "Why Do Parties Merge? The Case of the Conservative Party of Canada." *Parliamentary Affairs* 63 (1): 41–65. http://dx.doi.org/10.1093/pa/gsp041

Cairns, Alan C. 1977. "The Governments and Societies of Canadian Federalism." *Canadian Journal of Political Science* 10 (4): 695–726. http://dx.doi.org/10.1017/S0008423900050861

Careless, J.M.S. 1969. "'Limited Identities' in Canada." *Canadian Historical Review* 50 (1): 1–10. http://dx.doi.org/10.3138/CHR-050-01-01

Carty, R. Kenneth. 1991. *Canadian Political Parties in the Constituencies*. Vol. 23 of the Research Studies, Royal Commission on Electoral Reform and Party Financing. Toronto: Dundurn Press.

Carty, R. Kenneth. 2002. "The Politics of Tecumseh Corners: Canadian Political Parties as Franchise Organizations." *Canadian Journal of Political Science* 35 (4): 723–45. http://dx.doi.org/10.1017/S0008423902778402

Downs, Anthony. 1957. *An Economic Theory of Democracy*. New York: Harper.

EKOS. 2015. "Tie Continues." Poll conducted October 8–10 (N = 1,428). http://www.ekospolitics.com/wp-content/uploads/full_report_october_11_2015.pdf

Elkins, David J., and Richard Simeon. 1980. *Small Worlds: Provinces and Parties in Canadian Political Life*. Toronto: Methuen.

Ellis, Faron, and Peter Woolstencroft. 2004. "New Conservatives, Old Realities: The 2004 Election Campaign." In *The Canadian General Election of 2004*, edited by Jon H. Pammett and Christopher Dornan, 66–105. Toronto: Dundurn Press.

Ellis, Faron, and Peter Woolstencroft. 2006. "A Change of Government, Not a Change of Country: Conservatives in the 2006 Federal Election." In *The Canadian Federal Election of 2006*, edited by Jon H. Pammett and Christopher Dornan, 58–92. Toronto: Dundurn Press.

Ellis, Faron, and Peter Woolstencroft. 2011. "The Conservative Campaign: Becoming the New Natural Governing Party." In *The Canadian Federal Election of 2011*, edited by Jon H. Pammett and Christopher Dornan, 15–44. Toronto: Dundurn Press.

Eldersveld, Samuel J. 1964. *Political Parties: A Behavioral Analysis*. Chicago: Rand McNally & Company.

English, John. 1977. *The Decline of Politics: The Conservatives and the Party System, 1901–20*. Toronto: University of Toronto Press.

Flanagan, Tom. 2009. *Harper's Team: Behind the Scenes in the Conservative Rise to Power*. 2nd ed. Montreal: McGill-Queen's University Press.

Flanagan, Tom. 2014. *Winning Power: Canadian Campaigning in the Twenty-First Century*. Montreal: McGill-Queen's University Press.

Frenette, Yves. 2014. "Conscripting Canada's Past: The Harper Government and the Politics of Memory." *Canadian Journal of History* 49 (1): 49–65. http://dx.doi.org/10.3138/cjh.49.1.49

Glassford, Larry A. 1992. *Reaction and Reform: The Politics of the Conservative Party under R.B. Bennett, 1927–1938*. Toronto: University of Toronto Press.

Granatstein, J.L. 1967. *The Politics of Survival: The Conservative Party of Canada, 1939–1945*. Toronto: University of Toronto Press.

Key, V.O., Jr. 1955. "A Theory of Critical Elections." *Journal of Politics* 17 (1): 3–18. http://dx.doi.org/10.2307/2126401

Koop, Royce. 2011. *Organizing for Local and National Politics*. Vancouver: University of British Columbia Press.

Lipset, S.M. 1989. *Continental Divide: The Values and Institutions of the United States and Canada*. Toronto: C.D. Howe Institute.

Marland, Alex, and Tom Flanagan. 2013. "Brand New Party: Political Branding and the Conservative Party of Canada." *Canadian Journal of Political Science* 46 (4): 951–72. http://dx.doi.org/10.1017/S0008423913001108

Marland, Alex, and Tom Flanagan. 2015. "From Opposition to Government: Party Merger as a Step to Power." *Parliamentary Affairs* 68 (2): 272–90. http://dx.doi.org/10.1093/pa/gst015

Meisel, John. 1963. "The Stalled Omnibus: Canadian Parties in the 1960s." *Social Research* 30 (3): 367–90.

Morton, W.L. 1962. "Canadian Conservatism Now." In *Politics: Canada*, edited by Paul Fox, 286–90. Toronto: McGraw-Hill.

Newman, Peter C. 1963. *Renegade in Power: The Diefenbaker Years*. Toronto: McClelland and Stewart.

Pennington, Chris. 2012. *The Destiny of Canada: Macdonald, Laurier, and the Election of 1891*. Toronto: Viking Canada.

Perlin, George C. 1980. *The Tory Syndrome: Leadership Politics in the Progressive Conservative Party*. Montreal: McGill-Queen's University Press.

Plamondon, Bob. 2009. *Blue Thunder: The Truth about Conservatives from Macdonald to Harper*. Toronto: Key Porter Books.

Pruysers, Scott. 2014. "Reconsidering Vertical Integration: An Examination of National Political Parties and Their Counterparts in Ontario." *Canadian Journal of Political Science* 47 (2): 237–58. http://dx.doi.org/10.1017/S0008423914000407

Siegfried, André. 1907. *The Race Question in Canada*. London: Eveleigh Nash.

Stevenson, Garth. 1989. *Unfulfilled Union: Canadian Federalism and National Unity.* Toronto: Gage.

Stevenson, Garth. 2014. "The Mackenzie King of Our Time." *Inroads* 35 (Summer/Fall): 22–9.

Stewart, Gordon T. 1986. *Origins of Canadian Politics.* Vancouver: University of British Columbia Press.

Taylor, Charles. 1984. *Radical Tories*. Toronto: Formac Publishing.

Underhill, Frank. 1960. *In Search of Canadian Liberalism*. Toronto: Macmillan.

Walchuk, Bradley. 2008. "Intraparty Federalism and the Progressive Conservative Party in Alberta and Ontario, 1943 to 2003." Master's thesis, Brock University.

Walchuk, Bradley. 2012. "A Whole New Ballgame: The Rise of Canada's Fifth Party System." *American Review of Canadian Studies* 42 (3): 418–34. http://dx.doi.org/10.1080/02722011.2012.705867

Williams, John R. 1956. *The Conservative Party of Canada: 1920–1949*. Durham, NC: Duke University Press.

Wells, Paul. 2013. *The Longer I'm Prime Minister: Stephen Harper and Canada, 2006.* Toronto: Random House.

Woolstencroft, Peter. 1996. "The Progressive Conservative Party, 1984–1993: Government, Party, Members." In *Party Politics in Canada,* 7th ed., edited by Hugh G. Thorburn, 280–305. Toronto: Prentice-Hall.

Woolstencroft, Peter. 1997. "On the Ropes Again: The Campaign of the Progressive Conservative Party in the 1997 Federal Election." In *The Canadian General Election of 1997,* edited by Alan Frizzell and Jon H. Pammett, 71–90. Toronto: Dundurn Press.

Woolstencroft, Peter. 2001. "Staying Alive: The Progressive Conservative Party Fights for Survival." In *Party Politics in Canada,* 8th ed., edited by Hugh G. Thorburn and Alan Whitehorn, 248–63. Toronto: Prentice-Hall.

9

Ideological Moderation and Professionalization: The NDP under Jack Layton and Tom Mulcair[1]

DAVID McGRANE

COMPARED TO THE 1990s, THE FEDERAL New Democratic Party of Canada (NDP) has been quite successful over the past 15 years. When Jack Layton became the leader of the NDP in 2003, he inherited a party that had just won under 10 per cent of the popular vote in the previous federal election and had been relegated to fourth party status in the House of Commons. Less than 10 years later, the NDP scored a historic breakthrough in the 2011 federal election, forming the Official Opposition for the first time in its history and winning a large majority of the seats in Quebec. At the beginning of the 2015 federal election campaign, the NDP was riding high in the polls and was a legitimate contender to form government. While the Liberals eventually won a sizable majority and the NDP lost approximately half its seats, Tom Mulcair still led the party to one of the best electoral performances in its history, with 19.7 per cent of the national vote and 44 seats. Although the 2015 election results were disappointing to many in the party who dreamed of forming the first NDP federal government in Canadian history, the party was still successful in a certain sense. After almost drifting into irrelevance during the 1990s and early 2000s, it has firmly reasserted itself as an important player in Canadian politics and a party that impacts Canadian political discourse.

This chapter seeks to place the NDP's success during the Layton years and the party's loss of seats in the 2015 election into historical perspective. The main argument is that, under Layton and Mulcair, the NDP has simultaneously undergone the twin processes of ideological moderation and professionalization. The chapter begins with a section exploring the history of the NDP before Layton assumed leadership of the party, with a specific focus on ideology and internal organization. The sections that follow examine the professionalization of its campaign machinery and the transformation of the NDP's ideology during Layton's time as leader and during the first part of Mulcair's leadership. The chapter ends with an assessment of the party's position in Canadian politics following the 2015 federal election and a discussion of its prospects for the future.

Historical Roots: The Legacy of CCF-NDP (1932–2002)

During the 1920s, a large number of intellectuals, labour parties, farmers' movements, and Christian groups (known as *social gospellers*) who were critical of the existing inequality within the capitalist economic system emerged in Western Canada and Ontario (Penner 1992). Several Members of Parliament (MPs) from labour parties and farmer parties were subsequently elected to the House of Commons and eventually came together to form the "Ginger Group," which acted as an unofficial caucus of independent MPs who shared adhesion to socialism, social democracy, or left-leaning liberalism (McNaught 1959, 209–14). Eventually these MPs and groups critical of economic inequality came together to form the Co-operative Commonwealth Federation (CCF) as a "farmer-labour-socialist party" at a meeting in Calgary in 1932 (Lipset 1950, 114). Despite the fact that the CCF saw itself as a labour party, it is important to note that trade unions were almost completely absent at the founding of the party, and most unions continued to cooperate with the Liberals or maintain nonpartisan stances.

The ideology of the new party was outlined in the *Regina Manifesto,* which was adopted at the party's second convention in Regina in 1933. By today's standards, the manifesto employs what could be considered strident socialist language. The manifesto famously ends by promising that "No C.C.F. Government will rest content until it has eradicated capitalism and put into operation the full programme of socialized planning which will lead to the establishment in Canada of the Cooperative Commonwealth" (Young 1969, 313). Preceding this bold statement, the manifesto makes wide-ranging policy suggestions. Some of these suggestions are still considered quite radical today: state planning of the economy; government boards to control exports; state regulation of all wages; and the nationalization of all banks, natural resources, and the distribution systems for milk and bread. On the other hand, the manifesto makes some suggestions that have gradually came to be accepted by all political parties during the twentieth century, such as medicare, government-owned crop insurance, human rights for racial minorities, and unemployment insurance.

The CCF was organized as a "mass party" and prided itself as being controlled by its membership, in contrast to the autocratic Liberal and Conservative parties (Young 1969, 139–79). A *mass party* is issued from and affiliated to extra-parliamentary movements, such as churches or trade unions; encourages a large and active membership; ensures that party policy is determined by party members; possesses a rigid, doctrinaire ideology; and its election campaigns are run by volunteer local activists (Duverger 1963, 63–79). A *cadre party* has the opposite characteristics: parliamentary origins;

a small and inactive membership; party policy made by leaders; a flexible, catch-all ideology; campaigns run by a centralized group of professionals; and no formal affiliations to extra-parliamentary groups (Duverger 1963). In mass party fashion, CCF members were organized into local clubs that sent representatives to the national convention, where party policy was determined and the leader had to face re-election and could be challenged by any delegate from the floor of the convention. Since the CCF saw itself as a federation, it is important to note that power was very decentralized, with each province having its own self-functioning party that would send representatives to the CCF national convention, council, and executive.

The CCF contested seven federal elections from 1935 to 1958, averaging only 11 per cent of the popular vote and 16 seats per election. Its electoral high point was the 1945 election, when it received 16 per cent of the popular vote and 28 seats. The CCF's vote was highly regionalized. It obtained its highest popular vote and nearly all of its seats in British Columbia, Saskatchewan, and Manitoba. Its popular vote hovered just above 10 per cent in Ontario, but that support translated into only eight seats in that province over the party's history. East of Ontario and in Alberta, the party was simply not a factor in federal elections.

In 1958, the CCF was approached by the newly formed Canadian Labour Congress to form a political party that would combine "the CCF, the labour movement, farmer organizations, professional people and other liberally minded persons interested in basic social reform" (Knowles 1961, 127). It was hoped that the new party would attract more unionized voters through its official affiliation with the labour movement, represent a fresh image as a party that was embracing postwar prosperity as opposed to being mired in Depression-era thinking, and become a fully bilingual party that recognized the nationalist aspirations of the Québécois (Bickerton, Gagnon, and Smith 1999, 102; Erickson and Laycock 2014, 15). After extensive debate and consultation, the new party was finally created in 1961 and given the name "New Democratic Party" (Morton 1974, 27).

While it is difficult to summarize all of the nuances of the NDP's ideology from its founding to when Layton took over as leader, it is safe to say that the NDP struck a more moderate tone than the CCF. The language of the declaration adopted at the NDP's founding, the *New Party Declaration,* is noticeably more optimistic than the *Regina Manifesto.* Instead of condemning the evils of the existing economic system and aiming to eradicate capitalism, the purpose of the new party was to "achieve a fully free and just society in which all citizens participate, and all share equitably in its fruits" (Knowles 1961, 7).

From 1961 to 2000, the NDP's ideology could be summarized as embodying four elements. First, there was an emphasis on full employment achieved through direct subsidies to the private sector and Keynesian countercyclical spending on public goods such as infrastructure, hospitals, and schools (Evans 2012, 57). Countercyclical spending means that government spends heavily during times of weak economic growth to get the economy moving, even if it means going into deficit. Any public deficits incurred during times of slow economic growth could then be reduced once the economy regains strength. Second, public ownership remained an important part of the NDP's ideology, but its scope was constrained to selected industries, such as railways and the distribution of gasoline (Laycock 2014, 114). Third, the party favoured creating greater economic equality through the large-scale expansion of the welfare state financed by higher taxes on corporations and high-income earners (Whitehorn 1992). Fourth, the NDP came to embrace improvements to Canada's liberal rights regime to reduce the discrimination faced by women, Indigenous peoples, gay and lesbian individuals, the disabled, and visible minorities, as well as promoting the need for environmental protection (Wiseman and Isitt 2007, 583–84). As such, the NDP's ideology during this period was consistent with Moschonas's (2002, 15) classical formulation of postwar social democracy as "political liberalism + mixed economy + welfare state + Keynesian economic policy + commitment to equality."

While the Liberals and Conservatives are seen as cadre parties, the NDP has generally been considered the prototypical "mass party" of Canadian politics during the second half of the twentieth century (Sayers 1999; Whitehorn 1992). The NDP was explicitly linked to Canada's union movement through exchange of personnel, financial contributions, and formal affiliation, as well as unions wielding considerable influence over party policy through their large number of delegates at conventions (Archer 1990, 27–40). NDP members and candidates were expected to show a high level of commitment to the party, and NDP riding associations were very active between elections in terms of holding events, signing petitions, participating in local labour strikes, and organizing protests (Sayers 1999, 35–36). Like the CCF, the conventions of the NDP were the ultimate source of establishing party policy, and the NDP leader was required to stand for re-election at every convention and could face a challenge from any delegate (Whitehorn 1992, 113–14). The important role played by the convention in shaping party policy was meant to ensure that the NDP did not stray too far from its social democratic roots.

The campaign structure of the NDP before Layton was quite decentralized and volunteer driven, with each riding association running its local campaign and the staff of each provincial wing in charge of coordinating how the local campaigns were structured in their province. Nonetheless, beginning in the 1980s under the leadership of Ed Broadbent, more centrally controlled campaigns emerged. A small election planning committee made up of MPs, party staff, labour leaders, and members of the federal executive took over the creation of the election platform and overall election readiness. An even smaller group of key advisers surrounding the leader and officials in party headquarters were placed in charge of polling, campaign strategy, media relations, and the Leader's Tour (Whitehorn 1992).

Overall, the NDP was more electorally successfully than the CCF. During the federal elections held from 1962 to 2000, the NDP averaged 15 per cent of the popular vote and 23 seats per election. The party's electoral strength remained in British Columbia, Saskatchewan, and Manitoba, where over two-thirds of NDP MPs were elected during this time period. There was a marked improvement in Ontario, where the party won 81 seats from 1962 to 2000. However, the party was largely irrelevant in provincial and federal elections in Quebec, Alberta, and Atlantic Canada. It was not until the 1997 federal election that the NDP was able to establish a beachhead of seats in Atlantic Canada under the leadership of Nova Scotian Alexa McDonough.

Finally, it is important to note the ebbs and flows in the electoral support of the NDP from its inception to the 2000 election. With the exception of a tough 1974 election (when it received 15.6 per cent of the vote), the NDP's popular vote remained remarkably steady at 17 to 20 per cent from 1965 to 1988. This level of support produced anywhere from 21 to 43 seats in the House of Commons (again, in 1974 the NDP won only 16 seats). However, the 1990s were particularly hard on the NDP. Given its past electoral scores, the party was psychologically unprepared for the electoral disaster that it endured in the 1993 federal election, when its popular vote plummeted to 7 per cent and it won only nine seats. After bouncing back slightly in 1997, the NDP registered another disappointing result in the 2000 federal election, when it fell back to 9 per cent of the popular vote and secured only 13 seats.

Ideological Moderation of the NDP under Jack Layton

Koop and Bittner (2013, 320–21) and Pétry (2014, 145) have performed content analysis on recent federal NDP platforms. Content analysis involves assigning passages of text certain codes and then aggregating the codes together to identify patterns. Based on their coding schemes, both research-ers found that NDP platforms moved to the right during the time that Jack Layton was leader. However, this quantitative approach is summative and does not specify the ways in which NDP platforms moved to the right under Layton. This section briefly describes policies in the NDP's platforms from 2004 to 2011 to detect the manner in which Layton moderated the

NDP's ideology.[2] It then illustrates how the 2015 NDP platform moved the party slightly back to the left, even if it did not reverse the party's ideological moderation.

Some elements of NDP platforms from 2004 to 2011 were remarkably consistent. All of these platforms featured an activist state that would intervene in the economy through tax credits to companies that create jobs, orderly marketing in agriculture, restricting foreign takeovers, industrial strategies for priority sectors, and various subsidies to promote the green economy. With the exception of the suggestion of new Crown corporations to invest in renewable energy and to make prescription drugs in the 2004 platform, the creation of new public enterprises was not mentioned in any of the NDP's platforms from 2006 to 2011. The party's consumer protection policies consistently addressed proper food labelling and food inspection as well as the lowering of fees related to airlines, credit cards, cell phones, Internet service, and banking. The NDP's infrastructure ideas repeatedly stressed giving municipalities additional federal gas tax revenues to attend to public transit systems. The party's policies on women and minorities were consistent in their advocacy of better pay equity and greater funding for women's groups, more family reunification for immigrants, recognizing Indigenous self-government and increasing funding to on-reserve education, and more government programs for disabled Canadians. In intergovernmental affairs, there was a constant message of creating frameworks for national standards that nonetheless respected Quebec's autonomy.

On other policies, there were minor shifts that can be discerned from 2004 to 2011. The NDP's arts and culture policies initially focused heavily on better funding for the CBC and encouraging Canadian content. Later platforms supplemented these ideas with incentives to improve artists' incomes and the promotion of the French language and Quebec culture. There was a subtle shift in how the NDP platforms dealt with deficits. The 2004 platform promised balanced budgets "exempting years of extreme revenue shortfalls and disasters and acts of God," while the other platforms simply committed to a balanced budget in every year of NDP government. The NDP also dropped some of its more ambitious democratic reforms, such as lowering the voting age to 16 and designating seats for Indigenous peoples in the House of Commons. However, under Layton the party did remain committed to a mixed-member proportional representation electoral system, abolishing the Senate, and restricting the power of the prime minister and lobbyists. Similarly, in foreign affairs, the NDP dropped some of its more daring ideas, such as a "Tobin tax" (placing a small tax on all international monetary transactions) and forgiving debt of developing nations, but maintained a commitment to more conventional ideas like increasing foreign aid to 0.7 per cent of Canada's gross domestic product. While the NDP consistently advocated for higher corporate taxes, it did back away from its insistence on raising taxes on Canadians with higher incomes through initiatives like an inheritance tax. In terms of social policy, there remained a strong commitment to expanding social programs, but its scope was circumscribed. A few examples of the differences between the 2004 and 2011 platforms will suffice: the target of 200,000 new child-care spaces a year was reduced to 25,000 new child-care spaces a year; reducing tuition by 10 per cent and freezing it at that level was changed to making postsecondary education "more affordable" through increased transfer payments to provinces; a public prescription drug insurance program for all Canadians was replaced with an "aggressive" review of drug prices and hiring more doctors and nurses; and a 10-year strategy to build 200,000 new public housing units was reduced to a vague commitment of "new funding for affordable and social housing" and restoring funding to the residential rehabilitation assistance program.

The largest shifts in the NDP's policies during the Layton era took place in the areas of the environment, military, crime, labour policy, and trade policy. Earlier platforms stressed rehabilitation, restorative justice, and the underlying causes of crime, such as poverty. By contrast, the 2011 platform pledges tougher punishments and hiring more police officers as the primary mechanisms for reducing crime. On the environment, earlier platforms were stringent in calling for moratoriums on certain types of economic activity (e.g., new development of the oil sands) and completely removing government subsidies to the oil, gas, and nuclear sectors. Later platforms focused on the NDP's ideas for a cap-and-trade system as well as fostering research in green technology and renewable energy. The NDP's 2004 platform had a relatively strong emphasis on labour policy, with suggestions for anti-scab legislation, new national holidays, and a federal minimum wage. Similarly, the NDP called for the replacement of "undemocratic, corporate-driven trade deals" like the North American Free Trade Agreement and the World Trade Organization with fair trade agreements in 2004. However, the 2011 platform mentioned neither labour policy nor trade policy. When it comes to the military, earlier NDP platforms put forth minimalist and vague ideas of a stronger commitment to peacekeeping and increasing the pay of members of the Armed Forces. By 2011, the NDP's platform on the military had evolved considerably by identifying three priorities for Canada's military (peacekeeping, natural disaster relief, and defending Canada) and putting forth specific plans for purchasing more military equipment and improving services for Canadian veterans.

Overall, our examination of NDP platforms during the Layton years illustrates the moderation of the party's ideology. The party quietly removed many of its ambitious left-wing policies. As the 2000s progressed, NDP platforms also allocated more space to traditional concerns of right-wing parties like crime, infrastructure spending, and military policy while de-emphasizing traditional left-wing concerns like trade, labour, and the environment. There was a change in the tone of NDP platforms during the Layton era. The number of commitments involving "national" strategies, plans, and standards was steadily reduced and replaced with commitments that were introduced by expressions such as "as a practical first step toward" and "as finances permit."

However, it is not accurate to suggest that the NDP's ideology went through a wholesale transformation during the Layton years. Social policy and policies relating to women and minorities continued to make up large portions of the party's platform. Commitments to promoting economic equality, expanding social programs, and deepening Canada's liberal rights regime endured. Further, the 2011 platform did not represent a radical departure from previous platforms. Indeed, approximately 70 per cent of the policies in the 2011 platform can be found in the 2004, 2006, or 2008 NDP platforms. Rather than being a complete makeover of the party's ideology, the 2011 platform streamlined the party's focus and selected the most realizable and practical suggestions from previous platforms.

The NDP's 2015 platform was consistent with its 2011 platform and did not represent a major reversal of the party's ideological moderation. Policies around reducing small business taxation, raising the corporate tax rate, balancing the budget, introducing a mixed-member proportional representation system and a cap-and-trade system to reduce greenhouse gases, hiring more police officers, and hiring more nurses and doctors were virtually identical in 2011 and 2015. Nonetheless, in certain areas it could be argued that the NDP's platform in 2015 was more ambitious and left wing than the party's 2011 platform. The 2015 platform promised 1 million child care spaces over eight years at $15 a day compared to the 2011 promise of 100,000 spaces over four years with no mention of regulating the cost of those spaces. Whereas the 2011 platform contained a vague pledge to lower prescription drug costs when finances permitted, the 2015 platform boldly claimed that an NDP government would work toward universal public drug coverage for all Canadians that would lower prescription drug costs by 30 per cent. The 2011 NDP platform had been silent on labour policy, free trade agreements, and illicit drugs. The 2015 NDP platform committed to the decriminalization of marijuana and ensuring that trade agreements improved social, environmental, and labour standards in partner countries. The NDP also came out strongly against the Trans-Pacific Partnership during the final two weeks of the 2015 election campaign because it feared a loss of jobs in the dairy and auto sectors. Interestingly, the 2015 NDP platform pledged not only to repeal several pieces of labour legislation passed by the Harper government, but also to introduce anti-scab legislation and a $15 per hour federal minimum wage.

Professionalization of the NDP during the Layton and Mulcair Years

Professionalization has been a key concept in research on contemporary political parties. The basic premise of most research on professionalization is that a fundamental shift has occurred over the last 20 years. In the past, local volunteers and part-time party employees would gather together at election time to organize fundraising, identify supporters, and distribute campaign literature in the area in which they lived. The central party office dealt with national advertising like television commercials and organized a Leader's Tour, but generally let local volunteers and part-time employees run their campaigns how they saw fit (Plasser and Plasser 2002). Over the past two decades, campaigning has becoming increasingly organized by professionals employed full time at the central offices of parties. From fundraising to policy development to campaign strategy, these professionals have taken over tasks traditionally performed by volunteers and local party activists (Gibson and Rommele 2009).

The Layton era coincided with the acceleration of the professionalization of the federal NDP. The largest alteration in the party's organization was the decoupling of the federal and provincial NDP structures. Before the Layton era, provincial sections and local NDP riding associations were responsible for all fundraising, and these local entities were in charge of campaign organizations whenever a federal election rolled around. During Layton's time as leader, the federal NDP began to centrally fundraise out of its Ottawa headquarters using paid telemarketers and direct mailing; it also started receiving annual per-vote subsidies as part of the party financing reforms of the early 2000s.[3] With these increased revenues, the federal party hired field organizers in each region of the country reporting directly to Ottawa. New rules around party financing also forced NDP provincial offices to remove themselves from the organization of federal election campaigns as well as the daily operation of federal riding associations. The result was that the NDP headquarters in Ottawa assumed responsibility for all fundraising and local campaign readiness.

Local NDP activists traditionally organized the nomination of candidates with little interference from Ottawa. During Layton's years as leader, party headquarters became very involved in candidate searches. Starting in 2008, all candidates in NDP nomination races had to be "vetted" by party headquarters in Ottawa, and candidates could be prohibited from entering the nomination race if the central party office felt that they could embarrass the party or become a distraction during the election campaign. The central office was given the power to disallow a nomination race from proceeding until at least one candidate from an equity-seeking group had entered the race or it had been satisfied that an adequate search for such candidates had taken place.

In the past, NDP campaigns had been organized by an election planning committee (EPC) that was struck close to an election and made up of volunteer members of the party executive along with party staff, representatives from the labour movement, and a representative of the party's parliamentary caucus. As the election approached, the EPC would hire a national campaign manager and ensure that the provincial sections were ready with their individual campaigns. A subcommittee of the EPC would usually peruse the policy coming out of recent conventions to create the platform and embark on a consultation with the party membership. For instance, in 2004 the platform was approved by a meeting of the Federal Council on the eve of the election call (Whitehorn 2004, 111). During that campaign, the EPC convened three times to give advice to the national campaign manager.

Following the 2008 election, the NDP Federal Council passed a motion to simply designate the Party Executive as the EPC for the next election. While the Party Executive set the overarching goals, the real strategizing to achieve these goals was done by a coterie of professional party managers, referred to as the "senior campaign team." The advent of the senior campaign team meant that the NDP was in permanent campaign mode. The team met weekly and did not report to the caucus or anyone within the party's organization. The policy staff in the leader's office devised the 2011 and 2015 NDP platforms after minimal consultation with the Party Executive, Federal Council, caucus, and NDP provincial governments. The themes of the platform were extensively tested using market research techniques such as polling and focus groups. The final platforms were presented to Layton or Mulcair, who retained the power of final approval. In both 2011 and 2015, the senior campaign team ran the campaign out of party headquarters in Ottawa, and the EPC was not convened at any time.

Whereas volunteers like the presidents of local riding associations had traditionally been in charge of communicating with members, NDP headquarters increasingly took over this role by establishing an email subscription list that it used for fundraising appeals and "calls to action"—such as signing a petition being circulated by an NDP MP or mobilizing volunteers at election time. As social media and websites became more prominent at the end of the 2000s, staff at party headquarters became responsible for establishing

and monitoring the NDP's online presence. To create material to disseminate electronically, party headquarters hired paid staff to conduct opposition
research and formed a "rapid rebuttal unit" to combat the "spin" of other
parties within the social media sphere. Clearly, social media professionals had
replaced letters to the editor from rank-and-file party members. Similarly, in
contrast to the era when local NDP campaign managers kept paper records
of voter contacts from election to election in their basements, the party
office in Ottawa developed computerized voter contact databases that collected information from paid telemarketers in Ottawa as well as aggregated
all of the contacts made by local volunteers. By the 2015 election, the party
headquarters' database was able to provide lists for the sophisticated targeting of specific demographic groups of voters in priority ridings. As such,
decisions on key parts of local campaign strategies, such as which area of the
riding to prioritize, were increasingly being made in Ottawa.

For its part, the labour movement continued to support the federal
NDP during the 2000s (Jansen and Young 2009; Pilon, Ross, and Savage
2011). However, unions began running their own independent campaigns
during federal elections as opposed to being completely integrated with
the NDP's campaign. Some unions, such as the Canadian Auto Workers,
ran campaigns centred on encouraging their members to vote strategically
for the Liberal or NDP candidate that had the best chance of defeating
a Conservative in their riding. Other unions set up offices in targeted
ridings, independent from the NDP campaign, to communicate with local
union members to outline the reasons that they should vote for the NDP
(McGrane 2011, 97–98).

In sum, the professionalization of the NDP meant that it became more
of a cadre party and less of a mass party during Layton's and Mulcair's time
as leader. Professionals in Ottawa increasingly controlled the party's campaign machinery, and the labour movement became more of an independent
player during federal election campaigns, even to the point that some unions
embraced strategic voting. Still, the NDP maintained some characteristics of
a mass party. The NDP's central office worked hard to encourage a large and
active membership. As opposed to policy development or setting local campaign strategy, the activity that members were called to undertake involved
sharing NDP messages on their social media networks and forming neighbourhood teams of foot canvassers. While the NDP did make some adjustments to the ideas in its platform during the Layton era, it cannot be said to
have adopted a "flexible, catch-all" ideology. As Laycock (2014) argues, some
of the NDP's policy instruments to achieve its social democratic goals may
have been altered during the Layton era, but its core values, such as a commitment to equality, remained the same.

The Electoral Success of the NDP in the 2000s and the Disappointment of the 2015 Election

Table 9.1 depicts the electoral results of the NDP during Layton's and Mulcair's time as leader as well as the results from the 2000 election, which was Alexa McDonough's last election as leader of the party. In many ways, the degree to which the NDP's 2015 results were disappointing depends on if one compares them to the party's results from 2000 or the party's results from 2011.

Table 9.1 illustrates that the NDP improved its percentage of the popular vote and number of seats in every election that Layton contested as leader. The 2004, 2006, and 2008 elections gradually re-established the NDP to a level of electoral success that it had routinely experienced during the 1970s and 1980s. Evidently, the 2011 election represented a historic breakthrough for the party. The NDP established itself as the dominant party in Quebec. In English Canada, the 2011 election results mirrored closely the NDP's best-ever electoral performance, which was 1988. Whereas the CCF-NDP had always depended on its regional stronghold in Western Canada for a large

Table 9.1 Federal NDP Vote and Seats (2000–2015)

Province	2000		2004		2006		2008		2011		2015	
	Vote (%)	Seats	Vote (%)	Seats	Vote (%)	Seats	Vote (%)	Seats	Vote (%)	Seats	Vote (%)	Seats
NL	13	0	17	0	14	0	34	1	33	2	21	0
PE	9	0	12	0	10	0	10	0	15	0	16	0
NS	24	3	28	2	30	2	29	2	30	3	16	0
NB	12	1	21	1	22	1	22	1	30	1	18	0
QC	2	0	5	0	7	0	12	1	43	59	25	16
ON	8	1	18	7	19	12	18	17	26	22	17	8
MB	21	4	23	4	25	3	24	4	26	2	14	2
SK	26	2	23	0	24	0	25	0	32	0	25	3
AB	5	0	10	0	12	0	13	1	17	1	12	1
BC	11	2	27	5	29	10	26	9	33	12	26	14
YT	32	0	26	0	24	0	9	0	14	0	31	0
NT	27	0	39	0	42	1	41	1	46	1	27	0
NU	18	0	15	0	17	0	28	0	19	0	20	0
Total	9	13	16	19	17	29	18	37	31	103	20	44

Source: Elections Canada.

number of its seats, the 2011 election established the NDP as much more of a national party. As would be expected of a party with widespread support across the country, the NDP's caucus became increasingly dominated by MPs from Canada's three most populous provinces (Ontario, Quebec, and British Columbia). Further, under Layton the NDP became increasingly competitive in every province and even in the Northwest Territories. By 2011, the NDP scored less than 20 per cent of the popular vote only in Alberta and Prince Edward Island. With the Liberals relegated to third party status in the House of Commons and the NDP assuming the mantle of the Official Opposition, the prospect of a NDP federal government became a realistic possibility as the 2015 federal election approached. A poll taken on the day that the 2015 federal election campaign began was especially heartening for the party: the poll placed the NDP's support at 39 per cent, found Mulcair was the most preferred prime minister, and projected that the NDP was only 10 seats short of a majority government (Forum Research 2015).

However, the results of the 2015 federal election turned out to be bitterly disappointing for the NDP. The party saw its popular vote decrease in every province except PEI, and it lost over half of its seats. The NDP was wiped out in Atlantic Canada, where it lost all of its seats to the Liberals. Similarly, the party lost two-thirds of its seats in Ontario and saw its popular vote drop from 26 per cent to 17 per cent. In Quebec, the party lost 43 of its seats and placed second behind the Liberals in popular vote. The NDP's results in Western Canada were not as disastrous as its results in the rest of the country. While the NDP's popular vote decreased in all four Western Canadian provinces, it actually picked up a handful of new seats in Saskatchewan and British Columbia while retaining the same number of seats in Manitoba and Alberta. Nonetheless, holding no seats in Atlantic Canada and having its vote drop under 20 per cent in 6 out of 10 provinces makes it more difficult now to call the NDP a "national party."

What accounts for the NDP's loss of popular vote and seats in the 2015 federal election? While the answer to this question will become clearer as political scientists begin to analyze the election in greater depth, some preliminary conclusions can be made. In light of its lead in the polls, the NDP initially adopted a "government in waiting strategy" that presented itself as a safe and credible alternative to the Conservatives in contrast to the risky change represented by Trudeau and the Liberals. Party strategists decided not to initially attack the Liberals in the hopes of setting up the narrative of a two-way NDP/Conservative race (McGrane 2016). As the campaign wore on, the weaknesses of this strategy became apparent. In seeking to be seen as safe and credible, the NDP ended up not being able to clearly outline the differences between itself and the Liberals. Particularly after the NDP promised balanced budgets and the Liberals pledged to run deficits, the two parties may have appeared to voters to be equally progressive. In the middle of the campaign, the NDP's support in Quebec suffered because of the party's opposition to a ban on wearing a niqab at citizenship ceremonies. Polls found that 91 per cent of Quebecers supported the banning of niqabs at citizenship ceremonies, and the NDP suddenly appeared to be offside with commonly held values in Quebec (Blais 2015). As the NDP's support in Quebec eroded, the narrative of a two-way NDP/Conservative race seemed increasingly implausible. NDP party strategists noted that their party's support went into a downward spiral after the niqab episode, as the "Anyone but Conservative" voters who were hesitating between the NDP and the Liberals starting getting behind the idea that only Trudeau could stop another Harper majority (McGrane 2016). As such, the NDP entered the final phase of the campaign with little momentum and unable to differentiate itself from the Liberals, who appeared to represent a bolder and more exciting prospect of change from the way that the Conservatives had governed for the past 10 years. In short, it is possible that the NDP's poor strategic positioning at the end of the campaign really hurt the party as it battled with the Liberals for the votes of the large number of Canadians who had grown tired of Harper and were yearning for a change in government.

Appearing to be within the grasp of victory at the beginning of the 2015 election only to fall to third place by the end of the campaign was undoubtedly frustrating for NDP activists, candidates, and staff members. However, if one compares the NDP's 2015 results to the party's results in the 2000 election, the situation appears less grim. Following the 2000 election, the party barely clung to official party status in the House of Commons and it was the fourth party, holding only one more seat than the fifth-placed Progressive Conservatives. Now the NDP is firmly established as the third party in Parliament, and the Liberals and the Conservatives are the only other parties with official party status. Indeed, 44 seats is the second-highest seat total coming out of any federal election in history for the CCF-NDP. Most importantly, the NDP is competitive in Canada's three largest provinces. The party now has eight seats in Ontario compared to one in 2000 and fourteen seats in British Columbia compared to two in 2000. One out of every four Quebecers voted for the NDP in 2015, compared to only 2 per cent of Quebec voters in 2000.

In summary, the results of the 2015 election were certainly discouraging for the NDP. However, taking a longer-term view, the 2015 results can be characterized as a completion of the party's comeback in Canadian politics.

After coming close to extinction following the 2000 election and soaring to euphoric heights in 2011, the party has now returned to the level of electoral performance that it enjoyed during the 1980s, which previously had been the party's most electorally successful time period, with the notable difference between the current era and the 1980s being that the NDP is now electorally competitive in Quebec. Therefore, the party no longer flirts with irrelevance as it did in the 1990s and early 2000s. It has reasserted itself as Canada's only strong "third party" and re-established its importance to Canadian political discourse.

Conclusion

Layton was undeniably a successful politician. Under his leadership, the NDP went from nearly being wiped off the political map to a legitimate contender to form government. After Layton's death, Mulcair continued the professionalization and ideological moderation of the party that Layton had begun. However, he has not been nearly as electorally successful as Layton, as the 2015 election proved.

More research remains to be done to pinpoint the reasons for the NDP's loss of seats in 2015 and its return to its traditional position as the "third party" of Canadian politics. However, what is clear is that the party has undergone a transformation. Going into the future, the NDP is fundamentally different than it was in 2000. It is more independent from the labour movement and its provincial wings; it has retained an electoral base in Quebec in two consecutive elections; party headquarters in Ottawa has been thoroughly modernized and uses the latest campaign techniques and technology; and it adheres to a practical and moderate version of social democratic ideology. The party has much greater financial resources than in 2000, and it has developed a core of talented permanent political staff in the party. As one NDP political operative observed after the 2015 election, "We have learnt how to play with the big guys."[4] What remains to be seen is whether these changes can prevent a return to the electoral weakness of the 1990s, take it back to where it was in 2011, or simply allow it to maintain its current third party position.

Suggested Readings

Fournier, Patrick, Fred Cutler, Stuart Soroka, Dietlind Stolle, and Éric Bélanger. 2013. "Riding the Orange Wave: Leadership, Values, Issues, and the 2011 Canadian Election." *Canadian Journal of Political Science* 46 (4): 863–97.
Lavigne, Brad. 2013. *Building the Orange Wave: The Inside Story Behind the Historic Rise of Jack Layton and the NDP*. Madeira Park, BC: Douglas & McIntyre.

Laycock, David, and Lynda Erickson, eds. 2014. *Reviving Social Democracy: The Near Death and Surprising Rise of the Federal NDP*. Vancouver: University of British Columbia Press.

Lipset, Seymour. 1950. *Agrarian Socialism: The Co-operative Commonwealth Federation in Saskatchewan: A Study in Political Sociology*. Berkeley: University of California Press.

Whitehorn, Alan. 1992. *Canadian Socialism: Essays on the CCF-NDP*. Toronto: Oxford.

Young, Walter. 1969. *The Anatomy of a Party: The National CCF, 1932–1961*. Toronto: University of Toronto Press.

Notes

1   For more information on research on the federal NDP, visit the website of the Canadian Social Democracy Study at www.canadiansocialdemocracy.ca.
2   Federal NDP platforms can be downloaded from www.poltext.org.
3   For a description of the changes to federal party financing during the 2000s, see Young and Jansen (2011).
4   George Soule, director of media for the federal NDP during the 2015 election, interview with author.

References

Archer, Keith. 1990. *Political Choices and Electoral Consequences: A Study of Organized Labour and the New Democratic Party*. Montreal: McGill-Queen's University Press.

Bickerton, James, Alain-G. Gagnon, and Patrick J Smith. 1999. *Ties That Bind: Parties and Voters in Canada*. Toronto: Oxford University Press.

Blais, Annebelle. 2015. "Le Bloc juge 'grotesque' d'être comparé au Front national." *La Presse,* September 19. http://www.lapresse.ca/actualites/elections-federales/201509/19/01–4902055-le-bloc-juge-grotesque-detre-compare-au-front-national.php

Duverger, Maurice. 1963. *Political Parties: Their Organization and Activity in the Modern State*. Translated by Barbara and Robert North. New York: Wiley.

Erickson, Lynda, and David Laycock. 2014. "Party History and Electoral Fortunes, 1961–2003." In *Reviving Social Democracy: The Near Death and Surprising Rise of the Federal NDP,* edited by David Laycock and Lynda Erickson, 13–38. Vancouver: University of British Columbia Press.

Evans, Bryan. 2012. "From Protest Movement to Neoliberal Management: Canada's New Democratic Party in the Era of Permanent Austerity." In *Social Democracy after the Cold War,* edited by Bryan Evans and Ingo Schmidt, 45–98. Edmonton: Athabasca University Press.

Forum Research. 2015. "NDP Leads in First Post-Writ Poll." August 3. http://poll.forumresearch.com/post/334/new-democrats-headed-for-solid-minority/

Gibson, Rachel, and Andrea Rommele. 2009. "Measuring the Professionalization of Political Campaigning." *Party Politics* 15 (3): 265–93. http://dx.doi.org/10.1177/1354068809102245

Jansen, Harold, and Lisa Young. 2009. "Solidarity Forever? The NDP, Organized Labour, and the Changing Face of Party Finance in Canada." *Canadian Journal of Political Science* 42 (3): 657–78. http://dx.doi.org/10.1017/S0008423909990412

Knowles, Stanley. 1961. *The New Party*. Toronto: McClelland and Stewart.

Koop, Royce, and Amanda Bittner. 2013. "Parties and Elections after the 2011 Election: The Fifth Canadian Party System?" In *Parties, Elections, and the Future of Canadian Politics*, edited by Amanda Bittner and Royce Koop, 308–31. Vancouver: University of British Columbia Press.

Laycock, David. 2014. "Conceptual Foundations of Continuity and Change in NDP Ideology." In *Reviving Social Democracy: The Near Death and Surprising Rise of the Federal NDP*, edited by David Laycock and Lynda Erickson, 109–39. Vancouver: University of British Columbia Press.

Lipset, Seymour. 1950. *Agrarian Socialism: The Co-operative Commonwealth Federation in Saskatchewan: A Study in Political Sociology*. Berkeley: University of California Press.

McGrane, David. 2011. "Political Marketing and the NDP's Historic Breakthrough." In *The Canadian Federal Election of 2011*, edited by Jon Pammett and Christopher Dornan, 77–110. Toronto: Dundurn Press.

McGrane, David. 2016. "From Third to First and Back to Third: The 2015 NDP Campaign." In *The Canadian Federal Election of 2015*, edited by Jon Pammett and Christopher Dornan. Toronto: Dundurn Press.

McNaught, Kenneth. 1959. *A Prophet in Politics: A Biography of J. S. Woodsworth*. Toronto: University of Toronto Press.

Moschonas, Gerassimos. 2002. *In the Name of Social Democracy: The Great Transformation: 1945 to Present*. London: Verso Books.

Morton, Desmond. 1974. *The NDP: The Dream of Power*. Toronto: Hakkert.

Penner, Norman. 1992. *From Protest to Power: Social Democracy in Canada 1900–Present*. Toronto: James Lorimer & Company.

Pétry, François. 2014. "Ideological Evolution of the Federal NDP, as Seen through Its Election Campaign Manifestos." In *Reviving Social Democracy: The Near Death and Surprising Rise of the Federal NDP*, edited by David Laycock and Lynda Erickson, 140–64. Vancouver: University of British Columbia Press.

Pilon, Dennis, Stephanie Ross, and Larry Savage. 2011. "Solidarity Revisited: Organized Labour and the New Democratic Party." *Canadian Political Science Review* 5 (1): 20–37.

Plasser, Fritz, and Gunda Plasser. 2002. *Global Political Campaigning: A Worldwide Analysis of Campaign Professionals and Their Practices*. Westport: Praeger.

Sayers, Antony. 1999. *Parties, Candidates, and Constituency Campaigns in Canadian Elections*. Vancouver: University of British Columbia Press.

Whitehorn, Alan. 1992. *Canadian Socialism: Essays on the CCF-NDP*. Toronto: Oxford University Press.

Whitehorn, Alan. 2004. "Jack Layton and the NDP: Gains but No Breakthrough." In *The Canadian General Election of 2004*, edited by Christopher Dornan and Jon Pammett, 106–24. Toronto: Dundurn Press.

Wiseman, Nelson, and Benjamin Isitt. 2007. "Social Democracy in Twentieth Century Canada: An Interpretive Framework." *Canadian Journal of Political Science* 40 (3): 567–89. http://dx.doi.org/10.1017/S0008423907070448

Young, Lisa, and Harold Jansen. 2011. *Money, Politics, and Democracy: Canada's Party Finance Reforms*. Vancouver: University of British Columbia Press.

Young, Walter. 1969. *The Anatomy of a Party: The National CCF, 1932–1961*. Toronto: University of Toronto Press.

10

Third Parties in Canada: Variety and Success

ÉRIC BÉLANGER

> If someone were to give the proverbial political sociologist from Mars
> a list of Canadian election results, province by province, provincial
> as well as federal, from 1921 to the present, and ask him with that
> knowledge alone to guess what kind of country Canada is, I suspect
> that he would conclude that it is an extremely unstable nation, full
> of unresolved tensions, with a political system close to collapse. No
> other country has produced so many electorally effective minor
> parties in the same period of time.
> —*Seymour Martin Lipset (1990, 201)*

THE VARIABILITY AND DURABILITY OF THIRD parties have become traditional characteristics of Canadian party politics.[1] This is especially
intriguing given the fact that Canada offers an institutional environment that
is usually hostile to the emergence of third parties because of the first-past-
the-post electoral system, which introduces important distortions between
the number of votes and the number of seats won by minor parties (Harmel
and Robertson 1985). It is undoubtedly for this reason that an important body
of theoretical and empirical research on the rise of third parties comes from
Canadian political scientists and sociologists. It is the purpose of this chapter
to describe the extent to which Canada's federal and provincial political systems have provided fertile ground for third parties and for theories trying to
account for the varying degrees of success of these party movements.

Use of the term "third party" originally comes from the United States,
where it refers to a party other than the two major parties, the Democrats
and the Republicans. This also explains why these parties are often referred
to as "minor parties" as well. Maurice Pinard (1973, 455) proposes that
a third party "should be defined as any non-traditional party which has
not yet been in power. It thus remains in the eyes of the voters as an
untried alternative." This is the definition we adopt in this chapter. What
really differentiates these parties from the other ones is not so much their
numerical rank in terms of votes or seats as their institutional status within
the party system.[2] These are parties that are not part of the "governing
club," so to speak; that is, they are not considered as a natural (or traditional)

governing alternative because they are either new or they have been unable yet to enter the club.[3]

This definition can be generalized to any party system if we identify a set of conditions that have to be met for a party to become part of the "club" and thus lose its third-party status. We can think of three such conditions (see Martin 2007, 277–78). The party must first have the *will* to enter the club, in the sense that there are no debates within the party about the goal of winning office. It must also have the *ability* to enter the club. This requires that the party has enough electoral support to win office, but also that it is accepted by the other members of the club (the other government parties in a governing coalition, for instance). Finally, once it enters the club, the party must be able to *stay in*. The latter requires that the party's experience in office was not an overly negative one, meaning that it either did not quit the government, did not collapse in the following election, or was not excluded from the club by the other members. Unless this set of conditions is met, the party has to be considered as a third party, an outsider.

In this chapter, the terms "third party" and "minor party" are used interchangeably. It must also be stressed that this chapter deals with the rise (or emergence, or surge) of third parties *understood in terms of popular support in elections*. As such, we address only indirectly the factors behind the actual creation of these parties and their organizational development.[4] In effect, the success of third parties at election times may not always be entirely attributable to the same factors that initially led to their formation. One final precision is that a third party at the federal level may not necessarily be a third party at the provincial level. Federal and provincial party systems in Canada have to be considered separately in that respect. For example, the New Democratic Party, a third party in the federal party system, is currently considered an established governing alternative in the British Columbia provincial party system.

The next two sections present a brief survey of third parties in federal and provincial elections since 1945. This is followed by a review of the various theoretical arguments that have been proposed so far to account for third parties' electoral successes in Canada.

Third Parties in Canadian Federal Politics

There has rarely been a federal election where the two traditional governing parties, the Liberals and the Progressive Conservatives (PCs), were competing alone. Already by the 1920s, the Progressives, an agrarian protest party opposed to the tariff and freight rates imposed by the federal government, made substantial inroads in the prairie provinces, even to the point of holding the balance of power between 1921 and 1925. This third-party tradition continued throughout the rest of the twentieth century and into the twenty-first, as Table 10.1 shows. Here we will briefly look at the five minor parties that have attracted the most sizable portion of the vote in federal elections since World War II.[5]

The first of these parties is the Co-operative Commonwealth Federation (CCF). Created in Alberta in 1932, the CCF was a coalition of left-leaning

Table 10.1   Third Parties in Canadian Federal Elections, 1945–2015 (as Vote Percentages)

Election	CCF/ NDP	Bloc Québécois	Green Party	Reform/ Canadian Alliance	Social Credit	Créditistes	Bloc Populaire
1945	15.6	—	—	—	4.1	—	3.6
1949	13.4	—	—	—	3.7	—	—
1953	11.3	—	—	—	5.4	—	—
1957	10.7	—	—	—	6.6	—	—
1958	9.5	—	—	—	—	—	—
1962	13.5	—	—	—	11.7	—	—
1963	13.1	—	—	—	11.9	—	—
1965	17.9	—	—	—	3.7	4.7	—
1968	17.0	—	—	—	—	4.4	—
1972	17.7	—	—	—	7.6	—	—
1974	15.4	—	—	—	5.1	—	—
1979	17.9	—	—	—	4.6	—	—
1980	19.8	—	—	—	—	—	—
1984	18.8	—	—	—	—	—	—
1988	20.4	—	—	—	—	—	—
1993	6.9	13.5	—	18.7	—	—	—
1997	11.0	10.7	—	19.4	—	—	—
2000	8.5	10.7	—	25.5	—	—	—
2004	15.7	12.4	4.3	—	—	—	—
2006	17.5	10.5	4.5	—	—	—	—
2008	18.2	10.0	6.8	—	—	—	—
2011	30.6	6.1	3.9	—	—	—	—
2015	19.7	4.7	3.4	—	—	—	—

Sources: Gagnon and Tanguay (1996, 112) and Elections Canada.

Note: Only third parties obtaining at least 3 per cent of the national vote are included in the table.

groups that adopted a common socialist platform. After peaking in the 1945 federal election with 16 per cent of the popular vote, the party slowly declined. In 1961, CCF members decided to de-radicalize their policy positions, establish more formal links with organized labour, and relaunch the party under the label of the New Democratic Party (NDP) with a moderate social-democratic platform. The NDP enjoyed marked success in the 1980s before encountering some difficulties at the polls during the 1990s. The party then recovered significant ground under the leadership of Jack Layton and in part because of the weakening of the Liberal Party following the 2004 sponsorship scandal. But the best was yet to come. In the 2011 federal election, the NDP managed to supersede the Liberals and form the Official Opposition for the first time in its history, thanks to a wave of support in Quebec where it received 43 per cent of the vote (30 per cent at the national level). The CCF-NDP is currently one of the two parties occupying the political left on the Canadian federal scene. It has spawned several provincial wings, some of them having been successful to the point of forming governments on a regular basis (in Manitoba, Saskatchewan, and British Columbia).

The second party to occupy the federal political left is the Green Party of Canada. Obviously this minor party's main policy concerns involve the protection of the environment and the adoption of sustainable modes of economic development. But the Greens also defend several policy positions that reach beyond the environment and speak to issues of social justice and grassroots democracy. The federal Green Party was founded in 1983. Its support remained under 1 per cent until the 2004 federal election, where it tipped over 4 per cent. The party reached a peak of 6.8 per cent in the 2008 election. In 2011, its leader, Elizabeth May, became the first elected Green Party Member of Parliament (MP) in Canadian history, representing the riding of Saanich—Gulf Islands in British Columbia. In 2013, independent MP Bruce Hyer (formerly with the NDP) joined the Greens, thus increasing the party's parliamentary representation to two MPs up until the 2015 general election.

The Social Credit Party was formed in Alberta during the 1930s by William Aberhart. This movement was based on right-leaning ideas rooted in Major C.H. Douglas's radical monetary doctrine. Social Credit thus frequently used to attack federal monetary policies and decisions, a discourse that particularly appealed to farmers and small merchants from the West. The party also made a significant breakthrough in Quebec at the beginning of the 1960s under the leadership of populist Réal Caouette. Following tensions within the Social Credit federal caucus, Caouette created his own party in 1963, the Ralliement des Créditistes, which competed only in Quebec. Social Credit had several provincial wings, and two of them regularly formed governments in Alberta (between 1935 and 1971) and British Columbia (between 1952 and 1991). In spite of this, Social Credit vanished from the federal scene after 1980.

Created by Preston Manning in 1987, the Reform Party started as a Western populist party, catalyzing discontent with some of the Mulroney government's policy decisions that seemed to systematically favour the centre of the country over Western provinces. In addition, Reform was against the "old-line" parties and the pre-eminence of special interests in Canadian politics; it considered unions, feminist groups, and ethnic and linguistic lobbies as enemies of the people and obstacles to democracy. The Reform movement, however, quickly developed into a socially conservative party that sought to impose itself as a genuine national alternative to the ruling Liberals. In an attempt to shed its regional party image and to broaden its electoral appeal, the Reform Party changed its leader and platform and was renamed the Canadian Alliance a few months before the 2000 federal election. Still unable to break through in Ontario despite attracting the support of 25 per cent of the Canadian electorate, the party proposed a merger with the ailing PCs. The merger was endorsed in December 2003 by the two parties' memberships and led to the creation of the Conservative Party of Canada.

Finally, the Bloc Québécois was formed in 1990 by a handful of Progressive Conservative and Liberal MPs who were deeply dissatisfied with their parties' constitutional treatment of Quebec in the wake of the Meech Lake Accord debacle. The party soon became a sovereignist vehicle whose main objectives were to defend the interests of Quebec and to ease Quebec's eventual transition to independence. The Bloc was led to its first electoral success in 1993 by Lucien Bouchard with 49 per cent of the vote in Quebec (13.5 per cent of the national vote share), achieving Official Opposition status with a total of 54 seats in the House of Commons. The defeat of the sovereignty option in the October 1995 Quebec referendum weakened the party in the following two federal elections, but its electoral fortunes were rekindled in 2004 in the wake of the sponsorship scandal, which sullied the Liberal Party's reputation in Quebec. Over the years, in constantly pushing for Quebec's interests, the Bloc Québécois has ended up advocating distinctive positions on several important federal policy issues, such as fiscal imbalance, the preservation of a social safety net, and the treatment of criminal offenders. However, with the lack of constitutional disputes, a fatigue with the Bloc seems to have set in. That factor, together with the Bloc's development of a left-leaning policy agenda, has facilitated Quebecers' shift toward the NDP in 2011, resulting in the Bloc's collapse—the party kept only four seats in that election with all of its other seats going to the NDP. While in 2015 the party rebounded to 10 seats, its actual vote share continued on its declining path.

Popular support for these nontraditional parties has not always been constant over time. As Table 10.1 suggests, third parties have generally attracted around one-quarter (more or less) of the national vote share in federal elections since 1945. But there have also been important ups and downs in third-party support over that period, with the low points being the 1950s and the 1980s, and the high points the 1990s and the 2000s. These high points mostly reflect the rise of the Reform/Alliance and the Bloc Québécois. Third-party support reached its highest level ever in the 2000 federal election, where almost half of registered Canadian voters decided to support a party other than the Liberals or the PCs.

Third Parties in the Canadian Provinces

The presence of significant minor parties has also been a regular feature of provincial electoral politics in Canada. In effect, Canadian provinces offer a particularly rich and diversified environment to study third parties. Below we provide an overview of third-party successes in the country's 10 provinces since World War II, using Carty and Stewart's (1996) typology of Canadian provincial party systems as a guiding framework. These authors classify provincial party systems into four broad categories: one-party dominant systems, traditional two-party systems, three-party systems, and polarized party systems. Covering most of the same time period as ours, their typology also has the advantage of resting on the dynamics of party competition in each province, which is precisely our focus in this chapter. Table 10.2 provides a list of the most important third parties that have competed in the 10 provinces during the period 1945 to 2015.

The one-party dominant system category includes only one province, namely Alberta. This province probably represents the perfect example of a party system conducive to the emergence of third parties. It has been successively dominated by two parties for long periods (Social Credit from 1935 to 1971, followed by the PCs until 2015), which has had the result of preventing the Liberals and the NDP from taking office in that province since the 1930s. In addition, several other third parties have made important electoral inroads in that province over the past seven decades. Before 2015, the standout cases of success have been the Western Canada Concept Party in 1982 (12 per cent of the vote) and the NDP and Raymond Speaker's Representative Party in 1986 (29 per cent and 5 per cent of the vote, respectively). In the 2004 election, two small parties had relative success, the Green Party and especially the Alberta Alliance. Obtaining 9 per cent of the vote but no seats, this latter party, created by former supporters of Social Credit and the now-defunct Reform and Canadian Alliance federal parties, wished to offer

Table 10.2 Third Parties in Canadian Provincial Elections, 1945–2015

Party System	Province	Party	Best Score	
One-party dominant	Alberta	Alberta Alliance	2004	(9.1)
		CCF-NDP	2015★	(40.6)
		Green Party	2008	(4.6)
		Progressive Conservative Party	1971★	(46.4)
		Representative Party	1986	(5.1)
		Western Canada Concept	1982	(11.8)
		Wildrose Party	2012	(34.3)
Traditional two-party	Newfoundland	CCF-NDP	2011	(24.6)
	Nova Scotia	CCF-NDP	2009★	(45.2)
	Prince Edward Island	CCF-NDP	2015	(11.0)
		Green Party	2015	(10.8)
Three-party	Ontario	CCF-NDP	1990★	(37.6)
		Green Party	2007	(8.0)
	Manitoba	CCF-NDP	1969★	(38.1)
		Social Credit	1953	(13.1)
Polarized	New Brunswick	CCF-NDP	2014	(13.0)
		Confederation of Regions	1991	(21.0)
		Green Party	2014	(6.6)
		Social Credit	1956	(3.1)
	Quebec	ADQ	2007	(30.8)
		CAQ	2012	(27.1)
		Créditistes	1970	(11.1)
		Equality Party	1989	(3.7)
		Parti Québécois	1976★	(41.4)
		Parti Vert	2007	(3.9)
		Québec Solidaire	2014	(7.6)
		RIN	1966	(5.6)
		Ralliement National	1966	(3.2)
		Union des Électeurs	1948	(9.2)
	Saskatchewan	Progressive Conservative Party	1982★	(54.1)
		Independence Party	1982	(3.3)
		Saskatchewan Party	2007★	(50.9)
		Social Credit	1956	(21.5)
	British Columbia	CCF-NDP	1972★	(39.6)
		Green Party	2001	(12.4)

(*continued*)

Table 10.2 (Continued)

Party System	Province	Party	Best Score	
Polarized		Marijuana Party	2001	(3.2)
		Progressive Democratic Alliance	1996	(5.7)
		Reform Party	1996	(9.3)
		Social Credit	1952★	(30.2)
		Unity Party	2001	(3.2)

Sources: Feigert (1989), the *Canadian Parliamentary Guide* (annual), and the *Reports of the Chief Electoral Officer* from each province (selected years).

Notes: Figures in parentheses are vote percentages; only third parties obtaining at least 3 per cent of the vote were considered for inclusion in the table; ★ indicates the party took power that year and ceases to be considered a third party according to our definition.

a right-wing alternative to the dominant PCs. This new party formation came to be known a few years later as the Wildrose Party, and it achieved a breakthrough in the 2012 election with 34 per cent of the vote (20 per cent of seats) under the leadership of Danielle Smith. However, this result was a far cry from the predictions that were putting Wildrose into power, and the party started to lose steam after that relatively disappointing electoral performance. Since 1971, the most important third-party surge has been achieved by the NDP, which managed to form a majority government in the 2015 election, thus putting an end to more than 40 years of PC dominance in that province.

Conversely, the three provinces included in the traditional two-party systems category certainly represent good examples of party systems that are generally *not* conducive to third parties. Since the 1940s and generally since their inclusion in Canadian Confederation, Newfoundland and Labrador, Nova Scotia, and Prince Edward Island have all experienced strong competition between two traditional parties, the Liberals and the PCs, each having formed the government at various times over the past 70 years. In addition to fostering regular alternation between the two main parties, this particular environment has seen few successes from third parties, the NDP being one of the only two parties able to attract more than 3 per cent of the vote (the other one is the Green Party in the 2015 PEI election). Yet the NDP's scores frequently approach or even exceed 10 per cent of the vote in these three provinces. In Newfoundland and Labrador, the party experienced a sudden surge in the 2011 election with 25 per cent of the vote. In Nova Scotia since 1998, the NDP has proven to be a serious threat to the traditional parties, having forced three minority governments before finally taking power in 2009 with 45 per cent support.[6]

Ontario and Manitoba are the only Canadian provinces where a competitive three-party system can be found. In spite of a period of temporary weakness between 1985 and 1995, Ontario's PCs have generally dominated the legislature, but it is worth noting that no party in this province—not even the PCs—has been able to obtain a majority of votes during the entire period under study. This fact underlines the strong competitiveness of Ontario's party system—the Liberals and the NDP usually obtaining at least 20 per cent of the vote each, and each having formed the government at least once since 1945. The often slim legislative majorities in Manitoba also reflect a strong competition in this province between the PCs, the NDP, and the Liberals, even though the latter party has sometimes encountered electoral difficulties, especially during the early 1980s and since the end of the 1990s.[7] Apart from the three competitive parties, though, no other party has experienced any electoral breakthrough in those two provinces. For example, the Social Credit and the Confederation of Regions Party never obtained more than 3.5 per cent of the vote during the period, except Social Credit in the 1953 Manitoba election with 13 per cent support. The Ontario Family Coalition Party, a social conservative formation created in 1987 and opposed to abortion and gay rights, had its best score in the 1990 election with nearly 3 per cent of support. Some Manitoba Social Credit members joined the new Progressive Party[8] (created by former NDP members) at the beginning of the 1980s, but that party never received more than 2 per cent of the vote and was dissolved in 1995.

The four remaining provinces form the last category, polarized party systems, because they are characterized as provinces in which party competition is organized around a particular issue or cleavage. In the case of Saskatchewan and British Columbia, it is the traditional left–right cleavage: the NDP faces either Social Credit or the Liberals in British Columbia, and either the Liberals or the PCs in Saskatchewan.[9] Until recently, third parties rarely emerged in these two provinces. The exceptions are British Columbia's NDP and Saskatchewan's PCs, who formed a government for the first time in 1972 and 1982, respectively, and Social Credit in both provinces. The latter party had brief success in Saskatchewan during the 1950s (21 per cent and 12 per cent of the vote in the 1956 and 1960 elections, respectively) before merging with the PCs. In British Columbia, the Social Credit surged in the 1952 election with 30 per cent of the vote and went on to govern the province for the next 40 years with only one interruption (1972–75). However, the party disappeared at the beginning of the 1990s after most of its voters had shifted their support to the Liberals following Bill Vander Zalm's eccentricities and the numerous scandals that plagued his government. Former Social Credit members then joined the socially conservative but short-lived provincial Reform Party and Progressive Democratic Alliance in 1996 (9 per cent and 6 per cent, respectively) and Unity Party in 2001 (3 per cent). Recently, the Green Party has made significant electoral inroads, achieving 12 per cent of the vote in the 2001 British Columbia election and around 8–9 per cent ever since. We should finally point out the recent breakthrough of the Saskatchewan Party. Created in 1997 by right-leaning politicians to fill the void left by the collapse of the PCs following several scandals and fraud charges from the late 1980s,[10] the party received 39 per cent of the vote in both the 1999 and 2003 Saskatchewan elections before finally seizing power in 2007 with 51 per cent of the vote (it was re-elected in 2011 with a massive 64 per cent support).

While being correctly described by Carty and Stewart (1996) as "polarized" around the language issue, New Brunswick's party system closely resembles the other Atlantic systems, since it also is characterized by strong competition between the Liberals and the PCs that does not leave much room for third parties. Nevertheless, New Brunswick's NDP has regularly managed to get around 10 per cent of the vote since 1982, and the Confederation of Regions Party (CoR) experienced an electoral breakthrough in 1991 (21 per cent). This significant surge happened in a period of sudden weakness in the post–Hatfield PC Party,[11] but the CoR quickly disappeared from the provincial electoral map and was disbanded in 2002.

The case of Quebec is more particular. Polarized around the national question, this party system experienced a partisan realignment at the beginning of the 1970s when the Parti Québécois (PQ) replaced the Union Nationale as one of the two main contenders to form a government, which the PQ did for the first time in 1976. What is more, the province has seen many other third parties appear and disappear over the past 70 years: Réal Caouette's Union des Électeurs in 1948 (9 per cent of the vote), the Rassemblement pour l'Indépendance Nationale and the Ralliement National in 1966 (9 per cent combined), the Ralliement des Créditistes in 1970 and 1973 (11 per cent and 10 per cent, respectively), and the Equality Party in 1989 (4 per cent). The last two decades have seen a gradual fragmentation of Quebec's party system, with the appearance of several new parties, the most notable of these being the right-leaning Action Démocratique du Québec (which merged with the Coalition Avenir Québec in 2012) and the left-leaning and sovereignist Québec Solidaire. None of these third parties have yet been able to really shake the Liberal–PQ duopoly in the province, although the popular support for these two old-line parties (and especially the PQ) has been in constant decline since 1998, and the Action Démocratique was able to form the Official Opposition for a short period (2007–08).

To summarize, we can observe that third parties in Ontario and Manitoba have been rare and have had almost no success, whereas a variety of them have appeared on an almost regular basis in Quebec since the 1940s. The other seven provinces provide a mixed picture. Third-party support has been moderate but steady in Alberta and the four Atlantic provinces over the past seven decades. But since the 1990s, one can notice a relatively clear trend whereby minor parties gather a significantly growing share of the popular vote in provincial elections. In fact, nearly half of the parties listed in Table 10.2 have experienced their best electoral result in the past 15 years only. Some of these have been competing for most of the period under study but have just recently started to receive a greater share of the vote, like the NDP in Nova Scotia. Others are new party formations that have experienced a sudden rise, like the Saskatchewan Party, the Wildrose Party, and the British Columbia Green Party.

In fact, the relative success of the federal Green Party has been reflected at the provincial level. There is now a Green Party that competes in all of the Canadian provinces. Since 2001 the Greens have obtained between 2 and 4 per cent of the vote on a regular basis. They have been particularly successful in British Columbia, New Brunswick, and PEI: one Green Party candidate has been elected in each of these three legislative assemblies in their most recent elections (2013, 2014, and 2015, respectively). Thus, the slow rise of the Greens, at both the federal and provincial level, is an important feature of the last decade of Canadian electoral politics. It mirrors a similar Green surge in West European political systems (Spoon 2011).

The next section presents some of the theories that have been formulated to explain why third parties are such an important feature of Canada's political system.

Explaining the Electoral Success of Third Parties

What accounts for these ups and downs in third-party success in Canadian federal and provincial elections? The most important Canadian works on third-party support have often relied on a structural approach. However, several institutional or cultural counterarguments have also been proposed to account for the phenomenon. These theoretical divergences have led to a few important debates in the literature, the first of these having occurred during the 1950s between C.B. Macpherson and Seymour Martin Lipset.

In accounting for the impressive success achieved by the United Farmers of Alberta and the Social Credit Party in Alberta since the early 1920s, Macpherson (1953) proposed that two favourable conditions were behind these parties' rise. The first condition was the quasi-colonial relationship that existed between Alberta and the country's eastern region at the beginning of the twentieth century, when that province was mostly treated as a simple peripheral economic region. This relationship engendered a long-term feeling of alienation toward the Liberal and PC parties, which were seen, especially by the farmers, as political instruments of power controlled by Ontario's and Quebec's manufacturing and financial elites. The second condition was the relative class homogeneity among the group of Alberta farmers that started this protest movement and formed those new political parties. According to Macpherson, a majority of Alberta's society was composed at the time of one "petty bourgeois" class of agricultural producers that depended on a capitalist economy mostly controlled by Eastern Canadians. Sharing similar economic interests, this homogenous social class was easily able to organize itself politically and defend its interests against the menace of imperialism. This homogeneity of class also made the traditional parties useless, argued Macpherson, because the main function of a bipartisan system is to moderate class conflict.

It appears, however, that Macpherson may have overstated the homogeneity of class among Alberta's society, especially since Social Credit also drew strong support among the province's working class at that time (Bell 1993). Another weakness of Macpherson's approach is that it does not explain why the other prairie provinces, sociologically quite similar to Alberta, did not develop the same type of party system. According to the "fragment theory" (Hartz 1955; Horowitz 1966; McRae 1964), this difference might be explained by the differing political cultures that waves of immigrants brought with them (Wiseman 1981). The founding fragments thus brought a socialist touch in Saskatchewan and a populist touch in Alberta—hence the greater success of the CCF-NDP in Saskatchewan and of agrarian protest parties in Alberta.

The strongest critique of Macpherson came from Lipset (1954), who suggested that the conditions of third-party success in Western Canada had nothing to do with social structures, but were instead linked to two institutional factors: the parliamentary system and the electoral system in Canada. First, the party discipline inherited from British parliamentarianism tends to muffle dissent and protestation within the traditional political parties. It forces dissenting party members either to comply with the party line or exit the party and join (or create) a different party movement (see also Gerring 2005; Hauss and Rayside 1978). Whereas in the United States the system of primary elections allows the different factions within each major party to debate their views openly, party discipline in Canada leaves internal party cleavages unresolved and also prevents the creation of nonpartisan alliances in the House of Commons. The second factor identified by Lipset (1950; 1990, 203) is the electoral system. Based on constituencies, the first-past-the-post system favours the implantation and electoral success of local or regional parties (see also Cairns 1968; Gerring 2005).[12] This situation again contrasts with that of the United States, where the constituency has no real significance because the American electorate votes for a candidate at the national (the president) or state (the governor) level. According to Lipset, these institutional factors account for the Canadian specificity in terms of third-party success.

Lipset's institutional approach provides a compelling explanation as to why third parties have had more electoral success in Canada than in the United States. However, these factors cannot constitute sufficient conditions of success because they remain constant across all Canadian regions (Macpherson 1955). Yet, as we have seen in the preceding sections, there exist important differences across regions in Canada, not only in the number of third parties competing but also in the patterns of their success.[13]

The second debate in the Canadian literature on third parties revolved around Maurice Pinard's (1971) work. To account for the sudden breakthrough of Social Credit in Quebec in the 1962 federal election, Pinard proposed a general theory of third-party success that mostly relies on two structural factors. Together, these two variables should provide a third party with a substantial boost at election time. The first is the presence of specific grievances held against the government among some segments of the electorate. Such grievances are often economic in nature, but they can also be political, ethnic, linguistic, class, regional, or based on something else. What is important is that these grievances result from "gaps created between a group's expectations and its actual conditions" (Pinard 1971, 119), thus creating readiness among dissatisfied voters to vote against the government in an attempt to improve their conditions.

The second factor identified by Pinard is what he called "one-party dominance." What this really means is that the traditional opposition party has to be electorally weak. In such a situation, if angry voters want to cast their ballot for an opposition party, they will not consider the traditional "second" party as a viable alternative to the dominant governing party, and they will thus be more tempted (or predisposed) to turn toward a third party as a way to express their grievances. It is in this sense that the configuration of the party system, or its level of competitiveness, can act as a structural condition for the rise of a third party. According to Pinard, this is exactly what happened in 1962 in Quebec, where the rural population experienced serious economic hardship in the early 1960s; this dissatisfied portion of the electorate massively voted for Social Credit instead of the traditional federal PC Party because the latter had always been historically weak in Quebec.

The emphasis placed by Pinard on the condition of one-party dominance has led several scholars to criticize his theory. Using aggregate indicators of predominance different from Pinard's, both Lemieux (1965) and Blais (1973) were unable to confirm the theory. Blais argued that third-party success was due instead to the weakness of traditional party attachments, a view similar to that of Clarke and Kornberg (1996), who suggest that third-party support is mostly due to unstable party identification (i.e., partisan "dealignment") among the Canadian electorate. And according to Graham White (1973), one-party dominance does not help explain the success of minor "class parties" that arise at times of intense dissatisfaction within specific social classes toward the party system.

Following these critiques, Pinard reformulated his one-party dominance condition into "a more general condition of structural conduciveness, that of the political nonrepresentation of social groups through the party system" (Pinard 1973, 442). He also proposed to distinguish between two types of third parties: protest parties, such as Social Credit, and radical parties that propose an articulated ideology that integrates class or communal consciousness and values, like the farmers' and labour movements or the Parti Québécois. According to Pinard, one-party dominance would be a favourable condition for the rise of third parties of the protest type only. Minor radical parties, on the other hand, would be able to emerge even in a strongly competitive party system, as long as there was a significant portion of the electorate whose ideological positions were not represented through the existing parties.

More recent studies have confirmed the existence of a relationship between one-party dominance and third-party breakthrough. It seems that one-party dominance was a significant factor in the rise of the Reform Party in the West in the 1993 federal election (Bélanger 2004b; Michaud 1999), but not in the upsurge of the more "radical" Bloc Québécois in that same election (Bélanger 2004b). It also appears to have facilitated the sudden success of the NDP in Atlantic Canada in the 1997 federal election (S. White 2000), as well as the rise of the Social Democratic Party–Liberal Alliance in the 1983 British general election (Bélanger, Nadeau, and Lewis-Beck 2010; Eagles and Erfle 1993).

The role of grievances in the electoral breakthrough of third parties has also been confirmed recently. Perrella (2005, 2009) and Bélanger and Nadeau (2010) have shown that long-term economic hardship is related to voting for "nonmainstream" parties in federal elections, providing support to Pinard's argument about long-term economic grievances fuelling support for third parties. Analyzing the success of Reform and the Bloc Québécois in 1993, Bélanger (2004b) found that economic grievances had no effect on the vote for these parties but that support for both formations was instead linked to political grievances that rested on feelings of regional alienation that were exacerbated in Quebec and the West in the wake of the Meech Lake and Charlottetown constitutional debacles.[14] Given the often wide-spread perceptions in Quebec and the Western provinces that regional inter-ests receive insufficient attention from the federal government, such political grievances may partly account for the fact that third parties are usually more successful in those two regions of the country. Finally, a few studies have shown that the upsurge of the CoR in New Brunswick at the beginning of the 1990s was due to two "Pinardian" factors, namely the weakness of the provincial PCs and the development of grievances among the province's anglophone population regarding the Hatfield government's bilingualism policies (Belkhodja 1999; G. Martin 1998).

A different theoretical approach used to study the success of third parties in Canada has been to look at the varying political cultures found across the country. Several past studies have characterized the inhabitants of the Atlantic provinces as traditionalists and as inefficacious[15] people (Brym 1979; Clarke et al. 1979; Gidengil 1990; Leuprecht 2003; Simeon and Elkins 1974). Such cultural traits would make the mobilization of these people around a nontraditional minor party much more difficult; hence the low rate of third-party success in this region. However, this explanation remains unsatisfying, mainly because this rather naive picture of Atlantic political culture as mark-edly displaying political inefficacy appears to be mostly outdated (Hender-son 2004; I. Stewart 1994).

Another cultural argument that has been proposed is that the rise of some third parties, in particular that of the Reform Party during the 1990s, is a direct consequence of changing values among Canadian society. In other words, Reform would be the ideal vehicle for the "new politics" of the postmodern era (Sigurdson 1994). More generally, it is possible that the rise of new postmaterialist values might have encouraged support for new parties that promote better democratic participation for citizens (Inglehart 1998; Nevitte, Bakvis, and Gibbins 1989). But as Covell (1991) has argued, movements of the new politics in Canada have generally found a way of influencing politics through actions other than the creation of a political party. And while it is possible that these new values may influence electoral behaviour, it is unlikely that they would be a significant factor behind the sudden breakthrough of third parties. In addition, it seems that the established parties are usually successful at adapting themselves to the rise of postmaterialist values and at integrating these new issues into their political discourse and orientations (Pelletier and Guérin 1998).

The theoretical approaches discussed so far may lead one to believe that support for third parties lies solely in conditions that are external to them.

Yet these parties—just like major traditional party formations—are not simply passive actors of the political system. Several scholars have highlighted the importance of mobilization strategies in accounting for the success of third parties. For instance, Bell (1993) argues that Social Credit's organizational failures are the main reason why the party lost the 1971 Alberta election. The presence of a charismatic leader like Aberhart, Douglas, or Caouette can also help minor parties overcome the structural and institutional barriers facing them (Gagnon 1981). Likewise, the positive image of NDP leader Jack Layton over that of his opponents was one of the key factors explaining the party's surge in the 2011 federal election (Fournier et al. 2013).

Factors of a strategic nature have often been alluded to when accounting for the rise of the Reform Party in 1993. Some have argued that the party succeeded in constructing a sense of political identity among Canadian people by relying on a "modernized" populist discourse, which explains Reform's substantial electoral support at the time (Harrison 1995; Laycock 1994; Patten 1996). However, this hypothesis is usually developed based on an analysis of Preston Manning's writings and speeches, with the untested assumption that such a rhetoric had an important persuasive effect on public opinion and voter choice.

Whatever the case may be, these kinds of studies have the merit of focusing attention on the role of party strategies and rhetoric in mobilizing the vote (Hirano and Snyder 2007; Mair, Müeller, and Plasser 2004; Meguid 2008; Spoon 2011). Like every political party, minor party movements aim at getting their candidates elected and at promoting, if not enacting, their policy ideas. Recent work on the electoral success of extreme right-wing parties in Western Europe has shown the extent to which those parties' discourse, revolving around issues of declining economic conditions, immigration, insecurity, and national identity, has helped them build a relatively strong support base (e.g., Betz 1994; Delwit, De Waele, and Rea 1998; Golder 2003; Ignazi 1992; Jackman and Volpert 1996; Kitschelt 1995). Indeed, the choice of campaign issues and themes that parties make can explain part of their electoral appeal. During election campaigns, political parties tend to "prime" issues that will likely draw them popular support. For example, Jenkins (2002) has shown that the Reform Party's emphasis on cultural issues like bilingualism, multiculturalism, and immigration toward the end of the 1993 federal election campaign significantly contributed to its emergence.

Gagnon and Tanguay's (1996, 107, 127) account of the surprising 1993 election outcome briefly alludes to another potentially important factor that might explain the upsurge of Reform and the Bloc Québécois. They observe that significant electoral breakthroughs by third parties "are usually symptoms of a deeper malaise in the party system" and suggest that the two new parties' success coincided with "a wave of anger directed at the traditional mechanisms of political representation: the established political parties, politicians in general, bureaucrats, and legislatures" (see also Seidle 1994).

The Reform Party and the Bloc Québécois broke onto the electoral scene at the end of what Nevitte (1996) termed a "decade of turmoil," at a time when Canadians felt particularly disaffected from politics. As in other Western democracies, this sense of discontent with politics in Canada seems to go back a least a couple of decades. Even before the election of Brian Mulroney as prime minister in 1984, voters were starting to feel distrustful of their governing institutions (Bélanger and Nadeau 2005; Roese 2002) and were becoming increasingly disaffected from traditional party alternatives (Clarke and Kornberg 1993; Gidengil et al. 2002).

In effect, despite the role third parties' choices of campaign strategy and rhetoric might have on their individual electoral fortunes, it is striking that, in the past few decades, overall support for third parties has significantly grown in most advanced industrial democracies (see Dalton, McAllister, and Wattenberg 2000; Grofman, Blais, and Bowler 2009). We observed the same kind of phenomenon in the previous two sections of this chapter, where we concluded that third-party support reached new highs since the beginning of the 1990s, both at the federal and the provincial level. This strongly suggests that more general factors also greatly determine these parties' fate at the polls. One factor in particular—the rise of public discontent with politics (Dalton 2004; Dalton and Weldon 2005; Norris 1999; Pharr and Putnam 2000)—appears to be salient in explaining the recent success of third parties in several countries, including Canada. The impact of political disaffection on the rise of nontraditional parties can best be appreciated when one looks at the functions these parties fulfill in a political system.

One of these functions is the role of policy innovators that minor parties often play by bringing new ideas to the table and forcing the traditional parties to readjust their legislative agendas (Adams et al. 2006; Hesseltine 1962; Mallory 1954; Rosenstone, Behr, and Lazarus 1996) and even to modify some of their usual policy positions (Harmel and Svåsand 1997; Hirano and Snyder 2007; Meguid 2008). This is, for instance, the function often ascribed to the federal NDP, which most view as Parliament's "social conscience" and as an essential promoter of left-leaning policy ideas in Canada (Chandler 1977; Pétry 1988).

Another function of third parties is that they often spark large partisan realignments among the electorate (Key 1964, 256–62; P. Martin 2005; Rosenstone, Behr, and Lazarus 1996; Zingale 1978). When a third party attracts considerable support on the basis of a new salient issue dimension, it usually forces the major parties to adapt their own positions to the new dimension to recapture part of the electorate. In the process, the traditional parties lose some of their supporters but acquire new partisans, with the minor party acting as a temporary "way station." This explains, for example, the continued presence of the Republican and Democratic parties in the United States in spite of the occasional rise of a third party. Alternatively, an issue realignment can lead to the replacement of one of the traditional parties by the emerging party. This situation provides an accurate description of what happened in Quebec at the end of the 1960s. The appearance of the sovereignty issue on the political scene brought about a realignment in the party system, with the PQ replacing the Union Nationale as the main party alternative to the provincial Liberals (Bélanger and Nadeau 2009; Clarke 1983; Lemieux, Gilbert, and Blais 1970).

The function most relevant to our discussion here, however, is that third parties provide disaffected voters with a political vehicle to channel and voice their discontent (Fisher 1974, 175; Ranney and Kendall 1956, 458). This is close to the "tribunician" function ascribed to political parties by Georges Lavau (1969, 38–39; see also Hamel and Thériault 1975). Voters discontented with politics tend to turn toward nontraditional parties either to signal their dissatisfaction with the political process as an attempt to make things change and improve, or because they believe that a third party cannot make things worse than they already are under established party rule. In other words, a protest vote cast against the political system is not simply an expression of anger but also has an instrumentality to it: it aims at potentially improving the state of political affairs (Bélanger 2016; Hirschman 1970; Kang 2004).

Recent empirical work has shown that third parties, in the United States and elsewhere, mostly benefit from a widespread sense of malaise with politics and the institutions of governance (Bäck and Kestilä-Kekkonen 2014; Dalton and Weldon 2005; Hetherington 1999; Hibbing and Theiss-Morse 2002, 72–74; Hooghe, Marien, and Pauwels 2011; Miller and Listhaug 1990; Pattie and Johnston 2001; Peterson and Wrighton 1998). Political disaffection has to do with public expectations pertaining to government performance and to political parties as institutions linking citizens to the state and rests on a more or less systematic evaluation of the performance of established political institutions and parties (Dennis and Owen 2001). As Newton and Norris (2000, 61) put it, "Government institutions that perform well are likely to elicit the confidence of citizens; those that perform badly or ineffectively generate feelings of distrust and low confidence. The general public, the model assumes, recognizes whether government or political institutions are performing well or poorly and reacts accordingly." This entails that discontented voters may be significantly more prone to support nontraditional parties: "those low in trust . . . perceive the institutionalized alternatives as incapable of addressing their concerns, and hence they may welcome other options" (Hetherington 1999, 321).

Examining the phenomenon in Canada for the period 1984 to 1993, Bélanger and Nadeau (2005) have shown not only that "old-line" major parties suffer electorally from declining political trust but also that some third parties benefit more from this than others. Contrary to what was the case in the previous two elections, distrustful Canadian voters in 1993 were more likely to support the Reform Party or the Bloc Québécois than to vote for the NDP, suggesting that the transition from a three- to a five-party system had eroded the NDP's role as a vehicle for channelling citizen distrust. A similar situation has been observed with respect to another indicator of political cynicism, that of anti-party sentiment among the Canadian public (Bélanger 2004a; Gidengil et al. 2001). In their bid for voter support, third parties often tend to put all traditional parties together in the same bag and to exploit voters' hesitations to support old parties that appear disconnected from the needs and interests of the general population (Lemieux 1965, 188).

Some scholars have suggested that third parties construct or create feelings of discontent, arguing that voters become cynical toward politics only as a byproduct of first supporting the party for ideological reasons (e.g., Koch 2003; van der Brug 2003). While it is probably true that nontraditional party movements partly fuel feelings of discontent with their anti-establishment rhetoric, it has been shown that attitudinal measures such as political cynicism and distrust of government are sufficiently exogenous in nature to be considered as valid explanatory variables (Bélanger and Aarts 2006; Chanley, Rudolph, and Rahn 2001; Craig 1979; Hetherington 1998; Peterson and Wrighton 1998). It thus can be concluded that one of the important conditions for the recent rise of third parties in Canada, as well as in most advanced industrial democracies, is the existence of a significant reservoir of political disaffection among citizens.

Conclusion

This chapter has provided a comprehensive overview of the ups and downs of third-party support in Canadian politics over the past 70 years. These nontraditional parties have had considerable success at the polls, both at the federal and provincial levels. In a few provinces—British Columbia, Manitoba, Quebec, and Alberta—some third parties have even managed to realign the provincial party system and to become one of the major governing alternatives. Although they also reached impressive levels of success at times, especially during the 1990s and 2000s, federal third parties have not been able so far to fully displace one of the two traditional governing parties.

The fact that in 2003 the Reform Party/Canadian Alliance merged with the PCs is indicative of the resilience of a two-party competition between Liberals and Tories at the federal level in Canada.

Several theoretical approaches have been used to account for the electoral breakthroughs of Canadian third parties. Structural conditions such as class homogeneity, one-party dominance, and grievances have been proposed as important determinants of the rise of third parties. Others have pointed to institutional features such as Canada's strong party discipline and constituency-based electoral system as explanatory factors. Provincial political cultures have also been suggested as variables accounting for variations in third-party support. These cultural traits include founding ideological fragments, feelings of inefficacy, and emerging postmaterialist values. Another important factor that has to be taken into account is the actual behaviour of third parties, including their choices of campaign discourse and rhetoric. In some ways, political culture and party behaviour might best be considered as key intervening variables in the relationship between structural conditions and third-party success.

Finally, it appears that the recent rise in public discontent with politics, in Canada as in other Western democracies, has provided fertile ground for the electoral success of third parties. As stated in the introduction to this chapter, third parties occupy a special place in the party system because they are not part of the traditional party group. This confers on them a peculiar status that appeals to voters disaffected from government and the established party elites and who seek out new options in an attempt to voice their discontent. The current era of cynicism and distrust thus creates a situation not only of declining political participation but also of greater electoral volatility and openness to nontraditional party alternatives.

Suggested Readings

Cairns, Alan C. 1968. "The Electoral System and the Party System in Canada 1921–1965." *Canadian Journal of Political Science* 1 (1): 55–80. http://dx.doi.org/10.1017/S0008423900035228

Carty, R. Kenneth, William Cross, and Lisa Young. 2000. *Rebuilding Canadian Party Politics.* Vancouver: University of British Columbia Press.

Duverger, Maurice. 1951. *Les partis politiques.* Paris: Armand Collin.

Epstein, Leon D. 1964. "A Comparative Study of Canadian Parties." *American Political Science Review* 58 (1): 46–59. http://dx.doi.org/10.2307/1952754

Flanagan, Thomas. 2009. *Waiting for the Wave: The Reform Party and the Conservative Movement.* Montreal: McGill-Queen's University Press.

Lipset, Seymour Martin. 1950. *Agrarian Socialism: The Co-operative Commonwealth Federation in Saskatchewan.* Berkeley: University of California Press.

Macpherson, C.B. 1953. *Democracy in Alberta: The Theory and Practice of a Quasi-Party System*. Toronto: University of Toronto Press.
Martin, Pierre. 2005. *Dynamiques partisanes et réalignements électoraux au Canada (1867–2004)*. Paris: L'Harmattan.
Meguid, Bonnie M. 2008. *Party Competition between Unequals: Strategies and Electoral Fortunes in Western Europe*. Cambridge: Cambridge University Press. http://dx.doi.org/10.1017/CBO9780511510298
Rosenstone, Steven J., Roy L. Behr, and Edward H. Lazarus. 1996. *Third Parties in America: Citizen Response to Major Party Failure*. 2nd ed. Princeton, NJ: Princeton University Press.

Web Links

Centre for the Study of Democratic Citizenship: http://csdc-cecd.ca
Making Electoral Democracy Work: http://electoraldemocracy.com

Sites of the Provincial Chief Electoral Officers:

British Columbia: www.elections.bc.ca
Alberta: www.elections.ab.ca
Saskatchewan: www.elections.sk.ca
Manitoba: www.electionsmanitoba.ca/en
Ontario: www.elections.on.ca/en.html
Quebec: www.electionsquebec.qc.ca/english/
New Brunswick: www.electionsnb.ca/content/enb/en.html
Nova Scotia: https://electionsnovascotia.ca
Prince Edward Island: www.electionspei.ca
Newfoundland and Labrador: www.elections.gov.nl.ca/elections/

Notes

1 I thank Maryna Polataiko and Gaby González-Sirois for their research assistance. This chapter is an updated version of the one I published in the previous edition of this volume.
2 Laurent (1997) finely illustrates the degree to which a definition of "small parties" based on quantitative indicators such as votes and seats leads to complex and often inconsistent classifications.
3 Perrella (2005) calls those parties "non-mainstream," a label conceptually close to our definition.
4 Among others, see Harmel and Robertson (1985), Perkins (1996), Lucardie (2000, 2007), Hug (2001), Chhibber and Kollman (2004), Tavits (2006), and Lago and Martinez (2011) for accounts of the factors behind the organizational emergence, or formation, of party movements.
5 One other minor party received slightly over 3 per cent of the national vote share during the period under study, namely the Bloc Populaire in 1945 (a party from Quebec that was opposed to conscription).

6   Although Stewart and Carty (2006, 106) now consider Nova Scotia as a three-party system, the NDP's crushing defeat in the 2013 election following a single mandate suggests that it remains to be seen whether the recent NDP breakthrough will lead to a genuine three-party competition in Nova Scotia, or even to a party realignment in the province.

7   Note that the Liberals' steady decline since the 1999 election has led Stewart and Carty (2006, 106) to now classify Manitoba as a two-party system polarized around a left–right cleavage (NDP versus Progressive Conservative). The next few Manitoba elections should help clarify whether this party system has indeed evolved in that direction.

8   This party had no formal or historical connections with the Progressive Party that governed Manitoba in an alliance with the Liberals between 1932 and 1958.

9   Since the CCF-NDP won power in Saskatchewan in 1944, they are considered a major party. The same applies today for British Columbia's NDP, which came into power for the first time in 1972.

10   At the time, 14 PC members of the legislature and two caucus workers were convicted of fraud and breach of trust, which occurred between 1987 and 1991. Former PC Premier Grant Devine, however, was never criminally linked to the corruption, nor was he charged.

11   Richard Hatfield, as leader of the New Brunswick PC Party, was premier of the province for 17 consecutive years (1970–1987). In the wake of a series of personal scandals, he and his party lost all of their seats in the legislature in the 1987 provincial election.

12   According to what is now referred to as "Duverger's Law," the single-member plurality (or SMP, "first-past-the-post") electoral system favours a two-party system (Duverger 1951, 247). This is partly due to the psychological effect of this system: Because only one candidate can win the district seat with only a simple plurality of the votes, a third-party vote is somewhat wasted. In other words, SMP leads to strategic voting behaviour that systematically penalizes less competitive, smaller parties (Blais and Nadeau 1996; Cox 1997, 98). Duverger also proposed the hypothesis that proportional representation (PR) systems favour multi-partyism (Duverger 1951, 269). Empirical tests of this hypothesis have provided evidence of such a tendency toward multi-partyism in PR systems by showing that strategic voting decreases as district magnitude increases (Cox 1997; Willey 1998).

13   Note, however, that in provinces that have experimented with non-SMP electoral systems (for limited periods during the twentieth century) third parties have been significantly more successful. See the analysis presented by Bélanger and Stephenson (2014, 98–109).

14   In Quebec, the effect of regional grievances on support for the Bloc Québécois in 1993 still holds strong when one controls for sovereignty support (see Bélanger 2004b).

15   The concept of political inefficacy refers to the low degree of personal political empowerment an individual may feel.

References

Adams, James, Michael Clark, Lawrence Ezrow, and Garrett Glasgow. 2006. "Are Niche Parties Fundamentally Different from Mainstream Parties?

The Causes and the Electoral Consequences of Western European Parties' Policy Shifts, 1976–1998." *American Journal of Political Science* 50 (3): 513–29. http://dx.doi.org/10.1111/j.1540-5907.2006.00199.x

Bäck, Maria, and Elina Kestilä-Kekkonen. 2014. "Owning Protest but Sharing Distrust? Confidence in the Political System and Anti-Political-Establishment Party Choice in the Finnish 2011 Parliamentary Elections." *Research on Finnish Society* 7: 21–35.

Bélanger, Éric. 2004a. "Antipartyism and Third-Party Vote Choice: A Comparison of Canada, Britain, and Australia." *Comparative Political Studies* 37 (9): 1054–78. http://dx.doi.org/10.1177/0010414004268847

Bélanger, Éric. 2004b. "The Rise of Third Parties in the 1993 Canadian Federal Election: Pinard Revisited." *Canadian Journal of Political Science* 37 (3): 581–94. http://dx.doi.org/10.1017/S0008423904020554

Bélanger, Éric. 2016. "Voting Behaviour and Political Trust." In *Handbook on Political Trust,* edited by Sonja Zmerli and Tom van der Meer. Cheltenham, UK: Edward Elgar Publishing.

Bélanger, Éric, and Kees Aarts. 2006. "Explaining the Rise of the LPF: Issues, Discontent, and the 2002 Dutch Election." *Acta Politica* 41 (1): 4–20. http://dx.doi.org/10.1057/palgrave.ap.5500135

Bélanger, Éric, and Richard Nadeau. 2005. "Political Trust and the Vote in Multiparty Elections: The Canadian Case." *European Journal of Political Research* 44 (1): 121–46. http://dx.doi.org/10.1111/j.1475-6765.2005.00221.x

Bélanger, Éric, and Richard Nadeau. 2009. *Le comportement électoral des Québécois.* Montreal: Les Presses de l'Université de Montréal.

Bélanger, Éric, and Richard Nadeau. 2010. "Third-Party Support in Canadian Elections: The Role of the Economy." In *Voting Behaviour in Canada,* edited by Cameron D. Anderson and Laura B. Stephenson, 163–82. Vancouver: University of British Columbia Press.

Bélanger, Éric, Richard Nadeau, and Michael S. Lewis-Beck. 2010. "Forecasting the Vote for a Third Party: The British Liberals, 1974–2005." *British Journal of Politics and International Relations* 12: 634–43.

Bélanger, Éric, and Laura B. Stephenson. 2014. "The Comparative Study of Canadian Voting Behaviour." In *Comparing Canada: Methods and Perspectives on Canadian Politics,* edited by Luc Turgeon, Martin Papillon, Jennifer Wallner, and Stephen White, 97–122. Vancouver: University of British Columbia Press.

Belkhodja, Chedly. 1999. "La dimension populiste de l'émergence et du succès électoral du Parti Confederation of Regions au Nouveau-Brunswick." *Canadian Journal of Political Science* 32 (2): 293–315. http://dx.doi.org/10.1017/S0008423900010507

Bell, Edward. 1993. *Social Classes and Social Credit in Alberta.* Montreal: McGill-Queen's University Press.

Betz, Hans-Georg. 1994. *Radical Right-Wing Populism in Western Europe.* New York: St. Martin's Press. http://dx.doi.org/10.1007/978-1-349-23547-6

Blais, André. 1973. "Third Parties in Canadian Provincial Politics." *Canadian Journal of Political Science* 6 (3): 422–38. http://dx.doi.org/10.1017/S0008423900040014

Blais, André, and Richard Nadeau. 1996. "Measuring Strategic Voting: A Two-Step Procedure." *Electoral Studies* 15 (1): 39–52. http://dx.doi.org/10.1016/0261-3794(94)00014-X

Brym, Robert J. 1979. "Political Conservatism in Atlantic Canada." In *Underdevelopment and Social Movements in Atlantic Canada,* edited by Robert J. Brym and R. James Sacouman, 59–79. Toronto: New Hogtown Press.

Cairns, Alan C. 1968. "The Electoral System and the Party System in Canada, 1921–1965." *Canadian Journal of Political Science* 1 (1): 55–80. http://dx.doi.org/10.1017/S0008423900035228

Carty, R. Kenneth, and David K. Stewart. 1996. "Parties and Party Systems." In *Provinces: Canadian Provincial Politics,* edited by Christopher Dunn, 63–94. Peterborough, ON: Broadview Press.

Chandler, William M. 1977. "Canadian Socialism and Policy Impact: Contagion from the Left?" *Canadian Journal of Political Science* 10 (4): 755–80. http://dx.doi.org/10.1017/S0008423900050885

Chanley, Virginia A., Thomas J. Rudolph, and Wendy M. Rahn. 2001. "Public Trust in Government in the Reagan Years and Beyond." In *What Is It about Government that Americans Dislike?* edited by John R. Hibbing and Elizabeth Theiss-Morse, 59–78. Cambridge: Cambridge University Press.

Chhibber, Pradeep, and Ken Kollman. 2004. *The Formation of National Party Systems.* Princeton, NJ: Princeton University Press.

Clarke, Harold D. 1983. "The Parti Québécois and Sources of Partisan Realignment in Contemporary Quebec." *Journal of Politics* 45 (1): 64–85. http://dx.doi.org/10.2307/2130325

Clarke, Harold D., Jane Jenson, Lawrence LeDuc, and Jon H. Pammett. 1979. *Political Choice in Canada.* Toronto: McGraw-Hill Ryerson.

Clarke, Harold D., and Allan Kornberg. 1993. "Evaluations and Evolution: Public Attitudes toward Canada's Federal Political Parties, 1965–1991." *Canadian Journal of Political Science* 26 (2): 287–311. http://dx.doi.org/10.1017/S0008423900002961

Clarke, Harold D., and Allan Kornberg. 1996. "Partisan Dealignment, Electoral Choice and Party-System Change in Canada." *Party Politics* 2 (4): 455–78. http://dx.doi.org/10.1177/1354068896002004002

Covell, Maureen. 1991. "Parties as Institutions of National Governance." In *Representation, Integration and Political Parties in Canada,* edited by Herman Bakvis, 63–127. Vol. 14 of the Research Studies for the Royal Commission on Electoral Reform and Party Financing. Toronto: Dundurn Press.

Cox, Gary W. 1997. *Making Votes Count: Strategic Coordination in the World's Electoral Systems.* Cambridge: Cambridge University Press. http://dx.doi.org/10.1017/CBO9781139174954

Craig, Stephen C. 1979. "Efficacy, Trust, and Political Behavior: An Attempt to Resolve a Lingering Conceptual Dilemma." *American Politics Quarterly* 7 (2): 225–39. http://dx.doi.org/10.1177/1532673X7900700207

Dalton, Russel J. 2004. *Democratic Challenges, Democratic Choices: The Erosion of Support in Advanced Industrial Democracies.* Oxford: Oxford University Press. http://dx.doi.org/10.1093/acprof:oso/9780199268436.001.0001

Dalton, Russell J., Ian McAllister, and Martin P. Wattenberg. 2000. "The Consequences of Partisan Dealignment." In *Parties without Partisans: Political Change in Advanced Industrial Democracies,* edited by Russell J. Dalton and Martin P. Wattenberg, 37–63. Oxford: Oxford University Press.

Dalton, Russell J., and Steven A. Weldon. 2005. "Public Images of Political Parties: A Necessary Evil?" *West European Politics* 28 (5): 931–51. http://dx.doi.org/10.1080/01402380500310527

Dennis, Jack, and Diana Owen. 2001. "Popular Satisfaction with the Party System and Representative Democracy in the United States." *International Political Science Review* 22 (4): 399–415. http://dx.doi.org/10.1177/0192512101022004007

Delwit, Pascal, Jean-Michel De Waele, and Andrea Rea, eds. 1998. *L'Extrême droite en France et en Belgique*. Brussels: Éditions Complexe.

Duverger, Maurice. 1951. *Les partis politiques*. Paris: Armand Collin.

Eagles, Munroe, and Stephen Erfle. 1993. "Variations in Third/Minor Party Support in English Constituencies: One-Party Dominance and Community Cohesion Perspectives." *European Journal of Political Research* 23 (1): 91–116. http://dx.doi.org/10.1111/j.1475-6765.1993.tb00350.x

Feigert, Frank. 1989. *Canada Votes: 1935–1988*. Durham, NC: Duke University Press.

Fisher, Stephen L. 1974. *The Minor Parties of the Federal Republic of Germany: Toward a Comparative Theory of Minor Parties*. The Hague: Martinus Nijhoff. http://dx.doi.org/10.1007/978-94-010-2079-4

Fournier, Patrick, Fred Cutler, Stuart Soroka, Dietlind Stolle, and Éric Bélanger. 2013. "Riding the Orange Wave: Leadership, Values, Issues, and the 2011 Canadian Election." *Canadian Journal of Political Science* 46 (4): 863–97. http://dx.doi.org/10.1017/S0008423913000875

Gagnon, Alain-G. 1981. "Third Parties: A Theoretical Framework." *American Review of Canadian Studies* 11 (1): 37–63. http://dx.doi.org/10.1080/02722018109480719

Gagnon, Alain-G., and A. Brian Tanguay. 1996. "Minor Parties in the Canadian Political System: Origins, Functions, Impact." In *Canadian Parties in Transition*, 2nd ed., edited by A. Brian Tanguay and Alain-G. Gagnon, 106–34. Toronto: Nelson Canada.

Gerring, John. 2005. "Minor Parties in Plurality Electoral Systems." *Party Politics* 11 (1): 79–107. http://dx.doi.org/10.1177/1354068805048474

Gidengil, Elisabeth. 1990. "Centers and Peripheries: The Political Culture of Dependency." *Canadian Review of Sociology and Anthropology* 27 (1): 23–48. http://dx.doi.org/10.1111/j.1755-618X.1990.tb00443.x

Gidengil, Elisabeth, André Blais, Richard Nadeau, and Neil Nevitte. 2001. "The Correlates and Consequences of Anti-Partyism in the 1997 Canadian Election." *Party Politics* 7 (4): 491–513. http://dx.doi.org/10.1177/1354068801007004005

Gidengil, Elisabeth, André Blais, Neil Nevitte, and Richard Nadeau. 2002. "Changes in the Party System and Anti-Party Sentiment." In *Political Parties, Representation, and Electoral Democracy in Canada*, edited by William Cross, 68–86. Toronto: Oxford University Press.

Golder, Matt. 2003. "Explaining Variation in the Success of Extreme Right Parties in Western Europe." *Comparative Political Studies* 36 (4): 432–66. http://dx.doi.org/10.1177/0010414003251176

Grofman, Bernard, André Blais, and Shaun Bowler, eds. 2009. *Duverger's Law of Plurality Voting*. New York: Springer.

Hamel, Jacques, and Yvon Thériault. 1975. "La fonction tribunitienne et la députation créditiste à l'Assemblée nationale du Québec." *Canadian Journal of Political Science* 8 (1): 3–21. http://dx.doi.org/10.1017/S0008423900045200

Harmel, Robert, and John D. Robertson. 1985. "Formation and Success of New Parties: A Cross-National Analysis." *International Political Science Review* 6 (4): 501–23. http://dx.doi.org/10.1177/019251218500600408

Harmel, Robert, and Lars Svåsand. 1997. "The Influence of New Parties on Old Parties' Platforms: The Cases of the Progress Parties and Conservative Parties

of Denmark and Norway." *Party Politics* 3 (3): 315–40. http://dx.doi.org/
10.1177/1354068897003003003

Harrison, Trevor. 1995. *Of Passionate Intensity: Right-Wing Populism and the Reform
Party of Canada*. Toronto: University of Toronto Press.

Hartz, Louis. 1955. *The Liberal Tradition in America*. New York: Harcourt, Brace.

Hauss, Charles, and David Rayside. 1978. "The Development of New Parties in
Western Democracies since 1945." In *Political Parties: Development and Decay*,
edited by Louis Maisel and Joseph Cooper, 31–58. Beverly Hills, CA: Sage.

Henderson, Ailsa. 2004. "Regional Political Cultures in Canada." *Canadian Journal of
Political Science* 37 (3): 595–615. http://dx.doi.org/10.1017/S0008423904030707

Hesseltine, William B. 1962. *Third Party Movements in the United States*. Toronto: Van
Nostrand.

Hetherington, Marc J. 1998. "The Political Relevance of Political Trust." *American
Political Science Review* 92 (4): 791–808. http://dx.doi.org/10.2307/2586304

Hetherington, Marc J. 1999. "The Effect of Political Trust on the Presidential Vote,
1968–96." *American Political Science Review* 93 (2): 311–26. http://dx.doi.org/
10.2307/2585398

Hibbing, John R., and Elizabeth Theiss-Morse. 2002. *Stealth Democracy: Americans'
Beliefs about How Government Should Work*. Cambridge: Cambridge University
Press. http://dx.doi.org/10.1017/CBO9780511613722

Hirano, Shigeo, and James M. Snyder, Jr. 2007. "The Decline of
Third-Party Voting in the United States." *Journal of Politics* 69 (1): 1–16.
http://dx.doi.org/10.1111/j.1468-2508.2007.00490.x

Hirschman, Albert O. 1970. *Exit, Voice, and Loyalty: Responses to Decline in Firms,
Organizations, and States*. Cambridge, MA: Harvard University Press.

Hooghe, Marc, Sofie Marien, and Teun Pauwels. 2011. "Where Do
Distrusting Voters Turn if There Is No Viable Exit or Voice Option? The
Impact of Political Trust on Electoral Behaviour in the Belgian Regional
Elections of June 2009." *Government and Opposition* 46 (2): 245–73.
http://dx.doi.org/10.1111/j.1477-7053.2010.01338.x

Horowitz, Gad. 1966. "Conservatism, Liberalism, and Socialism in Canada: An
Interpretation." *Canadian Journal of Economics and Political Science* 32 (2): 143–71.
http://dx.doi.org/10.2307/139794

Hug, Simon. 2001. *Altering Party Systems: Strategic Behavior and the Emergence of
New Political Parties in Western Democracies*. Ann Arbor: University of Michigan
Press.

Ignazi, Piero. 1992. "The Silent Counter-Revolution: Hypotheses on the Emergence
of Extreme Right-Wing Parties in Europe." *European Journal of Political Research*
22 (1): 3–34. http://dx.doi.org/10.1111/j.1475-6765.1992.tb00303.x

Inglehart, Ronald. 1998. *Modernization and Postmodernization*. Princeton, NJ:
Princeton University Press.

Jackman, Robert W., and Karin Volpert. 1996. "Conditions Favouring Parties of the
Extreme Right in Western Europe." *British Journal of Political Science* 26 (4): 501–21.
http://dx.doi.org/10.1017/S0007123400007584

Jenkins, Richard W. 2002. "How Campaigns Matter in Canada: Priming and
Learning as Explanations for the Reform Party's 1993 Campaign Success."
Canadian Journal of Political Science 35 (2): 383–408. http://dx.doi.org/
10.1017/S0008423902778281

Kang, Won-Taek. 2004. "Protest Voting and Abstention under Plurality Rule Elections: An Alternative Public Choice Approach." *Journal of Theoretical Politics* 16 (1): 79–102. http://dx.doi.org/10.1177/0951629804038903

Key, V.O., Jr. 1964. *Politics, Parties, and Pressure Groups.* 5th ed. New York: Crowell.

Kitschelt, Herbert. 1995. *The Radical Right in Western Europe: A Comparative Analysis.* Ann Arbor: University of Michigan Press.

Koch, Jeffrey W. 2003. "Political Cynicism and Third Party Support in American Presidential Elections." *American Politics Research* 31 (1): 48–65. http://dx.doi.org/10.1177/1532673X02238579

Lago, Ignacio, and Ferran Martinez. 2011. "Why New Parties?" *Party Politics* 17 (1): 3–20. http://dx.doi.org/10.1177/1354068809346077

Laurent, Annie. 1997. "Définir les petits partis: le regard de l'électoraliste." In *Les petits partis: de la petitesse en politique,* edited by Annie Laurent and Bruno Villalba, 19–42. Paris: L'Harmattan.

Lavau, Georges. 1969. "Partis et systèmes politiques: interactions et fonctions." *Canadian Journal of Political Science* 2 (1): 18–44. http://dx.doi.org/10.1017/S0008423900024586

Laycock, David. 1994. "Reforming Canadian Democracy? Institutions and Ideology in the Reform Party Project." *Canadian Journal of Political Science* 27 (2): 213–47. http://dx.doi.org/10.1017/S0008423900017340

Lemieux, Vincent. 1965. "Les dimensions sociologiques du vote créditiste au Québec." *Recherches Sociographiques* 6 (2): 181–95. http://dx.doi.org/10.7202/055266ar

Lemieux, Vincent, Marcel Gilbert, and André Blais. 1970. *Une élection de réalignement: l'élection générale du 29 avril 1970 au Québec.* Montreal: Éditions du Jour.

Leuprecht, Christian. 2003. "The Tory Fragment in Canada: Endangered Species?" *Canadian Journal of Political Science* 36 (2): 401–16. http://dx.doi.org/10.1017/S000842390377869X

Lipset, Seymour Martin. 1950. *Agrarian Socialism: The Co-operative Commonwealth Federation in Saskatchewan.* Berkeley: University of California Press.

Lipset, Seymour Martin. 1954. "Democracy in Alberta." *Canadian Forum* 34 (November–December): 175–7, 196–8.

Lipset, Seymour Martin. 1990. *Continental Divide: The Values and Institutions of the United States and Canada.* London: Routledge.

Lucardie, Paul. 2000. "Prophets, Purifiers and Prolocutors: Towards a Theory on the Emergence of New Parties." *Party Politics* 6 (2): 175–85. http://dx.doi.org/10.1177/1354068800006002003

Lucardie, Paul. 2007. "Pristine Purity: New Political Parties in Canada." *American Review of Canadian Studies* 37: 283–300.

Macpherson, C.B. 1953. *Democracy in Alberta: The Theory and Practice of a Quasi-Party System.* Toronto: University of Toronto Press.

Macpherson, C.B. 1955. "Democracy in Alberta: A Reply." *Canadian Forum* 34 (January): 223–5.

Mair, Peter, Wolfgang C. Müeller, and Fritz Plasser, eds. 2004. *Political Parties and Electoral Change: Party Responses to Electoral Markets.* Thousand Oaks, CA: Sage.

Mallory, James R. 1954. *Social Credit and the Federal Power in Canada.* Toronto: University of Toronto Press.

Martin, Geoffrey R. 1998. "We've Seen It All Before: The Rise and Fall of the CoR Party of New Brunswick, 1988–1995." *Journal of Canadian Studies* 33: 22–38.

Martin, Pierre. 2005. *Dynamiques partisanes et réalignements électoraux au Canada (1867–2004)*. Paris: L'Harmattan.

Martin, Pierre. 2007. "Comment analyser les changements dans les systèmes partisans d'Europe occidentale depuis 1945?" *Revue Internationale de Politique Comparée* 14 (2): 263–80. http://dx.doi.org/10.3917/ripc.142.0263

McRae, Kenneth D. 1964. "The Structure of Canadian History." In *The Founding of New Societies,* edited by Louis Hartz, 219–74. New York: Harcourt, Brace and World.

Meguid, Bonnie M. 2008. *Party Competition between Unequals: Strategies and Electoral Fortunes in Western Europe.* Cambridge: Cambridge University Press. http://dx.doi.org/10.1017/CBO9780511510298

Michaud, Denis. 1999. *L'évolution du comportement électoral fédéral entre 1984 et 1997 dans les quatre provinces de l'ouest: une analyse des appuis au Reform Party à partir du modèle théorique de Maurice Pinard*. Master's dissertation, Université Laval.

Miller, Arthur H., and Ola Listhaug. 1990. "Political Parties and Confidence in Government: A Comparison of Norway, Sweden, and the United States." *British Journal of Political Science* 20 (3): 357–86. http://dx.doi.org/10.1017/S0007123400005883

Nevitte, Neil. 1996. *The Decline of Deference: Canadian Value Change in Cross-National Perspective.* Peterborough, ON: Broadview Press.

Nevitte, Neil, Herman Bakvis, and Roger Gibbins. 1989. "The Ideological Contours of 'New Politics' in Canada: Policy, Mobilization, and Partisan Support." *Canadian Journal of Political Science* 22 (3): 475–503. http://dx.doi.org/10.1017/S000842390001091X

Newton, Kenneth, and Pippa Norris. 2000. "Confidence in Public Institutions: Faith, Culture, or Performance?" In *Disaffected Democracies: What's Troubling the Trilateral Countries?* edited by Susan J. Pharr and Robert D. Putnam, 52–73. Princeton, NJ: Princeton University Press.

Norris, Pippa, ed. 1999. *Critical Citizens: Global Support for Democratic Governance.* Oxford: Oxford University Press. http://dx.doi.org/10.1093/0198295685.001.0001

Patten, Steve. 1996. "Preston Manning's Populism: Constructing the Common Sense of the Common People." *Studies in Political Economy* 50: 95–132.

Pattie, Charles, and Ron Johnston. 2001. "Losing the Voters' Trust: Evaluations of the Political System and Voting at the 1997 British General Election." *British Journal of Politics and International Relations* 3 (2): 191–222. http://dx.doi.org/10.1111/1467-856X.00057

Pelletier, Réjean, and Daniel Guérin. 1998. "Les nouveaux mouvements sociaux constituent-ils un défi pour les partis politiques? Le cas du Québec." *Canadian Journal of Political Science* 31 (2): 311–38. http://dx.doi.org/10.1017/S0008423900019818

Perkins, Doug. 1996. "Structure and Choice: The Role of Organizations, Patronage, and the Media in Party Formation." *Party Politics* 2 (3): 355–75. http://dx.doi.org/10.1177/1354068896002003004

Perrella, Andrea M.L. 2005. "Long-Term Economic Hardship and Non-Mainstream Voting in Canada." *Canadian Journal of Political Science* 38 (2): 335–57. http://dx.doi.org/10.1017/S0008423905040242

Perrella, Andrea M.L. 2009. "Economic Decline and Voter Discontent." *Social Science Journal* 46 (2): 347–68. http://dx.doi.org/10.1016/j.soscij.2009.02.002

Peterson, Geoff, and J. Mark Wrighton. 1998. "Expressions of Distrust: Third-Party Voting and Cynicism in Government." *Political Behavior* 20 (1): 17–34. http://dx.doi.org/10.1023/A:1024891016072

Pétry, François. 1988. "The Policy Impact of Canadian Party Programs: Public Expenditure Growth and Contagion from the Left." *Canadian Public Policy* 14 (4): 376–89. http://dx.doi.org/10.2307/3550410

Pharr, Susan J., and Robert D. Putnam, eds. 2000. *Disaffected Democracies: What's Troubling the Trilateral Countries?* Princeton, NJ: Princeton University Press.

Pinard, Maurice. 1971. *The Rise of a Third Party: A Study in Crisis Politics.* Englewood Cliffs, NJ: Prentice-Hall.

Pinard, Maurice. 1973. "Third Parties in Canada Revisited: A Rejoinder and Elaboration of the Theory of One-Party Dominance." *Canadian Journal of Political Science* 6 (3): 439–60. http://dx.doi.org/10.1017/S0008423900040026

Ranney, Austin, and Willmoore Kendall. 1956. *Democracy and the American Party System.* New York: Harcourt, Brace.

Roese, Neal J. 2002. "Canadians' Shrinking Trust in Government: Causes and Consequences." In *Value Change and Governance in Canada,* edited by Neil Nevitte, 149–63. Toronto: University of Toronto Press.

Rosenstone, Steven J., Roy L. Behr, and Edward H. Lazarus. 1996. *Third Parties in America: Citizen Response to Major Party Failure.* 2nd ed. Princeton, NJ: Princeton University Press.

Seidle, F. Leslie. 1994. "The Angry Citizenry: Representation and Responsiveness in Government." *Policy Options* 15 (6): 75–80.

Sigurdson, Richard. 1994. "Preston Manning and the Politics of Postmodernism in Canada." *Canadian Journal of Political Science* 27 (2): 249–76. http://dx.doi.org/10.1017/S0008423900017352

Simeon, Richard, and David J. Elkins. 1974. "Regional Political Cultures in Canada." *Canadian Journal of Political Science* 7 (3): 397–437. http://dx.doi.org/10.1017/S0008423900040713

Spoon, Jae-Jae. 2011. *Political Survival of Small Parties in Europe.* Ann Arbor: University of Michigan Press.

Stewart, David K., and R. Kenneth Carty. 2006. "Many Political Worlds? Provincial Parties and Party Systems." In *Provinces: Canadian Provincial Politics,* 2nd ed., edited by Christopher Dunn, 97–113. Toronto: University of Toronto Press.

Stewart, Ian. 1994. *Roasting Chestnuts: The Mythology of Maritime Political Culture.* Vancouver: University of British Columbia Press.

Tavits, Margit. 2006. "Party System Change: Testing a Model of New Party Entry." *Party Politics* 12 (1): 99–119. http://dx.doi.org/10.1177/1354068806059346

van der Brug, Wouter. 2003. "How the LPF Fuelled Discontent: Empirical Tests of Explanations of LPF Support." *Acta Politica* 38 (1): 89–106. http://dx.doi.org/10.1057/palgrave.ap.5500005

White, Graham. 1973. "One-Party Dominance and Third Parties: The Pinard Theory Reconsidered." *Canadian Journal of Political Science* 6 (3): 399–421. http://dx.doi.org/10.1017/S0008423900040002

White, Stephen. 2000. "Explaining the Rise of the NDP in Atlantic Canada." Paper presented at the annual meeting of the Canadian Political Science Association, Quebec City.

Willey, Joseph. 1998. "Institutional Arrangements and the Success of New Parties in Old Democracies." *Political Studies* 46 (3): 651–68. http://dx.doi.org/10.1111/1467-9248.00159

Wiseman, Nelson. 1981. "The Pattern of Prairie Politics." *Queen's Quarterly* 88: 298–315.

Zingale, Nancy H. 1978. "Third Party Alignments in a Two Party System: The Case of Minnesota." In *The History of American Electoral Behavior,* edited by Joel H. Silbey, Allan G. Bogue, and William H. Flanigan, 106–33. Princeton, NJ: Princeton University Press.

PART III

Representation and Democracy

11

Party Politics and Voting Systems in Canada

DENNIS PILON

THE VOTING SYSTEM COMPRISES A SET OF rules that determine how votes cast in an election will be converted into representation in a legislative body. The choice of voting system determines how voters will mark their ballot, how the ballots will be counted, and the method of determining winners. There are different kinds of voting systems in use around the world and even within present-day Canada. Though every Canadian voter has used a voting system, few are aware of the implications and repercussions of using any particular one. Indeed, for most Canadians it is like an invisible institution. Members of the public focus on how to mark their ballot, but the larger voting system within which such a vote is cast goes largely unnoticed. By contrast, politicians and political parties pay close attention to voting systems. They have been, and remain, the key players in their maintenance or reform.

This chapter will underscore the politics fuelling the origin, maintenance, and efforts to reform Canada's voting systems at all three levels of government. As will be made clear, interests of party have been paramount in such decisions, though not simply as a matter of electoral self-interest. Instead, the character of a given party system and the nature of the challenges it has faced have proven crucial in affecting decisions about institutional rules. Thus we must approach the question historically to assess the reasons why Canada's voting systems have been much contested but only rarely altered.

The argument will advance on three fronts. First, this chapter will set out what a voting system is and some of the key ideas about how they function. In addition, it will summarize the many different kinds of voting systems that have been used in Canada and are presently in use. Second, the chapter will explore the debate over where electoral institutions come from and why they are maintained or reformed. Finally, it will divide Canadian experience with voting system reform into three broad periods to highlight the factors contributing to the rise in reform interest as well as its ultimate success or failure.

Voting Systems and the Debate over Their Effects

Every voting system comprises three distinctive components: a districting rule, ballot design, and a voting formula (Rae 1971). The *districting rule* determines how many representatives will be elected from any given circumscribed geographic area, typically a distinction between a single- or multimember district. *Ballot design* refers to how voters mark their ballot, either through a nominal "X" or check mark, or via some ordinal preference method (e.g., 1, 2, 3). Finally, the *voting formula* refers to the rule applied to the raw votes setting out what level of support is required to secure representation. In some cases, a winner need only get more votes than any other candidate (a *plurality*); in others, a winner might need to gain a majority of votes cast to be declared elected; while in still others multiple winners might need only gain a certain proportion of the total votes to get a seat.

These three component elements can be combined in several ways to create different voting systems. For instance, the plurality formula can be combined with either single- or multimember districts. The first combination produces the voting system we typically use for provincial or federal elections in Canada, single-member plurality (SMP), while the second combination, multimember plurality, or "at large," is used for most municipal elections in British Columbia and a few other locales across Canada. Or we can see how the same ordinal ballot structure (where voters number their preferences) can be combined with different voting formulas and districting methods. For instance, Australia uses a preference ballot structure in two different ways. In the lower house, it is combined with single-member districts and a majority voting formula in a voting system called the *alternative vote* (AV). Meanwhile, in the upper house the preference ballot is combined with multimember districts and a proportional voting formula to create a voting system referred to as the single transferable vote (STV).

Voting systems can be defined and compared in several ways. For example, some scholars distinguish different voting systems in terms of their component parts (e.g., pure or mixed systems) or their impact on government formation (e.g., majoritarian or non-majoritarian) (Massicotte and Blais 1999; Norris 2004). But the academic approach that best aligns with how actual political actors have understood them organizes voting systems in terms of the kinds of results they produce (Law Commission of Canada 2004; Pilon 2007). Despite containing myriad unique elements, every voting system in use around the world can be fit within a fourfold typology of plurality, majority, proportional, and semi-proportional voting systems (see Table 11.1).

Why different countries developed or adopted different voting systems has been the subject of debate. Some have argued that voting systems were influenced by social cleavage structures (Lipset and Rokkan 1967) or political culture (Rokkan 1970) or the size of the party system (Lijphart 1999). Others have underlined the role of political parties in establishing rules that would benefit themselves electorally (Colomer 2005). But until recently

Table 11.1 Voting System Families

Voting System Family	Voting System Variants	Voting System Use by Country
Plurality	Single-member plurality	Canada, United States, United Kingdom
	Multimember plurality	Canada, United States (some local elections)
Majority	Double ballot	France
	Alternative vote	Australia
Proportional	Party list	Norway, Sweden, Finland, Denmark, Belgium, Netherlands, Italy
	Single transferable vote	Ireland, Malta, Australia (Senate)
	Mixed-member proportional	Germany, New Zealand
Semi-proportional	Limited vote	United States (some local elections)
	Cumulative vote	United States (some school board elections)
	Single nontransferable vote	Japan (1947–93)
	Parallel	Japan, Italy (1994–2004)

most work simply assumed—rather than explored—where voting rules came from, typically implying that any given voting system must have been sanctioned or approved by the public somehow, particularly when it has been in use for a long time (Katz 1997). Some commentators dispute that voting systems are really that important or influential in terms of affecting election results (Courtney 1999). Yet considerable debate arises whenever reforming a voting system is raised publicly.

All the debate over voting systems is really a debate about voting system effects. For most of the twentieth century, the discussion was rather unbalanced in North American political science. The region's own preferred voting system, SMP, was typically viewed as superior and promoted for providing local representation, a stable two-party system, majority government, a regular alternation in power between the different parties, and an efficient means of legislating policy (Lijphart 1977; Rustow 1950). The main alternative, various forms of proportional representation (PR), was characterized as fuelling political instability, party fragmentation, and legislative gridlock, largely on the basis of the experience in Weimar Germany, Israel, and postwar Italy (Hermans [1941] 1972; Wiseman 1997). More recent empirical research on the workings of these different voting systems across a wide range of countries in Western Europe and the Anglo-American countries has exposed most of these claims as myths. For instance, many of the countries using SMP have multiparty rather than two-party systems, while most countries using PR in Western Europe in the postwar period have been neither unstable nor unable to pass legislation (Lijphart 1994, 1999; Mair 1991; Norris 2004; Woldendorp, Keman, and Budge 2000).

To the extent that particular voting systems can be said to have specific effects, the claims must be narrowed or specified contextually. For instance, the French political scientist Maurice Duverger argued that voting systems have both mechanical and psychological effects. Mechanical effects are those that are directly observable, like the way that an SMP system will tend to over-reward regionally concentrated voters and fail to represent popular opinions that are spread too thinly across the polity. By contrast, psychological effects are harder to quantify but nonetheless real, as when voters decide to vote strategically for a less favoured choice for fear that their top preference may not be competitive in their geographic area (Duverger [1954] 1963). Another approach examines the results produced by particular voting systems in different locales over long periods, precisely to weigh the impact of the voting system against other important variables at work in any particular context. For instance, comparing the Western European and Anglo-American experience in the postwar period, one could say that SMP systems have tended to have smaller party systems, produce more single-party majority governments, and create significant barriers to the competitive entry of new parties, while PR systems have tended to have larger party systems, produce more coalition governments, and place fewer barriers to the entry of new parties (Blais 1991; Powell 2000). These "effects" are really broad tendencies, affected by the ebb and flow of political competition. As Peter Mair (1992, 85) once noted, voting systems "provide, at best, 'facilitating conditions,' the impact of which will also be mediated by a variety of other institutional cultural factors."

Over its history, Canada has experimented with a range of voting systems, sometimes briefly but in some cases for extended periods (Pilon 2006; see Table 11.2). Still, plurality voting systems, particularly the single-member variety, have remained the country's longest and most widely used voting methods. Federally, SMP has dominated, with some minor use of dual-member ridings from 1867 to 1966. Provincially, it was common to see SMP used in rural areas with multimember plurality used for urban seats well into the twentieth century. In the early to mid-part of the twentieth century, several provinces experimented with semi-proportional and proportional voting systems for urban centres, the latter usually in combination with majority voting used for rural areas. One province briefly introduced majority voting for both rural and urban areas in the early 1950s. Canadian municipalities have used both single-member ("wards") and multimember ("at large") plurality, with a few adopting proportional voting for varying periods.

Table 11.2 Nonplurality Voting Systems Used in Canada

Province	System	Adoption	Repeal	Application
Ontario	Limited vote	1885	1893	Toronto
Manitoba	Single transferable vote	1920	1955	Urban
	Alternative vote	1924	1955	Rural
Alberta	Single transferable vote	1924	1956	Urban
	Alternative vote	1924	1956	Rural
British Columbia	Alternative vote	1951	1953	All ridings

Municipality	System	Adoption	Repeal
Calgary	Single transferable vote	1916	1961
	Alternative vote	1961	1973
Lethbridge	Single transferable vote	1928	1929
Edmonton	Single transferable vote	1922	1928
Vancouver	Single transferable vote	1920	1923
Victoria	Single transferable vote	1920	1921
South Vancouver	Single transferable vote	1918	1928
West Vancouver	Single transferable vote	1917	1930
Nelson	Single transferable vote	1917	1919
Port Coquitlam	Single transferable vote	1917	1921
Mission City	Single transferable vote	1917	1921
New Westminster	Single transferable vote	1917	1919
Regina	Single transferable vote	1920	1926
Moose Jaw	Single transferable vote	1920	1925
Saskatoon	Single transferable vote	1920	1926
North Battlefield	Single transferable vote	1920	1924
Winnipeg	Single transferable vote	1920	1971
Transcona	Single transferable vote	c. 1941–44	1971
St. James	Single transferable vote	1922	1971
St. Vital	Single transferable vote	c. 1931–34	1971

Where "Democratic" Institutions Come From

The voting system is just one part of a larger set of rules—the electoral system—that shape the practice of elections. Scholars have explored the origins and reform of issues like voter registration (Smith and Courtney 1991), redistricting (Courtney 2001), and campaign finance in Canada (Paltiel 1966), but less attention has been given to the extension of the franchise, the voting system, and the achievement of even the minimum conditions of democracy. Queries about the origins of Canadian institutions are often directed to the preamble of the 1867 British North America Act, which states that Canada will have "a Constitution similar in Principle to that of the United Kingdom" (Leone 2006–07) or assumed to have simply arisen in response to what the public wants or has wanted. More recently, commentators have relied on political culture to explain Canadian use of different institutions, for instance, arguing that the failure of voting system reform efforts in Prince Edward Island, Ontario, and British Columbia reflect the public's attachment to a local member.

The problem with such views is that there is scant evidence to support them. Until the recent referenda on voting systems in several Canadian provinces, there had been almost no public input into the shape of the country's electoral institutions. Norman Ward (1950, vii–viii) noted more than a half century ago that the rules governing our elections have been the stuff of political battle, defined primarily by party self-interest. Even when reforms appeared to be animated by lofty goals—for example, with the creation of a national franchise and chief electoral officer in 1920, or the introduction of federal electoral boundary commissions in the 1960s—such endeavours were often "politics masquerading as principles," as Ward put it. And, as we shall see in the case of voting system reform, where politicians feared unpalatable political outcomes they often showed no hesitation in reforming long-standing institutional arrangements.

Canadian electoral institutions are fundamentally political compromises, representing the interests—and fears—of those designing them. In the Canadian context, many took shape amid a broader struggle for a minimally democratic state and then later alongside or in response to demands for a more substantive democratic process (McKay 2000). Comparative work on democratization has underscored that political struggle, as opposed to political culture or some kind of functional necessity, has defined institutional developments across Western countries as concerns the extension of franchise (Przeworski 2008, 2009), the parliamentarization of the executive (von Beyme 2000), and the end of corruption in electoral administration (O'Leary 1962; Ziblatt 2009). Indeed, several recent comparative volumes highlight how political struggle was responsible for most Western voting systems as well (Ahmed 2013; Pilon 2013). But Canadian electoral studies have largely eschewed both this approach and any study of some of these key breakthroughs in the democratization process (e.g., the nineteenth-century extension of the franchise, the adoption of the secret ballot, or the various struggles over voting systems). To understand where Canadian "democratic" institutions (like the voting system) come from, whom they serve, and what might animate their reform, we have to go back and look.

Canada's Three Eras of Voting System Reform

From 1867 to 1914, Canada's electoral system was a political battleground. All manner of electoral law was subject to often self-interested "reform," including balloting, districting, voter registration, and the franchise. Only the voting system remained untouched and largely unremarked upon. Plurality voting had been chosen for national and provincial elections in Canada without controversy, its adoption in 1867 often credited to British influence. But the imperial connection was, at best, indirect. More concretely influential were the decades of electoral experience in the pre-Confederation colonies themselves (Kerr 1970).

Internationally, voting system reform emerged as a reform issue in the mid- to late nineteenth century, often in culturally divided European countries (e.g., Switzerland) or to address coalition-making problems in Anglo-American party systems. But it made little headway. In all cases the political systems were either controlled by a small traditional or business elite or a tight two-party system. Those with the power to reform were uninterested in opening up the political system to the greater electoral competition (for more detail on these events, see Chapter 3 in Pilon 2013).

In Canada, a functioning two-party system emerged shortly after Confederation and remained in place, largely unchallenged, until the pressures of war forced a realignment of federal parties in 1917. The only successful voting system reform in this period was the adoption of semi-proportional limited voting in Ontario for provincial elections from the multimember riding of Toronto. Under this system, voters would be restricted to casting two votes in a multimember riding electing three representatives—the restriction would allow minority candidates a chance to be elected. Inspired by party self-interest (the ruling Liberals wanted a share of the urban representation that was dominated by the Conservatives), the experiment lasted for three elections, only to be repealed by the government when it appeared that the system might allow a labour rather than a Liberal candidate to win a seat (Pilon 2006). Federally and provincially, the dominance of two-party systems across the country during this period effectively sidelined any critical appraisal of the voting system.

The Reform Era, 1914 to 1956

The period from 1914 to 1956 witnessed the breakdown of Canada's traditional two-party system amid repeated challenges from new political forces perceived as threatening to the status quo. It was also the single most dynamic period of voting system reform in the country's history. New voting systems were adopted in more than two dozen municipalities across the country and given serious consideration in many more. Three provinces adopted new voting systems, and federal discussion of the issue emerged repeatedly in the 1920s, 1930s, and 1940s. Though the traditional plurality system would reassert itself in most locales by the late 1950s, the scope of the reform adoptions and the longevity of their use in a few cases refutes the oft-stated view that voting system reform has had little impact in Canada (this section draws from Phillips 1976 and Pilon 2006).

World War I would prove to be the catalyst for reform of all kinds, with progressives finding a home in both traditional and new political forces (Laycock 1990), but the conditions facilitating change had its roots in the previous decade. Prior to the war, progressives had gained a foothold in several provincial Liberal parties, securing promises to introduce a variety of institutional reforms, including proportional voting systems. Upon gaining office, they did pass permissive legislation allowing municipalities to adopt PR, either by vote of council or referenda. But few locales took up the option. Even where reformers were successful, their gains were often short-lived and quickly repealed.

The real impetus for reform was the general state of social upheaval following the end of the war and the challenges to the conventional party system that were then successfully mounted. Here the defining moment was the Winnipeg General Strike of 1919. The end of the war had led to considerable political uncertainty. Would the wartime coalition government hold together, signalling a reconfigured national party system, or would the old two-party system be revived? And how might farmers, organized labour, and returning soldiers influence the resulting policy mix? The Winnipeg General Strike proved the litmus test for the way the political wind was blowing, demonstrating a fairly high level of public support for the strikers and their demands for good jobs, housing, and social services.

In the aftermath of the revolts of 1919, conventional political operatives began scrambling for responses. This only intensified when labour candidates won all available seats on the Winnipeg city council later that fall, and a farmer/labour coalition captured power in Ontario. Now voting system reform emerged as a popular reform, with newspaper editors and political elites keen to make room for the "reasonable labour man." A wave of conversions at the municipal and provincial level followed. Manitoba's progressive Liberal administration, which had done little on voting system reform in its previous five years in office, now rushed through reforms for municipal and provincial voting to forestall what they feared was a coming labour sweep (Lightbody 1978a, 317–19). Alberta's farmers came to power in 1921 and introduced proportional voting for urban centres and the majoritarian alternative vote for rural areas, which conveniently had the effect of bolstering their support in rural areas while dividing their opponents in the cities. Manitoba would later introduce majority voting in rural areas as well.

By 1921, with the federal Liberal coalition in tatters, its former farmer and labour allies established in their own parties, there was a general consensus among the political competitors (except the Conservatives) that proportional voting would be a good thing. In many ways, political conditions in Canada did not appear terribly different than those in Western Europe, where a left–right polarization was squeezing centre parties and aiding the adoption of PR systems. But the character of the emerging Canadian party system would prove distinctive. Though the 1921 federal election produced a Parliament where a majority of members belonged to parties ostensibly committed to PR, the opportunity was quickly squandered. Labour and socialist politics did not make enough of a breakthrough in 1921 to appear threatening, while the more successful farmers were too tentative to seize the opportunity afforded by a Parliament where no party had a majority of seats. Mackenzie King's Liberals skilfully managed the challenges of minority government, avoiding any concession on voting system reform. The one vote held on the issue to mount a trial of PR in several large cities failed to pass in 1923. Where a fear of left electoral power remained, as in Calgary and Winnipeg, PR also remained in place. Where it faded, so too did the commitment to nonplurality voting systems.

The threat of radicalism would remain a reliable barometer of elite interest in voting system reforms, rising and falling with the left's electoral prospects. When the national party system appeared to be set to crumble again just before the 1935 Depression-era election, and support for the just formed socialist Co-operative Commonwealth Federation (CCF) appeared to be increasing, the Liberals again promised to introduce a proportional voting system if elected. But once safely ensconced back in power with a majority government, the Liberals' promise was dispatched to a parliamentary committee that eventually decided against any reform. Then, in the 1940s, as the socially levelling pressures of war again appeared set to benefit the CCF, various federal politicians in both the Liberal and Conservative parties anxiously raised voting system reforms as a necessary fix to block socialism. But when the CCF breakthrough never came, such discussion ceased.

The threat posed by the CCF did produce some voting system reforms during this period. In Vancouver, the rapid organization and immediate popularity of the CCF in the early 1930s moved Vancouver's Liberal mayor to engineer a shift from ward voting to voting at large in the hopes that the city's west side would swamp the CCF's voting base in the working-class east side. But, surprisingly, instead of sidelining the CCF, the reform led to an increase in CCF representation since they were the only coherent block of politicians running on one slate. Only when the city's business community organized a right-wing slate did they manage to push the CCF out of city hall (for more details, see Smith 1982). Fear that the CCF would capture government at the provincial level in British Columbia also motivated the rapid introduction of a new voting system in 1952, just before a scheduled provincial election. A coalition of the provincial Liberal and Conservative parties had run the province for a decade, winning two strong electoral victories by working together. But into the 1950s the political tensions of coalition were forcing the parties apart. The introduction of the majoritarian alternative vote was supposed to free the two parties to compete against each other without allowing the CCF to win power on a vote split between them. The plan worked—sort of. The CCF did not win the 1952 provincial election, but neither did the former coalition partners. Instead, an upstart, populist, right-wing party eked out a minority government, turning it into a majority one year later. Secure in government, Social Credit repealed the new voting system in 1955 (for more details, see Pilon 2010a).

By the mid-1950s, the left in Canada was appearing increasingly weak electorally, eclipsed by centrist parties that adopted just enough of their policy book to swing voters into their camp. Now voting system reform no longer appeared to be required to contain the left. Manitoba abandoned its unique PR/majority system in 1955, followed shortly by Alberta. Municipally, Calgary converted its STV system to AV in 1961, and then shifted to plurality in 1973, while Winnipeg dropped STV in a large municipal reorganization in 1972. Canada's key voting system reform era thus ended with a whimper, the reforms themselves quickly forgotten by the political class and largely ignored by political scientists.

Accommodating Difference, 1968–1992

The second period of interest in voting system reform in Canada would focus on accommodating political differences spatially. Alan C. Cairns opened the discussion in 1968, arguing that there was a major gap between the perception and reality of the workings of the SMP system as it functioned at the federal level. Canadian politics, he noted, was commonly held to be the "politics of moderation, or brokerage politics," an approach that would typically "minimize differences, restrain fissiparous tendencies, and thus over time help knit together the diverse interests of a polity weak in integration" (Cairns 1968, 63). But in reality Canada's voting system tended to balkanize the electoral support of the two traditional national governing parties, leaving them dominating some areas of the country with little or no representation elsewhere. In fact, with the rise of third parties after 1921, SMP regularly overrepresented parties with regionally concentrated support, thus seeming to reward politicians who made localist and sectional appeals (Cairns 1968; Jansen and Siaroff 2004).

Cairns's intervention anticipated the new wave of regional politics that arose in the 1970s in both Quebec and Western Canada. The initial catalyst for a serious discussion of voting system reform was the election of the separatist Parti Québécois (PQ) in Quebec in 1976. With the possibility that the country might break up, elements of Canada's political elite were prepared to examine how new institutional arrangements might help avoid that outcome. The Pépin-Robarts Task Force on Canadian Unity proposed a new semi-proportional voting system in 1979, one that would add a significant number of party list Members of Parliament (MPs) to those elected in single-member ridings to better reflect the regional strengths of different parties (Canada 1979). In the same year, political scientist William Irvine (1979) offered a more fully proportional version of the mixed system touted by Pépin-Robarts for many of the same reasons, namely better regional representation.

The events in Quebec were not the only spur to action on voting system reform. Nationally, declining representation for the federal Liberals in Western Canada, combined with the ongoing underrepresentation of the NDP, led to some discussion of the issue in 1978 and again in 1981. After the federal election in 1980, NDP leader Ed Broadbent gained some interest from Liberal Prime Minister Pierre Elliott Trudeau to pursue adding a small number of PR seats to the House of Commons. But neither national unity nor election results could push the issue any further. When Quebec voters rejected separation in 1980, the political pressure for any institutional reform visibly slackened. Meanwhile, Broadbent found his national proposals for voting system reform vetoed by his own provincial party elites in Western Canada, who benefited occasionally from the disproportionalities of SMP in British Columbia, Saskatchewan, and Manitoba (Blight 1981).

Consideration of voting system reform continued to emerge sporadically into the 1980s. The PQ in Quebec was committed to PR as party policy, a legacy of their dramatic underrepresentation in their first electoral contests in 1970 and 1973. After their re-election in 1981, the issue was delegated to a committee that eventually recommended an MMP form of PR, but opposition within the government caucus vetoed the proposal (Grenier 2002). Western Canadian grievances continued to fuel interest in institutional reform, though most interest settled on the Senate rather than the voting system (Canada 1985; McCormick, Manning, and Gibson 1981). Discussion of the voting system surfaced occasionally in the late 1980s and 1990s, linked mostly to proposals for Senate reform, but they went nowhere. A proposal to elect the senators by STV in the Charlottetown Accord did not survive a consultation with the premiers (Pierson et al. 1993, 327).

Where voting system reform did seem most likely to produce results during this period was in local politics, particularly in Vancouver and Winnipeg. Spatial issues played out at the municipal level in the late 1960s and early 1970s between suburbs and inner cities or between different neighbourhoods in terms of class, though not all focused their reform pressure on the voting system. In Montreal and Toronto, activists were able to stop various development projects by defeating the politicians who supported them (Magnusson and Sancton 1983). In other cases, like Winnipeg, a reforming provincial government sponsored a far-reaching local government reorganization to redress several historic grievances (Lightbody 1978b). In Vancouver, development and freeway issues led to the organization of a new urban political party—The Electors' Action Movement (TEAM)—that swept the mayoralty and council in the 1973 civic election. TEAM was also committed to replacing the city's "at large" multimember plurality voting system with a ward-based, SMP system, at least initially (Tennant 1980). Yet, despite considerable community organizing on the issue and six referenda over a span of three decades, various political forces were not able to reform the system (Pilon 2010a).

Concerns about national unity and regional/third-party underrepresentation at the federal level briefly put voting system reform on the agenda in the 1970s and early 1980s, but it did not lead to any changes. When Quebec voted to remain with Canada in 1980 and the West gained governing representation in the landslide federal Conservative majority in 1984, the twin crises fuelling the reform interest evaporated. The only reforms of the period occurred civically with the abolition of STV in Winnipeg and AV in Calgary, introduced by provincial governments less interested in voting systems than sweeping reforms to municipal governance.

Addressing the Democratic Deficit, 2000 to Present

A host of issues brought political reform back into the spotlight near the end of the twentieth century, though few singled out the voting system specifically. General complaints about a vague "democratic deficit" surfaced repeatedly. Critics pointed to a crisis of civic engagement with politics, specifically noting declining voter turnout and a seemingly broad public alienation from traditional political parties and politicians (Seidle 2002). These problems had been assessed in the far-reaching research reports of the Royal Commission on Electoral Reform and Party Financing (known colloquially as the Lortie

Commission) in 1991, but their proposed reforms (e.g., a new voter registration system) had done little to stem the criticisms (Canada 1991). Other reform suggestions—the reform of Parliament, a relaxation of party discipline, Senate reform—had failed to gain any traction with political elites. In light of such reform stasis, various political activists began calling for an examination of Canada's voting systems precisely to change the behaviour of the political parties. Between 1997 and 2000, three different organizations (Fair Voting BC, Mouvement démocratie nouvelle, and Fair Vote Canada) were founded in three different parts of the country (British Columbia, Quebec, and Ontario) to promote voting system reform.

Canadian activists were inspired by reforms occurring in other countries. The modern period of Western voting system reform arguably began with France in the mid-1980s. The governing left coalition government had gained power while challenging the emerging neoliberal economic consensus, but quickly split over just how to respond to it. The Socialist president turned to voting system reform as a strategy to remake his political coalition, allowing him to dump his left while reaching out to the centre. The strategy didn't work, and the voting system reform itself proved short-lived, but the essential elements of the drive to reform would be present in all subsequent efforts to remake voting systems in other countries (Pilon 2013, 194–97). In Japan and Italy, voting system reform emerged as a strategy adopted by neoliberal reformers to break the deadlock blocking economic reforms. However, in New Zealand, those opposed to neoliberal economics and the way it had apparently captured both major political parties latched onto voting system reform as a means of opening up the policy debate. Meanwhile, in the United Kingdom, Tony Blair used voting system reform at the sub- and supra-national level to divide and weaken regional competitors and further his control of his party's nomination process, all in the service of solidifying his ability to implement his neoliberal "third way" approach to social democracy (for more details, see Chapter 7 of Pilon 2013).

Ignoring the political and economic contexts that were fuelling them, reform activists in Canada simply took these international events as clear evidence that voting system change was possible. Grafting their reform proposals onto the various critiques of contemporary Canadian politics, reformers argued that a proportional voting system would improve political discourse, better represent what Canadians voted for, and improve the diversity of the representatives themselves (Fair Vote Canada 2003a). Several advocacy groups supported this latter theme, arguing that Canadian legislatures contained too few women and lagged in reflecting the racial and ethnic diversity of the country, particularly in urban areas (McPhedran and Speirs 2003). But arguably the key factor legitimizing this renewed focus on the voting system could be found in the results of the elections themselves throughout the 1990s, specifically the gap between the votes parties secured and the seats they won. From its formation in 2000, the nationally focused Fair Vote Canada would use every election result as an opportunity to hammer home such discrepancies (Fair Vote Canada 2003b, 2006). Still, public knowledge of or interest in the voting system remained low (Bricker and Redfern 2001).

Yet just a few years later the voting system had seemingly taken off as reform topic in Canada. In 2004 the Law Commission of Canada produced a report calling for Parliament to adopt a proportional system (Law Commission of Canada 2004). In 2005, Paul Martin's Liberal government agreed to allow a special committee of the House of Commons to investigate the issue and consult with the public. In the same period, five provinces were engaged in exploring whether or not to adopt a new voting system. Amid such a flurry of activity, the question of reform appeared to be not if but when Canadians would get a proportional voting system. Reform activists with organizations like Fair Vote Canada were also confident that Canadian voters would readily embrace a more proportional voting system, if given the chance. As such they lobbied to remove politicians from the equation and put the question directly to the public in binding referenda (Fair Vote Canada 2005).

Optimism about the inevitability of change or faith that instruments of "direct democracy" would clearly deliver reform soon appeared misplaced. Indeed, with the failure of the second STV referendum in British Columbia in 2009, the window for discussion of voting system reform anywhere in Canada rapidly closed. This was due primarily to the elite nature of the discussion on the issue. Despite some media attention and an attempt at grassroots organizing by voting system activists, public interest in or knowledge of voting systems remained low throughout the period (LeDuc 2011). Reformers had failed to reach the public directly. Instead, they had temporarily gained an audience with media and different political elites for reasons that differed considerably from the ones reformers presented to the public. The millennial revival of interest in the voting system in Canada was due largely to party system instability at both the federal and provincial level. It emerged within parties as one tentative response among many to their present insecurity and uncertainty amid rapidly changing circumstances. Even then, it was usually couched as just a possibility, as something for the party to explore, and then usually by those outside the leadership circles.

Reform at the Federal Level

At the federal level, the 1993 election introduced a competitive dynamic on the right of the political spectrum that would fuel some interest in voting system reform. In the 1993, 1997, and 2000 elections two right-wing parties vied for the same electorate, leading to vote-splits and losses for both. As both parties had geographic areas of strength and neither appeared willing to abandon the electoral field, right-wing supporters and activists across the country despaired that the Liberals would rule forever (Johnston 2001; Reid 2001). University of Calgary professor and Reform Party adviser Tom Flanagan promoted the majoritarian alternative vote as a strategy to allow right-wing voters to solve the problem (Flanagan 1999). Other right-wingers warmed to the idea of PR as a means of preserving pluralism on the right. Most on the right, however, advocated a merger of the two parties as the best solution. When that was accomplished in 2003, right-wing interest in voting system reform tapered off considerably.

The other federal parties faced different pressures to consider voting system reform. The federal NDP had previously exhibited some interest in the issue—not surprisingly given the party's perennial marginalization at the federal level. But attempts to speak to the issue in federal politics were usually checked by the Western provincial branches of the party that controlled the party's finances (and occasionally benefited from SMP). Instead, the party's strategy had always been to simply replace the Liberals as the alternative governing party at the federal level (see Blight 1981). The party's devastating result in the 1993 election—its weakest performance ever—seemed to expose how weak and unconvincing such a strategy was. Tensions arose throughout the 1990s as federal NDPers began to voice support for voting system reform despite opposition from provincial branches of the party. As such, the party's commitment to proportional voting remained weak at the turn of the century, even at the federal level, increasing somewhat only after federal election financing reforms effectively forced a separation of the provincial and federal wings of the party between 2004 and 2006 (Pilon, Ross, and Savage 2011). Under Jack Layton's leadership, the party's commitment to PR seemed to strengthen, with numerous attempts in the 2000s to raise the issue (MacDonald 2009; Wherry 2014). Surprisingly, as a regional party that benefited from SMP, the Bloc Québécois usually supported NDP motions for voting system reform, as did the Greens both outside Parliament and inside after their breakthrough in 2011.

As the beneficiaries of vote splitting on the right and the decline in support for the NDP, the federal Liberals were largely silent on the question of voting system reform throughout the 1990s. Occasionally this or that Liberal MP would voice support for the general principle (Bennett 2001), but on the whole Liberals defended SMP. Only when Paul Martin's Liberals were reduced to a minority government in 2004 and the party was wracked by internal divisions and embarrassing public scandals did they agree to examine the question at the urging of the NDP (Reid 2005). Various delays meant that Martin's Liberals were defeated before they could deliver on their promise (Canada 2005a, 2005b). The subsequent Harper Conservative minority government elected in 2006 honoured the Liberal commitment to examine the voting system but farmed out the public consultation to a think tank with a record of opposition to any reform (Cheadle 2007). Not surprisingly, their report in 2007 recommended sticking with the status quo (Compas/Frontier Centre for Public Policy 2007).

Since 2004, the NDP commitment to voting system reform appears to have strengthened. MPs have regularly used opposition days to forward motions calling for more proportional voting, and the issue has been featured more prominently in party literature and leadership debates (Wherry 2014). But the party's approach typically differed from the citizen assembly/referenda approaches pursued at the provincial level, arguing that politicians had an important expertise to contribute and that elected MPs should make the decision about whether or not to adopt a new system (Reid 2005). Some concerns arose that this new commitment to PR might fade with the party's breakthrough in 2011 when it became the Official Opposition and displaced the Liberals as the second-largest party in the House of Commons (Gillis 2011). Instead, the party came out with its strongest statement on the issue yet, promising that if elected to government in 2015 it would introduce a PR system during its term in time to be used in the following election (Bolen 2015). Since their historic fall into third place federally in 2011, the Liberals have also debated voting systems, but they remain divided between supporters of a majority "ranked ballot" approach and those favouring PR (Pilon 2015). Then, in the run-up to the federal election in 2015, Justin Trudeau announced that, if elected, his party would replace SMP with something else, but remained vague on just what it would be (Geddes 2015). After his surprise election victory, Trudeau reiterated the promise to replace SMP (Benzie 2015).

Reform at the Provincial Level

At the provincial level, the events that catalyzed interest in voting system reform took several different forms. The most obvious were a series of anomalous election results—wrong winners, lopsided victories, rapid party system change—that had the effect of drawing public attention to the voting system and mobilizing some party activists to consider possible alternatives. But behind the scenes, party elites had other reasons to take voting system reform seriously. In British Columbia, Ontario, and Quebec, the provincial Liberal parties had research that suggested each party faced an electoral disadvantage vis-à-vis their main rival in terms of converting their popular vote into seats (Massicotte 2006, 8). Indeed, both BC and Quebec Liberals had lost a provincial campaign to "wrong winners" in the 1990s for precisely that reason. Thus, even though in both cases Liberal parties got more votes than their main rival, the "wrong winner" managed to win more seats. Meanwhile, in PEI and New Brunswick, Conservative governments were concerned that a trend where opposition parties consistently gained only marginal representation despite considerable levels of support would compromise the legitimacy of the legislature and the actions it tried to take. They too thought some form of voting system reform might address this issue (Cross 2005).

British Columbia

The provincial revival began with British Columbia's anomalous 1996 election result, where the BC Liberals lost despite gaining more votes than the re-elected NDP. The stunning defeat led to significant internal party debate about how to build a bigger coalition, one that could entice the remaining populist right-wingers to join them. A package of democratic reform initiatives—including a proposal to examine alternative voting systems—was put together before the 2001 election (Pilon, forthcoming). Meanwhile, NDP attempts to broker disputes between environmentalists, resource companies, and their workers created a rift in their electoral coalition, bolstering support for the provincial Green Party. As the NDP weathered repeated scandal, resignations, and a largely hostile media, it too claimed to be interested in voting system reform (BC NDP 2001). As the next election approached, it appeared that all parties—BC Liberals, NDP, and Greens—were prepared to consider a new way to vote.

The 2001 provincial election featured another anomalous result, though with a different victim. The BC Liberals won 57 per cent of the popular vote and 77 of the province's 79 seats, while the NDP was reduced to just 2 seats. The Greens gained 12 per cent of the vote (up from 2 per cent in the previous election) but no representation. The results once again underlined seemingly perverse workings of the voting system in translating votes into seats. The governing Liberals moved quickly on several of their democratic reform promises, though the voting system reform issue was delayed until the government passed the halfway mark of their term. The BC Citizens' Assembly (BCCA) comprised randomly selected citizens who studied, debated, devised, and then proposed a new voting system for the province (Warren and Pearse 2008). As promised, the government agreed to put the proposal before the public in a referendum that would accompany the next provincial election. Premier Gordon Campbell was lauded by academics and pundits alike as a champion of democratic reform for sponsoring the BCCA and putting its STV proposal to the public (Pilon, forthcoming). But this ignored the government's fine print on the referendum process. For instance, after spending nearly $5 million on the BCCA process, the government refused to fund a serious public education campaign to let the public know what they would be voting on. In addition, the government insisted that reform would require a super-majority to pass—60 per cent of the total votes cast and a majority in 60 per cent of the ridings—despite the fact that previous voting system reforms in British Columbia had passed with a simple majority (Pilon 2010a). Confident that the public cared little about voting systems, few commentators thought the referendum would pass.

The referendum results surprised political elites—nearly 58 per cent of voters endorsed the BCCA's proposal. STV supporters quickly demanded that the government introduce the reform in light of such strong support (Gibson 2005), but critics complained that the public didn't understand what they were voting for and were simply using the referendum to strike a blow against the political class (Simpson 2005; Spector 2005). Survey research seemed to confirm that few voters understood what STV was or how it worked, with many voting in favour simply because they had positive feelings toward the BCCA (Cutler and Fournier 2008). But surveys also confirmed some interesting partisan trends. In 2005, STV gained strong support from Green and NDP voters, with a considerable number of Liberals also supporting change (Carty, Cutler, and Fournier 2009). Given the instability in BC's party system over the previous decade this was not surprising—supporters of all parties were worried about how SMP might wrong-foot their party, again. Meanwhile, the parties themselves had said little publicly about the BCCA or the referendum during the 2005 election campaign for fear of alienating the public, leaving their supporters with few partisan cues about how to vote.

The government would not budge on introducing STV but did agree to hold another referendum in 2009, this time with funding for public education. STV supporters celebrated, thinking they had four years to come up with another 2 per cent in support and win. But 2009 reversed the results of 2005—now only 39 per cent of voters were prepared to embrace change. Several factors contributed to this result. First, the public funding for education was ineffective, ending up in the hands of pro- and anti-STV campaigns that mostly attacked each other. Survey work would confirm that the public remained largely ignorant about the referendum options or the issues germane to their decision (Carty et al. 2009). Second, both Liberal and NDP politicians were less reticent about sharing their views about STV in 2009, with many clearly stating their opposition to change (Pilon 2010b). Finally, the election results of 2005, which had signalled a return to "normal" two-party competition, had gone some way to calming the fears of Liberal and NDP partisans. Voting system reform no longer seemed necessary as a kind of insurance against anomalous election results.

Quebec

Quebec had a similar starting point for its most recent explorations of voting system reform: an anomalous election result. In the 1998 provincial election, the Quebec Liberal Party got the most votes but lost to the Parti Québécois. But the previous election had also produced highly unrepresentative results: the Liberals trailed the PQ in 1994 by less than 1 per cent but won 30 fewer seats. As a result, several community groups organized publicly in the late 1990s to demand some form of PR be introduced provincially (Cliche 1999; Mouvement démocratie nouvelle 2014). By 2001 all three major parties claimed to be committed to reforming the voting system. In December 2001 the Standing Committee on Institutions of the National Assembly embarked on an exploration of the voting system, hearing from various experts about different possible models for reform, with many endorsing some form of compensatory additional member system. These pressures led the PQ government to agree to establish an Estates-General focused on the voting system. After much citizen and expert consultation, they too recommended the province adopt a compensatory voting system with some element of PR (Quebec 2003). However, three days after the report was submitted, the PQ called a provincial election—a contest they ultimately lost. Still, the momentum for reform survived as the new Liberal administration announced that they would reform the voting system during their term in office (Charest 2003).

Liberal interest in a new voting system was undoubtedly motivated by the party's struggle to regain power in the 1990s. The problem was their vote was too regionally concentrated, resulting in huge wins in some ridings and narrow losses in others. However, only four months later it was clear that the government's zeal for reform had weakened when it announced that a reformed voting system would not be in place for the next election. The Liberals did present a bill in December 2004 proposing a less-than-proportional mixed system of voting (Massicotte 2006, 21). Critics commended the government for bringing forward a concrete proposal but were unhappy that the system would not achieve more proportional results (Mouvement démocratie nouvelle 2004). A Select Committee on the Election Act was formed in June 2005 to review the legislation, and it in turn established a

Citizens' Committee to respond to the legislation and the work of the committee. Again, a significant amount of public and expert consultation took place. In April 2006, the Citizens' Committee presented their report, essentially arguing that the government's proposal was not proportional enough. A month later the Select Committee made its report, agreeing that a mixed compensatory system was desirable but admitting that committee members could not agree on precisely how proportional it should be (L'Écuyer and Lemay 2006). In opening a new session of the legislature in March 2006, Charest again underlined his government's commitment to introducing a new voting system with a "proportional element" (Charest 2006).

By the fall of 2006 opposition to reforming the voting system from within the Liberal caucus ground the process to a halt. Bolstering this position was strong opposition from local government officials who worried that PR would weaken the influence of regional interests (Cliche 2007). In December 2006, the government referred the issue to the province's chief electoral officer for input. After a year of study, his report basically supported the more proportional options promoted by the critics of the government's initial bill (Quebec 2007). However, while producing his report the political dynamics blocking reform appeared to shift considerably. In a provincial election held in March 2007, the Liberal government was reduced to a minority, thus at least theoretically increasing the chances that opposition parties could pressure the government to act on its promise to reform the voting system. As the three major parties elected in 2007 had previously publicly committed to some form of compensatory PR, reform seemed possible.

That reform did not occur can most likely be attributed to the increasing instability in the party system and some serious miscalculations on the part of a few key politicians. The rise of the Action démocratique du Québec (ADQ) did not please either the Liberals or the PQ, whose interest in voting system reform was primarily to bolster their own electoral position, not increase the competitive dynamic of the political system. In the late 1990s, the PQ thought the issue could corral a few more floating voters into their sovereignty camp, thus their party program commitment to a new voting system in 2001 was fairly straightforward. By 2006 the party was hedging its bets, suggesting that a new voting system would have to wait until after sovereignty was achieved. In 2011, the commitment to voting system reform was removed from the party program altogether. Meanwhile, the taste of power between 2003 and 2007 had tempered Liberal enthusiasm for voting system reform—Charest's inaugural speech as head of a minority government in 2007 failed to mention it (Mouvement démocratie nouvelle 2014).

Only the recent third party—the ADQ—had remained steadfast in their support, at least until the results of the 2007 election came in. Though born of frustration with the Quebec Liberal Party, the ADQ often drew protest votes from across the political spectrum, gaining a seat in the legislature in 1994 and moderately increasing its vote share in subsequent elections in 1998 and 2003. But in the 2007 contest its support spiked dramatically, jumping to 31 per cent of the popular vote, up from 18 per cent previously. More importantly, the surge in support allowed it to surpass the PQ as the Official Opposition. Now the party that had long been the strongest advocate of PR suddenly seemed less interested (Cliche 2007). Instead of using the minority government situation to secure voting system reform, the ADQ tried to solidify its position as the second party and potential alternative government to the Liberals. The strategy backfired when Charest called a snap election in December 2008 and regained his governing majority, while ADQ support slipped back to its traditional levels and the PQ returned to second place and the Official Opposition.

Post-2008 attempts by activist groups to get the reform moving failed to gain any traction with the major parties: both the Liberals and the PQ now refused to endorse voting system reform. Even the ADQ could not bring its historical commitment to PR with it in 2012 when it merged with the new third party—Coalition Avenir Québec (CAQ). At that point, only the small left-wing Québec solidaire continued to champion a more proportional voting system. Attempts to dislodge the voting system via various court challenges also failed (Mouvement démocratie nouvelle 2014). However, after losing ground in the 2014 election, the CAQ also called for a new voting system (Croteau 2015).

Ontario

Interest in voting system reform first emerged in the Ontario NDP in the late 1990s and then in the Ontario Liberal Party at the turn of century, both developments related to the dramatic party system changes witnessed in the province over the previous decade and half. The Ontario PCs' 42-year dynasty in government ended abruptly in 1985 when a Liberal minority, supported by the NDP, pushed them out of office. The Liberals later turned that into a majority in 1987, but then shockingly lost office to the NDP in 1990. The NDP term of government proved tumultuous, as the party found itself unable to fulfill the expectations of its own traditional supporters or the vote switchers that had help propel them into office, especially given the cuts to transfer payments for social programs from the federal government. The backlash against the party helped fuel a populist rebooting of the PCs under Mike Harris. As Harris enacted radical slash-and-burn cuts to government, with apparent public support (at least at first), both New Democrat and Liberal parties began to consider whether voting system reforms would benefit them.

For New Democrats, PR began bubbling up in various branches of the party in the mid- to late 1990s, first from those unhappy with the party's electoral strategy of moving closer to the political centre, but later from some of the "modernizers" as well as a way of disciplining its supporters and making coalitions with other parties more effective. Gilles Bisson and former Bob Rae cabinet minister Tony Silipo began raising the issue in caucus and with the party in 1998, and this was later passed as party policy in 1999 (Pilon 2004, 251–53). For Liberals, voting system reform emerged from policy workshops that preceded the 2002 provincial election. The party created five themes to campaign on, including democratic reform. Dalton McGuinty even appeared at a Fair Vote Canada event in 2003, publicly promising to sponsor a citizens' assembly on the issue and hold a referendum on a new proposed voting system if one was forthcoming (Pilon 2004, 256). Thus Liberal support amounted to agreeing to a process to consider reform; they did not endorse change or an alternative voting system. The SMP system had clearly not worked in their favour—they had barely gained office in the previous half-century despite nearly always being the main opposition. But as public opposition to the Harris PCs appeared to increase, Liberals were feeling confident that the coming election was winnable. Committing to a process allowed the party to claim the populist democratic reform mantle, and hopefully draw any voters keen on it without necessarily having to act on it.

After their election victory in 2003, the Liberals delivered on their promise of mounting a citizens' assembly and holding a referendum on the voting system. However, as in British Columbia, the fine print doomed the exercise to failure. Drawing from the BC experience, the Ontario Liberals also insisted on a super-majority rule for the referendum to pass, failed to educate the public about the vote or its substance, and blocked the parties from campaigning on the issue. In the end, Ontario's citizens' assembly recommended the province adopt an MMP form of PR. The media were relentless in their opposition to changing the voting system, discrediting the citizens' assembly and their work and failing to present a balanced view of the referenda or its choices during the 2007 provincial campaign (Pilon 2007, 103; 2009). Surveys demonstrated that the public was largely unaware a referendum was taking place, let alone what it was about (Cutler and Fournier 2007). With low information, only 37 per cent of voters in Ontario endorsed the change. With the result, the newly re-elected Dalton McGuinty announced that voting system reform was no longer a priority for his government, while the NDP would remain at least nominally supportive of the issue.

Prince Edward Island and New Brunswick

Voting system reform emerged in Prince Edward Island and New Brunswick from different parties and for different reasons than in other parts of the country. Conservatives rather than Liberals were the driving force in examining the voting system and were motivated by a different kind of anomalous election result. In both provinces, the previous few decades had produced several elections where the opposition parties barely achieved any representation in the legislatures. Indeed, in 1986 the opposition parties in New Brunswick were shut out entirely, despite gaining 40 per cent of the popular vote. The two provinces also chose to explore the question in different ways, eschewing the publicly driven citizens' assembly and Estates-General models used in other provinces for a more traditional expert-driven commission approach. Both processes produced recommendations for adopting the MMP form of PR and putting the choice before the public in a referendum.

Voting system reform first got a hearing in PEI as part of the reorganization of the province's electoral map in 1994. A court challenge had struck down the old map and its two-member district system that had survived since Confederation. The commission tasked with creating a new single-member riding system did hear from several participants that a proportional voting system would be a better option (Prince Edward Island 2003, 25). A special committee of the legislature in 2000 that reviewed the Election Act also recommended exploring PR (26). The legislature then directed the province's chief electoral officer to study and report back. This report (Prince Edward Island 2001) informed the government's decision to appoint a one-man commission in January 2003. In December of that year it recommended an MMP form of PR. The commissioner also called for further public consultation, perhaps in the form of a citizens' assembly, to work out the details of the model and a referendum process so the proposal could be put to a vote (Prince Edward Island 2003, 98–100). A year later the government chose instead to appoint a 10-member commission, which reported in May 2005 with the detailed model of an MMP voting system, the rules for a referendum, and the question that would be put to the public (Lea 2006).

At that point, under pressure from his caucus, the premier departed from the recommendations of his commissions and moved to hold the referendum in the fall of 2005, a nonelection year, with a super-majority rule for any change to pass (the second commission had recommended 50 per cent plus 1), no serious attempt to educate the public about the issue, and with only a fraction of the island's traditional voting locations open (Lea 2006). PEI political scientist Peter McKenna (2006) observed that it "looked like the entire electoral reform process—from start to finish—was more an exercise in public relations and political symbolism than an honest and forthright effort at purposeful and fundamental electoral reform on PEI." Not surprisingly, turnout for the referendum (unlike regular provincial elections) was low—only about 30 per cent—and the MMP proposal gained only 36 per cent of the vote.

New Brunswick appointed an eight-person commission in December 2003 to examine a host of issues related to modernizing the province's electoral system. A year later they submitted a report covering a broad range of topics and recommended reforms, including a proposal to adopt an MMP form of PR (New Brunswick 2004). The government responded in June 2006, agreeing to hold a referendum on the voting system proposal concurrent with the next provincial election, due in May 2008 (New Brunswick 2006). But a snap election in the fall of 2006 led to the defeat of the government before a referendum could be held. The new government offered its own responses to the commission's report in June 2007, arguing that reforming the voting system was too radical and opting instead to simply improve the existing system through better districting and by creating incentives for parties to diversify their candidates running for office (New Brunswick 2007).

The failure to carry out the different commission recommendations in New Brunswick and Prince Edward Island suggests that the proposals proved to be too radical for their sponsors. The Conservative premiers were looking for a way to secure a reliable representation of the opposition, not necessarily shift away from single-party majority governments or make their systems more competitive. When their commissions exceeded such modest expectations, caucus opposition and political self-interest subverted the process. Still, when the provincial elections in PEI and Nova Scotia produced anomalous results in 2015, the premiers of both provinces volunteered to examine different methods of voting as one response to public complaints, though expert commentators were not optimistic (McKenna 2015).

Reform at the Municipal Level

Municipal voting system reform since 2000 had been, until recently, mostly restricted to a debate between single-member and multimember plurality or a "ward" versus an "at large" system. Vancouver's seemingly never-ending debate over its voting system culminated in a stand-alone referendum on the issue in 2004. In the past, the results of different plebiscites on the issue had been marred by disagreement about the proper voting threshold to effect change and disputes between different political parties and levels of government (Berger 2004, 13–17). But by 2004 the referendum was sponsored by its long-time advocate, the Coalition of Progressive Electors (COPE) slate (which had won the mayoralty and control of council in 2002), without interference from the provincial government and with a threshold of just 50 per cent plus 1 to make the change. Yet the initiative failed, gaining only 46 per cent of the vote. COPE had to bear some of the blame for the loss—the decision to hold the referendum in a nonelection year pretty much ensured low voter turnout, particularly among their core working class and poor electorate. On the other hand, as was apparent in the previous referendum on the issue in the 1990s, the old consensus favouring wards as the sole alternative to the at large system had broken down, with some reformers now demanding a proportional system for the city (Tennant and West 1998a, 1998b). The issue of wards versus at large has also emerged in a few Ontario towns since 2000, notably Niagara Falls and Oshawa (Spiteri 2014; Zochodne 2014).

Perhaps the most surprising development at the local level was the grassroots campaign to change the voting system for Toronto city council from its traditional SMP system to the majoritarian alternative vote, dubbed "ranked ballots" by its promoters. The issue gained traction against a backdrop of ongoing mayoral misbehaviour on the part of the city's populist right-wing mayor, Rob Ford. The argument that a ranked ballot would ensure that the anti-Ford vote in any future election would not split between rival candidates was taken up approvingly by most political commentators and endorsed by media outlets like the *Globe and Mail* and *Toronto Star* (*Globe and Mail* 2014; *Toronto Star* 2013). Ranked ballot organizers secured high-level meetings with both municipal and provincial politicians, culminating in a promise from the premier to pass legislation allowing local councils to adopt ranked ballots (Benzie 2014), with the province preparing enabling legislation over the summer of 2015. Interestingly, with Rob Ford sidelined back to a council seat and his brother's loss in the mayoral contest, the pressure on Toronto city council to change its voting system seemed to slacken as the council suddenly (and surprisingly, to many observers) voted against adopting ranked ballots in October 2015 (*Toronto Star* 2015).

The modern period of voting system reform has been the most widespread the country has ever seen in terms of jurisdiction and geography. Five provinces invested considerable time and resources into researching the issue, and all produced reports that recommended dropping SMP in favour of some form of PR. At the national level, the voting system gained attention (at least in terms of debate) that it had not seen since the 1920s. But nowhere did reform actually occur. This is because the publicly stated rationales for reform—the democratic deficit, bettering demographic representation, making votes count—were not the real forces pushing consideration of new voting systems. The real impetus behind moving the issue up the agenda was party system instability at both the federal and provincial levels. And when the instability dissipated, or the price of reform appeared too high, politicians lost interest or put the brakes on the reform process.

Conclusion

Canada's voting system is a largely foreign device to most of its citizens, despite their regular interaction with it at every electoral opportunity. As William Irvine once noted, "Election results in Canada are usually accepted, if only because few Canadians bother to think that the results could have been other than what they were." Former BC politician and indefatigable STV proponent Nick Loenen (1995) cited this quote in an early foray into the most recent era of voting system reform as a call to educate the public and rally them to demand reform. Two decades later, despite gaining some attention from media and policymakers and securing four referenda on the issue, the reformers' efforts must be judged as a failure. Educating the public about voting systems and mobilizing them to action proved too difficult. The reformers were usually part-time activists, poorly resourced, and not well connected to the traditional elite channels of Canadian political discourse and organization. Meanwhile, their opponents—typically the media and the mainstream political parties—had considerable resources and connections to deploy when studied indifference wasn't enough. In the end, reformers could not do an end run around what the governing political parties wanted—and in each case what these parties wanted always proved to be most decisive.

Canada's traditional plurality voting system has been challenged throughout Canadian history, but rarely successfully. The character of the challenge has been crucial. The themes of reformers have changed, from demands for particular kinds of representation in the early twentieth century, to better regional representation in the 1970s and 1980s, to a remedy for the country's democratic deficit post-2000. But underlying the public rhetoric has always been party interests. Only in the first reform era would those interests feel threatened enough to agree to voting system reforms, and those threats involved competition from political forces perceived as economically threatening—not merely to this or that entity but to the political system as whole. By contrast, regionalism or democratic malaise or even considerable party system instability were storms to be weathered. They were not threatening enough to secure changes to the voting system.

Suggested Readings

Blais, André, ed. 2008. *To Keep or to Change First Past the Post?* Oxford: Oxford University Press. http://dx.doi.org/10.1093/acprof:oso/9780199539390.001.0001

Cairns, Alan C. 1968. "The Electoral System and the Party System in Canada, 1921–1965." *Canadian Journal of Political Science* 1 (1): 55–80. http://dx.doi.org/10.1017/S0008423900035228

Courtney, John. 2004. *Elections.* Vancouver: University of British Columbia Press.

Pilon, Dennis. 2007. *The Politics of Voting: Reforming Canada's Electoral System.* Toronto: Emond Montgomery.

References

Ahmed, Amel. 2013. *Democracy and the Politics of Electoral System Choice: Engineering Electoral Dominance.* Cambridge: Cambridge University Press.

Bennett, Carolyn. 2001. "Three Lenses for Judging Electoral Reform." *Policy Options* 22 (July–August): 61–5.

Benzie, Robert. 2014. "Ranked Ballot a Priority for 2018 Civic Elections, Kathleen Wynne Says." *Toronto Star,* September 30.

Benzie, Robert. 2015. "Electoral Reform Looms for Canada, Justin Trudeau Promises." *Toronto Star,* October 21.

Berger, Thomas R. 2004. *A City of Neighbourhoods: Report of the 2004 Vancouver Electoral Reform Commission.* Vancouver: Vancouver Electoral Reform Commission.

BC NDP. 2001. "Reform of BC's Electoral System: An Idea Whose Time Has Come." Committee to Review the Electoral Process. August.

Blais, André. 1991. "The Debate over Electoral Systems." *International Political Science Review* 12 (3): 239–60. http://dx.doi.org/10.1177/019251219101200304

Blight, Pat. 1981. *Report on Proportional Representation.* BC NDP Provincial Council Committee.

Bolen, Michael. 2015. "Mulcair Promises Proportional Representation if NDP Wins Next Election." *Huffington Post Canada,* January 2.

Bricker, Darrell, and Martin Redfern. 2001. "Canadian Perspectives on the Voting System." *Policy Options* 22 (July/August): 22–24.

Cairns, Alan C. 1968. "The Electoral System and the Party System in Canada, 1921–1965." *Canadian Journal of Political Science* 1 (1): 55–80. http://dx.doi.org/10.1017/S0008423900035228

Canada. 1979. *The Task Force on Canadian Unity: A Future Together: Observations and Recommendations.* Ottawa: The Queen's Printer.

Canada. 1985. *Royal Commission on the Economic Union and Development Prospects for Canada Report.* Volume III. Ottawa: Minister of Supply and Services Canada.

Canada. 1991. *Royal Commission on Electoral Reform and Party Financing Final Report.* Ottawa: Minister of Supply and Services Canada.

Canada. 2005a. "Forty-Third Report." Standing Committee on Procedure and House Affairs. Parliament of Canada.

Canada. 2005b. "Government Response to the Forty-Third Report of the Standing Committee on Procedure and House Affairs." Parliament of Canada.

Carty, R. Kenneth, Fred Cutler, and Patrick Fournier. 2009. "Who Killed BC-STV?" *The Tyee,* July 8.

Charest, Jean. 2003. "Address by the Prime Minister of Quebec, Jean Charest, on the Occasion of the Inauguration of the 37th Legislature." June 4.

Charest, Jean. 2006. "Notes for an Address by the Premier of Quebec on the Occasion of the Inauguration of the 2nd Session of the 37th Legislature National Assembly." March 14.

Cheadle, Bruce. 2007. "Tories Slammed over Vote Reform Contract." *Toronto Star,* March 22.

Cliche, Paul. 1999. *Pour réduire le déficit démocratique au Québec: le scrutin proportionnel.* Montreal: Les éditions du Renouveau québécois.

Cliche, Paul. 2007. "La réforme du mode de scrutin dans les limbes." *L'Aut' Journal,* July 17.

Colomer, Josep M. 2005. "It's Parties That Choose Electoral Systems (or, Duverger's Laws Upside Down)." *Political Studies* 53 (1): 1–21. http://dx.doi.org/10.1111/j.1467-9248.2005.00514.x

Compas/Frontier Centre for Public Policy. 2007. "Public Consultations on Canada's Democratic Institutions and Practices. A Report for the Privy Council Office." September 10.

Courtney, John. 1999. "Electoral Reform and Canada's Parties." In *Making Every Vote Count: Reassessing Canada's Voting System,* edited by Henry Milner, 91–100. Peterborough, ON: Broadview.

Courtney, John C. 2001. *Commissioned Ridings: Designing Canada's Electoral Districts.* Montreal: McGill-Queen's University Press.

Cross, William. 2005. "The Rush to Electoral Reform in the Canadian Provinces: Why Now?" *Representation* 41 (2): 75–84. http://dx.doi.org/10.1080/00344890508523292

Croteau, Martin. 2015. "François Legault veut réformer le mode de scrutin." *La Presse,* April 27.

Cutler, Fred, and Patrick Fournier. 2007. "Why Ontarians Said No to MMP." *Globe and Mail,* October 25.

Cutler, Fred, and Patrick Fournier. 2008. "Did the Citizens' Assemblies Affect Voting in BC and Ontario?" Paper prepared for "When Citizens Decide: The Challenge of Large Scale Public Engagement," Centre for the Study of Democratic Institutions at the University of British Columbia, May 1–2.

Duverger, Maurice. (1954) 1963. *Political Parties.* Translated by Barbara North and Robert North. New York: Wiley.

Fair Vote Canada. 2003a. "Can Fair Voting Systems Really Make a Difference? Research on Proportional Representation." December.

Fair Vote Canada. 2003b. "Dubious Democracy: Report on Provincial Elections 1980–2000." September.

Fair Vote Canada. 2005. "Proportional Representation in British Columbia, New Brunswick, Prince Edward Island, and Quebec: Assessments and Recommendations on Proposed Systems in Four Provinces." March.

Fair Vote Canada. 2006. "Dubious Democracy: Report on Federal Elections 1980–2004." January.

Flanagan, Tom. 1999. "The Alternative Vote: An Electoral System for Canada." In *Making Every Vote Count: Reassessing Canada's Voting System,* edited by Henry Milner, 85–90. Peterborough, ON: Broadview.

Geddes, John. 2015. "Can Justin Trudeau Fix the Vote with Electoral Reform?" *Maclean's,* June 27.

Gibson, Gordon. 2005. "Let's Get on with Electoral Reform." *Globe and Mail,* May 27, A19.

Gillis, Charlie. 2011. "Is Democratic Reform Dying Out? First-Past-the-Post Systems Are Proving Remarkably Durable." *Maclean's,* May 17.

Globe and Mail. 2014. "Ontario Points the Way with Ranked Ballots Experiment." October 2.

Grenier, André. 2002. "Le mode de scrutin: quelques jalons historiques." *Bulletin: Quebec Assemblée Nationale* 31–3 (4): 11–17.

Hermans, Ferdinand A. (1941) 1972. *Democracy or Anarchy? A Study of Proportional Representation.* New York: Johnson Reprint Corp.

Irvine, William P. 1979. *Does Canada Need a New Electoral System?* Kingston: Institute of Intergovernmental Relations, Queen's University.

Jansen, Harold, and Alan Siaroff. 2004. "Regionalism and Party Systems: Evaluating Proposals to Reform Canada's Electoral System." In *Steps Toward Making Every Vote Count: Electoral System Reform in Canada and Its Provinces,* edited by Henry Milner, ed. 43–63. Peterborough, ON: Broadview.

Johnston, Richard. 2001. "A Conservative Case for Electoral Reform." *Policy Options* (July–August): 7–14.

Katz, Richard. 1997. *Democracy and Elections.* New York: Oxford University Press. http://dx.doi.org/10.1093/acprof:oso/9780195044294.001.0001

Kerr, D.G.G. 1970. "The 1867 Elections in Ontario: The Rules of the Game." *Canadian Historical Review* 51 (4): 369–85. http://dx.doi.org/10.3138/CHR-051-04-01

Law Commission of Canada. 2004. *Voting Counts: Electoral Reform for Canada.* Ottawa: Department of Public Works and Government Services.

Laycock, David. 1990. *Populism and Democratic Thought in the Canadian Prairies, 1910 to 1945.* Toronto: University of Toronto Press.

Lea, Jennie. 2006. "The Prince Edward Island Plebiscite on Electoral Reform." *Canadian Parliamentary Review* 29 (1): 4–8.

L'Écuyer, Charlotte, and Martin Lemay. 2006. "The Select Committee on the Election Act and Reform of the Voting System in Quebec." *Canadian Parliamentary Review* 29 (3): 4–8.

LeDuc, Lawrence. 2011. "Electoral Reform and Direct Democracy in Canada: When Citizens Become Involved." *West European Politics* 34 (3): 551–67. http://dx.doi.org/10.1080/01402382.2011.555983

Leone, Rob. (2006–07). "Letter to the Editor: Keep Democracy out of the Court." *Canadian Parliamentary Review* 29 (4): 57–58.

Lightbody, James. 1978a. "Electoral Reform in Local Government: The Case of Winnipeg." *Canadian Journal of Political Science* 11 (2): 307–32. http://dx.doi.org/10.1017/S0008423900041111

Lightbody, James. 1978b. "The Reform of a Metropolitan Government: The Case of Winnipeg, 1971." *Canadian Public Policy* 4 (4): 489–504. http://dx.doi.org/10.2307/3549974

Lijphart, Arend. 1977. *Democracy in Plural Societies: A Comparative Exploration.* New Haven, CT: Yale University Press.

Lijphart, Arend. 1994. *Electoral Systems and Party Systems.* Oxford: Oxford University Press. http://dx.doi.org/10.1093/acprof:oso/9780198273479.001.0001

Lijphart, Arend. 1999. *Patterns of Democracy: Government Forms & Performance in Thirty-Six Countries.* New Haven, CT: Yale University Press.

Lipset, Seymour Martin, and Stein Rokkan. 1967. "Cleavage Structures, Party Systems and Voter Alignments: An Introduction." In *Party Systems and Voter Alignments: Cross-National Perspectives,* edited by Seymour Martin Lipset and Stein Rokkan, 1–64. New York: Free Press.

Loenen, Nick. 1995. "Proportional Representation Is a Must." *Canadian Parliamentary Review* 18 (2): 8–12.

MacDonald, L. Ian. 2009. "A Conversation with Jack Layton." *Policy Options* (October): 8.

Magnusson, Warren, and Andrew Sancton. 1983. *City Politics in Canada.* Toronto: University of Toronto Press.

Mair, Peter. 1991. "'The Electoral Universe of Small Parties in Postwar Western Europe." In *Small Parties in Western Europe: Comparative and National Perspectives,* edited by Ferdinand Müller-Rommel and Geoffrey Pridham, 41–70. London: Sage.

Mair, Peter. 1992. "The Question of Electoral Reform." *New Left Review* I (July–August): 194.

Massicotte, Louis. 2006. "Electoral Reform in Canada and its Provinces." Paper presented to the Plurality and Multiround Elections Conference, Montreal, June 17–18.

Massicotte, Louis, and André Blais. 1999. "Mixed Electoral Systems: A Conceptual and Empirical Survey." *Electoral Studies* 18 (3): 341–66. http://dx.doi.org/10.1016/S0261-3794(98)00063-8

McCormick, Peter, Ernest C. Manning, and Gordon Gibson. 1981. *Regional Representation: The Canadian Partnership.* Calgary: Canada West Foundation.

McKay, Ian. 2000. "The Liberal Order Framework: A Prospectus for a Reconnaissance of Canadian History." *Canadian Historical Review* 81: 617–45. http://dx.doi.org/10.3138/CHR.81.4.617

McKenna, Peter. 2006. "Opting Out of Electoral Reform—Why PEI Chose the Status Quo." *Policy Options* (June): 58–61.

McKenna, Peter. 2015. "Electoral Reform Redux a Charade in PEI." *The Chronicle Herald,* July 27.

McPhedran, Marilou, and Rosemary Speirs. 2003. *Reducing the Democratic Deficit through Equality-Based Electoral Reform.* Equal Voice submission to the Law Commission of Canada. Spring.

Mouvement démocratie nouvelle. 2004. "Gouvernement Charest le système de vote de la proposition est une bonne base de discussion décevante." Press release. December 16.

Mouvement démocratie nouvelle. 2014. "Historical Milestones 1998–2012." http://www.democratie-nouvelle.qc.ca/jalons-historiques/

New Brunswick. 2004. *Commission on Legislative Democracy Final Report and Recommendations.*

New Brunswick. 2006. "Province Releases Response to Commission on Legislative Democracy Report." Executive Council, June 20.

New Brunswick. 2007. "Government Response to Committee on Legislative Democracy Report." Executive Council Office, June 28.

Norris, Pippa. 2004. *Electoral Engineering: Voting Rules and Political Behavior.* Cambridge: Cambridge University Press. http://dx.doi.org/10.1017/CBO9780511790980

O'Leary, Cornelius. 1962. *The Elimination of Corrupt Practices in British Elections, 1868–1911.* London: Clarendon Press.

Paltiel, Khayyam Zev. 1966. *Studies in Canadian Party Finance: Committee on Election Expenses.* Ottawa: Queen's Printer.

Phillips, H.C.J. 1976. "Challenges to the Voting System in Canada, 1874–1974." Doctoral dissertation, University of Western Ontario, London, Ontario.

Pierson, Ruth Roach, Marjorie Griffin Cohen, Paula Bourne, and Philinda Masters. 1993. *Strong Voices,* vol. I. *Canadian Women's Issues.* Toronto: James Lorimer & Company.

Pilon, Dennis. 2004. "The Uncertain Path of Democratic Renewal in Ontario." In *Steps toward Making Every Vote Count,* edited by Henry Milner, 249–66. Peterborough, ON: Broadview Press.

Pilon, Dennis. 2006. "Explaining Voting System Reform in Canada, 1873–1960." *Journal of Canadian Studies* 40 (3): 135–61.

Pilon, Dennis. 2007. *The Politics of Voting.* Toronto: Emond Montgomery.

Pilon, Dennis. 2009. "Investigating Media as a Deliberative Space: Newspaper Opinions about Voting Systems in the Ontario Provincial Referendum." *Canadian Political Science Review* 3 (3): 1–23.

Pilon, Dennis. 2010a. "Democracy, BC Style." In *British Columbia Politics and Government,* edited by Michael Howlett, Dennis Pilon, and Tracy Summerville, 87–108. Toronto: Emond Montgomery.

Pilon, Dennis. 2010b. "The 2005 and 2009 Referenda on Voting System Change in British Columbia." *Canadian Political Science Review* 4 (2–3): 73–89.

Pilon, Dennis. 2013. *Wrestling with Democracy: Voting Systems as Politics in the Twentieth Century West.* Toronto: University of Toronto Press.

Pilon, Dennis. 2015. "Electoral Reform: Here's Your Evidence, Mr. Trudeau." *Inroads* 37 (Summer/Fall): 51–60.

Pilon, Dennis. Forthcoming. "Assessing Gordon Campbell's Uneven Democratic Legacy in British Columbia." In *The Campbell Revolution: Power and Politics in British Columbia from 2001 to 2011,* edited by Tracy Summerville and Jason Lacharite.

Pilon, Dennis, Stephanie Ross, and Larry Savage. 2011. "Solidarity Revisited: Organized Labour and the New Democratic Party." *Canadian Political Science Review* 5 (1): 20–37.

Powell, G. Bingham. 2000. *Elections as Instruments of Democracy: Majoritarian and Proportional Visions.* New Haven, CT: Yale University Press.

Prince Edward Island. 2001. *Report on Proportional Representation.* Elections Prince Edward Island.

Prince Edward Island. 2003. *Electoral Reform Commission Report.*

Przeworski, Adam. 2008. "Conquered or Granted? A History of Suffrage Extensions." *British Journal of Political Science* 39 (2): 291–321. http://dx.doi.org/10.1017/S0007123408000434

Przeworski, Adam. 2009. "Constraints and Choices: Electoral Participation in Historical Perspective." *Comparative Political Studies* 42 (1): 4–30. http://dx.doi.org/10.1177/0010414008324991

Quebec. 2003. "Citizen Participation at the Heart of Québec's Democratic Institutions." Organizing Committee of the Estates-General on the Reform of Democratic Institutions. Government of Quebec.

Quebec. 2007. "Characteristics of a Compensatory Mixed Member Voting System: Summary." Le Directeur général des élections du Québec. December.

Rae, Douglas. 1971. *The Political Consequences of Electoral Laws.* New Haven, CT: Yale University Press.

Reid, Scott. 2001. "Developing a Coalition for Electoral Reform." *Policy Options* (July–August): 76–77.

Reid, Scott. 2005. "The Road to Electoral Reform." *Canadian Parliamentary Review* 28 (3): 4–8.

Rokkan, Stein. 1970. *Citizens, Elections, Parties: Approaches to the Comparative Study of Processes of Development.* New York: David McKay Company.

Rustow, Dankwart A. 1950. "Some Observations on Proportional Representation." *Journal of Politics* 12 (1): 107–27. http://dx.doi.org/10.2307/2126090

Seidle, Leslie. 2002. "Electoral System Reform in Canada: Objectives, Advocacy, and Implications for Governance." CPRN Discussion Paper F/28. Ottawa: Canadian Policy Research Networks.

Simpson, Jeffrey. 2005. "A Vote for Something—Or Just Anything at All?" *Globe and Mail,* May 21, A19.

Smith, Andrea B. 1982. "The CCF, NPA and Civic Change: Provincial Forces behind Vancouver Politics 1930–1949." *BC Studies* 53 (Spring): 45–65.

Smith, David E., and John C. Courtney. 1991. "Registering Voters: Canada in a Comparative Perspective." In *Democratic Rights and Electoral Reform in Canada,* edited by Michael Cassidy, 343–461. Ottawa: Royal Commission on Electoral Reform and Party Financing.

Spector, Norman. 2005. "No Reason That B.C.'s Sore Losers Should Have Their Way." *Globe and Mail,* May 30, A13.

Spiteri, Ray. 2014. "Wards versus At Large: Falls Candidates Discuss." *Niagara Falls Review,* September 25.

Tennant, Paul. 1980. "Vancouver Civic Politics, 1929–1980." *BC Studies* 46 (Summer): 3–27.

Tennant, Paul, and Julian West. 1998a. "Half of Vancouver's Voters Go without Representation." *Vancouver Sun,* September 19: A23.

Tennant, Paul, and Julian West. 1998b. "Ward System Is No Better Than At-Large Democracy." *Vancouver Sun,* September 23: A17.

Toronto Star. 2013. "Toronto City Council Should Support Ranked Ballot Election System." June 10. http://www.thestar.com/opinion/editorials/2013/06/10/toronto_city_council_should_support_ranked_ballot_election_system_editorial.html

Toronto Star. 2015. "Toronto City Council Betrays Voting System Reform." October 5. http://www.thestar.com/opinion/editorials/2015/10/05/toronto-city-council-betrays-voting-reform-editorial.html

von Beyme, Klaus. 2000. *Parliamentary Democracy: Democratization, Destabilization, Reconsolidation, 1789–1999.* Houndsmills, UK: Palgrave. http://dx.doi.org/10.1057/9780230514393

Ward, Norman. 1950. *The Canadian House of Commons: Representation.* Toronto: University of Toronto Press.

Warren, Mark, and Hilary Pearse, eds. 2008. *Designing Deliberative Democracy: The British Columbia Citizens' Assembly.* Cambridge: Cambridge University Press. http://dx.doi.org/10.1017/CBO9780511491177

Wherry, Aaron. 2014. "Let's Debate Proportional Representation, Again." *Maclean's,* December 3.

Wiseman, Nelson. 1997. "Skeptical Reflections on Proportional Representation." *Policy Options* (November): 15–8.

Woldendorp, J.J., Hans Keman, and Ian Budge. 2000. *Party Government in 48 Democracies. Composition—Duration—Personnel.* London: Kluwer Academic Publishers.

Ziblatt, Daniel. 2009. "Shaping Democratic Practice and the Causes of Electoral Fraud: The Case of Nineteenth-Century Germany." *American Political Science Review* 103 (1): 1–21. http://dx.doi.org/10.1017/S0003055409090042

Zochodne, Geoff. 2014. "Wards versus At-Large, Take Two." *The Oshawa Express.* http://oshawaexpress.ca/viewposting.php?view=6006

12

Back to the Future: Encoding and Decoding Interest Representation Outside of Parties

JACQUETTA NEWMAN

[A] riot is clearly not an electoral rally, and both the participants and
the authorities know the difference.
—*Piven and Cloward 1995, 139*

IN 2011 AND 2012, many of us were excited by the seemingly spontaneous
uprising of mass action around the world. This had started earlier in 2009
when Icelanders rose in protest against their government's failure to secure the
economy after the 2008 financial collapse. In Greece, demonstrations against
austerity measures responding to the European sovereign debt crisis adopted
the title *Indignants,* from similar protests in Spain throughout 2011. The Arab
Spring hit, starting with the December 2010 self-immolation of Mohamed
Bouazizi in Tunisia and associated street protests, which melded into the Egyp-
tian Day of Revolt and the first day of the occupation of Tahrir Square on 25
January 2011. Protests then spread through Libya, Yemen, Bahrain, and Syria.

These protests were not lost on North America, where in February 2011
an editorial in *Adbusters* called for similar protests against Wall Street and a
business and political system that had allowed the financial collapse of 2008.
The Occupy Movement was born, peaking with occupations around the
world on 17 November 2011, the Global Day of Action. As Paul Mason
(2013) said in the title of his book on the 2011 protests (referencing a phrase
from 1968), it appeared *"it's still kicking off everywhere,"* and Manual Castells
(2012, 2), in *Networks of Outrage and Hope,* giddily said, "people from all ages
and conditions moved toward occupying urban space, on a blind date with
each other and with the destiny they wanted to forge, as they claimed their
right to make history—their history—in a display of self-awareness that has
characterized major social movements." By the end of the year, *Time* maga-
zine had named "The Protester" Man of the Year, and many were claiming
their membership in the "99 percent."

Canada was not immune from the 2011 social protest "contagion." Most
major Canadian cities had a least one park occupied for several weeks in the
fall of 2011, until city officials or cold weather cleared away all but the most

die-hard campers. In April 2011, responding to a Toronto police official's statement that what women wore increased their chance of being sexually assaulted, the first Slut Walk was held, spreading to other cities and countries as women protested the blaming of women for the violence perpetrated on them. Then in early 2012, the *Printemps érable* (Maple Spring) brought Quebec university students into the street to demonstrate and strike against tuition increases and the growing neoliberalization of postsecondary education. This was capped off at the end of 2012 with the Idle No More movement, as First Nations peoples not only protested the Harper Conservative Party government's treatment of Indigenous peoples, but also the ineffectiveness of the peak organization representing them, the Assembly of First Nations, in dealing with the government.

All this activity harkened back to the excitement felt around the world in 1968 when student, peace, feminist, civil rights, and nationalist protests spread worldwide, changing the way we view institutional politics and introducing the term new social movement (NSM). Why do we view these movements of mass collective action with excitement? We do so because such disruptions remind us of the true nature of politics and highlight the never-ending conflict between those inside the system and those outside, a status that is at the heart of interest group and advocacy politics.

This chapter is about the representation of citizen views and voices outside the formal institutions of parties and elections. By looking back, we hope to gather an understanding of why we reacted to the protests of 2011 with both excitement and trepidation and how interest representation outside of political parties has developed in the past half century. It is my intention to unpack this rather amorphous and nebulous collection of actors, discuss how representation has changed to normalize and accommodate elements of civil society once considered outside the system, and look at what consequences this normalization has for those participating in the system. The argument is that since 1968 there has been a normalization and accommodation of elements of civil society within the political system, and while our understanding of whose voices matter has substantially broadened to become more inclusive, the results have not necessarily become democratic or equal. Even in a world of participatory inclusion, age-old balances of power continue to replicate themselves. The conflict inherent in mass collective disruption reminds us that the status quo is not necessarily a consensus.

Politics by Other Means: Outsiders, a Hinterland Who's Who

Twenty-five years ago the tendency was to see participation by "outside" groups as inherently threatening to the system of good government. The first edition of this book (1989) talked of actors from outside the system: "parts of NSMs have institutionalized themselves, or have become pressure groups, [but] in general such movements, by definition, work at the margins of the political system" (Galipeau 1989). There was a clear division between the function of parties, which represented, articulated, and aggregated interests; ran for office to control the state; and gave expression to those interests through public policy, on the one hand, and organizations that emerged from civil society to represent and articulate interests. However, rather than being an indicator of alienation from the political system or a turning away from the democratic system, participation outside of political parties appears to increase the likelihood of engagement with the democratic and electoral process (see Phillips 1996; Young and Everitt 2004). Therefore, organizing within civil society is significant for the political system.

Definitionally I am casting a large net to cover a wide range of political participation that occurs outside formal government and party structures. Interest groups are organizations that focus their efforts on influencing the state and public policy from outside the "formal apparatus of the state" (Pross 1992). Young and Everitt (2004, 95) prefer the term *advocacy group*, because it encompasses groups acting for the best interests of members as well as groups acting to promote their opinions on an issue in which they do not have a direct interest. *Advocacy organizations* refer to a wide range of organizations, such as those formed by two or three individuals who live on the same street and lobby their municipal government to install a stop sign, as well as a group like the Council of Canadians, which claims thousands of members and lobbies the government on issues ranging from the environment to national sovereignty. It also includes industry associations and business lobby groups. Today we also add the term *third sector,* which refers to voluntary groups who are not "advocates" per se but are nonetheless intimately involved in politics and policy making. The focus is on the voluntary nature of a variety of organizations across civil society, such as charities, philanthropic foundations, and nonprofit groups. "Third sector" characterizes these voluntary organizations "as the third pillar of society, providing services and functions previously performed by government and the market" (Laforest 2011, 51).

The term *social movement* refers to a form of action where the collective actor (1) invokes and is defined by a sense of solidarity and shared meaning; (2) makes manifest a social, political, and cultural conflict; and (3) within that conflict presents a vision that contains an immanent critique of society (Melucci 1989). As such, social movements are often characterized as not being structurally specific and unified, but heterogeneous political, social, and cultural networks of groups and individuals working for a variety of aims and goals that fit within broader demands for change. However, in practice the distinction between advocacy groups and social movements is less than watertight (Newman and Tanguay 2002) because social movements create organizational structures—social movement organizations (SMOs)—that for all intents and purposes are advocacy organizations or volunteer service providers.

Significantly, NSMs articulate alternative visions of political, social, and economic activity, illustrating a concern with the "grammar of the forms of life" (Habermas 1981, 33). This idea of "the grammar of forms of life" is relevant because it highlights that the norms which govern our lives are a set of social constructions. In reflecting on the movements and events of 1968, Claus Offe (2002)[1] referred to the collective actions of the time as "the attempted subversion of some dominant 'code.'" If "code" is viewed as the social discourse that defines what society is and how it should be, then the activities of the social movements of 1968 can be viewed as efforts and struggles to disrupt the status quo code and, if not to bring a new world into being, at least to "distinguish between right and wrong, distinguish between those that mislead and those that enlighten and liberate and insist upon the validity of the latter and to expose the power content of the former" (Offe 2002, 83). There is an anti-systemic feature at the heart of social movements.

Similarly, McAdam, Tarrow, and Tilly's (2001) conception of "contention" reminds us of the opposition and challenge at the heart of social movements. While the borders between institutionalized and noninstitutionalized politics are hard to draw with precision, particularly as social movements and advocacy groups actively interact and involve similar processes of identity development, coalition-building, and strategic action, like Offe these authors see episodes of social movement contention as disrupting the status quo. These events create uncertainty and reveal fault lines in society that lead to opportunities for change and the possibility of realignment in the political system. This "leaves a residue of change not only in how social movements and advocacy organizations act, strategize and pursue their goals, but also in how state institutions react to these challenges" (McAdam et al. 2001, 9). In short, the oppositional contentious feature needs to be taken seriously, because occasionally it challenges and changes the rules of the game.

Normalization: Integrating the Outsiders into the Political Process

In the wake of the uprisings of 1968, demands were made for more open government and the direct participation of citizens in all stages of the political process. Citizenship and political participation were understood in a broad sense, encompassing not just large groups of mass public opinion expressed through voting and party support, but also actors from civil society and experts that have a stake in the wider implications of any policy. The result was the expansion of participation arenas and access points for citizens to express their interests and preferences, and when those openings did not materialize, concern was raised regarding a growing "democratic deficit." The year 1968 could be seen as the catalyst for this, and advocacy groups emerged as ready participants in this expanded political sphere.

In Canada before the 1970s, interest group/state relations were particularly privatized and exclusive, a shady private realm where individuals, corporate firms, or "fixers" from groups relied on personal connections to influence a small number of political and bureaucratic decision makers (Thorburn 2007, 386). As an example, the nineteenth-century campaign for women's suffrage was less prone to violence in Canada than in the United States and Great Britain, because middle class women not only relied on petitioning, lobbying, public appeals, and education, but also leveraging private connections with politicians, more often than not powerful and well-positioned husbands (Newman and White 2012; Prentice et al. 1988).

It was in the 1970s that the relationship between interest groups and the Canadian state became visible and the activities of advocacy groups grew exponentially. Thorburn (2007, 390) attributes the change to the election of Liberal Prime Minister Pierre Trudeau:

> [T]he Trudeau period championing the "Just Society" and "participatory democracy" called these emerging groups into being, just after the "quiet revolution" had rallied Quebec society to a new awareness of the real world interests of francophones in the power positions in its own society. Demands for "French Power" shaded into claims for recognition and empowerment of hitherto marginalized parts of society. Aboriginal peoples found their voice and sought new powers of self-government and support of their communities. Women's groups formed to demand status and rights. Gays and lesbians and transsexuals sought protection from discrimination and rights to full equality in the community. Immigrant groups, encouraged by government funding, set up organizations to make their claims to equality rights. Visible minorities were especially pressing in demanding freedom from discrimination in employment, housing, and treatment by law enforcement authorities.

We really can't attribute the emergence of these groups to one Canadian prime minister; for one thing, it doesn't account for the spread of similar social movements and demands for political rights and inclusion around the world in the same era. What it does describe, however, is Canada's experience of the challenging and changing of social "code" and discourse that occurred in the late 1960s and 1970s.

The decade of the 1960s represented a period of social and political tumult around the world; the "protest cycle of the 1960s" consisted of numerous social movements with international appeal, including student, anti-war, women's, gay and lesbian, and environmental movements (Staggenborg 2011). Large-scale socioeconomic and political changes in the decades following World War II had changed the "grammar of forms of life" and opened opportunities for groups to emerge and claim space in political life and make demands on the state. This was a period of national decolonization, as countries in the developing world, sometimes peacefully and other times not, declared their independence from European colonial powers. The civil rights movement emerged in the United States, providing a model of effective collective action along with a vision of freedom and equality that was emulated by movements worldwide.

This process was mirrored in Canada by the rise of francophone power and the Quiet Revolution within Quebec, which asserted the distinctiveness of Québécois society within Canada along with its attendant political autonomy, if not outright independence (Dufour and Traisnel 2008; Thorburn 2007). Across Canada, university students and academics became active in advocating for the protection of Canadian economic, cultural, and educational institutions against encroaching Americanization (Cormier 2004). The women's movement entered its second wave as Canadian women mobilized to change their situations across a broad spectrum of political, economic, and cultural structures. As a result of their demands, the government instituted the Royal Commission on the Status of Women, whose recommendations would in turn become a lightning rod for women's advocacy and political activism (Newman and White 2012). The period also saw Canada's Indigenous peoples use opening opportunities. The federal government's assimilationist White Paper on Indian Policy in 1969 was countered by the Indian Association of Alberta's release of the "Red Paper," a step in the creation of the National Indian Brotherhood (Ladner 2008; Ramos 2012): "The White Paper was a classical political opportunity which gave a rallying point to the Indigenous movement, encouraged mobilization, demanded the development of organizational capacities and provided access to the policy network" (Ladner 2008, 33). In the wake of other movements, particularly second wave feminism's rejection of the public–private distinction in its slogan, "the personal is political," and Pierre Trudeau's assertion that the state had "no place in the bedrooms of the nation," the gay and lesbian movement emerged demanding respect for their human rights and an end to discrimination (Rayside and Lindquist 1992; Smith 2008). Focus on human rights, equality, and anti-discrimination, along with the publication in 1969 of the fourth volume of the Royal Commission on Bilingualism and

Biculturalism, *The Cultural Contribution of the Other Ethnic Groups,* gave voice to and a growing political awareness of ethnocultural and racialized minority groups (Kobayashi 2008). These were combined with an active Canadian peace movement campaigning against nuclear weapons and the Vietnam War (Moffat 1982; Newman 1999) and an environmental movement entering its second wave (McKenzie 2008, 283), as people were mobilized by books such as Rachel Carson's (1962) *Silent Spring* to protest industrial pollution and a military–industrial–political complex seen to be out of control and unaccountable.

It was a "protest cycle" where social movements were the "early risers," opening up opportunities for others to impact the political system by taking advantage of and helping to create political opportunities (Tarrow 1998). These opportunities are features in the political environment that influence movement activity and success. The global contagion of those seeking national independence and individual rights certainly provided an open context; however, so did the actions of the Canadian government, such as establishing national inquiries into the status of French, English, and ethnic communities (Bilingualism and Biculturalism Commission) and women (Royal Commission on the Status of Women); legislation decriminalizing homosexuality; and formalizing federal approaches to individual rights in the Bill of Rights of 1960 without giving similar consideration for Indigenous peoples, as illustrated in the White Paper of 1969. As Audrey Kobayashi (2008, 151–52) points out in a discussion of minority ethnic movements in Canada, "whereas the movement for full and equal citizenship has been the basis for ethnocultural mobilization, the terms and the discourse are overwhelmingly influenced by the structural conditions set by public policy . . . within that space four main factors—political will, coalition-building, community support and public opinion—can create the most effective structure." Protest cycles are a dance between two partners: social movements and state.

As the participation of advocacy groups grew in light of the disruptions of the 1960s, there was a realignment of the Canadian state to accommodate and facilitate a more participatory relationship with these actors. Throughout the 1970s and 1980s the federal government launched a series of programs to support organizations representing and advocating in the name of particular segments of Canadian society—language minorities, Indigenous organizations, women, and ethnocultural minorities (Pal 1993; Smith 2008). The general focus was to expand the policy development process to include more actors, such as interest associations, advocacy groups, and various experts. Changes were made to Parliament to increase the role of individual Members of Parliament (MPs) as representatives of the people and encourage outside participation. Emphasis was put on public hearings and the role of participation in the policy-making process (Franks 1987, 177). As a result, more work was given over to committees and parliamentary task forces to undertake investigations, which brought together witnesses from both inside and outside government. Advisory councils were created, most notably the Canadian Advisory Council on the Status of Women (1973) and the Canadian Institute for Peace and Security (1985), with the purpose of having members appointed from both the government and the public advise the federal government on the effect public policy had on their specific issue area.[2] Funding was also made available to support civil society organizations in building the resources and institutional capacity to access and work with the state, and for groups seeking redress and confirmation of their rights through the courts. The Court Challenges Program was started in the 1970s to support minority-language cases and was expanded in the 1980s to include rights cases brought under the 1982 Charter of Rights and Freedoms. The intention was to enhance fairness and diversity in representation by ensuring resources for disadvantaged constituencies (Phillips 1991, 197).

This enabled groups to build organizational structures, grow their memberships, and develop expertise or hire policy experts and lawyers so that they were able to become active participants in the political process. Much greater use was made of advocacy advertising, opinion surveys, direct-mail solicitation, and coalition-building to facilitate political influence (Thorburn 2007). The result was a unique dynamic between the federal government and civil society—a dynamic that shaped civil society itself (Laforest 2013, 244). Groups gravitated to the federal level to gain political representation, resulting in the dominance in advocacy politics of umbrella organizations based and focused at the national level.

The close relationship between advocacy groups, civil society organizations, and the state was not without its critics, who asked why the government was funding groups that were ultimately critical of government policy. In 1992, the Mulroney Conservative government killed the Court Challenges Program, disbanded the Canadian Institute for International Peace and Security (CIIPS), and generally cut funding to advocacy groups. While the Chrétien Liberal government, which replaced the Mulroney government in 1993, reinstituted the Court Challenges Program (the CCP was finally cancelled in 2006 by the Harper Conservative government), it did not resurrect CIIPS and went on to dismantle the Canadian Advisory Council on the Status of Women in 1995. However, while the Chrétien government responded to growing public criticism and skepticism regarding "special interests biting the hand that fed them" by reducing funding to advocacy groups and regulating the growing number of lobbyists, as Thorburn (2007, 403) points out, during the same period the government was making "well-reported gestures" in favour of the voluntary sector (see also Laforest 2011; Phillips 2006). The argument was that the voluntary or third sector acted in the public interest in the broadest sense, and by offering public–private partnerships the legitimacy of both the third sector and the state would be enhanced and social programing delivered more efficiently.

The impetus was to shift from a more state-centred hierarchical control-based model of governing to a more networked collaborative approach—to develop a form of policy making and consultation characterized by individual social responsibility and a small state (Phillips 2006). This continued to include representatives from advocacy groups, because by the 1990s governments had become dependent on the substantial expertise and popular knowledge of the constituencies represented by groups and movements. Governments seldom develop policy in isolation from "stakeholders"; the term *stakeholder* itself is new and refers to those individuals, groups, or organizations seen to have an interest in or which are affected by certain policies.

Consequently, it has become unthinkable not to include a much wider range of participation from civil society. What is considered representation, how one's views or interests are expressed in the political system and how one is able to influence the political process, is much broader than was the view in the mid-twentieth century. While voting is still the dominant form of participation in democracies, conventional political participation cannot be reduced to it, and civic competence can no longer be considered merely having knowledge of the political field. Similarly, what is considered political activity is also much more broadly understood to include more than voting and electoral activities. Facetiously, one can argue that much more is expected from citizens today than in the past. This also holds for the inclusion of civil society and advocacy organizations in politics. As a recent article points out, "it is uncontroversial to suggest that the practice of government has changed in the past thirty years from a context in which the state was the dominant unitary actor to one in which power and influence are more horizontally distributed among state and non-state actors. There are a number of policy domains in Canada characterized by linked governance not only among levels of government but also in close policy deliberation with civil society representatives" (Doberstein and Millar 2014, 26).

In the world of policy making, there was a turn from "government" to "governance." Not unique to Canada, the concept of governance is applied to international relations, regional bodies, and individual states, particularly where greater involvement of civil society actors in multilevel governance structures is desired. Governance can be said to encompass a series of inter-related phenomena, including (1) the dispersal of policy-making power among a wide range of public and private actors, which often coordinate their actions in policy networks; (2) the increasing importance of multilevel governance decision-making structures because of the loss of powers by the state upwards (to supranational bodies such as the World Trade Organization, European Union, etc.), downwards (to regions and municipalities), and sideways (to corporations and nongovernmental organizations); and (3) the rise of new modes of governance that rely heavily on horizontal decision making or "self-steering" instead of hierarchical top-down command-and-control regulation (Palumbo 2010). In these arrangements civil society and state actors act collaboratively to serve a public interest. The expectation is that civil society organizations, as partners in governance structures, will bring a "diversity of interests and views" based on "down-to-earth citizen experiences" to the policy-making process, but will not exclusively pursue their own agendas (Kohler-Koch 2010; Offe 2009).

The modes of interaction associated with governance are argued to be "self-organizing, inter-organizational networks characterized by interdependence, resource exchange, rules of the game and significant autonomy from the state" (Rhodes 1997, cited in Phillips 2006, 11), which from the perspective of a Canadian political scientist strikes one as very similar to the definition of a policy community. *Policy communities* are collaborative networks of state and civil society actors who share a common "policy focus" and who, with varying degrees of influence, shape policy outcomes over the long run (Coleman and Skogstad 1990, 25). Within the policy community we find the subgovernment (which comprises government agencies, interest associations, and other social organizations that make public policy), the attentive public (made up of interest associations that are not regularly included in policy making), relevant media, and interested and expert individuals (Coleman and Skogstad 1990; Pal 1993; Pross 1992). As Thorburn (2007, 401) stated regarding the growth of relations between lobbyists and MPs in parliamentary law making, the reform of the parliamentary committee system "led to a kind of privatization of policy making in the hands of a policy community of MPs, governing officials, and interest lobbyists and the private interests they represented."

Professionalization: Governing the "Outsiders"

What we cannot overlook is the role of the state in setting the context and framework of policy communities. In conditions of advanced capitalist social and economic structures, the provision of semi-public functions to advocacy groups assigns them a status that ultimately regulates the type and scope of their activities. "Interest representation . . . tends to become predominantly a matter of 'political design' and thus in part a dependent rather than independent variable of public-policy making" (Offe 1981, 124–25). The institutionalization of interest representation is always two-sided in its effects: while the groups gain advantages and privileges, they have to accept certain constraints and obligations. Policy regimes or communities regularize the content of policy making, and as a result the member groups tend to become professional in nature and adopt institutionalized approaches to lobbying and pursuing policy change; this regulation and professional formality is characteristic of interest representation in Canada (Pross 1992; Staggenborg 2012).[3] It is the well-institutionalized and resourced groups that gain access and are seen as politically effective.

As new institutional levers, such as the courts, lobbyists, parliamentary committee hearings, public–private partnerships, and so on, became available after the 1960s, grassroots protest and loose civic organizations were replaced by professional advocacy and nongovernment organizations.[4] The tendency was for these more formal professional organizations to seek formal institutionalized access and eschew traditional protest activities. As Laforest (2013, 245) outlines, "contrary to EU processes access to governance arrangements in Canada was limited to organizations that were well versed in research. This helped to legitimate particular institutional forms and practices articulated around the importance of research and evidence-based practices for policy making." The expectation is that groups involved in policy communities and structures of shared governance will focus on contributing expertise, research, and services. This requires organization, and effective groups are characterized by efficient bureaucratic organizations that work within and adhere to the norms of the policy-making system, share a common knowledge base, are well versed in the issues involved, and share the same expert language.

Professionalization is closely tied to co-optation, the process of integrating new elements into the structures of an organization as a means of absorbing the threats to organizational stability or existence (Selznick 1966, 13). However, there is a tension. If the need for participation is ignored, the goal of cooperation may be jeopardized, but if participation is allowed to go too far, stable organizational leadership may be threatened (Selznick 1966, 261). There is a requirement to control participation and ensure that participating elements do not get out of hand and take advantage of their formal position to encroach on the actual arena of decision making. Consequently, it is government that determines the terms of access through the availability of resources and opportunities. Canadian governance structures, unlike the European Union's, have not institutionalized consultative arrangements; rather, they rely on a more ad hoc approach that is subject to changing government priorities (Laforest 2013, 246).

This goes back to the early incorporation of groups into the policy process in the 1970s and 1980s. "At the outset of policy making, the shape and nature of government's priorities certainly set the parameters of which types of groups will receive support and which not" (Pal 1993, 275). For example, Pierre Trudeau's "state-building initiatives" focused on incorporating "charter supporters and civil liberties groups" that rallied behind the Liberal Party's constitutional policy of the time. As governments and policy priorities changed, so did the groups involved. This is clearly seen in the change in policy and criteria of support for women's groups by the Women's Program. Within the program, the fortunes of the socially conservative REAL Women of Canada, which advocates more traditional views on gender, have tended to wax and wane with Conservative Party power in government, and during the 1980s moderate and small liberal groups were much more successful in applications to the program than those advocating on issue agendas perceived to be less socially acceptable, such as sexual orientation and abortion (Newman and White 2012, 133).

The most obvious area of control is through funding. As discussed earlier, part of the normalization of advocacy groups in Canada was the creation of funding programs to support civil society. This has afforded the state a great deal of control over groups who have accepted funds, such as the right to specify for what and by whom money will be spent, the right to demand proof that the funds have been spent in accordance with the stipulations first cited, and the right to withdraw or terminate the funds. Again, women's groups are a good example of this control. As state funding declined during the 1980s and 1990s, women's groups had to change their activities, focusing more on fundraising and less on political activities. Changes in funding criteria at the department of the Status of Women reduced funding for core organizations, which allows a degree of independence in pursuing program and organizational objectives, in favour of project-based funding, which leaves control in the hands of the funder on a case-by-case basis (Standing Committee on the Status of Women 2005, 2; 2007, 2–3).

A more egregious attempt at control was behind the controversy in 2009–10 over the defunding of KAIROS, an ecumenical social justice project of the Canadian Council of Churches, which undertakes programs of advocacy, education, and research on issues of Indigenous rights, sustainable environmentalism, women's empowerment, resource rights, and watershed protection. It appeared that funding was cut because of KAIROS's support of a boycott, divestment, and sanction campaign against Israel,[5] although officially it was stated that KAIROS's program no longer fit with that of the Canadian International Development Agency (CIDA; Whittington 2009). However, eventually it came to light that the decision had been made unilaterally by the Conservative Minister for International Cooperation, Bev Oda, overturning a decision from CIDA to continue funding (Clark 2011; KAIROS 2011).[6]

The allowance for groups to claim charitable status further enhances financial control. Charities receive preferential treatment under the Income Tax Act since their income is exempt from taxation and they are also able to give tax-deductible receipts as perquisites to elicit donors. This makes charitable status an enticing prospect for civil society organizations. However, charitable status comes with a *quid pro quo* tax exemption in return for promises to be "nonpolitical" and engage only in charitable services, which are defined as relief of poverty, the advancement of education and religion, and other purposes beneficial to the community. It is the role of the Canada Revenue Agency (CRA) to make a determination of whether a charity is engaging in political activities on a case-by-case basis by measuring the expenditures of charities to ensure that "substantially all" disbursements go to charitable activities. The CRA defines "substantially all" as 90 per cent (Kitching 2006). In July 2014, the *Toronto Star* reported that the Harper Conservative government had stepped up its scrutiny of political activities by charities, increasing money available to the CRA for audits (Canadian Press 2014a).[7] For the groups concerned, the effect is more than just losing its charitable status; the audit process itself represents a significant drain on resources that is further compounded if the issue goes to court. The use of CRA audits certainly distracts groups and ties up resources, but ultimately it works to stop the groups from pursuing an active political position or controversial solutions to the problems they address.

The point is that the normalization and institutionalization of civil society groups generally and advocacy groups in particular in structures of shared governance has resulted in their depoliticization. It would appear that Michels' ([1911] 1962) law of oligarchy is inescapable. As Piven and Cloward (1977, 30) found in their study of poor people's movements of the 1960s and 1970s, the focus of the state is to "channel the energies and angers of the protestors into more legitimate, less disruptive forms of political behaviour in part by offering incentives to movement leaders or, in other words, coopting them." Galipeau (1989, 414) made the same point in the first edition of this volume:

> [E]ven though the policy process has become more open in recent years, actual policy-making institutions seek to ensure stability by consensus-management. This is often accomplished by routinizing the presentation of interests, which in effect depoliticizes many issues, and in general, by seeking to organize certain issues out of the normal course of policy debates. . . .

> One can argue that stability is achieved by coopting those new interest groups which are willing to accept the dominant protocol of presentations—one based on discretion and non-ideological technical forms of discourses.

Phillips (2006, 250) describes this as occurring in the Voluntary Sector Initiative (VSI), where participants found it difficult to step outside the collaborative process to pursue more political actions because "they were consumed in the enormous operational details of the VSI, which left little time to deal with policy and because they were discouraged from pursuing a more political route until some of the contentious issues had been resolved within the VSI. As these were never resolved the political routes were not readily accessible." The integration of social movement politics into institutionalized politics while maintaining its critical anti-systemic edge has never been ensured or unproblematic. As Offe (1981, 241–42) identified, the integration of social movements like the German Greens into the formal political process would inevitably normalize their politics to fit with institutional political requirements. Similarly, as we have argued in this chapter, the integration of advocacy of organizations into policy communities has resulted in the co-optation and training of these organizations to a form of normal politics.

Further to this, the elevation in the status of participating groups in shared governance structures not only limits the tactics available to oppositional elements to those formally established political channels preferred by political elites, it also requires more marginalized groups to find additional resources since they have to compete with elites in their own movements who are attempting to protect their stakes in the system. "In other words, to use conventional methods of influence effectively, people must be able to muster the resources both to organize bureaucratically and to overcome the influence of other groups in regular political contests" (Piven and Cloward 1995, 153). The costs go up and the division between insiders and outsiders becomes much more rigid.

This has significant consequences for representation since it is no longer clear whose interests and voices are being represented or what the connection is between those being represented and those doing the representation. "The claim that CSOs [civil society organizations] are closer to the citizens than elected representatives because they have a short chain of delegation . . . just does not match reality. So if we think of representation as a social relationship we have to acknowledge that it is not built on direct personal encounters or on direct mandating. At best it is filtered through many layers of organizations—delivering synthetic or astroturf representation" (Kohler-Koch 2010, 111).

This is a particular problem in Canada, because representation in governance structures is based on individuals who are invited to join because they fulfill a certain language, regional, gender, racial, or ethnic criterion. "Such collections of individuals can be seen to be relatively inclusive and non-elitist, but there is little guarantee of—and there are often structural impediments to—their being able to connect to, negotiate on behalf of, or be accountable to real networks or actual communities" (Phillips 2006, 24). The result is the *look* of inclusivity, but not necessarily the practice of representation. The irony is that institutionalized civil society organizations presented as a democratic corrective to the layered and two- or three-times removed politics of political parties and elected representatives actually end up suffering from a similar fate.

Back to the Future: Viva la Revolución, or at Least the Political Riot

What can be done? If the problem is depoliticization, then the obvious solution is to bring "politics" back into the mix. This is Offe's (2009, 551) difficulty with the move to the discourse of governance: "most of the time *governance* is being used in contradistinction to *government* . . . the implication of this usage of the concept is often that *governance* as opposed to *government* is paradigmatically novel and somehow a more advanced, frictionless, voluntaristic-consensual and more freedom protecting approach to socio-political regulation." Similarly, Kohler-Koch (2010) sees the institutionalization of participatory governance as furthering what Chantal Mouffe (2005) refers to as the consensus ideology of postmodern democracy. Politics cannot be practised simply by making preconstituted identities cooperate, but by constituting those identities in confrontation (Mouffe 2013). Social change and the emergence of politics, far from requiring collective deliberation, requires disagreement, contentious interaction, and conflict. Therefore, the institutionalization of participatory democracy and the collaborative process underlying governance structures focusing on achieving common goals through consensus building, while intended to expand democratic participation, ultimately undermines its own capacity for politics.

In the first edition of this volume, Galipeau (1989) argued that social movements performed an innovative function by breaking the rigidity of the institutionalized system of interest representation. In this chapter we have seen how the normalization of expanded advocacy group participation within politics and associated policy communities became part of a turn from governing to governance, a code that not only cloaks hierarchies of control but depoliticizes politics itself. While the observation was made that it is hard to draw borders between institutionalized and noninstitutionalized politics, we can see that the normalization of advocacy politics has created a rigid and closed system of interest representation that sets firm boundaries between insider and outsider politics. It is the disruptions of "outsider politics" that breaks code. This was and is the message of 1968, or 1917, 1871, or 1789, if we want to go further back.

In the 1960s and 1970s, Piven and Cloward (1977) asked the question of how marginalized people, particularly those without conventional political resources, exert influence in politics. It was through the disruption of institutions and provocation of conflict that marginalized groups would have some possibility of influence:

> Rule-making is a strategy of power. Moreover, it is a strategy that creates new and lasting constraints on subsequent political action. Once objectified in a system of law, the rules forged by past power struggles continue to shape ongoing conflicts by constraining or enhancing the ability of actors to use whatever leverage their social circumstances yield them. That is why new power struggles often take the form of efforts to alter the parameters of the permissible by challenging or defying the legitimacy of prevailing norms themselves. . . . [P]rotest is indeed "outside of normal politics" and "against normal politics" in the sense that people break the rules defining permissible modes of political action. (Piven and Cloward 1995, 139)

Such forms of protest require less organization and integration and consequently have been the resort of powerless outsiders throughout history. "The riot" for example, "is the characteristic and ever-recurring form of popular protest" (Rudé 1964, 6).

This speaks to the excitement around the protests of 2011 and 2012: the possibility of worldwide efforts to break code, to disrupt the status quo and challenge dominant elite consensuses and invoke mass participation in politics; the volcanic "bubbling up of subterranean politics," where voices of all political types (Kaldor and Selchow 2012, cited in Mouffe 2013, 115) present a politics of mass hope and emancipation that is critical of both the state and the institutionalized representative groups. This was illustrated in 2011–12 by Occupy's critique of the World Social Forum, which some felt was too associated with the traditional institutionalized left (Mouffe 2013, 116). In Canada, looking at the Idle No More movement in 2012, we see a series of diffuse flash mobs, round dances, road and railway line blockages, mass marches, and rallies loosely organized and coordinated through social media–networked actors. The issues of focus were multiple government policies regarding land claims, funding to Indigenous peoples, and resource exploitation, tied to greater concerns regarding Indigenism and environmentalism. However, it was not only directed at the state but also at the main institutional organization that represents First Nations peoples in Canada, the Assembly of First Nations.

Idle No More's activities and evocation of Indigenous ways of knowing rooted in Indigenous sovereignty to protect water, air, land, and all creation for future generations (www.idlenomore.ca) represented the spirit of social movement. It invoked a sense of solidarity, making manifest a social, political, and cultural conflict based on a fundamental critique of society that could not be solved within the existing status quo. Idle No More represented a disruption of code and an attempt to break that code to bring about something else. As Drew Hayden Taylor (2014) said of it a year later, "it seemed like anything is possible . . ."

The problem is the temporary nature of these emancipatory disruptions. What bubbles up commonly simmers down, becomes dormant beneath the surface, and is then easily ignored. This is the distinction between movement mobilization and latency (Melucci 1989). Code is disrupted, but to what extent is it changed? Taylor (2014), commenting on Idle No More, is hopeful:

> It wasn't the big bang of aboriginal social protest, but one of the little bangs. Like the occupations of Alcatraz, Oka, Ipperwash and elsewhere, Idle No More was the right protest at the right time, the first to really use social media to get its story across. Today possibly because of it, native people are at the forefront of the fracking debate, they are calling for an inquest into missing and murdered aboriginal women. It's sort of like Idle 2.0, or maybe Idle No More Some More. And when those issues are done and finished something new and necessary will arise from it.

Out of the Idle No More protests a new advocacy group emerged. Founded by former prime ministers (Paul Martin and Joe Clark), Indigenous leaders (Ovide Mercredi), and the premier of the Northwest Territories (Stephen Kakfwi), Canadians for a New Partnership advocates for true reconciliation through a leadership initiative engaging Canadians and First Nations peoples in dialogue and relationship building (Levitz 2014; www.cfnp.ca). Is this a sign of the beginning of a new process of normalization in response to the disruptions of 2011 and 2012?

The excitement regarding the emergent voices of protest reflects the idea that civil society is a more attractive site of democratic action because it is relatively unconstrained (Dryzek 1996, 482). This unconstrained participatory democratic action is a significant feature tying the heterogeneous protests of 2010–12 together, along with the use of social media tools and the occupation of space, as the expression of "indignation" was not so much against the austerity policies of the period but a reflection of "profound political malaise vis-à-vis democratic institutions" (Mouffe 2013, 109) and "deep disappointment with the political system" (Kaldor and Selchow, 2012). However, just how unconstrained by or unconnected to institutions associated with the state these protests were is questionable. For example, the mobilization of the *Indignados* in Spain and the *Aganaktismenoi* in Greece expanded with the involvement of trade union organizations and the 2014 founding of the political party Podemos in Spain and the radical left coalition-party Syriza in Greece. Similarly in Canada, the 2012 Quebec student protests were joined by union organizations—the Confédération des syndicats nationaux and the Canadian Union of Public Employees (CUPE)—and provincial opposition parties—the Parti Québécois (PQ), Québec solidaire, and Option nationale (Shingler 2015; Radio-Canada 2014). In the election following the protests, Léo Bureau-Blouin, one of the student spokespersons, ran as a candidate for the PQ, which, after forming a minority government, cancelled the tuition increases.

The point is that the role of parties should not be overlooked. In the case of the 2011–12 protests, political parties were associated with the mass disruptions and in some cases became channels for the voices of indignation and frustration. This is seen in "the rise of non-mainstream parties like the Pirate Party in Germany and Sweden, *Jobbik* in Hungary and New [Golden] Dawn in Greece, the 5 Star movement in Italy [led by former comedian Beppe Grillo] in Italy, or Respect in Bradford, England" (Kaldor and Selchow 2012). We can also add Podemos in Spain. These parties represent both sides of the political spectrum, such as the left-wing Syriza in Greece, Respect in the UK, and the progressive freedom of information focus of the Pirate Party on the one side, and the right-wing nationalism, anti-globalism, and euro-skepticism of *Jobbik* and Golden Dawn on the other. What ties them together is their populist indignation and anti-establishment platforms. This has also appeared in more established political parties, for example, the popular appeal and success of "outsider" candidates such as Jeremy Corbyn, the maverick left winger elected leader of the UK Labour Party, or Bernie Sanders, the self-proclaimed democratic socialist, who ran against Washington insider elite Hillary Clinton for the 2016 Democratic presidential nomination. Both appear to have "tapped into a deep well of resentment against the mainstream political elite" (*Guardian Weekly* 2015).

Canada's version of this can be seen in the 2015 success of Alberta's New Democratic Party, not only defeating the 44-year dynasty of the Conservative Party, but also winning a decisive majority government. This success was based not only on the influx of Eastern and Central Canadian migrants to Alberta's urban areas and the vagaries of a first-past-the-post electoral system with two equally matched right-of-centre parties, the Progressive Conservatives and the Wildrose Party, but also a populist appeal based on the rejection of the old political establishment and its inability to reflect the needs of young and middle-class urban voters. This victory can be compared to the lack of success of the national New Democratic Party in the subsequent fall 2015 national election, a campaign where the NDP pursued the strategy of a front-runner established party that eschewed taking chances with civil society groups, for example, refusing to participate in the leaders' debate on women's issues proposed by the women's advocacy group Up For Debate. The NDP ended up overtaken by the populist, underdog, come-from-behind campaign of Justin Trudeau's Liberal Party, which more successfully portrayed itself as the agent of political change committed to wiping away the closed and undemocratic Harper Conservative government. While it remains to be seen if the populist, democratic, anti-establishment message of the successful Liberal Party will translate into policy, it is clear that the Liberal campaign's positioning of itself as the political outsider and channel of popular frustration in no small measure helped with the party's political success. The populism of unconstrained participatory democracy in this context is a powerful mobilizer.

While disruptions and protests motivate people to hope for and demand alternatives, this is only the beginning of effective transformation. The new consciousness borne of this hope must be brought into institutional channels (Mouffe 2013). It can be argued that parties like Podemos "represent new forms of politics that channel citizens' outrage and hope without having to clash daily with the police" (Castells 2012, 302), but this does not obviate the fact that there appears to be a process where the disruptive outsider expands into or associates with the traditional political insider, a political party. This is because, while movement protests and riots are strong in bringing issues to the fore and acting as agenda setters, decision taking and implementation is much better carried out by organizations like political parties. "Podemos is not and does not pretend to be 15M,[8] making a clear distinction between institutional politics and social movements" (Castells 2012, 303), much like in the 1970s when the Quebec independence movement split into a more anti-systemic wing, including the militant Front de libération du Québec faction and an institutional wing that became the Parti Québécois (Staggenborg 2012). This is the age-old dilemma faced by advocacy groups and social movements: some will take the plunge into the insider pool, risking co-optation and depoliticization in exchange for influence, while others will choose to continue in or be relegated to the outside.

Thus, we return to the assertion made at the outset of this chapter: that a conflict between insider and outsider status is at the heart of the social movement and advocacy politics. "Whether a group should choose the state, civil society, or both simultaneously depends on the particular configuration of movement interests and state imperatives" (Dryzek 1996, 486). What seems certain is that the agendas raised in moments of disruption will become normalized, assimilated, co-opted, or just forgotten. However, normalization has its own dynamic that feeds the frustration and exclusion expressed in disruption—hence the protest cycle. As stated earlier, these events create uncertainty and reveal fault lines in society and leave "a residue of change not only in how social movements and advocacy organizations act, strategize and pursue their goals, but also in how state institutions react to these challenges" (McAdam et al. 2001, 9).

Decoding the Future

It is the process of disruption and normalization that has been highlighted in this chapter. After the disruptions of 1968 we did see the expansion of our notions of political participation and rights, but these have been attenuated over time by the development of rigid, elitist forms of interest representation—normal politics. That politics for many might naturally be expressed as unconstrained emotional participation is suppressed by normal politics. Politics becomes the negotiation and networking of rational organized actors, and thus for the most part the study of social movements and advocacy politics has tended to emphasize this.

However, in periods of disruption "the impact of protest during these periods is not simply that it contributes to coalition-building and realignment . . . the role of disruptive protest in helping create political crisis . . . is the main source of political influence by lower stratum groups" (Piven and Cloward 1995, 160). This crisis emerges from the widespread expression of frustrated antagonism, which is profoundly populist. The coding of populism as emotional and therefore irrational or associated primarily with right-wing politics has tended to make political scientists uncomfortable with the emotional moralism of social movements and advocacy politics. However, it would be worthwhile to revisit the concept of populism and the role emotion plays in politics because the lack of avenues for the expression of emotion and passion underlies most protest (Jasper 1997; Laclau 2005; Mouffe 2013).

More study is needed to tease out the relationships between outsider and insider groups, including political parties. Are these relationships symbiotic, that is, mutually beneficial, or parasitic, where power imbalance results in the outsider, like a computer virus, being either quarantined and expelled or crashing the insider system? In other words, we need to revisit the tension that Selznick (1966) identified as arising in efforts at more inclusive participation and governance. It also needs to be established whether the divide between outsiders and insiders is insurmountable—a strong firewall that blocks all outside code—or if there is a degree of open source coding allowed through continued communications and cooperation between insider and outsider groups. This has always been a problem with the study of social movements and their associated advocacy groups, because in periods of latency it is much easier to study those organized groups who opt for or are accorded insider status within governance structures (or on the near periphery) than it is to examine those who become invisible, the "subterranean" political voices.

The protests of 2011 and 2012 do present us with an avenue into this subterranean world through the computer code of a digital world—that is, the technologies of communication behind the disruptions. Internet technologies help make visible the networks and communication that previously were much harder to access:

> The role of the Internet and wireless communication in the current networked social movements is crucial . . . but their understandings have been obscured by a meaningless discussion in the media and in academic circles denying that communication technologies are at the roots of social movements. This is obvious. Neither the Internet, nor any other technology for that matter, can be a source of social causation. Social movements arise from the contradictions and conflicts of specific societies, and they express people's revolts and projects resulting from their multidimensional experience. Yet at the same time, it is essential to emphasize the critical role of communication in the formation and practice of social movements, now and in history. (Castells 2012, 228–29)

As Castells above and Milner and Small in this book warn, we should be careful not to ascribe the powers of liberatory social causation to what are tools for political actors. However, we cannot ignore that our access to the digital world—to social media, the blogosphere, online zines, indie news sites, and a plethora of individually and group-run websites—gives us the opportunity, like social–political volcanologists (to switch metaphors at the end), to trace the tremors and relationships in the social zeitgeist portending emerging voices and disruptions, and giving us a way into the subterranean political world.

Suggested Readings

Politics and Protests of 2011:

Castells, Manuel. 2012. *Networks of Outrage and Hope: Social Movements in the Internet Age*. Cambridge: Polity Press.
Mouffe, Chantal. 2013. *Agonistics: Thinking the World Politically*. London: Verso.

Advocacy Groups in Canada:

Laforest, Rachel. 2011. *Voluntary Sector Organizations and the State.* Vancouver: University of British Columbia Press.
Staggenborg, Suzanne. 2012. *Social Movements.* 2nd Canadian ed. Toronto: Oxford University Press.

Outsider Politics Now and Then:

Coleman, Gabriella. 2014. *Hacker, Hoaxer, Whitleblower, Spy: The Many Faces of Anonymous.* London: Verso.
Piven, Francis Fox, and Richard A. Cloward. 1977. *Poor People's Movements: Why They Succeed, How They Fail.* New York: Vintage Books.

Notes

1   It should be noted that Offe appears to be inspired by the terminology and concept of "code as social discourse" found in Melucci's 1996 book, *Challenging Codes.*
2   Less politically controversial advisory councils, such as the Western Transportation Advisory Council, which brings together various participants from business, labour, and government to foster collaboration in transportation policy and practice (www.westac.com), were also created and continue today.
3   Looking at the participation programs of the late 1960s, Martin Loney concluded that government funding and involvement in the voluntary sector was a "conservatizing force" (cited in Pal 1993, 42). He argued that programs geared to bring Indigenous groups into mainstream society kept the discontented groups busy without threatening the underlying stability or division of wealth and power in Canada. Examining the federal government's Volunteer Sector Initiative (VSI), a public–private program that brought voluntary sector representatives and public servants together to consider programs to strengthen the sector so it could better serve Canadians, Phillips (2006, 25) found that the volunteer sector participants were frustrated because the process got bogged down in operational matters rather than addressing big policy issues. This was not only because the government had set limits on the mandate of the collaboration, but also because participants "were consumed with the enormous operational details of the VSI, which left little time to deal with policy, and because they were discouraged from pursuing a more political route until some of the contentious issues had been resolved within the VSI" (Phillips 2006)
4   Theda Skocpol (2003) traces this development in the United States and connects it with a diminishment of democracy.
5   This was announced by then Minister of Citizenship, Immigration, and Multiculturalism, Jason Kenney, during a visit to Israel (Whittington 2009).
6   Oda was accused of misleading Parliament by covering up that she had penciled the word "no" into the funding request sent from CIDA to her office (Clark 2011).

7   In the 1970s and 1980s, it was not uncommon for advocacy groups to create arm's-length foundations that focused solely on public education to claim a charitable taxation status for that arm of the organization. For example, the anti-nuclear weapons organization Operation Dismantle had an associated public education foundation, the Foundation for Global Peace. Today groups would be encouraged to create separate advocacy organizations to undertake public political advocacy. In this vein, ecologist David Suzuki resigned from his eponymous foundation, the Suzuki Foundation, because continuing to publicly present his political views jeopardized the status of the foundation (Boesveld 2012). At that time, 52 political activity audits were underway on organizations such as the Suzuki Foundation, Tides Canada, Équiterre, and the Environmental Defence Fund—all environmental organizations critical of the Harper government's policy on climate change and support for the Alberta oil sands. International issue groups, such as KAIROS and Amnesty International, were also included in the audited group (Canadian Press 2014a). In September 2014, it was reported that the Canadian Centre for Policy Alternatives, a left-wing research think tank, was also being audited because its research and educational material was deemed to be too one-sided and biased (Canadian Press 2014b).

8   15M was the original name of the movement in Spain, referring to the date of the first set of demonstrations on May 15. This is in the same manner that the protests against the World Trade Organization meetings in Seattle in 1999 (the Battle of Seattle) were referred to as N30 for 30 November 1999. Organized under the theme of "Real Democracy Now," the Spanish demonstrations were given the moniker *indignados* by the media, a name that characterized the frustration of the participants and that ended up being adopted by them.

References

Boesveld, Sarah. 2012. "David Suzuki Resigns to Save Foundation from 'Bully' Charitable Status Threats." *National Post,* April 14. http://news.nationalpost.com/news/canada/david-suzuki-resigns-to-save-foundation-from-bully-charitable-status-threats

Canadian Press. 2014a. "Canadian Charities in Limbo as Tax Audit Widens to New Groups." *CBC News,* July 10. http://www.cbc.ca/news/politics/canadian-charities-in-limbo-as-tax-audits-widen-to-new-groups-1.2703177

Canadian Press. 2014b. "CRA Audits CCPA Think Tank Due to Alleged Bias." *CBC News,* September 2. www.cbc.ca/news/business/cra-audits-ccpa-think-tank-due-to-alleged-bias-1.2752966

Carson, Rachel. 1962. *Silent Spring.* Boston: Houghton Mifflin.

Castells, Manuel. 2012. *Networks of Outrage and Hope: Social Movements in the Internet Age.* Cambridge: Polity Press.

Clark, Campbell. 2011. "Speaker Rebukes Bev Oda over Document in Kairos Case." *Globe and Mail,* February 10. www.theglobeandmail.com/news/politics/speaker-rebukes-bev-oda-over-document-in-kairos-case/article566676

Coleman, William G., and Grace Skogstad. 1990. *Policy Communities and Public Policy in Canada: A Structural Approach.* Mississauga, ON: Copp Clark Pitman.

Cormier, Jeffrey. 2004. *The Canadianization Movement: Emergence, Survival and Success.* Toronto: University of Toronto Press.

Doberstein, Cory, and Heather Millar. 2014. "Balancing a House of Cards: Throughput Legitimacy in Canadian Governance Networks." *Canadian Journal of Political Science* 47 (2): 259–80. http://dx.doi.org/10.1017/S0008423914000420

Dryzek, John S. 1996. "Inclusion and the Dynamics of Democratization." *American Political Science Review* 90 (3): 475–87. http://dx.doi.org/10.2307/2082603

Dufour, Pascale, and Christophe Traisnel. 2008. "Nationalism and Protest: The Sovereignty Movement in Quebec." In *Group Politics and Social Movements in Canada,* edited by Miriam Smith, 251–76. Peterborough, ON: Broadview Press.

Franks, S. 1987. *The Parliament of Canada.* Toronto: University of Toronto Press.

Galipeau, Claude. 1989. "Political Parties, Interest Groups, and New Social Movements: Toward New Representation?" In *Canadian Parties in Transition: Discourse, Organization, Representation,* edited by Alain-G. Gagnon and A. Brian Tanguay, 404–26. Toronto: Nelson Canada.

Guardian Weekly. 2015. "Corbyn Comes in from the Cold to Revive the Left." September 14–15, 193 (13): 4–10.

Habermas, Jürgen. 1981. "New Social Movements." *Telos* 49: 33–37. http://dx.doi.org/10.3817/0981049033

Jasper, James. 1997. *The Art of Moral Protest.* Chicago: University of Chicago Press. http://dx.doi.org/10.7208/chicago/9780226394961.001.0001

KAIROS. 2011. "Frequently Asked Questions: Kairos CIDA Funding Controversy." www.kairos.canada.org/wp-content/uploads/2011/10/GI-CIDA-KAIROS-FAQ-11-02-03.pdf

Kaldor, Mary, and Sabine Selchow. 2012. "The Bubbling up of Subterranean Politics in Europe." Opendemocracy.net, October 12.

Kitching, Andrew. 2006. "Charitable Purpose, Advocacy, and the Income Tax Act." February 28. Ottawa: Library of Parliament, Parliamentary Information and Research Service. www.parl.gc.ca/content/lop/researchpublications/prb0590-e.htm

Kobayashi, Audrey. 2008. "Ethnocultural Political Mobilization, Multiculturalism, and Human Rights in Canada." In *Group Politics and Social Movements in Canada,* edited by Miriam Smith, 131–57. Peterborough, ON: Broadview Press.

Kohler-Koch, Beate. 2010. "Civil Society and EU Democracy: 'Astroturf' Representation?" *Journal of European Public Policy* 17 (1): 100–16. http://dx.doi.org/10.1080/13501760903464986

Ladner, Kiera. 2008. "*Aysaka'paykinit:* Contesting the Rope around the Nations' Neck." In *Group Politics and Social Movements in Canada,* edited by Miriam Smith, 227–49. Peterborough, ON: Broadview Press.

Levitz, Stephanie. 2014. "Former PMs, Aboriginal Leaders Seek to Ease Tensions between Groups." *Canadian Press,* September 4. http://winnipeg.ctvnews.ca/former-pms-first-nations-leaders-seek-to-ease-tensions-between-groups-1.1991059

Laforest, Rachel. 2011. *Voluntary Sector Organizations and the State.* Vancouver: University of British Columbia Press.

Laforest, Rachel. 2013. "Shifting Scales of Governance and Civil Society Participation in Canada and the European Union." *Canadian Public Administration* 56 (2): 235–51. http://dx.doi.org/10.1111/capa.12016

Laclau, Ernesto. 2005. *On Populist Reason.* London: Verso.

Mason, Paul. 2013. *Why It's Still Kicking Off Everywhere: The New Global Revolutions.* London: Verso.

McAdam, Doug, Sidney Tarrow, and Charles Tilly. 2001. *Dynamics of Contention.* Cambridge: Cambridge University Press. http://dx.doi.org/10.1017/CBO9780511805431

McKenzie, Judith. 2008. "The Environmental Movement in Canada: Retreat or Resurgence?" In *Group Politics and Social Movements in Canada,* edited by Miriam Smith, 279–306. Peterborough, ON: Broadview Press.

Melucci, Alberto. 1989. *Nomads of the Present: Social Movements and Individual Needs in Contemporary Society.* Philadelphia: Temple University Press.

Melucci, Alberto. 1996. *Challenging Codes: Collective Action in the Information Age.* Cambridge: Cambridge University Press. http://dx.doi.org/10.1017/CBO9780511520891

Michels, Robert. (1911) 1962. *Political Parties: A Sociological Study of the Oligarchical Tendencies in Modern Democracy.* Translated by Eden and Dedar Paul. New York: Free Press.

Moffat, Gary. 1982. *A History of the Peace Movement in Canada.* Ottawa: Grapevine Press.

Mouffe, Chantal. 2005. *On the Political.* Abingdon, UK: Routledge.

Mouffe, Chantal. 2013. *Agonistics.* London: Verso.

Newman, Jacquetta. 1999. "Project Ploughshares: Surviving the End of the Cold War." *Peace Research: The Canadian Journal of Peace Studies* 31 (4): 44–58.

Newman, Jacquetta, and A. Brian Tanguay. 2002. "Crashing the Party: The Politics of Interest Groups and Social Movements." In *Citizen Politics: Research and Theory in Canadian Political Behaviour,* edited by Joanna Everitt and Brenda O'Neill, 387–412. Toronto: Oxford University Press.

Newman, Jacquetta, and Linda White. 2012. *Women, Politics, and Public Policy: The Political Struggles of Canadian Women.* 2nd ed. Toronto: Oxford University Press.

Offe, Claus. 1981. "The Attribution of Public Status to Interest Groups: Observations on the West German Case." In *Organizing Interests in Western Europe: Pluralism, Corporatism, and the Transformation of Politics,* edited by Suzanne D. Berger, 123–58. Cambridge: Cambridge University Press.

Offe, Claus. 2002. "1968 Thirty Years After: Four Hypotheses on the Historical Consequences of the Student Movement." *Thesis Eleven* 68 (February): 82–88. http://dx.doi.org/10.1177/0725513602068001006

Offe, Claus. 2009. "Governance an 'Empty Signifier'?" *Constellations* 16 (4): 550–62. http://dx.doi.org/10.1111/j.1467-8675.2009.00570.x

Pal, Leslie. 1993. *Interests of State: The Politics of Language, Multiculturalism and Feminism in Canada.* Montreal: McGill-Queen's University Press.

Palumbo, Antonino. 2010. "Introduction Governance: Meanings, Themes, Narratives and Questions." In *From Government to Governance,* edited by Richard Bellamy and Antonino Palumbo, xi–xxiii. Farnham, UK: Ashgate Publishing.

Phillips, Susan D. 1991. "Meaning and Structure in Social Movements: Mapping the Network of Canadian National Women's Organizations." *Canadian Journal of Political Science* 31: 311–88.

Phillips, Susan D. 1996. "Competing, Connecting, and Complementing: Parties, Interest Groups and New Social Movements." In *Canadian Parties in Transition* 2nd ed., edited by Alain-G. Gagnon and A. Brian Tanguay, 440–62. Toronto: Nelson Canada.

Phillips, Susan D. 2006. "The Intersection of Governance and Citizenship in Canada: Not Quite the Third Way." *IRPP Policy Matters* 7 (4): 1–31.

Piven, Francis Fox, and Richard A. Cloward. 1977. *Poor People's Movements: Why They Succeed, How They Fail*. New York: Vintage Books/Random House.

Piven, Francis Fox, and Richard A. Cloward. 1995. "Collective Protest: A Critique of Resource Mobilization Theory." In *Social Movements: Critiques, Concepts, Case Studies*, edited by Stanford M. Lyman, 137–67. New York: New York University Press. http://dx.doi.org/10.1007/978-1-349-23747-0_8

Prentice, Allison, Paula Bourne, Gail Cuthbert Brandt, Beth Light, Wendy Mitchinson, and Naomi Black. 1988. *Canadian Women: A History*. Toronto: Harcourt Brace Jovanovich.

Pross, Paul. 1992. *Group Politics and Public Policy*. 2nd ed. Toronto: Oxford University Press.

Radio-Canada. 2014. "Droits de scolarité au Québec: un débat de société." May 21. http://ici.radio-canada.ca/sujet/droits-scolarite

Ramos, Howard. 2012. "Aboriginal Protest." In *Social Movements*, 2nd Canadian ed., edited by Suzanne Staggenborg, 71–93. Toronto: Oxford University Press.

Rayside, David, and Evert Lindquist. 1992. "AIDS Activism and the State in Canada." *Studies in Political Economy* 39: 37–76.

Rhodes, R.A.W. 1997. *Understanding Governance*. Oxford: Oxford University Press.

Rudé, George. 1964. *The Crowd in History: A Study of Popular Disturbances in France and England, 1730–1848*. New York: Wiley.

Selznick, Philip. 1966. *TVA and the Grass Roots: A Study of Politics and Organization*. Berkeley: University of California Press.

Shingler, Benjamin. 2015. "Quebec Student Protests: What You Need to Know." *CBC Montreal*, April 2. www.cbc.ca/news/canada/montreal/quebec-student-protests-what-you-need-to-know-1.3018153

Skocpol, Theda. 2003. *Diminished Democracy: From Membership to Management in American Civic Life*. Norman: University of Oklahoma Press.

Smith, Miriam. 2008. "Identity and Opportunity: The Lesbian and Gay Rights Movement." In *Group Politics and Social Movements in Canada*, edited by Miriam Smith, 181–202. Toronto: University of Toronto Press.

Staggenborg, Suzanne. 2011. *Social Movements*, 2nd ed. New York: Oxford University Press.

Staggenborg, Suzanne. 2012. *Social Movements*. 2nd Canadian ed. Toronto: Oxford University Press.

Standing Committee on the Status of Women. 2005. *Funding through the Women's Program: Women's Groups Speak Out*. Ottawa: Author.

Standing Committee on Status of Women. 2007. *The Impact of Funding and Program Changes at Status of Women Canada*. 39th Parliament, 1st Session Report (May). Ottawa: Author.

Tarrow, Sidney. 1998. *Power in Movement: Social Movements and Contentious Politics*. 2nd ed. Cambridge: Cambridge University Press. http://dx.doi.org/10.1017/CBO9780511813245

Taylor, Drew Hayden. 2014. "Idle No More Isn't Dead, It's Just Resting." *Globe and Mail*, September 27. www.theglobeandmail.com/globe-debates/idle-no-more-isnt-dead-its-just-resting/article20795994

Thorburn, Hugh. 2007. "Interest Groups, Social Movements, and the Canadian Parliamentary System." In *Canadian Parties in Transition*, 3rd ed., edited by

Alain-G. Gagnon and A. Brian Tanguay, 385–410. Toronto: University of Toronto Press.

Whittington, Les. 2009. "'Anti-Semitic' Charge Angers Aid Group." *Toronto Star*, December 18. http://www.thestar.com/news/canada/2009/12/18/ antisemitic_charge_angers_aid_group.html

Young, Lisa, and Joanna Everitt. 2004. *Advocacy Groups*. Vancouver: University of British Columbia Press.

13

Party Politics in a Distinct Society: Two Eras of Block Voting in Quebec

ALAIN–G. GAGNON AND FRANÇOIS BOUCHER

Q UEBEC'S DISTINCT IDENTITY AND self-understanding as a minority nation within the larger Canadian federation are two of the central keys to understanding federal elections and party politics in the country.[1] Many authors advance the notion that Quebec exhibits distinctive electoral behaviour, which in turn has an important bearing on the outcome of federal elections. John McMenemy (1976, 14) remarked, "One of the more important electoral facts in Canadian history is that Quebec, the second most populous region and the only predominantly French and Catholic province, has a tendency to vote as a block." Several analysts also conclude that Quebec displays greater voter cohesion than that found in other provinces, and that it forms a monolithic voting block in federal elections. For instance, James Bickerton (2007) has convincingly argued that federal politics in Quebec can best be depicted as a one-party dominant system. Bickerton (2007, 426) advanced an explanation for this tendency to back a single party, arguing that "as a political minority, francophones in Quebec adopted a strategy of not fragmenting their vote among different parties."[2] Citing Marcel Rioux (1979), he claimed that greater electorate cohesion is explained by "the role of nationalist ideology in providing Quebeckers with common values and a shared frame of reference" (Bickerton 2007, 426). The view that Quebec votes as a block needs to be qualified, though, as Paul Thomas (1991, 199–200) stressed some time ago, "The idea of a Quebec block in national politics is part fact and part fiction, and it is also controversial."

In this chapter we will explore the view that Quebec ought to be analyzed apart from the other provinces because of its distinct electoral behaviour—namely its greater tendency to vote as a monolithic block in federal elections. We argue that this tendency is not caused by a natural or inherent characteristic of Quebecers, such as a greater homogeneity of political opinion or an aversion for disagreement or, as some misguided critics have suggested, a tendency betraying a herd-like instinct. Nor do we believe that the block voting phenomenon in Quebec is only an outcome of the electoral system. Rather, our understanding is that Quebec's distinct identity and self-understanding as a national community within the larger Canadian federation are likely to incite Quebecers to adopt voting strategies that result in greater voting cohesion. The claim that Quebecers tend to vote as a block needs to be qualified at the outset. It is only in federal elections that we can observe a clear and long-lasting tendency of block voting among Quebecers. Provincial elections in Quebec tend to be very competitive, and Quebec's vote is more fragmented in provincial elections than it is in federal ones (Bastien, Bélanger, and Gélineau 2013, 10–11).

It is quite understandable that Quebec voters have sought to protect themselves from Ottawa's centralizing initiatives by putting their trust in political parties that (1) valued provincial rights, (2) were sensitive and open to voters' policy preferences, and (3) showed less discomfort with the province's claims as a national community. The question, then, is whether Quebec's long-standing priorities and preferences have truly led the *belle province* to vote as a monolithic block in a way that other provinces have not.

We will argue that underneath the shifting dynamics of party politics in Quebec lies a greater continuity. We suggest that the Québécois, as a French-speaking minority nation integrated into a multinational federation, have fought to obtain representation within the Canadian parliamentary institutions by adopting different voting strategies from their counterparts in the rest of the country. For a long period, the Quebec electorate was able to remain largely cohesive and to rally behind the dominant party (the Liberal Party). This was particularly true during the dominance of the Liberals in Quebec—a period stretching from 1879 to 1980, where Quebec was overrepresented 24 times in the government, much more frequently than other Canadian regions (Bickerton 2007, 426; Bakvis and Macpherson 1995). It is important to point out that unilateral repatriation of the Constitution under Pierre Trudeau's Liberal government had an adverse effect on the historic ties between French-speaking Quebecers and the Liberals. Since then, as we argue below, despite great electoral volatility, Quebecers's voting behaviour seems to have been consistently dominated by the suspicion that federal parties are insensitive to their preferences. In this chapter we have identified what appear to be two durable features of Quebec party politics at the federal level:

1. Quebecers have tended to give their political support to parties that were able to present themselves as potential game changers and to speak on behalf of the province's distinct voice as a minority nation.
2. This has made Quebec a particularly fertile ground for third parties that build on a narrative of political transformation and rejection of the way mainstream parties do politics.

The general purpose of this chapter is to account for these two durable features of Quebec's political behaviour in federal elections and to offer our interpretation of recent electoral volatility in the province. First, to set the stage, we will assess the extent to which Quebec can be said to vote as a block. Next we discuss why Quebec has become a particularly fertile ground for the emergence of third parties at the federal level and as such constitutes a distinct electoral community. This is followed by an account of the period stretching from Meech Lake to the Orange Wave, along with an exploration of the current political situation in the province.

Quebec Voting as a Block?

One-party dominance in Quebec for the longest time favoured the Liberal Party of Canada, which for much of the twentieth century was able to attract large numbers of francophone and Catholic voters. However, since the 1980s, the Quebec electorate has tended to turn its back on the Liberal Party, its tendency to vote as a block has become significantly weaker, and voting behaviour in Quebec appears to be more volatile than ever, especially since the election of Stephen Harper's Conservative Party in 2006. The near collapse of the Bloc Québécois, the unexpected success of the New Democratic Party in 2011, and the return of the Liberals *en force* in 2015 illustrate quite well this new volatility of the Quebec electorate. How can one account for this turn of events? Is the decrease in electoral cohesion in Quebec due to a reduction in nationalist sentiment, as some contend when attempting to explain the electoral debacle of the Bloc? Can the apparent voter volatility be attributed entirely to political cynicism, which undermines individuals' party identification and loyalty and pushes them to vote strategically?

Block voting occurs when a region or a constituency consistently displays higher-than-average levels of electoral cohesion in support of a given party. When the largest party in a given region obtains 75 per cent or more of the seats or 55 per cent or more of the popular vote, block voting has occurred (L.G. Macpherson 1991; Thomas 1991, 200). The view that Quebec's electorate behaves as a monolithic voting block in federal elections takes root in the fact that, for a very long time (roughly 1896 to 1984), Quebecers overwhelmingly backed the Liberal Party (Bickerton 2014, 252–54). Thus, Quebec has been described as the Liberals' "solid South," referring to the role played in the early twentieth century by American Southern states in electing Democrats. Most importantly, the view that Quebec constitutes a voting block is usually explained by the fact that since French-speaking Quebecers form a minority nation within Canada, they tend to refrain, for strategic reasons, from fragmenting their vote among different parties and instead support a single party, often the governing one. As Paul Thomas (1991, 200) puts it, "As a political minority within the national political system, francophones in Quebec, it is suggested, have consciously adopted a strategy of not fragmenting their vote among different parties. Calculating which party will gain office nationally, they have placed their support behind that party to ensure their interests are not ignored."

This political behaviour explains a fair amount, but it does not tell the full story. Alan C. Cairns (1968) argued in a seminal article that the block voting thesis is misleading because it ignores the role of the first-past-the-post electoral system, which provides a bonus in seats to the party that wins the most votes in a region. For Cairns, Quebec's vote in federal elections was never as concentrated in favour of a political party as it was said to be, and it was only when looking at the number of seats won, in contrast with the percentage of the popular vote, that Quebec appeared to vote as a monolith. According to Cairns, Quebec's block voting was not a "social fact," but mainly an effect of the single-member plurality electoral system:

> It is only at the level of seats, not votes, that Quebec became a Liberal stronghold, a Canadian "solid South," and a one-party monopoly. The Canadian "solid South," like its American counterpart, is a contrivance of the electoral system, not an autonomous social fact which exists independent of it. (Cairns 1968, 67)

Cairns's argument is persuasive, but it nonetheless remains the case that Quebec has tended to send to Ottawa strong political delegations, usually on the side of the governing party, but also on the opposition side in times of political crisis—such as the two conscription crises or the rejection of the Meech Lake and Charlottetown accords. While the electoral system remains a constant variable, the changing political context can have a major impact on the final results.

Moreover, when we have a closer look, block voting appears both at the level of seats and the popular vote. Comparing federal election results in Ontario and Quebec from 1878 to 1991, Herman Bakvis and Laura Macpherson (1995) concluded that Quebec has a much greater tendency to vote as a block than Ontario, the only comparable province in terms of size. If we define block voting as a single party winning 75 per cent or more of the seats in a given region, then in the 31 federal elections held between 1878 and 1991 Quebec voted as a block in 23 of them; for the same period, Ontario voted as block only 4 times. Even when block voting is defined in terms of a single party capturing more than 55 per cent of the popular vote, Quebec reached that threshold on 12 occasions (22 when the threshold is lowered to 50 per cent), whereas Ontario did it only 4 times (Thomas 1991, Table 1, 200–1).

Since the arrival of the Bloc Québécois on the federal scene, block voting, paradoxically, seems to have been on the decline: still present but much weaker than before. Indeed, in the eight federal elections held between 1993 and 2015, the largest party in Quebec has never won 75 per cent or more of the seats or 55 per cent or more of the popular vote. However, on five occasions the largest party won two-thirds or more of the seats if one includes the 2008 election, when the Bloc won 49 out of 75 seats (65.3 per cent). Twice, in 1993 and 2004, the largest party was elected with almost 50 per cent of the popular vote in the province (see Table 13.1).

Table 13.1   Quebec's Block Voting in Federal Elections, 1867–2015

Party winning the highest percentage of seats and popular vote in Quebec

Election	Political Party	% of seats	% of votes
1867	**Conservative**	70.3★★	52.9
1872	**Conservative**	60.0★★	48.3
1874	**Liberal Party**	53.8	47.8
1878	**Conservative**	72.3★★	53.8
1882	**Conservative**	78.5★★	51
1887	**Conservative**	44.6★★	43.2
1891	Liberal Party★	50.8	45.3
1896	**Liberal Party**	75.4	53.5
1900	**Liberal Party**	87.7	55.9
1904	**Liberal Party**	81.5	56.4
1908	**Liberal Party**	80	52.5
1911	Liberal Party★	56.9★★	46.7
1917	Liberal Party (under Laurier)	95.4	69.7
1921	**Liberal Party**	100	70.2
1925	**Liberal Party**	90.8	60.4
1926	**Liberal Party**	92.3	63.2
1930	Liberal Party	61.5	53.1
1935	**Liberal Party**	84.6	54.4
1940	**Liberal Party**	93.8	74.1
1945	**Liberal Party**	86.2	51.1
1949	**Liberal Party**	93.2	61.8
1953	**Liberal Party**	90.7	64.7

(continued)

Table 13.1   (Continued)

Party winning the highest percentage of seats and popular vote in Quebec

Election	Political Party	% of seats	% of votes
1957	Liberal Party	85.3★★	62.3
1958	**Progressive Conservative Party**	66.7	49.6
1962	Liberal Party	46.7	39.8
1963	**Liberal Party**	62.7	45.6
1965	**Liberal Party**	74.7	45.6
1968	**Liberal Party**	75.7	53.6
1972	**Liberal Party**	75.7	49.1
1974	**Liberal Party**	81.1	54.1
1979	Liberal Party	89.3	61.6
1980	**Liberal Party**	98.7	68.2
1984	**Progressive Conservative Party**	77.3	50.2
1988	**Progressive Conservative Party**	84	52.7
1993	Bloc Québécois	72	49.3
1997	Bloc Québécois	58.7	37.9
2000	Bloc Québécois★	50.7	39.9
2004	Bloc Québécois	72	48.9
2006	Bloc Québécois	68	42.1
2008	Bloc Québécois	65.3	38.1
2011	New Democratic Party	78.7	42.9
2015	**Liberal Party**	51.3	35.7

★ The party has the highest number of seats but not the highest percentage of the votes.
★★ Number of seats includes one or more independent MPs having the same political allegiance.

Note: **Bold parties** indicate parties that formed the government.

Sources: For general elections from 1867–1921: Drouilly (1983, 937); for general elections from 1925–2006: Gagnon and Tanguay (2007, 574); for general elections from 2008–2011: Elections Canada (2015).

However, what emerges clearly from the data in Table 13.1 is that since the end of the dominance of the Liberals, block voting patterns seem to take shape in Quebec during political crises or phases of electoral realignment. With the Quebec referendum of 1980 and the ensuing patriation of the Constitution in 1982, Quebec francophones' trust in the Liberal Party was seriously eroded. This helped make Quebec's electorate much more volatile than it had previously been. Following patriation, most Quebec francophones in the 1984 federal election repudiated the federal Liberals and instead supported Brian Mulroney's Progressive Conservatives, a party that explicitly stated its desire to redress what it considered to be an unjust constitutional situation. Similarly, in 1993, Quebecers decided to support the newly born Bloc Québécois, which won 50 per cent of the popular vote and 72 per cent of the seats (54 out of 75). In 2011, francophone voters in Quebec helped generate the "Orange Wave," as they gave Jack Layton's NDP 43 per cent of the vote and 59 of the 75 seats (79 per cent) in the province (see Table 13.1). Finally, in 2015, it is worth pointing out that only one of the ten most francophone ridings in Quebec elected a Liberal candidate, whereas the Conservatives and the NDP elected six and three members, respectively (Letellier 2015).

What is striking about this period of intense electoral volatility in Quebec (1984–2015) is that these shifts in voting behaviour occurred at times when a large number of Quebecers felt that their interests as a distinct political community and their policy preferences within the Canadian state tended to be dismissed or even ignored in Ottawa. The Liberal Party's near death in Quebec in the 1984 federal election followed the unilateral patriation of the Constitution without Quebec's consent and the promises of Brian Mulroney to modify the Constitution to obtain Quebec's endorsement. After the failure of the Meech Lake Accord, with which Mulroney was trying to modify the Constitution to get Quebec's approval, Quebecers massively rallied behind the Bloc in the 1993 election.[3] In 2011, Quebecers withdrew their support for the Bloc and rallied to the NDP, which was perceived as the best option to defeat Harper's Conservatives. Importantly, at the outset of the campaign Jack Layton had stressed his party's 2005 Sherbrooke Declaration, which stated that Quebec constitutes a nation and that asymmetrical federalism was an appropriate measure to adopt to accommodate Quebec's social preferences. In addition—and even more importantly from Quebec's perspective—the NDP accepted the 50 per cent + 1 threshold for any future referendum. In 2015, the Quebec electorate is more fragmented than at any other time since the mid-1960s.

This shift in support, as we will see later, occurred once many Quebecers had stopped believing in Harper's "open federalism" and came to realize how antagonistic to their environmentalist and social democratic values the Conservative government had become. It thus seems that the main factor driving Quebecers' vote in federal elections is a distrustful and defensive posture vis-à-vis federal parties that were, in the end, generally insensitive to Quebec's policy preferences and identity claims.

There is a need to better understand the character of the Quebec electorate, which, despite its sociological transformation over many decades, continues to express itself as a strongly unified voice in the federal party system. In the following sections we will turn our attention to this specific question.

Quebec: A Fertile Ground for Third Parties

One of the most important repercussions of Quebec's block voting in federal elections is that Quebec, more than any other region with the exception of Alberta, constitutes fertile ground for the emergence of third parties. It is not our goal here to employ a restrictive definition of third parties. A classical definition of third parties is provided by Maurice Pinard (1973, 455), for whom a third party is a nontraditional party that has not yet been in power, thus remaining an untried alternative in the eyes of voters. Some authors have proposed a more technical definition of the term. For instance, André Blais (1973, 426) claims that "a third party is a non-traditional party that has not managed to obtain a minimum of 10 percent in each of the previous two elections." We will rather work with the general idea that a third party is a political formation that presents candidates in elections but usually fails to secure one of the two largest blocks of seats in the legislature and is perceived by voters as offering an original alternative to the dominant parties (see, for instance, Gagnon and Tanguay 1996, 108). Third parties have a tendency to present themselves as the vehicles for change and appeal to voters by claiming to offer real alternatives to the dominant parties, which are presented as old, disconnected from the social and political realities, and unresponsive to the concerns of ordinary citizens.

Several of the most important and enduring third parties in Canadian history have their roots in Quebec: the Bloc populaire canadien (1944–47), l'Union des électeurs/Parti du ralliement créditiste/Social Credit/Ralliement créditiste (1946/1958/1962/1963–80), and, more recently, the Bloc Québécois (1991–) have all left an imprint on political life (Gagnon and Tanguay 1996, 106–34; Bickerton, Gagnon, and Smith 1999). Considering that most single-member plurality electoral systems tend to favour bipartisanship, the continuing presence of third parties since the 1920s in Canada has been a distinctive feature of the federal party system (Gagnon and Tanguay 1996, 106). As Bickerton (2014, 257) stresses, "Canada has long been something of an exception among comparable political systems in terms of its propensity to support 'third parties.'"[4]

Third parties usually have a strong regional basis. The Co-operative Commonwealth Federation (CCF; Saskatchewan) and the Social Credit (Alberta) were born out of the Western rural region's discontent with dominant and centralist parties in Ottawa. Objectives pursued by these third parties consisted in furthering the interests of workers and farmers in the Prairies, regions that were hit especially hard during the Great Depression. As for the Bloc Québécois, its main *raison d'être* remains the promotion of Quebec's interests as a distinct nation within Canada while supporting the objective of Quebec's independence. Certain third parties, such as the CCF, the NDP, and the Reform Party, have had pan-Canadian ambitions, presenting candidates in every constituency across the country while their original support basis remains strongly associated with a region (the Prairies, to be sure; although as we will see, a surprising turn of events in the 2011 election was the sweeping victory of the NDP in Quebec). Other parties, such as the Bloc, are dedicated to furthering the interests of a particular region and present candidates only in that region.

There is an enduring debate over the main causes of the rise and success of third parties. Why have third parties been so present and successful in Canadian elections and not in the United States or in certain regions of Canada, such as the Maritimes? C.B. Macpherson and Maurice Pinard have provided seminal accounts of the rise of third parties in Canada. The former claimed that structural features, such as the quasi-colonial relationship between the West and Central Canada, along with the uniform class composition of Alberta in the 1920s (composed mainly of independent farmers), explains the rise of the Social Credit and of the United Farmers of Alberta (Macpherson [1953] 1962). Pinard argued that a period of one-party dominance followed by economic hardships affecting one segment of the population explains the sudden success of the Social Credit in Quebec during the 1962 general election and provides a general model explaining the rise or the failure of minor parties at different times and locations (Pinard 1975).[5]

Although it is debatable whether these precise factors can form the basis of a general theory of the rise and fall of third parties, it is fair to say that the explanation for the creation and endurance of such third parties involves the insensitivity or unresponsiveness of the federal party system to the claims and interests of different regions (Gagnon and Tanguay 1996). This failure to take into account regional voices and preferences of Canadians is exacerbated by different institutional factors rooted in the Canadian political system (Bickerton 2014, 257–59). For instance, the tendency of first-past-the-post electoral systems to generate an overrepresentation of the strongest parties in the House of Commons, the dominance of the executive, the strict party discipline found in a Westminster parliamentary democracy, and the inefficacy of the Senate as a means of regional representation all help reinforce the dominance of major parties. Yet these factors also fuel the perception that major parties at the federal level are unresponsive to the needs and claims of certain regions. Moreover, first-past-the-post electoral systems tend to reward parties with a regionally concentrated basis of support. This provides the conditions in which regionally based third parties become the vehicles for narratives of change and discontentment with established political elites.

As a result, regions with strong identities and distinctive claims are often the cradle of new parties, which can use regional identities and discontent to their advantage to modify the dominant party dynamics, possibly leading to significant changes and even realignment in the party system. Quebec is not, of course, the only province that can be depicted as a fertile ground for the emergence of third parties. As we have seen, Western provinces have had their share of enduring third parties (the CCF and Social Credit, especially). That being said, the interprovincial dynamics have profoundly changed during the last few decades. Economic and political power has migrated westward with the rise of the Conservative Party and of the oil-based economy in Alberta, to the extent that the vote of the residents of Western provinces can no longer be viewed as expressing the concerns of a relatively homogenous class of farmers whose interests are threatened by big corporations and banks established in Eastern Canada. On the other hand, the dynamics of identity have remained largely unchanged, as Quebec still expresses concerns as a minority nation within an English-speaking Canada. Quebecers still view their vote in federal elections as a way of protesting against Ottawa's unresponsiveness to their nationalist sentiments and concerns as a distinct nation within Canada. The monumental collapse of the Bloc Québécois in the 2011 election and continued troubles in the 2015 election (ending up in fourth position) might cause us to rethink the view that nationalist and identity-based considerations still play a major role in Quebec's voting behaviour. In the next section we suggest that the demise of the Bloc and the collapse of the Orange Wave are best understood in terms of continuity with Quebec's voting habits and historical patterns and, as such, do not constitute a radical change in the mindset of Quebec's electorate.

Two Decades in Search of a New Political Dynamic

One of the main recent distinctive features of party politics in Quebec is the low level of political trust Quebecers have in political institutions and political parties. Analyzing opinion surveys conducted in 2005 and 2010, Réjean Pelletier and Jérôme Couture (2012) have compared the respective levels of trust of Quebecers and residents from the rest of Canada. They found that Quebecers generally place less trust in political parties (federal and provincial) than other Canadians and that they put more trust in provincial public institutions (school and police, for example) than in federal public institutions (army and Supreme Court).

Different reasons can be invoked to explain Quebec's lower level of trust in federal political parties and institutions. According to Pelletier and Couture (2012, 240), although Quebec's distinct identity was the source of distrust reported in the survey they conducted in 2005, this factor has been replaced by regional alienation and cynicism—feelings that are shared by residents of the other provinces and are thus less specific to Quebec. In addition, over the years several key events on the federal political scene have acted as catalysts of distrust in Quebec by fuelling the perception that Quebec's demands, interests, and policy preference were not taken into account by federal politicians or that Quebecers were disliked by their fellow Canadians. For instance, in 1982 the repatriation of the Canadian Constitution without Quebec's consent led Quebec voters to turn their back on the Liberal Party of Canada, while the subsequent failure of Quebec's constitutional round, known as the Meech Lake Accord, as well as of the Canada round (the Charlottetown proposals), left many voters who had previously thrown their support to Mulroney's Conservatives feeling voiceless in Ottawa.

This constitutional debacle created the conditions for a major mobilization around a new political party in Ottawa—the Bloc Québécois—whose entry into federal politics in the 1993 election registered as a political earthquake. In its very first electoral campaign, the Bloc was able to win 54 seats and nearly half of Quebec's votes (49.3 per cent). Meanwhile, in Western Canada another new political formation, the Reform Party, displaced the Progressive Conservatives as the favoured alternative to the Liberal Party, with 18.7 per cent of the votes and 52 seats (Gagnon and Tanguay 1996, 106). The success of the Bloc Québécois and the Reform Party shook the existing party dynamics and was a major factor behind the decline of the Progressive Conservative Party. Those radical shifts in voting preferences made 1993 the most volatile election since Canada's founding (Carty, Cross, and Young 2000, 47).

The major and instantaneous success of the Bloc is mostly explained by its ability to attract voters who were tired of old parties and distrustful toward existing political elites. Since the Liberal Party and the Conservatives had been discredited in Quebec because of their inability to convince Quebecers to abandon their persistent constitutional claims (the Liberals) or to deliver on their promises (the Conservatives), it became easy for a new political force to open a political front constituted of disillusioned (when not alienated) voters. As Carty, Cross, and Young (2000, 48) explain, public dissatisfaction with the government and the desire for change and to break with "politics as usual" were so important that according to the Bloc's own account of its electoral success, frustration and discontent favoured the emergence of a new party so that the Bloc merely gathered the protest vote.

Not only were Quebec voters "free" to join a new political vehicle, various episodes connected to the re-emergence of nationalism in Quebec and to the insensitivity toward Quebec's political claims were instrumental in boosting support for the Bloc Québécois, especially during the 1997 election (Bernard 1997). The period following the 1995 Quebec referendum witnessed several episodes of Quebec-bashing in various parts of the country, which helped consolidate the Bloc's presence in the House of Commons. The Bloc also benefited from the fact that the Liberals were severely hurt in the federal elections of 2004, 2006, and 2008 by the sponsorship scandal (Gagnon and Hérivault 2004), which left the impression in the minds of many voters that the erstwhile "natural governing party" was a practitioner of a tired and corrupt style of politics.

Although the Bloc on its own had no chance to form the government in Ottawa, one ought to stress its impressive capacity to attract voters' support, at least until its near total collapse in the 2011 federal election and the unprecedented popularity of the New Democratic Party in Quebec. Just as Quebecers cast their votes in favour of the Progressive Conservative Party of Mulroney in 1984 following his promise to "reintegrate" Quebec into the Constitution—and withdrew their support after the failure of the Meech Lake Accord—they gave their support to the new Conservative leader Stephen Harper after his pledge to pursue a doctrine of "open federalism," but questioned this support once it appeared to many that there was little for Quebec in Harper's repackaged federalism. In fact, support for Harper's government within Quebec had been feeble in the years preceding the 2015 election, as many Quebecers saw his government as the very antithesis to their generally environmentalist and social democratic values.

On 2 May 2011, the Bloc Québécois suffered a major blow. It went from having 49 seats (with 38.1 per cent of popular support) after the 2008 election to only four after the 2011 election (23.4 per cent of support), bumping up slightly to ten MPs in 2015 with a still smaller share of the vote (19.4 per cent). The surprising collapse in 2011 did not benefit the Liberals or the Conservatives. Instead, a new player on the Quebec scene reaped the benefits of the demise of the Bloc: the NDP. After a successful campaign in the province led by the charismatic leader of the NDP, Jack Layton, who was able to appear during interviews and TV shows as the sympathetic and ordinary guy, the party won an unprecedented 59 seats in Quebec with 42.9 per cent of the votes. We argue below that the spectacular defeat of the Bloc Québécois can best be explained as a byproduct of the widespread distrust in the Harper government.

Many political analysts have claimed that the Bloc's catastrophic results in 2011 bear witness to the idea that the sovereignty project was, at the time, running out of steam and that the party's presence in Ottawa could be considered superfluous. Others simply point to the high level of popularity of Jack Layton in Quebec.

It is hard to deny that relatively weak support for Quebec's independence and the popularity of Jack Layton played an important role in the 2011 election. Nonetheless, although support for independence hit a historic low just before the 2011 federal election, it was far from having disappeared, and these polling results do not necessarily spell the end of nationalist aspirations in the province. Moreover, although many who shifted their vote from the Bloc to the NDP indicated that it was their trust in Jack Layton that motivated this change of electoral allegiance (20 per cent in a survey conducted by Leger Marketing just after the May 2 election), most voters who shifted their support from the Bloc to the NDP listed a desire for change (41 per cent) and the need to remove Harper's Conservatives from office (50 per cent) as the main reasons influencing their vote (Bélanger and Nadeau 2011, 131–32). Those survey results seem to indicate that the surprising results of the 2011 election were the effect of cynicism and distrust in old and established political parties—"we need a change"; "we need to do politics differently and give a chance to a party that hasn't been in office yet"—as well as to the perception, widely shared among Quebec voters, that the Conservative Party upheld values that clashed with those embraced by most Quebecers.

Although the NDP hardly qualifies as a new party (it was founded in 1961), it was never seen as a viable alternative in Quebec. Prior to the 2011 election, the NDP had never been able to win more than one seat in the province. Moreover, the NDP had never campaigned with such fervour and zeal inside Quebec as it did in the 2011 electoral campaign. Thus, although the NDP had existed for roughly five decades, it remained largely unknown to many Quebecers until the 2011 electoral campaign, during which it was perceived as a "new" alternative and a fresh option. To be fair, the NDP was already well-known and to a certain extent quite popular among Quebec intellectuals in the 1960s (when Charles Taylor ran for the NDP in Plateau Mont-Royal) and had short episodes of popularity among the whole population in the mid-1980s under the capable leadership Ed Broadbent (Leebosh 2011). Nonetheless, the NDP remained either a party whose roots were in the West or a not very well-known option in the eyes of most Quebecers during the 1990s and 2000s.

Not only was the NDP perceived as a new option during the 2011 electoral campaign, it was also perceived by Quebecers as a viable one. First, the party's ideology was already naturally aligned with the environmental and social values of many Quebecers. Second, the NDP expressed sympathy for Quebec's concerns for provincial autonomy and, following its Sherbrooke Declaration in 2005 (New Democratic Party [Québec Section] 2005), self-understanding as a distinct nation. At that time, the NDP committed itself to (1) recognize Quebec's national character, (2) promote asymmetrical federalism, and (3) respect Quebec's right to self-determination. In the 2011 campaign, Layton remained sympathetic to Quebec's claims to nationhood, to provincial autonomy, and to asymmetrical federalism. For example, in a gathering with the *Globe and Mail* editorial board on 21 April 2011, Layton remarked:

> I noticed that Stephen Harper is talking about asymmetrical federalism. That's a concept we've used for a very long time in our party.
>
> And not only that—it's represented in some of our most successful programs nationally. Like our medicare program, that has a Quebec version. Our Canadian Pension Plan, which has a Quebec version. That's asymmetrical federalism. And we proposed the same thing when it came to our national childcare legislation. Quebec already has, by far, one of the most advanced.
>
> . . . So, we have worked this thing out before and our childcare legislation represents the same thing. And in fact was supported by both the Liberals and the Bloc Québécois. It of course didn't get adopted because the Conservatives were opposed to the approach of a national childcare program. (*Globe and Mail*, 2011)

Despite voting for a federalist party, Quebecers did so because of concerns about the unresponsiveness of the federal government to its distinctive values and identity (environmentalist and social democrat leanings) and out of a sense that a new alternative needed to be tried. The Bloc failed in 2011 not so much because nationalism might be outdated, but rather because it was no longer seen as an effective alternative able to stop the Conservatives and perhaps (although this remains to be fully appraised) because it had run its course as a third party and was already perceived as an old party that had had its chance and seemed no longer able to influence the policy process in Ottawa in the eyes of Quebec voters. In 2015 we witnessed a similar trend, with a Quebec electorate that was searching for the best available option to remove the Conservatives from office as they proved to be less and less sensitive to Quebec's political demands in various domains (language politics, national security regulation, accrued political autonomy, infrastructure, gun registry, international relations).

This was particularly well rendered by NDP slogans used during the 2011 campaign, such as "Politics is going nowhere in Ottawa" and "It is time for that to change." Brad Lavigne (2013, 222–23) raised the point that the NDP could change things in Ottawa whereas the Bloc could not get things done. The NDP even mocked the Bloc's slogan, "Let's Talk about Quebec," and made the point that the only thing the Bloc could do in Ottawa was to talk; it was failing to obtain concrete results. Layton said he wanted results for all of Canada and for Quebec. During the 2011 campaign, he made the point that "I cannot promise not to be nice, but we need to improve our health care system, build a green economy, bring our troops home, support the arts, support culture, protect the French language. Let's work together for families. There is a lot of work to do" (cited in Lavigne 2013, 222). Through these kinds of speeches and arguments, Layton continued to make significant inroads into francophone territory. His positions in favour of culture, arts, and the French language attracted a lot of positive feedback in Quebec. Shortly after the 2011 general elections, and considering the NDP's unprecedented success in Quebec, Layton told Quebecers that they could count on him to defend their interests (Bellavance 2011). Tom Mulcair, the new NDP leader, was never able to make the same connection with the Quebec electorate, although the party managed to secure 25.4 per cent of the vote and to elect 16 MPs in 2015, in contrast with their unprecedented 42.9 per cent of the vote and 59 seats in 2011.

From the beginning of Confederation to the early 1980s, Quebecers overwhelmingly voted as a block and consistently supported the Liberal Party. Supporting the biggest party in Ottawa to achieve some representation within a dominant party was viewed as a viable option for Quebecers up to the unilateral repatriation of the Constitution. Following this, Quebecers have from time to time given and withdrawn their support to federal political parties according to their capacity to take into account Quebec's aspirations as a distinct society. This has led Quebecers to be especially prone to support newly arrived third parties that emphasize change and promise to be more responsive to Quebec's distinct identity. Paradoxically, the near collapse of the Bloc Québécois does not constitute so much of a radical shift in Quebec's voters' attitudes as a confirmation of Quebec's desire to have a federal party that can be effective in expressing its distinct political identity and values.

Conclusion

The last few elections confirm that political trust and a sense of political efficacy matter a lot in the way Quebecers cast their votes and explain in good part why they are so easily mobilized by third parties. Quebec's level of trust in federal political parties is highly contextual and can easily evolve in response to unfriendly or tense intergovernmental and interprovincial relations. For instance, as was sharply illustrated by Herman Bakvis and Brian Tanguay (2012, 109), "the 2008 election and the prorogation that followed later that year brought to a standstill the Conservatives' foray in Quebec and their longer term strategy of building a sufficiently large base in the province to form a majority government. The prorogation also resulted in a further deterioration of trust within the House of Commons and heightened what was already a highly charged partisan atmosphere."

Building on Russell Hardin's concept of encapsulated interest, Peter Russell (2010, 9) suggests that trust feeds on trust: "Below the surface of politics, the embers of distrust on the Québécois side remained warm, and were occasionally inflamed as in the conscription crises of both world wars. Any trust that existed between Canadian and Quebec provincial leaders was of the *encapsulated interest* kind"—that is to say, trust in this form suggested it was in the interests of both parties to act in a trustworthy manner. Russell's observation can be extended to many other cases, among which we can find various constitutional bouts, economic decisions, and public policies that were said to have disfavoured Quebec: energy politics, automobile industry policies, economic development, forestry, agriculture, fiscal policy, infrastructure, and the like. The implementation of such decisions helped predispose Quebec voters to new political movements that were able to make electoral inroads based on a politics of discontent toward the governing party.

The political analysis in this chapter suggests that Quebecers have tended to vote as a block in federal elections, steadily supporting for long periods the party most inclined to hear and express their voice, but abruptly withdrawing such support when their political interests and self-understanding were ignored. In light of political developments over the last few decades, it is much harder to maintain that Quebec constantly votes as block, mobilizing itself to support the largest party and avoiding the fragmentation of its vote to rally behind the governing party. Since 1993, the most successful party in Quebec has obtained more than 75 per cent of the seats only once and never obtained more than 55 per cent of the popular vote. In addition, Quebec has tended to support parties in the opposition. The 2015 election suggests a continued fragmentation of voters' support, with four parties obtaining 709,185 votes (Conservatives, 12 seats), 821,140 votes (Bloc, 10 seats), 1,075,365 votes (NDP, 16 seats), and 1,515,631 votes (Liberals, 40 seats). This new pattern suggests that the Quebec electorate is highly volatile and can still be mobilized by parties based on emerging political issues and leadership capability.

Suggested Readings

Bakvis, Herman, and Laura G. Macpherson. 1995. "Quebec Block Voting and the Canadian Electoral System." *Canadian Journal of Political Science* 28 (4): 659–92. http://dx.doi.org/10.1017/S000842390001934X

Bélanger, Éric. 2004. "The Rise of Third Parties in the 1993 Canadian Federal Election: Pinard Revisited." *Canadian Journal of Political Science* 37 (3): 581–94. http://dx.doi.org/10.1017/S0008423904020554

Bickerton, James, Alain-G. Gagnon, and Patrick Smith. 1999. *Ties That Bind: Parties and Voters in Canada.* Toronto: Oxford University Press.

Cairns, Alan C. 1968. "The Electoral System and the Party System in Canada, 1921–1965." *Canadian Journal of Political Science* 1 (1): 55–80. http://dx.doi.org/10.1017/S0008423900035228

Macpherson, C.B. (1953) 1962. *Democracy in Alberta.* 2nd ed. Toronto: University of Toronto Press.

Pelletier, Réjean, ed. 2012. *Les partis politiques québécois dans la tourmente.* Quebec: Les Presses de l'Université Laval.

Pinard, Maurice. 1973. "Third Parties in Canada Revisited." *Canadian Journal of Political Science* 6 (3): 439–60. http://dx.doi.org/10.1017/S0008423900040026

Notes

1   The research assistance of Julien Verville, graduate student in the department of political science at the Université du Québec à Montréal, is gratefully acknowledged. Many thanks to Brian Tanguay for his insightful comments on an earlier version of this chapter.

2   The 19 October 2015 general election constitutes an exception to the trend.

3   As Bélanger and Nadeau (2009, 153) remark: "when Quebec voters had their own agenda, as was the case in the wake of the Meech Lake Accord failure (in 1993) or the sponsorship scandal (in 2004 and, to a lesser extent, in 2006), the Bloc obtained its highest scores (49 percent, 49 percent, and 42 percent respectively). But when Quebecers showed less interest in constitutional matters (1997 and 2000), the federalist parties usually fared better (62 percent of the vote in 1997 and 60 in 2000)."

4   By contrast, third parties in the United States have been utterly unsuccessful: "all third parties in American politics in the twentieth century have been transitory, rarely lasting more than one election and usually fading into political oblivion along with their founders" (Gagnon and Tanguay 1996, 108).

5   For an assessment of Pinard's theory of the sudden rise of third parties in light of more recent elections in Quebec, see Bélanger (2004), as well as his chapter in this edition.

References

Bakvis, Herman, and Laura G. Macpherson. 1995. "Quebec Block Voting and the Canadian Electoral System." *Canadian Journal of Political Science* 28 (4): 659–92. http://dx.doi.org/10.1017/S000842390001934X

Bakvis, Herman, and A. Brian Tanguay. 2012. "Federalism, Political Parties, and the Burden of National Unity: Still Making Federalism Do the Heavy Lifting." In *Canadian Federalism,* 3rd ed., edited by Herman Bakvis and Grace Skogstad, 96–115. Toronto: Oxford University Press.

Bastien, Frédérick, Éric Bélanger, and François Gélineau. 2013. "Une élection extraordinaire?" In *Les Québécois aux urnes: les partis, les médias et les citoyens en campagne,* edited by Frédérick Bastien, Éric Bélanger, and François Gélineau, 9–20. Montreal: Presses de l'Université de Montréal.

Bélanger, Éric. 2004. "The Rise of Third Parties in the 1993 Canadian Federal Election: Pinard Revisited." *Canadian Journal of Political Science* 37 (3): 581–94. http://dx.doi.org/10.1017/S0008423904020554

Bélanger, Éric, and Richard Nadeau. 2009. "The Bloc Québécois: Victory by Default." In *The Canadian Federal Election of 2008,* edited by Jon H. Pammett and Christopher Dornan, 136–61. Toronto: Dundurn Press.

Bélanger, Éric, and Richard Nadeau. 2011. "The Bloc Québécois: Capsized by the Orange Wave." In *The Canadian Federal Election of 2011,* edited by Jon H. Pammett and Christopher Dornan, 111–39. Toronto: Dundurn Press.

Bellavance, Joël-Denis. 2011. "Vous pouvez compter sur moi pour défendre vos intérêts, dit Layton." *La Presse,* May 25.

Bernard, André. 1997. "The Bloc Québécois." In *The Canadian General Election of 1997,* edited by Alan Frizzell and Jon H. Pammett, 135–48. Toronto: Dundurn Press.

Bickerton, James. 2007. "Between Integration and Fragmentation: Political Parties and the Representation of Regions." In *Canadian Parties in Transition,* 3rd ed., edited by Alain-G. Gagnon and A. Brian Tanguay, 411–36. Toronto: University of Toronto Press.

Bickerton, James. 2014. "Competing for Power: Parties and Elections in Canada." In *Canadian Politics,* 6th ed., edited by James Bickerton and Alain-G. Gagnon, 249–79. Toronto: University of Toronto Press.

Bickerton, James, Alain-G. Gagnon, and Patrick Smith. 1999. *Ties That Bind: Parties and Voters in Canada.* Toronto: Oxford University Press.

Blais, André. 1973. "Third Parties in Canadian Povincial Politics." *Canadian Journal of Political Science* 6: 422–38.

Cairns, Alan C. 1968. "The Electoral System and the Party System in Canada, 1921–1965." *Canadian Journal of Political Science* 1 (1): 55–80. http://dx.doi.org/10.1017/S0008423900035228

Carty, R. Kenneth, William Cross, and Lisa Young. 2000. *Rebuilding Canadian Party Politics.* Vancouver: University of British Columbia Press.

Drouilly, Pierre. 1983. *Statistiques électorales fédérales du Québec 1867–1980.* Montreal: Université du Québec à Montréal.

Elections Canada. 2015. "Élections passées." http://www.elections.ca/content.aspx?section=ele&dir=pas&document=index&lang=f

Gagnon, Alain-G., and Jacques Hérivault. 2004. "The Bloc Québécois: The Dynamics of a Distinct Electorate." In *The Canadian General Election of 2004,* edited by Jon H. Pammett, and Christopher Dornan, 139–69. Toronto: Dundurn Press.

Gagnon, Alain-G., and A. Brian Tanguay. 1996. "Minor Parties in the Canadian Political System: Origins, Functions, Impact." In *Canadian Parties in Transition,* 2nd ed., edited by A. Brian Tanguay and Alain-G. Gagnon, 106–34. Toronto: Nelson.

Gagnon, Alain-G., and A. Brian Tanguay, eds. 2007. *Canadian Parties in Transition.* 3rd ed. Toronto: University of Toronto Press.

Globe and Mail. 2011. "Jack Layton, on the Record." April 21.

Lavigne, Brad. 2013. *Building the Orange Wave: The Inside Story behind the Historic Rise of Jack Layton and the NDP.* Madeira Park, BC: Douglas & McIntyre.

Leebosh, Derek. 2011. "NDP Hits the Jack-Pot in Quebec: From Decades of Work to Overnight Success." *Policy Options* (June–July): 113–18.

Letellier, Antoine. 2015. "Comment les Canadiens ont voté?" *L'Actualité*, October 22. http://www.lactualite.com/actualites/politique/comment-les-canadiens-ont-vote/

Macpherson, C.B. (1953) 1962. *Democracy in Alberta.* 2nd ed. Toronto: University of Toronto Press.

Macpherson, Laura G. 1991. "Quebec Block Voting." Honours Political Science Essay. Department of Political Science, Dalhousie University, Halifax, Nova Scotia.

McMenemy, John. 1976. "Parliamentary Parties." In *Political Parties in Canada,* edited by Conrad Winn and John McMenery, 10–28. Toronto: McGraw-Hill Ryerson.

New Democratic Party [Québec Section]. 2005. "Québec's Voice and Choice for a Different Canada: Federalism, Social-Democracy and the Québec Question." http://www.pierreducasse.ca/IMG/pdf/Declaration_Sherbrooke_ENG_V2.pdf

Pelletier, Réjean, and Jérôme Couture. 2012. "La confiance dans les partis politiques au Canada et au Québec: Un Québec distinct?" In *Les partis politiques québécois dans la tourmente: mieux comprendre et évaluer leur rôle,* edited by Réjean Pelletier, 225–46. Quebec City: Les Presses de l'Université Laval.

Pinard, Maurice. 1973. "Third Parties in Canada Revisited." *Canadian Journal of Political Science* 6 (3): 439–60. http://dx.doi.org/10.1017/S0008423900040026

Pinard, Maurice. 1975. *The Rise of a Third Party.* Enlarged ed. Montreal: McGill-Queen's University Press.

Rioux, Marcel. 1979. "The Development of Ideologies in Quebec." In *The Canadian Political Process,* 3rd ed., edited by Richard Schultz, Orest M. Kruhlak, and John C. Terry, 98–114. Toronto: Holt, Rinehart, Winston.

Russell, Peter. 2010. "Trust and Distrust in Canada's Multinational Constitutional Politics." Seminar, Research Group on Plurinational Societies (GRSP), Université du Québec à Montréal, Montreal, June 4.

Thomas, Paul G. 1991. "Parties and Regional Representation." In *Research Studies of the Royal Commission on Electoral Reform and Party Financing,* vol. 14, edited by Herman Bakvis, 179–252. Toronto: Dundurn Press.

14

Where Are the Women in Canadian Political Parties?

JOANNA EVERITT

POLITICAL PARTIES HAVE LONG BEEN recognized as playing an important role in the aggregation and representation of diverse political interests. Some of these political concerns are based on region, language, or racial or cultural interests that may or may not evolve from territorial identities. Others are less territorial based, constructed instead as a result of characteristics such as gender, race, or sexual orientation. This chapter focuses on the latter set of interests, specifically exploring how federal parties in Canada have attempted to acknowledge and incorporate women into their internal organizational structures (committees or commissions) and ensure the representation of women's interests in their decision-making positions (executives) and processes (conventions). Finally, this chapter will examine the degree to which national parties have facilitated or promoted women as party leaders, candidates, and elected officials.

Patterns of Women's Participation within Political Parties

Following the Report of the Royal Commission on the Status of Women (RCSW) in 1970, which found that women played primarily a supporting role within party structures, researchers such as Sylvia Bashevkin (1985, 1993), Janine Brodie (1985), and Lisa Young (2000, 2002) have consistently found that Canadian political parties remain difficult for women to enter. Bashevkin's work in the 1980s and early 1990s provided the groundwork for the study of women in political parties. Her study, *Toeing the Lines: Women and Party Politics in English Canada,* revealed two important axioms that govern women's party participation: (1) the higher, the fewer, and (2) the more competitive, the fewer. The first denotes the fact that although women's involvement in party activity has increased over time, the number of women in elite levels of the party hierarchy remains limited. Women have been more likely to assume grassroots and support roles within political parties, working in election offices rather than managing campaigns, and taking on positions of riding association secretaries rather than riding association presidents. The higher one moves up the ladder of authority within the party, the fewer women one is likely to find.

The second axiom of party politics suggests that the more competitive a position is, or the more likely it is to actually wield power, the less likely it is that a woman will hold the position. In other words, studies have found that the higher the chance that a party will elect their candidate to office, the more likely it is that they will run a male candidate (Thomas and Bodet 2013). Similarly, the more likely the party is to form the government, the more likely it is to select a male party leader (Bashevkin 2010). Because of this tendency, women tend to hold the position of candidate, riding association president, or even party leader in areas where their parties are electorally weak or vulnerable.

While all parties follow this pattern to some extent or another, parties on the left, such as the NDP, are more ideologically predisposed to establishing procedures to ensure the representation of women and other underrepresented groups. Those on the right, such as the current Conservative Party of Canada, are less willing to acknowledge structural barriers to political engagement and are thereby much less willing to provide special measures to enable underrepresented groups to overcome them. These underlying values are reflected in the structures and opportunities created within each of the main Canadian political parties that have allowed or restricted women's greater involvement in decision-making processes or positions of power and influence.

History of Women within Canadian Political Parties

Women have long been involved in political parties through separate auxiliaries or committees. These organizations were established in connection with the Liberal and Conservative parties in the 1920s and 1930s to provide political education to the newly enfranchised female electorate (Royal Commission on the Status of Women 1970, 345). Their roles were primarily to serve and support the "men's" associations by performing numerous routine activities such as organizing meetings, canvassing during elections, staffing campaign offices, and sponsoring events to raise funds that enabled parties to function. In other words, they performed many of the domestic and secretarial roles that women were assigned in society at that time and, because they involved a separate membership from the main wing of the party, women were often left out of decision-making roles within the main structures of these political parties.

The NDP and the Co-operative Commonwealth Federation (CCF) before it differed from these two older parties in that they never had separate women's auxiliaries; instead they had women's committees that were standing committees of the party. As a result, right from their establishment, women were always full members of the constituency, provincial, or federal CCF/NDP associations. Nonetheless, these committees often played the same roles within the CCF/NDP as the auxiliaries did within the Liberals or Conservatives (Young 2000, 134).

Because the auxiliaries in the Liberal and Conservative parties were perceived as diverting women's attention away from mainstream party discussions about policy or candidate selection, one of the many recommendations of the RCSW was that they "be amalgamated with the main bodies of these parties" (RCSW 1970, 348). Parties slowly adopted this recommendation throughout the 1970s. In 1973, the old Women's Liberal Federation of Canada was transformed into the National Women's Liberal Commission, and in 1977 the NDP's Participation of Women Committee was reconstituted to give it increased influence (Bashevkin 1993, 125). By the end of the decade, even the National PC Women's Association had seen some reforms to reflect the changing roles that women were assuming within the party, and by 1984 it had become the National Progressive Conservative Women's Federation (Bashevkin 1993, 130).

Throughout the 1970s and 1980s, women's organizations within the parties pressured their organizations to do more to increase women's level of party participation, and the parties responded by creating internal structures aimed at enhancing the engagement of women and other underrepresented groups, as well as using less formal methods to attract them to the party (Bashevkin 1985, 84). Not surprisingly, it was the NDP who made the greatest strides in this area. In 1983 they adopted an affirmative action resolution, based on an earlier Ontario NDP resolution that required at least 50 per cent of riding executive and provincial council executive members to be women (Bashevkin 1985, 86–87). This policy dramatically changed the gender balance of these bodies. The Liberal Party of Canada, pushed by the example of the NDP, subsequently established an ad hoc committee on affirmative action in 1982, but proposals for the establishment of specific targets or quotas were rejected by the party executive in favour of relying on strategies involving less prescribed recruitment and training of women for elite positions (Young 2000, 147–48). The Progressive Conservatives showed the least interest in making formal efforts to increase women's participation (Young 2000).

These efforts resulted in small gains in the numeric representation of women within party structures throughout this period, with the NDP making the greatest strides toward equality and the Liberals and PCs more moderate ones. Following the example of the NDP, in 1986 the Liberals introduced a constitutional amendment requiring that half of the party's vice-presidential positions be held by women (Bashevkin 1993, 99; Young,

2002, 188). However, since no such restrictions were attached to the regional presidential positions, the number of women holding senior decision-making positions within the party was smaller in 1990 than in 1986. This regulation was later dropped in 1990 on the initiative of the National Women's Liberal Commission, as members supported voluntary efforts rather than formal quotas to encourage and promote women's political engagement (Bashevkin 1993, 100). The Progressive Conservatives had women from the executive of their women's federation sitting on the executive of the National PC Association and many federal party committees; however, no other gender-designated positions were mandated in the party's constitution during this period (Bashevkin 1993, 100).

The impact of these changes appeared to have only moderate effects on the representation of women at the riding association level, but the research that has been conducted suggests that women remain excluded from leadership positions within their parties. In her cross-time comparison of women's participation in local riding associations in Ontario at the provincial level, Bashevkin (1993, 69) found that for most parties women were more likely to be a riding association president in 1990 than they were in the early 1980s—but the improvement was only about nine percentage points during this period. Her subsequent analysis of parties at the federal level across the country found that in 1990 approximately 24 per cent of riding association presidents in the Liberal Party and the NDP were held by women, compared to 14 per cent of the same positions in the Progressive Conservatives (Bashevkin 1991). Similar results continued to be found into the late 1990s (Tremblay and Pelletier 2001).

Where parties appeared to feel most comfortable in the adoption of targeted strategies to enhance representation was in the selection of delegates to national conventions. During the 1980s and 1990s, the numbers of female delegates at Canadian party conventions came close to parity with men because of stipulations surrounding the number of delegate spots reserved for women. The Liberals required that 50 per cent of their elected delegates be women, while the Progressive Conservatives had a policy that at least two of the six riding delegates be women (Bashevkin 1993, 100). Although this ensured that during this period almost one-third of the elected delegates were female, the actual number fluctuated depending on the importance and size of the convention. At regular national party conventions the percentage of delegates who were women was higher than at the higher stakes leadership conventions (see Table 1 in Young 2000, 164). Numbers were also affected by the high proportion of male *ex officio* delegates that attended conventions because of their positions on national executives, as riding association presidents, and as elected Members of Parliament or unsuccessful candidates. Ironically, the NDP, the party that typically went the furthest to ensure gender equality, never instituted any gender-based representational guarantees for its party conventions (Courtney 1995, 147; Young 2000, 162). Nonetheless, even without designated delegate spots the participation rate of women in NDP conventions during this period matched that of the other parties.

Canadian Political Parties in Recent Decades

Lisa Young (2002, 190) has described the years between 1957 and 1993 as a period in which the three main political parties sought to accommodate women's interests and addressed their political exclusion through an acceptance of a group-based conception of representation. This approach was driven by strategies pursued by the NDP, a party that she referred to as the "dynamic element" of this system. In adopting affirmative action approaches along with other tactics to increase women's representation and attract them to their party, the NDP pushed the Liberals and Conservatives to take their own steps in the same direction. However, the collapse of the third party system (see Patten, Chapter 1 in this volume) and the rise of two new parties (the Reform Party and the Bloc Québécois) in the early 1990s shifted the focus from group representation to territorial representation. With the 1993 election the new dynamic element in Canadian politics became the Reform Party and its successors, the Canadian Alliance and the Conservative Party of Canada, all of which have adopted a policy of undifferentiated citizenship (Young 2002). These parties have contended that women have the same opportunity to participate in party activities as men, and it is only their lack of interest rather than systemic barriers that prevents them from doing so. As a result, they have argued that no special measures are necessary to augment women's engagement, as such measures would discriminate against men.

While the Bloc Québécois was similar to the NDP in its approach to issues of representation, its focus on the province of Quebec has meant that it has had a much more limited impact than the Reform and subsequently the Canadian Alliance in setting the agenda regarding gender representation. It was not, however, until the early 2000s that the Bloc developed a focused strategy to increase the representation of women both within the party and in the electorate. This approach grew out of a workshop at the party's 2003 convention that produced several proposals to enhance women's engagement, including a special fund and training opportunities to assist female candidates, measures to increase parity within the bodies of the Bloc, and the alternation of women and men in positions of leadership at all levels of the party (Tremblay 2010, 168). Steps were taken over the next few years to implement these initiatives.

Unfortunately, there has been little research on the gender composition of political parties since the creation of the Conservative Party of Canada out of the former Progressive Conservative and Canadian Alliance parties. However, a 2000 study of Canadian party members conducted before this merger found that while almost two-thirds of party members are men, the proportions vary from party to party (Young and Cross 2003). In parties that are prepared to adopt some affirmative action approaches to promote gender equality within their structures (to be discussed below), such as both the New Democratic and the Liberal parties, women made up just slightly less than 50 per cent of the membership. This figure dropped to about a third in the Bloc Québécois and the Progressive Conservative and Canadian Alliance parties, the latter two having been more resistant to steps to enhance women's involvement. The study also found that women were more likely than men to have been recruited into the party, in particular to support a leadership candidate or a candidate for a riding nomination (Young and Cross 2003, 94).

Furthermore, these results indicate that women engaged in many of the grassroots activities, such as volunteering in election campaigns, attending association meetings, or attending national conventions, at rates that equalled those of men (Young and Cross 2003, 98). It was only in terms of serving on a riding executive that real gender differences appeared. As might be expected from Bashevkin's (1993) previous work, women were less likely than men to sit on these bodies. This tendency for women to hold fewer positions of authority was reflected in their perception of the influence they held within their party. In all parties, save for the Canadian Alliance, there was a statistical difference between the amount of influence that women thought they had and the amount they thought they should have (Young and Cross 2003, 101). These findings are noteworthy as women in constituency leadership roles have been found to play a key role in recruiting and promoting female candidates (see Cheng and Tavits 2009; Tremblay and Pelletier 2001).

To date there has been no update to Bashevkin's (1993) research in the early 1990s on the type of roles played by women in Canadian political parties. However, a quick review of the national executives of these parties in the summer of 2015 suggests that her earlier observations about the higher the fewer and the more powerful the fewer still hold true today, since the majority of positions on national party executives continue to be occupied by men (see Table 14.1). This was most obvious among the governing Conservatives, where only four of the 19-member National Council were women and neither the position of president nor chair of the Conservative Fund of Canada, the most powerful positions within the party, were held

Table 14.1   Positions Held by Women on National Party Executives (2015)

	Conservative	Liberal	NDP	Bloc Québécois
President	0/1	1/1	1/1	0/1
Vice-President	1/3	1/2	1/2	1/1
Regional Director/ President/Councillors	4/19	2/13	6/12	2/6
Treasurer/CFO	0/1	0/1	1/1	0/1
Policy Chair	0/1	1/1		
Secretary	0/1			
Membership Secretary	0/1	1/1		
Chair Youth Commission/ Committee		0/1	0/1	0/1
Chair Aboriginal Peoples' Commission		1/2	1/1	
Chair Women's Commission/Committee		1/1	1/1	
Chair Senior Commission		1/2		
Chair Visible Minority Committee			0/1	
Chair LGBT Committee			0/1	
Chair Disability Rights Committee			1/1	
Chair Council of Presidents		1/1		
Labour Representatives			1/2	
National Campaign Chair	1/2	1/2	1/2	
Total	6/24 (25%)*	11/28 (39%)	14/26 (54%)	3/10 (30%)

* Many of the executive positions in the Conservative Party of Canada are held by regional directors.

Source: Party websites, accessed June 2015.

by women. One-third of the executive positions within the Liberal Party, in third place in terms of seats in the House of Commons in the lead up to the 2015 federal election, were held by women, including the role of president, policy chair, membership secretary, and chair of the Council of Presidents. However, only two of the presidents of the 13 provincial or territorial wings of the party are women, significantly reducing the gender balance. Similarly, only one-fifth of the positions on the National Bureau of the Bloc were held by women, with positions such as president and treasurer both occupied by men, despite the fact that its statutes have enshrined a policy originally proposed in 2003 that favours and encourages the "alternation between women and men in its bodies and on its local riding executives" and that "the bodies of the Bloc Québécois aim for the objective of parity representation for all of its bodies and committees" (Tremblay 2010, 168). The NDP's National Council, which includes the regional councillors and chairs of its various equity committees, is the only governing body to actually achieve a gender balance: 54 per cent of its members are women. This can be attributed to the constitutional provisions requiring them to ensure gender diversity on their executive and among the various committees.

One of the most significant changes to have occurred in political parties over the past few decades is in how they select their leaders. Since the early 1900s this has been done at party conventions where riding delegates and party elites gather to choose among competing leadership contenders. Over time the process has become increasingly more open to grassroots involvement as parties have succumbed to pressures, first from the left and later from the right, to enhance member participation (Cross 2004). As noted above, by the 1980s the Liberals and Progressive Conservatives had designated delegate spots for women (as well as youths, Indigenous persons, and later seniors) in an effort to ensure their involvement in this process.

Popular pressure and arguments for enhanced democracy began to appear in the last decades of the century as more parties, primarily at the provincial level, began to explore direct election methods to select their leaders. At the national level, this one member, one vote (OMOV) leadership selection method was promoted by the Reform Party and later adopted by the Canadian Alliance. The Bloc Québécois was also quick to adopt this direct election method in 1997. The Progressive Conservatives, in an effort to revitalize the party after their disastrous showing in the 1993 election, initially adopted a direct leadership selection process in 1995 but then returned to a hybrid system after the election of Joe Clark as leader in 1998. Under this hybrid system the results of each riding were assigned an equal weight regardless of the number of party members who voted. This means that ridings with large memberships do not dominate the selection processes. The new Conservative Party of Canada continued this system after the merger of the Progressive Conservatives and the Canadian Alliance in 2003. The NDP also adopted an OMOV selection process in 2003. In this first leadership selection process, which saw the election of Jack Layton, the voting results were weighted so that the votes of labour delegates counted for 25 per cent of the total result, and riding delegates count for 75 per cent. However, for the 2012 race, won by Thomas Mulcair, a strict OMOV rule was in place: affiliated labour groups had no special status. The Liberals were the last national party to introduce an OMOV process, voting in 2009 to adopt a system similar to that of the Conservatives.

While these changes to who can participate in the selection of party leaders have had the effect of enabling more individuals to be involved in the choice of party leaders, there is also some evidence that it has reduced the influence of women in these decisions. Under the delegated systems used in the 1980s and 1990s, the quotas established to ensure the involvement of women resulted in women comprising approximately 40 per cent of the total delegates (Brodie 1988, 176; Courtney 1995, 336). While there is some evidence from Alberta that universal ballots have increased the number of women participating in leadership processes (Stewart 2002), there is other evidence that suggests that this is not always true, and in some cases OMOV rules have resulted in a decline (Stewart and Stewart 2007, 31). Simply the fact that the majority of party members are men translates into a situation where the majority of the votes cast in leadership selection processes will be cast by men. This is particularly a concern with parties like the Conservative Party of Canada and the Bloc Québécois, where women remain significantly underrepresented even at the grassroots level.

Party Elites: Leaders, Candidates, and Elected Representatives

In the last two decades, attention by party organizations and by academics to the numeric representation of women within political parties has declined in favour of a focus on women as party leaders or as political candidates and elected officials. The highest office in a political party is that of leader. These are also positions that have remained elusive for women, unless their parties were in a weak electoral position or were experiencing an electoral decline. While women have regularly sought their party's leadership ever since Rosemary Brown came in second in the NDP leadership race of 1975, in reality they have made little progress over the past few decades. Brown's challenge to the NDP was followed by Flora MacDonald, who came in fifth in a field of 10 other candidates, dropping out after the second ballot of the Progressive Conservative leadership contest in 1976. The Liberal and Progressive Conservative leadership races of the early 1980s saw no female candidates run, and while in most every campaign since, except for those among the parties of the right, there have been female contenders, few of these individuals had any chance of success. As Table 14.2 indicates, only a small number of these candidates have received more than 10 per cent of their party's votes, and only two (Audrey McLaughlin and Kim Campbell) received a majority of support. Alexa McDonough, who won the 1995 NDP leadership, would have also likely won a majority, but the race ended after third-place candidate

Table 14.2 Female Candidates for Party Leadership

Party	Year	Candidate	Position in Race	Number of Candidates	Per cent of Vote at End of Race
NDP	1975	Rosemary Brown	2nd	5	41.1
	1989	**Audrey McLaughlin**	1st	7	55.1
	1995	**Alexa McDonough**	1st	3	32.6
	2003	Bev Meslo	6th	6	1.1
	2012	Peggy Nash	4th	8	16.8
		Niki Ashton	8th	8	5.7
Liberal	1990	Shelia Copps	3rd	5	10.7
	2003	Shelia Copps	2nd	2	6.1
	2006	Martha Hall Findlay	8th	8	2.7
	2009	None		1	
	2013	Joyce Murray	2nd	6	10.16
		Martha Hall Findlay	3rd	6	5.72
		Debra Coyne	5th	6	0.7
		Karen McCrimmon	6th	6	0.68
Progressive Conservative	1976	Flora MacDonald	5th	11	10.2
	1983	None			
	1993	**Kim Campbell**	1st	5	52.7
	1995	None		1	
	1998	None		5	
	2003	None		5	
Canadian Alliance	2000	None		5	
	2003	Diane Ablonczy	3rd	4	3.8
Conservative Party of Canada	2004	Belinda Stronach	2nd	3	34.5
Bloc Québécois	1996	Francine Lalonde	2nd	2	32.9
	1997	Francine Lalonde	4th	6	5.1
		Pierrette Venne	6th	6	1.12
	2011	Maria Mourani	2nd	3	38.7
	2014	None		2	

Note: Names in **bold** indicate eventual winners of the leadership race.

Lorne Nystrom was forced to withdraw from the ballot and Svend Robin-son, the first-place candidate, withdrew from the race as he determined he would not have enough votes to win on a second ballot.

It is clear from Table 14.2 that party members among the NDP and the Bloc have been slightly more willing than those in other parties to seriously consider female candidates as their leaders. Not only did women run in almost every one of these parties' leadership campaigns over the past couple of decades, several of these women either won or came in second among the field of candidates, obtaining a third or more of the party vote. This level of support is important to acknowledge, since the Liberal Party could also claim to be open to female leadership candidates until closer attention is paid to where these candidates are ranked and how much of the vote share they received on their last ballot. Despite coming in second in their respective leadership races, neither Sheila Copps in 2002 nor Joyce Murray in 2014 received more than 10 per cent of the final vote. These poor results undermine their positions as real contenders in these races and reinforce the perception that the Liberal Party, as one of Canada's traditionally strongest parties, remains closed to women at the highest levels.

Similarly, the experience of female candidates running for the leadership of Progressive Conservatives supports Bashevkin's (2010, 72) findings that women are more likely to be selected to fill elite party positions when the parties are in decline. Such was the case for Kim Campbell when she succeeded Brian Mulroney, an unpopular prime minister at the end of two terms in office. Campbell was presented as a fresh face and the party's only hope to reverse a precipitous decline in the public opinion polls. Needless to say, she was unable to accomplish such a Herculean task, and no other woman stepped forward to seek the party's leadership in the next three races.

Due to their newness, the Canadian Alliance has only had two leadership races and the Conservative Party of Canada has had one. Diane Ablonczy ran a distant third in the 2003 Canadian Alliance leadership, and Belinda Stronach, a high-profile celebrity businesswoman, came in second in the Conservative Party campaign (Trimble 2007; Trimble and Everitt 2010). As was the case with the Progressive Conservatives, these parties' right-wing ideological approach makes them less open to arguments about the need to enhance diversity within their party structures.

Although this chapter has concentrated primarily on the opportunities for women to engage in four main national parties, a brief comment should be made about the Green Party of Canada. Since 2006 it has been led by Elizabeth May, who won the party's leadership with 65 per cent of the vote on the first ballot in a field of three candidates. Of the 10 individuals who have led the party since its founding in 1983, four have been women. While this record makes it the party that has been most open to female leadership, it also reinforces the finding that women are able to break into positions of power when in fact the positions possess little power.

The main focus of this chapter has been on women within parties at the national level. However, recent successes and failures of women in leadership positions at the provincial level demand some comment. Over the past several decades, an increasing number of women were elected to the leadership of provincial parties. As is the case at the national level, their presence has been the greatest in parties of the left, but some have also led provincial Liberal or Conservative parties, usually when those parties have been out of office, though. This seemed to have changed by 2013 when six of the 13 provincial and territorial leaders were women. Yet claims that women were beginning to make real breakthroughs into party leadership quickly appeared to be premature. Within a few months the resignations of Alison Redford and Kathy Dunderdale, the electoral defeats of Eva Aariak and Pauline Marois, and the near defeat of Christy Clark in her own seat in the 2013 election all point to the lack of internal party support for women in leadership positions or the uncompetitiveness of the parties led by women (Everitt 2015). Kathleen Wynne's experience in Ontario, where she took over the leadership of a party struggling in the polls after several years in office, or Rachel Notley's unexpected success in Alberta, where her New Democratic Party had been sitting in fourth place in the legislature at the time of her leadership selection, while important milestones, do little to negate Baskevkin's arguments about the more competitive the fewer.

Even greater than the increase in the number of women who are running for leadership positions within political parties is the number of women who are contesting general elections as the chosen candidates for their political parties. Only 71 women ran as candidates in the 1972 federal election. In 1984 this number had increased to 213, and in 1993 it had grown to 476. By the 2015 election the total number of female candidates for all parties had climbed to 525 (29.3 per cent), but whereas in earlier elections women were often nominated for minor parties with little hope of winning their seat, as Table 14.3 indicates, in recent elections women have been securing a larger share of the nominations for major political parties.

As might be expected by their policies regarding women within their party offices, the main national parties all take very different approaches to the level of effort that they put into encouraging women's candidacies. As in other areas, the NDP have gone the furthest to promote women as candidates for election. In the late 1980s, their original approach was to group federal ridings together and require that a target of 50 per cent of the candidates in these clusters were women. When this strategy proved unsuccessful in producing significant change (see Table 14.3), they put in place a policy in the early 1990s that gave the Federal Council the right to not allow a nomination contest to occur until the riding association had presented a diverse

Table 14.3 Percentage of Female Candidates by Party, 1984–2015

	NDP	Liberal	Progressive Conservative	Reform/ Canadian Alliance/ Conservative	Bloc Québécois
1984	23	16	8		
1988	28	18	13	11	
1993	38	22	23	11	13
1997	36	28	19	10	21
2000	30	22	13	11	24
2004	31	24		12	24
2006	35	26		12	31
2008	34	37		21	27
2011	40	29		22	32
2015	43	29		19	28

slate of candidates (Young 2002, 188). This put pressure on riding search committees to seek out qualified female and minority candidates where none came forward on their own. Their goal was to ensure that 60 per cent of the winnable ridings would be contested by female candidates (Young 2013, 264). The party also maintains an affirmative action fund that is intended to assist candidates from marginalized groups with their election expenses. The impact of these efforts has varied from election to election; however, women have typically comprised at least one-third of NDP candidates, with the level reaching 43 per cent in the 2015 election.

The Liberals have tended to rely on less formal forms of intervention, which have been more or less successful depending on the leader of the party. This approach has included mentorship programs linking new candidates with those with more experience, campaign colleges and training for female candidates, and financial support for female candidates from the Judy LaMarsh Fund (Young 2000). In 1990, the party gave the leader the constitutional authority to appoint candidates, which Jean Chrétien used in the following elections to appoint more women in winnable ridings (Young 2002); he appointed 11 in 1993 and four in 1997 (Goodyear-Grant 2013, 132). Over the last several elections the party has nominated women in at least one-quarter of all ridings. The highest proportion of women (37 per cent) ran in 2008 when the party leader, Stéphane Dion, publicly committed to running women in one-third of the seats. This put pressure on riding associations to seek out female candidates, sometimes at the expense of male candidates (Bryden 2007). While the party committed once again to having one-third of their candidates as women in 2011, it was less of a priority to Michael Ignatieff, the new leader, and it only reached 29 per cent. In the lead up to the 2015 election, Liberal leader Justin Trudeau once again committed to increasing the number of female candidates by ensuring that riding associations have search committees with a least one woman who were tasked with actively seeking out women who wanted to run. Despite these actions the Liberals only managed to recruit women to fill just under 30 per cent of their candidacies in the 2015 election.

The Bloc Québécois first adopted a concerted strategy to enhance women's representation in the lead up to the 2004 election. Prior to this, their efforts were limited and uncoordinated. These new initiatives included a fund to support female candidates by covering personal expenses that did not already fall under the provisions of the Canada Elections Act and the hiring and training of staff to support their campaigns. At that time the party also sent letters to local executives encouraging them to seek out female candidates, particularly in ridings that had previously been held by Bloc incumbents (Tremblay 2010, 169).

The importance of parties actively seeking out potential female candidates to run for office should not be underestimated. In the lead up to the 2008 election, all parties except for the Conservatives made a commitment to Equal Voice, a multipartisan organization dedicated to electing more women in Canada, that one-third to one-half of their candidates would be women (Thomas and Young 2014, 380). As a result, two-thirds of the female Liberal and NDP candidates who were surveyed after the 2008 election said that they were approached to run by a member of their local association executive (Cross and Young 2013, 29), whereas only just over half of the male candidates indicated such a move. Only 18 per cent of the women indicated that they decided to run without being encouraged to do so; 30 per cent of men ran for their party's nomination with no party recruitment. Women (47 per cent) were even more likely than men (31 per cent) to be recruited by someone at the national party level. In addition, it is clear that women's associations within the parties played an important role in candidate recruitment as almost 10 per cent of those surveyed indicated that they had been encouraged to run by their party's women's association. These findings reflect the results of past studies in Canada (Erickson 1991), or more recently in the United States (Lawless and Fox 2010), that highlight the critical role that recruitment plays in getting women and other underrepresented groups to run for office.

Although the Progressive Conservatives adopted many similar approaches to the Liberals, save for the appointment of candidates, the Reform Party and later the Canadian Alliance refused to implement any special measures to encourage women to run for their party. The Conservative Party of

Canada has followed the latter's lead and has not committed to any public efforts to increase the participation of women (Goodyear-Grant 2013, 132). While some authors have speculated that the slight increase in the number of female candidates (12 per cent in 2004 to 22 per cent in 2011) who have run in the past few elections may be due to behind-the-scenes strategies "to address a potentially embarrassing absence of women from its caucus" (Young 2013, 265), the drop to 19 per cent in the 2015 election suggests that this was a short-lived effort.

One way that the major parties have been slightly more responsive to questions of gender representation is in their appointment of key election campaign officials. The Conservatives, Liberals, and NDP all appointed women as chairs or co-chairs of their 2015 national election campaigns. While there is no doubt that these individuals play critical roles in determining the strategies their parties employ during the election, there is little evidence that similar levels of gender equity are reached at the constituency level, where local riding campaign teams are more often than not led by men.

While the number of female candidates a party runs in election campaigns is a good indicator of how open they are to the representation of diversity, an even better measure is the number of women who get elected because they ran in winnable seats. This is an important distinction, since Thomas and Bodet (2013) have argued there is evidence that parties (save for the Bloc) are more likely to nominate women in vulnerable swing or lost-cause ridings. As Bashevkin (1985, 1993) noted decades ago, the more competitive a position is (i.e., a candidate in a winnable riding) the less likely it is that it will be held by a woman. This would suggest that without concerted efforts on the part of parties to ensure that women are considered as candidates in ridings where their party has traditionally been strong, the number of women who win elections will be lower than the number who run as candidates. It is for this reason that Young (1991) has argued that increases in the number of women holding elected office often accompany elections that see a party making unexpected gains in regions of the country where the party had previously been politically weak (such as the Progressive Conservatives in 1984 or the NDP in 2011).

Despite efforts on the part of parties to appear more open and supportive of women within their ranks, little change has occurred over the past several decades in the numeric representation of women in the House of Commons. In 1993 women held 18 per cent of the seats, increasing slightly to 21 per cent in 1997. This number did not really change over the next four elections, and it was not until 2011 that it rose to 25 per cent of the seats, primarily due to the unexpected wins by NDP candidates in Quebec. In 2015 that number increased only slightly to 26 per cent.

Table 14.4 Percentage of Women by Party Caucus, 1984–2015

	NDP	Liberal	Progressive Conservative	Reform/Canadian Alliance/ Conservative	Bloc Québécois	Total Number of Seats
1984	10	13	9			10
1988	12	16	12			13
1993	11	20	50	13	15	18
1997	38	24	10	7	25	21
2000	38	23	8	11	26	21
2004	26	25		12	26	21
2006	41	20		11	33	21
2008	32	25		16	31	22
2011	39	18		17	35	25
2015	42	27		17	20	26

Much of the explanation for this stagnation in the election of women can be attributed to the growing popularity of the Conservatives. As can be seen from Table 14.4, although women regularly made up approximately one-third of the caucuses of the NDP and the Bloc and close to a quarter of the Liberal caucus, they represented a much smaller percentage of the Conservative caucus. Because of this, the increased electoral success of the Conservatives throughout the 2000s had a depressing impact on the overall number of women holding seats in the House of Commons. With the results of the 2015 election, the percentage of the seats held by women did not increase substantially despite the dramatic gain by the Liberals, since the increased number of Liberal women winning was countered by the loss of seats by NDP women.

Conclusion

Despite advances made by women in other areas of Canadian life, the last few decades have seen few improvements in the roles they play within political parties at the national level. Change has been incremental and slow. Few new initiatives to reduce the structural barriers to women's political engagement have been introduced since the 1980s, and the participation of women in elite positions within the parties still remains substantially lower than their numbers in the population and in the grassroots of their parties warrant.

In part, this has been due to the expectation that the advances made during the 1970s and 1980s would continue and women would assume an increasingly greater role within party organizations. In addition, the growing strength of the Reform, Canadian Alliance, and ultimately the Conservative Party of Canada—whose ideological orientation made them unwilling to make gender representation a priority—took pressure off the Liberals and the weakening Progressive Conservatives to do more on this issue.

This is not to say that breakthroughs have not occurred. Women have been selected as party leaders or as party presidents, and there is much celebration when a party fields a record number of female candidates. However, these successes have been temporary, and within a short period are undermined by the fact that at the next election parties often fall back to past levels of representation. As a result, the situation in Canada today looks quite similar to that of the early 1990s, with only marginal improvements. Perhaps even more telling of how much further we still have to go to reach gender parity is the attention given to Justin Trudeau's first cabinet after the 2015 election. The fact that he had to explain why half of his new ministers were women speaks to parties' traditional approach of symbolic or small incremental increases in representation rather than a course of openly engaging women as active participants in the political process. When women are active they tend to be present in parties of the left, which have structures in place to guarantee their representation, or in parties that are electorally weak and thereby have limited access to power. Right-wing parties and those that have been politically dominant are less likely to have women in positions of leadership, either at the riding level or on the national executive. Similarly, they are less likely to have women seek out and win the leadership of their parties, run as candidates, and sit as elected officials. In other words, Bashevkin's (1985) observations that the higher, the fewer and the more competitive, the fewer ring as true today as they did when they first appeared in print 30 years ago.

Suggested Readings

Bashevkin, Sylvia. 1993. *Toeing the Lines: Women in Party Politics in English Canada.* 2nd ed. Toronto: Oxford University Press.

Thomas, Melanie, and Lisa Young. 2014. "Women (Not) in Politics: Women's Electoral Participation." In *Canadian Politics,* 6th ed., edited by James Bickerton and Alain-G. Gagnon, 373–93. Toronto: University of Toronto Press.

Tremblay, Manon. 2010. *Quebec Women and Legislative Representation.* Vancouver: University of British Columbia Press.

Young, Lisa. 2000. *Feminists and Party Politics.* Vancouver: University of British Columbia Press.

Young, Lisa. 2002. "Representation of Women in the New Canadian Party System." In *Political Parties, Representation, and Electoral Democracy in Canada,* edited by William Cross, 181–200. Toronto: Oxford University Press.

Web Links

Equal Voice:

www.equalvoice.ca
A multipartisan Canadian organization committed to increasing women's political
participation and representation.
The Inter-Parliamentary Union: Women in National Parliaments: www.ipu.org/
wmn-e/classif.htm
The Inter-Parliamentary Union is an international organization of the parliaments
of sovereign states. It regularly maintains a website documenting the percentage
of seats held by women in national legislatures.
Report of the Royal Commission on the Status of Women (1970): http://epe.lac-bac.
gc.ca/100/200/301/pco-bcp/commissions-ef/bird1970-eng/bird1970-eng.htm
This report documented the status of Canadian women in the early 1970s and made
numerous recommendations related to their engagement in political life.

References

Bashevkin, Sylvia. 1985. *Toeing the Lines: Women in Party Politics in English Canada.*
Toronto: Oxford University Press.
Bashevkin, Sylvia. 1991. "Women's Participation in Political Parties." In *Women in
Canadian Politics: Toward Equity in Representation,* edited by Kathy Megyery,
61–97. Vol. 6 of the Research Studies of the Royal Commission on Electoral
Reform and Party Financing. Toronto: Dundurn Press.
Bashevkin, Sylvia. 1993. *Toeing the Lines: Women in Party Politics in English Canada.*
2nd ed. Toronto: Oxford University Press.
Bashevkin, Sylvia. 2010. "When Do Outsiders Break In? Institutional Circumstances of
Party Leadership Victories by Women in Canada." *Commonwealth and Comparative
Politics* 48 (1): 72–90. http://dx.doi.org/10.1080/14662040903444525
Brodie, Janine. 1985. *Women and Politics in Canada.* Toronto: McGraw-Hill.
Brodie, Janine. 1988. "The Gender Factor and National Leadership Conventions in
Canada." In *Party Democracy in Canada: The Politics of National Party Conventions,*
edited by George Perlin, 172–87. Scarborough, ON: Prentice Hall.
Bryden, Joan. 2007. "Liberals Set to Bar Men in Some Ridings in Bid to Boost
Female Candidates." *New Brunswick Telegraph Journal* (Saint John), February 9.
Cheng, Christine, and Margit Tavits. 2009. "Informal Influences in Selecting Female
Political Candidates." *Political Research Quarterly* 20 (10): 1–12.
Courtney, John. 1995. *Do Conventions Matter? Choosing National Party Leaders in
Canada.* Montreal: McGill-Queen's University Press.
Cross, William. 2004. *Political Parties.* Vancouver: University of British Columbia
Press.
Cross, William, and Lisa Young. 2013. "Candidate Recruitment in Canada: The Role
of Political Parties." In *Parties, Elections, and the Future of Canadian Politics,* edited
by Amanda Bittner and Royce Koop, 24–45. Vancouver: University of British
Columbia Press.
Erickson, Lynda. 1991. "Women and Candidacies for the House of Commons." In
Women in Canadian Politics: Toward Equity in Representation. Vol. 6 of the Research

Studies of the Royal Commission on Electoral Reform and Party Financing, edited by Kathy Megyery, 111–37. Toronto: Dundurn Press.

Everitt, Joanna. 2015. "Gender and Sexual Identity in Provincial Election Campaigns." *Canadian Political Science Review* 9 (1): 177–92.

Goodyear-Grant, Elizabeth. 2013. "Women Voters, Candidates, and Legislators." In *Parties, Elections, and the Future of Canadian Politics,* edited by Amanda Bittner and Royce Koop, 119–39. Vancouver: University of British Columbia Press.

Lawless, Jennifer, and Richard Fox. 2010. *It Still Takes a Candidate: Why Women Don't Run for Office.* New York: Cambridge University Press. http://dx.doi.org/10.1017/CBO9780511778797

Royal Commission on the Status of Women. 1970. *Report of the Royal Commission on the Status of Women.* Ottawa: Information Canada.

Stewart, David. 2002. "Electing a Premier." In *Citizen Politics: Research and Theory in Canadian Political Behaviour,* edited by Joanna Everitt and Brenda O'Neill, 321–37. Toronto: Oxford University Press.

Stewart, Ian, and David Stewart. 2007. *Conventional Choices: Maritime Leadership Politics.* Vancouver: University of British Columbia Press.

Thomas, Melanie, and Marc André Bodet. 2013. "Sacrificial Lambs, Women Candidates and District Competitiveness in Canada." *Electoral Studies* 32 (1): 153–66. http://dx.doi.org/10.1016/j.electstud.2012.12.001

Thomas, Melanie, and Lisa Young. 2014. "Women (Not) in Politics: Women's Electoral Participation." In *Canadian Politics,* 6th ed., edited by James Bickerton and Alain-G. Gagnon, 373–93. Toronto: University of Toronto Press.

Tremblay, Manon. 2010. *Quebec Women and Legislative Representation.* Vancouver: University of British Columbia Press.

Tremblay, Manon, and Réjean Pelletier. 2001. "More Women Constituency Party Presidents: A Strategy for Increasing the Number of Women Candidates in Canada?" *Party Politics* 7 (2): 157–90. http://dx.doi.org/10.1177/1354068801007002002

Trimble, Linda. 2007. "Gender, Political Leadership and Media Visibility: *Globe and Mail* Coverage of Conservative Party of Canada Leadership Contests." *Canadian Journal of Political Science* 40 (4): 969–93. http://dx.doi.org/10.1017/S0008423907071120

Trimble, Linda, and Joanna Everitt. 2010. "Belinda Stronach and the Gender Politics of Celebrity." In *Mediating Canadian Politics,* edited by Shannon Sampert and Linda Trimble, 50–74. Toronto: Pearson.

Young, Lisa. 1991. "Legislative Turnover and the Election of Women to the Canadian House of Commons." In *Women in Canadian Politics: Toward Equity in Representation,* edited by Kathy Megyery, 81–100. Vol. 6 of the Research Studies of the Royal Commission on Electoral Reform and Party Financing. Toronto: Dundurn Press.

Young, Lisa. 2000. *Feminists and Party Politics.* Vancouver: University of British Columbia Press.

Young, Lisa. 2002. "Representation of Women in the New Canadian Party System." In *Political Parties, Representation, and Electoral Democracy in Canada,* edited by William Cross, 181–200. Toronto: Oxford University Press.

Young, Lisa. 2013. "Slow to Change: Women in the House of Commons." In *Stalled: The Representation of Women in Canadian Governments,* edited by Linda Trimble,

Jane Arscott, and Manon Tremblay, 253–72. Vancouver: University of British Columbia Press.

Young, Lisa, and William Cross. 2003. "Women's Involvement in Canadian Political Parties." In *Women and Electoral Politics in Canada,* edited by Manon Tremblay and Linda Trimble, 92–109. Toronto: Oxford University Press.

15

The Promise of Direct Democracy: Is That All There Is?

A. BRIAN TANGUAY

RECENT STUDIES HAVE SHOWN THAT THE use of the various mechanisms of direct democracy—referendums,[1] citizen initiatives, and recall—has increased markedly since the 1950s, peaking in the 1990s (Strøm 2000, 187; see also Mendelsohn and Parkin 2001, 3) and tapering off slightly after 2000, though "still at a higher level than before the 1990s" (Qvortrup 2013a, 247; see also Altman 2011, 63–65; Qvortrup 2013b, 128). If we include not just the use of referendums but all mechanisms that "allow for direct popular decision-making," such as universal membership votes for party leaders and the direct election of city mayors, we can see a noticeable shift over the past several decades toward greater formal citizen involvement in governance in most of the established democracies (Scarrow 2001).[2]

These trends are understandable at a time when political parties are widely perceived to be failing to perform many of the functions ascribed to them in democratic theory.[3] The idea of direct democracy is most attractive to voters when anti-party sentiment is strong, as it is now and as was the case, for example, in the United States during the Progressive Era, in Western Canada during the 1920s and 1930s, or in Canada during the divisive constitutional debates that dominated public life from the mid-1980s to the end of the century. When political parties are viewed as "narrow sects concerned as much with self-preservation as with the public good" (Bogdanor 1981, 4), then direct democracy can be seen, in its strongest version, as a means of circumventing political parties altogether. In its weaker form, direct democracy offers citizens the possibility of reining in the sovereignty of parties, limiting their room to manoeuvre, and increasing their responsiveness to citizens' demands.

Through an examination of historical and contemporary experiments with direct democracy in Canada, this chapter will show that there is little likelihood that these techniques will replace political parties and traditional representative institutions in the foreseeable future. Populists of all stripes, like Canada's Reform Party in the 1990s, almost always downplay or overlook entirely the paradoxes of direct democracy, which historically has promised far more—in terms of facilitating the unmediated expression of the popular will—than it has been able to deliver. In many cases (though not always), the techniques of direct democracy are no more successful than traditional intermediary organizations in creating the conditions for joint deliberation and dialogue among citizens that are the hallmarks of a true democracy. Nor does direct democracy always place limits on the influence of so-called special interests, if by this term we understand organizations with money and influence, such as large corporations or pressure groups.

The remainder of the chapter is divided into four sections. In the first, I examine the historical antecedents of direct democracy in populist and neopopulist thought in both Canada and the United States. The second and third sections provide overviews of the actual use of referendums, initiatives, and recall, first at the provincial level and then at the national level in Canada. A brief concluding section will explore the prospects for direct democracy in this country.

A Brief History of the Idea of Direct Democracy in the United States and Canada

The basic idea underpinning direct democracy derives from the notion, expressed most forcefully by Jean-Jacques Rousseau (1973, 242), that the sovereignty of a people can neither be alienated nor represented: "the moment a people allows itself to be represented, it is no longer free: it no longer exists." In Rousseau's view, representative government was a modern invention, first coming into existence under feudalism, an "iniquitous and absurd system which degrades humanity and dishonours the name of man" (Rousseau 1973, 240). In a representative political system, individual citizens fancy themselves to be free, but this is true only for the brief moment when they are actually casting a ballot, once every four years or so. During the lifetime of a representative parliament, however, citizens are effectively barred from engaging in the common deliberation and debate needed to formulate the laws under which they live. Face-to-face dialogue and deliberation are the hallmarks of true citizenship, in Rousseau's eyes, and for this reason he believed that democracy was possible only in states small enough to allow all citizens to assemble together, as in his native city of Geneva (Birch 1971, 35).

In his writings, Rousseau invoked the democratic ideal of the ancient Greek city-states, Athens in particular, where meetings of the Assembly were open to all citizens who wished to attend, open votes were held on important matters of public policy, and members of the political executive were selected randomly by lot from a list of citizens over the age of 30 who allowed their names to stand. Frequent rotation of public officials and limits on their terms in office were also the norm in ancient Athens (Finley 1983, 71–74).[4] By the late eighteenth century, however, most societies had grown far too large and complex to permit the kind of face-to-face decision making extolled by Rousseau. Representative government easily won out over Rousseau's idealized republican city-state (Smith 1991, 19–21). In some of these polities, however—the Swiss cantons, for example, and the American colonies, both of which had a lengthy tradition of exercising legislative and executive power in open assemblies (like the New England town hall)—the use of the referendum to ratify important decisions gradually became entrenched. Whether used to adopt or alter constitutions, as in the American states after 1778, or to decide almost any matter of public policy, as in some Swiss cantons after 1800, the referendum eventually evolved into the most important tool in the arsenal of modern direct democracy (Butler and Ranney 1978, 5).[5]

The ideal of direct democracy was never more in vogue (outside of Switzerland) than during the populist and Progressive eras in the United States—roughly from the 1880s to the end of World War I. The populist movement emerged out of a political revolt among disaffected farmers in the American Midwest who traced the economic oppression of the "common man" to the baleful influence of the railroads, the banks, and monopolies or "trusts." In the populist worldview, corporations exploited their privileged political ties to the state, largely through corrupt party machines and ward bosses, to divert economic benefits to themselves. According to the populists, economic power derived from political privilege, not the reverse (Goebel 2002, 20–24).

The Progressives, a much more broadly based movement than the populists, with strength in such states as New York (Theodore Roosevelt), New Jersey (Woodrow Wilson), and Wisconsin (Robert La Follette), took up many of the same themes that had been articulated by their populist predecessors, in particular the urgent need to reduce the influence of special interests in American political life. For the Progressives, use of direct legislation (a term then used to encompass both the referendum and the citizen initiative) and provisions for recall of elected officials, along with the regulation of election financing and the use of direct primaries to select party candidates for office, would ultimately allow for the accurate expression of the uncorrupted will of the people. For these reformers, it was intermediary organizations themselves—parties and pressure groups—that were perverting democracy (Butler and Ranney 1978, 27–33). Allow citizens to bypass these obstacles to democracy, and not only would political life be purified, but political engagement and participation would also be sure to blossom.

Between 1898 and 1933, over 20 American states—most of them in the South (Arkansas and Oklahoma, for example) and Midwest (North and South Dakota, Montana, Missouri, and others)—enacted legislation permitting the use of referendums or citizen initiatives (Cronin 1989, 51). During that same period, 12 states passed laws allowing voters to recall most elected officials in the event that a certain percentage of electors in the juris-diction (anywhere from 10 to 40 per cent) signed a petition calling for the removal of the incumbent. Despite the lofty hopes of the reformers, however, this profusion of direct democracy measures in the early twentieth century failed to alter the political status quo appreciably, let alone usher in a new democratic commonwealth. Moneyed interests frequently adapted quite easily to the new legislative regimes, even if they were sometimes placed on the defensive by citizen initiatives and referendums. Pressure groups contin-ued to play a prominent role in the electoral process. The professionalization of election campaigns and the political consultant industry were stimulated by the spread of direct legislation in some American states, notably Califor-nia (Goebel 2002, 8). In most cases, John and Jane Q. Public were no more engaged in political life after the advent of direct legislation than they had been previously, and as a result voter turnout did not increase significantly. One study of this era in American history concludes on a decidedly sombre note: direct democracy did not "contribute in any meaningful way to the revival of democracy in America" (Goebel 2002, 198).

As in the United States, direct democracy in Canada in the first half of the twentieth century was largely a Western phenomenon. Fuelled by resentment of the banks and big manufacturers, chafing at the quasi-colonial political relationship between the West and Ottawa, and convinced that the national parties were mere pawns of the Central Canadian economic elites, prairie populists mobilized between 1900 and 1935, creating such organiza-tions as the Saskatchewan Grain Growers' Association, the United Farmers of Alberta, the Co-operative Commonwealth Federation, and the Social Credit League. Each of these groups was nominally committed to the principles of direct democracy, although their commitment seemed to diminish the closer they got to exercising power. Spurred on by populist factions within their ranks, Liberal governments in Alberta (1912), Saskatchewan (1913), and Manitoba (1916) passed laws to allow the use of referendums and initiatives. None of these provincial laws included provisions for the recall of elected officials, and grain growers' associations in Manitoba and Saskatchewan were particularly "disappointed with the limited scope of these enabling bills" (Laycock 1990, 38). Saskatchewan held a province-wide referendum on its direct legislation bill in 1913, which failed to garner the required support of 30 per cent of registered voters because of low turnout. The legislation was subsequently repealed. In Manitoba, the provincial Court of Appeal ruled that the government's direct legislation act was beyond the constitutional authority of the provincial legislature, a ruling ultimately upheld by the

Judicial Committee of the Privy Council in 1919. In its decision, the Manitoba Court of Appeal articulated the widely held constitutional view that direct democracy is incompatible with British-style responsible government: "In Canada there is no sovereignty in the people; . . . it is in the Parliament at Westminster, and our powers to legislate are such, and only such, as that Parliament has given us" (cited in Laycock 1990, 40).

Among the more unusual expressions of prairie populism in Canada was the Alberta Social Credit League, which won a landslide victory in the provincial election of 1935, less than a year after its creation. Under the charismatic leadership of William ("Bible Bill") Aberhart, Social Credit's attacks on the "money power," the economic "big shots," the federal government, central planners, and socialists appealed to those categories of voters who felt most threatened by the relentless centralization and concentration of economic production under capitalism: farmers, small merchants, teachers, and other elements of the petty bourgeoisie.[6] Unlike previous populist movements in the Prairies, Social Credit had only a tenuous commitment to direct democracy. In fact, as Macpherson (1962, 158) has shown, Aberhart's leadership style was highly authoritarian: decision-making power within the party was so centralized that every candidate running in the provincial election was selected by Aberhart and his advisory committee from lists supplied by the constituency association. According to the Albertan variant of social credit doctrine, the role of "the people" was to express their general desires for economic security and prosperity; it was up to the "experts" like Aberhart and other elected representatives to act on these desires. If the experts failed to deliver results, then the people ought to have a means of dismissing them, and so Alberta Social Credit included a provision for recall in its 1935 electoral program.[7] Interestingly, the Aberhart government retroactively repealed the Recall Act in 1937, at the moment when a petition to recall the premier himself was gathering signatures in his own riding of Okotoks-High River (Laycock 1990, 231–32; Macpherson 1962, 153; McCormick 1991, 275–76).

Macpherson characterized Social Credit's political philosophy as a form of plebiscitarian democracy. The term *plebiscite* derives from the Latin *plebis scitum,* used to describe a decree of the common people in ancient Rome. Napoleon Bonaparte organized a series of plebiscites in France at the beginning of the nineteenth century to ratify his proposals for constitutional change and to install himself as dictator ("consul for life"). In all cases, voters were presented with a *fait accompli;* their role was passive, simply to express their faith in the leader. In effect, Bonaparte legitimized his dictatorship by direct appeal to the people.[8] Over the course of the twentieth century, Adolf Hitler, Juan Perón, Charles de Gaulle, Augusto Pinochet, Ferdinand Marcos, and other authoritarian rulers would employ similar techniques to manipulate gullible, desperate, or cowed voters and consolidate their stranglehold on power (Laycock 1990, 203, 338n; LeDuc 2003, 46–47).

The experience of Social Credit in power in Alberta points to one of the central paradoxes of direct democracy: it is championed as a means whereby the popular will can be expressed and ordinary citizens can rein in elected representatives, yet in practice it has often been used by the prince—authoritarian or charismatic leaders—to manipulate and control the people. This paradoxical quality of direct democracy was evident in the ideology and practice of the most recent expression of prairie populism, the Reform Party of Canada. Founded in 1987 with the slogan "The West Wants In," the Reform Party advocated the "trinity of direct democracy" (Goebel 2002, 110): binding referendums on major issues of public policy, citizen initiatives, and a recall procedure that could be used by constituents to unseat Members of Parliament (MPs) that they felt had violated their oath of office (Reform Party 1991, 11). In its "Statement of Principles," the party asserted: "We believe in the common sense of the common people, their right to be consulted on public policy matters before major decisions are made . . . and their right to directly initiate legislation for which substantial public support is demonstrated" (Reform Party 1991, 3). According to leader Preston Manning, these techniques of direct democracy would complement Canada's traditional representative institutions, not replace them. They would provide voters with a powerful weapon for preventing elected officials and "special interests" from ignoring or subverting the wishes of the majority (Manning 1992, 326).

The party program also enshrined the notion of delegate democracy, which had been at the core of Social Credit ideology: "We believe . . . the duty of elected members to their constituents should supersede their obligations to their political parties" (Reform Party 1991, 3). However, Reform MPs had a great deal of difficulty overcoming the logistical and philosophical obstacles to determining the exact nature of their constituents' wishes. Party leaders were also not always willing to bend before constituents if their opinions differed from long-standing party policy on key issues, such as the right to assisted suicide or gun control. While it is true that Reform went much further than any of its federal counterparts in experimenting with electronic town halls and other forms of "teledemocracy," the results of their efforts were often quite meagre. In June 1994, for instance, Reform MP Ted White (North Vancouver) held a referendum on the Young Offenders Act in which only 6 per cent of his riding's registered voters actually took part. White nonetheless trumpeted the views of this minority as representative of the constituency—perhaps because they overwhelmingly endorsed a tougher line on young offenders.[9] Val Meredith, Reform MP from Surrey,

British Columbia, voted against the Liberal government's gun-control legislation on the basis of a telephone survey of her constituents. Only 3 per cent (2,800) of the riding's approximately 100,000 voters took part in the survey, and a solid majority of those participating actually favoured the registration of handguns, a position loudly opposed by Meredith and many other Reformers.

Preston Manning himself participated in an electronic town hall in April 1994 on the issue of doctor-assisted suicide, to which he was personally opposed. A random telephone survey of 700 people in five Calgary ridings revealed a strong majority (70 per cent) in favour of medically assisted suicide, but Manning balked at interpreting this as the "will of the people." He indicated that he would have to determine the exact breakdown of views in his own constituency, rather than for all of Calgary. If a solid majority—say, 60 to 65 per cent—supported this type of euthanasia, he acknowledged, he would be obliged to accede to his constituents' wishes, although he still indicated that he would argue and discuss the issue with the voters to convince them that this was not a good idea. Manning's actions in this case betrayed an almost Burkean conception of the role of the elected representative. Or as Tom Flanagan (1995, 32), the former chief policy adviser to Manning and the Reform Party, put it, "Manning's populism is fluid. He speaks in the name of 'the common sense of the common people,' but he is the only one who is authorized to express it, and he has various and not necessarily compatible ways for discovering that elusive wisdom."

To sum up, from the late 1800s to the start of the Great Depression a variety of populist thinkers in the United States and Canada advocated greater reliance on direct democracy to allow the voice of the "common man" to be heard over the din of special interests and money power. The populists had no faith whatsoever in party organizations, viewing them as hopelessly corrupted pawns of big business and its dutiful servants in government. To the extent that these populists were able to put their ideas into action, however—whether in several state governments or at the provincial level in Canada—the results fell disappointingly short of the wildly optimistic predictions of the most fervent advocates of direct democracy. In some cases, the tools of direct democracy—referendum, initiative, and recall—were simply co-opted by those same special interests that the populists were most interested in rendering powerless. In other cases, as with the Alberta Social Credit League under the charismatic leadership of William Aberhart and the Reform Party under Preston Manning, the movement's idiosyncratic notions of delegate democracy translated into substantial power for the leader over the grassroots. In both cases, it was difficult to make the argument that the version of direct democracy touted by the populists represented a substantial improvement over traditional representative government. It was certainly a very limited version of the Rousseauian ideal.

The next two sections examine the actual use of referendums, initiatives, and recall in Canada, first among the provinces then at the federal level. This will help us assess whether these tools do in fact hold out the prospect not only of reining in the power and purview of political parties, but of actually improving the quality of democracy in this country.

Direct Democracy in the Provinces

Despite the fact that some politicians and constitutional experts have long been convinced that referendums are "un-Canadian," or at best at odds with British parliamentary tradition, every province has conducted at least one referendum or plebiscite since Confederation, as have two of the three territories (Nunavut and the Northwest Territories) and the federal government.[10] Although some political scientists and constitutional experts distinguish between referendums as binding votes and plebiscites as merely consultative, in practice the terms have been used interchangeably (Marquis 1993, 8).[11] Six provinces—Prince Edward Island, New Brunswick, Quebec, Saskatchewan, Alberta, and British Columbia—all three territories, and the federal government have enacted legislation specifically governing the conduct of referendums and plebiscites. Ontario, Manitoba, Alberta, and Yukon have adopted taxpayer protection legislation that compels the provincial government to call a referendum before introducing a bill that would create a new tax or raise existing tax rates (no such votes have yet been called in any of these jurisdictions). Manitoba has adopted legislation stipulating that the government may not pass legislation to privatize Manitoba Hydro or the Manitoba Public Insurance Corporation without first putting "the question of the advisability of the privatization to the voters of Manitoba in a referendum" (Manitoba 2001, 2004). In the remaining provinces, referendums are regulated by the same statutes that govern the conduct of elections.

Below is a list of the most recent referendums conducted in each of the provinces since 1990:[12]

- Newfoundland (1997): The referendum asked voters whether they favoured the creation of a single school system to replace the denominational boards in the province. Just over 72 per cent voted yes.
- Nova Scotia (2004): 55 per cent voted against Sunday shopping.
- New Brunswick (2001): 53 per cent voted in favour of continuing to permit the legal operation of video lottery terminals in the province.

- Prince Edward Island (2005): 64 per cent rejected the proposal to adopt a mixed-member proportional (MMP) electoral system in the province; turnout was very low, at about one-third of registered voters (Tanguay 2014, 300).
- Quebec (1995): A bare majority, 50.6 per cent, voted "No" to the proposal that Quebec become a sovereign nation after having made a formal offer of economic and political partnership to the rest of Canada.
- Ontario (2007): A referendum on electoral system reform was held in conjunction with the provincial election of 10 October 2007. Just over 63 per cent—turnout was 50 per cent of registered voters—rejected the proposal to adopt an MMP system in the province (Stephenson and Tanguay 2009).
- Manitoba (1952): The last referendum was on the marketing of barley and oats in the province.
- Saskatchewan (1991): Three questions were put to the province's voters. First, almost 80 per cent voted in favour of balanced budget legislation. Second, almost 80 per cent endorsed the idea that any proposed changes to the Canadian Constitution be subject to approval in a provincial referendum. And third, almost 63 per cent rejected the proposal that the provincial government pay for abortion procedures.
- Alberta (1971): The last referendum was held on the adoption of daylight savings time.
- British Columbia (2011): Elections BC (2016a) notes that five referendums have been held in the province since 1991, on the recall and initiative process (1991), treaty negotiations (2002), electoral reform (2005 and 2009), and the harmonized sales tax (HST; 2011). The most recent referendum involved a mail-in ballot that was distributed to the province's registered voters. Just under 55 per cent of those who voted[13] expressed their desire to extinguish the HST and reinstate the PST (provincial sales tax) in conjunction with the GST (goods and services tax). Turnout for this referendum was 52.7 percent (Elections BC 2011, 3, 28).
- Northwest Territories (1992): 54 per cent of voters endorsed the creation of a new territory, which would eventually become Nunavut, in the eastern portion of the existing territory.
- Nunavut (1997): 57 per cent of voters rejected the proposal to have an equal number of men and women Members of the Legislative Assembly (MLAs), with one man and one woman elected from each electoral district.

Table 15.1 summarizes the various legislative provisions for referendums and plebiscites at both levels of government in Canada. It shows that a total of 68 referendums have been held at the provincial or territorial level since

1867 and three at the national level. The first "wave" of referendum activity among the provinces occurred in the first two decades of the twentieth century, when nearly one referendum was held each year, most of them dealing with the sale of alcoholic beverages (Belkhodja 2007, 222; Boyer 1992, Appendix 1; Mowrey and Pelletier 2001, 19). Since the start of World War II, over 30 referendums have been held in the provinces on a wide range of issues, including the adoption of daylight savings time in British Columbia, Alberta, and Saskatchewan; the creation of a nondenominational school system in Newfoundland; Quebec's constitutional future; the creation of the new territory of Nunavut; and several moral–economic issues, such as Sunday shopping and the legalized use of video lottery terminals. The peak of this second "wave" of experimentation with direct democracy occurred during the 15-year period that coincided with the constitutional distemper that roiled the country as a result of the abortive Meech Lake Accord and the extensive political repercussions that attended its failure.

Since 2000, largely in an effort to address the perceived "democratic deficit," three provinces—British Columbia, Ontario, and Prince Edward Island—have held four referendums[14] on the adoption of a more proportional electoral system, and another two (Quebec and New Brunswick) contemplated doing so. British Columbia and Ontario travelled furthest down the road toward providing a workable model of public consultation on the issue of electoral reform. Both created citizens' assemblies consisting of individuals randomly drawn from each constituency in the province. These assemblies were tasked with learning about the advantages and drawbacks of the various electoral systems in use around the world and making recommendations for reform, if the existing single-member, simple-plurality system (familiarly known as "first-past-the-post") was deemed in need of change. In both cases, the citizens' assemblies recommended that alternative electoral systems be put to a vote in province-wide referendums—mixed-member proportional (in use in Germany and Scotland among other jurisdictions) in the case of Ontario, and single transferable vote (STV, currently employed in the Republic of Ireland) in the case of British Columbia.

With one exception, all of the proposals for electoral reform were defeated decisively, garnering the support of only 36 per cent of voters in Prince Edward Island (November 2005), 37 per cent in Ontario (October 2007), and 39 per cent in British Columbia (May 2009). The sole exception was the first referendum held in British Columbia in May 2005, when 58 per cent of voters endorsed STV, with majorities in 77 of the province's 79 constituencies. This impressive result nonetheless failed to meet one element of the super-majority (60 per cent of valid votes cast in at least 60 per cent of the ridings)

Table 15.1 Overview of Federal and Provincial Referendum Legislation

Province	Name of Act	Topic	Binding?	Number Held Since 1867
Newfoundland and Labrador	Elections Act	Any matter of public concern	No	5
Nova Scotia	Liquor Plebiscite Regulations Elections Act	Operation of liquor store or licenced premises	Yes	4
New Brunswick	Referendum Act Elections Act	Any matter	Yes, if more than 50 per cent of the ballots validly cast in a referendum are cast for the same response to the referendum question and at least 50 per cent of all qualified electors cast votes	2
Prince Edward Island	Elections Act Plebiscites Act	Any matter of public concern	No	7
Quebec	Referendum Act	On a question approved or bill adopted by the National Assembly	No	5
Ontario	Taxpayer Protection Act Election Act	Establishing a new tax or increasing tax rates	Yes*	5
Manitoba	Balanced Budget, Fiscal Management and Taxpayer Accountability Act Elections Act Manitoba Hydro Act and Manitoba Public Insurance Corporation Act**	Any proposed tax increase	Yes	7
			Yes	
Saskatchewan	Referendum and Plebiscite Act†	Any matter of public concern	Yes, if more than 60 per cent of ballots validly cast vote the same way and at least 50 per cent of eligible voters vote	7

	Election Act			
	Time Act/Local Government Election Act††		Yes	
Alberta	Constitutional Referendum Act	Any proposed changes to provincial constitution	Yes, if more than 50 per cent of ballots validly cast vote the same way	7
	Alberta Taxpayer Protection Act	Imposition of provincial sales tax	Yes	
	Election Act			
British Columbia	Referendum Act	Any matter of public interest	Yes	15
	Recall and Initiative Act‡	Any matter within jurisdiction of the legislature	Yes, if supported by at least 50 per cent of registered voters in the province and 50 per cent of registered voters in at least two-thirds of the ridings vote in favour of the initiative	
	Election Act			
Northwest Territories	Elections and Plebiscites Act	Any matter	No	3
Nunavut	Plebiscites Act	Any matter	Yes, if clearly indicated in writ	1
Yukon	Plebiscite Act	Any matter	No	0
	Taxpayer Protection Act	New taxes or tax increases	Yes	
Federal Government	Referendum Act	Constitutional issues	No	3
	Canada Elections Act			

*The act states that a subsequent government formed by a different political party is not required to implement the results of the referendum.

**These acts stipulate that the Manitoba government may not pass legislation to privatize Manitoba Hydro or the Manitoba Public Insurance Corporation without first putting "the question of the advisability of the privatization to the voters of Manitoba in a referendum."

†Saskatchewan's legislation directs the minister of justice to hold a plebiscite when 15 per cent of electors sign a petition requesting that an issue be put to voters.

††This act (Chapter T-14 of The Revised Statutes of Saskatchewan, 1978, effective 26 February 1978) allows for municipalities in western and northwestern Saskatchewan to hold "votes" (the legislation avoids the use of both the terms referendum and plebiscite) to determine which time zone—Mountain Standard or Central Standard—they will observe, and (in the case of northwestern Saskatchewan only) for which part of the year.

‡BC legislation allows registered voters to propose new laws or changes to existing laws if they can obtain the signatures of at least 10 per cent of the registered voters in each of the province's electoral districts.

Sources: Adapted from Boyer (1992); Elections Canada (2015); Kaye (2000); Mowrey and Pelletier (2001).

established by the Liberal government of Gordon Campbell to make the results binding.

In his analysis of the BC referendums on electoral reform, Dennis Pilon (2010, 74; see also his chapter in this volume) argues that political elites erected "numerous innovative . . . barriers against change," in particular the unprecedented and unreasonable requirement for a super-majority, when ballot laws have been changed on numerous occasions in the past at both the provincial and municipal level with a simple *legislative* majority. In addition, the parties themselves sometimes played a deliberately confusing game during the referendum campaigns, sending out mixed signals to their supporters and members on the desirability of electoral reform—even when they themselves had introduced the reforms (Stephenson and Tanguay 2009). In one of the most significant studies to date of the citizens' assembly process, Fournier et al. (2011, 157) concluded on a somewhat pessimistic note, arguing that while the citizens' assemblies themselves were examples of "intense participatory, deliberative, and epistemic democracy," much of their good work was undone in the referendums that followed by the mass of voters, many of whom "lacked the contextual background information that could allow them to recognize the option that conformed to their interests."

As for the remaining two elements of the "trinity of direct democracy," only two provinces—Saskatchewan and British Columbia—have enacted legislation to allow citizen initiatives. Both bills were adopted by right-wing administrations—in Saskatchewan by the Progressive Conservative government of Grant Devine, and in British Columbia by the Social Credit government of Bill Vander Zalm. In Saskatchewan, the minister of justice must direct a plebiscite on any issue of public concern when he or she receives a petition signed by at least 15 per cent of the province's voters. No such province-wide plebiscites have been held since the passage of the law in 1991. In British Columbia, any citizen can apply to have a legislative proposal put to a province-wide vote if he or she gathers signatures from at least 10 per cent of the registered voters in each of the province's ridings. There have been nine applications for initiatives in British Columbia since the legislation came into effect in 1995,[15] on such issues as a prohibition on bear hunting and the adoption of a proportional electoral system. Only one of them—launched by former Premier Bill Vander Zalm in 2010 to abolish the HST, which critics had dubbed the "Hated Sales Tax" (Stueck 2013)—obtained a sufficient number of valid signatures (557,383 in this case, well in excess of the 299,611 signatures required by the law) to trigger a province-wide vote, which succeeded in reinstating the PST/GST (Elections BC 2016b).

This lone instance of a successful citizens' initiative does highlight some of the putative benefits of direct democracy: the campaign brought together an unlikely coalition of citizens' groups representing the middle class, the hospitality industry, organized labour, and the poor, all of whom argued that the HST disproportionately benefited big business in the province and their allies in the political class (*CBC News* 2011). Gordon Campbell—who announced his resignation as premier in November 2010 as a result of the controversy—was excoriated for having introduced the tax in 2009 without any prior warning or consultation and in spite of his party's silence on the issue during the 2009 provincial election campaign (Postmedia News 2011). By overcoming the relatively high threshold required to trigger a province-wide vote on an issue of public policy, the successful campaign against the HST in British Columbia demonstrated that the mechanisms of direct democracy can indeed be used to sanction political elites who stray too far from their electoral promises or who treat the electorate with disdain.[16]

Finally, British Columbia is the only province that permits the recall of elected officials if an applicant (called a "proponent") gathers signatures from at least 40 per cent of the registered voters in the legislative member's (MLA's) riding. In that case, a by-election will be called, in which the recalled MLA can run again as a candidate. Since 1995 there have been 26 such applications under the Recall and Initiative Act, but only one gathered the required number of signatures to trigger a by-election. The target was Liberal MLA Paul Reitsma in the riding of Parksville-Qualicum in 1998. Reitsma, who used a pseudonym to write letters to the editors of several local newspapers in which he criticized his opponents and heaped praise on his own work, resigned before the by-election could be held (O'Neill 2002, 285).

In summary, recent provincial experiences with referendums, initiatives, and recall yield mixed lessons for the proponents of direct democracy. The first lesson is that these tools—even referendums—are rarely used in the provinces, and this is unlikely to change in the foreseeable future now that the democratic distemper of the 1990s has subsided somewhat and the Reform Party—the most consistent and vocal partisan advocate of the advantages of direct democracy—has been absorbed into the mainstream. However, when these mechanisms are used they can, in rare instances (as with the campaign to rescind the HST in British Columbia), provide one of the principal benefits of direct democracy touted by its advocates, namely "restricting the sovereignty of the political parties" and limiting their room to manoeuvre vis-à-vis the voters who put them in power (Bogdanor 1981, 2; compare to Manning 1992, 326).

Despite this, there are very real limitations to the effectiveness of the most frequently used tool of direct democracy: referendums. As the history of electoral reform efforts in both British Columbia and Ontario demonstrates, the referendum process does not insulate voters from the effects of the "special interests"; it does not provide the opportunity for voters to educate themselves about the various options under discussion, nor does it filter out the often ambiguous or equivocal role played by party elites in sending cues to those who are deciding the issue. As Amy Lang (2007, 66) has convincingly argued, randomly drawn assemblies of "ordinary" citizens, or what she and others have labelled "randomocracy," represent "a substantial improvement over consultation processes that limit citizen involvement to making expressive statements, or that ask citizens to select from a narrow set of pre-defined options."

Direct Democracy at the Federal Level

Only three national referendums have been held since Confederation. The first, in 1898, was on the issue of the prohibition of sales of alcoholic beverages. Turnout was low, about 44 per cent of eligible voters, and a bare majority (just over 51 per cent) of ballots were cast in favour of prohibition. The proposal carried in every province except Quebec, where an overwhelming 83 per cent of voters rejected prohibition. This national referendum, like the next one held in 1942 on the Mackenzie King government's request to be released from its pre-war pledge not to impose conscription, exposed one of the most serious limitations of direct democracy as a decision-making technique: its divisiveness and its tendency to allow majorities to bulldoze over the wishes of important minority groups, like francophone Quebecers (MacDonald 1991, 309). In the 1942 plebiscite, over 70 per cent of Quebecers opposed Mackenzie King's manoeuvre to impose conscription, while 80 per cent of voters outside of Quebec supported it (Beck 1968, 244). This result could have had fatal consequences for national unity had it not been for Mackenzie King's assiduous efforts to bridge the linguistic divide in the country. King managed to delay the implementation for another two years after the plebiscite, during which time he worked to portray the Liberal Party as the only organization that could successfully knit the country together, a strategy that ultimately won him a third successive majority in the 1945 general election (Beck 1968, 248–49; Boyer 1992, 42). In this case, direct democracy had done virtually nothing to solve the crisis of national unity and, in fact, had exacerbated the divisions over conscription. It was traditional brokerage politics practised by the Liberal Party and its leader that managed to avert disaster.

Popular interest in direct democracy in this country peaked in the late 1980s and early 1990s as Canada lurched from one political crisis to another and faith in national representative institutions and trust in the political class plummeted. The acrimonious debate over free trade with the United States, the imposition of the widely reviled GST, the armed stand-off between Mohawk Warriors and the Canadian army at Oka, and the collapse of the Meech Lake Accord: all of these exacted a severe toll on the health of Canadian democracy. The Citizens' Forum on Canada's Future,[17] established by Prime Minister Brian Mulroney in 1990 in the wake of the failure of the Meech Lake constitutional package and given the mandate of "listen[ing] to the people to find out what kind of country they wanted for themselves and their children" became a sounding board for a cranky electorate. A group from Quebec neatly encapsulated one of the report's recurrent themes: "It is time the individual becomes actively involved in the future of Canada and not leave it to the politicians" (Canada, Citizens' Forum on Canada's Future 1991, 15, 105). Among the instruments proposed by various individuals and groups to overhaul what they saw as our ineffective, elitist, and unresponsive political system were greater use of referendums on major issues of public policy; citizen initiatives; the creation of a constituent assembly to explore options for constitutional renewal; a mechanism for recalling sitting MPs in the event that a sufficient number of citizens in a riding wanted to remove the incumbent; a means of impeaching an incumbent prime minister; limitations on the number of terms in office for elected representatives; direct election of the prime minister; an elected or abolished Senate; more free votes in the House of Commons and a relaxation of party discipline (Canada, Citizens' Forum on Canada's Future 1991, 102–5, 134–37).

Voter disenchantment with "politics as usual" culminated in the decisive rejection of the Charlottetown Accord in the third national referendum to be held in Canada on 26 October 1992. A majority of voters in six of the ten provinces—from 51 per cent in Nova Scotia to 68 per cent in British Columbia—rebuffed the last attempt by the Mulroney government to bring Quebec into the Canadian constitutional fold. Overall, 55 per cent of Canadians voted "no" to the proposed changes. For many voters, this referendum offered them the opportunity to thumb their nose at the political class, especially Prime Minister Brian Mulroney, who by that point was probably "the most unpopular prime minister in Canadian history. . . . [Voters] were allowed to indulge themselves in a negativism that was partly tribal, partly . . . anti-elite" (Johnston et al. 1996, 277, 285).

While some observers applauded this spasm of voter anger as a salutary repudiation of a remote, self-absorbed, and unresponsive political elite, the result nonetheless raised serious questions about the utility of referendums for facilitating significant institutional changes. Banting and Simeon (1985, 25; see also Dion 1996, 272) observed more than 30 years ago that "constitutional change is not easy to bring about." These sorts of changes are usually necessitated by a lack of consensus about existing institutional arrangements among the various constituents of a polity, but this very absence of consensus means there are simply too many different ways to say "no" to a referendum question: "all parties may consider the constitutional status quo preferable to the adoption of their opponent's position" (Banting and Simeon 1985, 25). This dynamic was certainly visible during the referendum campaign on the Charlottetown Accord: an initially popular (but very complex) constitutional proposal was defeated when women's groups, Westerners, Quebecers, and others mobilized public opinion in favour of the "no" vote—all of them for differing reasons. Other scholars (Darcy and Laver 1990, 10; Magleby 1984) have noted this tendency for referendum voters to behave "conservatively," to opt for the status quo over proposed institutional changes. Qvortrup (2013a, 249) confirms this tendency, but sees it as beneficial: "In Western Europe, North America and Australia, the referendum has often—but not exclusively—performed the function of a constitutional safeguard, which has prevented politicians from enacting institutional changes at a faster pace than favoured by the electors." He cites the referendum on the Charlotte-town Accord as an illustration of direct democracy's role as constitutional safeguard, and also points out that "in Australia fewer than 25 per cent of all referendums have been passed."

The most recent controversy over direct democracy at the federal level has swirled around the issue of electoral reform. During the federal election campaign of 2015, both the Liberals and the NDP pledged to replace the "antiquated" and "unfair" first-past-the-post system with a new ballot law in time for the next federal election, slated for October 2019. Thomas Mulcair and the NDP favoured a mixed-member proportional system similar to the one advocated by the Law Commission of Canada (2004) in its report *Voting Counts*.[18] The Liberals promised, if elected, to "convene an all-party Parliamentary committee to review a wide variety of reforms, such as ranked ballots, proportional representation, mandatory voting, and online voting" and to pass legislation enacting electoral reform "within 18 months of forming government" (Liberal Party of Canada 2015, 27). After winning a resounding majority in the 2015 election, the Liberals announced in December 2015 that they would implement electoral reform without holding a referendum on the matter. In a television interview, Prime Minister Justin Trudeau was asked about the need to hold a referendum before any modifications are made to the system, and he "responded by asking the interviewer whether it is necessary to have a referendum on everything that matters to the future of the country. 'You have to make choices at one point,' he said, 'and we are committed to holding full, engaged consultations. And we'll see where that takes us'" (Galloway 2015, A2).

This stance has produced differing degrees of apoplexy in conservative opponents of electoral reform—the federal Conservative Party has promised to "use any means necessary, including a Senate blockade," to prevent any modification of the existing system unless a national vote is held (Ibbitson 2015)—as well as among certain sympathizers of proportional representation, who fear that reform without referendum will jeopardize the legitimacy of the entire project (Gibson 2015). Connoisseurs of irony will appreciate the reversal of traditional positions on the issue of direct democracy as an instrument of social and political change. While the Conservative Party—no doubt emboldened by the failure of three (or four, depending on one's definition of failure) previous public consultations on the matter—has unfurled the standard of "no electoral reform without a referendum," Fair Vote Canada (2015), which in the past strongly supported a national consultation on the question of electoral reform, now contends that

> referendums are not binding on governments under the Westminster system. There's absolutely no legal or constitutional requirement to hold a referendum. . . . Proportional representation is about our equality as citizens. We should never have referendums on extending basic democratic rights. Should there have been a referendum in Canada to decide whether or not to give women the vote?

This issue will be played out over the course of the Liberal mandate. What is relevant for the purposes of this chapter is the evident loss of faith among some civil society groups militating for significant institutional reforms in the traditional tools of direct democracy as agents of such change.

Conclusion: Assessing the Prospects for Direct Democracy in Canada

The ideal of direct democracy—the unmediated expression of the "will of the people"—was most forcefully articulated in the writings of Jean-Jacques Rousseau. We have seen that support for this ideal, in both Canada and the United States, has reached a peak during periods of intense anti-party sentiment, as during the populist revolts in the prairie provinces in the first half of the twentieth century and the distempered 1990s. This chapter has raised questions about the translation of the ideal into practice, however: often, populist administrations—like William Aberhart's Social Credit government in Alberta and the crypto-populist Liberal governments in Alberta, Saskatchewan, and Manitoba before World War I—have been reluctant to abandon traditional representative institutions in favour of the mechanisms of direct democracy. When they have used the tools of direct democracy, it was for their own self-interest, to shore up their legitimacy and extend elite control over their citizens.

This is not to say that the use of direct democracy has had no appreciable benefits at either the provincial or the federal level in Canada. From the historical overview provided in this chapter, we can glean at least two advantages of direct democracy in practice. First, as the 1995 vote on sovereignty in Quebec demonstrated, referendum campaigns can be galvanizing moments in a nation's existence. In certain circumstances—as Stephen Tierney (2015) has shown in the case of the Scottish referendum of 2014—they can also dilute elite control of key political issues and encourage widespread public engagement. Second, as the one successful instance of a citizen initiative (British Columbia's vote on the HST) demonstrated, these mechanisms can be used effectively to rein in political elites, provided that the thresholds required to trigger such votes are high enough to discourage frivolous campaigns.

On the other hand, there are some obvious limitations to the various mechanisms of direct democracy. In the first place, government and party elites are often tempted to manipulate the decision rules to their advantage: witness the differing thresholds required to make the results binding in the case of Quebec—50 per cent + 1 in a vote to determine the future of an entire nation—versus the super-majorities needed in the referendums on electoral reform, which involved a comparatively minor modification of ballot laws.

Second, one of the most intractable problems associated with direct democracy is the impact these decision-making tools have on minorities. In his study of direct democracy in the American states, Lewis (2013, 2) argues that "the ability of citizens to directly create public policy increases governmental responsiveness to the preferences of the majority. In cases where the majority prefers policies that restrict the rights of political minorities, this enhanced responsiveness works to the detriment of these groups." This "tyranny of the majority" was visible in the two referendums held at the federal level in Canada on prohibition and conscription. It is difficult to envisage the frequent resort to direct democracy to decide key constitutional and moral issues in a multinational state like Canada, when majoritarian decisions might have a deleterious impact on the rights and status of significant minority groups, such as Indigenous peoples, Québécois, anglophones in Quebec, or the LGBT community.

Perhaps the most serious drawback to direct democracy has been highlighted by Fournier et al. (2011) in their examination of the citizens' assemblies on electoral reform created in British Columbia, Ontario, and the Netherlands. Referendum campaigns simply do not offer an adequate opportunity for average voters to educate themselves about the issues in play, and they remain vulnerable to the often equivocal or ambiguous cues provided by the parties themselves. Yes, in certain circumstances direct democracy can serve to constrain the sovereignty of the parties, as Vernon Bogdanor (1981) argued in his seminal book on the subject, but it nonetheless appears as though the promise of direct democracy will almost always outstrip its performance.

Suggested Readings

Bogdanor, Vernon. 1981. *The People and the Party System: The Referendum and Electoral Reform in British Politics*. Cambridge: Cambridge University Press.

Bookchin, Murray. 2015. *The Next Revolution: Popular Assemblies and the Promise of Direct Democracy*. London: Verso.

Bruce, Iain, ed. 2004. *The Porto Alegre Alternative: Direct Democracy in Action*. London: Pluto Press.

Fournier, Patrick, Henk van der Kolk, R. Kenneth Carty, André Blais, and Jonathan Rose. 2011. *When Citizens Decide: Lessons from Citizen Assemblies on Electoral Reform*. Toronto: Oxford University Press. http://dx.doi.org/10.1093/acprof:oso/9780199567843.001.0001

Qvortrup, Matt. 2013. *Direct Democracy: A Comparative Study of the Theory and Practice of Government by the People*. Manchester: Manchester University Press. http://dx.doi.org/10.7228/manchester/9780719082061.001.0001

Notes

1   A note on usage: Qvortrup (2013c, 2) notes that it "is generally agreed" that the term *referendums* is "grammatically more correct than" *referenda*. This view is also held by Butler and Ranney (1978, 4–5) and by Fowler (1965, 511), who points out that *referenda* is confusing, since its original sense was "questions to be referred," for which we now use *terms of reference* in English.

2   However, Scarrow (2001, 660–61) added the important caveat that political elites often retain control over the timing of popular consultations, along with the conditions under which they are held.

3   See Peter Mair's (2013, 1) *Ruling the Void* for a brilliant diagnosis of what he calls the end of the "age of party democracy."

4   The term in office for the Council of 500, the most important component of the Athenian executive, was limited to one year. A man (women, like slaves, were excluded from citizenship) could serve on the Council only twice in his lifetime (see Finley 1983).

5   As Aubert (1978, 39) points out, the referendum was used in some Swiss cantons, Bern in particular, as early as the late Middle Ages, only to be suppressed during the seventeenth and eighteenth centuries by a return to oligarchic rule. By 1830, however, "most cantons, including the conservative ones, accepted the custom of submitting their constitutions to the people—and some of their laws as well."

6   Laycock (1990) notes, however, that "many skilled and semi-skilled workers supported and participated in the Social Credit movement, particularly in Calgary," attracted in part by the party's promise of a $25 dividend to each citizen.

7   "The Social Credit government when in power will pass legislation to the effect that candidates submit to the voters' right of recall if they fail to carry out the proposals made prior to the election" (quoted in Irving 1959, 351).

8   One study of Napoleon points out that the path toward authoritarian rule in post-revolutionary France was "punctuated at every stage by a plebiscite, in which Bonaparte invited the French people to approve or reject the institutions he proposed. . . . Bonapartism was not a military dictatorship, in the sense that Napoleon derived his power chiefly from the support of the army. His was rather a civilian dictatorship because it drew its legitimacy from direct consultation with the people, in the form of a plebiscite" (Lyons 1994, 111).

9   See the insightful discussion of this and other efforts at electronic democracy by the Reform Party in Barney 1996.

10   This does not take into account the numerous local and municipal referendums and plebiscites that have been held in all of the provinces.

11   Given the pejorative connotations that have been attached to the term *plebiscite,* it might be thought that *referendum* would be preferred for both binding and nonbinding votes. As Butler and Ranney (1978, 4) observe, however, if one examines the practice of a number of countries, and not just the Anglo-American democracies, "there does not seem to be any clear or generally acknowledged line that can be drawn to distinguish the subject matter, the intent, or the conduct of a referendum from that of a plebiscite." Saskatchewan is the only province to draw a legal distinction between referendums and plebiscites in its Referendum and Plebiscite Act, which stipulates that referendums can only be called by cabinet while plebiscites can be called either by cabinet or by the minister of justice, if the latter receives a petition with a sufficient number of signatures on it. Elections BC (2016b) notes that referendums are "usually binding on the government," while plebiscites *may* be binding.

12   This list is compiled mainly from Mowrey and Pelletier (2001), along with information gleaned from the websites of the individual provincial governments.

13   Technically, this did not meet the threshold established by the government's own Recall and Initiative Act, which requires that 50 per cent of registered voters vote the same way for a referendum to be binding. However, prior to the vote on the HST, then Premier Gordon Campbell stipulated that his government would "accept a simple majority of those who cast ballots, a break future referendums might not be as likely to catch" (Dhillon 2011).

14   The vote in PEI was called a plebiscite. British Columbia held two referendums (as will be discussed in greater detail below) on electoral reform, in 2005 and 2009. See Tanguay (2014, 296–301) for an analysis of these experiments with electoral reform.

15   Initiative and recall were endorsed in a province-wide referendum in 1991. Over 80 per cent of those voting supported the idea of recall, and 83 per cent endorsed citizen initiatives (Mowrey and Pelletier 2001, 20). Legislation authorizing initiatives and recall received Royal Assent in 1994 and took effect in 1995.

16 This is not to say that the policy outcome of this initiative was necessarily optimal. There are many compelling economic reasons—even from a social democratic perspective—to prefer the HST over the PST/GST. See Stueck (2013) and Postmedia News (2011).

17 Better known as the Spicer Commission after its chairman, Keith Spicer, the former commissioner of official languages.

18 "The NDP will ensure every vote counts, and that this will be the last unfair election Canadians participate in. As government, the NDP will: Make your vote truly count by bringing in a system of mixed-member proportional representation that is appropriate for Canada in our first mandate" (NDP 2015, 56).

References

Altman, David. 2011. *Direct Democracy Worldwide*. Cambridge: Cambridge University Press.

Aubert, Jean-François. 1978. "Switzerland." In *Referendums: A Comparative Study of Practice and Theory,* edited by David Butler and Austin Ranney, 39–66. Washington, DC: American Enterprise Institute for Public Policy Research.

Banting, Keith G., and Richard Simeon. 1985. "Introduction: The Politics of Constitutional Change." In *Redesigning the State: The Politics of Constitutional Change,* edited by Keith G. Banting and Richard Simeon, 1–29. Toronto: University of Toronto Press.

Barney, Darin. 1996. "Push-Button Populism: The Reform Party and the Real World of Teledemocracy." *Canadian Journal of Communication* 21 (3). http://www.cjc-online.ca/index.php/journal/article/view/956

Beck, J. Murray. 1968. *Pendulum of Power.* Scarborough, ON: Prentice-Hall.

Belkhodja, Chedly. 2007. "The Referendum Experience in New Brunswick." In *Democratic Reform in New Brunswick,* edited by William Cross, 221–39. Toronto: Canadian Scholars' Press.

Birch, A.H. 1971. *Representation: Key Concepts in Political Science.* London: Macmillan.

Bogdanor, Vernon. 1981. *The People and the Party System: The Referendum and Electoral Reform in British Politics.* Cambridge: Cambridge University Press.

Boyer, Patrick. 1992. *Direct Democracy in Canada: The History and Future of Referendums.* Toronto: Dundurn Press.

Butler, David, and Austin Ranney, eds. 1978. *Referendums: A Comparative Study of Practice and Theory.* Washington, DC: American Enterprise Institute for Public Policy Research.

CBC News. 2011. "B.C. Votes 55 Per cent to Scrap HST." August 26. http://www.cbc.ca/news/canada/british-columbia/b-c-votes-55-to-scrap-hst-1.1011876

Citizens' Forum on Canada's Future. 1991. "Report to the People and Government of Canada." Ottawa: Minister of Supply and Services.

Cronin, Thomas E. 1989. *Direct Democracy: The Politics of Initiative, Referendum, and Recall.* Cambridge, MA: Harvard University Press. http://dx.doi.org/10.4159/harvard.9780674330092

Darcy, R., and Michael Laver. 1990. "Referendum Dynamics and the Irish Divorce Amendment." *Public Opinion Quarterly* 54 (1): 1–20. http://dx.doi.org/10.1086/269180

Dhillon, Sunny. 2011. "After the HST: What Will Happen to the Referendum Process in BC?" *Globe and Mail*, August 26. http://www.theglobeandmail.com/news/british-columbia/after-the-hst-what-will-happen-to-the-referendum-process-in-bc/article4181751/

Dion, Stéphane. 1996. "Why Is Secession Difficult in Well-Established Democracies? Lessons from Quebec." *British Journal of Political Science* 26 (2): 269–83. http://dx.doi.org/10.1017/S0007123400000466

Elections BC. 2011. "Report of the Chief Electoral Officer on the 2011 HST (Harmonized Sales Tax) Referendum." June 13–August 26.

Elections BC. 2016a. "Referendum/Plebiscite/Recall/Initiative." http://www.elections.bc.ca/index.php/referendum-plebiscite-recall-initiative/

Elections BC. 2016b. "Summary of Initiative Petitions, 1995–2013." http://www.elections.bc.ca/docs/init/Summary-Initiatives-1995–2013.pdf

Elections Canada. 2015. *A Compendium of Election Administration in Canada: A Comparative Overview.* http://www.elections.ca/content.aspx?section=res&dir=loi/com&document=index&lang=e

Fair Vote Canada. 2015. "The 2015 Election Will Be the Real Referendum." https://m.facebook.com/permalink.php?story_fbid=995712260489613&id=122787891115392

Finley, M.I. 1983. *Politics in the Ancient World.* Cambridge: Cambridge University Press. http://dx.doi.org/10.1017/CBO9780511612893

Flanagan, Tom. 1995. *Waiting for the Wave: The Reform Party and Preston Manning.* Toronto: Stoddart.

Fournier, Patrick, Henk van der Kolk, R. Kenneth Carty, André Blais, and Jonathan Rose. 2011. *When Citizens Decide: Lessons from Citizen Assemblies on Electoral Reform.* Toronto: Oxford University Press. http://dx.doi.org/10.1093/acprof:oso/9780199567843.001.0001

Fowler, H.W. 1965. *A Dictionary of Modern English Usage.* 2nd ed. Revised by Sir Ernest Gowers. New York: Oxford University Press.

Galloway, Gloria. 2015. "Ottawa Rules Out Referendum on Electoral Reform." *Globe and Mail,* December 28, A1–A2.

Gibson, Gordon. 2015. "Changing Our Voting System Demands a Public Referendum." *Globe and Mail,* December 29. http://www.theglobeandmail.com/globe-debate/why-canadians-must-be-consulted-directly-on-how-they-vote/article27951364/

Goebel, Thomas. 2002. *A Government by the People: Direct Democracy in America, 1890–1940.* Chapel Hill: University of North Carolina Press.

Ibbitson, John. 2015. "Conservatives Vow to Block Electoral Reform without Referendum." *Globe and Mail,* December 30. http://www.theglobeandmail.com/news/politics/conservatives-vow-to-block-electoral-reform-without-referendum/article27968324/

Irving, John A. 1959. *The Social Credit Movement in Alberta.* Toronto: University of Toronto Press.

Johnston, Richard, André Blais, Elisabeth Gidengil, and Neil Nevitte. 1996. *The Challenge of Direct Democracy: The 1992 Canadian Referendum.* Montreal: McGill-Queen's University Press.

Kaye, Philip. 2000. "Overview of the Federal/Provincial/Territorial Referendum Legislation." Backgrounder 18. Toronto: Office of the Legislative Assembly of Ontario.

Lang, Amy. 2007. "But Is It for Real? The British Columbia Citizens' Assembly as a Model of State-Sponsored Citizen Empowerment." *Politics & Society* 35 (1): 35–70. http://dx.doi.org/10.1177/0032329206297147

Law Commission of Canada. 2004. *Voting Counts: Electoral Reform for Canada.* Ottawa: Minister of Justice.

Laycock, David. 1990. *Populism and Democratic Thought in the Canadian Prairies, 1910 to 1945.* Toronto: University of Toronto Press.

LeDuc, Lawrence. 2003. *The Politics of Direct Democracy.* Peterborough, ON: Broadview Press.

Lewis, Daniel C. 2013. *Direct Democracy and Minority Rights.* New York: Routledge.

Liberal Party of Canada. 2015. *A New Plan for a Strong Middle Class.*

Lyons, Martyn. 1994. *Napoleon Bonaparte and the Legacy of the French Revolution.* New York: St. Martin's Press. http://dx.doi.org/10.1007/978-1-349-23436-3

MacDonald, David. 1991. "Referendums and Federal General Elections in Canada." In *Democratic Rights and Electoral Reform in Canada,* edited by Michael Cassidy, 301–42. Vol. 10 of the Research Studies for the Royal Commission on Electoral Reform and Party Financing. Toronto: Dundurn Press.

Macpherson, C.B. 1962. *Democracy in Alberta: Social Credit and the Party System.* 2nd ed. Toronto: University of Toronto Press.

Magleby, David. 1984. *Direct Legislation: Voting on Ballot Propositions in the United States.* Baltimore: Johns Hopkins University Press.

Mair, Peter. 2013. *Ruling the Void: The Hollowing Out of Western Democracy.* London: Verso.

Manitoba. 2001. Manitoba Hydro Amendment Act. S.M. c.3.

Manitoba. 2004. Manitoba Public Insurance Corporation Amendment Act (Protection of Crown Assets). S.M. c.7.

Manning, Preston. 1992. *The New Canada.* Toronto: Macmillan.

Marquis, Pierre. 1993. *Referendums in Canada: The Effect of Populist Decision-Making on Representative Democracy.* Ottawa: Library of Parliament, Political and Social Affairs Division. http://www.lop.parl.gc.ca/content/lop/researchpublications/bp328-e.htm

McCormick, Peter. 1991. "Provision for the Recall of Elected Officials: Parameters and Prospects." In *Democratic Rights and Electoral Reform in Canada,* edited by Michael Cassidy, 269–300. Vol. 10 of the Research Studies for the Royal Commission on Electoral Reform and Party Financing. Toronto: Dundurn Press.

Mendelsohn, Matthew, and Andrew Parkin. 2001. "Introducing Direct Democracy in Canada." *Choices: Strengthening Canadian Democracy* 7 (5): 3–35.

Mowrey, Tim, and Alain Pelletier. 2001. "Referendums in Canada: A Comparative Overview." *Electoral Insight* 3 (1): 18–22.

NDP. 2015. *Building the Country of Our Dreams: Tom Mulcair's Plan to Bring Change to Ottawa.*

O'Neill, Brenda. 2002. "Democracy in Action: Elections, Referendums, and Citizens' Power." In *Studying Politics,* edited by Rand Dyck, 262–89. Toronto: Thomson Nelson.

Pilon, Dennis. 2010. "The 2005 and 2009 Referenda on Voting System Change in British Columbia." *Canadian Political Science Review* 4 (2–3): 73–89.

Postmedia News. 2011. "BC Votes to Scrap HST." *National Post,* August 26. http://news.nationalpost.com/news/canada/b-c-votes-to-scrap-hst

Qvortrup, Matt. 2013a. "Conclusion." In *Referendums around the World: The Continued Growth of Direct Democracy,* edited by Matt Qvortrup, 246–51. Houndmills, UK: Palgrave Macmillan.

Qvortrup, Matt. 2013b. *Direct Democracy: A Comparative Study of the Theory and Practice of Government by the People.* Manchester: Manchester University Press. http://dx.doi.org/10.7228/manchester/9780719082061.001.0001

Qvortrup, Matt. 2013c. "Introduction: Theory, Practice and History." In *Referendums around the World: The Continued Growth of Direct Democracy,* edited by Matt Qvortrup, 1–16. Houndmills, UK: Palgrave Macmillan.

Reform Party. 1991. *Principles and Policies: The Blue Book.* Calgary.

Rousseau, Jean-Jacques. 1973. *The Social Contract and Discourses.* Translated by G.D.H. Cole. London: J.M. Dent and Sons.

Scarrow, Susan. 2001. "Direct Democracy and Institutional Change: A Comparative Investigation." *Comparative Political Studies* 34 (6): 651–65. http://dx.doi.org/10.1177/0010414001034006003

Smith, Jennifer. 1991. "The Franchise and Theories of Representative Government." In *Democratic Rights and Electoral Reform in Canada,* edited by Michael Cassidy, 3–27. Vol. 10 of the Research Studies for the Royal Commission on Electoral Reform and Party Financing. Toronto: Dundurn Press.

Stephenson, Laura, and A. Brian Tanguay. 2009. "Ontario's Referendum on Proportional Representation: Why Citizens Said No." *IRPP Choices* 15 (10): 1–30.

Strøm, Kaare. 2000. "Parties at the Core of Government." In *Parties without Partisans: Political Change in Advanced Industrial Democracies,* edited by Russell J. Dalton and Martin P. Wattenberg, 180–207. Oxford: Oxford University Press.

Stueck, Wendy. 2013. "HST: Gone but Hardly Forgotten in B.C." *Globe and Mail,* April 19. http://www.theglobeandmail.com/news/british-columbia/hst-gone-but-hardly-forgotten-in-bc/article11436043/

Tanguay, A. Brian. 2014. "The Limits to Democratic Reform in Canada." In *Canadian Politics,* 6th ed., edited by James Bickerton and Alain-G. Gagnon, 281–308. Toronto: University of Toronto Press.

Tierney, Stephen. 2015. "Reclaiming Politics: Popular Democracy in Britain after the Scottish Referendum." *Political Quarterly* 86 (2): 226–33. http://dx.doi.org/10.1111/1467-923X.12161

PART IV

New Paths for Research

16

From Brokerage to Boutique Politics: Political Marketing and the Changing Nature of Party Politics in Canada

ALEX MARLAND AND THIERRY GIASSON

Introduction

The long-held conceptualization of brokerage politics in Canada is now entwined with political marketing. In the past, party elites could rely on information from regional heavyweights, media coverage, gut instinct, and basic in-house survey data to assess the regional dimensions that were so important in campaign strategy. However, in recent decades the intensity associated with accommodating regional interests, which had been such a formidable component of brokerage politics, seems to have waned. Area-based grievances still exist, but the media environment has eroded the importance of mollifying regional appeals and new technology has facilitated the ability to appeal to narrow segments of the electorate. Political parties are treating durable and flexible partisans as consumers and are attempting to unify them into political coalitions that are not based on regional clusters but rather on marketing approaches. None other than R.K. Carty (2013), arguably the dean of Canadian political party scholarship, questions whether the 2006 federal election marked the end of brokerage politics, an election that marked the emergence of retail marketing in Canadian politics.

We contend that the old style of politicking is changing, and that the brokerage model is changing with it. Communication technologies have gone through immense evolution in a short period. Advances in hardware (e.g., digital cameras, tablets, smartphones, bandwidth, computing power) and software (e.g., websites, social media, blogging, video streaming) digital technologies have profoundly and irrevocably changed the way that humans communicate. This has sped up the flow of information and altered what is communicated, at a cost of squeezing out those who are least engaged. Local party members and representatives are still fed regional messages, but they now have little leeway to diverge from the national party line. This is in part because digital technologies allow the media and ordinary citizens to instantly report on any area of divergence from the party centre's message.

Party politics is also adjusting to a new playing field where technological advances make it easier to gather research intelligence about the electorate. The once prohibitive costs of public opinion surveys have gone down since data can now be collected through low-cost platforms such as computer-assisted telephone interviewing and online polls. Expertise in statistical analysis and advanced computer modelling increases the ability to understand audiences and identify subsets. Government data sources such as the census are supplemented by the party's own voter information databases and media consumption behaviour data. The combination of new ways of communicating and new ways of identifying the electorate's needs and wants has given way to new marketing practices in political parties. Brokerage parties and political marketers both ignore the ideological fringes. Normally, we interpret a brokerage approach as seeking policy compromise to accommodate the national interest or regional interests. Conversely, marketing considers individual-level interests, including the ability to strategically design and more efficiently promote "boutique" policies that are targeted at clusters of the electorate based on their values and lifestyles.

In this chapter we introduce readers to the theoretical and practical aspects of political marketing. We argue that Canadian political parties and their brokerage behaviours of the past have been transformed. To be competitive in elections, it has always been essential to embrace new approaches. While all three of Canada's major federal parties have ideological underpinnings that preclude them from being truly market oriented, the practice of marketing is increasingly a routine component of their campaigning and interactions with the electorate.

Regional Placation and National Unity: The Old Maxims of Brokerage Politics

For a generation, students of Canadian politics have prioritized a brokerage lens to explain party behaviour. Regrettably, brokerage politics is often used as a synonym for vote maximizers that undergo internal change in an effort to appeal to the median voter. Both approaches concern the mobilization of a coalition by proposing resolutions to policy disagreements of public opinion between the left and right without satisfying the hardline demands of ideologues on either side. But the Canadian nuance is that a brokerage party uses short-term electioneering tactics to accommodate social cleavages and stabilize national unity. Historically this approach has been the domain of the Liberal Party of Canada, which won the most seats in 21 of the 31 general elections held between 1896 and 2004 and again in 2015.

Defining brokerage politics is a difficult proposition, one that Steve Patten tackles in Chapter 1 of this book. Carty and Cross (2010, 193) have defined brokerage parties as seeking to placate "the potentially destructive internal tensions of a weakly integrated national community [and] . . . to obscure differences and muffle conflicting interests." They believe that the dominant features of a brokerage party are electoral pragmatism, antipathy to coalition politics, party allegiance, and domination by the leader. This underplays the long-standing premise that brokerage politics propose to resolve regional agitation by making election promises that appease premiers and other localized interests. Brokerage parties have historically attempted to mollify political flashpoints of ethnolinguistic tensions, religion, and regional identities that have threatened the fragile union, in particular Quebec nationalism. The single-member plurality electoral system is a mitigating factor. Regional parties can concentrate their campaigning in a geographical area and ride a wave of anger about regional grievances. The stunning success of the Bloc Québécois (54 seats on 13.5 per cent of the national vote) and the Western-based Reform Party (52 seats on 18.7 per cent of the vote) in the 1993 federal election, contrasted with the inability of the governing Progressive Conservative Party to translate votes into seats (two seats on 16 per cent of the vote), is the epitome of how regional parties profit from the electoral system compared with pan-Canadian parties that appeal to national interests. Historically, regional political parties stirring local disenchantment is a recipe for fracturing the party system, and pan-Canadian brokerage parties that propose to placate regional anger are attractive to those voters who are concerned about regional unrest.

These dynamics have implications for how Canadian political parties practise political marketing, the nuances of which will be explained shortly. Brokerage party leaders have historically emphasized select messaging in different parts of the country to appease regional interests (Carty, Cross, and Young 2000, 180–81; Neatby 1973). Operating in the pre-Internet age, they did so unbeknownst to residents in other regions, and regional party representatives could freely put a local spin on the party platform. Equally, a brokerage party's policy positions are muted on matters that may inflame regional tensions, leading to "vague platforms" and "token commitments" (Stevenson 1987, 814). The ideological malleability of brokerage parties increases the breadth of their appeal but reduces the durability of their partisans' attachment (Bélanger and Stephenson 2010; Brodie and Jenson 1996; but for a contrasting view see Sniderman, Forbes, and Melzer 1974). One of the prevailing heuristics for voters is the party label, which has been shown to act as an information cue for ideological parties but not for brokerage parties whose policies shift with the political winds (Merolla, Stephenson, and Zechmeister 2008).

This is not to say that brokerage parties do not have durable partisans—they do. But their "big tent" ideology is more likely to attract the sort of people who are not averse to supporting different parties, meaning that they can be poached by rivals. In this way the brokerage party model is a fluid Canadian variation of Otto Kirchheimer's catch-all party (Kirchheimer 1966; Krouwel 2003): both welcome an array of political interests to optimize the chances of winning votes. As a vote-seeker, leaders of these parties use the mass media to communicate with a diverse electorate. They search for policy compromise among a coalition of independent interests over valence issues—that is, those policies that all electors should support in theory, such as a stronger economy or better health care. Party members are united by their desire to improve society and act as cheerleaders of the leadership circle. Over time, the participatory role of the party's membership declines because of the organization's ideological flexibility, the outsourcing of electioneering to professionals, and increased emphasis on expensive communication practices.

The view of brokerage parties as being uniquely Canadian because of their role as national unifiers is not universal, but it is the most salient point of demarcation from Kirchheimer's catch-all party model. Janine Brodie and Jane Jenson (1996, 61) have emphasized a brokerage party's ability to respond to social fragmentation and attract a diverse coalition of supporters, albeit in a manner that considers national unity concerns. Clarke, Jenson, LeDuc, and Pammett (1991, 9–10) have added that brokerage parties build new coalitions in every election. Party elites tinker with existing policy rather than introduce grand visions, are not shackled by their past positions, and expect the party leader to negotiate policy compromises. This notion should give us pause, for as Clarke, Kornberg, and Scotto (2009, 22) have recently pointed out, party politics encompasses more than electoral behaviour, and so-called brokerage parties have contested several issue-based elections, such as free trade in 1988.

Brokerage is an oscillating concept, one whose definition appears to shift along with its practice. This leads us to believe that an overarching characteristic of a modern Canadian brokerage party is its willingness to adopt new strategies and tactics along the lines of an electoral–professional party. Increasingly, this includes gravitating toward the business firm model of parties. This is because Canadian political parties are contracting out tasks, treating electors as consumers, and invoking marketing practices (Hopkin and Paolucci 1999).

A potential barrier to the practice of political marketing in Canada is the increasing prioritization of the national party's messages, coupled with the rigidity of party discipline that inhibits the ability of local representatives to respond to local demands. The centralization of Canadian politics has been hastened by a combination of emergent communications technologies and the infusion of election campaigning practices into daily political life. In this leader-centric environment, operating in a country as physically vast and diverse as Canada, how can a competitive democratic party be anything other than a broker of competing demands? The necessary flexibility might be akin to political parties operating as franchise organizations. In his franchise model of party politics, Carty finds similarities with the private sector approach of major retail brands like McDonald's restaurants, which provide local operators with the limited ability to customize the menu of product offerings in response to local audiences' tastes. However, he too wrestles with the complexity of neatly bundling political parties into categories and concedes that it is unclear to what extent the franchise model is an evolution of cadre, mass, catch-all, or electoral–professional parties (Carty 2004, 12). What matters is that the description synthesizes a new way of looking at how parties work and what they do.

We need not get bogged down by an obsession over classifying parties into dichotomies. What concerns us is the behaviour of party elites and the indicators of such behaviours. It is our contention that brokerage party elites have adapted to new ways of politicking, which for our purposes here we shall group together as political marketing.

Individualism and Political Marketing: The New Characteristics of Brokerage Politics

Marketing is not a synonym for publicity, advertising, sales, media relations, communications, branding, and so on. Above all, it is a philosophical approach to the marketplace. A marketing orientation holds that there are competitive advantages to be gained if organizations listen to what consumers say they want and need, consider these insights, and respond by changing what is offered for sale. This entails a deep-seated commitment to collecting market intelligence through focus groups, opinion surveys, and other available information such as census data. Newer techniques include web scraping, where information appearing on websites and social media sites is collected online by humans and software programs and assembled into a database. In addition to informing changes to the product itself, the data are analyzed to identify which audiences are most likely to want a product and to guide communication decisions to reach them in an effective and persuasive manner. Marketing is an attractive proposition to executives because it is more efficient than offering a product that fewer people want or investing in communications that reach people who are unlikely to be customers. In theory, this philosophical approach can be practised by political parties. In *Political Marketing in Canada*, we defined political marketing as

> the application of business marketing concepts to the practice and study of politics and government. With political marketing, a political organization uses business techniques to inform and shape its strategic behaviours that

are designed to satisfy citizens' needs and wants. Strategies and tools include branding, e-marketing, delivery, focus groups, GOTV [get-out-the-vote activities], internal marketing, listening exercises, opposition research, polling, public relations, segmentation, strategic product development, volunteer management, voter-driven communication, voter expectation management, and voter profiling. (Marland, Giasson, and Lees-Marshment 2012, 262)

What distinguishes marketing as a concept, therefore, is the collection of research intelligence, the analysis of that data, and an ability to change in response to that intelligence. Not long ago, quantitative public opinion research was prohibitively expensive, the skills and tools for statistical analysis of the data were more limited, and there was less capacity to communicate new developments to existing and prospective buyers. Recent technological developments have further automated the administration of opinion surveys, which has profoundly reduced the cost and speed of data collection, transmission, and analysis. Polls can now be administered through interactive voice response, which uses automated dialling and provides respondents with a recorded message that asks them to press numbers to indicate their answer, or through Internet-based technologies, which deploy an online survey to a large assembled panel. There have been some methodological issues with the technologies—for example, data weighting problems leading to inaccurate predictions in recent Alberta and British Columbia provincial elections—causing some to advocate for a return to computer-assisted telephone interviewing that uses human interviewers, although as people opt against landlines this too becomes prone to error. Nevertheless, the advantages of computerization of surveys are attractive: not only are they less expensive, they are easy to set up and data sets are automatically generated when respondents input their responses themselves. For political parties, opinion surveys used to be so expensive and time consuming that the governing party held a formidable advantage, and they all had to supplement their own research with data gleaned from the periodic surveys that were commissioned by the news media. Now all political parties can afford to administer surveys.

This ability to collect reams of information about electors has led to the so-called age of "big data" and "data analytics." Big data may conjure visions of supercomputers, but the term actually describes advanced analysis using off-the-shelf computers and online connectivity. It refers to a new playing field where data sets have become so large that they can be difficult to manage. In the past, data sets were so small that little more than frequency analysis and limited multivariate analysis was feasible. This meant that pollsters focused on party standings across basic sociodemographic indicators such as gender, age, education, religion, employment status, income, and geography.

The low number of cases meant that regional clustering was commonplace, with breakouts clustering the four easternmost and westernmost provinces into monolithic Atlantic and Western regions, with some oversampling in British Columbia to distinguish it from the three prairie provinces. Ontario and Quebec each had to be treated as a unified whole; there were simply not enough respondents to distinguish, say, the opinions of Torontonians from other Ontarians within a reasonable margin of error. Such regional breakdowns continue to be practised, but the integration of rolling samples and online survey methodologies means that marketers are no longer constrained in the way they once were. Instead, they can employ regression analysis to identify relationships between variables and trends analysis to identify the direction that public opinion is headed. Increasingly, information is freely collected from website-browsing behaviour and Internet search habits, opening interesting possibilities for the future of data analytics.

The main area of data analytics that is becoming mainstream in Canada is the segmentation of audiences into narrow target groups. Writing in the 1950s, when scientific public opinion polling was growing in popularity, marketing consultant Wendell Smith explained that segmentation had resulted from understanding consumer demand and from the adjustment of the product and its communications to meet consumer preferences. He argued that up to that point, organizations had been differentiating themselves by striving for a "horizontal share of a broad and generalized market" and going after "a layer of the market cake" (Smith 1956, 5). In contrast, organizations that practised market segmentation were prioritizing a deep penetration of a narrowly defined aspect of the market, thereby securing "one or more wedge-shaped pieces" of the market cake. Smith was observing that by understanding audiences it was possible to shift from a mass market approach that satisfied a wide swath of homogenous consumers to a more narrow approach that instilled a deep brand loyalty among a collection of like-minded but diverse clusters.

Until recently, political elites had to base their targeting decisions on the aforementioned demographic data, such as Conservatives tailoring their offering to older upper-income men in Western Canada. But after the 2004 federal election campaign the party went through something of a marketing epiphany. Pouring through public opinion data, including psychographics that consider people's values and lifestyles, Conservative strategists began to apply marketing segmentation to the Canadian electorate. They pinpointed subgroups that research suggested would be inclined to support the party if their attention could be drawn to policy matters and issues where they would judge the Conservative Party favourably compared with its rivals. That is, Conservative marketers identified clusters of voter groups based on data about consumers' everyday lives and aspirations as well as party elites' intuitions. They then matched policies and messages that were acceptable to the elites with the voter segments that appeared likely to respond positively to what the Conservatives were offering. The strategists identified what they believed were the best places to promote select messages, such as on specialty channels like Discovery and The Sports Network instead of networks like CBC, CTV, or Global. A tradeoff of this narrow focus was that the party would knowingly ignore certain segments of the electorate and media. The triage approach was colourfully described by journalist Paul Wells (2006) in *Right Side Up: The Fall of Paul Martin and the Rise of Stephen Harper's New Conservatism* and has been retold by others. The story goes that Stephen Harper's marketing analysts used avatars to help the party's executives visualize their target groups. As is well known to students of Canadian political marketing, the party decided to concentrate their efforts on connecting with tradespeople like "Dougie," a fictional construction worker in rural Nova Scotia who did not always vote, and to ignore people who would never support the Conservatives, like the fictional "Zoë" who was single, in her late twenties, lived in a downtown Toronto condo, and ate at trendy restaurants (Wells 2006, 214). In that case it was reasoned that pitching a tax credit on tradesperson tools would resonate on an individual level with the Dougies of Canada, while abandoning people like Zoë to consider other choices. While we might be inclined to think that this approach was imported from American Republicans, in fact it was the Australian Liberal Party's electoral strategy that had considerable influence on Conservative strategic thinking at the time, notably the techniques outlined in *The Victory: The Inside Story of the Takeover of Australia* (Williams 1997). The Conservatives were inspired by the success of the centre-right Australian Liberals, who used marketing techniques to mobilize a coalition of voters on a policy of economic liberalism.

Whether or not the Conservative Party operated in a market-oriented fashion is open for debate, as is the question of whether they were a brokerage party. As noted, marketing holds that an organization must demonstrate an ability to change in response to public opinion data. The Conservatives chose to emphasize aspects of their ideological agenda that were deemed palatable to a minimum winning coalition (e.g., low taxes, law and order, accountability) and opted to jettison the hot-button aspects of conservatism that would jeopardize their electability (e.g., abortion, same-sex marriage, privatization of health care). They applied marketing principles to the political arena without sacrificing their core economic liberalism product while calculating that most social conservatives would be resigned that the Conservatives remained the best available option. Conservative Party marketing strategists had approached the electorate vertically and bundled together slices of the electoral cake. The calculation worked in three successive elections, but failed to break through in 2015.

In Canadian politics we have been conditioned to think of a brokerage party as approaching politics in a horizontal manner (i.e., seeking a thick layer of electoral cake). This raises questions about whether a brokerage party must operate as a mass market party and pretend to appeal to everyone, or if a brokerage party can alternatively practise market segmentation to bring together like-minded voters who were identified vertically. As Lawrence LeDuc (2014) has observed, it is a popular misconception that Stephen Harper did not lead a brokerage party. The Conservatives did, after all, form a majority government in 2011 on the basis of broadening their appeal to segments of the electorate who previously supported the Liberals. The Conservatives' retrenchment in 2015, which included stirring elector unease about Muslim women wearing the niqab in Canada, gave several electors reason to support Justin Trudeau and the renewed Liberal Party. Once back in government, the so-called natural governing party's brokerage style was on display as it set about dismantling the many boutique tax credits installed by the Conservative government (Cheadle 2016).

Just as Canadian political parties do not fit neatly into theoretical models of political parties, nor do they fit neatly into political marketing models. Take, for example, the models posited by two leading scholars in the subfield. American Bruce Newman (1994) has applied the managerial marketing model of commercial goods to the American presidential system. At its core, the model follows the notion of exchange between producers (parties/candidates) and consumers (voters). In theory, marketing within the political market prioritizes the needs and wants of certain clusters of the electorate when developing policy to render a political product more attractive to them. Newman explains that political parties seeking to form government must avail themselves of marketing techniques to identify messages that will appeal to a targeted segment of flexible partisans and to position themselves in the voter's mindset in a manner that is favourably differentiated from the competition. This requires the adoption of policies that are not uniformly popular while maintaining sufficient flexibility to reposition should changing circumstances warrant.

A related but expanded conceptualization is presented in Jennifer Lees-Marshment's (2001) application to the British parliamentary system of managerial marketing theory. Through the use of three ideal types, her model posits that parties either act as businesses that are manufacturing products they expect an inherent demand for, are bombarding consumers with persuasive advertising to generate demand, or are using market research to design products that fulfill what consumers say they want and need. Lees-Marshment's classifications distinguish product-oriented parties to describe those that are unconcerned with public opinion research (usually ideological or programmatic parties); sales-oriented parties to refer to those that use communication, advertising, and media management to persuade electors and shape public opinion; and market-oriented parties who use market intelligence to adapt their offer to meet voters' demands and to communicate with them. Early attempts to apply her taxonomy to Canadian politics suggest that it is an instructive way of looking at political party behaviour, but that the rigidity of each category's characteristics limits their applicability. In evaluating the Conservative Party's use of marketing in the 2006 federal election, Daniel Paré and Flavia Berger (2008, 59) questioned whether "the electorate is getting what it needs and wants as a result of the Conservatives having apparently become more market oriented or whether this change in party behaviour reflects, foremost, a strategy aimed at enabling the party to get what *it* wants and needs." Moreover, there is no empirical evidence that the practice of political marketing in itself secures votes, and numerous questions are levied in the literature about its democratic consequences (Johansen 2012; Lilleker 2005; Savigny 2008).

At the core of the treatment of political parties as market oriented lies the debate over the professionalization of their campaign organization and electioneering. For political scientist Margaret Scammell (1999), this involves more than assessing the extent to which a political organization has adopted American-style techniques. Rather, the practice of political marketing has come to be seen as an innovative development in campaigning, and what was once new becomes old with the passing of each electoral cycle. Tactics normally associated with elite parties are deemed to be amateur; practices that were cutting edge in the 1990s and early 2000s are now semi-professional; while techniques advanced by the Conservative Party circa 2006 that were seen as path-breaking and professional (Table 16.1) have since become common practice among all three major Canadian parties. These classifications are not absolute; for instance, while it is suggested that right-of-centre parties are early adopters of innovative marketing tactics, other political parties do catch on. The point is that innovations and indicators of marketing professionalism are prone to shift over time. The United States remains the dominant laboratory for new techniques despite Scammell's protestations. In the 1992 presidential election, the introduction of a campaign "war room" to coordinate rapid response communication was a competitive advantage, but this is now commonplace in campaigns everywhere. Likewise, Barack Obama's 2012 re-election campaign introduced "the cave," where data analysts could provide evidence-based strategy recommendations, and soon we should expect to find the same in Canadian campaigns. What is instructive

Table 16.1 Types of Political Campaigns by Early 2000s Standards

	Amateur	Semi-professional	Professional
Ideology	Strong	Mainstream	Right of centre
Preparation	Short term, ad hoc	Long term	Permanent campaign
Decision making	Local-centric, party leader and staff	National-centric, party campaign managers and external communications experts	Local-/national-centric, bifurcation, special party units, specialized political consultants
Resources	Volunteer labour, low budget	Capital intensive, increasing spending	Spiralling spending
Market intelligence	Meetings	Polls, focus groups	Computer databases, opposition research
Targeting	Loyal partisans, cleavage- and group-based, stable voting behaviour	Loyal and floating partisans, rising volatility	Consumers, issue based, highly volatile voting behaviour
Positioning	Ideological, party messages	Persuasion, spin, sound bites, image management	Product adjustment, issue specific, micromessages
Strategy	Interpersonal, unprofessional, mobilization	Mediated, indirect, converting and mobilizing	Marketed, targeted, continuous, interactive
Tactics	Print media, posters, rallies, door knocking, leafleting, radio	National TV spots, broadcast TV news coverage and spots, colour print adverts, mass direct mailings	TV narrowcasting, targeting direct mail, telemarketing, continuous campaigning
Execution	Error prone	Bureaucratic	Military-like efficiency

Source: Marland (2012, 60, Table 4.1), itself an amalgamation of tables and figures from other sources.

is that brokerage parties seem to show an interest to be at the forefront of technological innovations in electioneering and politicking in their goal to better understand the electorate and broker needs and wants.

New forms of e-communication are especially subject to rapid displacement from being innovative and exclusive. For instance, the major Canadian political parties have all now incorporated direct marketing and relationship marketing into their e-campaigning repertoire. Direct marketing entails customized communication that bypasses the mainstream media to reach voters directly, such as personalized letters, robocalls, email, or social media postings. It ties into relationship marketing, where an organization engages in communication activities aimed at nurturing a two-way relationship and strengthened loyalty with its supporters. This is achieved through regular

354 MARLAND AND GIASSON

contact via direct marketing that professes a mutual friendship, invites customer consultations or retroaction, and urges repeat transactions. In politics this involves asking party members and sympathizers alike to take immediate action to achieve a shared goal, such as by adding their name to an online petition, making a small donation, getting involved with the party grassroots, or sharing a message on social media.

To reach supporters the marketer needs to store information electronically and regularly update the database. This is known as database marketing, whereby data collected about electors are maintained in a central depository and are drawn on to profile the electorate. All three of Canada's major parties have developed voter databases that are information warehouses about people who have donated to the party, entered their name on a party website, contacted an elected official, taken a lawn sign during an election, attended a campaign event, and other such behavioural monitoring. The data are routinely used to communicate with selected segments through direct personalized marketing, such as emails with requests that recipients demonstrate their support for a recent undertaking by making a tiny donation of as low as $3. The Conservatives' Constituency Information Management System (CIMS) has been the dominant force in database marketing, but in recent years the NDP and Liberals have also developed their own in-house data management systems: NDPVote—which was recently replaced by a novel platform named Populus—and Liberalist. These are similarly aimed at cultivating deep brand loyalty with loyalists and prospective supporters. The software is trickling down to provincial campaigns, where provincial New Democrats and some provincial Liberal Party organizations are participating in building and using the databases. Across Canada, party politics has entered an age of data-driven permanent campaigning.

The American connections to Canadian political parties' database marketing may surprise some. As hinted earlier, the Conservative brand has often been associated with the United States, whereas the NDP has publicly tut-tutted American campaign approaches and, in the early 1990s, generated some internal rancour over the hiring of an American pollster. Yet to our knowledge CIMS is custom-built software. By comparison, Liberalist was created by Voter Activation Network (VAN), the American firm behind VoteBuilder, the data management system developed for the Democratic National Committee and the Obama campaign in the months preceding the 2008 presidential election (Kreiss 2012, 103–19). The open access online tool is presented as an "identification and relationship management system." It allows users (party personnel, campaign managers, communication staffers) to tap into the Liberal database to carry geographically and demographically targeted communications and mobilization activities.

Less is known about the NDP platform. The Populus database, designed for insider use, is not readily accessible through the party's website, but it represents the culmination of the NDP's adoption of marketing practices that began following the arrival of Jack Layton as leader. Through this transformation, the party engaged in data collection, segmentation and targeting, message repositioning, and manifesto simplification (Delacourt 2013, 286–98; Wesley and Moyes 2014). Data management became a key strategic function for the party following the 2008 federal election. In *Shopping for Votes: How Politicians Choose Us and We Choose Them,* Susan Delacourt (2013, 297) explains that "the NDP knew the neighbourhoods where people were paying the highest cellphone costs and so knew which homes would be most receptive to demands from Layton to bring down the cellphone charges." This was one focused outcome of the party purchasing massive amounts of information from numerous sources to better target voters about specific issues.

This quote reveals how data management and microtargeting techniques are used by parties to better reach segments of electors expected to react positively to their message, positions, or promises, but also for policy development. Canadian parties now design their manifestos and platforms by following the needs and wants of target voters highlighted in their research. They prioritize issues that will mobilize key segments needed to assemble their minimum winning coalition of voters. This includes promises aimed at precise segments and the promotion of wedge issues that create divisions in voting coalitions of opponents. Wedge issues are social issues instrumentalized by a party to create a political dilemma in segments of opposing voters; the niqab issue during the 2015 campaign is a good example. This dilemma confronts voters with the cross-pressure of having to re-evaluate their partisan loyalty if an issue position about which they disagree with their party becomes salient during a campaign.

The Conservatives were keen at engaging in these tactics in the period before they won a majority of seats in 2011. First, in their campaign platforms they introduced a promise for sales tax reduction (GST from 7 to 5 per cent), tax credits (for children's physical activities, tradespersons' equipment, or property renovation), and disbursements ($100 monthly payments for child care) aimed at middle-class suburban Canadian families. Second, they engaged in wedge politics by introducing divisive issues like the repeal of the long-gun registry. That issue was of little significance for most Canadians but of high importance for a minority of NDP and Liberal rural voters that the Tories were courting, located in ridings outside of Quebec where opposition to the gun registry was strong (Giasson and Dumouchel 2012). In the past, brokerage politics was about the aggregation of regional interests. Its current incarnation imposes the aggregation of segmented individual interests that parties achieve by crafting specialized boutique policies for specific niches of voters. Changes in technology and communications strategy are displacing the brokerage of regional grievances in favour of the brokering of individualized consumer interests.

The vertical cultivation of brand loyalty among voters who are not clustered in regions complicates the tradition of a national-oriented brokerage party approaching the electorate horizontally. The formula of national coalitions to achieve majority mandates is no longer in fashion. Political parties' electoral strategy is much more about a permanent campaign of "triage and concentration" of resources aimed at swing voters who, in the Conservatives' case at least, are brought into a minimum winning coalition through the "promises of rewards" (Flanagan 2014, 70–71). In the age of political marketing, elections are waged by mobilizing smaller groups of voters who share socioeconomic profiles by pitching electoral promises customized to their needs. In their electoral messaging, Canadian parties may seem to be addressing the needs of all voters in promises geared at protecting the common good and national interest. However, closer analysis reveals that their platforms and persuasion strategies are aimed at specific microsegments of volatile voters who make or break governing mandates. This means that the priorities of opponents' core supporters are intentionally ignored and bypassed. This is an anathema to the concept of brokerage politics. It is not new, but it has become possible because of the increasing precision of being able to identify, understand, and reach voter cohorts. This is changing the way that the electoral game is played.

How Political Marketing Is Changing Canadian Party Politics

Political marketing was emerging at the time of Kirchheimer's thesis about the catch-all party, and the two concepts are surprisingly similar. That's because in discussing the evolution of mass-integration parties to catch-all parties, he was cataloguing the transformation of political parties that espoused a selling concept into market-oriented organizations (Henneberg and Eghbalian 2002). Moreover, a catch-all or brokerage philosophy treats all electors as a homogenous group in what is analogous to a mass marketing approach. To stretch the analogy further, the cadre party model is akin to a product-oriented party; a mass party is similar to a sales-oriented party; and electoral–professional parties and business firm parties are more likely to draw on marketing. In the Canadian context, leading parties seem to have moved away from traditional brokerage catch-all organizations to become more market oriented, franchise, or "boutique" formations. Some Canadian party scholars are suspicious of political marketing. Indeed, the American import generates apprehensions of a so-called Americanization or presidentialization of the Canadian political system. But one apprehension is uniquely Canadian: its disruption of the brokerage model of politicking. And as this chapter suggests, the introduction and adoption of a marketing philosophy by Canadian parties has modified the way they approach campaign preparedness, strategy design, voter contact, policy development, and electoral communication. Adaptation to political marketing has also affected how parties function as institutions by impacting their inner life and their role as interest representatives.

As electoral machines, political parties have considerably transformed how they use research, data, and communications for strategic purposes. In the past, the larger share of a party's expenses was dedicated to developing and broadcasting national campaigns of persuasive advertising; that still holds today, but data collection and communication technologies can focus on subsegments of the electorate more efficiently. Moreover, this is occurring in a context of permanent campaigning, whereby parties invest in constant market analysis and tracking to improve their voter profiling, segmentation, and targeting procedures. This ongoing research is now the foundation of their policy development and issue positioning strategies. Persuasive communication, fundraising, data collection, and other forms of electioneering are now perpetual rather than foremost a function of an official election campaign.

The growing obsession with data-driven politics brings several consequences for parties. First, it reaffirms the importance of raising funds. Political marketing and associated tactics require money. Data collection and analysis is an expensive business and, as with the Liberal/VAN joint venture for the creation of the Liberalist database, expertise is drawn from outside party ranks. The availability of funds provides parties with a strategic advantage to hire marketing consultants who can deliver increasingly precise and efficient data and counsel. Consultants brought in for their proficiency in data management have considerable influence on paramount party orientations regarding, for instance, voter targeting, policy design, and persuasion tactics. Their role could dilute the influence of party insiders and membership on decision-making processes, including in the NDP, which at one time guarded against outside influence. The evolving function of brokerage politics and the prevalence of data-driven decisions may erode the traditional function of intraparty democracy. For instance, the party members who debate policy at party conventions may be considered as little more than participants in a giant focus group if their leader is prone to overrule their resolutions based on the advice of political marketing strategists.

The practice of political marketing generates other concerns for the quality of interest representation in Canada. When parties jockey for the support of swing voters by offering them boutique tax credits and other forms of "free money," they prioritize the needs and wants of some voters over others. This creates a classist and divisive system of interest representation within the electorate, where a first-tier of desirable swing voters is aggressively courted, but which casts aside the residual segments of voters whose decision is fixed. The social and political interests of the economically disadvantaged, of young Canadians or of Indigenous peoples, for instance, could be added to this unfortunate second category. The brokering of some individual interests, which is the driving principle of consumer politics, may not ultimately serve the national interest or the common good. Such an approach risks creating a sense of alienation from politics and increased cynicism coupled with decreased mobilization among left-behind electors. Conversely, if ignored long enough, they may become sufficiently frustrated to rally behind a political movement that promises change.

Some might view these developments as ironic, given that political marketing and the premium it imposes on opinion research has been described as inherently democratic (see, for instance, Lees-Marshment 2011). Canadians have never been more consulted, probed, and questioned by political parties than they are today. Having to define and promote intangible products, more akin to commercial services than consumer goods, political parties engage in ongoing market research that informs how they can respond to the electorate's stands on issues and policies. This constant consultation through polling, focus groups, and media monitoring implies that parties listen and understand (some) voters rather than guess or assume. Finally, political marketing is said to impose the delivery of policy commitments more strongly, because parties winning power actively seek to realize (or to give the impression of moving forward with) their core engagements to stimulate voter confidence, which is motivated by their ability to demonstrate accountability and responsiveness when they seek re-election (Esselment 2012; Lees-Marshment 2011). To offer one example, the Harper Conservatives barrelled forward with several controversial bills—prostitution, mandatory minimums for gun crimes, assisted suicide, time-served sentencing (Hopper 2015)—that they may well have predicted would be struck down by the courts as unconstitutional. This strategy allowed them to promote "tough on crime" messaging that resonated with their core constituency and to present wedge issues that boxed in their opponents. Through this lens, political marketing and brokerage politics are synonymous insofar as they embody the spirit of vote maximization. The point of demarcation is that political marketing edges aside the perceived viability of the big tent catch-all party model.

At issue is whether marketing is used idealistically and altruistically by political parties. We need look no further than negative political advertising and the downward trend of voter turnout to recognize that the notion of marketing as a democratic panacea is a romanticized fiction. As consumer politics has grown in practice, higher levels of democratic malaise have been observed in every postindustrial democracy, including Canada, bringing scholars to hypothesize about a possible "marketing malaise" explanation (see, for instance, Cappella and Jamieson 1997; Patterson 1994; Savigny 2008). Bruce Newman (1994) has cautioned about the increasing reliance on opinion polls by political leaders and the engagement of political consultants in image management. His concerns are echoed by marketing skeptic Heather Savigny (2008, 117–20), who has warned that marketing depoliticizes politics by removing ideologies, which are useful analytical frames for citizens and historically important mobilizing factors for parties. Ideological disengagement for strategic electoral gains, Savigny laments, should lead to voter disengagement and its correlate of diminished legitimacy for the democratic system. For his part, critic Nicholas O'Shaughnessy (2004) flatly dismisses political marketing as a modern form of political propaganda that allows political elites to achieve their own ends through sophisticated persuasive techniques. From these realists' point of view, there is nothing noble about how political marketing is practised.

Political marketing still seems to offer several positive opportunities for Canadian political parties. Nevertheless, apprehensions should be top of mind when analyzing the state and extent of marketing practices in the Canadian party system, particularly given the sizable share of flexible voters in Canada who party elites are courting through boutique politics as the traditional model of brokerage politics fades away.

Emerging Areas of Practice and Research in Political Marketing

Political marketing is an emerging and growing subfield of party politics and electioneering. As party strategists adopt new practices, we anticipate that media and scholarly attention will follow. To date, the limited research on political marketing in Canada has largely revolved around the Conservative Party, which is credited for introducing new ways of politicking beginning with the 2006 federal election campaign. Interest in other parties' practices will follow as they copy these behaviours and introduce innovative ways of politicking. A serious challenge for researchers toward understanding the strategic rationale behind party marketing decisions means locating strategists who are willing to disclose competitive secrets. To get around this limitation to the study of political marketing, elsewhere we have argued in favour of a mixed-method approach that blends elite interviews with spending data filed with Elections Canada (Marland and Giasson 2013).

It is tempting to lump new forms of political communication and persuasion activities under the political marketing umbrella. We must be mindful that marketing involves changing in response to consumer preferences as identified through research. To understand electors, the era of big data analytics is on its way, which will bring a greater demand for quantitative data and information collected through web scraping. The segmentation of electors will move from a preoccupation with demographic and geographic data to analyses of behavioural and lifestyle values. More precise ways of reaching targeted electors will be practised, for instance cable addressability, which allows digital cable providers to expose viewers of an identical television program to different advertising. Database marketing is already taking hold, as political parties collect email addresses to add supporters to a listserv, who are then subjected to a barrage of fundraising appeals. Negative communication will intensify as political parties place more emphasis on opposition research and on exposing opponents' blunders and as tactics once confined to the official campaign take shape during the interelection period. Finally, scholarly attention to the practice of branding will increase as political parties recognize the strategic value of wrapping simplified communications into a consistent, cohesive offering. Throughout, researchers will be well-advised to turn descriptive documentation of what is happening into high-level analysis that informs theory to help us understand the implications of political marketing on Canadian democracy regardless of which political party is practising it.

Suggested Readings

CBC Radio. 2013. "The Rise of Political Marketing." October 7. http://www.cbc.ca/player/Shows/ID/2410929804/

Delacourt, Susan. 2016. *Shopping for Votes: How Politicians Choose Us and We Choose Them,* 2nd edition. Madeira Park: Douglas & McIntyre.

Journal of Political Marketing. http://www.tandfonline.com/toc/wplm20/current

Marland, Alex, Thierry Giasson, and Jennifer Lees-Marshment, eds. 2012. *Political Marketing in Canada.* Vancouver: University of British Columbia Press.

Political Marketing Study and Teaching Resources. http://www.political-marketing.org

References

Bélanger, Éric, and Laura B. Stephenson. 2010. "Parties and Partisans: The Influence of Ideology and Brokerage on the Durability of Partisanship in Canada." In *Voting Behaviour in Canada,* edited by Cameron D. Anderson and Laura B. Stephenson, 107–38. Vancouver: University of British Columbia Press.

Brodie, Janine, and Jane Jenson. 1996. "Piercing the Smokescreen: Stability and Change in Brokerage Politics." In *Canadian Parties in Transition*, 2nd ed., edited by A. Brian Tanguay and Alain-G. Gagnon, 33–53. Toronto: Nelson Canada.

Cappella, Joseph N., and Kathleen Hall Jamieson. 1997. *Spiral of Cynicism: The Press and the Public Good*. Oxford: Oxford University Press.

Carty, R. Kenneth. 2004. "Parties as Franchise Systems: The Stratarchical Organizational Imperative." *Party Politics* 10 (1): 5–24. http://dx.doi.org/10.1177/1354068804039118

Carty, R. Kenneth. 2013. "Has Brokerage Politics Ended? Canadian Parties in the New Century." In *Parties, Elections, and the Future of Canadian Politics*, edited by Amanda Bittner and Royce Koop, 10–23. Vancouver: University of British Columbia Press.

Carty, R. Kenneth, and William Cross. 2010. "Political Parties and the Practice of Brokerage Politics." In *The Oxford Handbook of Canadian Politics*, edited by John C. Courtney and David E. Smith, 191–207. Toronto: Oxford University Press. http://dx.doi.org/10.1093/oxfordhb/9780195335354.003.0011

Carty, R. Kenneth, William Cross, and Lisa Young. 2000. *Rebuilding Canadian Party Politics*. Vancouver: University of British Columbia Press.

Cheadle, Bruce. 2016. "Finance Minister Morneau Says Review of Federal Tax Breaks Is Coming." *CBC News*, March 25. http://www.cbc.ca/news/canada/calgary/finance-minister-tax-code-mintz-review-1.3507374

Clarke, Harold D., Jane Jenson, Lawrence LeDuc, and Jon H. Pammett. 1991. *Absent Mandate: Interpreting Change in Canadian Elections*. 2nd ed. Toronto: Gage Publishing.

Clarke, Harold D., Allan Kornberg, and Thomas J. Scotto. 2009. *Making Political Choices: Canada and the United States*. Toronto: University of Toronto Press.

Delacourt, Susan. 2013. *Shopping for Votes: How Politicians Choose Us and We Choose Them*. Toronto: Douglas & McIntyre.

Esselment, Anna. 2012. "Market Orientation in a Minority Government: The Challenges of Product Delivery." In *Political Marketing in Canada*, edited by Alex Marland, Thierry Giasson, and Jennifer Lees-Marshment, 123–38. Vancouver: University of British Columbia Press.

Flanagan, Tom. 2014. *Winning Power: Canadian Campaigning in the 21st Century*. Montreal: McGill-Queen's University Press.

Giasson, Thierry, and David Dumouchel. 2012. "Of Wedge Issues and Conservative Politics in Canada." Paper presented at the Annual Meeting of the Midwest Political Science Association. Chicago, April.

Henneberg, Stephen C., and Stefan Eghbalian. 2002. "Kirchheimer's Catch-All Party: A Reinterpretation in Marketing Terms." In *The Idea of Political Marketing*, edited by Nicholas J. O'Shaughnessy and Stephen C. Henneberg, 67–91. London: Praeger.

Hopkin, Jonathan, and Caterina Paolucci. 1999. "The Business Firm Model of Party Organization: Cases from Spain and Italy." *European Journal of Political Research* 35 (3): 307–39. http://dx.doi.org/10.1111/1475-6765.00451

Hopper, Tristin. 2015. "A Scorecard of the Harper Government's Wins and Losses at the Supreme Court of Canada." *National Post*, April 15. http://news.nationalpost.com/news/canada/scoc-harper-gov-scorecard-741324

Johansen, Helene P.M. 2012. *Relational Political Marketing in Party-Centred Democracies*. Farnham, UK: Ashgate.

Kirchheimer, Otto. 1966. "The Transformation of the Western European Party Systems." In *Political Parties and Political Development,* edited by Joseph LaPalombara and Myron Weiner, 177–200. Princeton, NJ: Princeton University Press.

Kreiss, Daniel. 2012. *Taking Our Country Back: The Crafting of Networked Politics from Howard Dean to Barack Obama.* New York: Oxford University Press. http://dx.doi.org/10.1093/acprof:oso/9780199782536.001.0001

Krouwel, André. 2003. "Otto Kirchheimer and the Catch-All Party." *West European Politics* 26 (2): 23–40. http://dx.doi.org/10.1080/01402380512331341091

LeDuc, Lawrence. 2014. "The Canadian Voter in a New Conservative Era." In *Society in Question,* 7th ed., edited by Robert J. Brym, 229–44. Toronto: Nelson.

Lees-Marshment, Jennifer. 2001. *Political Marketing and British Political Parties.* Manchester: Manchester University Press.

Lees-Marshment, Jennifer. 2011. *The Political Marketing Game.* Basingstoke, UK: Palgrave-MacMillan. http://dx.doi.org/10.1057/9780230299511

Lilleker, Darren G. 2005. "Political Marketing: The Cause of an Emerging Democratic Deficit in Britain?" *Journal of Nonprofit & Public Sector Marketing* 14 (1–2): 5–26. http://dx.doi.org/10.1300/J054v14n01_02

Marland, Alex. 2012. "Amateurs versus Professionals: The 1993 and 2006 Canadian Federal Elections." In *Political Marketing in Canada,* edited by Alex Marland, Thierry Giasson, and Jennifer Lees-Marshment, 59–75. Vancouver: University of British Columbia Press.

Marland, Alex, and Thierry Giasson. 2013. "Investigating Political Marketing Using Mixed Method: The Case for Campaign Spending Data." *Journal of Public Affairs* 13 (4): 391–402. http://dx.doi.org/10.1002/pa.1492

Marland, Alex, Thierry Giasson, and Jennifer Lees-Marshment, eds. 2012. *Political Marketing in Canada.* Vancouver: University of British Columbia Press.

Merolla, Jennifer L., Laura B. Stephenson, and Elizabeth J. Zechmeister. 2008. "Can Canadians Take a Hint? The (In)effectiveness of Party Labels as Information Shortcuts in Canada." *Canadian Journal of Political Science* 41 (3): 673–96. http://dx.doi.org/10.1017/S0008423908080797

Neatby, H. Blair. 1973. *Laurier and a Liberal Quebec: A Study in Political Management.* Toronto: McClelland and Stewart.

Newman, Bruce I. 1994. *The Marketing of the President: Political Marketing as Campaign Strategy.* Thousand Oaks, CA: Sage.

O'Shaughnessy, Nicholas J. 2004. *Politics and Propaganda: Weapons of Mass Seduction.* Ann Arbor: University of Michigan Press.

Paré, Daniel J., and Flavia Berger. 2008. "Political Marketing Canadian Style? The Conservative Party and the 2006 Federal Election." *Canadian Journal of Communication* 33 (1): 39–63.

Patterson, Thomas E. 1994. *Out of Order.* New York: Vintage.

Savigny, Heather. 2008. *The Problem of Political Marketing.* London: Continuum.

Scammell, Margaret. 1999. "The Model Professionals? Political Marketing in the United States and the Prospects of Americanization of Global Campaigning." *Journal of Euromarketing* 7 (2): 67–89. http://dx.doi.org/10.1300/J037v07n02_05

Smith, Wendell R. 1956. "Product Differentiation and Market Segmentation as Alternative Marketing Strategies." *Journal of Marketing* 21 (1): 3–8. http://dx.doi.org/10.2307/1247695

Sniderman, Paul M., H.D. Forbes, and Ian Melzer. 1974. "Party Loyalty and Electoral Volatility: A Study of the Canadian Party System." *Canadian Journal of Political Science* 7 (2): 268–88. http://dx.doi.org/10.1017/S0008423900038336

Stevenson, H. Michael. 1987. "Ideology and Unstable Party Identification in Canada: Limited Rationality in a Brokerage Party System." *Canadian Journal of Political Science* 20 (4): 813–50. http://dx.doi.org/10.1017/S0008423900050423

Wells, Paul. 2006. *Right Side Up: The Fall of Paul Martin and the Rise of Stephen Harper's New Conservatism.* Toronto: McClelland and Stewart.

Wesley, Jared J., and Mike Moyes. 2014. "Selling Social Democracy: Branding the Political Left in Canada." In *Political Communication in Canada: Meet the Press and Tweet the Rest,* edited by Alex Marland, Thierry Giasson, and Tamara A. Small, 74–91. Vancouver: University of British Columbia Press.

Williams, Pamela. 1997. *The Victory: The Inside Story of the Takeover of Australia.* Sydney: Allen and Unwin.

17

Political Campaigning

RICHARD NADEAU AND FRÉDÉRICK BASTIEN

E LECTION CAMPAIGNS CAN BE SEEN as one of the highpoints of democratic life. Beyond their most immediately noticeable and publicized manifestations, such as rallies, debates, and public appearances (all of which the media diligently follow), campaigns are highly strategic operations. They require that each party have in-depth knowledge of not only their opponents, but also the preferences of the electorate and how the media works, all topped off with a good dose of preparation. This chapter focuses on the strategic choices that Canadian political parties made during the most recent federal election. In turn, these strategic decisions influence which issues parties emphasize to maximize their electoral support, the angle from which they will approach them, and how they will convey these messages through the media.

First, we will introduce some important concepts for understanding why Canadian federal parties have chosen to focus on certain issues during election campaigns. We will then briefly discuss strategies that parties use for ensuring that their political positions are visible in the public space. From this we draw two major conclusions: (1) in Canada as elsewhere, strategic choices about the issues and means of communication used to carry out these choices are the cornerstones of political campaigning; and (2) these choices partly explain political party success and failure in recent Canadian federal elections.

Political Campaigning and Issues

Political parties use election campaigns to draw voters' attention to characteristics that paint them in the best possible light. A party's objective is relatively simple: it aims to focus the debate on issues for which it has a positive image and to convince voters to view these issues as being important so that a vote will be cast for the party on the basis of that important issue come election day. For example, a voter who believes that the economy is the biggest challenge facing the country and sees a particular political party as being more competent than others to deal with the economy is more likely to support this party than someone who thinks that another issue is important or who believes that another party is better able to deal with this issue.

Scholars in political science and communication sciences have called these efforts by parties to draw attention to specific questions *agenda building*. A related concept, that of *agenda setting*, refers to the relationship between the importance given to a question by the media and the importance given to the same question by voters. Finally, a *priming effect* occurs when a process leads a voter to not only attach importance to a question, but also to make it a decisive criterion in voting (Iyengar and Kinder 1987; Nadeau and Bastien 2003; Nadeau, Pétry, and Bélanger 2010; Norris et al. 1999; Vavreck 2009).

The use of issue-based strategies in election campaigns rests on the idea that some parties have a more favourable image with regard to certain issues than their competitors; this idea has resulted in the concept of "issue ownership" (Petrocik 1996). For example, rightist parties have a reputation as being the best to deal with issues of inflation, crime, or defence, while leftist parties are perceived as more competent to deal with issues such as unemployment, health, and education (Blais et al. 2002; Budge and Farlie 1983; Egan 2013; Trilling 1976). The reputation that parties have with regard to the issues is related to two factors: (1) the intensity of their commitment to certain problems, and (2) their performance on these issues when they were in government (Petrocik 1996). Thus, a party's image on the issues is relatively stable, but not immutable. The Conservative Party in the United Kingdom has long enjoyed the reputation of being more competent than the Labour Party in dealing with economic issues. However, in the 1990s an economic crisis tarnished the party's image and paved the way for the Labour Party's return to power in 1997 (Norris et al. 1999). Similarly, the reputation of the Republican Party in the United States on the same issue also suffered because of the severe financial crisis during George W. Bush's presidency (Lewis-Beck and Nadeau 2009).

What about the image of Canadian political parties? Do they have distinct advantages on certain issues that might guide their strategic choices with regard to issues during electoral campaigns? The oldest study on the topic concludes that there are none. In the mid-1960s, Howard Scarrow proposed that Canadian parties' reputations with regard to issues were primarily due to projection effects, that is to say, the percentage of people attributing a competence to a party to deal with a particular issue being linked to how popular it is at the moment. Speaking about the results of his survey that sought to identify the image of Canadian political parties, Scarrow (1965, 73) stated that "The party thought of as best for meeting these problems is the one which happens to be popular at the time, and ... as the popularity decreases the party is perceived less able to meet these problems." For him, this is unique to Canada. "This pattern," he wrote, "represents a contrast with the United States where for example, when Eisenhower's popularity was at its peak, the Democratic party was still thought of as best to meet the problem of unemployment" (Scarrow 1965, 73).

Scarrow's thesis was challenged by Nadeau and Blais in the early 1990s and Bélanger in the early 2000s. By using data from the Gallup polling firm collected since the 1950s, Nadeau and Blais (1990) showed that the Liberal Party of Canada has enjoyed a marked advantage when it comes to issues of international affairs and national unity. Analyses by Bélanger (2003), which include data for the 1990s, come to the same conclusion. Nadeau and Blais's study also shows that parties' images on economic issues have fluctuated over time. The Conservative Party suffered for decades because of its poor management of the economic crisis of the 1930s. In 1956, Canadians still massively opted for the Liberal Party (45 per cent) over the Conservative Party (22 per cent) to manage the Canadian economy if economic difficulties were to arise. The rise in unemployment during the Diefenbaker administration consolidated these perceptions. It was not until the crisis of 1982–83 under a Liberal government, followed by a period of prosperity during the Mulroney years, that Canadians had a more favourable opinion of the Conservative Party's economic competence.

Bélanger's study shows that in the wake of the recession of 1992–93 at the end of the Mulroney era, the Liberal Party emerged once again as the party of the economy (Bélanger 2003). The economic growth of the 1990s and the recovery of public finances under the leadership of Jean Chrétien and Paul Martin gave the Liberal Party a clear advantage over its opponents for nearly a decade. However, this advantage would tilt toward the Conservative Party in the mid-2000s. The relatively good performance of the Canadian economy during the difficult context of the economic crisis of the late 2000s and skepticism toward the Liberal "Green Shift" strategy in 2008 brought a clear majority of Canadians to believe that the Conservative Party was most adept at dealing with the economy in the 2008 and 2011 elections (Bélanger and Nadeau 2014, 2015).

The remarks above show that Canadian voters' perceptions about the reputation of different parties to deal with different issues are sufficiently distinct and stable enough to guide the electoral strategy of the parties. The Liberal Party still continues to be perceived as best able to handle foreign policy and maintain national unity. The Conservative Party is seen as better able to tackle crime and reduce the debt, as well as being seen for nearly a decade as the most competent in developing the economy. The NDP continues to be seen as the party most able to adequately address social policy in general, and in particular the health care system (Blais et al. 2002; Gidengil et al. 2012; Nevitte et al. 2000).

These rather distinct images guide party strategies, because Canadian voters are sensitive to them when deciding for which party to vote. Nadeau et al. (2001) systematically analyzed this issue and concluded that there is a significant and substantial link between the support received by a party and perceptions about its competence to deal with various issues. Pushing the analysis further, Bélanger and Meguid (2008) showed, using Canadian data, that this effect was especially noticeable when voters attached greater importance to the issues in question. Thus pursuing a strategy based on issues in Canada can be beneficial. By attracting voters' attention to certain issues, political parties manage to do two things at once. First, they persuade more voters to believe that a given issue is a priority for the country. Then, they make them remember very clearly that the party has a good reputation with regard to this issue. The ideal issue for a party is one that is seen as a priority and on which they are seen as extremely competent.

Therefore, the objective for parties is to ensure that the media give strong visibility to these issues to get voters to consider them to be priorities (i.e., agenda-setting effects) and ultimately to make these issues decisive in choosing which party they support.[1] However, several factors obstruct the implementation of this strategy. First, there is the difficulty of being heard. When faced with several opponents who are all trying to impose their own issues on the agenda, it can be difficult for a party to ensure that their message becomes the dominant signal to which voters will pay attention (Iyengar and Simon 2000). The second obstacle is resistance from the media, who are anxious to assert their independence and work according to their own logic. As we will see, the media tends to avoid becoming a simple transmission belt for political parties' messages (Zaller 1999). The third (but not least) obstacle is the inertia of voters' priorities during the relatively short period of an election campaign. Table 17.1 shows the priorities of Canadian voters at the beginning and the end of the four federal elections from 1997 to 2006. The conclusion is clear: the priorities of voters vary little during campaigns. There are seldom changing short-term realities with which parties must contend. For example, during the 2000 election it was virtually impossible for parties to dodge the issue of health care and divert voters' attention to other issues. The data in Table 17.1 show that this inertia in voter priorities is the rule rather than the exception in Canadian elections, which is a conclusion that could be extended to most parliamentary democracies characterized by relatively short electoral campaigns.

The above remarks suggest that the battling issues model is probably incomplete, if not inadequate, in explaining the strategic choices that Canadian political parties make with regard to issues during election campaigns. In fact, analyses of party behaviour show that they tend to address the same issues in elections in a trend called *convergence* (Damore 2005; Nadeau, Pétry, and Bélanger 2010; Sigelman and Buell 2004). However, the parties

Table 17.1   Change in Issue Salience during Four Canadian Federal Elections

	Beginning Weeks	Ending Weeks	Change	Ranking	
				Beginning	End
A. 1997 Election					
Creating jobs	82.9	80.4	−2.5	1	1
Fighting crime	72.9	68.7	−4.2	2	2
Protecting social programs	60.9	60.1	−0.8	3	4
Reducing the deficit	59.7	60.6	0.9	4	3
B. 2000 Election					
Improving health care	81.4	85.7	4.3	1	1
Fighting crime	71.5	71.4	−0.1	2	2
Creating jobs	65.1	66.3	1.2	3	3
Protecting the environment	56.7	58.7	2.0	4	4
C. 2004 Election					
Health care	47.9	50.0	2.1	1	1
Corruption in government	25.1	22.0	−3.1	2	2
Taxes	15.1	15.0	−0.1	3	3
Social welfare programs	7.6	7.1	−0.5	4	4
D. 2006 Election					
Health care	44.8	40.4	−4.4	1	1
Corruption in government	28.2	32.0	+3.2	2	2
Taxes	13.0	11.7	−1.3	3	3
Social welfare programs	8.8	10.6	1.8	4	4

Format questions for 1997 and 2000: "To you personally, in this Federal election, [Issue], is it very important, somewhat important, or not very important?" Entries are the percentages selecting "very important." Format for the 2004 and 2006 question: "Which of the following five issues is the most important to you personally in this election? [Issue]." Entries are the percentages corresponding to the various categories. Beginning and ending weeks correspond to the first and last two weeks of the campaign.

Source: Data are from the Canadian Election Study (1997, 2000, 2004, 2006).

differentiate themselves not only by addressing different issues, but also by presenting the same issues in different ways. Parties can propose a certain reading of the same issues (or a certain "frame") that is favourable to them (Druckman 2010; Entman 2004). In this context, the struggle between parties lies not in increasing the visibility of an issue, but rather in ensuring the widest possible dissemination of an interpretation about the issue. For example, if the economy is bad and this issue is a concern to voters, then all parties will have to address this issue, but each party will do so differently. For example, the incumbent party will insist that its policies have allowed Canada to do relatively well in a difficult economy. Opposition parties will argue that the government's economic mismanagement has made things worse. If the first interpretation is prevalent in the media and is latched onto by voters, the incumbent government has a good chance of being re-elected. Otherwise, it is likely to be defeated. Thus, what is at the heart of electoral battles between political parties is less their ability to impose a particular issue than the interpretation of the issue.

Thus, parties engaged in election campaigns both promote specific issues (strategic outcome priming) and specific interpretations about these issues (strategic issue framing). This idea is the topic of an article published by Nadeau, Pétry, and Bélanger (2010), where they show that the issue of health care was a key issue in the 2000 federal election (see Table 17.1) at a time when satisfaction with the Liberal government on this issue was barely 18 per cent. In this context, a debate centred on the government's overall performance could have been damaging to the incumbent government. But the Liberal Party successfully reframed the election as a choice between maintaining the Canadian public health care system or switching to a US-style two-tiered system under its main rival, the Canadian Alliance. Nadeau, Pétry, and Bélanger show that the penetration of this frame within the electorate favoured the Liberal Party's re-election.

Political Parties' Strategic Issues in Canadian Federal Elections

We will now look at strategic choices with regard to issues that Canadian political parties have adopted ever since the appearance of the Bloc Québécois at the federal level in 1993. It is around these choices that parties organized their campaign, showed their political positions, and sought to project a positive image of themselves and their leaders. The promotion of certain issues and their framing are the cornerstones of political campaigning both in Canada and around the world.[2]

The case of the Bloc Québécois is interesting. This party has centred all its campaigns on the theme of defending Quebec's interests, and this choice is understandable. In poll after poll, the Bloc Québécois have always been seen as the party best able to fulfill this task, and analyses show that this factor contributed significantly to consolidating and increasing Bloc support (Nadeau et al. 2001). In spite of its position as a one-issue party, the Bloc has tried over time to expand its message by addressing other issues. For example, it proposed measures to fight motorcycle gangs in the 1990s and fought against reforming employment insurance. Issues of criminalization of young offenders and federal funding of cultural policies allowed the party to rein-vigorate its campaign in 2008. The most explicit linkage between the Bloc position and an issue specific to a particular election campaign happened in 2004, when this party skilfully exploited the sponsorship scandal by posing as "*un parti propre au Québec*."[3]

The effectiveness of the Bloc's positioning depended on its opponents and the political context. The Bloc had its greatest successes against the Liberal Party in 1993 during the constitutional debates and in 2004 during the spon-sorship scandal. With the accession of the Conservatives to power in 2006 and a lull in the constitutional debate, the Bloc had to retool its message from being the defender of Quebec's powers to being a bulwark against the rise of con-servative values embodied by the Harper government. The Bloc used issues such as environmental protection, criminalization of young offenders, support for culture, and the long-gun registry to illustrate the gap between the Con-servative Party's values and those of Quebec, with the aim of emphasizing the Bloc's importance in defending them. While this worked in 2008, it has proven less effective since. In 2011, the Bloc found itself faced with an opponent who was perceived as conveying the same progressive values: the NDP (Bélanger and Nadeau 2011). In a political juncture where the constitutional issue was virtually absent from the election campaign, the Bloc lost its footing.

The issues that the NDP emphasized were a reflection of the party's tra-ditional positions, perceived by many as the social conscience of Parliament. Data from the Canadian Election Study (Blais et al. 2002; Gidengil et al. 2012; Nevitte et al. 2000) show clearly that the NDP is seen as the party best able to handle health care and social policy in general. The expression of this political stance, which makes the NDP out to be more of a pressure group within Parliament than a party that could eventually come into power, cul-minated in the 1993, 1997, and 2000 elections, during which the NDP suf-fered heavy defeats and lost its official party status. Perhaps its lowest point was during the 1997 election, in which the party's advertisements explic-itly conceded victory to the Liberal Party and asked voters to support the NDP to be the watchdog for progressive values in Parliament.[4] The arrival of Jack Layton as party head resulted in a change of political stances, but the NDP's favourite issues remained essentially the same: adequate financ-ing of the health system, establishing a drug plan and a child-care system similar to Quebec's,[5] fairer taxation, and preserving the main provisions of employment insurance were at the heart of the party's positions during elec-tion campaigns of the 2000s. Unlike the Liberal Party, the NDP managed to maintain its unity on foreign policy, including the Canadian mission in Afghanistan, by adopting a critical position. However, divisions appeared within the NDP caucus on the issue of gun control.

The issues emphasized by the NDP during election campaigns mirror both its strengths and weaknesses. The NDP is clearly seen as a progressive party that may put in place a more efficient tax system and bolder social policies. But the party's main difficulty is that it is not perceived as being particularly competent in dealing with issues such as national unity, foreign affairs (including defence policy), public finance, and especially the economy. For example, in the 2011 election, where the NDP got nearly 31 per cent of the vote, only 11 per cent of Canadians perceived the party as being the best suited to deal with the economy (Bélanger and Nadeau 2014, 2015). The NDP is therefore faced with a dilemma: if it addresses economic issues in the next campaign, it risks drawing attention to an issue on which its opponents (and the Conservative Party in particular) enjoy a distinct advantage. However, if it does not, it may be seen as a party uninterested in an issue that matters to many Canadians.

The choice of issues addressed by conservative political parties in Canada can be divided into two periods: the elections of 1993, 1997, and 2000, which were dominated first by the Reform Party and then by the Canadian Alliance; and the 2004 through 2011 elections, when these forces recombined with the defunct Progressive Conservative Party under the new banner of the Conservative Party of Canada. Three themes were at the centre of Reform and Canadian Alliance campaigns: economic conservatism focused on significantly reducing both the tax burden and the size of the state; alienation felt by the Western provinces, leading to demands to give less attention to the grievances of the central provinces (and Quebec in particular); and the introduction of mechanisms to increase transparency of parliamentary work and accountability of elected officials. The Reform Party's opposition to the GST in 1993, demands for an elected Senate whose composition reflects the weight of Canadian regions, opposition to Quebec's distinct society status, and establishment of a "recall" mechanism for federal Members of Parliament constitute policy positions that clearly reflect the party's political positioning. The same concerns were generally at the heart of the 1997 Reform campaign, the highlight of which may have been an advertisement denouncing the dominant role played by Quebec politicians on the federal scene.[6] Reform's disappointing results in Ontario during that election would later lead party officials to want to project a more moderate image for the party to make inroads beyond the Western provinces. The creation of the Canadian Alliance and the arrival of a new leader (Stockwell Day) realized this goal. However, controversial positions taken by Alliance candidates (notably on the death penalty and morality questions), and the Liberal Party's skillful exploitation of the Alliance's apparent willingness to privatize the Canadian health care system, helped consolidate the perception among Canadians that the party advocated extremist measures, which brought about its defeat.

The choice of issues addressed by the Conservative Party in the 2004–11 elections demonstrates an explicit desire to project a more moderate image to appeal to centrist voters, especially in Ontario, which had overwhelmingly supported the Liberal Party for a decade. The most significant effort to refocus the Conservative Party came after the partial success of the 2004 election, which resulted in a minority Liberal government. During this election, Conservative efforts focused on two main themes: fiscal conservatism and economic competence. The most significant sign that the Conservative Party wanted to be seen more in terms of its tax policies than its stance on moral issues was its promise to reduce the GST by two percentage points, which was introduced at the beginning of their successful 2006 election campaign. Following the election, the Conservative Party would go on to propose policies mobilizing its conservative base, such as a proposal to hold a free vote on same-sex marriage, the dismantling of the long-gun registry, a timid environmental protection policy, and a foreign policy more in line with that of the United States. The Conservative Party would also try to maintain a balance on constitutional issues through its (unsuccessful) efforts to reform the Senate and to accept some of Quebec's demands (e.g., open federalism, a reserved place for Quebec in the Canadian delegation to UNESCO, and harmonization of the GST and QST). But these positions are secondary in the Conservatives' electoral strategy. Conservative campaigns will focus mainly on the issues of public finance and reducing the tax burden, thereby securing its image in Canadian voters' minds as the party of the economy. This image was at the centre of the 2008 and 2011 campaigns, with the following rhetorical question addressed to voters: "Which is the best party to take care of the economy in the current economic situation?" Figures from the Canadian Election Study show that the Conservatives were able to convince a substantial portion of voters that they were best suited to lead the Canadian economy. Outside of Quebec, 43 per cent of voters chose the Conservative Party, versus 25 per cent for the Liberals and only 12 per cent for the NDP. Conservative dominance on this issue was more pronounced in 2011, as the responses were 44 per cent for the Conservatives, 20 per cent for the Liberals, and 11 per cent for the NDP.

For the Liberal Party, their strategic choices are characterized by two well-defined directions. First, true to its tradition, the Liberal Party ran as a centrist party whose moderate positions, close to the views of Canadians, provide an appropriate balance between the radicalism (left or right) of its opponents. Then, the Liberal Party presented itself as a party of responsible public finances and job creation. These choices are easily explained. The Liberal Party returned to power in 1993 after a long economic recession and faced a federal government deficit of over $40 billion. Thus, the Conservative's reputation for economic competence was at an all-time low during their historic defeat in 1993. Economic recovery in the mid-1990s, combined with fiscal consolidation by Paul Martin, allowed the Liberal Party to project competence with regard to the economy and public finances. This gave the party a decisive advantage in the 1997 and 2000 elections. This same advantage, coupled with fears about the radicalism of the Conservative Party, would allow the Liberal Party to be victorious in 2004 in spite of the sponsorship scandal. However, the persistence of the theme of integrity in the public debate, the relative economic calm (which made this theme less important for voters), and the Conservatives' more moderate image combined with their promise to reduce the GST by two percentage points finally overcame the Liberals in 2006. This meant that the 2008 election was going to be very difficult.

The new leader, Stéphane Dion, chose to focus the campaign on a policy reconciling economic development and environmental protection called "The Green Shift." This choice would prove to be detrimental for two reasons. First, it would be difficult for the Liberals to explain that the plan's main provision, a tax on carbon emissions, would not result in a higher tax burden. The Conservative Party was quick to describe this as a simple tax, which allowed it to stand out even more as the party most concerned with defending taxpayers. Second, this strategy made the party look like a progressive party rather than a centrist one. By abandoning its centrist positioning, the Liberal Party conceded electoral space that its main opponent swooped in to occupy. Finally, the Liberal Party would have great difficulty in imposing these issues in the 2008 and 2011 elections, which were dominated by the issue of the economy. The dominance of the Conservative Party on economic and public finance issues created problems for a now centre-left Liberal Party, which found itself competing with the NDP and led to one of the most severe electoral defeats in its history.

Strategic Framing of Issues by Political Parties

This overview of the strategic choices made by parties in the most recent federal elections allows us to see what issues they emphasized and for what purposes. A closer reading of these strategies also shows that parties often promote not just an issue itself but also a certain interpretation of the issue. For example, in 1993, all parties agreed that Canada was facing two problems: a large deficit and a difficult economic situation after emerging from a deep recession. The solutions to these problems would lead to opposite results. Lowering spending to fight the deficit could delay an economic recovery, while introducing measures to stimulate the economy could increase the deficit. All federal political parties would go on to address both of these issues during the election campaign but propose different solutions. As a result, the battle between parties would focus on these frames. The Reform Party proposed a rapid elimination of the deficit in three years. The Progressive Conservative Party promised a return to a balanced budget in five years. The NDP suggested first addressing unemployment and postponing tackling the deficit. The Liberal Party proposed a more balanced solution: gradually reducing the federal deficit to about 3 per cent of gross domestic product, which would reduce the deficit without jeopardizing an economic recovery.

The 1997 election would once again be fought along the same lines. However, the most pressing question at that time was how to use the federal government budget surplus. The Reform Party and the Progressive Conservative Party proposed using the money to cut taxes and reduce the debt, while the NDP advocated for using this flexibility to fund public services. Polls showed that while Canadians wanted tax cuts, they were also anxious to see properly funded public services. The Liberal Party's solution sought to address these concerns. It would use half of the budget surplus to reduce taxes and the debt, with the other half used to finance the health care system, the fight against child poverty, and job creation programs.

Other elections would also be the site of framing battles. In the 2000 election the issue of health care came to the fore. Again, the Liberal Party managed to frame the debate in its favour by presenting itself as the defender of the public health care system. The elections after that would then be fought over what the interpretive frame of the main issues should be. Most striking is the case of the 2008 election, which was called by a minority Conservative government because of the effects of the US financial crisis. At this point the economy was the main concern of Canadians, and the Harper government decided to make it the central theme of its campaign. However, unemployment had been increasing in Canada since the Harper government came to power in 2006, making the incumbent government vulnerable. But the Conservatives were successful by arguing that Canada, thanks to Conservative economic policies, still fared better than the United States and European countries. Advantaged by the Liberal Party's Green Shift, the Conservatives won out as the most competent party to handle the economy. This image would greatly contribute to their re-election in 2008, and with this reputation still intact, if not strengthened, would go on to play a significant role in securing a majority government in 2011.

Adopting a frame that compares Canada's economic situation with that of other countries is not always successful, as evidenced by the severe defeats of the Liberal Party in 1984 and the Conservative Party in 1993 after periods of recession. However, it has also been successfully used in 1974, when Canada was faced with high inflation. The Liberal government of the time was able to convince a majority of voters that the root causes of this situation were international and that Canada was in a better situation than most countries. In all these cases, the economy has been at the centre of political parties' strategies, but it is ultimately the interpretation of the situation that has been at the heart of the electoral battle.

The Mediatization of Political Campaigning

The strategic choices of political parties—selecting which issues to emphasize and how to frame them being among the most critical—are deployed in a mediatized environment that has become increasingly intense and complex in recent decades. Mediatization, which Hjarvard (2008, 113) has defined as "the process whereby society, to an increasing degree is submitted to, or becomes dependent on, the media and their logic," affects institutions, organizations, and political actors by imposing upon them a media logic to which they must adapt. Strömbäck and Esser (2014a, 246) argue that "media and politics constitute two different institutional systems that serve different purposes and that each has its own set of actors, organizations and institutions, rules and procedures, and needs and interests. These institutional rules and procedures can be formal as well as informal, and together form a certain 'logic of appropriateness.'" In a seminal article, Strömbäck (2008) distinguished four dimensions of the mediatization of politics, where (1) the media are the most important source of information about politics and society, (2) the media are semi-independent from other social and political institutions, (3) media content is guided by media logic instead of political logic, and (4) political institutions, organizations, and actors are guided by media logic instead of political logic.

Canadian political parties are faced with this mediatization of politics. For Canadians, obtaining political information is most often mediated and done so through a complex network of information sources. With increased commercialization and decreased regulation, news media outlets are more autonomous from political forces. Furthermore, journalists have become more "interventionist" in the production of information. As a result, political parties are making significant efforts to adapt to the growing challenges of political journalism while also trying alternative ways to directly connect with Canadians and get their message out, notably by taking advantage of online communications technologies.

Mediation, Autonomy, and Journalistic Intervention

In Canada, as in other industrialized countries, citizens mainly learn about politics through the media. In fact, how Canadians collect information about

Table 17.2   Canadians' Most Important Source of Information about
Federal Elections or Political News (%)

	1993	2008	2014
Television	52.6	57.4	46.6
Newspapers	20.6	20.2	17.4
Radio	15.6	8.6	7.4
Internet	—	7.5	24.1
Friends and family	11.1	3.8	2.7
None, other	—	2.5	1.8
Number of respondents	3,699	3,651	1,968

Note: Data are from the 1993 and 2008 Canadian Election Studies and the 2014 Canadian Online Citizenship Survey. All data were collected by phone. Questions asked respondents about their most important source of information about federal elections (in 1993 and 2008) or political news (in 2014). In the 2014 survey, the "newspapers" item clearly referred to print news in newspapers or magazines.

politics and electoral campaigns has changed over the past century, and even over the past two decades. Interpersonal networks (i.e., information obtained from family, friends, and co-workers) have declined in importance as Canadians inform themselves via a set of increasingly complex media sources. This is what is suggested by using data from both the 1993 and 2008 Canadian Election Studies (before and after the popularization of the Internet), along with another survey carried out in 2014 as part of the *Online Citizenship* project (Table 17.2).[7]

Television remains the main source of information for a large number of Canadians (about half), but this proportion has clearly declined in recent years, as has the percentage of Canadians who are primarily informed via print newspapers and radio. In 2014, nearly one in four respondents said that online platforms were their most important source of political information, whether news websites (17 per cent) or other sources less clearly related to journalism, such as social networking sites (7 per cent). The proportion of respondents who said that nonmediated interpersonal networks (such as family or friends) were their main source of information on politics is minimal (3 per cent) and confirms the importance of the media in the flow of political information. The data also confirm the central role of the news media in transmitting political information to citizens. Canadians mostly learn about politics through television journalists and newspapers. It is therefore not surprising that political parties pay particular attention to the news media during campaigns.

Unlike the days of the partisan press, the role of the news media is more critical, as they are more focused on maximizing profits than supporting an ideology or a political party. Political actors and organizations can no longer rely on them as much as in the past for support.[8] In addition, ethical codes to which journalists subscribe (at least implicitly, since journalism is not formally governed by an order, as is the case with most professions), collective agreements where they exist, and the Broadcasting Act (for the CBC) all emphasize independence from media owners and political power and promote their role as watchdogs. A survey conducted in the late 1990s showed that professional autonomy was the characteristic of their job deemed most important by Canadian journalists (Pritchard and Sauvageau 1999).

Citizens are rarely directly exposed to political speeches; instead, they rely on the media to inform them about what political parties are proposing. However, as journalists enjoy their professional autonomy and newspaper companies are relatively independent from federal political parties, the media do not so readily play the role of a simple transmission belt. In addition, the pressure to get and keep the audience's attention in an environment where competition between messages of all kinds is intense encourages journalists and news organizations to adopt an accelerated pace and offer easily intelligible content that does not necessarily match the attributes of political discourse, which often lasts a long time and is full of complex considerations. Therefore, the media's agenda is likely to differ from that of political parties and, even when the two converge toward the same issues, journalists can choose to substitute other frames to replace those selected by parties.

Recent research testifies to these transformations. In an oft-cited US study, Hallin (1992) measured the average length of presidential candidates' sound bites in major television newscasts and found that it decreased from 43 seconds during the 1968 campaign to 9 seconds in 1988. We do not have comparable statistics for federal candidates on Canadian television, but it is likely that the figures and, above all, the trend would be the same. In a study of the French-language press in Quebec from 1945 to 1995, Charron (2006) observed a substantial reduction in the average length of quotes and a transformation of their role in journalistic discourse: these quotes are used less to inform the public about what the political actor said, as was the case before, and more to establish the validity of the reporter's interpretation about the political events of the day.

In this sense, interpretive journalism has an important role in media coverage during election campaigns. More specifically, it is commonly recognized that Canadian journalists tend to cover the campaigns as if they were sports events (hence the term *horserace journalism*), emphasizing the performance and strategies of political actors. This interpretive framework is different from that developed by the political parties, which focuses more on issue definition and solving problems that concern (or *should* concern, according to the parties) citizens. Although the proportion of horserace coverage varies according to country, it is quite prevalent and increases as election day approaches. We also note that the tone of horserace coverage tends to be negative; in addition to politicians who criticize their opponents, journalists themselves introduce a certain amount of negativity (Soroka and Andrew 2010). It is especially when talking about the race between parties that journalists' tones are more pointed. For example, journalists rarely weigh in on the feasibility of election promises, but frequently argue about the impact of these promises on voting intentions (Marcotte and Bastien 2012).

As stated earlier, we do not have longitudinal data that allow us to show the growth in horserace journalism or the negative tone of election coverage in Canada, but such trends have been well-documented by our American neighbours, including Patterson (1994) and Zaller (1999). Moreover, election polling, which is an important part of horserace journalism, is becoming more prevalent in Canada. In the introduction to their study of news coverage of polls during the 2008 election campaign, Pétry and Bastien (2013) note that the results of more than 200 national polls on voting intentions (including the almost daily reports of four rolling polls) were broadcast by polling firms and published by the media during the 37 days of the campaign. In contrast, Johnston et al. (1992, 121) had identified only 22 polls during the 51 days of the 1988 campaign.

Political Parties Who Adapt

This increase in the mediatization of politics compels political parties to adapt to (and some might say adopt) the media logic that colours the coverage of election campaigns and politics more broadly. In theory, mediatization of parties "implies (and becomes visible through) changes in organizational structure (rules and resources for communication) and behavior (degree and form of communication output)" (Donges and Jarren 2014, 188–89). These changes can be seen through a variety of indicators: an intensification of media monitoring, increased human and financial resources devoted to communication activities, repositioning of these activities to the top of the organizational hierarchy, a more intense use of press relations tools, and so on. Political public relations tactics, such as the provision of information subsidies by parties that the media can use (e.g., press releases, photo opportunities, pseudo-events, videos) are deemed necessary for agenda building and the strategic framing of issues (Lieber and Golan 2011; Tedesco 2011). Furthermore, if it has already been established that elected representatives need the media to govern (Cook 2005), then parties obviously need publicity to win elections. Some have also proposed the hypothesis that "vote-seeking parties

[are] more likely to adapt to news media logic than policy-seeking parties ... that do not see a great need to influence public opinion" (Strömbäck and Esser 2014b, 20–21).

In practice, this transformation is noticeable among Canadian parties, especially the parties that have made the most substantial gains since 1993: the Conservatives and the NDP, preceded by the Liberal Party. These parties' efforts are not limited to election campaigns or to their press relations. In fact, they illustrate the development of a permanent election campaign and a large-scale mobilization of resources to bypass news media to speak directly to the public, notably through advertising and online communications tools. These tactics reflect the rise of political marketing in these political parties (Marland 2012).[9] Although government communications were a concern for Jean Chrétien's Liberal government, control over communications was not as advanced as it later became under Stephen Harper, given the context of minority governments and the Conservatives' greater mistrust of civil servants and the press. Data from 2014 indicate that the Prime Minister's Office (PMO) employed 34 people in its divisions devoted to communications and touring activities, whereas these employees numbered 19 under Jean Chrétien in 2001 and only 18 under Paul Martin in 2006 (Esselment 2014).

These changes have been extensively documented in the case of the Conservative Party, notably by Tom Flanagan, a political science professor at the University of Calgary who has organized several campaigns for the party. Communication activities occupy a prominent role in the story he presents about the rise of the Conservative Party under Stephen Harper. In contrast to the traditional ad hoc organizations set up in the year preceding an election, the party seems to be engaged in a perpetual election campaign, consisting of advertisements targeting opponents (e.g., Stéphane Dion, Michael Ignatieff, and Justin Trudeau) broadcast at great expense by the mass media, mailings and automated phone messages targeting microsegments of the electorate, and the use of information technologies to collect donations from a large number of supporters, all coordinated by a team reporting directly to the party head (Flanagan 2012). Toward the end of his book *Harper's Team: Behind the Scenes in the Conservative Rise to Power,* Flanagan reveals the "Ten Commandments of Conservative Campaigning," of which one is self-discipline, considered essential in the face of an adversarial press: "The media can be savage with any party that lacks discipline, but they are particularly suspicious of conservatives" (Flanagan 2009, 284). It is in this spirit that specific instructions are sent to candidates and activists, notably to avoid contact with the media and to speak only of the party platform, not their personal convictions.

Upon the election of a Conservative government in 2006, the search for better control over "the message" resulted in considerable tension with journalists of the Canadian Parliamentary Press Gallery in Ottawa. The full story presented by Paré and Delacourt (2014) on the relationship between the members of the Press Gallery and the PMO shows how the PMO changed the routines of parliamentary journalists to increase its power with the press by selecting journalists who were allowed to ask questions at press conferences from a list, banning access to spaces bordering on the cabinet meeting room, unveiling several public policies outside the federal capital (and consequently, far from the Parliamentary Press), and requiring any government communication to the press to be authorized by the PMO.

Having long been a third party, the NDP saw its vote share surpass that of the Liberals as it went on to become the Official Opposition in the 2011 election. According to McGrane (2011), this breakthrough was preceded by significant adjustments to make better use of political marketing, including a more tactical management of its communications. Under the leadership of Jack Layton, these communications were professionalized and centralized within work teams operating on a permanent basis and acting strictly within the party executive rather than a larger federal committee, as was previously the case. Most notably, this committee coordinated the microtargeting polling and communications activities aimed at demographic groups prevalent in specific neighbourhoods. Online advertising efforts yielded the email addresses of a large number of supporters who were asked during the campaign to participate in events, watch live-streamed speeches, and contribute financially to the party. Already in 2008 the party had made available to supporters, in its "Orange Room," a set of digital tools that could be used through social media (e.g., Facebook, Flickr, YouTube, and blogs). All in all, the party devoted half a million dollars and 16 people to its web campaign, including 10 solely responsible for processing emails (Erickson and Laycock 2009). Following the decline of the NDP in the 2015 election, the long-term success of this strategy remains to be seen.

Some of these communication tactics are discussed further in other chapters of this book, especially microsegmentation (see Alex Marland and Thierry Giasson's Chapter 16) and use of the Internet and social media (see Tamara A. Small's Chapter 18). Similar to advertising and talk shows on television, these channels of communication allow political parties to bypass the journalistic filter and get their message out to citizens by avoiding constraints imposed by news media logic.

Conclusion

The strategic choices that parties make with regard to issues—that is, their framing and media coverage of their messages—lie at the heart of political campaigning in Canada. Parties aim to promote the issues for which they have a competent reputation, offer interpretations (or frames) on important issues to show that their solutions are the most appropriate, and exercise greater control over their communications activities so that their messages are directly relayed to citizens despite the autonomy claimed by journalists and the media. The strategic use of issues also serves to highlight the qualities of a leader (competence, empathy, etc.) or a party's positioning (progressive, centrist, or conservative). In all cases, the purpose of these strategic choices is the same: to present a party in the best possible light to maximize its electoral support.

Some dimensions of party image are more durable than others. For example, the Liberal Party has long been perceived as more competent in dealing with issues of national unity and international affairs. Canadians believe that the NDP is best able to deal with social programs in general and health care. The Conservative Party is seen as the most committed to reducing the tax burden and fighting crime. However, these images are not immutable. The Liberal Party had historically been perceived as the most competent party to look after public finances and economic issues, but it ceded its title to the Conservative Party in the most recent elections. The NDP has often suffered from a lack of credibility in this matter.

Parties use issues to mobilize their constituencies and to try to make gains by positioning themselves advantageously compared to their opponents. In the past, the Liberal Party has often used its positions to project the image of a moderate party, competent on economic and financial issues and whose values were similar to those of most Canadians. However, the Conservative Party has increasingly been centring its campaigns on issues of the economy and public finances to consolidate its reputation on these matters and to rally moderate voters drawn in more by the party's fiscal conservatism than its moral conservatism. This same party also always takes care to promote, but with less emphasis, conservative positions on topics such as crime, internal affairs, moral issues, and environmental protection to mobilize its electoral base. The NDP has always benefited from its reputation among some voters as being the social conscience of Parliament. Its issue positioning aims to consolidate this support while projecting the image of a true government party that is also able to deal with international issues along with Canada's economic and financial problems.

Even with the controversy surrounding the right to wear the niqab at Canadian citizenship ceremonies popping up as an unexpected issue during the campaign, the 2015 election largely followed the above characterization. Relying on the fact that the economy remained the most important issue for voters (EKOS 2015; Ipsos 2015), the Conservative Party touted its economic record and stressed that proper management in this domain allowed them to lower taxes. The NDP sought to capitalize on its socially conscious image by promising to raise the minimum wage to $15 per hour and implement a nationwide child-care plan. However, the party was also eager to win credibility on questions of the economy and finance, so they promised a balanced budget if elected. This seems to have turned some progressive-minded voters away from the party. As for the Liberals, they seem to have played the centrist card by presenting themselves as champions of the middle class and relied on citizens' desire for change. They promised more transparent government and emphasized that the party's values and its stances on international issues were more in line with the views of Canadians.

In 2015, the battle between parties seemed to revolve around the economy. Due to the deteriorating economic situation resulting from falling oil prices and also possibly due to voters being drawn to the Liberals' expansionist strategy emphasizing major infrastructure projects, the Conservative Party was not able to benefit from a decisive advantage on the issue of the economy, as was the case in 2008 and 2011 (EKOS 2015; Ipsos 2015). This stalemate on the issue of the economy seems to have led to a defeat for the Conservatives, and in turn it has allowed the Liberals to regain credibility on economic issues. Coupled with the ability to capitalize on Canadians' desire for change, they are now coming into power after ten years in opposition.

It is likely that the next campaigns will see the federal political parties strategically using issues in the way described above. But given that this strategy of using issues to project a favourable image can come up against numerous challenges, such as the resistance of the news media and a lack of voter interest, we can also predict that the parties will continue to further refine their tactics when it comes to their relationships with journalists while continuing to invest in alternative communications channels, especially online communications technologies, as citizens further integrate these sources into their information consumption habits.

Suggested Readings

Bélanger, Éric, and Richard Nadeau. 2015. "Issue-Ownership of the Economy: Cross-Time Effects on Vote Choice." *West European Politics* 38 (4): 909–32. http://dx.doi.org/10.1080/01402382.2015.1039373

Egan, Patrick J. 2013. *Partisan Priorities: How Issue Ownership Drives and Distorts American Politics.* Cambridge: Cambridge University Press. http://dx.doi.org/10.1017/CBO9781107337138

Marland, Alex, and Thierry Giasson, eds. 2015. *Canadian Election Analysis 2015: Communication, Strategy, and Democracy.* Vancouver: University of British Columbia Press. http://www.ubcpress.ca/canadianelectionanalysis2015/CanadianElectionAnalysis2015.pdf

Nadeau, Richard, François Pétry, and Éric Bélanger. 2010. "Issue-Based Strategies in Election Campaigns: The Case of Health Care in the 2000 Canadian Federal Election." *Political Communication* 27: 367–88. http://dx.doi.org/10.1080/10584609.2010.516797

Nadeau, Richard, André Blais, Elisabeth Gidengil, and Neil Nevitte. 2001. "Perceptions of Party Competence in the 1997 Election." In *Party Politics in Canada,* 8th ed., edited by Hugh G. Thorburn and Alan Whitehorn, 413–30. Toronto: Prentice-Hall.

Vavreck, Lynn. 2009. *The Message Matters: The Economy and Presidential Campaigns.* Princeton, NJ: Princeton University Press. http://dx.doi.org/10.1515/9781400830480

Notes

1   This chapter's focus on issues seems to leave little room for strategy on leader image. Political scientists have long argued that the strategy of political parties was to take ambiguous positions on issues and instead focus their campaigns on leader image. In addition to Jacobs and Shapiro's (1994) pioneering study, more recent works have instead shown that parties use issues to bring attention to a leader's strengths. For example, the issue of the economy can be used to emphasize a leader's competence, while issues such as health care and social policies can serve more to highlight their empathy and compassion (see Nadeau and Lewis-Beck 2015).

2   This section draws on material gathered in the following studies: Blais et al. (2002), Clarke, Kornberg, and Scotto (2009), Gidengil et al. (2012), LeDuc et al. (2010), Nevitte et al. (2000), as well as books on the 2006, 2008, and 2011 elections edited by Pammett and Doran (2006, 2009, 2011).

3   In French, this slogan is a play on words. While it can mean "Québec's own party," with *propre* meaning "of one's own," it can also be interpreted to mean "a clean party in Québec," with *propre* also having the meaning of "clean" or "free of corruption."

4   The clearest example is an advertisement that bears the title "Wake up Liberals!"

5   The rhetoric of the NDP often presented Quebec as a model for social policy, which may have contributed to the idea that the party's values corresponded largely with those of Quebecers.

6   During the campaign, the Reform Party aired a controversial ad that crossed out the faces of four Quebecers prominent in Canadian politics (Prime Minister Jean Chrétien, Bloc Québécois leader Gilles Duceppe, Progressive Conservative leader Jean Charest, and Quebec Premier Lucien Bouchard) with a message saying that the province's politicians had dominated government for too long and that the Reform Party would put an end to Quebec favouritism.

7   We do not present data from the 2011 Canadian Election Study because there was no question on the most important source for information about the election; data from the 2015 Canadian Election Study were not available at the time of press. Online Citizenship/Citoyenneté en ligne is a Social Sciences and Humanities Research Council–funded project exploring online political activity and democratic citizenship in Canada, led by Harold Jansen (Lethbridge), with Frédérick Bastien (Montreal), Thierry Giasson (Laval), Royce Koop (Manitoba),

and Tamara A. Small (Guelph). This phone survey was conducted between February and May 2014 by the Institute for Social Research at York University. For more information about the project, visit www.oc-cel.ca.

8   Paul Nesbitt-Larking (2009) offers a more detailed historical description of the development of the press in Canada.

9   Alex Marland and Thierry Giasson present a more complete discussion of political marketing in Chapter 16 of this book.

References

Bélanger, Éric. 2003. "Issue Ownership by Canadian Political Parties." *Canadian Journal of Political Science* 36 (3): 539–58. http://dx.doi.org/10.1017/S0008423903778755

Bélanger, Éric, and Bonnie M. Meguid. 2008. "Issue Salience, Issue Ownership, and Issue-Based Vote Choice." *Electoral Studies* 27 (3): 477–91. http://dx.doi.org/10.1016/j.electstud.2008.01.001

Bélanger, Éric, and Richard Nadeau. 2011. "The Bloc Québécois: Capsized by the Orange Wave." In *The Canadian Federal Election of 2011,* edited by Jon H. Pammett and Christopher Dornan, 111–37. Toronto: Dundurn Press.

Bélanger, Éric, and Richard Nadeau. 2014. "Economic Crisis, Party Competence, and the Economic Vote." *Acta Politica* 49 (4): 462–85. http://dx.doi.org/10.1057/ap.2014.13

Bélanger, Éric, and Richard Nadeau. 2015. "Issue Ownership of the Economy: Cross-Time Effects on Vote Choice." *West European Politics* 38 (4): 909–32. http://dx.doi.org/10.1080/01402382.2015.1039373

Blais, André, Elisabeth Gidengil, Richard Nadeau, and Neil Nevitte. 2002. *Anatomy of a Liberal Victory: Making Sense of the Vote in the 2000 Canadian Election.* Peterborough, ON: Broadview Press.

Budge, Ian, and David Farlie. 1983. *Explaining and Predicting Elections.* London: Allen and Unwin.

Charron, Jean. 2006. "Journalisme, politique et discours rapporté: évolution des modalités de la citation dans la presse écrite au Québec, 1945–1995." *Politique et Sociétés* 25 (2–3): 147–81. http://dx.doi.org/10.7202/015932ar

Clarke, Harold D., Allan Kornberg, and Thomas J. Scotto. 2009. *Making Political Choices: Canada and the United States.* Toronto: University of Toronto Press.

Cook, Timothy E. 2005. *Governing with the News: The News Media as a Political Institution.* 2nd ed. Chicago: University of Chicago Press. http://dx.doi.org/10.7208/chicago/9780226026688.001.0001

Damore, David F. 2005. "Issue Convergence in Presidential Campaigns." *Political Behavior* 27 (1): 71–97. http://dx.doi.org/10.1007/s11109-005-3077-6

Donges, Patrick, and Otfried Jarren. 2014. "Mediatization of Political Organizations: Changing Parties and Interest Groups?" In *Mediatization of Politics: Understanding the Transformation of Western Democracies,* edited by Frank Esser and Jesper Strömbäck, 181–99. Basingstoke, UK: Palgrave Macmillan. http://dx.doi.org/10.1057/9781137275844.0017

Druckman, James N. 2010. "Competing Frames in a Political Campaign." In *Winning with Words: The Origins and Impact of Framing,* edited by Brian F. Schaffner and Patrick J. Sellers, 101–20. New York: Routledge.

Egan, Patrick J. 2013. *Partisan Priorities: How Issue Ownership Drives and Distorts American Politics*. Cambridge: Cambridge University Press. http://dx.doi.org/10.1017/CBO9781107337138

EKOS. 2015. "Three-Way Tie as Voters Try to Sort Out Who Can Solve the Economy." Poll conducted between August 26 and September 1 (N = 3,243). http://www.ekospolitics.com/wp-content/uploads/full_report_september_4_2015.pdf

Entman, Robert M. 2004. *Projections of Power: Framing News, Public Opinion, and U.S. Foreign Policy*. Chicago: Chicago of University Press.

Erickson, Lynda, and David Laycock. 2009. "Modernization, Incremental Progress, and the Challenge of Relevance: The NDP's 2008 Campaign." In *The Canadian Federal Election of 2008,* edited by Jon H. Pammett and Christopher Dornan, 98–135. Toronto: Dundurn Press.

Esselment, Anna. 2014. "The Governing Party and the Permanent Campaign." In *Political Marketing in Canada,* edited by Alex Marland, Thierry Giasson, and Jennifer Lees-Marshment, 24–38. Vancouver: University of British Columbia Press.

Flanagan, Tom. 2009. *Harper's Team: Behind the Scenes in the Conservative Rise to Power.* 2nd ed. Montreal: McGill-Queen's University Press.

Flanagan, Tom. 2012. "Political Communication and the 'Permanent Campaign.'" In *How Canadians Communicate IV: Media and Politics,* edited by David Taras and Christopher Waddell, 129–48. Edmonton: Athabasca University Press.

Gidengil, Elisabeth, Neil Nevitte, André Blais, Joanna Everitt, and Patrick Fournier. 2012. *Dominance and Decline: Making Sense of Recent Canadian Elections.* Toronto: University of Toronto Press.

Hallin, Daniel. 1992. "Sound Bite News: Television Coverage of Elections 1968–1988." *Journal of Communication* 42 (2): 5–24. http://dx.doi.org/10.1111/j.1460-2466.1992.tb00775.x

Hjarvard, Stig. 2008. "The Mediatization of Society: A Theory of the Media as Agents of Social and Cultural Change." *Nordicom Review* 29 (2): 105–34.

Ipsos. 2015. "What's Driving Who Canadians Will Vote for on Election Day: Economy, Taxes and Desire for Change 'Absolutely Critical.'" Poll conducted between October 9 to 13 on behalf of *Global News* (N = 1,349). http://www.ipsos-na.com/news-polls/pressrelease.aspx?id=7025

Iyengar, Shanto, and Donald K. Kinder. 1987. *News That Matters: Television and American Opinion.* Chicago: University of Chicago Press.

Iyengar, Shanto, and Adam F. Simon. 2000. "New Perspectives and Evidence on Political Communication and Campaign Effects." *Annual Review of Psychology* 51 (1): 149–69. http://dx.doi.org/10.1146/annurev.psych.51.1.149

Jacobs, Lawrence R., and Robert Y. Shapiro. 1994. "Issues, Candidate Image, and Priming: The Use of Private Polls in Kennedy's 1960 Presidential Campaign." *American Political Science Review* 88 (3): 527–40. http://dx.doi.org/10.2307/2944793

Johnston, Richard, André Blais, Henry E. Brady, and Jean Crête. 1992. *Letting the People Decide: Dynamics of a Canadian Election.* Montreal: McGill-Queen's University Press.

LeDuc, Lawrence, Jon H. Pammett, Judith I. McKenzie, and André Turcotte. 2010. *Dynasties and Interludes: Past and Present in Canadian Electoral Politics.* Toronto: Dundurn Press.

Lewis-Beck, Michael S., and Richard Nadeau. 2009. "Obama and the Economy in 2008." *PS, Political Science & Politics* 42 (3): 479–83. http://dx.doi.org/10.1017/S1049096509090775

Lieber, Paul S., and Guy J. Golan. 2011. "Political Public Relations, News Management, and Agenda Indexing." In *Political Public Relations: Principles and Applications,* edited by Jesper Strömbäck and Spiro Kiousis, 54–74. New York: Routledge.

Marcotte, Philippe, and Frédérick Bastien. 2012. "L'influence du mode de financement des médias audiovisuels sur le cadrage des campagnes: le cas des élections canadiennes de 2005–2006 et 2008." *Canadian Journal of Political Science* 45 (2): 313–36. http://dx.doi.org/10.1017/S0008423912000340

Marland, Alex. 2012. "Amateurs versus Professionals: The 1993 and 2006 Canadian Federal Elections." In *Political Marketing in Canada,* edited by Alex Marland, Thierry Giasson, and Jennifer Lees-Marshment, 59–75. Vancouver: University of British Columbia Press.

McGrane, David. 2011. "Political Marketing and the NDP's Historic Breakthrough." In *The Canadian Federal Election of 2011,* edited by Jon H. Pammett and Christopher Dornan, 77–109. Toronto: Dundurn Press.

Nadeau, Richard, and Frédérick Bastien. 2003. "La communication électorale." In *La communication politique: État des savoirs, enjeux et perspectives,* edited by Anne-Marie Gingras, 160–88. Quebec City: Presses de l'Université du Québec.

Nadeau, Richard, and André Blais. 1990. "Do Canadians Distinguish between Parties? Perceptions of Party Competence." *Canadian Journal of Political Science* 23 (2): 317–33. http://dx.doi.org/10.1017/S0008423900012270

Nadeau, Richard, André Blais, Elisabeth Gidengil, and Neil Nevitte. 2001. "Perceptions of Party Competence in the 1997 Election." In *Party Politics in Canada,* 8th ed., edited by Hugh Thorburn and Alan Whitehorn, 413–30. Toronto: Prentice-Hall.

Nadeau, Richard, and Michael Lewis-Beck. 2015. "Between Leadership and Charisma, the Importance of Leaders." In *Personality in Politics? The Role of Leader Evaluations in Democratic Elections,* edited by Marina Costa Lobo and John Curtice, 169–90. Oxford: Oxford University Press.

Nadeau, Richard, François Pétry, and Éric Bélanger. 2010. "Issue-Based Strategies in Election Campaigns: The Case of Health Care in the 2000 Canadian Federal Election." *Political Communication* 27: 367–88. http://dx.doi.org/10.1080/10584609.2010.516797

Nesbitt-Larking, Paul. 2009. *Politics, Society, and the Media.* 2nd ed. Toronto: University of Toronto Press.

Nevitte, Neil, André Blais, Elisabeth Gidengil, and Richard Nadeau. 2000. *Unsteady State: The 1997 Canadian Federal Election.* Toronto: Oxford University Press.

Norris, Pippa, John Curtice, David Sanders, Margaret Scammel, and Holli A. Semetko. 1999. *On Message: Communicating the Campaign.* London: Sage.

Pammett, Jon H., and Christopher Dornan, eds. 2006. *The Canadian Federal Election of 2006.* Toronto: Dundurn Press.

Pammett, Jon H., and Christopher Dornan, eds. 2009. *The Canadian Federal Election of 2008.* Toronto: Dundurn Press.

Pammett, Jon H., and Christopher Dornan, eds. 2011. *The Canadian Federal Election of 2011.* Toronto: Dundurn Press.

Paré, Daniel J., and Susan Delacourt. 2014. "The Canadian Parliamentary Press Gallery: Still Relevant or Relic of Another Time?" In *Political Communication in Canada: Meet the Press and Tweet the Rest,* edited by Alex Marland, Thierry Giasson, and Tamara A. Small, 111–26. Vancouver: University of British Columbia Press.

Patterson, Thomas E. 1994. *Out of Order.* New York: Vintage.

Petrocik, John R. 1996. "Issue Ownership in Presidential Elections, with a 1980 Case Study." *American Journal of Political Science* 40 (3): 825–50. http://dx.doi.org/10.2307/2111797

Pétry, François, and Frédérick Bastien. 2013. "Follow the Pollsters: Inaccuracies in Media Coverage of the Horse-Race during the 2008 Canadian Election." *Canadian Journal of Political Science* 46 (1): 1–26. http://dx.doi.org/10.1017/S0008423913000188

Pritchard, David, and Florian Sauvageau. 1999. *Les journalistes canadiens: un portrait de fin de siècle.* Sainte-Foy, QC: Presses de l'Université Laval.

Scarrow, Howard A. 1965. "Distinguishing between Political Parties: The Case of Canada." *Midwest Journal of Political Science* 9 (1): 61–76. http://dx.doi.org/10.2307/2109214

Sigelman, Lee, and Emmett H. Buell, Jr. 2004. "Avoidance or Engagement? Issue Convergence in US Presidential Campaigns, 1960–2000." *American Journal of Political Science* 48 (4): 650–61. http://dx.doi.org/10.1111/j.0092-5853.2004.00093.x

Soroka, Stuart, and Blake Andrew. 2010. "Media Coverage of Canadian Elections: Horse-Race Coverage and Negativity in Election Campaigns." In *Mediating Canadian Politics,* edited by Shannon Sampert and Linda Trimble, 113–28. Toronto: Pearson.

Strömbäck, Jesper. 2008. "Four Phases of Mediatization: An Analysis of the Mediatization of Politics." *International Journal of Press/Politics* 13 (3): 228–46. http://dx.doi.org/10.1177/1940161208319097

Strömbäck, Jesper, and Frank Esser. 2014a. "Introduction: Making Sense of the Mediatization of Politics." *Journalism Studies* 15 (3): 243–55. http://dx.doi.org/10.1080/1461670X.2014.897412

Strömbäck, Jesper, and Frank Esser. 2014b. "Mediatization of Politics: Towards a Theoretical Framework." In *Mediatization of Politics: Understanding the Transformation of Western Democracies,* edited by Frank Esser and Jesper Strömbäck, 3–28. Basingstoke, UK: Palgrave Macmillan. http://dx.doi.org/10.1057/9781137275844.0006

Tedesco, John C. 2011. "Political Public Relations and Agenda Building." In *Political Public Relations: Principles and Applications,* edited by Jesper Strömbäck and Spiro Kiousis, 75–94. New York: Routledge.

Trilling, Robert J. 1976. *Party Images and Electoral Behavior.* New York: Wiley.

Vavreck, Lynn. 2009. *The Message Matters: The Economy and Presidential Campaigns.* Princeton, NJ: Princeton University Press. http://dx.doi.org/10.1515/9781400830480

Zaller, John. 1999. *A Theory of Media Politics: How the Interests of Politicians, Journalists and Citizens Shape the News.* Chicago: University of Chicago Press.

18

Two Decades of Digital Party Politics in Canada: An Assessment

TAMARA A. SMALL

CANADIAN POLITICAL PARTIES HAVE BEEN online, in some way or another, for more than two decades. The purpose of this chapter is to assess the relative impact that digital technologies have had on political parties in Canada. From the earliest online politics literature, there have been two dichotomized perspectives about the value of digital technologies in democratic politics: the innovation[1] and normalization hypotheses. In the first perspective, digital technologies fundamentally change politics in a more positive and participatory manner, while the latter perspective sees the impact in a much more muted way. This chapter asks if Internet and social media use by Canadian political parties has been innovative or normalized. The chapter develops in several sections. We begin by providing a brief history of digital party politics in Canada, focusing on federal politics. Next we outline the innovation and normalization hypotheses. The chapter then explores several dimensions of the innovation hypothesis as identified by Eva Schweitzer (2008) to assess how they have played out in Canadian party politics. Research is drawn from both federal and provincial politics. The chapter argues that, on the whole, normalization has taken place; the evidence from federal and provincial politics shows that there has not been a fundamental shift in the political communication of Canadian parties because of digital technologies.

A Brief History of Digital Party Politics in Canada

While parties use digital technologies during and between elections, most research focuses on the e-campaign. The federal Liberals were one of the first Canadian parties to enter cyberspace. The Liberals created their first website in 1993, which was used in the campaign held that year (Kippen 2000). On one level, the 1997 federal election can be regarded as the inaugural cyber-campaign in Canada in the sense that all major parties and one minor one engaged in Internet-based campaigning. However, the impact of this cyber-campaign was limited. First, party use of the Internet was still in its "infancy" (Carty, Cross, and Young 2007), and second, the digital divide was a real concern in Canada at this time. The digital divide refers the availability of digital technologies between those with access and those without (Norris 2001). Where divides exist, the benefits of the Internet, political or otherwise, will not be equally distributed.[2] In the mid- to late 1990s, Internet penetration in Canada was around 20 per cent, which means that most Canadians were unable to access the online campaign content provided in the 1997 election. By the next federal election in 2000, the digital divide had begun to narrow, in part due to a commitment to improve communications infrastructure by the federal government. A slim majority of Canadians were online, and therefore a good part of the electorate had access to online politics. The e-campaign was still limited, with the websites of the major Canadian parties being described as "lacklustre" offerings that had not taken advantage of the political value of the technology (Attallah and Burton 2001). The 2004 federal election is probably Canada's first real Internet election. By this time, the Internet had begun to permeate all aspects of economic and cultural life. While the digital divide remained an issue, around three-quarters of the Canadian population were using the Internet from home with a high-speed connection. Also by this time, the Internet was no longer a political novelty but a necessity. All registered political parties, both major and minor, were online. Many local candidates also operated campaign websites during this election. While the use of the Internet likely had a minor impact on the outcome of the 2004 election, the Internet was well integrated into the overall campaign strategies of the federal parties (Small 2004).

Today party websites have become standardized at the federal and provincial levels. While there are party variations in terms of colour, design, and categorization, sites tend to offer personal information (e.g., biographies of leaders, candidates, or parliamentarians), policy information (e.g., election platform, policy statements, speeches, news releases), and mobilization opportunities (e.g., membership/donation/volunteer forms, e-newsletters, event calendars). Sites tend to be redesigned every couple of years, usually to coincide with an election, changes in party leadership, or technological innovations.

While websites remain a key hub of digital party politics and e-campaigning, the rise of social media has added a new dynamic. Social media such as blogs, Facebook, Twitter, and YouTube are online applications that facilitate users' ability to "create and share content and collaborate and communicate with users" (Marland, Giasson, and Small 2014, 254). After the success of blogging in the 2004 presidential election in the United States, some Canadian parties and candidates created campaign blogs during the 2006 election (Chen and Smith 2010), as did many parliamentarians in the interelection period. However, blogs were soon replaced by Facebook and Twitter, which have been consistently used since the 2008 campaign.

Indeed, the 2011 federal election was hailed as "Canada's first social media election" (Curry 2011), with the parties making extensive use of Facebook, YouTube, and especially Twitter (Francoli, Greenberg, and Waddell 2011). Federal and provincial political parties typically use social media to broadcast party-related information to the public, including news releases, stories from official websites, and YouTube videos. While much is known about how Canadian parties use some aspects of social media, our understanding of other social media, such as YouTube or photo-sharing sites, is still quite limited.

Today, there is a virtual omnipresence of parties—that is, they can be found all over the Internet. In the early days of the Internet a single website was sufficient. But now, just like individuals, organizations, and businesses, political actors create accounts on all the newest and latest technologies available. For instance, Table 18.1 lists all the online presences related to the Conservative Party of Canada in late 2014. This list does not include the numerous web presences of Stephen Harper as prime minister that were operated by the Prime Minister's Office (PMO) within the Government of Canada, or those of Conservative Members of Parliament (MPs). Similar lists could be created for the NDP, Liberals, Greens, and many provincial parties. For instance, current Prime Minister Justin Trudeau has accounts on Twitter, Facebook, Instagram, and Flickr that are separate from the many sites operated by the main party.

Not only do parties use numerous online applications to communicate, different organizational aspects of the party are represented. First, there are sites/accounts related to the party, which serve extra-parliamentary and

Table 18.1   The Virtual Omnipresence of the Conservative Party (as of October 2014)

Websites	*YouTube*
• www.conservative.ca • www.StephenHarper.ca	• cpcpcc
Facebook	*Photo Sharing*
• Conservative Party • Stephen Harper	• cpcpcc (Flickr) • pmharper (Flickr) • pmstephenharper (Instagram)
Email listserv	*Google Plus*
• Conservative Party	• StephenHarper
Twitter	*Microsites*
• CPC_HQ • pmharper	• www.justinoverhishead.ca • mulcairsndp.ca • scrappedtheregistry.ca

caucus functions. These sites/accounts are quite partisan; they promote accomplishments of the leadership and caucus while attacking other parties or their leaders. They also play an organizational role by being a hub for media relations, financial donations, and registration for membership or party conventions. Canada's leader-oriented politics is also well represented on the Internet. While party websites have always been heavily focused on leadership, the rise of social media has led to an online division between the leader and the party. As Table 18.1 shows, Stephen Harper had just as many accounts as the Conservative Party. In fact, leaders are much more popular than parties online. For instance, in the 2011 federal election, the ratio of Twitter followers for leader feeds compared to party feeds was 11:1 (Small 2014). That means that for every 11 people who followed one of the five leaders, only one person followed one of the five parties.

Perspectives on Online Politics

As mentioned, from the earliest studies of online politics, there have been two opposing perspectives on digital technologies in democratic politics. The first perspective, the innovation hypothesis, sees the Internet contributing to a "fundamental change in the way politics is presented to the public" (Schweitzer 2008, 450). This is because the Internet offers political actors and the public what Sara Bentivegna (2002, 54) calls "democratic potentials." Unlike previous communications technologies, especially television, the Internet is interactive, inexpensive, decentralized, hypertextual,[3] and has great informational capabilities and is a multimedia. These features present new opportunities in politics for citizens and political actors, including positive developments in citizen engagement and participation (Vergeer, Hermans, and Sams 2013) that were impossible in the era of mass communications technologies. According to this perspective, more people will participate because the barriers to politics (financial, time, skill) are reduced. That is, the Internet and social media make it easier for people to become involved. This is particularly beneficial for young people and political minorities, who otherwise tend to be politically disengaged from offline politics.

Specific to political parties, Schweitzer's (2008, 53) review of the literature identifies six major changes to the structure and the quality of political communications wrought by the Internet and social media. She suggests that digital technologies will allow for

1. more rapid and unmediated information dissemination;
2. substantial policy discussion;
3. less candidate-focused communication;

4. positive campaigning;
5. direct and interactive communication; and
6. narrowcasting and individual customization of political messages.

Together these would benefit the relationship between parties and citizens—making party politics more open and participatory.

Many question the deterministic view of Internet politics presented by the innovation hypothesis. The normalization hypothesis, developed by Michael Margolis and David Resnick (2000), contends that despite the unique features of Internet technologies, offline structures and forces will shape political uses of the Internet (Larsson 2013, 174). Rather than the Internet positively influencing political behaviour and practices, politics influences how the Internet is used and online political activity comes to resemble that of the real world (Margolis and Resnick 2000). Instead of altering levels of participation and the efficacy of citizens, those that benefit politically in the offline world will continue to benefit online. For normalizers, politics on the Internet is nothing new—it is "politics as usual" (Margolis and Resnick 2000). Normalization rejects the changes to party communication and behaviour suggested by the innovation hypothesis. Instead, the online and offline communication practices of political parties will converge, and traditional patterns of communication will be favoured (Schweitzer 2008).

Given that Canadian political parties have been online for quite some time, these two perspectives provide a useful tool for assessing the relative impact of the Internet on party politics. In what follows, we use the dimensions of the innovation hypothesis as identified by Schweitzer to assess whether parties' communication practices have shifted fundamentally due to the employment of digital technologies such as websites and social media.

Dimensions 1–3: Quantity and Quality of Online Information

The Internet has the capacity to change the quantity and quality of information that parties produce. Given that the first three components identified by Schweitzer are related to information dissemination, it is useful to discuss them all at once. To say that there is an enormous amount of information on the Internet is an understatement. Google, the world's most popular website, indexes more than 30 trillion individual pages (Koetsier 2013). The Internet greatly reduces the costs of producing, transmitting, storing, and sorting information. In the pre-Internet age, global media companies had a monopoly on the dissemination of information and cultural products to mass audiences; now regular people and nontraditional organizations are on a more level playing field. In terms of politics, websites and social media undoubtedly increase the amount and diversity of political information available to citizens. This can be seen as a benefit to democracy, given how vital information is to citizenship and political decision making, especially during elections. Political actors and academics often allege that political issues are not treated fairly or given sufficient depth of coverage by traditional news organizations. For instance, when covering Canadian elections, the media often use the "strategy frame," which focuses on opinion polling, party strategy, the performance of leaders, and dramatic confrontations (Trimble and Sampert 2004). Research has found that the focus on strategy is at the expense of substantive discussion of policy and issues in media reports (Cross et al. 2015). The democratic implication of this phenomenon is that citizens may have little understanding of the complex political issues of the day (and the party's stances on them), and voters may focus their evaluation of parties on strategic factors (Mendelsohn 1993). Digital technologies are seen as being able to change this. According to the innovation hypothesis, the increased informational capacities of the Internet mean that parties have greater control over the information provided to citizens. Information will be unmediated—that is, through websites and social media, parties can communicate directly with the public without journalistic intervention. Since the information comes directly from the party, it is more likely to have a greater policy focus and less likely to focus on strategic factors like personality.

From the beginning, Canadian political parties have capitalized on the informational capabilities of the Internet. Parties use websites and social media to broadcast and control official messages and to have direct and quicker contact with the public. For political junkies, digital technologies are a cornucopia of unmediated information produced by the large parliamentary parties and the smaller fringe parties. As mentioned, party websites feature policy documents, leader statements and speeches, statements made by MPs, blog posts, and press releases. For instance, prior to the 2015 federal election, the Conservative website featured a page called "Where We Stand" that listed three key policy areas; the Liberals' "What We Stand For" provided seven policy planks, while the NDP made a 28-page policy book available online. Moreover, all major parties have email updates to which people can subscribe. In addition to financial contribution appeals, party emails are often timely, in that they respond directly to the issues of the day. For instance, recently (November 2015) the federal Liberals sent an email with the subject line "Canada's message at COP21." The email briefly discussed the issue of climate change, suggesting that both Conservative and Liberal governments have done little in terms of concrete action. The email then asked the subscriber to sign a petition on the Liberal website. Such emails highlight policy and also encourage mobilization on the part of the public.

Parties also use social media to provide information to citizens. Indeed, research has found that the main use of Twitter by parties is to provide political information. In the 2011 federal election, the leaders of the three major parties[4] sent 269 tweets over the 36-day campaign, where 80 per cent of the tweets were informational (Small 2014). Just over 50 per cent of the informational tweets were about campaign issues. For instance, most of the tweets by the Conservative leader communicated party information, including policy planks and press releases. Provincial parties, too, use Twitter in this manner. The vast majority of tweets by the three main Ontario parties were informational in the 2011 provincial election (Cross et al. 2015), while 60 per cent of tweets by political parties in the 2012 Quebec campaign were focused on providing information to voters. Similar to the federal numbers, more than 50 per cent of the informational tweets by Quebec parties focused on providing political information and news (Giasson et al. 2013).

Information dissemination on social media is both rapid and unmediated. Parties use Twitter to provide information instantaneously to followers. For instance, there was live-tweeting during the 2011 federal election debates. In real-time, several parties provided "reality checks" on comments made by opponents and provided more details on policy statements made by the leader. Green Party leader Elizabeth May tweeted throughout the English-language debate, as she was not allowed to participate because the Greens did not have a seat in the House of Commons. Social media and email are particularly useful for parties to provide unmediated communication because they are subscription based. This means that the messages of the parties go directly and instantly into inboxes or social media feeds. Online video is also used to disseminate information. In addition to political ads, many Canadian parties post videos from events, media interviews, and Question Period to websites and YouTube.

Nevertheless, the increase in policy discussion online by parties has not necessarily led to a decline in the focus on candidates or candidates' personality. Like offline politics, Canadian party leaders are important in online communications. As mentioned, federal and provincial leaders have their own social media feeds and websites that are far more popular than the sites of the parties they represent. While these sites are politically focused, they do allow for some level of personalization. Leader images are also important in the Internet age. The Internet is a multimedia technology that brings together text, audio, and video. While the textual aspects of the Internet contribute to the extensive amounts of information online, the Internet is increasingly image-centric. Good images and videos grab attention and can encourage site visitors to explore content. Digital political photography, for instance, is crucial to the branding of a party leader and a party's communication strategy (Marland 2012). Thus the images of leaders often dominate party websites, especially if the leader is popular. Pictures of other key party members, including cabinet ministers, MPs, or candidates are far less common. Images and video of party leaders are regularly included in tweets or Facebook posts. Most parties now operate a photo-sharing site like Instagram or Flickr, and some party leaders, such as Justin Trudeau and Tom Mulcair, have their own. These sites feature numerous photos of the leader in various situations, including speaking in the legislature, at party events, giving speeches, in meetings, and talking with supporters. The photos are meant to tell a particular story about a leader. For instance, Marland (2014) showed that the PMO's Photos of the Day page framed Harper as a hard-working head of government, both nationally and internationally, who is also a personable, regular family man (there are many photos of Harper's wife, children, and cats). In this way, it does not appear that digital technologies have made party politics less candidate focused. Rather, the visual imperatives of the Internet have created new opportunities to promote and brand party leaders to the public and the media.

While there is evidence that Canadian parties do use digital technologies to provide substantive policy information, a couple of caveats need to be made. First, despite all the political information put online by parties, it is questionable whether Canadians are consuming it. Data from the 2014 Canadian Online Citizenship Survey[5] find that very few Canadians actually go to the websites and social media pages of parties and politicians. Only 13 per cent of survey respondents had visited a political party's or politician's website in the year previous (Jansen et al. 2014). The numbers for social media are even lower: 6 per cent of respondents friended or followed a political actor on Facebook, while less than 4 per cent followed one on Twitter. Given that surveys such as this tend to overrepresent the politically interested, these are probably optimistic projections. This brings us to the second caveat: even though parties can bypass the traditional media through digital technologies and communicate directly with the public, this does not necessarily mean that parties want to or should. The fact that so few Canadians are visiting parties' websites and social media means that the traditional media are important targets of digital information produced by parties. The tweets, policy statements, emails, and photos are just as much for journalists as they are for citizens. For instance, Marland (2012, 222) suggests that the objective of the prime minister's photo website is to "achieve pickup in national media, in community publications, on news aggregators and on blogs, as well as to attract visits to the PM's Web site."

In terms of the quantity and quality of online information produced by Canadian parties, evidence of both innovation and normalization exist. To be sure, Canadian parties produce a lot of political content on a lot of digital platforms, and much of that content is policy oriented. In some ways, digital technologies do have the ability to counteract the limited issue focus found in the traditional media. For those who want information about party politics, it is available online. At the same time, however, there has not been a reduction in candidate-focused communication in the Internet age. Leaders are important offline on television and in the print media and they remain important online. Indeed, parties themselves have become the purveyors of online leader-focused content, especially on social media.

Dimension 4: Positive Campaigning

Negativity has always been an important aspect of Canadian party politics. In negative campaigning, the candidate focuses on the opposition, both in terms of policy or leadership, rather than his or her own positive attributes or polices (Buell and Sigelman 2008). Recent election campaigns have been dominated by negative television ads, and parties are also now going negative in between elections as well (Rose 2012). If the innovation hypothesis were true, the level of attack politics would be dramatically reduced online as compared to television or radio; online, parties and candidates would engage in positive and self-referential communication. If negative campaigning on television alienates voters, as some claim, digital technologies would increase the quality of political communication (Klotz 2004). Other scholars suggest a normalization of negative campaigning (i.e., similar levels of off- and online negativity) is more likely to occur. Druckman, Kifer, and Parkin (2010) suggest that since websites are targeted to supporters rather than the general public, candidates may go negative because it may stimulate donating, volunteering, and voting.

Contrary to the expectations of the innovation hypothesis, Canadian parties have long used websites to target opponents (Small 2012b). One of the first such sites was www.mikeharris.com, created by the Ontario Liberal Party in the 1999 provincial election. The site targeted then-Premier Mike Harris. The address of the Liberal site was similar to Harris's actual website (www.mikeharrispc.com). Visitors who typed in the wrong address would find an anti-Harris message. Negative microsites have been a feature of Canadian political communication ever since. At the federal level, the Liberal Party has created StephenHarperSaid.ca (2004), Scandalpedia (2008), and Cheque Republic (2010). Every leader of the federal Liberal Party has been targeted by a federal Conservative Party microsite: TeamMartinSaid.ca (2004), Not a Leader (2008), The Dion Tax Trick (2008), Ignatieff Me! (2010), and Justin Over His Head (2012). In the 2011 Ontario election, the provincial Liberals created three attack sites while the Progressive Conservatives created one

(Cross et al. 2015). Negative microsites feature things such as negative online ads, excerpts of media articles that critique the leader (usually taken out of context), and snippets of comments made by the targeted party member or leader (usually with little context). The sites are branded differently than regular party websites, avoiding traditional party colours or logos.

Canadian parties have also used online videos and YouTube to go negative. While ads on television are the norm in electoral politics, online videos have become an alternative venue for political ads. The free posting of online videos on sites like YouTube allows parties, candidates, interest groups, and the public to post professionally made or amateur video at any time. The 2006 federal election provides an infamous example. The federal Liberals "inadvertently" posted an ad on its website that claimed the Conservative Party wanted to increase the military presence by putting soldiers "with guns" in Canadian cities. Even though the "Soldiers" ad never aired on television, it became a national news story and the Liberal campaign was painted as incompetent and disorganized (Clarkson 2006, 193). Despite being removed from the Liberal website almost immediately, the ad can still be viewed on YouTube.[6] Negative YouTube videos that were never aired on television were also created in recent campaigns in Nova Scotia, British Columbia, and Quebec. While academic research on online negativity in Canada is scant, there is much anecdotal evidence to suggest that Canadian parties have been engaging in this behaviour almost as long as they have been using the Internet. Digital technologies have not innovated or changed the behaviour of Canadian parties; the negative tone of offline politics has simply moved online.

Dimension 5: Interactivity

One of the fundamental advantages that digital technologies have over traditional media is interactivity (Mossberger and Tolbert 2012). In traditional media, such as television, radio, and newspapers, information flows from one to many in a single direction, from top to bottom. Digital information is multidirectional. Like the traditional media, online information can flow from top to bottom but it can also flow from bottom to top. And information may be shared from one to many (e.g., a blog), one to a few (e.g., Facebook), or one to one (e.g., email or texting). In politics, interactivity may lead to "more direct communication and a higher responsiveness" between political actors and the public (Schweitzer 2008, 451). For some, interactivity is a tool for plebiscitary or direct democracy by allowing citizens to initiate, deliberate, and vote online. Others, however, look to interactivity as a way of revitalizing representative institutions by facilitating direct communication between the public and governments and political parties (Norris 2001).

In one of the earliest published works on Canadian digital politics, Darin Barney (2005, 140) concluded that Canadian political parties were "very reluctant to pursue with vigour and creativity" the interactive potential of the Internet. In the early years of the Internet, parties did not engage in online participatory exercises with the public. Subsequent research on party websites in elections confirmed this finding. Studies of major party websites in the 2004 and 2006 federal elections found that interactive elements such as discussion boards, online polls, and blogs were uncommon (Kernaghan 2007; Small et al. 2008), although smaller parties, such as the Bloc Québécois and the Green Party, were more interactive. For instance, on the Bloc site in 2004, there was a comment section at the conclusion of campaign stories similar to what is found on media sites today.

Similar findings exist in provincial politics. Jansen's (2004) analysis of candidate websites in the 2001 Alberta and British Columbia elections found that only the most rudimentary forms of interactivity, like online contact forms, were made available, while deeper interactive tools were extremely rare. In a study of the 2007 Quebec provincial election, Bastien and Greffet (2009) analyzed the websites of parliamentary and nonparliamentary parties on three dimensions: information, interactivity, and mobilization. They found that Quebec's parties, whether they had a seat in the National Assembly or not, scored lowest on interactivity compared to information and mobilization.[7]

We are now in the era of social media. Social media allows users to create, share, collaborate, and communicate with other users. Whereas websites are "read only," social media are "read–write." This does not mean that collaboration, participation, and interactivity were nonexistent online before social media, it is just that these characteristics are now built directly into the architecture of social media. Consider how easy it is for a person to take a photo with a smartphone and instantly upload the photo to Instagram, Facebook, or Twitter. Social media sites are thought to have inherent democratic capabilities. Effing, van Hillegersberg, and Huibers (2011, 30) suggest that governments, politicians, and political parties could use social media to "create opportunities for political participation" and "enabling, engaging and empowering" the public. Barack Obama's 2008 presidential campaign may be the textbook social media campaign. In addition to his own social networking site MyBo (My.BarackObama.com), the Obama campaign used a multitude of other social media sites such as Twitter and Facebook. The Obama campaign turned social media into a "virtual organization" that enabled them to "get out the vote," solicit much-needed financial contributions, and identify and mobilize the grassroots supporters, especially young people (Cogburn and Espinoza-Vasquez 2011, 209).

With regards to interactivity, many researchers have explored whether the introduction of social media has made Canadian parties more open. The answer is not straightforward—it can depend on the type of social media being used and the type of political party using it. Let's start with Facebook. In some ways, Facebook does force parties to open up and be more interactive. The "News Feed" function on Facebook operates the same whether you are an individual or an organization. This means that when a party posts to the News Feed, supporters and friends are able to "Like" it or leave a comment. Comments made to Canadian parties on Facebook include posts of support or criticism, broader discussions of the post, questions, and responses by commenters to previous comments. Canadians do seem to take advantage of the opportunity to provide feedback to parties. For instance, Small (2012a) conducted a two-month analysis of the use of Facebook by four federal parliamentary parties and their leaders in 2010. During the analysis period, supporters liked or commented more than 9,000 times. However, the study did not laud Facebook interactivity. Despite all the comments and questions posted by friends, parties tended not to respond to them. The interaction or conversation was strictly one sided, creating what Sweetser and Lariscy (2008, 193) call a dialogic façade. The analysis even found that some parties disabled the "Post" function, which allows others to "Write something on this page," thus also limiting interactivity. Indeed, at the time of writing, most of the Facebook pages of the major federal parties and leaders did not allow friends to "Write something on this page." By removing or limiting this feature, the parties can remain in control of the political message. Similar results were found in the 2011 Ontario provincial election, where Facebook friends contributed 47,000 likes and more than 20,000 comments on the pages of the three main Ontario party leaders (Cross et al. 2015). The Facebook pages of the Ontario Liberal and Progressive Conservative leaders were unresponsive and limited independent posts, though the NDP leader's page was far more interactive. The NDP campaign (not the leader) responded to a select few comments, and supporters/friends were able to post their own thoughts. So Facebook can force parties to be more open. This is because the ability to comment on and like a post is native to Facebook, which means that friends can provide feedback whether the parties like it or not. At the same time, there is evidence of parties' pre–social media behaviour. Deep interaction between parties and the public does not occur regularly on Facebook.

Interactivity on Twitter by Canadian parties is also not straightforward. Here it is not about how interactive tools are built into the site; rather, there is some evidence that suggests the type of party using Twitter will indicate how open or closed the Twitter feed is. At first glance there appears to be a good level of interactivity in the 2011 federal election. One in three tweets made by the five main party leaders was considered interactive or social (Small 2014). However, on closer inspection the data show that one leader—Elizabeth May of the Green Party—significantly skews the level of interaction in the campaign. Fifty-five per cent of May's tweets are interactive, compared to an average of 18 per cent for the other four leaders. While more than half of the tweets produced by the Green leader were attempts to engage followers, the number of interactive tweets for the other leaders ranged from as low as 13 per cent (Gilles Duceppe of the Bloc) to a high of 24 per cent (Michael Ignatieff of the Liberals). Typically a social tweet involves the party/leader answering a specific question posed by a follower, usually providing links to related information, including the election platform or event calendar. Other social tweets acknowledge and thank the followers for their well wishes. While the Green leader may be an outlier in Canada, she is not internationally. Previous research shows that Green parties worldwide are more advanced and interactive online than other parties (Ward, Gibson, and Nixon 2003). Indeed, in the 2011 Ontario election 32 per cent of tweets by the Green Party of Ontario were interactive compared to 18 per cent of interactive tweets by the NDP and 7 per cent by the Liberals (Giasson and Small, 2014). The precarious electoral position of Green parties or their progressive ideology provides them with a greater incentive to use digital technologies effectively and innovatively (Vaccari 2013; Ward et al. 2003). As noted, the main purpose of Twitter for parties is information provision, not interaction; when it comes to federal politics in Canada, Twitter is the "not-so-social network" (Small 2014, 102).

The hypothesis that different types of parties use Twitter differently has also been tested in the province of Quebec. Giasson et al. (2013) examined the Twitter feeds of parties in the 2012 provincial election. While information provision was central, they found that 40 per cent of tweets were social or interactive. Like the federal parties, some parties were considerably more interactive than others. The three major parties in that campaign were more cautious in their social use of Twitter; less than 10 per cent of tweets by the governing Parti libéral du Québec were social, compared to 25 per cent for the Coalition Avenir Québec (CAQ) and 40 per cent for the Parti Québécois (PQ). Like Elizabeth May, more than half of the tweets of the two smaller parties, Québec solidaire (QS) and Option nationale (ON), were interactive, at 64 and 62 per cent respectively. In fact, the two minor parties are twice as likely to be interactive compared to the major parties. While there are similarities between these findings and the findings of the federal leaders discussed earlier, Giasson and colleagues also note party differences that are specific to the Quebec party system. Left-leaning and mass parties

(PQ, ON, QS) all make more social use of Twitter than right-of-centre and elite-based parties (QLP and CAQ). Overall, they conclude that ideology and electability affect how Quebec parties used Twitter during the campaign.

It would be a mistake to suggest that deep interactive events never happen in Canadian politics. For instance, former Conservative leader Stephen Harper held a Q&A session on YouTube in 2010. More recently, in 2014, Liberal leader Justin Trudeau participated in an online video chat with students in Ontario. It is nevertheless fair to suggest that these events are few and far between. Despite the introduction of social media, the level of engagement between the parties and supporters remains relatively low. To be sure, social media opens up the opportunity for citizens to provide comments and feedback to parties, allowing them to interact with other members of the public about political issues. But the major political parties, the ones that most people vote for and have an affiliation with, tend to be unresponsive on social media.

Dimension 6: Narrowcasting

Narrowcasting or *targeting* refers to the practice of "sending particular political messages to particular people" (Howard 2005, 158). This occurs all the time on digital technologies. If you search for a product on Google, you may subsequently get ads on other websites for that product. Narrowcasting can also occur through personalization or customization. That is, websites can offer tools that allow for personalized content to be displayed. According to the innovation hypothesis, narrowcasting would empower users by increasing their control over content.

Canadian parties narrowcast offline. For instance, Turcotte (2012) notes that the Conservative Party of Canada has engaged in a process called "hypersegmentation," where the party determines segments of voters using data mining and opinion polling and then targets specific campaign messages to them. The NDP did similar narrowcasting of messages in the lead up to its massive success in the 2011 election (Lavigne 2013). Canadian parties operate very sophisticated voter databases, such as Liberalist, Populus, and the Conservatives' Constituent Information Management System. And the growth of robocalling[8] by political parties, between and during campaigns, is another example of offline narrowcasting.

Of all the areas discussed in this chapter, online narrowcasting by Canadian political parties is the least researched by scholars. This is in part because it is difficult to systematically assess individualized information and content on digital technologies. One exception is another study exploring the 2012 Quebec election, where the researchers conducted interviews with political operatives within the Quebec parties to learn about the goals and objectives for digital technologies (Giasson et al. 2014). The interviews indicate that there was some online targeting or narrowcasting in the campaign. For instance, the CAQ invested heavily in targeted ads on Facebook. However, the authors do note that when interviewees discussed online voter targeting and voter data collection, it was usually in reference to what they wanted to do in the future rather than what actually occurred in the 2012 campaign. While narrowcasting or targeting is central to party politics in Canada, we simply do not know enough about it in the online context to reach some conclusion.

Conclusion: The Normalization of Digital Party Politics in Canada

This chapter assessed the relative impact that digital technologies have on party politics in Canada. We have used the dimensions of the innovation hypothesis to determine whether digital technologies have profoundly shifted how Canadian parties do what they do. In other words, has the Internet and social media been innovative in Canadian party politics? On the whole, the evidence from federal and provincial politics shows that Canadian parties are using digital technologies to do what they have always done—normalization has taken place. On several dimensions examined, online politics has done little to transform the quality of political communication in this country. Digital technologies have not contributed to a decrease in candidate or leader-focused politics; in fact, it seems that social media have brought greater attention to party leadership. Nor have digital technologies contributed to a decrease in negative campaigning; rather, Canadian parties have taken advantage of this cheap and efficient way to go negative. Finally, even in the age of social media, the Internet has not made parties more open and participatory. Canadian parties have never really been effective vehicles for citizen participation (Cross 2004). Opportunities for the public to get involved in party affairs are typically limited to leadership races, candidate selection, and policy conventions—all of which are infrequent. The opportunities for public participation in digital party politics are also rare. The one area where there has been a significant innovation is in policy-oriented information dissemination. From websites to tweets to YouTube, parties talk about policy and ideas online. There can be little doubt that digital technologies allow parties to make political information available to those who want it.

The rise of digital politics may not have fundamentally changed the communication practices of Canadian parties, but parties *are* different in the Internet age. Two decades ago, when Canadian parties first began to use digital technologies, television was the dominant medium for reaching the public and the Internet was a novelty. The Internet was seen as something outside the central core of a party's communication strategy. Today, digital technologies are part and parcel of the political, marketing, and communication objectives of Canadian parties (Giasson et al. 2014). To be sure, digital technologies have not replaced television, but it certainly challenges its dominance. Indeed, we are now witnessing a growing integration or hybridization of the old and new media (Chadwick 2013). Canadian parties employ television, media events, websites, social media, radio, pamphlets, and live speeches concurrently and concordantly; digital technologies are just one segment of a vastly complex political communication context in which Canadian parties now operate.

This chapter has drawn on numerous studies on federal and provincial digital politics in Canada. While this literature is growing, it lags far behind research in other Western democracies (especially the United States), and there are many gaps. Perhaps not surprising, most Canadian research focuses on campaigning. However, Canadian parties make use of the Internet and social media each and every day. There has been far less examination into nonelection uses of digital technologies, including during parliamentary sessions, leadership/policy conventions, and in internal party politics. We also know little about digital politics at the subnational levels. Beyond federal politics, digital politics in Quebec has received considerable scholarly attention. Nevertheless, Manitoba, Saskatchewan, Atlantic Canada, and the North are understudied, as are municipal politics. Finally, the use of websites and Twitter has been examined over several campaigns, but less is known about other digital applications. This is not necessarily a Canadian problem but one for the broader study of digital politics. The Internet, as a tool for campaigning, is a moving target and the cool, new app tends to change from election to election. Online videos, especially on YouTube, and email have not yet received scholarly attention despite being used by Canadian parties for many years. We are not convinced that if such gaps did not exist our conclusions regarding the normalization of Canadian politics would be different. Normalization does appear to be taking hold in other political contexts.[9] However, we would certainly benefit from a more complete understanding of digital politics and how Canadian parties engage with digital technologies.

Web Links

Enpolitique.com: www.enpolitique.com
A comparative study of the political web within the French presidential and legislative elections of 2012 and the Quebec elections.

Online Citizenship/Citoyenneté en ligne:

www.oc-cel.ca
Online Citizenship is a project exploring online political activity and democratic citizenship in Canada.

Pew Research Center:

www.pewinternet.org
The Pew Research Center conducts research on the use of digital technologies during American election campaigns.

Politwitter:

http://politwitter.ca
A site that indexes the social media accounts of Canadian federal and provincial politicians.

Notes

1   Aspects of the innovation hypothesis are also referred to as the equalization hypothesis or mobilization hypothesis in the literature.
2   Pippa Norris (2001) points to three types of digital divides. The *global divide* is the divide between industrial and developing countries. The *social divide* refers to divisions within a country, usually related to socioeconomic factors. The *democratic divide* refers to those within a country that use the Internet to engage in politics and those who do not.
3   Hypertext refers to text displayed on an electronic document (e.g., a website, email, or social media site) that is (hyper)linked to other information on another electronic document that the reader can immediately access. Hypertext is a crucial component of the World Wide Web.
4   The leaders were Stephen Harper, Michael Ignatieff, and Jack Layton.
5   The 2014 Canadian Online Citizenship Survey was conducted by Online Citizenship/Citoyenneté en ligne, a project exploring online political activity and democratic citizenship in Canada.
6   The video can be found at www.youtube.com/watch?v=uMsqEph7a8I.
7   The interactivity scale featured 15 items, such as a discussion forum or email link. Twenty-nine items were on the information scale, including party information, speeches, and press releases. Online volunteers, membership, and donations were items included on the mobilization scale of eight items.
8   *Robocalling* refers to prerecorded political messages via telephone. It has been used in Canada with controversy for more than a decade. However, robocalling was linked to voter suppression in the 2011 federal election, with calls to voters falsely telling them that the location of their polling stations had changed. In 2014, a former junior Conservative Party staffer, Michael Sona, was found guilty of violating the Canada Elections Act.
9   See Chapter 4 in Lilleker and Jackson (2013) for a summary of research on the normalization hypothesis.

References

Attallah, Paul, and Angela Burton. 2001. "Television, the Internet, and the Canadian Federal Election of 2000." In *The Canadian General Election of 2000*, edited by Jon H. Pammett and Christopher Dornan, 215–42. Toronto: Dundurn Press.

Barney, Darin. 2005. *Communication Technology*. Vancouver: University of British Columbia Press.

Bastien, Frédérick, and Fabienne Greffet. 2009. "Les campagnes électorales sur Internet: une comparaison entre la France et le Québec." *Hermes* 2: 211–19.

Bentivegna, Sara. 2002. "Politics and New Media." In *The Handbook of New Media*, edited by Leah A. Lievrouw and Sonia Livingstone, 50–61. London: Sage.

Buell, Emmett H., and Lee Sigelman. 2008. *Attack Politics: Negativity in Presidential Campaigns since 1960*. Lawrence: University Press of Kansas.

Carty, R. Kenneth, William Cross, and Lisa Young. 2007. *Rebuilding Canadian Party Politics*. Vancouver: University of British Columbia Press.

Chadwick, Andrew. 2013. *The Hybrid Media System: Politics and Power*. Oxford: Oxford University Press. http://dx.doi.org/10.1093/acprof:oso/9780199759477.001.0001

Chen, Peter John, and Peter Jay Smith. 2010. "Adoption and Use of Digital Media in Election Campaigns: Australia, Canada and New Zealand Compared." *Public Communication Review* 1 (1): 3–26.

Clarkson, Stephen. 2006. "How the Big Red Machine Became the Little Red Machine." In *The Canadian Federal Election of 2006*, edited by Christopher Dornan and Jon H. Pammett, 24–56. Toronto: Dundurn Press.

Cogburn, Derrick L., and Fatima Espinoza-Vasquez. 2011. "From Networked Nominee to Networked Nation: Examining the Impact of Web 2.0 and Social Media on Political Participation and Civic Engagement in the 2008 Obama Campaign." *Journal of Political Marketing* 10 (1–2): 189–213. http://dx.doi.org/10.1080/15377857.2011.540224

Cross, William. 2004. *Political Parties*. Vancouver: University of British Columbia Press.

Cross, William, Jonathan Malloy, Tamara A. Small, and Laura Stephenson. 2015. *Fighting for Votes: Parties, the Media, and Voters in the 2011 Ontario Election*. Vancouver: University of British Columbia Press.

Curry, Bill. 2011. "Canada's First Social Media Election Is on, but Will People Vote?" *Globe and Mail*, March 21. http://www.theglobeandmail.com/news/politics/canadas-first-social-media-election-is-on-but-will-people-vote/article574263/

Druckman, James N., Martin J. Kifer, and Michael Parkin. 2010. "Timeless Strategy Meets New Medium: Going Negative on Congressional Campaign Web Sites, 2002–2006." *Political Communication* 27 (1): 88–103. http://dx.doi.org/10.1080/10584600903502607

Effing, Robin, Jos van Hillegersberg, and Theo Huibers. 2011. "Social Media and Political Participation: Are Facebook, Twitter and YouTube Democratizing Our Political Systems?" Third IFIP WG 8.5 International Conference, ePart 2011, Delft, The Netherlands, August 29–September 1. http://dx.doi.org/10.1007/978-3-642-23333-3_3

Francoli, Mary, Josh Greenberg, and Christopher Waddell. 2011. "The Campaign in the Digital Media." In *The Canadian Federal Election of 2011,* edited by Jon H. Pammett and Christopher Dornan, 219–46. Toronto: Dundurn Press.

Giasson, Thierry, Frédérick Bastien, Mireille Lalancette, and Gildas Le Bars. 2014. "Is Social Media Transforming Canadian Electioneering? Hybridity and Online Partisan Strategies in the 2012 Quebec Election." Annual Meeting of the Canadian Political Science Association, Brock University, St. Catharines, Ontario, May 27–29.

Giasson, Thierry, Gildas Le Bars, Frédérick Bastien, and Mélanie Verville. 2013. "Qc2012: L'utilisation de Twitter par les partis." In *Les Québécois aux urnes: Les partis, les médias et les citoyens en campagne,* edited by Frédérick Bastien, Éric Bélanger, and François Gélineau, 133–46. Montreal: Les Presses de l'Université de Montréal.

Giasson, Thierry, and Tamara A. Small. 2014. "#elections: The Use of Twitter by Provincial Political Parties in Canada." British Association of Canadian Studies, London, UK, April 25.

Howard, Philip N. 2005. "Deep Democracy, Thin Citizenship: The Impact of Digital Media in Political Campaign Strategy." *Annals of the American Academy of Political and Social Science* 597 (1): 153–70. http://dx.doi.org/10.1177/0002716204270139

Jansen, Harold. 2004. "Is the Internet Politics as Usual or Democracy's Future? Candidate Campaign Web Sites in the 2001 Alberta and British Columbia Provincial Elections." *Public Sector Innovation Journal* 9 (2): 1–20.

Jansen, Harold, Frédérick Bastien, Thierry Giasson, Royce Koop, and Tamara A. Small. 2014. "The Digital Divide Meets the Democratic Divide: The Internet and Democratic Citizenship in Canada." 23rd World Congress of Political Science, Montreal, July 19–24.

Kernaghan, Kenneth. 2007. "Moving Beyond Politics as Usual? Online Campaigning." In *Digital State at the Leading Edge,* edited by Sandford F. Borins, Kenneth Kernaghan, David Brown, Nick Bontis, Perri 6, and Fred Thompson, 183–223. Toronto: University of Toronto Press.

Kippen, Grant. 2000. *The Use of Information Technologies by a Political Party.* Vancouver: SFU-UBC Centre for the Study of Government Business.

Klotz, Robert. 2004. *The Politics of Internet Communication.* Lanham: Rowman & Littlefield Publishers.

Koetsier, John. 2013. "How Google Searches 30 Trillion Web Pages, 100 Billion Times a Month." *Venture Beat,* March 13. http://venturebeat.com/2013/03/01/how-google-searches-30-trillion-web-pages-100-billion-times-a-month/

Larsson, Anders Olof. 2013. "'Rejected Bits of Program Code': Why Notions of 'Politics 2.0' Remain (Mostly) Unfulfilled." *Journal of Information Technology & Politics* 10 (1): 72–85. http://dx.doi.org/10.1080/19331681.2012.719727

Lavigne, Brad. 2013. *Building the Orange Wave: The Inside Story Behind the Historic Rise of Jack Layton and the NDP.* Madeira Park, BC: Douglas & McIntyre.

Lilleker, Darren, and Nigel Jackson. 2013. *Political Campaigning, Elections and the Internet: Comparing the US, UK, France and Germany.* London: Routledge. http://dx.doi.org/10.1093/oxfordhb/9780199589074.013.0019

Margolis, Michael, and David Resnick. 2000. *Politics as Usual: The Cyberspace Revolution.* Thousand Oaks, CA: Sage.

Marland, Alex. 2012. "Political Photography, Journalism, and Framing in the Digital Age the Management of Visual Media by the Prime Minister of Canada." *International Journal of Press/Politics* 17 (2): 214–33. http://dx.doi.org/10.1177/1940161211433838

Marland, Alex. 2014. "The Branding of a Prime Minister." In *Political Communication in Canada: Meet the Press and Tweet the Rest,* edited by Alex Marland, Thierry Giasson, and Tamara A. Small, 55–73. Vancouver: University of British Columbia Press.

Marland, Alex, Thierry Giasson, and Tamara A. Small. 2014. *Political Communication in Canada: Meet the Press and Tweet the Rest.* Vancouver: University of British Columbia Press.

Mendelsohn, Matthew. 1993. "Television's Frames in the 1988 Canadian Election." *Canadian Journal of Communication* 18 (2): 149–71.

Mossberger, Karen, and Caroline J. Tolbert. 2012. "How Politics Online Is Changing Electoral Participation." In *The Oxford Handbook of American Elections and Political Behavior,* edited by Jan E. Leighley, 200–18. New York: Oxford University Press.

Norris, Pippa. 2001. *Digital Divide: Civic Engagement, Information Poverty, and the Internet Worldwide.* New York: Cambridge University Press. http://dx.doi.org/10.1017/CBO9781139164887

Rose, Jonathan. 2012. "Are Negative Ads Positive? Political Advertising and the Permanent Campaign." In *How Canadians Communicate IV: Media and Politics,* edited by David Taras and Christopher Waddell, 159–68. Athabasca, AB: Athabasca University Press.

Schweitzer, Eva Johanna. 2008. "Innovation or Normalization in e-Campaigning? A Longitudinal Content and Structural Analysis of German Party Websites in the 2002 and 2005 National Elections." *European Journal of Communication* 23 (4): 449–70. http://dx.doi.org/10.1177/0267323108096994

Small, Tamara A. 2004. "Parties@canada: The Internet and the 2004 Cyber-Campaign." In *The Canadian General Election of 2004,* edited by Jon H. Pammett and Christopher Dornan, 203–34. Toronto: Dundurn Press.

Small, Tamara A. 2012a. "Are We Friends Yet? Relationship Marketing on the Internet." In *Political Marketing in Canada,* edited by Alex Marland, Thierry Giasson, and Jennifer Lees-Marshment, 193–208. Vancouver: University of British Columbia Press.

Small, Tamara A. 2012b. "E-ttack Politics: Negativity, the Internet, and Canadian Political Parties." In *How Canadians Communicate IV: Media and Politics,* edited by David Taras and Christopher Waddell, 169–88. Athabasca, AB: Athabasca University Press.

Small, Tamara A. 2014. "The Not-so-Social Network: The Use of Twitter by Canada's Party Leaders." In *Political Communication in Canada: Meet the Press and Tweet the Rest,* edited by Alex Marland, Thierry Giasson, and Tamara A. Small, 92–108. Vancouver: University of British Columbia Press.

Small, Tamara A., David Taras, and Dave Danchuk. 2008. "Canada: Party Websites and Online Campaigning during the 2004 and 2006 Federal Election." In *Making a Difference: A Comparative View of the Role of the Internet in Election Politics,* edited by Stephen Ward, Diana Owen, Richard Davis, and David Taras, 113–31. Lanham, MD: Lexington Press.

Sweetser, Kaye D., and Ruthann Weaver Lariscy. 2008. "Candidates Make Good Friends: An Analysis of Candidates' Uses of Facebook." *International Journal of Strategic Communication* 2 (3): 175–98. http://dx.doi.org/10.1080/15531180802178687

Trimble, Linda, and Shannon Sampert. 2004. "Who's in the Game? The Framing of Election 2000 by the *Globe and Mail* and the *National Post*." *Canadian Journal of Political Science* 37 (1): 51–71. http://dx.doi.org/10.1017/S0008423904040028

Turcotte, André. 2012. "Under New Management: Market Intelligence and the Conservative Party's Resurrection." In *Political Marketing in Canada,* edited by Alex Marland, Thierry Giasson, and Jennifer Lees-Marshment, 76–90. Vancouver: University of British Columbia Press.

Vaccari, Cristian. 2013. *Digital Politics in Western Democracies: A Comparative Study.* Baltimore: Johns Hopkins University Press.

Vergeer, Maurice, Liesbeth Hermans, and Steven Sams. 2013. "Online Social Networks and Micro-Blogging in Political Campaigning: The Exploration of a New Campaign Tool and a New Campaign Style." *Party Politics* 19 (3): 477–501. http://dx.doi.org/10.1177/1354068811407580

Ward, Stephen, Rachel Gibson, and Paul Nixon. 2003. "Parties and the Internet: An Overview." In *Political Parties and the Internet: Net Gain?*, edited by Rachel Kay Gibson, Paul G. Nixon, and Stephen J. Ward, 11–38. London: Routledge.

19

Participation, Mobilization, and the Political Engagement of the Internet Generation

HENRY MILNER

HOW HAVE STRUCTURAL TRANSFORMATIONS, AND in particular the advent of the digital age, affected how young people relate to politics? In answering this question in this chapter, the focus will be on Canada, but this is a phenomenon common to the Internet generation in all developed democracies. While people of all ages use the Internet, only one generation so far grew up with it (see Milner 2010). From what we know, compared to the rest of the population, the Internet generation is less attentive to politics and participates in it less. While the generation gap in informed political participation predates the Internet, there is good reason to believe that the gap has grown significantly with the arrival of the Internet generation—a paradoxical state of events given the proficiency of the Internet generation at accessing information.

This suggests that we are witnessing two contradictory developments. On the one hand, among young people there are proportionally more political dropouts (those excluded from informed political participation) than in the other age cohorts. On the other, the minority of young people who are interested in politics have in the Internet a basis for being more easily and fully informed than previous generations of youth. The result is that a new and deeper digital divide has emerged. No longer primarily one of access to digital communications, it is rather a gap between those for whom it provides a bridge to informed political participation and those for whom it is a moat.

If this is so, given that the Internet is here to stay, the challenge is to narrow the digital divide by finding ways to use digital technologies for the purposes of civic education. This is a fundamental challenge for contemporary democracies since, ultimately, it is the choices of emerging generations that will determine the future of our democratic systems.

Forms of Political Participation

Political participation is viewed in the literature under two commonly accepted headings: conventional and unconventional. When it comes to conventional participation—that is, through parties and elections—almost all contemporary democracies have experienced a clear secular decline in recent decades. This is the result of several simultaneous developments. Transformations in family and community have made the young citizen's civic duty to vote and otherwise participate politically less compelling. Associations that tie young people to their local community are being replaced by electronically linked networks that bypass traditional information gatekeepers and authorities. More widely, as we shall see, changes in the communications media have, on balance, impeded attentiveness to political developments.

A particular and early victim of these developments has been party membership. Youth party membership has been dropping for several decades in almost all mature democracies (Scarrow and Gezgor 2010). Canada is certainly no exception (Cross and Young 2008). There is every indication that this tendency toward "professionalization" of party membership— party involvement dwindling to those contemplating careers in politics and members of their networks—will continue with emerging generations.

If party-related activities are relegated to a small insider group of young people, we are left with voting as the expression of conventional political participation. Such political participation is dependent on a politically knowledgeable citizenry, what I term *civic literacy* (Milner 2002). While compulsory voting can boost the number of voters, there is no real indication that it raises the number of informed citizens (Loewen, Milner, and Hicks 2008). Attaining a minimal familiarity with the relevant institutions of decision making, combined with a basic knowledge of the key positions on relevant issues and some ability to distinguish the key political actors holding them, entails attentiveness to the political world primarily via the information media. It is the schools, through civic education, that must increasingly replace the family in nurturing the habits and skills needed for effective media attentiveness.

Establishing the link between Internet use and informed political participation is difficult, since we are trying to pin down a moving and largely invisible target. We can use surveys to ask a sample of people about their Internet usage or quantify certain kinds of "hits," but we can only speculate on how these reflect the overall gamut of relevant activities in cyberspace. On the other side of the equation, apart from turnout, we rely on tests of political knowledge to capture the information/attentiveness dimension of informed political participation. It is the least imperfect of such indicators since, unlike other survey-based measures such as interest in politics or political efficacy, it is objective.

As far as unconventional participation is concerned, the inherent difficulties in quantifying and thus comparing it to conventional modes of political participation have become even greater with the advent of the digital age. There is no clear, agreed-upon line between what is political and what is not. As Aaron Smith et al. (2009) put it: "A social networking site like Facebook is more a forum for political talk than for organized political effort ... 'Friending' a candidate is not the same as working in a campaign." However it is defined, a crucial element of unconventional political participation is still political knowledge. For example, if signing a petition on the environment is to be meaningful, it must involve some knowledge of the relevant parties' record and position on environmental issues.

One thing we do know from numerous empirical studies is that unconventional participation is not meaningfully compensating for declining conventional participation[1] (see Kavadias, Elchardus, and De Groof 2011; Quinlan 2011) and cannot be expected to do so. Hence the emphasis here is on the latter. We thus use reported and registered turnout as our indicator of conventional participation, while we treat indicators of political knowledge as reflecting unconventional as well as conventional participation. Since the point of any meaningful political involvement is to affect political reality, uninformed unconventional participation is ultimately a contradiction. In saying this, we need to add that the questions used to measure political knowledge tend to be skewed toward conventional forms, something to which comparative analysis must be sensitive.

Declining Youth Turnout

There is no shortage of data showing a worrisome gap between the electoral participation of current and previous generations. Even allowing for the possibility that the young, overall, are less likely to report voting when they have not done so, the gap in reported voting well exceeds any estimate of overreporting turnout by adults (see, for example, Garcia Albacete 2014). While not all countries quite fit this depiction, the overall generational data provide a picture of how turnout has been declining over three generations, a development independent of the normal life cycle pattern.[2] (We return to the factors explaining this generational decline below.)

Detailed Canadian turnout data confirm this trend, though the decline is more gradual. As we can see in Table 19.1, from a paper published for Elections Canada (Blais and Loewen 2011), compared to the generation reaching voting age before the 1990s, the Internet generation votes significantly less at 18 *and* continues to do so at 35.

Table 19.1   Percentage of Voter Turnout by Election Cohort

	Election Cohort												
	1965	1968	1974	1979	1980	1984	1988	1993	1997	2000	2004	2006	2008
1965	69	71	71	79	75	82	84	85	81	78	79	80	76
1968	70	71	80	75	83	85	85	82	79	80	81	77	
1972	60	71	65	75	78	79	75	72	73	75	70		
1974	56	68	62	73	76	77	74	70	72	74	69		
1979	60	54	66	70	72	68	64	66	68	63			
1980	45	57	62	64	61	57	59	62	56				
1984	58	63	65	62	58	60	63	58					
1988	54	57	53	50	53	56	50						
1993	53	49	46	49	52	47							
1997	43	40	43	47	42								
2000	34	37	41	36									
2004	34	38	34										

Note: Dates on the horizontal axis represent the year each cohort reached voting age. Those on the vertical axis represent election years.

Source: Blais and Loewen (2011, 13).

The decline is concentrated among young people of low education. US data confirming this can be found in a recent article by Owen and Soule (2011), while for Europe, a recent study found that

> In general, the young vote at much lower rates than the age-group between 30 and 65. At the same time, however, turnout differences are much more pronounced for those below 30. . . . Young adults with low levels of education are the most likely abstainers in national elections, whereas the highly educated participate at much higher rates everywhere. In countries such as Great Britain, France and Switzerland, only one out of three of those with low education below the age of 30 reports to have voted in the last general election, whereas at least 60 percent of the highly educated claim to have done so. In countries with high average turnout rates, almost nine of 10 of those with higher education report to have voted—even among the young. (Abendschön, Roßteutscher, and Schäfer 2014, 9)

The relationship with education is telling. Clearly, turnout decline is simultaneously age and knowledge related. In the rest of the chapter I focus on political knowledge as an indicator of informed political participation, though anyone in doubt as to the close relationship between the two, when

Figure 19.1 Association between Political Knowledge and Voting Behaviour, Canada 2011

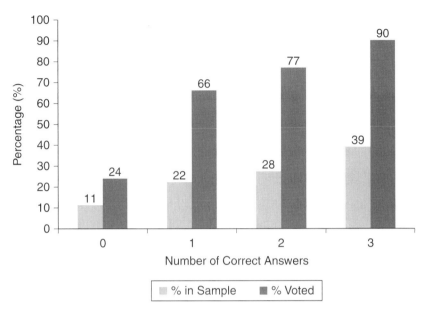

Respondents (aged 18 to 34) to the National Youth Survey were asked three questions to test their political knowledge:

- "Which party won the most seats in the general election held on May 2?"
- "What level of government has primary responsibility for education (federal, provincial, or municipal)?"
- "What is the name of your provincial (territorial) premier?"

Of the sample asked, 39 per cent answered all three questions correctly; 11 per cent answered none correctly. The percentage of respondents who answered no questions right and who voted was 24. Among those who answered all the questions correctly, 90 per cent voted.

Source: National Youth Survey, http://www.elections.ca/content.aspx?section=res&dir=rec/part/nysr&document=p3&lang=e#a55

it comes to young people, should find Figure 19.1, from a study for Elections Canada (2011), instructive.

In a recent paper using data from the Australian Election Studies 2001, 2007, and 2010, Gibson and McAllister (2014) measured the political knowledge gap[3] over three Australian elections, finding that while usage of the Internet is becoming more socially dispersed, use of the Internet to follow election news is becoming more socially concentrated and contributes to a wide and growing knowledge gap. In 2001, the knowledge gap associated with Internet usage was around one question out a total of six; by 2010 it had increased to one-and-a-half questions. Moreover, the rise in the mean level of knowledge of those most actively consuming political information online was only marginal (0.13 on the 0–6 scale) between 2001 and 2010. The real change was among those with low to no consumption of such information, whose average level of political knowledge actually declined in absolute terms from a mean of 1.96 questions to 1.64, a difference of 0.32. In other words, while Internet use has grown, with the exception of those who use it expressly to acquire political knowledge, it has contributed to a measurable decline in political knowledge. As the authors put it, "These results provide strong support for the hypothesis that greater media choice, reflected particularly in the availability of political information through the Internet, is fostering a growing gap in political knowledge across the electorate." They add that those who make little to no effort to source information online are increasingly falling behind in the information acquisition stakes, while those who "know more" are continuing to accumulate and increase their store of knowledge. As suggested above, the Internet, while not necessarily causing the gap, is significantly contributing to it by discriminating ever more strongly between uninformed and informed voters in their choice of online content.

Political knowledge questions have been included in the national election surveys associated with the Comparative Study of Electoral Systems (CSES)[4] since the first wave was conducted in the 1990s through to the ongoing fourth wave, in which there are four standardized political knowledge questions. We do not have data beyond the 2008 election for Canada, but the overall trend did not differ significantly from the general one of CSES countries portrayed in Figure 19.2 below (see Milner 2014a). Starting with the 1997 election, we already see low and declining levels of political knowledge among both 18–25-year-old Canadians and 26–65-year-olds. With individual scores ranging from 0 to 3 correct answers, the average for the younger cohort declined from roughly 1.3 to 1.0 correct answers, while the average for the older group declined slightly less, from 1.6 to 1.4 correct answers.

We now have the results of the three completed rounds as well as several surveys from the ongoing fourth round. This allows us to be more selective, comparing like with like. Taking together all the responses through the four rounds in the long-standing democracies in the CSES (Australia, Austria, Canada, Finland, France, Germany, Great Britain, Iceland, Ireland, Israel, Japan, Netherlands, New Zealand, Norway, Portugal, Spain, Sweden, Switzerland, Taiwan, and the United States) yields a total of 102,783 respondents.

The CSES data fit neatly into five-year intervals for the first three rounds, with a final category composed of the current fourth round that began in 2011. Because each period contains the results of many different countries, the effect of these fluctuations is significantly diminished. Figure 19.2 sums

Figure 19.2 Knowledge Gap between Young (18–25) and Older (26–65) Voters, 1996–2013

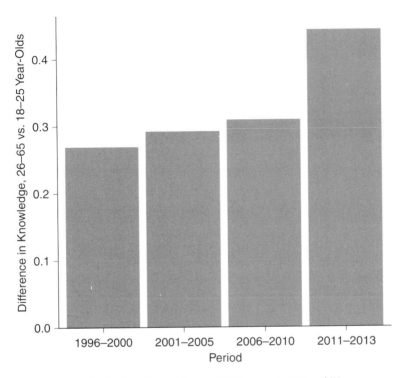

Source: Comparative Study of Electoral Systems (CSES), waves I, II, III, and IV.

up the data in this manner, setting out the average difference between the two age groups for all the surveys carried out in each period.[5] As expected, we can see a steady increase, with the generational difference rising from about a quarter of a question to almost half a question from the earliest to the latest period.

The Media: Old and New

We now turn to explaining the developments captured in charts like those in Figures 19.1 and 19.2. As noted, it is in the area of communications media that the most important changes affecting the informed participation of young citizens have taken place. Young people reaching adulthood in the 1990s grew up in a world fundamentally transformed by the revolution in communications technology from that of earlier generations. The digital revolution in information and communications technology, combining the home computer, wireless links, mobile devices, and the high-speed Internet, radically transformed the patterns of media use. This latest transformation is unique—indeed revolutionary—in its comprehensive and multidimensional character and its simultaneous and integrated transformation of the medium of communication and the nature of the content.

As a medium of information, the Internet is sometimes compared to television, but the analogy only holds with the arrival of the remote control device and the expansion of viewing options through cable and satellite transmission. It is at this point that the effect of watching TV on political knowledge and political participation emerges. Prior (2007, 126) found that the choice presented by cable TV fundamentally altered the effect of TV watching on political knowledge and political participation for those for whom television was a medium of entertainment rather than information. The "political knowledge of respondents without access to cable or Internet is unrelated to their degree of preference for entertainment; for those with access to cable television, on the other hand, moving from low to high entertainment preference corresponds to a 20 percent drop in political knowledge." In a complementary earlier study, Bellamy and Walker (1996) found that pre–remote control generations were more deliberate in choosing what to watch. And newspaper readers who really were only interested in sports or the social pages were exposed to news headlines in much the same way that TV consumers before the advent of the remote control would be tuned to network news even when they were only interested in Ed Sullivan. With the invention of the remote control this changed.

The remote control, video cassettes, and the personal channel repertoires that cable and satellite TV providers offered subscribers allowed viewers, with minimal or no effort, to avoid political news. This resulted in a deeper political knowledge gap between those who seek news and those who avoid it. Combined with a decline in newspaper readership, there was a fundamental shift in information dissemination. As Internet-based communications technologies emerged, the process widened. TV watching is to some extent a social activity: others take notice when one family member watches the news. Connecting to the Internet is a private activity. Over time, an externally imposed order associated with the linear logic of the newspaper as well as pre-remote television—especially public television and radio—increasingly gave way to one where the content is internally selected, ordered, and potentially created.

The new digital information and communications technologies have brought about a more comprehensive and multidimensional transformation in the very nature of the content (combining sound, text, and graphics), which has led to vastly expanded choice and, consequently, even greater ease at news-avoiding choice. Low-cost, high-speed Internet access provides the physical capacity to retrieve and exchange digital content as text, sounds, still and moving pictures, and various types of graphics—anytime, anywhere, with anyone. Beyond emails and text messaging, users can manoeuvre effectively through blogs, podcasts, social networking services, digital petitions, and wikis (online documents written and edited by volunteers), choosing to join certain online communities, message boards, and so on.

Despite hopes of closing this skill-based digital divide, the positive effects of such initiatives seem to have largely been confined to young people of higher social class and educational attainment (Sloam 2007). Di Gennaro and Dutton (2006) found that Internet experience and proficiency had a significant impact on whether one becomes politically engaged online, but that online political participation reinforced and, in some cases, exacerbated existing social inequalities in offline political participation. So far, cross-national research suggests that the hopes of creators of youth-oriented civic and political sites—that the Internet would re-engage the young in the public sphere—have not been realized.

All in all, it would appear that daunting obstacles remain to the Internet becoming a source of political information for as wide a segment of the population as were newspapers and (pre-multichannel) television, obstacles no longer primarily in the form of access. The skills involved in making judgments using digital information and tools are unequally distributed along the usual class lines. Moreover, there appear to be important cross-national differences, which are largely based on efforts to narrow the gap through policies designed to disseminate the needed knowledge and skills. When asked (in the 2000 Canadian Election Study) if they ever used the Internet to inform themselves about politics, by far the most important discriminating factor was education, with income second (Gidengil et al. 2004, 33).[6] The limited evidence suggests a parallel to Prior's above-noted finding of the effects of the widened choice provided by cable television, namely that increased Internet access widens the gap in informed political participation between people looking for news and those looking for other things.

Even those actively seeking information are not certain to find it if they lack the necessary skills to do so. Consumers of information are flooded with free content produced by amateurs, much of it consciously blurring the line between news and opinion. We cannot expect a generation that downloads its music and other media content for free to be willing to pay what is required to sustain professional news reporting. Hence, increasingly freed of the "gatekeepers" in the professional media, how can ordinary web users be assumed to be able to distinguish the "facts" that the many conspiracy theorists purvey on the web from real facts? While it is true that the Internet facilitates the fact-checking of dubious assertions, it is not at all clear that we can count on young citizens to be sufficiently motivated or sophisticated to check assumptions against facts. The Internet makes it easier than either television or radio to emulate the prototypical Fox News watcher and talk-show listener, selecting online sources that skew information to reinforce assumptions and prejudices.[7]

What is not in question is that the Internet is here to stay as the basic media information environment for emerging generations. Thus the fundamental challenge is to ensure that those lacking an information-rich family or community environment—the potential political dropouts—gain the skills appropriate for that environment. Before addressing this question, we need to consider another dimension of young people's reliance on Internet-based communications, namely political mobilization.

Political Mobilization and the Internet Generation

Returning to what the academic literature describes as "unconventional" political participation, we turn briefly to youth-focused activities that in an earlier time were termed *extra-parliamentary* or simply *protest politics*. Leaving aside the passive elements of unconventional participation, such as signing online petitions (which allow for no clear line between what is political and what is not), here we are interested in what is most commonly defined as *political mobilization*. In the "old" model of such mobilization, activists, a distinct minority of the population, seek to win over public opinion through demonstrations, protests, boycotts, and the like that place pressure on political actors (legislators, parties, candidates, etc.). Such activities constitute a legitimate dimension of democratic participation, means by which popular concerns disregarded by conventional actors enter the political arena. But extra-parliamentary movements must be capable of refining goals and tactics in the context of evolving developments that they need to be informed about.

While it is true that, overall, survey data show no generalized replacement of conventional by unconventional forms of participation on the part of the Internet generation, there is another dimension to this issue, namely instances of rapid and intense mobilization. This is not the place to try to evaluate the extent of this phenomenon, a matter on which there is nothing even close to an established consensus in the literature. We can say that such mobilization, once it reaches a certain point of intensity, takes on a logic of its own, a logic of self-expression. The process is both more individualized and immediate, with those involved defining and identifying goals and means in personal terms based on their own experiences at the moment. Attention is focused more on events that are visually engaging on a screen (and therefore typically conflictual) and less on the relevant facts, objectives, and means of attaining them. In the social networks, content that is immediately striking to people rises to the top via "liking," "retweeting," and so on. And apparently once the mobilization ends, it leaves little trace in the form of future informed political participation.

We can see these tendencies in a particularly relevant case: the Quebec student strike of spring 2012, which closed down college and university faculties (see Milner 2014b). In the beginning it appeared to be a straightforward demand by students to defend accessibility against a tuition boost. But the logic of politics was soon replaced by another dynamic, one of intensification that was unrelated to any negotiations or concessions. The changing and at times contradictory, but immediate and intense, demands are the natural expression of what might be termed *social media politics*. What was constant and consistent was maintaining mobilization. In their interviews with some of the students, Dufour and Savoie (2013) found a strong emotional response: many reacted with rage, and some evoked guilt in the face of mounting social pressure to be even more involved. Though sympathetic to the strikers, Dufour and Savoie admit that the students' tactics alienated many Quebecers:

> At the start of the strike, the population is divided equally between supporting the Government of Quebec and the students. . . . However, throughout the period that follows, marked among other things by the first offers of negotiations, the issue of violence and several events marked by clashes . . . the government rose to enjoy 60 per cent support on May 10. This despite the fact that 71 per cent of Quebecers believed that the Charest government had mismanaged the student conflict. (Dufour and Savoie 2013, 13–14, my translation)

The various tactics of the students clearly served more as self-expression than as a means of placing pressure on political actors. There appeared to be a disconnect between the issues at stake and the mobilization taking place. The conflict ended when, after the government resigned, the opposition Parti Québécois (PQ) squeaked through to form a minority government and cancelled the tuition hike by decree. Relative calm was restored, but the question was left open of what would have happened, given the unwillingness of the student organizations to accept the verdict of the people, had the composition of the government reflected the 58 per cent who voted for parties that opposed the students' demands.

More profoundly, while the conflict boosted turnout in the 2012 election, the effect was short lived. In the election hastily called by the PQ in April 2014, there was no sign of any lasting effect of the mobilization—quite the contrary, in fact. The PQ lost to the Liberals, the party that had brought in the tuition hike, utterly failing to remobilize the youth support from 2012. The PQ ran two student leaders from the 2012 campaign, Léo Bureau-Blouin and Martine Desjardins, both of whom were defeated. A Leger poll in late March in the *Journal de Montréal* showed PQ support among those over 55 to be 13 percentage points higher than among 18–35-year-olds. And very few of the votes lost by the PQ went to the left-wing, pro-student Québec solidaire, whose vote rose from 6 to 7.6 per cent (see Milner 2014a).[8]

While we should be careful not to draw conclusions from a single case, there may be a lesson in this for political parties. But it should lead political parties to pose the question more pointedly as to the kind of political engagement we can expect from a generation that relies on digital sources of information. We return to this question in the final section of this chapter.

Measures to Promote Informed Political Participation of Young Citizens

The challenge is thus to begin to plug the deeper digital divide that has emerged among the Internet generation, to reduce the number of political dropouts via Internet-based technologies, and to boost informed political participation among the Internet generation. There are many projects seeking to bring the public into contact and potential partnership with decision makers in setting agendas and designing policies, implementing them, and monitoring their outcomes. Instruments include e-voting, e-petitions, deliberative polling, electronic town hall meetings, participatory budgeting, and citizen juries. More directly focused on young people are sites that encourage social networking, where young people can find others with similar political interests, vote on posted resolutions, sign petitions, and engage in online discussion of political issues. Cross-national research so far has not found that the hopes of these civic and political sites to re-engage the young in the public sphere have been realized. Overall, their positive contribution is limited by a process of self-selection that favours citizens with superior resources.

Hence we are interested in measures that are targeted widely at the emerging generation—ones that seek to include rather than exclude the potential political dropouts. In the rest of this chapter we summarize what we know about the most important of these, focusing on the experience of countries that have implemented them.

Voting at 16

The most straightforward measures are reforms to the electoral institutions designed to encourage the participation of young people. The most discussed is that of reducing the voting age to 16, especially after the vote in the 2014 Scottish referendum was extended to 16-year-olds. We are not interested here in the issue as one of principle, whether 16- and 17-year-olds are entitled to vote. What concerns us is whether, as argued notably by Franklin (2004), voting is habit forming.[9] We can now draw on the experience of Austria, which has allowed this cohort to vote since 2007. This case shows that, once the novelty has subsided, 16- and 17-year-olds tend to turn out in roughly the same numbers and with the same level of interest—though somewhat lower political knowledge—as 18- and 19-year-olds (Wagner, Johann, and Kritzinger 2012).

We also now have more detailed data emerging from what constitutes a natural experiment taking place in Norway, which allowed 16- and 17-year-olds to vote in 20 municipalities in the 2011 and 2015 local elections. Moreover, data tracing the effects of this participation on turnout in the national election of 2013 in the relevant municipalities have been made available. The evidence is positive insofar as increasing the turnout of first-time voters is concerned: young people are more likely to vote at 16 and 17 than at 18 and 19, though the novelty aspect cannot yet be ruled out entirely (Ødegård, Bergh, and Saglie 2014). However, there is no indication that they are any more informed, and there is real doubt as to any kind of habit being formed based on their experience in voting at 16 and 17 (Bergh 2014). We know that young people are more likely to vote if their parents vote, and that this is more likely to be the case at 16 and 17 when still at home than at 18 and 19 when they are in a state of transition. So we must be skeptical of any claim that voting at 16, in itself, will have any long-term beneficial effect.

Civic Education

This brings us to civic education. There are two key factors that emerge when considering civic education. First, it must make use of digital communications familiar to the Internet generation. And it must not be limited to, or even concentrated on, an elite that has access to the needed resources in the family and community. Wilkenfeld (2009) identifies a "civic engagement gap" among adolescents in the United States associated with students' demographic characteristics. The most disadvantaged are male, black, American Indian, immigrant, and low socioeconomic status (SES) youth, with a cumulative effect on low-SES black males in particular. Moreover, attending a school with a high-SES population is associated with higher civic knowledge even after the individual's own socioeconomic status has been taken into account.[10]

These studies suggest that in a low-civic-literacy country like the United States, civic education is a means by which schools can narrow the informed participation gap between different groups of students. This, however, is less the case for a high-civic-literacy country like Sweden. Ekman and Zetterberg (2010) found that the different school contexts had little effect on the political knowledge or anticipated political participation of 14 year-old Swedish high school students.

Election Simulations

The best known simulations are mock elections. Mock elections were initiated in North America in 1988 by Kids Voting USA, a nonprofit, nonpartisan program in which teachers help students gather information about the candidates and issues. On Election Day, students cast their ballots in special booths, the younger ones going to the polls with their parents. The first such simulation in Canada, known as Student Vote, was conducted in Ontario: students in Grades 9 to 12 in about three-quarters of public high schools cast ballots supplied by Election Ontario identical to those used in the October 2003 provincial election.[11] This was followed by the Canada-wide Student Vote 2004 in 1,168 schools, in which participation was hampered by the fact that the election took place at the end of June, when schools were out.[12] Since then simulations have taken place at both the federal and provincial level. In British Columbia, the fact that the voting date was fixed in advance clearly facilitated Student Vote BC, which took place on 16 May 2005 in 350 schools. Overall, compared to the examples below, Student Vote has had its efforts hampered by uncertainty as to funding as well as unfixed election dates.

Norway, a high-civic-literacy country that has faced a serious generation gap in turnout, provides a contrasting case. The Norwegian *Skolevalg* has been running mock elections since 1989 for parliamentary and local elections. It also carries out a survey of students with a similar survey among a representative population sample before the election. Approximately 70 per cent of all high school students participate in *Skolevalg*, and 30 per cent participate in the election survey (which allows for longitudinal comparison of age differences in attitudes). Overall results are reported online, while school results are distributed to the schools so students can compare their choices with those of their peers. This is also the case in the Swedish version, *Skolval* (School Vote). Here election committees are formed to represent the various parties, with candidates invited to schools to debate the issues. Ballots identical to the official ones are counted in the same fashion as the national vote. In both cases funding is guaranteed and election dates are fixed, so planning can proceed well in advance. In addition, as we shall see below, these and other simulations are integrated into civic education classes.

Parliamentary Simulations

The Scandinavian countries figure prominently among those that have developed youth parliaments. The most innovative aspect of certain of these mock parliaments was the inventive use of committees combined with use of the Internet. Still, direct participation was limited to a relatively small number of young people. Even more promising, therefore, is a parliamentary simulation instrument based on committees. Like here, efforts to bring students into contact with legislative institutions traditionally took the form of student tours of parliamentary buildings combined with lectures informing them about what goes on there. With indications of growing passivity among young people toward traditional forms of political participation, such visits were seen as inadequate.

The response arrived at could serve as a model for democracies like Canada facing even larger democratic deficits. The parliaments of Sweden, Norway, and Denmark created and funded interactive centres that offer students typically aged 15 and 16 the opportunity to experience, through role-playing, the parliamentary committee decision-making process. The centres, located next to the parliaments, include places for party caucus meetings, areas set up to resemble committee rooms, and a larger area for plenary meetings. After suitable preparation in their civics classes before the visit, students meet trained animators (who also work as parliamentary press or information officers) who guide them through a three-hour simulation of a key aspect of the work of an MP. Each student is assigned a card with the first name of an individual MP and his or her party, and is placed on a committee responsible for dealing with one or two issues. During my own Swedish visit, one committee was considering whether the punishment for graffiti should be made harsher and another was examining whether boxing should be outlawed; both matters had come up in Parliament. In Norway, students have looked at legislative bills proposing that domestic animals should be fenced in and whether there should be compulsory identity chips, among other issues.

The students first get a chance to express their own opinion, then they are asked to express those of the legislator whose persona they have taken on. (The card gives information about his or her party affiliation, age, gender, professional background, and so on. The parties are fictitious, but their names and positions are based on those of the existing parties. The size of the party groups varies to reflect the real political situation.) The game begins when students in each committee go to their parties' caucus rooms (specially designed booths) and work out a position on the legislative issue under consideration. Students are guided in their deliberations by instructions provided to them by the animator and via a computer screen in the booth. In the party booths, students also have access to newspaper articles and excerpts from TV and radio coverage. Their deliberations are frequently interrupted by telephone calls and computer screen messages from "interested persons" (lobbyists, constituents, party activists, etc.). In the Norwegian role-play, a press conference scenario is also incorporated into the game.

Discussions on the bills are carried out alternatively in the party caucuses and in all-party committee meetings. This means that the students not only have to arrive at a common party position, but must work with other parties to form alliances or compromises to win majority support in the committee, keeping in mind that the proposals will need to pass in the plenary composed of all the students present. When the drafted bills come to the plenary floor in a mock-up session of Parliament overseen by the animator acting as Speaker, there are speeches for and against, and a vote is taken. In some of the scenarios the prime minister, the spokesperson for the governing party/coalition, asks for a vote of confidence, and the members must re-evaluate their views and take a stand on whether they want to support the government or bring it down. Finally, the students are asked to vote based on their own personal views on the issue and to reflect on whether their decisions have changed over the course of the simulation, and if so how. This discussion is followed up back home in the civics classroom. Of course, even with three such groups every day of the school year, not all classes can be accommodated. Nevertheless, the many schools that do participate, unlike the case with mock parliaments, constitute a cross-section rather than a politically sophisticated minority of young people.

Outside the classroom, several projects can be seen as contributing to civic education. The Netherlands is a country where innovations in this area have flourished, in particular from the work of the Instituut voor Publiek en Politiek (IPP, the Dutch Centre for Political Participation). Since 1994, the IPP has organized election simulations for secondary school students in the two days before the day of the election. Linked to these are diverse educational projects targeted at youth participation, including *Wegwijs op het Gemeentehuis,* in which young people fill the role of a member of the municipal council for a day. The IPP also provides electronic information about the position of the various political parties on issues such as health care, the economy, and education, and even tests election knowledge.

Testing electoral knowledge is the mission of voter advice applications (VAAs), which are websites that help voters determine which party or candidate their views are most in line with. We cannot be sure what effect such VAAs may have: participation in no other country has come close to attaining the rate of 75 per cent of Dutch citizens 18–24 who used VAAs in the 2006 election (Ruusuvirta and Rosema 2009).[13] The best known Dutch VAA is the *StemWijzer*. It was as an application of another Dutch VAA, *Kieskompas*, that the VAAs in Canada known as Vote Compass were initiated for the 2011 Canadian federal election campaign in partnership with the CBC, attracting nearly 2 million respondents. It has since been used for the 2011 Ontario election, the 2012 Alberta election, the 2012 Quebec election, the 2013 BC election, and most recently the 2015 federal election. Like other VAAs, visitors to the sites are asked to give their opinions on about 30 propositions. The site calculates which party program most corresponds to their answers and provides information about the positions held by the political parties.

Other Measures

Elections Canada is the independent body that administers federal elections. Since 2000, in response to the especially low turnout that year, Elections Canada has made reaching young people a priority, beginning with efforts to get those turning 18 on the National Register of Electors. The main initiatives include simulations; contests; special events; games such as crossword puzzles containing democratic words such as "Vote," "Assembly," and "Elections"; and a trivia game on the Internet that involves players answering questions about Parliament and elections. One contest asked students to create public service announcements telling their peers why democracy is important and why it is important to vote. Another contest, held during the 2004 election in partnership with four student associations, was to produce posters that were displayed on campuses across Canada. More recently, winners to a contest (by sending in a video) were invited to participate in a televised debate among Canadians aged 18 to 25 about the qualifications and aptitude needed to be "The Next Great Prime Minister."[14]

Several initiatives were based on collaboration with civil society organizations—apart from Student Vote. Elections Canada contributed to a youth voter education kit for an education and media initiative launched by the Dominion Institute. Along with the latter and other public and private donors, it supported a series of surveys carried on by Innovative Research on issues related to youth political participation as well as 63 all-candidates debates organized at high schools and universities. Elections Canada also funded musical events in Ottawa, Toronto, and Edmonton organized by "Rush the Vote,"[15] at which performers encouraged voting and democratic involvement. In addition, we should note the efforts of voluntary organizations acting in this area, especially Apathy is Boring.

While continuing low turnout figures (61 per cent in the 2011 election) suggest that these measures have had limited effects in Canada, the fact that the Conservatives, a party with notably more support from the old than the young, unsuccessfully sought (with Bill c-23 in 2014) to restrict Elections Canada's role in public information efforts at stimulating electoral participation indicates that we should not be so quick to dismiss them. Indeed, we need to learn from countries like Norway how we can do them better.

Conclusion

How do political parties fit into all of this? In Canada, unfortunately, not especially well. Here as in most democratic countries youth involvement in political parties is low and declining. Given the orientation of the Internet generation, it is unrealistic for parties to expect to compete with single-issue organizations in recruiting young activists. Moreover, as organizations with limited resources, it is also unrealistic to expect political parties to give priority to the interests and needs of a group where the majority does not even turn out to vote for their electoral platforms. Nevertheless, we can gain useful insights from some of the above cases into ways in which political parties can be more closely integrated into the process of promoting civic literacy among young people. A good starting point is the Scandinavian initiative in which classes of 15- and 16-year-old students simulate parliamentary committees. We noted that each student is assigned a role as an individual MP representing the position of his or her party and defends the stance of the party on the bill under consideration. Moreover, the student receives advice via the computer screen, from actual party leaders, and others. Those from a given party meet in caucus to decide on strategy to take to the committee, seeking to arrive at a position that could win majority support in the committee. We should add that the legitimacy of party politics in student life is also reflected in the fact that, unlike in Canada, it is quite common for elected Nordic party representatives to be invited to present their positions to civic classes.

In my view, it is here that the challenge for Canada lies. The initiatives along these lines described above, such as Vote Compass, though useful, are limited to individuals who are already interested in politics. Only Student Vote has the potential to transcend this limitation, but it has a long way to go to live up to the potential as reflected in the experience of the Nordic countries. Canada requires a state-funded independent organization with the mandate and resources to help establish a framework for such efforts to gain traction. Narrowing the mandate of Elections Canada to measures that directly assist and encourage voting is exactly the wrong direction in which to go. To set the context for efforts to promote the acquisition of practical political knowledge, political research should focus on comparative and longitudinal analyses of political knowledge, rather than relying on subjective indicators such as political interest, political trust, or even media use to provide us with an accurate picture of just where we stand.

Web Links

Elections Canada:
http://inspirerlademocratie-inspiredemocracy.ca/index-eng.asp

Student Vote:
 http://studentvote.ca
CIRCLE (Center for Information and Research on Civic Learning and Engagement): http://civicyouth.org

UNDP: Enhancing Youth Political Participation throughout the Electoral Cycle:
www.undp.org/content/undp/en/home/librarypage/democratic-governance/
    electoral_systemsandprocesses/enhancing-youth-political-participation-
    throughout-the-electoral.html

Notes

1   Some observers claim that unconventional forms of political participation are substituting for traditional ones, but when we try to find evidence of this we seldom succeed. An analysis of the results of a survey of 14-year-olds in the 24-nation International Energy Agency study found "no overall shift in post-materialist societies from voting to more active, issue-specific forms of participation" (Amnå, Munck, and Zetterberg 2004, 35). Overall, the data suggest that in certain countries a measure of substitution is taking place among a small group of well-educated young citizens, but as Gallego Dobón (2007, 1) notes, it is the concentration rather than the substitution hypothesis that "is more appropriate in regard to poorly educated citizens who are increasingly withdrawing from political activity."

2   For a detailed study of the evolution of youth political participation in Europe, see Garcia Albacete (2014).

3   The respondents were presented with a series of six statements regarding the operation of Australia's political institutions asked consistently in the 2001, 2007, and 2010 surveys.

4   The CSES is a collaborative program of cross-national research among election studies conducted in over 50 states. Its design allows researchers to conduct cross-level as well as cross-national analyses, addressing the effects of electoral institutions on citizens' attitudes and behaviour, the presence and nature of

social and political cleavages, and the evaluation of democratic institutions across different political regimes.

5   I wish to thank Eric Guntermann for his assistance in assembling these data.

6   A 2007 survey (Anduiza Perea, Gallego Dobón, and Jorba 2009) of 3,700 respondents used three political knowledge items and found the expected strong, positive, and linear relationship between level of education and political interest with political knowledge. The highly educated and highly interested in politics averaged twice the correct answers of the least educated and interested, with the political knowledge gap between the well-educated and the poorly educated larger for Internet users than for non-Internet users.

7   A study cited by Sunstein (2007) revealed that web political bloggers rarely highlight opposing opinions: of 1,400 blogs surveyed, 91 per cent of links were to like-minded sites. In an interview with salon.com, Sunstein expresses the fear that "when it comes to the Internet, we demand the right to reinforce our own beliefs without embracing the responsibility to challenge them."

8   The Liberals, while not reinstating the tuition hike, embarked in the fall of 2014 on a series of severe funding cuts for universities.

9   Franklin (2004) maintains that the costs of learning to vote are higher if one's first election falls in a period when one is only starting to establish the social networks that will frame future choices, including political ones. Those aged 18 to 20 years are typically in a period of transition, in the process of withdrawing from their home and traditional school environment without fully settling into another. Since voting is to an important degree habitual, turnout decline will accelerate as newly eligible-to-vote cohorts, set in their nonvoting ways, replace older cohorts with developed voting habits. Hence the decline when eligibility was reduced from 21 to 18. Given that raising the voting age back to 21 is politically unfeasible, Franklin concludes that reducing it to 16 is preferable to the status quo.

10   Wilkenfeld controlled for inequalities in civic experiences in school and the overall school environment, finding that the civic engagement gaps between racial minority low-SES, and higher-SES white students was greatly reduced. In neighbourhoods with high poverty levels, the school confidence in future political participation was positively associated with students' civic knowledge. While higher levels of school civic curriculum related to overall increases in the civic outcome, the relationship was most pronounced in high-poverty neighbourhoods.

11   In all, the ballots of over 43 per cent of Ontario high school students were collected and tabulated. The results were broadcast live alongside the official adult vote on CBC.

12   Surveys across Canada were carried out by Student Vote 2004 to test the impact of the simulation. The pre-election survey had 14,344 responses, but only 2,841 responded to the post-election survey. While in the pre-election survey 71 per cent said they would vote if they had the opportunity, this rose to 88 per cent among those who had participated in the program (Student Vote 2004).

13   Other innovative VAAs have emerged in a number of European countries, including the Swiss *Smartvote,* which operates independently of government, as opposed to some others, for example, *Wahlomat* in Germany, which is operated by the BB (*Bundeszentrale für politische Bildung*), the federal agency responsible for civic education materials and for whom young voters are a priority. Despite

Germany's relatively strong showing with regard to youth participation, efforts during the election campaign are clearly warranted. Huber and Schafar (2014) found that the age gap in political knowledge got wider during the 2009 and 2013 federal campaigns. *Smartvote* too has sought to reach out to the young with a shorter, more simply worded version known as *Myvote*. It seems to have had a positive effect. Whereas the general voter turnout increased between 1995 and 2007 from 42 per cent to 48 per cent, the electoral participation of young voters (18–24 years of age) has increased to a much higher degree, from 21 per cent to 35 per cent.

14 This took place in an *American Idol* type of format with former prime ministers as judges.
15 This is an organization that aims to increase youth voter turnout and political awareness through "edutainment" and is affiliated with the American program "Rock the Vote."

References

Abendschön, Simone, Sigrid Roßteutscher, and Armin Schäfer. 2014. "Young People's Political Participation in Europe—The Rise of Political Inequality?" Paper prepared for the Conference Youth, Politics and Society, Leuwen, Belgium, September 9–10.

Amnå, Erik, Ingrid Munck, and Pär Zetterberg. 2004. "Meaningful Participation: Political Efficacy of Adolescents in 24 Countries." Paper presented at the European Consortium for Political Research (ECPR) Joint Sessions of Workshops, Uppsala University, Sweden.

Anduiza Perea, Eva, Aina Gallego Dobón, and Laia Jorba. 2009. "New Media Exposure, Knowledge and Issue Polarization." Paper presented at the European Consortium for Political Research (ECPR) Joint Sessions of Workshops, University of Lisbon, April.

Bellamy, Robert V., and James R. Walker. 1996. *Television and the Remote Control: Grazing on a Vast Wasteland*. New York: Guilford Press.

Bergh, Johannes. 2014. "Is Voting a Habit? An Analysis of the Effects of the Norwegian Voting-Age Trial." Paper presented at the ECPR General Conference, Glasgow, September.

Blais, André, and Peter Loewen. 2011. *Youth Electoral Engagement in Canada*. Elections Canada.

Cross, William, and Lisa Young. 2008. "Factors Influencing the Decision of the Young Politically Engaged to Join a Political Party: An Investigation of the Canadian Case." *Party Politics* 14 (3): 345–69. http://dx.doi.org/10.1177/1354068807088126

Di Gennaro, Corinna, and William Dutton. 2006. "The Internet and the Public: Online and Offline Political Participation in the United Kingdom." *Parliamentary Affairs* 59 (2): 299–313. http://dx.doi.org/10.1093/pa/gsl004

Dufour, Pascale, and Louis-Philippe Savoie. 2013. "Quand les mouvements sociaux changent le politique: Le cas du mouvement étudiant de 2012 au Québec." Paper presented in the Framework Convention of the Canadian Political Science Association, Victoria, June.

Ekman, Joakim, and Par Zetterberg. 2010. "Making Citizens in the Classroom? Family Background and the Impact of Civic Education in Swedish Schools." Paper presented at IPSA RC21: Political Socialization and Education, Seminar, Arlberg, Denmark, September.

Elections Canada. 2011. *National Youth Survey.* http://www.elections.ca/content. aspx?section=res&dir=rec/part/nysr&document=p3&lang=e

Franklin, Mark N. 2004. *Voter Turnout and the Dynamics of Electoral Competition in Established Democracies since 1945.* Cambridge: Cambridge University Press. http://dx.doi.org/10.1017/CBO9780511616884

Gallego Dobón, Aina. 2007. "Changing Repertoires of Political Action: Which Impact on Equality in Participation?" Paper presented at the European Consortium of Political Research (ECPR) Biennial Conference, University of Pisa, Italy.

Garcia Albacete, Gema. 2014. *Young People's Political Participation in Western Europe: Continuity or Generational Change?* London: Palgrave Macmillan.

Gibson, Rachel K., and Ian McAllister. 2014. "New Media, Elections and the Political Knowledge Gap in Australia." *Journal of Sociology:* 1–17.

Gidengil, Elisabeth, André Blais, Neil Nevitte, and Richard Nadeau. 2004. *Citizens.* Vancouver: University of British Columbia Press.

Huber, Sacha, and Anne Schafar. 2014. "Media and Political Learning during the 2009 and 2013 German Federal Election Campaigns: A Study of Moderating Effects." Paper presented at the European Consortium for Political Research (ECPR) Joint Sessions of Workshops, University of Salamanca, Spain.

Kavadias, Dimitrikos, Mark Elchardus, and Saskia De Groof. 2011. "The Importance of Conventional Citizenship Compared: An Empirical, Comparative Analysis of Young People's Political and Civic Engagement." Paper presented at the 6th ECPR General Conference, Reykjavik, Iceland, August.

Loewen, Peter, Henry Milner, and Bruce Hicks. 2008. "Does Compulsory Voting Lead to More Informed and Engaged Citizens? An Experimental Test." *Canadian Journal of Political Science* 41 (3): 655–72. http://dx.doi.org/10.1017/S000842390808075X

Milner, Henry. 2002. *Civic Literacy: How Informed Citizens Make Democracy Work.* Hanover, MA: University Press of New England.

Milner, Henry. 2010. *The Internet Generation: Engaged Citizens or Political Dropouts?* Hanover, MA: University Press of New England.

Milner, Henry. 2014a. "The Political Engagement of the Internet Generation." Paper presented at the Youth, Politics and Society Conference, Leuven, Belgium, September 9.

Milner, Henry. 2014b. "Social Media Politics and Youth Participation." Paper presented at the ECPR Conference, Bordeaux, France, September.

Ødegård, Guro, Johannes Bergh, and Jo Saglie. 2014. "Why Did They Vote? Voter Turnout and the Mobilisation of 16-Year-Olds in the Norwegian Local Elections of 2011." Paper presented at the ECPR General Conference, Glasgow, September.

Owen, Diana, and Suzanne Soule. 2011. "Civic Education and Knowledge of Government and Politics." Paper presented at the Annual Meeting of the American Political Science Association, Seattle, Washington, September 1–4.

Prior, Markus. 2007. *Post-Broadcast Democracy: How Media Choice Increases Inequality in Political Involvement and Polarizes Elections.* New York: Cambridge University Press. http://dx.doi.org/10.1017/CBO9781139878425

Quinlan, Stephen. 2011. "Youth Electoral Participation: 'Crisis' for Democracy or a New Model of Political Participation?" Paper presented at the 2011 Annual Meeting of the European Political Science Association, Dublin, June 16–18.

Ruusuvirta, Outi, and Martin Rosema. 2009. "Do Online Selectors Influence the Direction and Quality of the Vote?" Paper presented at the European Consortium of Political Research (ECPR) Biennial Conference, University of Potsdam, Germany, September.

Scarrow, Susan, and Burcu Gezgor. 2010. "Declining Memberships, Changing Members? European Political Party Members in a New Era." *Party Politics* 16 (6): 823–43. http://dx.doi.org/10.1177/1354068809346078

Sloam, James. 2007. "Rebooting Democracy: Youth Participation in Politics in the UK." *Parliamentary Affairs* 60 (4): 548–67. http://dx.doi.org/10.1093/pa/gsm035

Smith, Aaron, Kay Lehman Schlozman, Sidney Verba, and Henry Brady. 2009. *The Internet and Civic Engagement*. Washington, DC: Pew Research Center.

Student Vote. 2004. Post-Election Report. www.studentvote.ca

Sunstein, Cass R. 2007. *Republic.com 2.0*. Princeton, NJ: Princeton University Press.

Wagner, Markus, David Johann, and Sylvia Kritzinger. 2012. "Voting at 16: Turnout and the Quality of Vote Choice." *Electoral Studies* 31 (2): 372–83. http://dx.doi.org/10.1016/j.electstud.2012.01.007

Wilkenfeld, Britt. 2009. "Civic Contexts: How Schools and Neighborhoods Influence Youth Political Engagement." Paper presented at the Conference on Youth and Politics: Strange Bedfellows? Comparative Perspectives on Political Socialization, Bruges, Belgium, July.

20

Municipal Political Parties: An Answer to Urbanization or an Affront to Traditions of Local Democracy?[1]

KRISTIN R. GOOD

Introduction

Municipal politics and governance is a different form of political life than at other orders of government in Canada. Many Canadians became aware of some of these differences when former Toronto Mayor Rob Ford (2010–14) refused to resign in a scandal surrounding allegations that he had, among other indiscretions, smoked crack cocaine. As the media frenzy put Toronto on the international map for all the wrong reasons, the debacle also brought to light fundamental questions about the nature of local democracy and lines of accountability in municipal politics. Ford's critics lamented the lack of effective recourse to address what was seen as a democratic crisis. In the end, in what could be seen by some as a political compromise and by others as a stalemate, council decided to dramatically curtail Ford's powers and office budget, leaving the more fundamental question of removal to voters in the next election. Ford argued that council's actions violated the principles of local democracy and that only voters should be able to circumscribe the mayor's power. On the surface, this argument carried some weight, since Ford had been elected to office with more votes than any other leader in Canada; he was elected at large, receiving more direct votes (rather than indirect endorsement of leadership through partisan voting) than the prime minister or premiers who are elected in single ridings. Nevertheless, the argument loses ground when one considers the legal basis for mayoral leadership in Toronto and, one might argue, also the long-standing tradition of the decentralization of power on local councils.

Despite popular perception, Canadian mayors legally have few additional powers beyond those of ordinary councillors. The broadened powers that Ford possessed were relatively recent and were delegated by council as part of a less-than-decade old reform initiative whereby the province of Ontario encouraged the city to strengthen the mayor's ability to lead as part of the negotiations surrounding the passage of a more empowering legislative basis for the city in 2006. Thus, since the mayor's powers are neither inherent (constitutionally based) nor anchored in provincial legislation, but rather had been delegated voluntarily by council, that same council was also empowered to remove those powers. In essence, the scandal illuminated the significantly weaker basis of mayoral powers than at other levels of government, where leaders exercise powers based on deeply entrenched constitutional conventions associated with Westminster-style parliamentary government.[2]

As the outrage grew, a more fundamental tension in local democracy arose. More specifically, the question of whether the Ontario Liberal government under Kathleen Wynne might intervene was also raised, since the power to remove a sitting mayor was not established in the City of Toronto Act (2006). This element of the debate brought to the surface yet another distinctive element of local accountability structures—the role of the province as an "overseer" of municipal government and a sort of "accountability" of municipalities and their councils to provinces.[3]

A final difference in the model of democratic accountability at the local level illuminated by the Ford scandal, and which is the focus of this chapter, is the generally nonpartisan basis of municipal elections (at least formally). Where parties do compete at the municipal level, they are locally based rather than branches of national or provincial parties. The absence of political parties removes a layer of accountability for municipal leaders in between elections. At other levels of government, parties play a crucial role in selecting, reviewing, and removing leaders.[4] Nevertheless, a crucial difference at the local level is that municipal mayors are elected at large and, therefore, even if removed as leader of a local party controlling a plurality or majority of seats on council, the mayor would continue to lead (although with more difficulty) since his or her electoral mandate to lead is completely independent of fellow party members. In this way, Canadian municipalities combine elements of presidential and parliamentary systems (Quesnel 1986, 67). In parliamentary democracies, a leader's (and government's) legitimacy is tied to their ability to maintain the confidence of their legislature, which is structured by party support. In contrast, municipal mayors and councillors are directly responsible to the electorate and, although in tension with this principle, institutionally they are also accountable to their province. Thus, somewhat paradoxically, municipal mayors' electoral and democratic legitimacy is strong, but in a highly decentralized legislature characterized for the most part by the absence of parties, as well as municipalities' institutional subordination to provinces, their ability to lead is weak. The leadership challenge is especially difficult for mayors in nonpartisan contexts since they must build coalitions on council informally.

Canada's tradition of nonpartisan municipal government stands out as an exception among Western liberal democracies. Only two provincial jurisdictions, British Columbia and Quebec,[5] allow partisan affiliations to be listed on local elections ballots, a common measure used to distinguish between partisan and nonpartisan elections since even in formally nonpartisan contests political parties may play a role (Siegel 2009, 35).[6] In Europe, although there is some recent discussion of the emergence of nonpartisan politics and local parties, national political parties dominate local elections (Copus et al. 2012, 211).[7] Like Canada, the United States is exceptional among liberal democracies insofar as the nonpartisan tradition is strong at the local level. In the United States, 77 per cent of city elections employ the nonpartisan ballot, and parties compete in only 10 of the 30 most populous American cities, including New York, Chicago, and Houston (National League of Cities 2015). However, unlike in Canada where municipal parties are independent, in the United States it is *national* political parties that compete, which, as will be discussed further below, has significantly different implications for both municipal politics and relations among governments.

As Canada has become more urban[8] and ethnoculturally diverse, debates about the fundamental role of municipal governments in the Canadian intergovernmental system have emerged. Rather than reducing the salience of territory to economic exchanges, globalization has led to the reterritorialization of capitalism, with cities becoming the places that increasingly drive countries' economic growth. Furthermore, with economic change Canadian cities and urban municipalities have become important sites and actors of not only immigrant settlement (Good 2005, 2009; Tolley and Young 2011; Tossutti 2012) but also of linguistic and national identity politics (Boudreau 2006; Bourgeois and Bourgeois 2005, 2011; Good 2014). There is also evidence to suggest that major Canadian cities have become increasing socially polarized and that these divisions intersect in many instances with ethnic and racial diversity (Walks 2014).

The 1990s were a time of significant reform to and contention about municipal systems. Some reforms, like provincially imposed municipal amalgamations, for instance, reflected the influence of traditional constitutional doctrines such as the "creatures of provinces" doctrine or "Dillon's rule."[9] These constitutional principles emphasize municipalities' lack of independent constitutional status and the province's unfettered discretion over municipal affairs at the expense, some would argue, of citizens' right to local government (see Magnusson 2005). Amalgamations generated significant citizen opposition (Horak 1998; Milroy 2002; Trent 2012). Other reforms were inspired by changing notions of municipal democracy and increased autonomy. In the aftermath of amalgamation in Toronto, a powerful and diverse movement for municipal autonomy emerged, with calls for empowerment ranging from the introduction of a more enabling legislative framework (with an implicit commitment to a roughly similar division of power) to radical decentralization of the powers of a province to the municipality (Good 2009, Chapter 7; Keil and Young 2003). Although many would describe the reforms to date as modest, beginning in Alberta in 1994 many provinces began empowering municipalities through more permissive municipal legislation (Tindal and Tindal 2009, 179) and, more recently, by establishing asymmetrical arrangements with major cities, usually through the passage of a separate statute to govern the city—called a *city charter* in municipal circles. For instance, the strategically named Stronger City of Toronto for a Stronger Ontario Act (2006) placed Canada's largest city among its charter cities.[10] The direction in municipal systems is toward empowering cities (Garcea 2014), and this arguably creates the conditions for a more complex, "creative" politics at the municipal level.

As municipal populations grow and provinces loosen legal constraints, questions also arise about whether municipalities are up to the challenge of governing. All Canadian councils are versions of "council–mayor" or "weak mayor" systems whereby executive and legislative authority is shared by the mayor and ordinary councillors. Mayors' positions are vaguely defined; major executive functions such as preparing the budget, providing leadership over a legislative agenda, and appointing top-level administrators are all shared in such systems. There is some variation in mayors' powers; "in no instances, however, do heads of council in Canada possess significant executive power" (Tindal and Tindal 2004, 263). Furthermore, as discussed above, unlike the Westminster convention of "responsible government"—whereby the political executive (the first minister and cabinet) must retain the confidence of the House—at the municipal level, council is collectively responsible to the electorate for municipal operations.

There are a variety of statutory and nonstatutory executive committees on local councils that strengthen their leadership capacity to varying degrees (Tindal et al. 2013, 307–10). Among the strongest is Winnipeg's, where the mayor appoints the entire executive policy committee (Leo and Piel 2005, 117; Sancton 2015, 231; Tindal et al. 2013, 293). More recently, as part of a broader reform initiative that led to the passage of a "city charter" to govern Toronto, Toronto council adopted a 13-member executive committee. Nevertheless, although such reforms provide a stronger institutional footing than many organizational models associated with Canada's weak mayoral systems, none provides the strong executive leadership characteristic of Canada's Westminster-style parliamentary governments. The reason is simple: for the most part, Canadian municipal elections and governance are nonpartisan. As the historical example of the reign of former Montreal Mayor Jean Drapeau and his Civic Party (1960–86)[11] suggests, it is the combination of executive committees and political parties that appears to confer significant power on mayors (Sancton 1994, 182). In the absence of political parties or exceptional leadership, power remains highly decentralized on local councils, raising the question of whether municipalities are capable of providing the requisite leadership to govern urban communities, in particular Canada's largest cities.

Thus, the question of whether political parties would be desirable at the local level constitutes one of the most important contemporary questions of municipal governance. Furthermore, the debate is inextricably connected to other fundamental reform debates, including those about municipal autonomy, mayoral power, and questions of municipal size raised by amalgamations in some provinces. The purpose of this chapter is to introduce the reader to the debate about municipal parties in Canada. Since the roots of nonpartisanship lie in the ideas of the American reform movement that attempted to take "politics" out of municipal decision making, as well as in Canadian municipalities' constitutional status and institutional development, we begin by discussing the relationship between one's view on the nature, purpose, and democratic potential of municipal governments and one's position on the merits of the nonpartisan approach. As will become apparent below, in many ways the debate about parties is really about whether and the extent to which municipal politics matter. Furthermore, the chapter asks whether Canada's nonpartisan municipal tradition has a "neutral" impact on local politics or whether it is biased toward a right-wing, conservative position. The chapter then turns to a discussion of the claim that parties would increase the number of women and ethnic minorities on council. Following that, the chapter explores arguments about how parties might alter the conduct of local politics, including elections and municipal decision making as well as intergovernmental relations. The chapter concludes by arguing that a partisan ballot should be permitted at the local level, arguing that such a system should remain flexible and independent from party politics at the provincial and especially federal levels.

Nonpartisan Municipal Government: Apolitical and Neutral or the Institutionalization of Bias?

Normative assumptions about municipalities' *purpose and potential as democratic governments* are crucial to the debate about parties at the municipal level. Most fundamentally, those who argue against municipal partisan elections tend to downplay the political aspects of municipal decision making. There are at least three reasons why one might argue that local politics are unimportant and apolitical.

The first is rooted in the historical American reform movement that argues municipalities ought to be run like a business. In 1972, J.D. Anderson wrote that experts writing on local government were "almost unanimous" in ascribing the origins of municipal nonpartisanship in Canada to the influence of ideas from the American reform movement in the late nineteenth century (Anderson 1972, 5).[12] This late nineteenth century reform or "Progressive" movement developed in reaction to what was perceived as widespread corruption in American cities where party politics had resulted in powerful political machines or monopolies. Reformers were inspired by conceptions of municipalities as publicly run businesses. Thus, they proposed to attempt to make a clear separation between politics and administration and to empower expert managers to manage local service delivery. Reforms proposed and implemented by the Progressives included the nonpartisan ballot, the city manager or council manager system, and the at-large election (Anderson 1972, 16). The influence of these ideas on Canadian municipal systems can be seen in the pervasiveness of nonpartisan ballots, weak mayoral systems, and the prevalence of the ideal of nonpartisanship in local political cultures. British Columbia also adopted the reformers' at-large method[13] of electing both mayors and councillors. Reformers' conception of politics envisioned local councils as a sort of board of directors charged with making decisions in the interests of effective administration and efficiency. Partisan divisions have no place in such a system. This is the strongest "apolitical" stance. This idea is famously expressed in the phrase that "there is no Conservative or Liberal way to pave a road" (Lightbody 2006, 239).

The second reason is rooted in municipalities' lack of independent constitutional status—as "creatures of provinces"—and a corresponding conception of municipalities as administrative extensions of provincial governments whose limited autonomy is insufficient to generate and maintain partisan divisions. Strict traditionalists even question whether one should view municipalities as "governments" at all (Sancton 2012, 303). Andrew Sancton (2006, 313) argues that municipal political parties do not exist both because of institutional limitations (which he also stresses) and because the political divisions among citizens themselves are insufficient to sustain a local party system. Municipalities' parochial politics flow to a certain extent from their responsibilities for planning and zoning decisions; for instance in the prevalence of Not In My BackYard (NIMBY) movements at the local level, which "are rarely capable of building an ongoing city-wide coalition of like-minded people" (Sancton 2006, 314). However, Sancton also points out that the reform movement of the 1970s, a time that some associate with a resurgent interest in local democracy in Canada, were not entirely or even mainly directed at municipalities (Sancton 2006), which is consistent with his multilevel perspective on local politics and a normative preference for a strong provincial role in governing cities (see Sancton 2008). Sancton also points out that the "sharp divisions between new reformers and old-guard pro-development politicians" that characterized the 1970s reform movement no longer exist (Sancton 2006, 314).

A third line of reasoning for why local parties do not exist in Canada stresses the constraining nature of the political economy of cities (Sancton 2006). Whereas the conception of municipalities as "creatures of provinces" has been pervasive in the Canadian urban politics literature, the image of the city limited by its competitive position in a fragmented urban system is more common in the United States. American federalism and local government scholar Paul Peterson's (1981) *City Limits* is a seminal contribution that downplays the importance of local politics (and therefore the value of political parties). He argues that municipalities focus on "developmental policies," policies that are in their "economic interest" because of the limited nature of local politics in relation to the state and federal governments as well as competitive dynamics within horizontally fragmented municipal systems at the local level (Peterson 1981). This rational choice perspective leads one to expect convergence among municipalities; in other words, partisan divisions would not matter in such a model.

There is also a body of American literature that asks about the nature of local power, with an important strain that stresses structural constraints on municipal autonomy. In the 1950s and 1960s,[14] the "community power" debate between pluralists and elitists offered competing answers regarding the extent to which the electoral arena influences local decision making. Theories that followed this unresolved debate about community power, such as "growth machine" theory (Logan and Molotch 1987) and "urban regime" theory (Stone 1989), changed the analytical focus but seemed to suggest (with the elitists) a strong bias toward business interests. Logan and Molotch (1987) argue that property owners, what they call the "rentiers," are most influential in local politics and that "growth" dominates local agendas. They theorize why a broad group of local actors in local politics share a common interest in growth, referring to cities as "growth machines." In such systems ideological differences do not matter and politicians accept that their role is to encourage unfettered development. Urban regime theorists also assert that local power structures are biased toward the business community because they possess resources that are vital to the capacity to govern (Stone 1989). However, urban regime theorists argue that *local politics matter* because it is through the process of coalition-building across the public and private sectors that the resources necessary to govern are brought to bear to address local challenges. This theoretical paradigm that focuses on governance became the dominant theoretical paradigm in the urban politics literature (Mossberger and Stoker 2001). The urban regime literature tends to downplay the significance of the electoral arena to local governance and therefore also traditional intermediaries such as political parties. Furthermore, I am unaware of a study that examines the influence of partisan and nonpartisan or other institutional features of municipal governments on the nature of governance arrangements in the United States.

Nevertheless, although the focus on governance continues, more recent American urban politics literature suggests a revival of interest in the effects of institutions and traditional arenas like elections on local politics in the United States (see, for instance, Hajnal 2010; Hajnal and Trounstine 2014; Trounstine 2008). Furthermore, this literature establishes that preferences for policies are not uniform among local residents, that there are several important cleavages in American urban politics, and that governing coalitions make different policy decisions.[15] In other words, it establishes that local politics matter. Moreover, contributions to this literature explore the biases in municipal institutions challenging both the notion that local politics do not generate significant political divisions and that nonpartisan institutions have a neutral impact on these politics (see Hajnal 2010).

Although the literature on the effects of municipal institutions on local politics and policy choices is limited in Canada, supporters of partisan politics argue that nonpartisan government has a right-wing and conservative bias. As James Lightbody (2006, 225) argues, "the ideological bias of nonpartisanship lies in its appeal to a status quo in which the debate is more around how well run the process of governing is than into normative questions as to what public policies that process should be about." Similarly, Charles Adrian (1952, 774), one of the foremost students of nonpartisan politics in North America, noted the following in his classic article on the characteristics of nonpartisan politics in the United States: "nonpartisanship produces a legislative body with a relatively high percentage of experienced members, making for conservatism." This reality is in turn a product of the advantages conferred on incumbents in nonpartisan elections, which are rarely based on issues and thereby frustrate protest voting (Adrian 1952, 773–74). More specifically, in the absence of an issue-based campaign and parties as cues, voters vote on the basis of name recognition (Schaffner, Streb, and Wright 2001). The importance of name recognition and, relatedly, the costs of running independent elections as well as the depressive effects of nonpartisan elections on voter turnout have all been cited as reasons for a right-wing bias (see, for instance, Welch and Bledsoe 1986, 129–30).

The tendency of political actors on the right to be in favour of a nonpartisan municipal politics also suggests a conservative and "right-wing" bias. In the United Kingdom, the Maud Commission found that "anti-partyism" was "associated with rural, suburban, and more conservative councillors generally" (Lightbody 2006, 235). The American urban politics literature of the 1960s offered strong support for a Republican bias in nonpartisan elections (Lee 1960, cited in in Welch and Bledsoe 1986, 129; Hawley 1968, cited in Welch and Bledsoe 1986, 129). In the 1980s, a general Republican bias in nonpartisan elections was largely disconfirmed in an important study by Welch and Bledsoe, who found that such a bias was limited to communities that combined nonpartisan elections with at-large systems of election and to small American cities with populations between 50,000 and 100,000 (Welch and Bledsoe 1986, 136–37). In Canada, evidence of a bias is apparent in that the tradition is popular among political actors on the right of the political spectrum, including, for instance, the Non-Partisan Association in Vancouver (Lightbody 2006, 235). Furthermore, an examination of the historical development of civic parties in Canada suggests that parties on the right enter civic politics reactively—when a worker-based party of the left organizes (Filion 1999, 92). This could suggest that those who benefit from the right-wing biases in nonpartisan institutions do not organize until the status quo is threatened.

Moreover, if one were to adopt either a strong elitist perspective or weaker regime perspective, one might expect that in nonpartisan elections such a community bias would be accentuated. Expanding the local agenda in the context of a civic arena dominated by the business community would require a strong electoral coalition that political parties could express and channel. The ability of councils to influence local agendas in collaboration with actors in civil society is further weakened in weak mayoral systems where executive power is diffuse. Strengthening the influence of the electoral arena in relation to the civic arena of local politics is crucial to democratizing local politics. This perspective is supported by Peter John's (2001) contention that, in many European cities, the business community's role in governance is reactive rather than proactive, as is the case in American cities. He attributes this in part to the strength of social–democratic parties in many European cities that have, in his words, "governed many cities and . . . transformed political institutions to reflect both the development of working class ideologies and a belief in the public intervention in social affairs" (John 2001, 48). Thus, although the evidence is somewhat uncertain, it is notable that to the extent that biases do exist, the literature agrees that a nonpartisan politics would work to the advantage of the "right."

Some American research continues to assert that a partisan politics would not lead to different policy choices because of the constraints inherent in the political economy of cities. For instance, writing in the American context, Ferreira and Gyourko (2009, 420) find that partisanship doesn't matter at the local level—it doesn't affect level of spending, funding allocations, or rates of property and violent crimes. They argue that "Tiebout competition,"[16] which emphasizes the effects of competition among jurisdictions and the possibility of exit, explains convergence among municipalities regardless of the partisanship of their mayors. Nevertheless, they temper their conclusions by noting that contextual factors matter, including, most importantly, the extent to which the urban system is horizontally fragmented (Ferreira and Gyourko 2009, 401). The authors also acknowledge that their study does not address the dynamics of many important municipal policy areas. Such a perspective contradicts a growing body of research on American local elections cited above that finds that the electoral arena matters to local decision making.

In Canada, even in the absence of parties, there is evidence of variation in municipal policies in areas that could be important sources of partisan division, including immigration and multiculturalism (Good 2009) and environmental policies (Gore, Robinson, and Stren 2012). Furthermore, significant variations in municipal responsiveness to immigrants also exist *within* city regions (Good 2009). This variation suggests that partisanship (and more fundamentally politics) might not be irrelevant in all policy areas and political contexts and, more fundamentally, that local agency and politics matter.

Municipal Political Parties and the Representation of Women and Ethnoracial Minorities

Some proponents of municipal political parties suggest that they would result in more equitable representation of ethnic minorities and women (Lightbody 1999, 178). This argument has intuitive appeal, since the tendency for nonpartisan elections to favour incumbency means that as ethnic demographics change political turnover might be particularly slow. It is possible that political parties would be more responsive to such changes since they would have a long-term incentive to attract new ethnic constituencies' support. Nevertheless, this incentive would only exist in competitive party systems (Jones-Correa 1998), and there is reason to believe that one-party dominant systems could develop in many cities (Bish 2001, 7).

The urban politics literature does not offer straightforward lessons with respect to the effect of partisan politics on the political incorporation of ethnoracial minorities at the municipal level. In their seminal study of the political incorporation of blacks and Hispanics into local politics in California, Browning, Marshall, and Tabb (1984, 243) argue that political incorporation occurs when minorities are included in the governing coalition of a liberal coalition and, in party terms, with "more Democrats on council." Advocates of municipal parties, like Lightbody (1999, 178), argue that they will both encourage a more innovative, "creative" politics and increase the representation of ethnoracial minorities. Nevertheless, since the Conservative Party has made significant inroads among immigrants, especially in suburban areas of major cities in Canada, it is questionable whether greater representation of immigrants and ethnoracial minorities would be associated with such a "left-wing" politics. Romain Garbaye's (2004) work on the political incorporation of minorities in Birmingham, Lille, and Roubaix also leads one to question the connection between left-wing politics and the political incorporation of minorities. In his study conducted in Lille, the attitudes of the governing Socialist Party and its institutional power base on council contributed to the city's poor levels of incorporation of North African immigrants (Garbaye 2004, 50–51). Susan Clarke and Keeley Stokes's (2014, 271) analysis of the political incorporation of ethnocultural minorities in London also finds a multitude of paths to political incorporation and challenges the assumption that "the Labour Party—or any traditional party—is the primary vehicle for BME [black and minority ethnic] immigrant incorporation."

The most recent and comprehensive study of ethnic minorities and women's political incorporation in Canadian cities argues that the bias in local elections toward incumbency contributes to the underrepresentation of both ethnic minorities and women, especially in combination with municipal amalgamations, which increase the size of constituencies and reduce the number of seats up for election (Andrew et al. 2008, 263). Nevertheless, it is not clear that party politics would lead women to overcome these barriers. For instance, Gavan-Koop and Smith (2008) found that women were more underrepresented in those municipalities in British Columbia where parties competed. Clearly, the extent to which parties facilitate women's political incorporation also depends on a multitude of factors. The extent to which women and ethnic minorities would have greater success in a local partisan politics depends fundamentally on which parties compete as well as their internal practices.

Local Parties, Democratic Accountability, and Municipal Decision Making

Decision making on local councils has been likened to "herding cats." One of the most important arguments for the introduction of political parties at the local level is that it would create more decisive leadership by establishing stable coalitions on council. According to some, this stability would also clarify lines of accountability and eliminate the practice of logrolling—allowing councillors whose wards are against a particular development or issue to vote against it knowing full well that the support exists on council to have it pass (Lightbody 2006, 239). Nevertheless, as Lightbody admits, at least one local party—Winnipeg's Citizens' Election Committee (1921–86)—has also engaged in such practices (Lightbody 1999, 174). However, party caucuses would undoubtedly limit logrolling.

Where they exist, executive committees can encourage greater attention to city-wide issues, prioritize agenda items, and strengthen mayoral leadership. However, in the absence of a stable coalition to support them, their ability to do so is highly limited. Therefore, in the current nonpartisan context, unlike leaders at other levels of government, as Andrew Sancton notes, "many mayors in Canada are often on the losing sides of important votes" (Sancton 2015, 229). In a dramatic example of this phenomenon, a study of the 2010–13 term of council in Calgary reported that its mayor (Naheed Nenshi) was on the winning side of only 60.3 per cent of 73 important votes taken on council (Farkas 2013, 5). What is even more telling is that of the 15-member council, 11 members were on the winning side more often than the mayor, and only three were less likely to win votes than he was (Farkas 2013, 5). The analysis of voting patterns on council in this study illustrates how decentralized power is on municipal councils in Canada. It also raises questions about how difficult it could be for voters to know how their councillor and even the mayor voted on particular issues and, therefore, makes it more difficult for them to hold elected officials accountable for their decisions.

Thus, supporters of parties argue that they would clarify lines of accountability. According to this argument, accountability would be enhanced since councillors would vote for issues based on party, allowing voters to reward or punish them more clearly at election time. Parties would become the relevant cues for voters in elections rather than name recognition or incumbency, which tends to be the dominant cue in nonpartisan elections (Schaffner, Streb, and Wright, 2001).

Advocates of municipal party politics also argue that by simplifying voter choice during elections parties increase voter turnout. Although extensive empirical research on this question has not been conducted in Canada, Canadian academics both for and against (or possibly ambivalent about) the question of nonpartisan elections give credence to this point (Lightbody 2006, 231; Siegel 1987, 27; Young 2009, 497). The American literature suggests that nonpartisan elections do indeed depress voter turnout. For instance, in his study of the effects of institutional design on local democracy and the representation of racial minorities in the United States, Zoltan Hajnal (2010, 159) finds that "cities that hold partisan primaries and that place party labels on their ballots tend to garner 3 percent more voters than cities that do not allow parties to be involved in the electoral process."[17] He attributes this to the role that parties play in mobilizing voters as well as the importance of party labels as a method of easing voter choices (Hajnal 2010, 159). Nevertheless, according to Hajnal, it is the combination of reform institutions that produces the most remarkable depressive effect on voter turnout in local elections in the United States and therefore also has the most potential to address deficits in the quality of local democracy: "Taken together, movement to the mayor/council form of government, non-staggered council elections, partisan contests, and the elimination of direct democracy could ... increase registered voter turnout in a typical [American] city by 18 percent" (Hajnal 2010, 160). His work suggests that when leadership is strengthened on local councils and councils are empowered to make important decisions for local communities, elections are given more serious attention by voters.

Furthermore, to the extent that parties facilitate an issue-based or ideological campaign as well as increase the competitiveness of local elections, they could increase citizen engagement in local affairs. The competitiveness of local elections could be particularly enhanced if campaign financing laws accompanied such changes (Young and Austin 2008). Moreover, according to Lightbody (1999, 178), the introduction of party politics would "facilitate" the issue of ethical campaign funding since "party funds reduce expectations of *quid pro quo* falling on individual candidates." Currently, developers (who have strong stakes in municipal decisions) are "heavily inclined" toward incumbents (Young and Austin 2008, 96). Campaign financing is another element of the institutional foundations of local politics that supports the above-discussed "conservative" or right-wing bias in local politics. Introducing parties could therefore broaden the local agenda to include different approaches to urban development and sustainability (Lightbody 1999, 177).

Those against party politics at the local level value the direct link of accountability between the electorate and their councillor (Siegel 1987, 27). Furthermore, they value the openness of debates in council rather than the closed decision making in party caucuses. In a party system, councillors' positions would be determined by partisanship rather than their constituents' views, unless partisanship were weak, in which case some of the benefits of parties would no longer hold (Siegel 1987, 27).

Others argue that adversarial norms would be introduced into local politics, undermining the ability for compromise. Copus et al.'s (2012, 217) review of the literature on party politics, particularly in Europe, supports this view. They argue that in England national parties have introduced Westminster norms into local councils, including the adversarial nature of the system. They disparagingly refer to local governments as local "partocracies" rather than "democracies." More generally, there seems to be a great deal of interest in the rise of independent local politics in Europe as a possible remedy to the perceived ills of local party politics. The extent to which Westminster norms have permeated local politics in England should be taken especially seriously in Canada, considering the particularly strict norms of party discipline that have evolved at other orders of government in Canada, even in relation to other Westminster systems (Aucoin, Jarvis, and Turnbull 2011).

According to Lightbody (1999, 177), a key benefit to partisan politics at the local level is that "systematic opposition will be entrenched." Nevertheless, given the greater homogeneity of city electorates, the question arises whether a one-party dominant system might develop. This is especially the case if one assumes that the current norm of a single-member plurality and ward-based system would remain constant. Such a council could indeed provide strong leadership. However, it could also limit debate on council significantly. As Robert Bish (2001) notes, this is what happened in the northeastern US states where party competition exists. Nevertheless, such generalizations must be considered in light of a broader American literature that suggests political monopolies arise in both partisan and nonpartisan contexts (see Trounstine 2008). There is some historical evidence to suggest that one-party dominant systems could develop at the local level in Canadian cities. For instance, Vancouver's Non-Partisan Association—which formed in 1937 after the socialist Co-operative Commonwealth Federation (CCF) won three seats on Vancouver's council in 1936—managed to control majorities on council "for most of the twentieth and early twenty-first centuries," leading Smith and Stewart (2009, 300) to call it "a juggernaut."

Former Montreal Mayor Jean Drapeau's reign as mayor and leader of the Civic Party from 1960 to 1986 is the other relevant example here. His tenure as mayor is often invoked in the debate about local parties in Canada. On the one hand, some consider his tenure an example of the possibilities of what a mayor can accomplish with the support of a disciplined coalition on council. They note that it was under his tenure that the Montreal subway system was built and Montreal hosted two major events that brought international attention to the city—Expo 67 and the 1976 Olympic Summer Games. According to Sancton (2015, 181), others would characterize Drapeau's Montreal "as the horrible example of how strong local parties eliminate meaningful local participation." Tom Urbaniak (2014, 215) suggests that Drapeau's leadership is not so much a reflection of the impact of party politics on local political dynamics and leadership as an exceptional case whereby a leader was able to create a party around his own political aspirations. More broadly, Urbaniak (2009) has begun to theorize the conditions under which political monopolies might develop in nonpartisan contexts. In Mississauga, during the "McCallion era," the "de facto Hazel McCallion Party . . . held virtually every seat on [Mississauga] council" (Urbaniak 2009, 226). The pervasiveness of her influence was also apparent insofar as her personal position on the city's role in multiculturalism was considered "policy" by some civil servants, despite the lack of a formal policy (Good 2009, 102–3). Urbaniak's point reinforces the idea that political monopolies could develop in both partisan and nonpartisan contexts.

Nevertheless, power on councils in both Vancouver and Montreal today is more diffuse because party systems have fragmented. In Vancouver in the last decade, the left-wing Coalition of Progressive Electors (COPE) governed from 2002 to 2005, providing support to independent Mayor Larry Campbell. Former Mayor Sam Sullivan governed as a Non-Partisan Association (NPA) mayor from 2005 to 2008. Vision Vancouver formed from moderate COPE members and took control of council in 2008 (winning re-election in 2011), with Gregor Robertson as mayor; the party now holds six of ten seats on Vancouver council (Vision Vancouver 2015). Similarly, since Drapeau's reign Montreal's party system has opened up dramatically. Three different parties have held majorities on Montreal's council. The current mayor, Denis Coderre, who created yet another party or slate called "Team Coderre," is in a minority position on council (holding 27 out of 65 seats) with Project Montreal, a party focused on environmental issues, holding the balance of power at 20 seats. This leads Sancton (2015, 180) to conclude that "Montreal's municipal party system could well be in the process of breaking down." Such a development would put Montreal more in line with other municipalities in the province.[18]

Moreover, to the extent that advocates of parties have a Westminster model in mind, such a system would require additional reforms. The only councils that have institutions to support "municipal parliamentarianism" in place are in Quebec—including a cabinet with portfolios assigned to members of executive committees that correspond to municipal administrative departments, an institutionalized opposition, and a Speaker to chair debates (Belley et al. 2009, 111–12). Still, even with such reforms in place the model would be very different than at other orders of government if the fundamental convention of responsible government would not apply.

Many institutional configurations are possible, and outlining them is beyond the scope of this chapter.[19] However, a brief mention of the American strong mayoral system is warranted. This system is used in many jurisdictions, including Chicago, New York City, Philadelphia, and Indianapolis. Like government structures at the state and federal levels in the United States, such systems separate executive and legislative authority clearly and rigidly. In such systems, the mayor does not sit in the legislature (council) and has clear authority to provide executive direction to the city, acting as its chief executive officer.[20] Under such a system a mayor could be elected from a different political party than the majority on council, which could lead to legislative deadlock depending on the nature of the mayoral veto. Although such a system is foreign to Canadian political practice, the tradition of electing Canadian mayors separately is a point of commonality. Thus, in current municipal systems in Canada, it is possible that a mayor will be elected from a party that is different than the legislative plurality on council, an institutional feature that makes it more difficult for parties to penetrate local politics (Clarkson 1972, 166) and adds yet another layer of complexity to the debate about parties' effect on municipal democracy.

In strong mayoral systems, the mayor's power flows from control over the municipal administration (Sancton 2015, 229). Thus, a brief mention of the administrative aspect of leadership is warranted, especially since it is not addressed sufficiently in the literature on municipal political parties. David Siegel's (1994, 11; 2010; 2015, Chapter 1) work has illuminated the many unique challenges faced by municipal administrators (including city managers and other top-level administrators) in a nonpartisan, "weak mayor" environment. In such systems, administrators receive vague and sometimes conflicting direction from council, since their direction comes not only from the mayor or a political executive but from all of council. Municipal administrators also operate in a more public environment. Thus, one might argue that by concentrating power in a political executive and centralizing power over the administration, political parties could contribute to greater administrative coherence and overall leadership.

Local Autonomy and Intergovernmental Relations

In their review of Europe's experience with party politics at the local level, Copus et al. (2012, 212) argue that the introduction of national parties into local elections has stifled local diversity and, essentially, "nationalized" local politics, increasing uniformity through the adoption of national standards with respect to service provision. Nevertheless, there are good reasons to hypothesize that nationalization might not result from the introduction of partisan politics at the local level in Canada. One reason is that, with the possible exception of the CCF-NDP, national parties do not appear to have shown a great deal of interest in local politics. To my knowledge, the only example of the Liberal Party fielding candidates in a local election was the 1969 election in Toronto, in which its success was limited and its mayoral candidate (Stephen Clarkson) was defeated. According to Siegel (2009, 35), in Ontario the 1969 loss "is frequently cited as a lesson to all national parties that the gains in obtaining local office are not as great as the downside embarrassment of losing." Nevertheless, as Clarkson (1972) argues, there were many institutional barriers to the introduction of party politics that, if removed, could lead to different results should parties at upper levels of government be interested in municipal contests.

Canada's regionalism and its status as a multinational federation would be particularly strong barriers to national party involvement in local affairs. First, federal and provincial parties are currently not integrated. Second, it is difficult to imagine national (federal) parties running in Quebec elections without significant backlash from the Quebec National Assembly. If federal parties were to express a desire to compete in Quebec elections, this could be perceived as an infringement on Quebec's responsibility for municipal government and urban affairs.

More generally, given the strength of regionalism in Canadian politics and the independence of provincial parties (with some exceptions), the nationalization of municipal politics is unlikely, especially in Quebec and Western provinces, where unique provincial parties have emerged and governed. Canada's party system is highly "confederal" (Riker 1964, cited in Bakvis and Tanguay 2012, 98) or decentralized (Dyck 1996; Smiley 1987, 117; both cited in Bakvis and Tanguay 2012, 98). For these reasons, it is more likely that if partisan politics were to emerge in Canada more generally at the local level, they would take an independent form. This point is reinforced by the fact that where parties do compete in municipal elections in Canada—namely in British Columbia and Quebec—they are generally locally based and unaffiliated with parties at upper levels of government.

Although the nationalization of local politics is unlikely, it is worth mentioning that if it were to occur it could enhance local politics and governance in some respects. In particular, it could increase the pool of candidates willing to run in local elections, thereby increasing the quality of political representation. Furthermore, by facilitating the progression of political careers from the local to the provincial and federal levels, the quality of local representation could be enhanced at all levels. In particular, were a member of a provincial legislature or federal Parliament to have experience as a mayor or councillor of an urban municipality, she or he would bring that sensitivity of urban and municipal issues to other levels of government. In federal–provincial relationships this function is described as strengthening institutions of intrastate federalism.[21]

In the urban politics literature, to the extent that parties' effects on intergovernmental relations are discussed, it is in relation to "interstate" rather than "intrastate" dimensions.[22] In the intergovernmental sphere, municipalities are represented by provincial associations or unions of municipalities and, at the federal level, by the Federation of Canadian Municipalities. Some argue that the nonpartisan nature of local politics facilitates a positive and productive relationship between municipalities and provinces. As former mayor of Westmount, Quebec, W.D. Lighthall put it in a speech delivered to the (American) National Municipal League in 1917, "the chief advantage is that [nonpartisan elections] sever the municipal policy from all sorts of state and federal considerations. It thus enables a municipality to come before its legislature standing on the merits of its demands" (Lighthall 1917, republished in Anderson 1972, 31). Lightbody (2006, 240) argues that the introduction of parties wouldn't undermine localities' ability to cooperate with other levels of government or have a significant negative impact upon them, both because federal and provincial parties aren't integrated and because a great deal of provincial legislation that applies to municipalities is general in scope. It would therefore be difficult for a provincial government to punish any one city. The diversity and sheer number of municipalities would have the same effect, a situation that led Stefan Dupré (1968) to conclude that municipalities were only in a position of "hyper-fractionalized quasi-subordination" rather than complete subordination to their provincial creators. To a large degree, Lightbody is likely correct on this point, since a great deal of intergovernmental relations has been conducted through municipal associations and laws and policies governing municipalities have largely been general in scope.

Nevertheless, there is reason to believe that intergovernmental relations could become more complex as cities are delegated more power and financial responsibility. The trend toward establishing city charters for major cities in provincial municipal systems is an acknowledgement that provincial–municipal relationships will become increasingly asymmetrical and could logically lead to demands for more government-to-government interaction, especially with municipalities representing core areas of major cities.[23] As the interests and responsibilities of a province's largest city or cities diverge from other urban and rural municipalities, and possibly also among such cities, it becomes difficult for provincial associations to represent them in intergovernmental negotiations. It is precisely this source of tension that led to the withdrawal of the City of Toronto from the Association of Municipalities Ontario (AMO) in the midst of negotiations surrounding a memorandum of understanding to guide relations between the AMO and the province (Siegel 2009, 47–48). The City of Toronto's new charter also legislates the municipality's ability to enter into intergovernmental negotiations and agreements with the federal government without the province's involvement or consent.[24] Although the extent to which provinces would be willing to accept direct federal–municipal interaction varies significantly across the country,[25] the more general point here is that intergovernmental relations are becoming more complex, and to the extent that government-to-government relations become the norm, party politics could either introduce barriers to or facilitate intergovernmental cooperation.

Furthermore, the question of the relationship between parties and intergovernmental relations does not only arise in "vertical" relations. It also has important horizontal dimensions, which are rarely mentioned. Cooperation among municipalities within city regions could be compromised by the introduction of party politics, especially if the parties were national parties with clear ideological positions. According to Alan Walks (2005), there is evidence of the emergence of an urban–suburban cleavage in Canadian cities. Accentuating such a cleavage could complicate cooperation in important areas of common concern in city regions, especially in major cities with fragmented urban systems, such as Toronto and Vancouver. In Vancouver, parties (called *elector organizations* officially and sometimes *slates* on the ground) are local and independent in two senses: horizontally and vertically. For instance, independent parties compete in many of the municipalities in Greater Vancouver that surround the City of Vancouver, including in the City of Richmond and the City of Surrey (Good 2009, 148–51; Smith and Stewart 2009, 301). Although to my knowledge there is nothing written on the subject, there is no evidence to suggest that parties influence city region dynamics there.

Adrian (1952) offers a final hypothesis concerning the consequences of nonpartisan elections, arguing that they appear to contribute to weakening political parties at other levels of government by reducing the number of offices controlled by parties as well as by cutting parties away from their local "roots" and thereby weakening local party organizations and their ability to campaign effectively. As discussed above, they also weaken parties by segregating candidate recruitment pools among levels of government. More generally, nonpartisan elections could contribute to the decline of partisan ties at other levels by reducing the salience of party in voters' minds. Arguably, many of the same effects on parties at other levels would apply in the cases where independent local parties compete; in that case "split-ticket" voting—whereby voters opt for one party in one electoral arena, and for another party in another electoral arena"—(Mair 2013, 36) would be the culprit responsible for weakening general levels of partisanship. Nevertheless, this argument loses ground when one considers that "split-ticket" voting, which is well established and growing in Canada, is also increasing in other countries, such as Australia, Sweden, and the United States (Mair 2013, 36–37).

Furthermore, how one ought to measure the "stability" of partisan attachments in Canada is highly contested among scholars of Canadian voting behaviour. In particular, the notion that people with strong, stable (but different) partisan attachments at the federal and provincial levels should be considered "flexible partisans" with weaker partisan attachments than "durable" partisans is questioned (Gidengil et al. 2012, Chapter 4). As Gidengil et al. (2012, 55) observe, "having different party attachments at the federal and provincial levels may be less a matter of inconsistency than a case of dual identifications in a highly decentralized federal system, especially given that some provincial parties have no federal counterparts." Thus, at least in this way, Anglo-democracies and European countries where local parties are well established seem to be moving in a more Canadian direction with respect to splitting the ticket. In sum, tri-level splitting in Canada simply extends Canadian political practices from other levels of government; whether this practice weakens partisanship in general is highly contested by scholars of Canadian voting behaviour.

Conclusion: Are Municipal Political Parties the Answer?

Local political parties and debates about them have tended to emerge in times of political turmoil and perceived crisis in urban places. In the 1970s, the decade of urban reform debates, several academics who studied local parties seemed to believe that local political parties were inevitable (Anderson 1972, 21). Andrew Sancton (2006, 311–15) argues that, if anything, we are further away from having party politics at the local level.

The direction of both institutional and social change suggests otherwise. Reform of municipal systems in provinces—toward greater legislative and fiscal power as well as asymmetry—suggests that the importance of municipalities to urban governance is gaining increased recognition. Similarly, the changing social conditions of cities calls into question the image of the homogeneous city characterized by middle class and neighbourhood-based NIMBY movements alone. The increasing social polarization of cities, the racialization of poverty, and more generally the changing ethnocultural demographics of cities is an international phenomenon that has introduced a new politics of identity and forms of political pluralism, and Canadian cities are no exception (Björkdahl and Strömbom 2015; Gagnon and Jouve 2009; Good, Turgeon, and Triadafilopoulos 2014). Research on federalism suggests that sociological diversity leads to decentralization (Erk 2007; Erk and Koning 2010). As cities increasingly become the places driving economic growth, where questions of social and environmental sustainability arise, and where identity politics is negotiated, one might argue that, were the institutional context right, municipalities' political importance could continue to grow. Indeed, advocates of greater municipal autonomy stress the importance of cities' ethnocultural diversity to the debate (see, for instance, Andrew 2001; Broadbent 2008; and Good 2009).

One of the most powerful forces against the introduction of party politics at the local level is ideational. It appears as though many Canadians still adhere to the ideal of nonpartisan local elections without questioning why. Referring to Ontario's political culture, David Siegel (2009, 35) notes a strong "stigma" attached "to any form of party involvement in local politics," which he views as "a hangover from the turn-of-the-century reform movement." And this stigma is not limited to Ontario. For instance, during a visit to Toronto to address the Toronto Region Board of Trade that took place during the City of Toronto election campaign in 2014, Calgary Mayor Naheed Nenshi offered his thoughts on ideological and party divisions in municipal politics: "Is removing the snow a right-wing or left-wing idea? Is fixing potholes more New Democrat or Conservative? . . . It's ridiculous" (cited in Gerster 2014). What is more ridiculous is that a mayor of a major city in Canada with a master's degree from Harvard University's Kennedy School of Government would imply that municipalities do nothing more than fix potholes and remove snow. The irony of minimizing the city's role in such a way and suggesting that ideological differences wouldn't matter to decision making, in the context of a trip to Toronto to sell the virtues of investment in Calgary to Toronto's business community, also speaks to a point that Lightbody and others have made with respect to the conservative and ultimately right-wing bias of nonpartisan local politics. Although party politics might not result in left-wing politics, as the NPA party's historic dominance in Vancouver attests, explicit party labels would at least put an end to claims that municipal politics are "neutral." Like all politics, municipal politics is a coalitional politics and, to the extent possible, voters ought to know how politicians "herd" (Leo 2006; Lightbody 1999, 172).

In the late twentieth and early twenty-first centuries, debates about the fundamental purpose of municipal governments and local politics have again been raised. Somewhat unexpectedly, these debates were raised most forcefully in Ontario following Conservative Premier Mike Harris's tenure (Lightbody 1999, 172). Forced municipal amalgamations and "disentanglement" exercises raised fundamental questions of local democracy, including the "quasi-constitutional" questions of the division of power between provinces and municipalities as well as the legitimacy of altering political boundaries unilaterally. One reform movement to develop was the "New Deal for Cities" (Bradford 2004), a movement that, while diverse, unlike past reform movements centred on these fundamentally *constitutional* questions. While motivated by questions of autonomy (defined in various ways), this debate also raised fundamental questions about the nature of municipalities as political institutions. What kind of decision-making institutions are appropriate to the local scale? To what extent are municipalities able to provide leadership on questions of importance in cities and in a possibly growing list of formal responsibilities? Where one stands on the question of political parties is shaped fundamentally by one's position on the nature and purpose of municipal government.

It is an inherently conservative position to suggest that because local parties haven't emerged or because citizens do not seem to care about municipal politics, urban communities could not support a vibrant municipally based partisan politics. Current local political cultures and institutions have been shaped by their historical paths, including their history of a limited franchise, strong connection to property (still reflected in municipal electoral laws that permit property owners to vote in all municipalities in which they own properties), and provincial control. There are significant institutional disincentives to the emergence of party politics at the local level in Canada (Clarkson 1972). The more radical debate concerns whether municipalities are fundamentally a form of democratic government, what powers municipalities ought to have to facilitate authentic community-based governance, and whether political parties would be a useful way to organize such politics.

As the above discussion suggests, the effect that parties would have on local politics is not clear. A great deal of research is needed to fill gaps in our understanding of both partisan and nonpartisan local politics. Based on experience with party government at other levels, one might argue cynically that parties do not always implement their platforms. Others might say that their marketing techniques and practices in government (such as strict party discipline) contribute to voter disengagement. It might therefore seem out of touch to suggest that parties could contribute to a vibrant local democracy at the municipal level. However, as compared with the alternative—nonpartisan politics—several clear virtues of partisan politics seem apparent. Parties would simplify municipal ballots for voters and could introduce greater discussion of issues in local campaigns. It is difficult to imagine how this wouldn't be the case in relation to the status quo, which is dominated by individual notoriety. Furthermore, an issue-based politics could be encouraged with the introduction of political parties by clarifying where the mayor and individual councillors stand on issues during election campaigns as well as by facilitating the implementation and evaluation of electoral mandates through the establishment of relatively stable coalitions on council. The research also suggests that partisan elections could contribute to increasing voter turnout at the local level, especially if combined with other democratic reform measures, including reforms to strengthen the executive power of mayors (see Hajnal 2010, 160). Finally, there is ample reason to believe that party politics at the local level would not suffer from the same pathologies of parties at other levels (admittedly, different ones might manifest, though). In both Montreal and Vancouver, the core municipalities in Canada's second- and third-largest cities respectively, party systems have become more decentralized and fragmented.

In my view, a party system in which parties could easily enter and exit the system could provide a way of introducing some stability and transparency into local political coalitions without sacrificing the openness of the system to citizen participation. Although independent local parties could be a welcome addition to the municipal sphere, the entry of national (federal) parties would be unfortunate and destined to increase intergovernmental conflict. For the many reasons discussed above, there is also cause to believe that independent, locally based party systems would be the norm. The evidence includes past failures of national parties to enter local politics, the fragmented and highly decentralized nature of Canada's party system at other levels, as well as the social foundations of decentralization. Locally based parties would also arguably be more appropriate given the political culture of nonpartisanship that exists at the local level.

It seems illegitimate from a democratic perspective to forbid local candidates from running as teams in local elections and, more specifically, to disallow partisan affiliations on municipal ballots.[26] Although the burden to make the case for reform always seems to be on the reformers, advocates of the status quo have yet to make a strong case that nonpartisan politics enhances the quality of municipal democracy. One clear conclusion to be reached here is that there is much work to be done in the largely unexplored empirical terrain of nonpartisan and independently partisan politics in Canada. This research ought to address fundamental questions about the quality of local democracy in Canada through comparative analysis combining both subnational and cross-national comparisons. In particular, comparisons should incorporate municipal contexts that are nonpartisan—cities where independent parties compete (like Vancouver and Montreal)—as well as cases where national parties compete, such as in some American cities and most European cities.

Systematic research is needed on all of the fundamental questions concerning the relationship between parties and the quality of local democratic governance, including how councillors and residents view elected officials' roles (and whether they are in harmony), whether lines of accountability are clear, municipal responsiveness to citizens, municipal policy capacity, voter turnout and citizen engagement, and others. Moreover, in light of the dominant focus of the urban politics literature on governance to the neglect of the electoral arena (see Clark and Krebs 2012, 87), a research agenda that investigates the consequences of partisan and nonpartisan politics within the context of broader community power structures are sorely needed. This is where small-*n* comparative research designs and case studies could make a significant contribution to our understanding of municipal democracy and the political institutions that might best sustain it. Ultimately, this empirical research ought to take place within an explicit normative debate about the fundamental purpose of municipalities within Canada.

This is an exciting time to study cities. Canada's many cities and variations of partisan and nonpartisan politics provide a laboratory in which to test and compare the effects of parties on local democracy. Although we are accustomed to thinking about municipal politics not only as a different form of political life but also as the "lowest" form of political life (Clarkson 2002, 103), it could be at the grassroots that we find insights into how to improve democratic politics—including a party-based democratic politics—at other levels as well.

Suggested Resources

Good, Kristin R. 2009. *Municipalities and Multiculturalism: The Politics of Immigration in Toronto and Vancouver*. Toronto: University of Toronto Press.

Lightbody, James. 1999. "Finding the Trolls under Your Bridge: The New Case for Party Politics in Canadian Cities." *Journal of Canadian Studies* 34 (1): 172–83.

Munger, Andrew, dir. 2004. *Campaign: The Making of a Candidate* [Film]. National Film Board. https://www.nfb.ca/film/campaign_the_making_of_a_candidate

Siegel, David. 2015. *Leaders in the Shadows: The Leadership Qualities of Municipal Chief Administrative Officers*. Toronto: University of Toronto Press.

Tindal, Richard C., Susan Nobes Tindal, Kennedy Stewart, and Patrick J. Smith. 2013. *Local Government in Canada*. 8th ed. Toronto: Nelson.

Urbaniak, Tom. 2009. *Her Worship: Hazel McCallion and the Development of Mississauga*. Toronto: University of Toronto Press.

Notes

1   The author would like to thank Lionel Feldman as well as the editors, Alain-G. Gagnon and Brian Tanguay, for their helpful feedback on this work.

2   Had the basis for these mayoral powers been established in provincial legislation, an amendment to the City of Toronto Act (2006) would have been necessary. Unlike the federal and provincial governments, which are sovereign in their areas of jurisdiction, municipalities' governance structures, elections, as well as legislative and fiscal powers are all established through provincial legislation. This fundamental condition is rooted in municipalities' lack of independent constitutional status and provinces' exclusive responsibility to make laws regarding municipalities and municipal institutions. The legal debates are somewhat more complex than this. For instance, there is debate about whether some of council's

motions to limit Ford's powers (including the limits on his budget) influenced the mayor's ability to perform even the limited tasks established in the City of Toronto Act (2006) (see Flynn-Guglietti et al. 2013). These nuances aside, the general principle of councils being collectively responsible for leadership and delegation of their authority is well established in Canadian municipal law.

3   Although for Ford's supporters and others the spectre of a premier empowering a council to remove a democratically elected mayor from office would seem clearly undemocratic, Canada's fundamental (constitutional) law would permit such action, just as provinces can unilaterally amalgamate and disband municipal institutions. In 2006, Karen Casey, minister of education in Nova Scotia, dismissed the entire (democratically elected) Halifax Regional School Board for failure to "act in a professional manner" (Nova Scotia 2006), replacing the 13-member board with a single appointee.

4   Leaders at the provincial and federal levels in Canada are more difficult to remove than in other Anglo-parliamentary democracies insofar as they are not subject to removal by elected members of their parliamentary caucus, as is the case in Britain and Australia, for instance (Cross and Blais 2012). Nevertheless, history shows that Canadian parties find ways to remove leaders who have lost their party's support. It is unlikely that a government leader could maintain the support of their own party members under circumstances similar to the Ford scandal unless voters were clearly on their side. Furthermore, in federal and provincial parliaments/legislatures, if a leader of a government plagued by a scandal similar to the Ford fiasco refused to resign, as a last resort the parliament could withdraw its confidence and an election would be called—although, admittedly, in a majority government situation, a vote of nonconfidence would be unlikely. The Reform Act introduced as a private member's bill by Conservative MP Michael Chong in the last session of the 41st Parliament empowers caucuses to decide whether, among other powers, they would like the power to review and remove their leader as well as to select an interim leader.

5   Although partisan politics in British Columbia has a much longer history, partisan ballots were introduced by the NDP government led by Michael Harcourt (1991–96) in 1992 (Smith and Stewart 2009, 300). Legislation recognizing municipal political parties in Quebec municipalities with populations greater than 100,000 was passed in 1978 and its scope was broadened in both 1979 and 1998 (Belley et al. 2009, 108). According to Louise Quesnel (1986, 69), who identifies 1979 as the legislative turning point (likely because the law's applicability was extended considerably to include municipalities with populations above 20,000), municipal parties emerged in about 30 municipalities between 1982 and 1985 as a consequence of these legal changes.

6   For instance, in Toronto, where elections are fought on a formally nonpartisan basis, some refer to the existence of "shadow" parties; the coalitions on the left are sometimes "dubbed the 'NDP' by media" (Siegel 2009, 35). This is the case in smaller provinces and cities as well, including some in New Brunswick (Bourgeois and Strain 2009, 205).

7   For instance, in England over 92 per cent of council seats are held by national parties (Copus et al. 2012, 214).

8   In 1921, there were only six urban areas in Canada with a population over 100,000 and no metropolitan area had more than 1 million residents (Bradford 2002, 4).

Today, 33 urban areas have populations of more than 100,000, and six have populations over 1 million (Statistics Canada 2015).

9   Dillon's Rule "was set down by Iowa Supreme Court Judge John F. Dillon in the 1860s; Dillon equated municipalities with business corporations, both of them limited to the powers expressly granted through their incorporation. Like Canadian municipalities being 'creatures of the province' (under section 92.8), Dillon described local governments as 'tenants at will' of the states" (Tindal et al. 2013, 203).

10   Charters exist for most of Canada's largest and most provincially significant cities, including Vancouver, Winnipeg, Montreal, Toronto, and Halifax. Negotiations are underway for the establishment of city charters for Calgary and Edmonton.

11   As discussed later in this chapter, the Drapeau years in Montreal are often cited as an example of both what can be accomplished with a strong concentration of power on a municipal council and the potential costs to local participation of such centralization.

12   Since corrupt local political machines did not exist at the local level in Canada, clearly its historical "path" to nonpartisan politics differed. According to Anderson (1972), these "indigenous factors" include Canada's slower rate of urbanization, the relative homogeneity of its cities, and the greater level of provincial control over municipalities in Canada than of state control over municipalities in the United States (Anderson 1972, 9). Furthermore, the later adoption of the universal municipal franchise in Canada than in the United States was also a significant factor (Taylor 2014, 60).

13   In at-large systems, the city is not divided into wards or districts (territorial subdivisions) for the purposes of electing councillors, but rather is treated as a single constituency for the election of both the mayor and councillors. Thus, in such systems, voters vote for as many councillors as there are positions on council. In theory, such systems encourage councillors (and not only the mayor) to adopt a city-wide perspective on issues since the link between a particular neighbourhood or geographical area of the city and councillors is absent. Nevertheless, among the most important critiques of such systems is that they dilute minority votes.

14   Two seminal contributions to this debate between the elitist and pluralist perspectives, respectively, are Floyd Hunter's (1953) *Community Power Structure* and Robert A. Dahl's (1961) *Who Governs?*

15   For instance, in their quantitative study of local election exit polls, Hajnal and Trounstine (2014) found that race, party, and ideology are all significant in explaining voting behaviour, with race being the deepest political cleavage in American cities.

16   In his path-breaking article, Charles Tiebout (1956) argued that in a fragmented metropolitan system (in other words, a metropolitan area with multiple municipalities) residents would vote with their feet and settle or move to the jurisdiction that offers the best mix of services and tax rates, eventually resulting in an equilibrium. This spatial sorting leads municipalities to compete for residents and leads to a convergence in their politics. In fact, strong versions of the model view Tiebout competition as an alternative to politics (Kollman, Miller, and Page 1997, 977).

17　As part of this study's remarkably comprehensive research design, a survey was sent to every American city with more than 2,500 residents. The response rate was 66 per cent (Hajnal 2010, 31).

18　According to Collin and Robertson (2004), like other provinces in Canada Quebec's nonpartisan tradition is strong and parties in the province are more like slates that are organized around issues at election time and then fade away (see also Belley et al. 2009, 109).

19　See Feldman and Graham (2005) for an overview of possible reforms to strengthen municipal mayors' powers.

20　The mayor's office is responsible for the preparation and administration of the city budget as well as having control over the administration. Strong mayors also sometimes possess a veto that may be overridden by council.

21　Herman Bakvis and Brian Tanguay (2012, 98) make this point in relation to assessing the effects of party systems on integrating regional perspectives into Canada's institutions of intrastate federalism. Because the relationship between municipalities and other levels of government is not one of constitutional equals, the language of "intrastate federalism" doesn't apply.

22　*Interstate* relations refer to relations among governments, whereas *intrastate* relations refer to the extent to which the representation of subunits is incorporated into a central government's political institutions.

23　A government-to-government relationship and an acknowledgement of significant asymmetry in municipal systems is also the principle underlying urban development agreements like the Vancouver Agreement (2000–10). However, intergovernmental agreements generally lack legal enforceability and depend on the ongoing goodwill of the partners in contrast to city charters, which establish the legal basis of a distinct relationship with provinces.

24　The process of negotiating the Stronger City of Toronto for a Strong Ontario Act (2006) also reflects this turn toward government-to-government relations. Siegel (2009, 25) describes the process as "groundbreaking."

25　For instance, municipal law in Quebec states that municipalities cannot accept funding from the federal government without the province's consent. This law was passed shortly after the 1982 patriation of the Constitution without the Quebec National Assembly's consent. The extent to which provinces insist on relationships with the federal government being mediated by provinces varies, with "have less" provinces more likely to allow municipalities to seek money from the federal government (Garcea and Pontikes 2006).

26　A fringe mayoral candidate who ran (unofficially, of course) as a member of the "Toronto Party" in the 2014 election launched a court challenge of the province's electoral law that bans the inclusion of partisan affiliations on municipal ballots (Barber 2014).

References

Adrian, Charles R. 1952. "Some General Characteristics of Nonpartisan Elections." *American Political Science Review* 46 (3): 766–76. http://dx.doi.org/10.2307/1952283

Anderson, J.D. 1972. "Nonpartisan Urban Politics." In *Emerging Party Politics in Urban Canada,* edited by Jack K. Masson and James D. Anderson, 5–25. Toronto: McClelland and Stewart.

Andrew, Caroline. 2001. "The Shame of (Ignoring) the Cities." *Journal of Canadian Studies* 35 (4): 100–10.

Andrew, Caroline, John Biles, Myer Siemiatycki, and Erin Tolley. 2008. "Conclusion." In *Electing a Diverse Canada: The Representation of Immigrants, Minorities, and Women,* edited by Caroline Andrew, John Biles, Myer Siemiatycki, and Erin Tolley, 255–69. Vancouver: University of British Columbia Press.

Aucoin, Peter, Mark D. Jarvis, and Lori Turnbull. 2011. *Democratizing the Constitution: Reforming Responsible Government.* Toronto: Emond Montgomery.

Bakvis, Herman, and A. Brian Tanguay. 2012. "Federalism, Political Parties, and the Burden of National Unity: Still Making Federalism Do the Heavy Lifting?" In *Canadian Federalism: Performance, Effectiveness and Legitimacy,* 3rd ed., edited by Herman Bakvis and Grace Skogstad, 96–115. Toronto: Oxford University Press.

Barber, John. 2014. "A Partisan Conspiracy." *Torontoist,* January 9. http://torontoist. com/2014/01/a-partisan-conspiracy/

Belley, Serge, Laurence Bherer, Guy Chiasson, Jean-Pierre Collin, Pierre Hamel, and Mathieu Rivard, with Julie Archambault. 2009. "Quebec." In *Foundations of Governance: Municipal Government in Canada's Provinces,* edited by Andrew Sancton and Robert Young, 70–137. Toronto: University of Toronto Press.

Bish, Robert L. 2001. "Local Government Amalgamations: Discredited Nineteenth-Century Ideals Alive in the Twenty-First." *The Urban Papers* no. 150, C.D. Howe Institute Commentary (March).

Björkdahl, Annika, and Lisa Strömbom, eds. 2015. *Divided Cities: Governing Diversity.* Lund, Sweden: Nordic Academic Press.

Boudreau, Julie-Anne. 2006. "Intergovernmental Relations and Polyscalar Social Mobilization: The Cases of Montreal and Toronto." In *Canada: The State of the Federation 2004,* edited by Robert Young and Christian Leuprecht, 161–80. Montreal: McGill-Queen's University Press.

Bourgeois, Daniel, and Yves Bourgeois. 2005. "Territory, Institutions and National Identity: The Case of Acadians in Greater Moncton, Canada." *Urban Studies* 42 (7): 1123–38. http://dx.doi.org/10.1080/03056240500121123

Bourgeois, Daniel, and Yves Bourgeois. 2011. "Les municipalités canadiennes et les langues officielles." *Canadian Journal of Political Science* 44 (4): 789–806. http:// dx.doi.org/10.1017/S0008423911000758

Bourgeois, Daniel, and Frank Strain. 2009. "New Brunswick." In *Foundations of Governance: Municipal Government in Canada's Provinces,* edited by Andrew Sancton and Robert Young, 186–222. Toronto: University of Toronto Press.

Bradford, Neil. 2002. "Why Cities Matter: Policy Research Perspectives for Canada." CPRN, Discussion Paper No. F23. Ottawa: Canadian Policy Research Networks.

Bradford, Neil. 2004. "Canada's Urban Agenda: A New Deal for Cities?" In *Canadian Politics,* 4th ed., edited by James Bickerton and Alain-G. Gagnon, 425–46. Peterborough, ON: Broadview Press.

Broadbent, Alan. 2008. *Urban Nation: Why We Need to Give Power Back to the Cities to Make Canada Strong.* Toronto: HarperCollins.

Browning, Rufus P., Dale R. Marshall, and David H. Tabb. 1984. *Protest Is Not Enough: The Struggle of Blacks and Hispanics for Equality in the United States.* Berkeley: University of California Press.

Clark, Alistair, and Timothy B. Krebs. 2012. "Elections and Policy Responsiveness." In *The Oxford Handbook of Urban Politics,* edited by Karen Mossberger, Susan E. Clarke, and Peter John, 87–113. New York: Oxford University Press.

Clarke, Susan E., and Keeley W. Stokes. 2014. "Social Cohesion and Democratic Voice: Path to Political Incorporation." In *Segmented Cities? How Urban Contexts Shape Ethnic and Nationalist Politics,* edited by Kristin R. Good, Luc Turgeon, and Triadafilos Triadafilopoulous, 250–76. Vancouver: University of British Columbia Press.

Clarkson, Stephen. 1972. "Barriers to Entry of Political Parties into Toronto's Politics." In *Emerging Party Politics in Urban Canada,* edited by Jack K. Masson and James D. Anderson, 158–81. Toronto: McClelland and Stewart.

Clarkson, Stephen. 2002. *Uncle Sam and Us: Globalization, Neoconservatism, and the Canadian State.* Toronto: University of Toronto Press.

Collin, Jean-Pierre, and Mélanie Robertson. 2004. "Metropolitan Change and Related Political Behaviour in a Canadian Metropolis." Working paper presented at the meeting of the International Metropolitan Observatory, Université de Bordeaux, January 9–10.

Copus, Colin, Melvin Wingfield, Kristof Steyvers, and Herwig Reynaert. 2012. "A Place to Party? Parties and Nonpartisanship in Local Government." In *The Oxford Handbook of Urban Politics,* edited by Karen Mossberger, Susan E. Clarke, and Peter John, 210–30. New York: Oxford University Press. http://dx.doi.org/10.1093/oxfordhb/9780195367867.013.0011

Cross, William P., and André Blais. 2012. *Politics at the Centre: The Selection and Removal of Party Leaders in the Anglo Parliamentary Democracies.* New York: Oxford University Press.

Dahl, Robert A. 1961. *Who Governs? Democracy and Power in an American City.* New Haven, CT: Yale University Press.

Dupré, Stefan. 1968. *Intergovernmental Finance in Ontario: A Provincial-Level Perspective.* Toronto: Ontario Commission on Taxation, Government of Ontario.

Dyck, Rand. 1996. "Relations between Federal and Provincial Parties." In *Canadian Parties in Transition,* 2nd ed., edited by A. Brian Tanguay and Alain-G. Gagnon, 160–89. Toronto: Nelson.

Erk, Jan. 2007. *Explaining Federalism: State, Society and Congruence in Austria, Belgium, Canada, Germany and Switzerland.* New York: Routledge.

Erk, Jan, and Edward Koning. 2010. "New Structuralism and Institutional Change: Federalism between Centralization and Decentralization." *Comparative Political Studies* 43 (3): 353–78. http://dx.doi.org/10.1177/0010414009332143

Farkas, Jeromy Anton. 2013. "Growing the Democratic Toolbox: City Council Vote Tracking." September 20. Calgary: The Manning Foundation for Democratic Education.

Feldman, Lionel D., and Katherine A. Graham. 2005. "Background Paper: Discussion Papers on Selected Urban Governance Models." Prepared for consideration by the Governing Toronto Advisory Panel, November.

Ferreira, Fernando, and Joseph Gyourko. 2009. "Do Political Parties Matter? Evidence from US Cities." *Quarterly Journal of Economics* 124 (1): 399–422. http://dx.doi.org/10.1162/qjec.2009.124.1.399

Filion, Pierre. 1999. "Civic Parties in Canada: Their Diversity and Evolution." In *Local Political Parties in Political and Organizational Perspective,* edited by Martin Saiz and Hans Geser, 77–100. Boulder, CO: Westview Press.

Flynn-Guglietti, Mary, Annik Forristal, Adam D.H. Chisholm, and Ciaron Burke. 2013. "Did the City of Toronto Council Have the Right to Strip the Mayor of His Powers?" *Municipal Law Bulletin* (December). Toronto: McMillan LLP.

Gagnon, Alain-G., and Bernard Jouve, eds. 2009. *Facing Cultural Diversity: Cities under Stress.* Lyon: University of Lyon Press.

Garbaye, Romain. 2004. "Ethnic Minority Local Councillors in French and British Cities: Social Determinants and Political Opportunity Structures." In *Citizenship in European Cities: Immigrants, Local Politics and Integration Policies,* edited by Rinus Penninx, Karen Kraal, Marco Martiniello, and Steven Vertovec, 39–56. Hants, UK: Ashgate.

Garcea, Joseph. 2014. "The Empowerment of Canadian Cities: Classic Canadian Compromise." *International Journal of Canadian Studies* 49: 81–104. http://dx.doi.org/10.3138/ijcs.49.81

Garcea, Joseph, and Ken Pontikes. 2006. "Federal-Municipal-Provincial Relations in Saskatchewan: Provincial Roles, Approaches and Mechanisms." In *Canada: The State of the Federation 2004,* edited by Robert Young and Christian Leuprecht, 333–67. Montreal: McGill-Queen's University Press.

Gavan-Koop, Denisa, and Patrick Smith. 2008. "Gendering Local Governing." *Canadian Political Science Review* 3 (3): 152–71.

Gerster, Jane. 2014. "Calgary Mayor Offers Toronto Candidates Some Advice." *Toronto Star,* February 28. http://www.thestar.com/news/gta/2014/02/28/calgary_mayor_offers_toronto_candidates_some_advice.html

Gidengil, Elizabeth, Neil Nevitte, André Blais, Joanna Everitt, and Patrick Fournier. 2012. *Dominance and Decline: Making Sense of Recent Canadian Elections.* Toronto: University of Toronto Press.

Good, Kristin R. 2005. "Patterns of Politics in Canada's Immigrant-Receiving Cities and Suburbs: How Settlement Patterns Shape the Municipal Role in Multiculturalism Policy." *Policy Studies* 26 (3–4): 261–89. http://dx.doi.org/10.1080/01442870500198312

Good, Kristin R. 2009. *Municipalities and Multiculturalism: The Politics of Immigration in Toronto and Vancouver.* Toronto: University of Toronto Press.

Good, Kristin R. 2014. "Governing Immigrant Attraction and Retention in Halifax and Moncton: Do Linguistic Divisions Impede Cooperation?" In *Comparing Canada: Methods and Perspectives on Canadian Politics,* edited by Luc Turgeon, Martin Papillon, Jennifer Wallner, and Stephen White, 292–316. Vancouver: University of British Columbia Press.

Good, Kristin R., Luc Turgeon, and Triadafilos Triadafilopoulos, eds. 2014. *Segmented Cities? How Urban Contexts Shape Ethnic and Nationalist Politics.* Vancouver: University of British Columbia Press.

Gore, Christopher, Pamela Robinson, and Richard Stren. 2012. "Governance and Climate Change: Assessing and Learning from Canadian Cities." In *Cities and Climate Change: Responding to an Urgent Agenda,* edited by Daniel Hoornweg et al., 498–523. Washington, DC: World Bank.

Hajnal, Zoltan L. 2010. *America's Uneven Democracy: Race, Turnout, and Representation in City Politics.* New York: Cambridge University Press.

Hajnal, Zoltan L., and Jessica Trounstine. 2014. "What Underlies Urban Politics? Race, Class, Ideology, Partisanship, and the Urban Vote." *Urban Affairs Review* 50 (1): 63–99. http://dx.doi.org/10.1177/1078087413485216

Horak, Martin. 1998. "The Power of Local Identity: C4LD and the Anti-Amalgamation Mobilization in Toronto." Research Paper No. 195. Toronto: Centre for Urban and Community Studies.

Hunter, Floyd. 1953. *Community Power Structure: A Study of Decision Makers*. Chapel Hill: University of North Carolina Press.

John, Peter. 2001. *Local Governance in Western Europe*. London: Sage.

Jones-Correa, Michael. 1998. *Between Two Nations: The Political Predicament of Latinos in New York City*. Ithaca, NY: Cornell University Press.

Keil, Roger, and Douglas Young. 2003. "A Charter for the People? A Research Note on the Debate about Municipal Autonomy in Toronto." *Urban Affairs Review* 39 (1): 87–102. http://dx.doi.org/10.1177/1078087403253055

Kollman, Ken, John H. Miller, and Scott E. Page. 1997. "Political Institutions and Sorting in a Tiebout Model." *American Economic Review* 87 (7): 977–92.

Leo, Christopher. 2006. "What's Wrong with Municipal Political Parties?" Blog entry. November 19. http://christopherleo.com/2006/11/19/whats-wrong-with-municipal-political-parties/#more-2861

Leo, Christopher, and Mark Piel. 2005. "Municipal Reform in Manitoba: Homogenizing, Empowering, and Marketing Municipal Government." In *Municipal Reform in Canada: Reconfiguration, Re-empowerment, and Rebalancing,* edited by Joseph Garcea and Edward C. LeSage, Jr., 106–26. Toronto: Oxford University Press.

Lightbody, James. 1999. "Finding the Trolls under Your Bridge: The New Case for Party Politics in Canadian Cities." *Journal of Canadian Studies* 34 (1): 172–83.

Lightbody, James. 2006. *City Politics, Canada*. Peterborough, ON: Broadview Press.

Lighthall, W.D. 1917. "The Elimination of Political Parties in Canadian Cities." *National Municipal Review* 6 (2): 207–9. http://dx.doi.org/10.1002/ncr.4110060203

Logan, John R., and Harvey L. Molotch. 1987. *Urban Fortunes: The Political Economy of Place*. Berkeley: University of California Press.

Magnusson, Warren. 2005. "Are Municipalities Creatures of the Provinces?" *Journal of Canadian Studies* 32 (2): 5–29.

Mair, Peter. 2013. *Ruling the Void: The Hollowing Out of Western Democracy*. London: Verso.

Milroy, Beth. 2002. "Toronto's Legal Challenge." In *Urban Affairs: Back on the Policy Agenda,* edited by Caroline Andrew, Katherine A. Graham, and Susan D. Phillips, 157–78. Montreal: McGill-Queen's University Press.

Mossberger, Karen, and Gerry Stoker. 2001. "The Evolution of Urban Regime Theory: The Challenge of Conceptualization." *Urban Affairs Review* 36 (6): 810–35.

National League of Cities. 2015. "Partisan vs. Nonpartisan Elections." Accessed January 17. http://www.nlc.org/build-skills-and-networks/resources/cities-101/city-officials/partisan-vs-nonpartisan-elections

Nova Scotia. 2006. "Minister Moves to Take Control of Halifax Regional School Board." News Release. Department of Education, December 19.

Peterson, Paul E. 1981. *City Limits*. Chicago: University of Chicago Press. http://dx.doi.org/10.7208/chicago/9780226922645.001.0001

Quesnel, Louise. 1986. "La démocratie municipal au Québec." *Démocratie et libéralisme* 9: 61–97.

Riker, William. 1964. *Federalism: Origin, Operation, Significance*. Boston: Little, Brown.

Sancton, Andrew. 1994. "Mayors as Political Leaders." In *Leaders and Leadership in Canada,* edited by Maureen Mancuso, Richard Price, and Ronald Wagenberg, 174–89. Toronto: Oxford University Press.

Sancton, Andrew. 2006. "City Politics: Municipalities and Multi-level Governance." In *Canadian Cities in Transition: Local through Global Perspectives,* 3rd ed., edited by Trudi Bunting and Pierre Filion, 306–19. Toronto: Oxford University Press.

Sancton, Andrew. 2008. *The Limits of Boundaries: Why City-Regions Cannot Be Self-Governing.* Montreal: McGill-Queen's University Press.

Sancton, Andrew. 2012. "The Urban Agenda." In *Canadian Federalism: Performance, Effectiveness and Legitimacy,* 3rd ed., edited by Herman Bakvis and Grace Skogstad, 302–19. Toronto: Oxford University Press.

Sancton, Andrew. 2015. *Canadian Local Government: An Urban Perspective.* 2nd ed. Toronto: Oxford University Press.

Schaffner, Brian F., Matthew Streb, and Gerald Wright. 2001. "Teams without Uniforms: The Nonpartisan Ballot in State and Local Elections." *Political Research Quarterly* 54 (1): 7–30.

Siegel, David. 1987. "City Hall Doesn't Need Parties." *Policy Options* (June): 26–27.

Siegel, David. 1994. "Politics, Politicians, and Public Servants in Non-partisan Local Governments." *Canadian Public Administration* 37 (1): 7–30. http://dx.doi.org/10.1111/j.1754-7121.1994.tb00845.x

Siegel, David. 2009. "Ontario." In *Foundations of Governance: Municipal Government in Canada's Provinces,* edited by Andrew Sancton and Robert Young, 20–69. Toronto: University of Toronto Press.

Siegel, David. 2010. "The Leadership Role of the Municipal Chief Administrative Officer." *Canadian Public Administration* 53 (2): 139–61. http://dx.doi.org/10.1111/j.1754-7121.2010.00122.x

Siegel, David. 2015. *Leaders in the Shadows: The Leadership Qualities of Municipal Chief Administrative Officers.* Toronto: University of Toronto Press.

Smiley, D.V. 1987. *The Federal Condition in Canada.* Toronto: McGraw-Hill Ryerson.

Smith, Patrick J., and Kennedy Stewart. 2009. "British Columbia." In *Foundations of Governance: Municipal Government in Canada's Provinces,* edited by Andrew Sancton and Robert Young, 282–313. Toronto: University of Toronto Press.

Statistics Canada. 2015. "Population of Metropolitan Areas." February 11. http://www.statcan.gc.ca/tables-tableaux/sum-som/l01/cst01/dem005a-eng.htm

Stone, Clarence. 1989. *Regime Politics: Governing Atlanta 1946–1988.* Lawrence: University Press of Kansas.

Taylor, Zack. 2014. "If Different, Then Why? Explaining the Divergent Political Development of Canadian and American Local Governance." *International Journal of Canadian Studies* 49: 53–80. http://dx.doi.org/10.3138/ijcs.49.53

Tiebout, Charles. 1956. "A Pure Theory of Local Expenditures." *Journal of Political Economy* 64 (5): 416–24. http://dx.doi.org/10.1086/257839

Tindal, Richard C., and Susan Nobes Tindal. 2004. *Local Government in Canada.* 6th ed. Toronto: Nelson.

Tindal, Richard C., and Susan Nobes Tindal. 2009. *Local Government in Canada.* 7th ed. Toronto: Nelson.

Tindal, Richard C., Susan Nobes Tindal, Kennedy Stewart, and Patrick J. Smith. 2013. *Local Government in Canada*. 8th ed. Toronto: Nelson.

Tolley, Erin, and Robert Young, eds. 2011. *Immigrant Settlement Policy in Canadian Municipalities*. Montreal: McGill-Queen's University Press.

Tossutti, Livianna S. 2012. "Municipal Roles in Immigrant Settlement, Integration and Cultural Diversity." *Canadian Journal of Political Science* 45 (3): 607–33. http://dx.doi.org/10.1017/S000842391200073X

Trent, Peter F. 2012. *The Merger Delusion: How Swallowing Its Suburbs Made an Even Bigger Mess of Montreal*. Montreal: McGill-Queen's University Press.

Trounstine, Jessica. 2008. *Political Monopolies in American Cities: The Rise and Fall of Bosses and Reformers*. Chicago: University of Chicago Press. http://dx.doi.org/10.7208/chicago/9780226812830.001.0001

Urbaniak, Tom. 2009. *Her Worship: Hazel McCallion and the Development of Mississauga*. Toronto: University of Toronto Press.

Urbaniak, Tom. 2014. "Studying Mayoral Leadership in Canada and the United States." *International Journal of Canadian Studies* 49: 205–28. http://dx.doi.org/10.3138/ijcs.49.205

Vision Vancouver. 2015. "Gregor and the Vision Team." Accessed June 15. http://www.votevision.ca/gregor_and_the_vision_team

Walks, Alan. 2005. "The City-Suburban Cleavage in Canadian Federal Politics." *Canadian Journal of Political Science* 38 (2): 383–413. http://dx.doi.org/10.1017/S0008423905030842

Walks, Alan. 2014. "Gentrification, Social Mix, and the Immigrant-Reception Function of Inner-City Neighbourhoods: Evidence from Canadian Globalizing Cities." In *Segmented Cities? How Urban Contexts Shape Ethnic and Nationalist Politics,* edited by Kristin R. Good, Luc Turgeon, and Triadafilos Triadafilopoulos, 81–114. Vancouver: University of British Columbia Press.

Welch, Susan, and Timothy Bledsoe. 1986. "The Partisan Consequences of Nonpartisan Elections and the Changing Nature of Urban Politics." *American Journal of Political Science* 30 (1): 128–39. http://dx.doi.org/10.2307/2111297

Young, Lisa, and Sam Austin. 2008. "Political Finance in City Elections: Toronto and Calgary Compared." *Canadian Political Science Review* 2 (3): 88–102.

Young, Robert. 2009. "Conclusion." In *Foundations of Governance: Municipal Government in Canada's Provinces,* edited by Andrew Sancton and Robert Young, 487–99. Toronto: University of Toronto Press.

Statistical Appendix[1]

Table A.1 Valid Votes Cast (%) and Candidates Elected (N) by Political Party at Canadian General Elections, 1925–1935

Party	1925	1926	1930	1935[2]
Liberal	40.4	43.6	43.9	44.4
	99	116	88	171
Conservative	46.6	46.2	49.0	29.8
	116	91	137	39
Progressive	8.8	6.2	2.3	—
	24	22	5	2[3]
Labour/CCF	1.6	1.5	1.2	8.9
	2	3	3[4]	7
United Farmers	—	1.9	2.2	—
	—	11	10	1[5]
Social Credit	—	—	—	4.1
	—	—	—	17
Reconstruction	—	—	—	8.7
	—	—	—	1
Others	2.6	0.6	1.4	4.1
	4	2	2	7[6]
Total valid votes	**3,144,337**	**3,256,508**	**3,898,995**	**4,406,854**
Total seats	**245**	**245**	**245**	**245**

Table A.2 Valid Votes Cast (%) and Candidates Elected (N) by Political Party at Canadian General Elections, 1940–1962

Party	1940	1945[7]	1949	1953	1957	1958	1962
Liberal	54.9	41.4	50.1	50.0	42.3	33.8	37.4
	181[8]	127	193	172	106	48	99
PC	30.6	27.7	29.7	31.0	39.0	53.7	37.3
	40	68	41	51	112	208	116
CCF/NDP	8.5	15.7	13.4	11.3	10.8	9.5	13.4
	8	28	13	23	25	8	19
Social Credit	2.7	4.1	3.9[9]	5.4	6.6	2.6	11.7
	10	13	10	15	19	—	30
Bloc Populaire	—	3.3	—	—	—	—	—
	—	2	—	—	—	—	—
Others	3.3	7.8	2.9	2.3	1.3	0.4	0.2
	6[10]	7[11]	5	4[12]	3[13]	1[14]	1[15]
Total valid votes	**4,620,260**	**5,246,130**	**5,848,971**	**5,641,272**	**6,605,980**	**7,287,297**	**7,690,134**
Total seats	**245**	**245**	**262**	**265**	**265**	**265**	**265**

Table A.3 Valid Votes Cast (%) and Candidates Elected (N) by Party at Canadian General Elections, 1963–1988

Party	1963	1965	1968	1972	1974	1979	1980	1984	1988
Liberal	41.7	40.2	45.5	38.5	43.2	40.1	44.3	28.0	31.9
	128	131	155	109	141	114	147	40	83
PC	32.8	32.4	31.4	34.9	35.4	35.9	32.5	50.0	43.0
	95	97	72	107	95	136	103	211	169
NDP	13.1	17.9	17.0	17.7	15.4	17.9	19.8	18.8	20.4
	17	21	22	31	16	26	32	30	43
Ralliement des Creditistes	—	4.6	4.4	—	—	—	—	—	—
	—	9	14	—	—	—	—	—	—
Social Credit	11.9	3.7	0.8	7.6	5.0	4.6	1.7	0.1	**
	24	5	0	15	11	6	0	0	0
Bloc Québécois	—	—	—	—	—	—	—	—	—
	—	—	—	—	—	—	—	—	—
Reform	—	—	—	—	—	—	—	—	2.1
	—	—	—	—	—	—	—	—	—
Others	0.4	1.2	0.9	1.2	0.9	1.5	1.7	3.0	2.6
	1	2	1	1	1	0	0	1	0
Total valid votes	7,894,076	7,713,316	8,125,996	9,667,489	9,505,908	11,455,702	10,947,914	12,548,721	13,175,599
Total seats	265	265	264	264	264	282	282	282	295

** Less than 0.1

Table A.4 Valid Votes Cast (%) and Candidates Elected (N) by Political Party at Canadian General Elections, 1993–2015

Party	1993	1997	2000	2004	2006	2008	2011	2015
Liberal	41.3	38.5	40.8	36.7	30.2	26.3	18.9	39.5
	177	155	172	135	103	77	34	184
PC	16.0	18.8	12.2	—	—	—	—	—
	2	20	12	—	—	—	—	—
Reform Party/Canadian Alliance[16]	18.7	19.4	25.5	—	—	—	—	—
	52	60	66	—	—	—	—	—
Conservative[17]	—	—	—	29.6	36.3	37.7	39.6	31.9
	—	—	—	99	124	143	166	99
NDP	6.9	11.0	8.5	15.7	17.5	18.2	30.6	19.7
	9	21	13	19	29	37	103	44
Bloc Québécois	13.5	10.7	10.7	12.4	10.5	10.0	6.1	4.7
	54	44	38	54	51	49	4	10
Green[18]	—	—	—	—	—	—	3.91	3.4
	—	—	—	—	—	—		1
Others	3.6	1.6	2.3	5.6	5.5	7.8	1	0.7
	1	1	0	1	1	2	0	0
Total valid votes	13,667,671	12,985,964	12,857,773	13,564,702	14,817,159	13,834,294	14,723,980	17,591,468
Total seats	295	301	301	308	308	308	308	338

Figure A.1 Federal Voter Turnout, 1867–2015

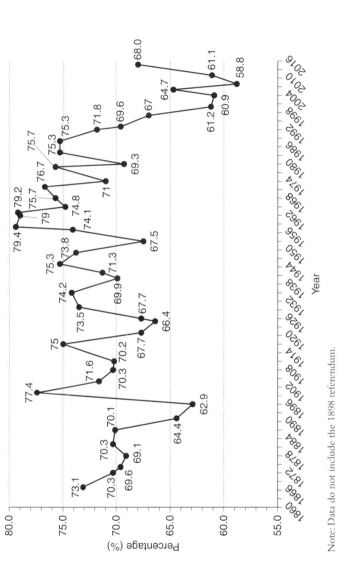

Note: Data do not include the 1898 referendum.

Source: Elections Canada. (2015). Voter Turnout at Federal Elections and Referendums.
http://www.elections.ca/content.aspx?dir=turn&document=index&lang=e&section=ele

Table A.5   Federal Voter Turnout, 1867–2015

Election/ Referendum	Population	Number of Electors on Lists	Total Ballots Cast	Voter Turnout (%)
1867	3,230,000	361,028	268,387	73.1
1872	3,689,000	426,974	318,329	70.3
1874	3,689,000	432,410	324,006	69.6
1878	3,689,000	715,279	534,029	69.1
1882	4,325,000	663,873	508,496	70.3
1887	4,325,000	948,222	724,517	70.1
1891	4,833,000	1,113,140	778,495	64.4
1896	4,833,000	1,358,328	912,992	62.9
1900	4,833,000	1,167,402	958,497	77.4
1904	5,371,000	1,385,440	1,036,878	71.6
1908	5,371,000	1,463,591	1,180,820	70.3
1911	7,204,527	1,820,742	1,314,953	70.2
1917	7,591,971	2,093,799	1,892,741	75.0
1921	8,760,211	4,435,310	3,139,306	67.7
1925	8,776,352	4,608,636	3,168,412	66.4
1926	8,887,952	4,665,381	3,273,062	67.7
1930	8,887,952	5,153,971	3,922,481	73.5
1935	10,367,063	5,918,207	4,452,675	74.2
1940	10,429,169	6,588,888	4,672,531	69.9
1942	11,494,627	6,502,234	4,638,847	71.3
1945	11,494,627	6,952,445	5,305,193	75.3
1949	11,823,649	7,893,629	5,903,572	73.8
1953	14,003,704	8,401,691	5,701,963	67.5
1957	16,073,970	8,902,125	6,680,690	74.1
1958	16,073,970	9,131,200	7,357,139	79.4
1962	18,238,247	9,700,325	7,772,656	79.0
1963	18,238,247	9,910,757	7,958,636	79.2
1965	18,238,247	10,274,904	7,796,728	74.8
1968	20,014,880	10,860,888	8,217,916	75.7
1972	21,568,311	13,000,778	9,974,661	76.7
1974	21,568,311	13,620,353	9,671,002	71.0
1979	22,992,604	15,233,653	11,541,000	75.7

1980	22,992,604	15,890,416	11,015,514	69.3
1984	24,343,181	16,774,941	12,638,424	75.3
1988	25,309,331	17,639,001	13,281,191	75.3
1992	20,400,896	13,725,966	9,855,978	71.8
1993	27,296,859	19,906,796	13,863,135	69.6
1997	27,296,859	19,663,478	13,174,698	67.0
2000	28,846,761	21,243,473	12,997,185	61.2
2004	30,007,094	22,466,621	13,683,570	60.9
2006	30,007,094	23,054,615	14,908,703	64.7
2008	31,612,897	23,677,639	13,929,093	58.8
2011	33,476,688	24,257,592	14,823,408	61.1
2015	35,749,600★	26,044,131	17,711,983	68.0

★estimate as of April 1, 2016.

References

Beck, Murray J. 1968. *Pendulum of Power: Canada's Federal Elections*. Scarborough, ON: Prentice-Hall.

Canadian Encyclopedia. 1988. Edmonton: Hurtig Publishers.

Mackie, Thomas T., and Richard Rose. 1982. *The International Almanac of Electoral History*. 2nd ed. New York: Facts on File.

Pinard, Maurice. 1975. *The Rise of a Third Party: A Study in Crisis Politics*. Montreal: McGill-Queen's University Press.

Notes

1   The authors would like to thank Emily Mann (University of Waterloo) for her invaluable work in revising these tables for the fourth edition.

2   The first electoral appearance of the Co-operative Commonwealth Federation (CCF) at the national level was in 1935.

3   The votes obtained that correspond to these seats (2 Liberal Progressive) are included under Liberal.

4   Includes 1 Independent Labour and 2 Labour.

5   The votes obtained that correspond to this seat (1 United Farmer of Ontario-Labour) are included under Other.

6   Includes 5 Independent Liberal, 1 Independent Conservative, and 1 Independent.

7   The election of 1945 was the first in which the name Progressive Conservative Party was used. The New Democratic Party (NDP) first participated in the election of 1962.

8   This total includes 3 Liberal Progressives.

9   Includes 1.5 per cent of votes received by the Union des Electeurs, the French-Canadian affiliate of Social Credit. Although more frequently referred to as

Social Credit's Quebec wing (Canadian Encyclopedia 1988, 532; Mackie and Rose 1982, 76; Pinard 1975, 53), the Union des Électeurs ran candidates in New Brunswick (1) and Ontario (4) as well as Quebec (50). See Beck (1968, 272).

10 Consists of 1 Independent Liberal, 1 United Reform, 1 Unity, and 1 Independent.

11 Consists of 1 Labour Progressive, 1 Independent Progressive, and 5 Independent.

12 Consists of 1 Liberal Labour and 3 Independent.

13 Consists of 1 Liberal Labour and 2 Independent.

14 Liberal Labour.

15 Liberal Labour.

16 The Canadian Reform Conservative Alliance replaced the Reform Party of Canada in the 2000 election.

17 The Conservative Party of Canada was formed from the merger of the Progressive Conservative and Canadian Alliance parties in December 2003.

18 As of 2011 the Green Party appears separate from the "Other" category in Elections Canada statistics.

Contributors

The Editors

Alain-G. Gagnon holds the Canada Research Chair in Quebec and Canadian Studies at the Université du Québec à Montréal. His most recent books include, as author, *The Case for Multinational Federalism* and *Minority Nations in the Age of Uncertainty;* as co-author, *Federalism, Citizenship, and Quebec;* and as co-editor, *Federal Democracies* with Michael Burgess, *Political Autonomy and Divided Societies* with Michael Keating, as well as *Canadian Politics,* Sixth Edition, with James Bickerton.

A. Brian Tanguay is Professor of Political Science at Wilfrid Laurier University. He was the lead author of the Law Commission of Canada's report *Voting Counts: Electoral Reform for Canada,* and the co-author (with Laura B. Stephenson) of a study of the outcome of the 2007 Ontario referendum on electoral reform. He writes extensively about Quebec party politics and published a study of the Action démocratique du Québec in *Conservatism in Canada,* edited by James Farney and David Rayside.

The Contributors

Grant Amyot is Professor in the Department of Political Studies at Queen's University, Kingston, Ontario. His areas of expertise are comparative politics and political economy, with a particular focus on Italy, Western Europe, and the European Union. His first book was *The Italian Communist Party: The Crisis of the Popular Front Strategy* (London: Croom Helm, 1981), and he has continued to teach and write on political parties.

Frédérick Bastien is Assistant Professor of Political Science at the Université de Montréal and Associate Director of the Centre for the Study of Democratic Citizenship. His research focuses on the mediatization of politics, political journalism, and online technologies. He has published on politics and infotainment television programs (*Tout le monde en regarde!* Montreal: Presses de l'Université Laval, 2013) and he was the lead editor of *Les Québécois aux urnes: les partis, les médias et les citoyens en campagne* (Montreal: Presses de l'Université de Montréal, 2013).

Éric Bélanger is Professor in the Department of Political Science at McGill University and is a member of the Centre for the Study of Democratic Citizenship. His research interests include political parties, public opinion, voting behaviour, as well as Quebec and Canadian politics. His work has been published in several scholarly journals, including *Comparative Political Studies, Political Research Quarterly, Electoral Studies, Publius: The Journal of Federalism,* the *European Journal of Political Research,* and the *Canadian Journal of Political Science.* He is also the co-author of a book on Quebec politics, *Le comportement électoral des Québécois* (Montreal: Presses de Université de Montréal, 2009), which won the 2010 Donald Smiley Prize.

James Bickerton is Professor of Political Science at St. Francis Xavier University. He is co-author of *Ties That Bind: Parties and Voters in Canada* (Toronto: Oxford University Press, 1999) and co-editor of *Canadian Politics,* Sixth Edition (Toronto: University of Toronto Press, 2014), and *Governing: Essays in Honour of Donald J. Savoie* (Montreal: McGill-Queen's University Press, 2013). His research interests are in the areas of Canadian federalism, regionalism, and party politics.

François Boucher is a Postdoctoral Fellow at the Centre de recherche en éthique, Université de Montréal. His research focuses mainly on the philosophical and normative foundations of multiculturalism with special attention to issues related to the accommodation of ethnoreligious minorities and to the critical analysis of normative models of secularism. He has also worked on nationalism and federalism. He recently published various book chapters on those topics, as well as articles in *Criminal Law and Philosophy, Philosophy and Public Issues,* and *Revue Catholique de Louvain.*

Joanna Everitt is the Dean of Arts at the University of New Brunswick in Saint John. She specializes in Canadian politics, gender differences in public opinion, media coverage of male and female party leaders and its impact on leadership evaluations, and voting behaviour in Canadian elections.

Thierry Giasson is Professor of Political Science and the Director of the Research Lab on Political Communication at Université Laval in Quebec City. He is the co-editor (with Alex Marland) of the series *Communication, Strategy, and Politics* (Vancouver: University of British Columbia Press), which examines elite decision making and political communication in today's hyper-mediated political arena. His research focuses on political marketing practices and strategies, web politics, and the mediatization of politics. His recent work has been published in the *Journal of Public Affairs, Politique* *et Sociétés, About Journalism,* the *Canadian Journal of Political Science,* and the *Canadian Journal of Communication.*

Kristin R. Good is Associate Professor in the Department of Political Science at Dalhousie University. She is author of *Municipalities and Multiculturalism: The Politics of Immigration in Toronto and Vancouver* (2009), which received the Canadian Political Science Association's Donald Smiley Prize in 2010. Her contributions include an edited volume (with Luc Turgeon and Triadafilos Triadafilopoulos) entitled *Segmented Cities? How Urban Contexts Shape Ethnic and Nationalist Politics* (Vancouver: University of British Columbia Press, 2014) and a guest-edited special issue of *International Journal of Canadian Studies* (vol. 49) entitled "Reopening the Myth of the North American City Debate: On Comparing Canadian and American Cities."

Brooke Jeffrey is Political Science Professor at Concordia University and a former policy adviser to the Liberal Party. She is the author of *Dismantling Canada: Stephen Harper's New Conservative Agenda* (Montreal: McGill-Queen's University Press, 2015) as well as *Divided Loyalties: The Liberal Party of Canada, 1984–2008* (Toronto: University of Toronto Press, 2010).

Richard Johnston is Professor of Political Science and Canada Research Chair Public Opinion, Elections, and Representation at the University of British Columbia. He specializes in the study of elections and voting behaviour, mainly in Canada and the United States. He is author or co-author of five books, co-editor of four books, and has written 90 articles and book chapters. He led the Canadian Election Study in 1988 and 1992–93 and the National Annenberg Election Survey at the University of Pennsylvania in 2000 and 2008.

Alex Marland is Associate Professor of Political Science and Associate Dean of Arts at Memorial University of Newfoundland. He was the lead editor, with Thierry Giasson and others, of *Political Marketing in Canada* (Vancouver: University of British Columbia Press, 2012) and *Political Communication in Canada* (Vancouver: University of British Columbia Press, 2014). Work is underway on new volumes about permanent campaigning and political elites in Canada. He is the author of a forthcoming book about the practice of branding and centralized communication in Canadian politics and government.

David McGrane is Associate Professor of Political Studies at St. Thomas More College and the University of Saskatchewan. He has published articles in several academic journals, and his most recent research is a book entitled *Remaining Loyal: Social Democracy in Quebec and Saskatchewan* (Montreal: McGill-Queen's University Press, 2014). His research interests include multiculturalism, provincial elections, and child care. He currently holds a Social Sciences and Humanities Research Council grant to write a book on the federal NDP.

Henry Milner is a Research Fellow and the Chair in Electoral Studies in the Department of Political Science at l'Université de Montréal and has been a Visiting Professor in Sweden, Finland, France, Australia, New Zealand, and the United States. He has published eight books and edited four others, recently focusing on comparative political participation. He has contributed to numerous journals, including *Inroads* (http://inroadsjournal.ca), which he co-publishes.

Richard Nadeau is Professor of Political Science at the Université de Montréal. His interests include voting behaviour, public opinion, political communication, and quantitative methodology. A Fulbright Scholar and a former chief adviser to the premier of Quebec, he has authored or co-authored over 170 articles (published in prestigious political science journals), chapters, and books, including *Le vote des Français de Mitterrand à Sarkozy, Unsteady State, Anatomy of a Liberal Victory, Citizens, French Presidential Elections, The Austrian Voter, Health Care Policy and Opinion in Canada and the United States,* and *Le comportement électoral des Québécois,* which won the Donald Smiley Award in 2010.

Jacquetta (Jacquie) Newman is Associate Professor of Political Science at King's University College at Western University. Her research is primarily focused on feminist issues, social movements, and identity politics. She is co-author with Linda White of *Women, Politics, and Public Policy: The Political Struggles of Canadian Women* (Toronto: Oxford University Press, 2012).

Steve Patten is Associate Professor in the Department of Political Science at the University of Alberta. His research and teaching focus on contemporary Canadian and Alberta politics, with a particular emphasis on the evolving character of Canadian conservatism, party politics, public policy, and the challenges of deepening democracy in policymaking. He is co-editor (with Lois Harder) of *Patriation and Its Consequences: Constitution-Making in Canada* (Vancouver: University of British Columbia Press, 2015) and author of several other publications, including "The Politics of Alberta's One-Party State" in *Transforming Provincial Politics: The Political Economy of Canada's Provinces and Territories in a Neoliberal Era,* edited by Bryan Evans and Charles

Smith (Toronto: University of Toronto Press, 2015) and "The Triumph of Neoliberalism within Partisan Conservatism in Canada" in *Conservatism in Canada,* edited by James Farney and David Rayside (Toronto: University of Toronto Press, 2013).

Dennis Pilon has been Associate Professor in the Political Science Department at York University since 2011. From 2006 to 2011, he was Assistant Professor at the University of Victoria. His research has focused on democratic reform at the provincial and federal level in Canada as well as across Western industrialized countries. He is the author of two books, *The Politics of Voting: Reforming Canada's Electoral System* (Toronto: Emond Montgomery, 2007) and *Wrestling with Democracy: Voting Systems as Politics in the Twentieth Century West* (Toronto: University of Toronto Press, 2013).

Tamara A. Small is Associate Professor in the Department of Political Science at the University of Guelph. Her research focus is digital politics: the use and impact of the Internet by Canadian political actors. She is the co-author of *Fighting for Votes: Parties, the Media, and Voters in an Ontario Election* (Vancouver: University of British Columbia Press, 2015) and the co-editor of *Political Communication in Canada: Meet the Press, Tweet the Rest* (Vancouver: University of British Columbia Press, 2014) and *Mind the Gaps: Canadian Perspectives on Gender and Politics* (Halifax: Fernwood Press, 2013). Her work has been published in the journals *Information Communication and Society, Party Politics,* and the *Canadian Journal of Political Science.*

Nelson Wiseman is Professor of Political Science and the Director of the Canadian Studies Program at the University of Toronto. His most recent book is *The Public Intellectual in Canada* (Toronto: University of Toronto Press, 2013). He fields inquiries from various local, national, and international media on Canadian politics and is a columnist for *The Hill Times,* Canada's politics and government newsweekly.

Peter Woolstencroft, while retired from the Department of Political Science at the University of Waterloo, is still teaching courses and advising students. A specialist in Canadian politics, he has published essays on education, political geography, party leadership elections, Ontario's political culture, election campaigns, and the federal and Ontario Progressive Conservative parties.

Lisa Young is Professor of Political Science and Vice-Provost and Dean of Graduate Studies at the University of Calgary. Her research has focused on Canadian political parties and party systems, political finance, and gender and politics.

Index